The Standard Encyclopedia of

American Silverplate

Flatware and Hollow Ware

Identification &
Value Guide

Frances Bones & Lee Roy Fisher

COLLECTOR BOOKS

A Division of Schroeder Publishing Co., Inc.

The current values in this book should be used only as a guide. They are not intended to set prices, which vary from one section of the country to another. Auction prices as well as dealer prices vary greatly and are affected by condition as well as demand. Neither the Authors nor the Publisher assumes responsibility for any losses that might be incurred as a result of consulting this guide.

Cover Design: Michelle Dowling
Book Design: Benjamin R. Faust

On the Cover: Vintage Pattern Jelly Knife, 1847 Rogers Bros., Group 1, $58.00 – 68.00
First Love Pattern Cold Meat Fork, 1847 Rogers Bros., Group 2, $18.00 – 28.00
Remembrance Coffee Pot, 1847 Rogers Bros., Group 2, $113.00 – 128.00

Searching For A Publisher?

We are always looking for knowledgeable people considered to be experts within their fields. If you feel that there is a real need for a book on your collectible subject and have a large comprehensive collection, contact Collector Books.

COLLECTOR BOOKS
P.O. Box 3009
Paducah, KY 42002-3009
www.collectorbooks.com

Contents

Acknowledgments

We wish to acknowledge those who so generously gave of their time, expertise, and materials: Mark Balay; Lisa Derrick Bones; Carolyn of Carman's Collectibles; Ken Deibel; Sandy Findley of Oneida Silversmiths; Karen and Nan Fisher; Fran Jay; Lydia Bones Thompson; and Diane Williams.

About the Authors

Frances Bones and Lee Roy Fisher have pooled their knowledge and catalog materials so that collectors and dealers may have a better understanding of American silverplate patterns. Both authors are dedicated silver collectors and are always delighted to share their knowledge with collectors of like interest.

Lee Roy Fisher is a nationally known silverplate dealer. He and his wife Nan operate Fishers Silver Exchange in Huntsville, Texas, and are widely known on the antiques show circuit. Lee Roy specializes in the older fancier patterns and is a recognized authority on all of the grape patterns. Since the late 1950s, Fishers Silver Exchange has advertised continuously in *The Antique Trader Weekly*.

Frances Bones is a dealer in both silver and glass. She published *Collectibles of the Depression* in 1971 and *The Book of Duncan Glass* in 1973.

This identification guide is easy to use. The American firms are listed alphabetically. The patterns we have chosen to feature are also listed alphabetically under their manufacturer. Since few collectors are fully aware of the variety of silverplate made by American silver artisans, we anticipate this compilation of catalogs will expand the collectors' appreciation for these wonderful patterns.

Dealers and collectors of silverplate will find many pieces in this guide that are new to them. Hopefully, a new wave of collecting American silverplate will occur. We have placed particular emphasis on the patterns that were produced in both flatware and hollow ware, since these patterns are especially collectible.

Throughout the book, patterns are assigned to Groups 1, 2, and 3 by the authors. Group 1 is generally the period from the early 1900s up to World War I, and is characterized by ornate patterns with many pieces offered. This group is highly collectible because of the beauty and exquisite die-work. Groups 2 and 3 are of the period from World War I through the 1970s, and are characterized by less ornate patterns, with fewer pieces offered. Group 2, however, was generally offered with an increased number of hollow ware pieces. Group 3 is generally the less collectible group of its time period.

The prices presented in the Price Guide on pages 6 – 13 are presented only as a rough guide for the reader. They represent the market experience of the authors at the time of publication. As with other things, the dynamics of supply and demand change with time. One should recognize also that condition is a great factor in determining price. The prices listed represent excellent condition. Many of the catalog illustrations retain the original selling prices. This gives the collector a perspective as to which patterns were introduced as quality products at the time, and which ones were offered at lower prices.

Group 1

These suggested prices are for items in excellent condition. Items must not have serious scratches, dings, dents, acid spots, or obvious wear. Blades in excellent condition will be void of scratches and acid spots. Reproductions and resilvered items are not covered in this guide.

Add 50% to the suggested prices for these patterns: Charter Oak, Columbia, Floral, Moselle, and Vintage.

Forks

Asparagus	.75.00 – 95.00
Baby fork, indv., short handle	.10.00 – 15.00
Berry/strawberry fork, indv.	.12.00 – 18.00
Berry fork, server, flat or hollow handle	.50.00 – 65.00
Cake/cold meat fork, server, long handle	.35.00 – 45.00
Carving fork, bird, hollow handle	.20.00 – 25.00
Carving fork, roast, hollow handle	.27.00 – 32.00
Carving fork, steak/game, hollow handle	.22.00 – 27.00
Child/youth fork, indv.	.12.00 – 16.00
Chipped beef, small cold meat fork, server	.20.00 – 30.00
Cold meat fork, server, 1-tine larger	.38.00 – 48.00
Dinner/table (medium) fork, indv.	.16.00 – 21.00
Dinner/table (medium) fork, indv., hollow handle	.25.00 – 30.00
Fish fork, indv.	.30.00 – 40.00
Fish fork, server, flat or hollow handle	.65.00 – 80.00
Ice cream fork, indv.	.25.00 – 30.00
Lettuce fork, server	.42.00 – 58.00
Lobster fork, indv.	.20.00 – 26.00
Luncheon/dessert fork, indv.	.12.00 – 16.00
Luncheon/dessert fork, indv., hollow handle	.20.00 – 25.00
Olive fork, server, long handle	.30.00 – 38.00
Oyster/cocktail/seafood fork, indv.	.12.00 – 18.00
Pickle fork, server, twist handle	.32.00 – 40.00
Pickle fork, server, long handle	.32.00 – 40.00
Pickle fork, server, short handle	.20.00 – 27.00
Pickle fork, server, short handle, cutting tine	.18.00 – 25.00
Pie fork, indv., 1-cutting tine larger	.20.00 – 30.00
Salad fork, indv.	.20.00 – 30.00
Salad fork, server, large, fancy bowl, tines	.60.00 – 75.00
Salad fork, server, regular tines	.25.00 – 35.00
Salad fork, server, hollow handle, w/olive wood	.25.00 – 32.00
Sardine fork, server	.35.00 – 43.00
Sandwich fork, server, flat or hollow handle	.55.00 – 65.00

Knives

Bread/cake knife, server, hollow handle . . . . .40.00 – 50.00
Butter knife/spreader, indv., 1-piece, flat handle . . . . .12.00 – 18.00
Butter knife/spreader, indv., hollow handle .15.00 – 23.00
Butter knife, server, twist handle . . . . .20.00 – 30.00
Butter knife, server . . . . .8.00 – 12.00
Cake knife, server, flat handle, saw-back blade . . . . .60.00 – 75.00
Cake knife, server, hollow handle, saw-back blade . . . . .50.00 – 65.00
Cake knife server, hollow handle, tined blade . . . . .45.00 – 55.00
Carving knife, bird, hollow handle . . . . .20.00 – 25.00
Carving knife, roast, hollow handle . . . . .27.00 – 32.00
Carving knife, steak/game, hollow handle . . . . .22.00 – 27.00
Cheese knife, server, hollow handle, trowel blade . . . . .25.00 – 30.00
Cheese knife, server, flat handle . . . . .25.00 – 30.00
Child's/youth knife, indv., flat handle . . . . .12.00 – 17.00
Child's/youth knife, indv., solid handle . . . . .11.00 – 13.00
Dinner/table knife, indv., hollow handle . . . . .12.00 – 18.00
Dinner/table knife, indv., solid/modeled handle . . . . .8.00 – 12.00
Fish knife, indv., hollow handle . . . . .25.00 – 30.00
Fish knife, indv., flat handle, pointed/blunt blade . . . . .25.00 – 30.00
Fish knife, server, flat handle, pointed blade . . . . .60.00 – 75.00
Fruit/orange knife, indv., hollow handle, saw-back . . . . .20.00 – 25.00
Fruit/orange knife, indv., hollow handle, blunt blade . . . . .20.00 – 25.00
Fruit knife, indv., hollow handle, pointed blade . . . . .20.00 – 25.00
Fruit knife, indv., solid handle . . . . .15.00 – 21.00
Ice cream knife/slicer, server, flat handle . . . . .60.00 – 75.00
Ice cream knife, server, hollow handle, cleaver blade . . . . .65.00 – 75.00
Ice cream/pastry knife, server, hollow handle, trowel . . . . .35.00 – 50.00
Jelly knife, server, flat handle, trowel blade . . . . .40.00 – 50.00
Luncheon/dessert knife, indv., hollow handle . . . . .15.00 – 20.00
Luncheon/dessert knife, indv., solid handle .6.00 – 8.00
Orange/fruit knife, indv., hollow handle, saw-back . . . . .20.00 – 25.00
Pie/pastry knife, server, hollow handle . . . . .35.00 – 45.00
Pie/pastry knife, server, flat handle, trowel blade . . . . .45.00 – 55.00
Pudding knife, server, flat handle, trowel blade . . . . .45.00 – 55.00

Spoons

After dinner/demi-tasse spoon, indv. . . . . .9.00 – 12.00
Baby spoon, indv., curved handle . . . . .15.00 – 20.00
Berry spoon, server, fancy bowl . . . . .55.00 – 70.00
Berry/nut spoon, server, long handle . . . . .35.00 – 40.00
Bon bon/nut scoop, server . . . . .30.00 – 45.00
Child's spoon, indv., short handle . . . . .12.00 – 17.00
Coffee/five o' clock/youth spoon, indv. . . . . .10.00 – 15.00
Dessert spoon (oval bowl), indv. . . . . .8.00 – 12.00
Egg spoon, indv. . . . . .15.00 – 20.00
Honey spoon, server . . . . .20.00 – 25.00
Horseradish spoon, server . . . . .30.00 – 40.00
Iced tea/beverage spoon, indv. . . . . .12.00 – 18.00

Ice cream spoon, indv. ....20.00 – 30.00
Ice spoon/pea server, pierced bowl ....70.00 – 80.00
Jelly/preserve spoon, server ....22.00 – 30.00
Mustard spoon, server ....30.00 – 38.00
Olive spoon, server, pierced bowl ....30.00 – 40.00
Olive spoon, server, open bowl ....35.00 – 45.00
Orange/citrus spoon, indv. ....15.00 – 28.00
Salt spoon, indv. ....16.00 – 22.00
Salt spoon, master server ....20.00 – 25.00
Soup spoon, bouillon, indv. ....12.00 – 18.00
Soup spoon, cream, indv. ....14.00 – 20.00
Soup spoon/dessert, indv., oval bowl ....8.00 – 12.00
Salad spoon, server, fancy bowl ....55.00 – 65.00
Salad spoon, server, hollow handle, w/olive wood .....25.00 – 32.00
Sifter, sugar, server ....35.00 – 45.00
Sugar shell, spoon, server ....12.00 – 22.00
Teaspoon, indv. ....8.00 – 13.00
Tablespoon, server ....15.00 – 20.00

Miscellaneous Pieces

Asparagus server, hollow handle ....75.00 – 95.00
Asparagus tongs, server, hollow handle ....70.00 – 80.00
Bon bon/cracker scoop, server ....35.00 – 45.00
Butter pick ....22.00 – 32.00
Bottle opener ....27.00 – 37.00
Cheese scoop server, flat or hollow handle ....60.00 – 75.00
Cheese server, disc-type bowl ....55.00 – 60.00
Cucumber/tomato, server ....60.00 – 80.00
Food pusher, indv. ....25.00 – 35.00
Ladle, cream, server ....20.00 – 30.00
Ladle, gravy, server ....25.00 – 35.00
Ladle, medium/soup, server ....55.00 – 65.00
Ladle, mayonnaise, server ....20.00 – 30.00
Ladle, mustard, server ....25.00 – 35.00
Ladle, oyster stew, server ....55.00 – 65.00
Ladle, punch/frappe, server, solid handle ....60.00 – 80.00
Ladle, punch, server, hollow handle ....90.00 – 110.00
Ladle, tureen, server ....60.00 – 75.00
Lobster pick, indv., hollow handle ....18.00 – 25.00
Macaroni/veg., server, flat or hollow handle, trowel ...55.00 – 65.00
Napkin ring ....22.00 – 32.00
Nut crack, indv., solid or hollow handle ....25.00 – 35.00
Nut pick, indv. ....12.00 – 18.00
Pie server, hollow handle ....60.00 – 80.00
Roast holder, server ....55.00 – 65.00
Sharpener (carving set), any size ....22.00 – 28.00
Tomato/cucumber, server ....60.00 – 80.00
Tongs/bon bon, server ....25.00 – 35.00
Tongs, ice, server ....30.00 – 40.00
Tongs, sugar, server ....27.00 – 37.00

Groups 2 & 3

These suggested prices are for items in excellent condition. Items must not have serious scratches, dings, dents, acid spots, or obvious wear. Blades in excellent condition will be void of scratches and acid spots. Reproductions and resilvered items are not covered in this guide.

Add 50% to the suggested prices for these Group 2 patterns: Coronation, Daffodil, Eternally Yours, First Love, Grosvenor, Heritage, and Remembrance.

Deduct 50% from the suggested prices for all Group 3 patterns.

Forks

Baby fork, indv., short handle	9.00 – 11.00
Cake fork, server	27.00 – 37.00
Carving fork, bird, hollow handle	20.00 – 24.00
roast, hollow handle	27.00 – 32.00
steak, solid/modeled handle	15.00 – 18.00
steak/game, hollow handle	22.00 – 27.00
Child's/youth fork, indv.	8.00 – 10.00
Chipped beef/small cold meat fork, server	15.00 – 18.00
Cold meat fork, server	15.00 – 20.00
Dinner/table fork, indv.	8.00 – 12.00
Dinner/table fork, indv., solid/modeled handle	5.00 – 8.00
Ice cream fork, indv.	18.00 – 22.00
Lemon fork, server, small	12.00 – 15.00
Luncheon/dessert/breakfast form, indv., solid/modeled handle	5.00 – 8.00
Oyster/cocktail/seafood fork, indv.	8.00 – 11.00
Pickle/olive fork, server, short handle	13.00 – 16.00
Pie fork, indv., cutting tine	15.00 – 19.00
Salad/pastry form, indv.	8.00 – 13.00
Salad fork, server, fancy bowl	15.00 – 20.00
Salad fork, server, plain bowl	11.00 – 16.00
Salad fork, server, tined and pierced	19.00 – 23.00
Salad fork, server, hollow handle, w/olive wood	20.00 – 24.00
Viande/grill fork, indv., long handle	7.00 – 10.00

Knives

Bread/cake knife, server, hollow handle	15.00 – 20.00
Bread/cake knife, server, solid handle	11.00 – 13.00
Butter knife/spreader, indv., hollow handle	8.00 – 11.00
Butter knife/spreader, indv., hollow handle, round-end blade	12.00 – 14.00
Butter knife, server	6.00 – 9.00
Cake knife, server, hollow handle	22.00 – 27.00
Carving knife, bird, hollow handle	20.00 – 24.00
roast, hollow handle	27.00 – 32.00
steak, solid/modeled handle	15.00 – 18.00
steak/game, hollow handle	22.00 – 27.00

Cheese knife, server, hollow handle, trowel type blade . . . . .15.00 – 20.00
Cheese knife, server, flat handle . . . . .9.00 – 13.00
Dinner/table knife, indv., hollow handle . . . . .8.00 – 12.00
Dinner/table knife, indv., solid/modeled/embossed handle . . . . .5.00 – 8.00
Dinner/table knife, indv., "jeweled" (colored) handle . . . . .15.00 – 20.00
Fruit/orange knife, indv., hollow handle, round-end blade . . . . .10.00 – 14.00
Fruit knife, hollow handle, pointed blade . . . . .12.00 – 17.00
Fruit knife, indv., saw-back blade . . . . .10.00 – 14.00
Jelly knife, server . . . . .15.00 – 20.00
Luncheon/dessert/breakfast knife, indv., solid/modeled handle . . . . .5.00 – 8.00
Luncheon/dessert/breakfast knife, indv., hollow handle . . . . .8.00 – 10.00
Luncheon/dessert/breakfast knife, indv., "jeweled" (colored) handle . . . . .10.00 – 15.00
Pie/pastry knife, server, hollow handle . . . . .18.00 – 22.00
Pie/pastry knife, server, flat handle, trowel type blade . . . . .16.00 – 19.00
Salad/tea/youth knife, indv., hollow handle . . . . .12.00 – 14.00
Viande/grill knife, indv., hollow handle . . . . .7.00 – 10.00
Youth/child knife, indv., flat handle . . . . .10.00 – 12.00
Youth/tea/salad knife, indv., solid/modeled handle . . . . .8.00 – 10.00
Youth/tea salad knife, indv., hollow handle . . . . .12.00 – 14.00

Miscellaneous pieces

Bon bon/nut server, small . . . . .15.00 – 20.00
Cheese server, hollow handle, small . . . . .15.00 – 20.00
Jelly server . . . . .10.00 – 12.00
Jelly server, pierced . . . . .15.00 – 20.00
Ladle, cream/mayonnaise, server . . . . .14.00 – 17.00
Ladle, gravy server . . . . .17.00 – 22.00
Ladle, punch, server . . . . .75.00 – 80.00
Ladle, punch, server, hollow handle . . . . .85.00 – 100.00
Ladle, soup tureen, server . . . . .55.00 – 65.00
Ladle, soup tureen, server, hollow handle . . . . .65.00 – 75.00
Napkin ring, place piece . . . . .25.00 – 35.00
Pie server, hollow handle, trowel type . . . . .20.00 – 25.00
Poultry/game shears, hollow handle . . . . .25.00 – 35.00
Roast holder server . . . . .30.00 – 35.00
Sharpener, for carving sets, any size . . . . .15.00 – 18.00
Tomato/cucumber, server, usually pierced . . . . .20.00 – 25.00
Tomato/cucumber, server, hollow handle . . . . .20.00 – 25.00
Tongs, bon bon/sugar, server . . . . .20.00 – 25.00

Spoons

After dinner/demi-tasse spoon, indv. . . . . .8.00 – 11.00
Baby spoon, indv., curved handle . . . . .9.00 – 13.00
Baby/child spoon, indv., short handle . . . . .9.00 – 13.00
Berry spoon, server . . . . .20.00 – 25.00
Berry/jam/conserve spoon, server, small . . . . .16.00 – 19.00
Bon bon/nut spoon, server, pierced . . . . .16.00 – 19.00
Coffee/5 o' clock/youth spoon, indv. . . . . .8.00 – 12.00
Dessert spoon, indv. . . . . .5.00 – 8.00

Honey spoon, server, small . . . . .12.00 – 15.00
Ice tea/beverage/parfait spoon, indv. . . . . .9.00 – 12.00
Jam/conserve/small berry spoon, server . . . . .16.00 – 19.00
Olive spoon, server, pierced or open bowl . . . . .16.00 – 22.00
Pabulum/infant/feeding spoon, sm. bowl, long handle . . . . .9.00 – 12.00
Salt spoon, indv. . . . . .8.00 – 12.00
Soup spoon, bouillon, indv. . . . . .10.00 – 13.00
Soup spoon, cream, indv. . . . . .10.00 – 13.00
Soup/dessert spoon, indv., oval bowl . . . . .4.00 – 7.00
Salad/berry spoon, server, fancy bowl . . . . .28.00 – 33.00
Salad/berry spoon, server, plain bowl . . . . .20.00 – 24.00
Salad/berry spoon, server, w/olive wood . . . . .20.00 – 24.00
Salad/berry spoon, server, pierced bowl . . . . .28.00 – 33.00
Sugar spoon/shell, server . . . . .7.00 – 10.00
Teaspoon, indv. . . . . .3.00 – 5.00
Tablespoon, server . . . . .9.00 – 13.00
Tablespoon, server, pierced . . . . .20.00 – 25.00

Hollow Ware

Prices suggested are for Group 2 patterns only. Very few Group 1 patterns have matching hollow ware. Proper grading of condition is essential. These suggested prices are for pieces in very fine condition. Items must not have serious scratches, dings, dents, acid spots, or obvious wear. Resilvered items are not covered in this guide. Patterns reviewed for this guide were manufactured by Community, Holmes & Edwards, and 1847 Rogers Bros. Plainer patterns sell for less than the fancier ones.

Add 50% to the suggested prices for these Group 2 patterns: Coronation, Daffodil, Eternally Yours, First Love, Grosvenor, Heritage, and Remembrance.

Deduct 50% from the suggested prices for all Group 3 patterns.

Bowls/Dishes

Bowl, all purpose, rect., 4-footed, 14½" x 10½" .60.00 – 70.00
Bon bon, small, 4-footed, or on a base . . . . .20.00 – 25.00
Bon bon/tidbit, small . . . . .12.00 – 17.00
Buffet Dish, cov., 2-handled, 13" . . . . .70.00 – 80.00
Butter Dish, cov., with glass liner . . . . .28.00 – 33.00
Casserole, cov., deep, with glass liner . . . . .50.00 – 60.00
Center bowl, 4-footed, or on base . . . . .60.00 – 70.00
Centerpiece, pierced, covered, footed . . . . .60.00 – 70.00
Centerpiece/flower, cov., small . . . . .22.00 – 28.00
Chafing dish, cov. w/warmer, 1 handle . . . . .75.00 – 90.00
Child's dish/porringer, 1 handle . . . . .13.00 – 18.00
Finger bowl/child . . . . .13.00 – 16.00
Ice bowl . . . . .50.00 – 60.00
Ice bowl, vacuum liner, covered . . . . .65.00 – 75.00
Instant coffee jar, glass w/silver lid and spoon . . . . .30.00 – 40.00
Mayonnaise bowl, footed. . . . . .25.00 – 35.00

Punch bowl, footed. . . . . .195.00 – 215.00
Shell dish, up to 11" . . . . .25.00 – 30.00
Serving bowl (bottom to double dish) . . . . .22.00 – 28.00
Sugar, with lid . . . . .20.00 – 28.00
Sugar, dessert/indv. . . . . .16.00 – 19.00
Vegetable dish, cov., double, 2-handle . . . . .60.00 – 70.00
Vegetable dish, cov., 1 handle on top of lid .50.00 – 60.00
Waste bowl . . . . .17.00 – 22.00

Miscellaneous

Basket, footed, handle . . . . .50.00 – 60.00
Box, cigarette/jewelry . . . . .40.00 – 50.00
Candelabrum, 2 – 3 lights . . . . .95.00 – 125.00
Candelabrum, 4 – 6 lights . . . . .150.00 – 180.00
Candlestick, short, 4" – 5" . . . . .28.00 – 33.00
Candlestick, tall, 6" – 9" . . . . .45.00 – 52.00
Coffee pot, covered . . . . .80.00 – 90.00
Cocktail mixer, handled, covered . . . . .70.00 – 80.00
Compotier . . . . .40.00 – 50.00
Creamer . . . . .18.00 – 23.00
Creamer, dessert/indv. . . . . .13.00 – 16.00
Cup, child's . . . . .13.00 – 19.00
Cup, punch . . . . .18.00 – 23.00
Food warmer, covered, w/burner, rect. . . . . .140.00 – 150.00
Gravy boat/sauce dish w/tray . . . . .40.00 – 50.00
Kettle, on stand w/warmer . . . . .150.00 – 175.00
Napkin ring . . . . .25.00 – 35.00
Pepper shaker . . . . .15.00 – 20.00
Pitcher, water/beverage . . . . .60.00 – 70.00
Salt dip . . . . .12.00 – 15.00
Salt shaker . . . . .15.00 – 20.00
Tea pot, covered . . . . .75.00 – 85.00
Tureen, soup, covered . . . . .135.00 – 155.00
Urn, coffee, w/burner, large . . . . .170.00 – 190.00
Vase, short . . . . .16.00 – 21.00
Vase, tall . . . . .19.00 – 27.00
Wine cooler, large . . . . .100.00 – 110.00

Plates

Bread and butter, round, square, 6" – 7" . . . . .11.00 – 13.00
Cake/sandwich, large center, round, 12" – 13" . . . . .32.00 – 38.00
Cake/sandwich, small center, round, 11" – 12" . . . . .30.00 – 35.00
Relish/chop, glass inserts . . . . .60.00 – 70.00
Relish/chop, without inserts . . . . .50.00 – 60.00
Service plate, large center, round, square, 10½" – 11" . . . . .30.00 – 38.00
Tea, salad, round, 7" – 8" . . . . .13.00 – 16.00

Trays

Tray/basket, oval, handle . . . . .32.00 – 42.00
Tray/bread/roll, oblong, 12" – 15" . . . . .28.00 – 38.00
Tray, bon bon, oval . . . . .22.00 – 30.00
Tray, chafing dish, round, no handle, 17" . . . . .75.00 – 85.00
Tray, gravy boat, oval, oblong, rect., 9" . . . . .25.00 – 35.00
Tray, lazy susan, glass div., w/center covered bowl . . . . .85.00 – 105.00
Tray, individual cream, sugar/cold meat, oval, 12¾" . . . . .28.00 – 38.00
Tray, meat, oval, rect., 18" – 20" . . . . .70.00 – 80.00
Tray, meat, with well, oval, oblong, 16" – 19" . . . . .80.00 – 90.00
Tray, meat with well, oval, oblong, 20" – 22" .100.00 – 120.00
Tray, olive/pickle, oval, 7½" and longer . . . . .20.00 – 25.00
Tray, punch, round, 22" . . . . .100.00 – 120.00
Tray, relish, glass divider, round, oval . . . . .70.00 – 80.00
Tray, sandwich, oval 12¾" – 13½" . . . . .32.00 – 42.00
Tray, sandwich, square, 10" – 12" . . . . .28.00 – 35.00
Tray/waiter, no handles, round, 15" – 17" . . . . .75.00 – 85.00
Tray/waiter, no handles, oval or rect., 16" – 18" .75.00 – 85.00
Tray/waiter, no handles, oval or rect., 20" or more . . . . .90.00 – 100.00
Tray/waiter, oval, 2-handled, 16" – 21" . . . . .100.00 – 120.00
Tray/waiter, oval, 2-handled, 22" – 28" . . . . .110.00 – 150.00
Tray/waiter, rect., 2-handled, 20" to 28" . . . . .110.00 – 150.00

Alvin Manufacturing Company

Brides Bouquet

Patented 1908. Orange/citrus spoons and seafood cocktail fork.

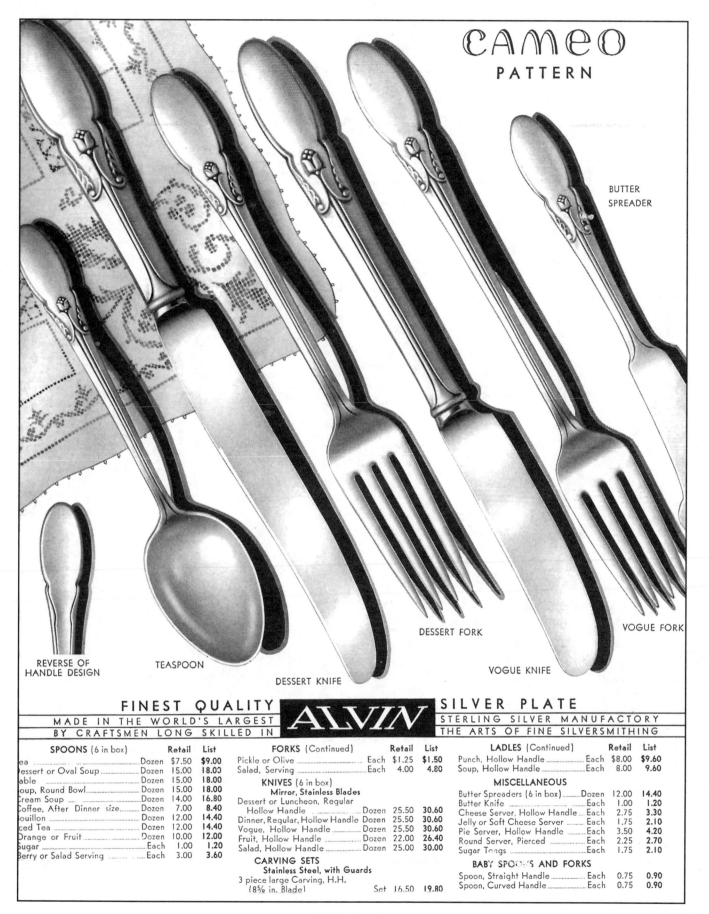

Alvin Mfg. Co.

CAMEO PATTERN

BUTTER SPREADER

REVERSE OF HANDLE DESIGN

TEASPOON

DESSERT KNIFE

DESSERT FORK

VOGUE KNIFE

VOGUE FORK

FINEST QUALITY **ALVIN** SILVER PLATE

MADE IN THE WORLD'S LARGEST STERLING SILVER MANUFACTORY
BY CRAFTSMEN LONG SKILLED IN THE ARTS OF FINE SILVERSMITHING

SPOONS (6 in box)		Retail	List
...ea	Dozen	$7.50	$9.00
...essert or Oval Soup	Dozen	15.00	18.00
...able	Dozen	15.00	18.00
...oup, Round Bowl	Dozen	15.00	18.00
...ream Soup	Dozen	14.00	16.80
...offee, After Dinner size	Dozen	7.00	8.40
...ouillon	Dozen	12.00	14.40
...ced Tea	Dozen	12.00	14.40
...range or Fruit	Dozen	10.00	12.00
...Sugar	Each	1.00	1.20
...erry or Salad Serving	Each	3.00	3.60

FORKS (Continued)		Retail	List
Pickle or Olive	Each	$1.25	$1.50
Salad, Serving	Each	4.00	4.80

KNIVES (6 in box)
Mirror, Stainless Blades

		Retail	List
Dessert or Luncheon, Regular Hollow Handle	Dozen	25.50	30.60
Dinner, Regular, Hollow Handle	Dozen	25.50	30.60
Vogue, Hollow Handle	Dozen	25.50	30.60
Fruit, Hollow Handle	Dozen	22.00	26.40
Salad, Hollow Handle	Dozen	25.00	30.00

CARVING SETS
Stainless Steel, with Guards

3 piece large Carving, H.H. (8⅝ in. Blade)	Set	16.50	19.80

LADLES (Continued)		Retail	List
Punch, Hollow Handle	Each	$8.00	$9.60
Soup, Hollow Handle	Each	8.00	9.60

MISCELLANEOUS

Butter Spreaders (6 in box)	Dozen	12.00	14.40
Butter Knife	Each	1.00	1.20
Cheese Server, Hollow Handle	Each	2.75	3.30
Jelly or Soft Cheese Server	Each	1.75	2.10
Pie Server, Hollow Handle	Each	3.50	4.20
Round Server, Pierced	Each	2.25	2.70
Sugar Tongs	Each	1.75	2.10

BABY SPOONS AND FORKS

Spoon, Straight Handle	Each	0.75	0.90
Spoon, Curved Handle	Each	0.75	0.90

1936 Catalog

THE CLASSIC
GRAY FINISH

THE following illustrations show our "Long Life" Quality Plate which will satisfy the most particular customer. It is produced with the same care, skill and attention to details as Sterling silver. Each piece is heavily plated with a uniform weight and thickness of pure silver to resist the hardest wear and insure the longest life.

SPOONS

		List	Retail
Baby, Nursery Rhyme	each	$1.23	$1.00
Baby, Short Handle	each	1.23	1.00
Baby, Curved Handle	each	1.23	1.00
Berry	each	3.99	3.25
Berry, Small (*Louisiana only*)	each	3.38	2.75
Bouillon	set of six	8.87	7.25
Coffee	set of six	4.59	3.75
Dessert	per dozen	18.36	15.00
Ice Cream (*Louisiana and Classic only*)	per dozen	13.52	11.00
Iced Tea	set of six	7.36	6.00
Olive	each	2.15	1.75
Orange or Grapefruit	set of six	6.45	5.25
Salad Serving (*Louisiana, Classic and Dawn*)	each	3.99	3.25
Soup	per dozen	18.36	15.00
Sugar	each	1.53	1.25
Table	per dozen	18.36	15.00
*Tea, 5 o'Clock	per dozen	9.80	8.00
Tea, Regular	per dozen	9.18	7.50

FORKS

		List	Retail
Baby, Nursery Rhyme	each	$1.23	$1.00
Baby, Short Handle	each	1.23	1.00
Child's	each	1.23	1.00
Cold Meat, large	each	2.46	2.00
Cold Meat, medium (*George Washington and Luxor only*)	each	2.15	1.75
Dessert	per dozen	18.36	15.00
Dinner	per dozen	18.36	15.00
Ice Cream (*Classic, Louisiana and Dawn only*)	per dozen	14.72	12.00
Ind. Salad or Pastry	set of six	9.18	7.50
Oyster	set of six	5.82	4.75
Pickle or Olive	each	1.84	1.50
Salad Serving (*Louisiana, Classic and Dawn only*)	each	4.91	4.00

KNIVES

		List	Retail
Butter Knife	each	$1.53	$1.25
Butter Spreaders	set of six	7.68	6.25
Jelly Knife	each	2.15	1.75
Pastry Server, F. H. (*Classic and Louisiana only*)	each	5.22	4.25
Sugar Tongs	each	2.46	2.00
Cucumber or Tomato Server F. H.	each	3.99	3.25

LADLES

		List	Retail
Cream, large	each	$2.46	$2.00
Gravy	each	3.07	2.50
Soup, Hollow Handle	each	6.26	5.00
Punch, Hollow Handle	each	7.84	6.25

HOLLOW HANDLE CUTLERY

		List	Retail
Baby Knife, S. S., Nursery Rhyme	each	$2.15	$1.75
Bread Knife, Hollow Handle	each	5.22	4.25
Cheese Cutter, Hollow Handle S. S.	each	3.38	2.75
Child's Knives, S. S. Blades	each	2.15	1.75
Carving Set, 3 pcs. S. S. Knife and Fork, with Guards	per set	22.94	18.50
Dessert Knives, H.H., S.S.F.B.	per dozen	31.30	24.00
Dinner Knives, H.H., S.S.F.B.	per dozen	31.30	24.00
Fruit Knives, H.H., S.S.	set of six	14.35	11.00
Game Set, 2 pcs. S.S. Knife and Fork, with Guards	per set	16.68	13.50
Game Shears	each	13.04	10.00
Pie Server, Hollow Handle S.S.	each	5.52	4.50
Steak Set, 2 pcs. S.S. Knife and Fork, no Guards	per set	10.74	8.50
Tomato Server or Egg Server, S.S. Blades	each	6.67	5.50

SETS

		List	Retail
Baby, 3 pcs. Nursery Rhyme	per set	$4.60	$3.75
Baby Spoon and Fork, Short Handle	per set	2.46	2.00
Butter Knife and Sugar Spoon	per set	3.06	2.50
Child's, 3 pcs. H.H. Knife S.S. Blades	per set	4.20	3.50
Olive Set, 2 pcs.	per set	4.00	3.25
Salad, Olive Wood Fork and Spoon, H.H.	per set	9.20	7.50
Salad, F.H. (*Classic, Louisiana and Dawn*)	per set	8.90	7.25
6 Dinner Forks, F.H., 6 Knives, H.H.S.S.F. Blades	per set	25.44	19.80
6 Dessert Forks, F.H., 6 Knives, H.H.S.S.F. Blades	per set	25.44	19.80
26-Piece Dinner Size, Knives with S.S.F. Blades		41.70	33.25
26-Piece Dessert Size, Knives with S.S.F. Blades		41.70	33.25

* Not made in the Dawn.

1930 Catalog

Alvin Mfg. Co.

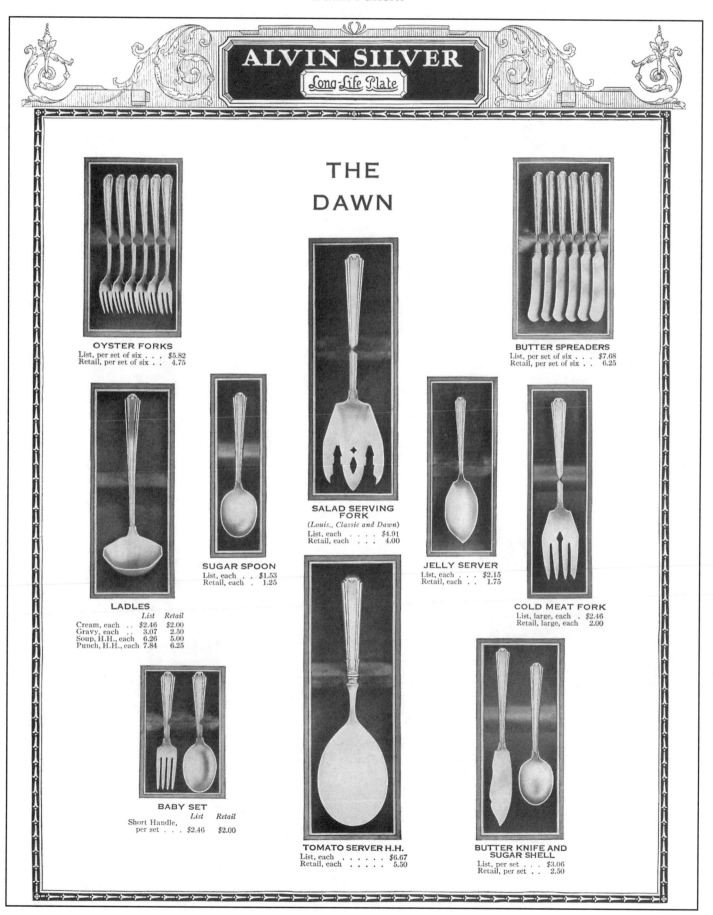

ALVIN SILVER
Long-Life Plate

THE DAWN

OYSTER FORKS
List, per set of six . . . $5.82
Retail, per set of six . . 4.75

BUTTER SPREADERS
List, per set of six . . . $7.68
Retail, per set of six . . 6.25

SALAD SERVING FORK
(Louis., Classic and Dawn)
List, each $4.91
Retail, each . . . 4.00

SUGAR SPOON
List, each . . $1.53
Retail, each . 1.25

JELLY SERVER
List, each . . . $2.15
Retail, each . . 1.75

COLD MEAT FORK
List, large, each . $2.46
Retail, large, each 2.00

LADLES
	List	Retail
Cream, each ..	$2.46	$2.00
Gravy, each ..	3.07	2.50
Soup, H.H., each	6.26	5.00
Punch, H.H., each	7.84	6.25

BABY SET
	List	Retail
Short Handle, per set . . .	$2.46	$2.00

TOMATO SERVER H.H.
List, each $6.67
Retail, each 5.50

BUTTER KNIFE AND SUGAR SHELL
List, per set . . . $3.06
Retail, per set . . 2.50

ALVIN SILVER
Long-Life Plate

THE
DAWN

THE following illustrations show our "Long Life" Quality Plate which will satisfy the most particular customer. It is produced with the same care, skill and attention to details as Sterling silver. Each piece is heavily plated with a uniform weight and thickness of pure silver to resist the hardest wear and insure the longest life.

SPOONS

		List	Retail
Baby, Nursery Rhyme	each	$1.23	$1.00
Baby, Short Handle	each	1.23	1.00
Baby, Curved Handle	each	1.23	1.00
Berry	each	3.99	3.25
Berry, Small (*Louisiana only*)	each	3.38	2.75
Bouillon	set of six	8.87	7.25
Coffee	set of six	4.59	3.75
Dessert	per dozen	18.36	15.00
Ice Cream (*Louisiana and Classic only*)	per dozen	13.52	11.00
Iced Tea	set of six	7.36	6.00
Olive	each	2.15	1.75
Orange or Grapefruit	set of six	6.45	5.25
Salad Serving (*Louisiana, Classic and Dawn*)	each	3.99	3.25
Soup	per dozen	18.36	15.00
Sugar	each	1.53	1.25
Table	per dozen	18.36	15.00
*Tea, 5 o'Clock	per dozen	9.80	8.00
Tea, Regular	per dozen	9.18	7.50

FORKS

		List	Retail
Baby, Nursery Rhyme	each	$1.23	$1.00
Baby, Short Handle	each	1.23	1.00
Child's	each	1.23	1.00
Cold Meat, large	each	2.46	2.00
Cold Meat, medium (*George Washington and Luxor only*)	each	2.15	1.75
Dessert	per dozen	18.36	15.00
Dinner	per dozen	18.36	15.00
Ice Cream (*Classic, Louisiana and Dawn only*)	per dozen	14.72	12.00
Ind. Salad or Pastry	set of six	9.18	7.50
Oyster	set of six	5.82	4.75
Pickle or Olive	each	1.84	1.50
Salad Serving (*Louisiana, Classic and Dawn only*)	each	4.91	4.00

KNIVES

		List	Retail
Butter Knife	each	$1.53	$1.25
Butter Spreaders	set of six	7.68	6.25
Jelly Knife	each	2.15	1.75
Pastry Server, F. H. (*Classic and Louisiana only*)	each	5.22	4.25
Sugar Tongs	each	2.46	2.00
Cucumber or Tomato Server F. H.	each	3.99	3.25

LADLES

		List	Retail
Cream, large	each	$2.46	$2.00
Gravy	each	3.07	2.50
Soup, Hollow Handle	each	6.26	5.00
Punch, Hollow Handle	each	7.84	6.25

HOLLOW HANDLE CUTLERY

		List	Retail
Baby Knife, S. S., Nursery Rhyme	each	$2.15	$1.75
Bread Knife, Hollow Handle	each	5.22	4.25
Cheese Cutter, Hollow Handle S. S.	each	3.38	2.75
Child's Knives, S. S. Blades	each	2.15	1.75
Carving Set, 3 pcs. S. S. Knife and Fork, with Guards	per set	22.94	18.50
Dessert Knives, H.H., S.S.F.B.	per dozen	31.30	24.00
Dinner Knives, H.H., S.S.F.B.	per dozen	31.30	24.00
Fruit Knives, H.H., S.S.	set of six	14.35	11.00
Game Set, 2 pcs. S.S. Knife and Fork, with Guards	per set	16.68	13.50
Game Shears	each	13.04	10.00
Pie Server, Hollow Handle S.S.	each	5.52	4.50
Steak Set, 2 pcs. S.S. Knife and Fork, no Guards	per set	10.74	8.50
Tomato Server or Egg Server, S.S. Blades	each	6.67	5.50

SETS

		List	Retail
Baby, 3 pcs. Nursery Rhyme	per set	$4.60	$3.75
Baby Spoon and Fork, Short Handle	per set	2.46	2.00
Butter Knife and Sugar Spoon	per set	3.06	2.50
Child's, 3 pcs. H.H. Knife S.S. Blades	per set	4.20	3.50
Olive Set, 2 pcs.	per set	4.00	3.25
Salad, Olive Wood Fork and Spoon, H.H.	per set	9.20	7.50
Salad, F.H. (*Classic, Louisiana and Dawn*)	per set	8.90	7.25
6 Dinner Forks, F.H., 6 Knives, H.H.S.S.F. Blades	per set	25.44	19.80
6 Dessert Forks, F.H., 6 Knives, H.H.S.S.F. Blades	per set	25.44	19.80
26-Piece Dinner Size, Knives with S.S.F. Blades		41.70	33.25
26-Piece Dessert Size, Knives with S.S.F. Blades		41.70	33.25

* Not made in the Dawn.

Alvin Mfg. Co.

ALVIN SILVER
Long-Life Plate

THE
DAWN

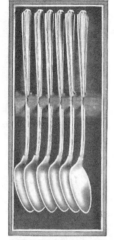

ICED TEA SPOONS
List, per set of six . . . $7.36
Retail, per set of six . . 6.00

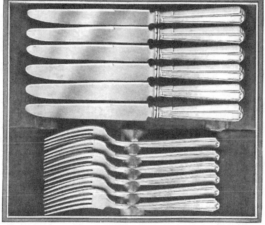

KNIFE AND FORK SET

	List	Retail
6 Dinner Forks, F.H., and Knives, H.H. Stainless Steel Blades, per set	$25.44	$19.80
6 Dessert Forks, F.H., and Knives, H.H. Stainless Steel Blades, per set	25.44	19.80

IND. SALAD FORKS
List, per set of six . . . $9.18
Retail, per set of six . . 7.50

OLIVE SPOON
List, each . . . $2.15
Retail, each . . 1.75

BUTTER KNIFE
List, each . . . $1.53
Retail, each . . 1.25

COFFEE SPOONS
List, per set of six . . . $4.59
Retail, per set of six . . 3.75

PICKLE OR OLIVE FORK
List, each . $1.84
Retail, each 1.50

TOMATO SERVER
Flat Handle, List . $3.99
Retail, each 3.25

SUGAR TONGS
List, each . . . $2.46
Retail, each . . 2.00

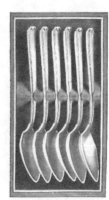

ORANGE OR GRAPE FRUIT SPOONS
List, per set of six . . . $6.45
Retail, per set of six . . 5.25

GEORGE WASHINGTON

FINEST QUALITY **ALVIN** SILVERPLATE

A pattern in the finest quality of silver plate, especially designed for those who desire dignity and restraint in their silver. The lines, being classical, are forever young and in good taste. The design is particularly appropriate for the beautiful, bright finish now so fashionable. Guaranteed to give complete satisfaction without limit of years.

SPOONS

		Retail	List
Baby, Nursery Rhyme	each	$1.00	$1.22
Baby, Short Handle	each	1.00	1.22
Baby, Curved Handle	each	1.00	1.22
Berry	each	3.25	4.00
Bouillon	set of six	7.25	8.87
Coffee	set of six	3.75	4.59
Dessert	per dozen	15.00	18.36
Iced Tea	set of six	6.00	7.36
Olive	each	1.75	2.14
Orange or Grapefruit	set of six	5.25	6.45
Soup	per dozen	15.00	18.36
Sugar	each	1.25	1.54
Table	per dozen	15.00	18.36
Tea, 5 o'clock	per dozen	8.00	9.80
Tea, Regular	per dozen	7.50	9.18

FORKS

Baby, Nursery Rhyme	each	1.00	1.22
Baby, Short Handle	each	1.00	1.22
Child's	each	1.00	1.22
Cold Meat, Large	each	2.00	2.46
Cold Meat, Small	each	1.75	2.15
Dessert	per dozen	15.00	18.36
Dinner	per dozen	15.00	18.36
Ind. Salad or Pastry	set of six	7.50	9.18
Oyster	set of six	4.75	5.82
Pickle or Olive	each	1.50	1.84

KNIVES

All cutlery has Hollow Handles unless otherwise specified.

Baby, Nursery Rhyme	each	1.75	2.14
Bread	each	4.25	5.22
Butter, Flat Handle	each	1.25	1.54
Child's, S. S. Blade	each	1.75	2.14
Dessert, S. S. Blade	per dozen	24.00	31.30
Dessert, Mirror Finished Blade	per dozen	28.00	36.28
Dinner, S. S. Blade	per dozen	24.00	31.30
Dinner, Mirror Finished Blade	per dozen	28.00	36.28
Fruit, S. S. Blade	set of six	11.00	14.35
Salad, Mirror Finished Blade	per dozen	27.00	35.44

LADLES

Cream or Sauce	each	2.00	2.46
Gravy	each	2.50	3.06
Soup, Hollow Handle	each	5.00	6.26
Punch, Hollow Handle	each	6.25	7.84

MISCELLANEOUS

Butter Spreaders	set of six	6.25	7.68
Cheese Server, H. H.	each	2.75	3.38
Cucumber or Tomato Server, Flat Handle	each	3.25	3.98
Game Shears, Hollow Handle	each	10.00	13.04
Jelly Server	each	1.75	2.14
Pie Server, H. H.	each	4.50	5.52
Sugar Tongs	each	2.00	2.46
Tomato or Egg Server, H. H.	each	5.50	6.68

SETS

Baby, 3 pcs., Nursery Rhyme, H. H.	per set	3.75	4.58
Baby Spoon and Fork, Short Handle	per set	2.00	2.44
Butter Knife and Sugar Spoon	per set	2.50	3.08
Child's, 3 pcs., H. H., S. S. Knife	per set	3.50	4.20
Game, 2 pcs., H. H., S. S. with guards	per set	13.50	16.68
Carving, 3 pcs., H. H., S. S. Knife and Fork with guards	per set	18.50	22.94
Olive, 2 pcs.	per set	3.25	3.98
Salad, 2 pcs., Olive Wood, Hollow Handle	per set	7.50	9.20
Steak, 2 pcs., H. H., S. S. with guards	per set	8.50	10.74
26 pcs., Dessert or Dinner size, S. S. Blades	per set	33.25	41.70
With Mirror Finished Blades	per set	35.25	44.18
29 pcs., Dessert or Dinner size, S. S. Blades	per set	33.25	41.70
With Mirror Finished Blades	per set	35.25	44.18
34 pcs., Dessert or Dinner size, S. S. Blades	per set	43.50	54.54
With Mirror Finished Blades	per set	46.25	57.86
50 pcs., Dessert or Dinner size, S. S. Blades	per set	64.00	80.28
With Mirror Finished Blades	per set	68.00	85.26

DESSERT FORK

DESSERT KNIFE

BUTTER SPREADER

TEASPOON

INDIVIDUAL SALAD FORK

1931 Catalog

Alvin Mfg. Co.

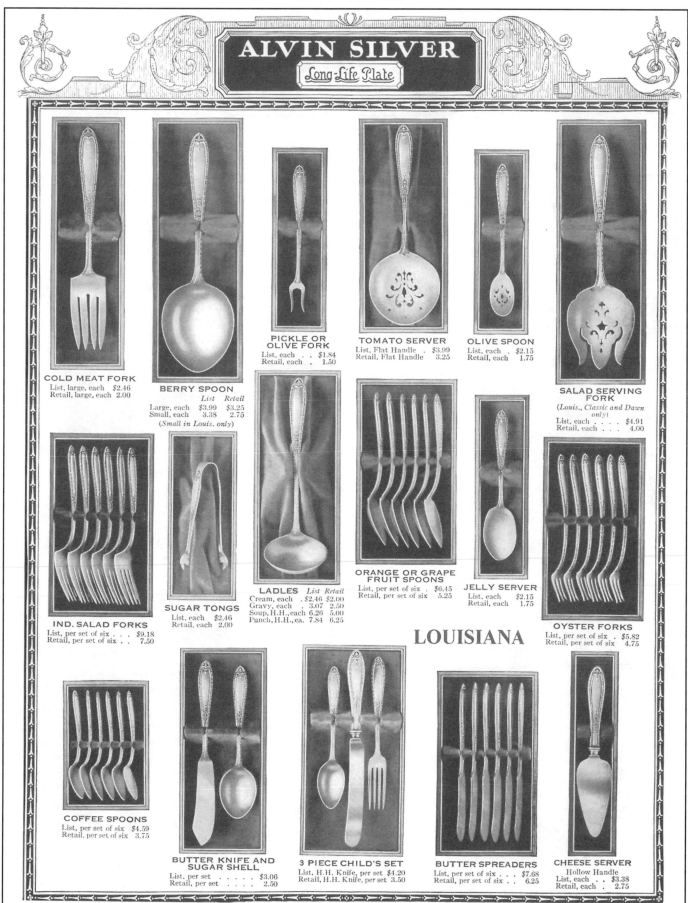

ALVIN SILVER
Long-Life Plate

COLD MEAT FORK
List, large, each $2.46
Retail, large, each 2.00

BERRY SPOON
	List	Retail
Large, each	3.99	3.25
Small, each	3.38	2.75
(Small in Louis. only)

PICKLE OR OLIVE FORK
List, each . . $1.84
Retail, each . 1.50

TOMATO SERVER
List, Flat Handle . $3.99
Retail, Flat Handle 3.25

OLIVE SPOON
List, each . $2.15
Retail, each 1.75

SALAD SERVING FORK
(*Louis., Classic and Dawn only*)
List, each $4.91
Retail, each . . . 4.00

IND. SALAD FORKS
List, per set of six . . . $9.18
Retail, per set of six . . 7.50

SUGAR TONGS
List, each $2.46
Retail, each 2.00

LADLES *List Retail*
Cream, each . $2.46 $2.00
Gravy, each . 3.07 2.50
Soup, H.H., each 6.26 5.00
Punch, H.H., ea. 7.84 6.25

ORANGE OR GRAPE FRUIT SPOONS
List, per set of six . $6.45
Retail, per set of six 5.25

JELLY SERVER
List, each . $2.15
Retail, each 1.75

OYSTER FORKS
List, per set of six . $5.82
Retail, per set of six 4.75

LOUISIANA

COFFEE SPOONS
List, per set of six $4.59
Retail, per set of six 3.75

BUTTER KNIFE AND SUGAR SHELL
List, per set $3.06
Retail, per set 2.50

3 PIECE CHILD'S SET
List, H.H. Knife, per set $4.20
Retail, H.H. Knife, per set 3.50

BUTTER SPREADERS
List, per set of six . . . $7.68
Retail, per set of six . . 6.25

CHEESE SERVER
Hollow Handle
List, each . . $3.38
Retail, each . 2.75

1930 Catalog

See Price Guide — Group 3

ALVIN SILVER
Long-Life Plate

LOUISIANA
GRAY FINISH

THE following illustrations show our "Long Life" Quality Plate which will satisfy the most particular customer. It is produced with the same care, skill and attention to details as Sterling silver. Each piece is heavily plated with a uniform weight and thickness of pure silver to resist the hardest wear and insure the longest life.

SPOONS

		List	Retail
Baby, Nursery Rhyme	each	$1.23	$1.00
Baby, Short Handle	each	1.23	1.00
Baby, Curved Handle	each	3.99	3.25
Berry	each	3.38	2.75
Berry, Small (*Louisiana only*)	each	8.87	7.25
Bouillon	set of six	4.59	3.75
Coffee	per dozen	18.36	15.00
Dessert	per dozen	13.52	11.00
Ice Cream (*Louisiana and Classic only*)	set of six	7.36	6.00
Iced Tea	each	2.15	1.75
Olive	set of six	6.45	5.25
Orange or Grapefruit	each	3.99	3.25
Salad Serving (*Louisiana, Classic and Dawn*)	per dozen	18.36	15.00
Soup	each	1.53	1.25
Sugar	per dozen	18.36	15.00
Table	per dozen	9.80	8.00
*Tea, 5 o'Clock	per dozen	9.18	7.50
Tea, Regular			

FORKS

Baby, Nursery Rhyme	each	$1.23	$1.00
Baby, Short Handle	each	1.23	1.00
Child's	each	1.23	1.00
Cold Meat, large	each	2.46	2.00
Cold Meat, medium (*George Washington and Luxor only*)	each	2.15	1.75
Dessert	per dozen	18.36	15.00
Dinner	per dozen	18.36	15.00
Ice Cream (*Classic, Louisiana and Dawn only*)	per dozen	14.72	12.00
Ind. Salad or Pastry	set of six	9.18	7.50
Oyster	set of six	5.82	4.75
Pickle or Olive	each	1.84	1.50
Salad Serving (*Louisiana, Classic and Dawn only*)	each	4.91	4.00

KNIVES

Butter Knife	each	$1.53	$1.25
Butter Spreaders	set of six	7.68	6.25
Jelly Knife	each	2.15	1.75
Pastry Server, F. H. (*Classic and Louisiana only*)	each	5.22	4.25
Sugar Tongs	each	2.46	2.00
Cucumber or Tomato Server F. H.	each	3.99	3.25

LADLES

Cream, large	each	$2.46	$2.00
Gravy	each	3.07	2.50
Soup, Hollow Handle	each	6.26	5.00
Punch, Hollow Handle	each	7.84	6.25

HOLLOW HANDLE CUTLERY

Baby Knife, S. S., Nursery Rhyme	each	$2.15	$1.75
Bread Knife, Hollow Handle	each	5.22	4.25
Cheese Cutter, Hollow Handle S. S.	each	3.38	2.75
Child's Knives, S. S. Blades	each	2.15	1.75
Carving Set, 3 pcs. S. S. Knife and Fork, with Guards	per set	22.94	18.50
Dessert Knives, H.H., S.S.F.B.	per dozen	31.30	24.00
Dinner Knives, H.H., S.S.F.B.	per dozen	31.30	24.00
Fruit Knives, H.H., S.S.	set of six	14.35	11.00
Game Set, 2 pcs. S.S. Knife and Fork, with Guards	per set	16.68	13.50
Game Shears	each	13.04	10.00
Pie Server, Hollow Handle S.S.	each	5.52	4.50
Steak Set, 2 pcs. S.S. Knife and Fork, no Guards	per set	10.74	8.50
Tomato Server or Egg Server, S.S. Blades	each	6.67	5.50

SETS

Baby, 3 pcs. Nursery Rhyme	per set	$4.60	$3.75
Baby Spoon and Fork, Short Handle	per set	2.46	2.00
Butter Knife and Sugar Spoon	per set	3.06	2.50
Child's, 3 pcs. H.H. Knife S.S. Blades	per set	4.20	3.50
Olive Set, 2 pcs.	per set	4.00	3.25
Salad, Olive Wood Fork and Spoon, H.H.	per set	9.20	7.50
Salad, F.H. (*Classic, Louisiana and Dawn*)	per set	8.90	7.25
6 Dinner Forks, F.H., 6 Knives, H.H.S.S.F. Blades	per set	25.44	19.80
6 Dessert Forks, F.H., 6 Knives, H.H.S.S.F. Blades	per set	25.44	19.80
26-Piece Dinner Size, Knives with S.S.F. Blades		41.70	33.25
26-Piece Dessert Size, Knives with S.S.F. Blades		41.70	33.25

* Not made in the Dawn.

ALVIN

LUXOR

Here is a pattern that might have excited the admiration of a sculptor of ancient Greece. The purity of line, the delicacy of ornamentation, the feeling of balance of harmony backed by master craftsmanship in silversmithing, have made LUXOR one of America's most popular patterns in silver plated flatware. Its soft gray finish adds that final touch sure to please the most discriminating hostess. Guaranteed to give entire satisfaction without limit of years.

SPOONS

		Retail	List
Baby, Nursery Rhyme	each	$1.00	$1.22
Baby, Short Handle	each	1.00	1.22
Baby, Curved Handle	each	1.00	1.22
Berry	each	3.25	4.00
Bouillon	set of six	7.25	8.87
Coffee	set of six	3.75	4.59
Dessert	per dozen	**15.00**	**18.36**
Iced Tea	set of six	6.00	7.36
Olive	each	1.75	2.14
Orange or Grapefruit	set of six	5.25	6.45
Soup	per dozen	**15.00**	**18.36**
Sugar	each	1.25	1.54
Table	per dozen	**15.00**	**18.36**
Tea, 5 o'clock	per dozen	8.00	9.80
Tea, Regular	per dozen	**7.50**	**9.18**

FORKS

Baby, Nursery Rhyme	each	1.00	1.22
Baby, Short Handle	each	1.00	1.22
Child's	each	1.00	1.22
Cold Meat, Large	each	**2.00**	**2.46**
Cold Meat, Small	each	1.75	2.15
Dessert	per dozen	**15.00**	**18.36**
Dinner	per dozen	**15.00**	**18.36**
Ind. Salad or Pastry	set of six	7.50	9.18
Oyster	set of six	4.75	5.82
Pickle or Olive	each	1.50	1.84

KNIVES

All cutlery has Hollow Handles unless otherwise specified.

Baby, Nursery Rhyme	each	1.75	2.14
Bread	each	4.25	5.22
Butter, Flat Handle	each	**1.25**	**1.54**
Child's, S. S. Blade	each	1.75	2.14
Dessert, S. S. Blade	per dozen	**24.00**	**31.30**
Dessert, Mirror Finished Blade	per dozen	28.00	36.28
Dinner, S. S. Blade	per dozen	**24.00**	**31.30**
Dinner, Mirror Finished Blade	per dozen	28.00	36.28
Fruit, S. S. Blade	set of six	11.00	14.35
Salad, Mirror Finished Blade	per dozen	27.00	35.44

LADLES

Cream or Sauce	each	2.00	2.46
Gravy	each	**2.50**	**3.06**
Soup, Hollow Handle	each	5.00	6.26
Punch, Hollow Handle	each	6.25	7.84

MISCELLANEOUS

Butter Spreaders	set of six	**6.25**	**7.68**
Cheese Server, H. H.	each	2.75	3.38
Cucumber or Tomato Server, Flat Handle	each	3.25	3.98
Game Shears, Hollow Handle	each	10.00	13.04
Jelly Server	each	1.75	2.14
Pie Server, H. H.	each	4.50	5.52
Sugar Tongs	each	2.00	2.46
Tomato or Egg Server, H. H.	each	5.50	6.68

SETS

Baby, 3 pcs., Nursery Rhyme, H. H.	per set	3.75	4.58
Baby Fork and Spoon, Short Handle	per set	2.00	2.44
Butter Knife and Sugar Spoon		2.50	3.08
Child's, 3 pcs., H. H., S. S. Knife	per set	3.50	4.20
Game, 2 pcs., H. H., S. S. with guards	per set	13.50	16.68
Carving, 3 pcs., H. H., S. S. Knife and Fork with guards	per set	18.50	22.94
Olive, 2 pcs.	per set	3.25	3.98
Salad, 2 pcs., Olive Wood, H. H.	per set	7.50	9.20
Steak, 2 pcs., H. H., S. S. with guards	per set	8.50	10.74
26 pcs., Dessert or Dinner size, S. S. Blades	per set	33.25	41.70
With Mirror Finished Blades	per set	35.25	44.18
29 pcs., Dessert or Dinner size, S. S. Blades	per set	33.25	41.70
With Mirror Finished Blades	per set	35.25	44.18
34 pcs., Dessert or Dinner size, S. S. Blades	per set	43.50	54.54
With Mirror Finished Blades	per set	46.25	57.86
50 pcs., Dessert or Dinner size, S. S. Blades	per set	64.00	80.28
With Mirror Finished Blades	per set	68.00	85.26

1931 Catalog

See Price Guide — Group 3

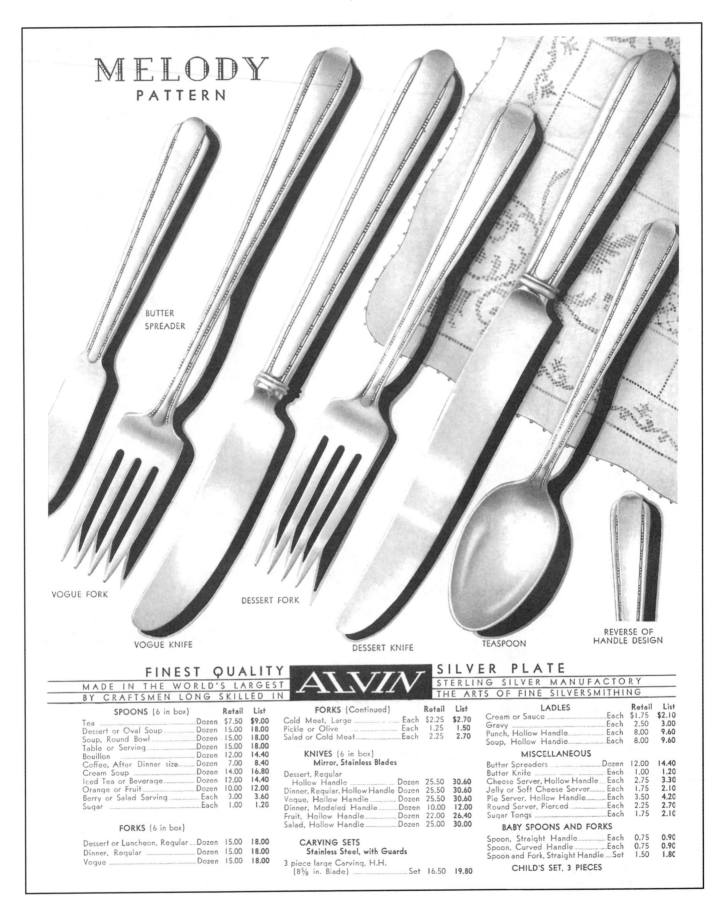

MELODY PATTERN

BUTTER SPREADER

VOGUE FORK

VOGUE KNIFE

DESSERT FORK

DESSERT KNIFE

TEASPOON

REVERSE OF HANDLE DESIGN

FINEST QUALITY ALVIN SILVER PLATE

MADE IN THE WORLD'S LARGEST — STERLING SILVER MANUFACTORY
BY CRAFTSMEN LONG SKILLED IN — THE ARTS OF FINE SILVERSMITHING

SPOONS (6 in box)		Retail	List
Tea	Dozen	$7.50	$9.00
Dessert or Oval Soup	Dozen	15.00	18.00
Soup, Round Bowl	Dozen	15.00	18.00
Table or Serving	Dozen	15.00	18.00
Bouillon	Dozen	12.00	14.40
Coffee, After Dinner size	Dozen	7.00	8.40
Cream Soup	Dozen	14.00	16.80
Iced Tea or Beverage	Dozen	12.00	14.40
Orange or Fruit	Dozen	10.00	12.00
Berry or Salad Serving	Each	3.00	3.60
Sugar	Each	1.00	1.20

FORKS (6 in box)		Retail	List
Dessert or Luncheon, Regular	Dozen	15.00	18.00
Dinner, Regular	Dozen	15.00	18.00
Vogue	Dozen	15.00	18.00

FORKS (Continued)		Retail	List
Cold Meat, Large	Each	$2.25	$2.70
Pickle or Olive	Each	1.25	1.50
Salad or Cold Meat	Each	2.25	2.70

KNIVES (6 in box)
Mirror, Stainless Blades

Dessert, Regular			
Hollow Handle	Dozen	25.50	30.60
Dinner, Regular, Hollow Handle	Dozen	25.50	30.60
Vogue, Hollow Handle	Dozen	25.50	30.60
Dinner, Modeled Handle	Dozen	10.00	12.00
Fruit, Hollow Handle	Dozen	22.00	26.40
Salad, Hollow Handle	Dozen	25.00	30.00

CARVING SETS
Stainless Steel, with Guards

3 piece large Carving, H.H.			
(8⅝ in. Blade)	Set	16.50	19.80

LADLES		Retail	List
Cream or Sauce	Each	$1.75	$2.10
Gravy	Each	2.50	3.00
Punch, Hollow Handle	Each	8.00	9.60
Soup, Hollow Handle	Each	8.00	9.60

MISCELLANEOUS			
Butter Spreaders	Dozen	12.00	14.40
Butter Knife	Each	1.00	1.20
Cheese Server, Hollow Handle	Each	2.75	3.30
Jelly or Soft Cheese Server	Each	1.75	2.10
Pie Server, Hollow Handle	Each	3.50	4.20
Round Server, Pierced	Each	2.25	2.70
Sugar Tongs	Each	1.75	2.10

BABY SPOONS AND FORKS			
Spoon, Straight Handle	Each	0.75	0.90
Spoon, Curved Handle	Each	0.75	0.90
Spoon and Fork, Straight Handle	Set	1.50	1.80

CHILD'S SET, 3 PIECES

1936 Catalog

American Silver Company

Moselle Pattern

Moselle is the queen of all American grape patterns and it is possibly the most desired of all silverplate patterns. The American Silver Company produced the wonderful design and it was patented in 1906. Grape motifs were the rage during this period and American glass companies produced many grape patterns that coordinated with Moselle. This pattern was offered in two qualities, and many items could also be purchased with a gilded bowl. Lee Roy and Nan Fisher have collected Moselle since the 1960s and the pieces photographed are from their set. Two items they do not have are the little bonbon and the individual ice cream forks. They have seen the bonbon but were unable to purchase it. The orange/citrus spoons came both with and without the fancy bowl. There are at least two salad serving spoons, one is 8¾", the other is 8½" (illustrated). The motif in the bowl part is different on these two. Also ranking as rarities are the mustard spoon (ladle), ice teas, and hollow handle cheese scoop.

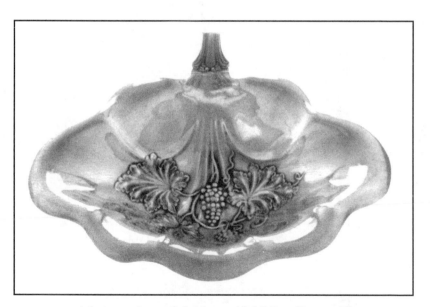

A better view of the beautiful Moselle motif.

Backstamp of American Silver Company pieces.

See Price Guide — Group 1

Left to right: 7" gravy ladle, 14⅕" punch ladle, 6³⁄₁₀" cream ladle.

Left to right: 7½" dinner fork, 6" teaspoon, 5¾" mustard ladle, 4⅞" 5 o'clock coffee spoon, 9⁹⁄₁₀" hollow handle dinner knife with replaced stainless steel blunt blade, 8⅕" tablespoon. Bottom: 4¼" sugar tongs.

Moselle Pattern

Top left to right: 6⁹⁄₁₀" cream soup, 4½" gilded demi-tasse spoon, 7⅕" ice tea spoon. Bottom left to right: 4⅝" bouillon spoon, 3" individual salt spoon, 6" orange/citrus spoon.

Moselle Pattern

Left to right: 12" x 4½" soup ladle, 6⅛" sugar shell, 10½" oyster ladle.

See Price Guide — Group 1

Moselle Pattern

Left to right: 8⁷⁄₁₀" salad serving spoon, 9¹⁄₁₀" salad serving fork, 7⅞" preserve serving spoon.

Left to right: 8⅕" long handle pickle fork, 5¾" individual butter spreader, 6⅝" hollow handle individual fruit knife, 7½" hollow handle individual orange knife, 7⅘" cold meat fork.

Moselle Pattern

Left to right: 7⁷⁄₁₀" tomato/cucumber server, 5⁵⁄₈" sardine serving fork, 7⁷⁄₈" cake serving fork, 8³⁄₁₀" jelly knife server.

Moselle Pattern

Left to right: 6⅜" salad fork, 5⁵⁄₁₆" oyster cocktail fork, 4¾" berry fork, 7¾" hollow handle dinner fork, 7" pastry fork with cutting tine.

See Price Guide — Group 1

Community Silver

Adam Pattern

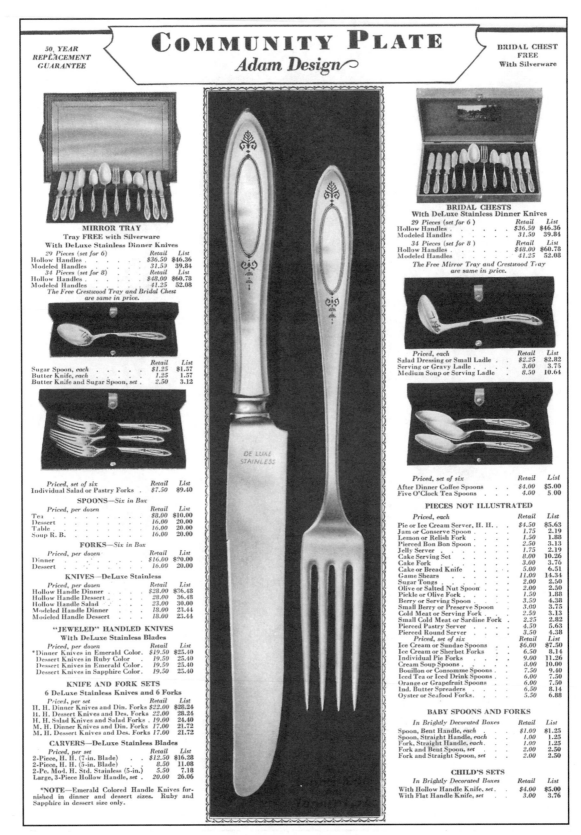

COMMUNITY PLATE
Adam Design

50, YEAR
REPLACEMENT
GUARANTEE

BRIDAL CHEST
FREE
With Silverware

MIRROR TRAY
Tray FREE with Silverware
With DeLuxe Stainless Dinner Knives

29 Pieces (set for 6)	Retail	List
Hollow Handles	$36.50	$46.36
Modeled Handles	31.50	39.84
34 Pieces (set for 8)	Retail	List
Hollow Handles	$48.00	$60.78
Modeled Handles	41.25	52.08

The Free Crestwood Tray and Bridal Chest are same in price.

	Retail	List
Sugar Spoon, *each*	$1.25	$1.57
Butter Knife, *each*	1.25	1.57
Butter Knife and Sugar Spoon, set	2.50	3.12

Priced, set of six	Retail	List
Individual Salad or Pastry Forks	$7.50	$9.40

SPOONS—Six in Box
Priced, per dozen	Retail	List
Tea	$8.00	$10.00
Dessert	16.00	20.00
Table	16.00	20.00
Soup R. B.	16.00	20.00

FORKS—Six in Box
Priced, per dozen	Retail	List
Dinner	$16.00	$20.00
Dessert	16.00	20.00

KNIVES—DeLuxe Stainless
Priced, per dozen	Retail	List
Hollow Handle Dinner	$28.00	$36.48
Hollow Handle Dessert	28.00	36.48
Hollow Handle Salad	23.00	30.00
Modeled Handle Dinner	18.00	23.44
Modeled Handle Dessert	18.00	23.44

"JEWELED" HANDLED KNIVES
With DeLuxe Stainless Blades
Priced, per dozen	Retail	List
*Dinner Knives in Emerald Color.	$19.50	$25.40
Dessert Knives in Ruby Color	19.50	25.40
Dessert Knives in Emerald Color.	19.50	25.40
Dessert Knives in Sapphire Color.	19.50	25.40

KNIFE AND FORK SETS
6 DeLuxe Stainless Knives and 6 Forks
Priced, per set	Retail	List
H. H. Dinner Knives and Din. Forks	$22.00	$28.24
H. H. Dessert Knives and Des. Forks	22.00	28.24
H. H. Salad Knives and Salad Forks	19.00	24.40
M. H. Dinner Knives and Din. Forks	17.00	21.72
M. H. Dessert Knives and Des. Forks	17.00	21.72

CARVERS—DeLuxe Stainless Blades
Priced, per set	Retail	List
2-Piece, H. H. (7-in. Blade)	$12.50	$16.28
2-Piece, H. H. (5-in. Blade)	8.50	11.08
2-Pc. Mod. H. Std. Stainless (5-in.)	5.50	7.18
Large, 3-Piece Hollow Handle, set	20.00	26.06

NOTE—Emerald Colored Handle Knives furnished in dinner and dessert sizes. Ruby and Sapphire in dessert size only.

DE LUXE
STAINLESS

BRIDAL CHESTS
With DeLuxe Stainless Dinner Knives

29 Pieces (set for 6)	Retail	List
Hollow Handles	$36.50	$46.36
Modeled Handles	31.50	39.84
34 Pieces (set for 8)	Retail	List
Hollow Handles	$48.00	$60.78
Modeled Handles	41.25	52.08

The Free Mirror Tray and Crestwood Tray are same in price.

Priced, each	Retail	List
Salad Dressing or Small Ladle	$2.25	$2.82
Serving or Gravy Ladle	3.00	3.75
Medium Soup or Serving Ladle	8.50	10.64

Priced, set of six	Retail	List
After Dinner Coffee Spoons	$4.00	$5.00
Five O'Clock Tea Spoons	4.00	5.00

PIECES NOT ILLUSTRATED
Priced, each	Retail	List
Pie or Ice Cream Server, H. H.	$4.50	$5.63
Jam or Conserve Spoon	1.75	2.19
Lemon or Relish Fork	1.50	1.88
Pierced Bon Bon Spoon	2.50	3.13
Jelly Server	1.75	2.19
Cake Serving Set	8.00	10.26
Cake Fork	3.00	3.76
Cake or Bread Knife	5.00	6.51
Game Shears	11.00	14.34
Sugar Tongs	2.00	2.50
Olive or Salted Nut Spoon	2.00	2.50
Pickle or Olive Fork	1.50	1.88
Berry or Serving Spoon	3.50	4.38
Small Berry or Preserve Spoon	3.00	3.75
Cold Meat or Serving Fork	2.50	3.13
Small Cold Meat or Sardine Fork	2.25	2.82
Pierced Pastry Server	4.50	5.63
Pierced Round Server	3.50	4.38

Priced, set of six	Retail	List
Ice Cream or Sundae Spoons	$6.00	$7.50
Ice Cream or Sherbet Forks	6.50	8.14
Individual Pie Forks	9.00	11.26
Cream Soup Spoons	8.00	10.00
Bouillon or Consomme Spoons	7.50	9.40
Iced Tea or Iced Drink Spoons	6.00	7.50
Orange or Grapefruit Spoons	6.00	7.50
Ind. Butter Spreaders	6.50	8.14
Oyster or Seafood Forks	5.50	6.88

BABY SPOONS AND FORKS
In Brightly Decorated Boxes	Retail	List
Spoon, Bent Handle, *each*	$1.00	$1.25
Spoon, Straight Handle, *each*	1.00	1.25
Fork, Straight Handle, *each*	1.00	1.25
Fork and Bent Spoon, set	2.00	2.50
Fork and Straight Spoon, set	2.00	2.50

CHILD'S SETS
In Brightly Decorated Boxes	Retail	List
With Hollow Handle Knife, set.	$4.00	$5.00
With Flat Handle Knife, set	3.00	3.76

1930 Catalog

Left to right: 8⅜" pastry serving fork, 6³⁄₁₆" individual salad fork, 7½" ice tea spoon, 10" hollow handle carving fork, 12¼" hollow handle carving knife. By 1930 Adam hollow ware had been discontinued.

Adam Pattern

Left to right: 11½" hollow handle, plated blade bread knife, 6¼" individual butter spreader, 6¼" individual butter spreader, 6¹⁄₁₆" sugar server, 7⅛" gravy server, 10⁵⁄₁₆" pie server. Patented 1917.

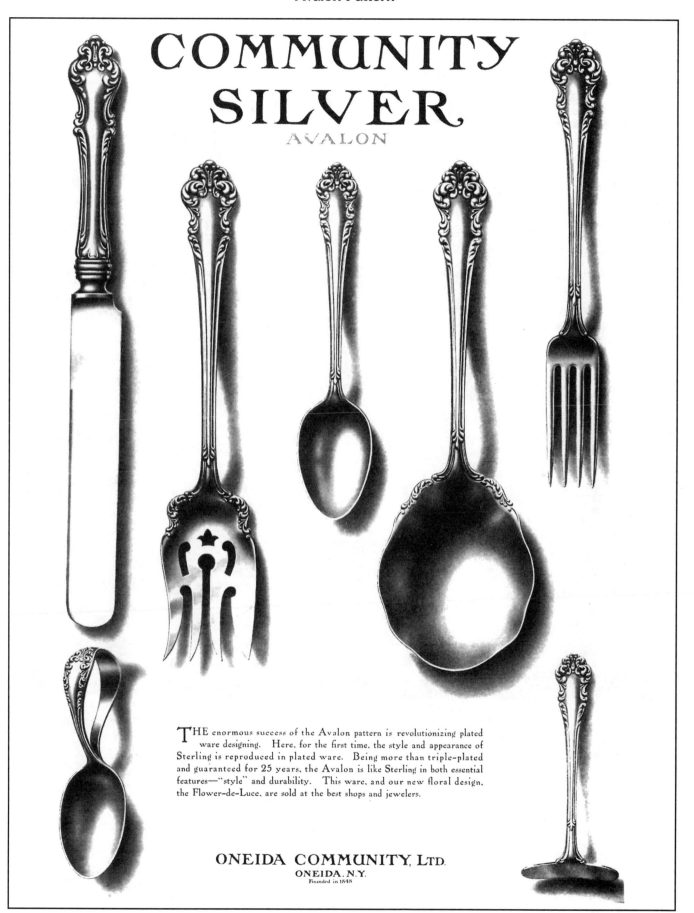

COMMUNITY SILVER

AVALON

T HE enormous success of the Avalon pattern is revolutionizing plated ware designing. Here, for the first time, the style and appearance of Sterling is reproduced in plated ware. Being more than triple-plated and guaranteed for 25 years, the Avalon is like Sterling in both essential features—"style" and durability. This ware, and our new floral design, the Flower-de-Luce, are sold at the best shops and jewelers.

ONEIDA COMMUNITY, LTD.
ONEIDA, N.Y.
Founded in 1848

'Ballad'* IN COMMUNITY*
The Finest Silverplate

Ballad brings a touch of brilliant elegance in an era of gracious living. In complete harmony with Ballad flatware, each piece carries the beautiful Ballad design-motif. Luxurious and timely, in keeping with today's trend in home appointments.

TEA AND COFFEE SERVICES	Consumer	List
25611 4-Piece Tea and Coffee Set...........	$115.00	$138.00
(Tea, Coffee, Sugar, Cream)		
25603 3-Piece Tea Set (Tea, Sugar, Cream)....	77.50	93.00
25607 3-Piece Coffee Set..................	77.50	93.00
(Coffee, Sugar, Cream)		

INDIVIDUAL ITEMS	Consumer	List
25010 Tea Pot, Capacity 8 Cups.............	$37.50	$45.00
(Insulated Handle)		
25020 Coffee Pot, Capacity 9 Cups..........	37.50	45.00
(Insulated Handle)		
25060 Sugar Bowl, with Cover..............	22.00	26.40
25070 Cream Pitcher, Gold Lined...........	18.00	21.60
25600 Sugar Bowl and Cream Pitcher Set.....	40.00	48.00
252120 Oblong Tray or Waiter, Length 20 ins.	35.00	42.00

1958 Catalog

Ballad Pattern

25031 Beverage Pitcher . . . Ideal for serving beverages on any occasion, perfect pouring lip with ice guard. Capacity 2 quarts. Each $35.00

25500 2-Light Candelabrum . . . Perfect for mantel and dinner table. Height 5 7/16 inches. Spread 9 1/4 inches. Each $13.50

SPECIAL REINFORCEMENT . . . In addition to Balanced Plating, 15 of the most-used Community Spoons and Forks are scientifically reinforced with a pure silver overlay where the bowl or tines rest on the table. The pieces so reinforced are:

A. D. Coffee Spoon	Table Spoon	Grille Fork
5 O'clock Tea Spoon	Round Bowl Soup Spoon	Dessert Fork
Teaspoon	Iced Drink Spoon	Oyster Fork
Cream Soup Spoon	Sugar Spoon	Cold Meat Fork
Dessert Spoon	Dinner Fork	Salad Fork

No other manufacturer reinforces so many pieces.

SCIENTIFIC TEMPER, HARD SURFACES . . .

Light-weight silverware, or silverware not made by scientific methods, may bend in use—or may nick and scratch too easily. Fork tines in particular are likely to bend—and spoon bowls become dented.

Community pieces are correctly tempered in the most up-to-date, especially built furnaces so that they are—*Strong* to resist bending and denting—and *Hard*, to resist cuts, nicks and scratches.

Every piece of Community, even the most dainty and delicate of patterns, is strong enough to be used every day—for a lifetime.

25140 Community Double Vegetable Dish . . . Ballad Design Length 12 3/4inches. Each $30.00

25501 3-Light Candelabrum . . .A rich decorative accent for living or dining area. Height 6 inches, Spread 9 1/4 inches. Each $15.00

1958 Catalog

See Price Guide — Group 2

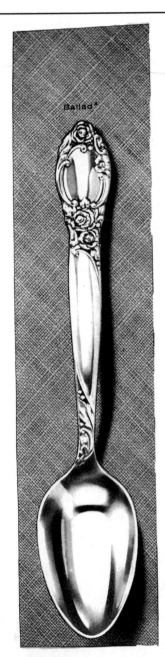

Ballad*

Ballad

25 08/B **Buffet Server,** With Hardwood Well and Tree Carving Board.
Length 20 inches.   Retail...**$45.00**

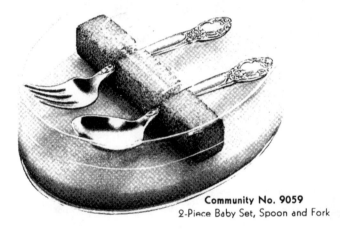

Community No. 9059
2-Piece Baby Set, Spoon and Fork

Ballad

25 13 **Sauce Bowl and Tray**
Capacity 14 ounces. Length of Tray 10 inches.
Retail...**$25.00**

25801 Ballad Child's Cup
Consumer...**$3.75**

Ballad Pattern

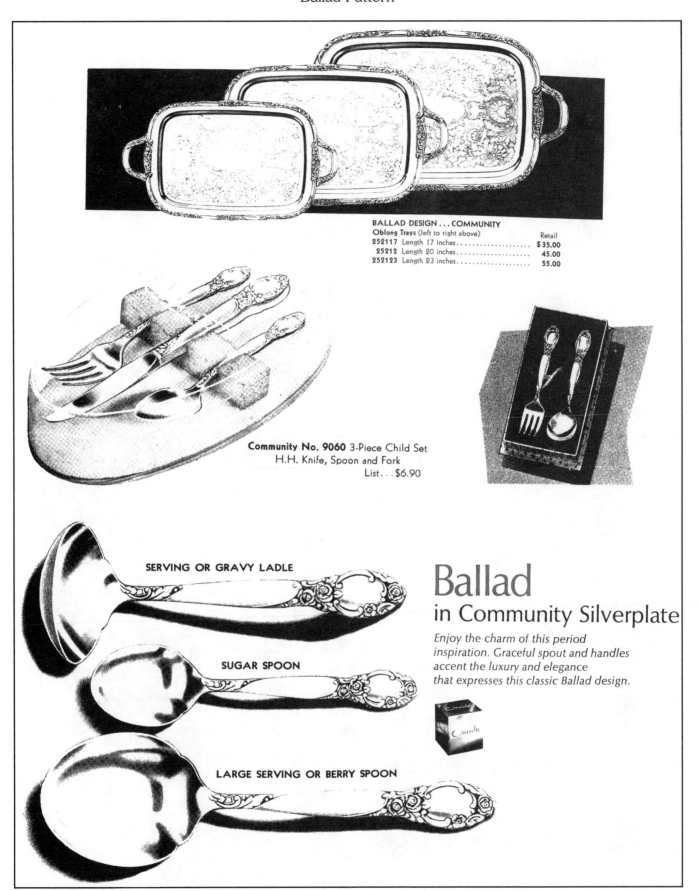

BALLAD DESIGN . . . COMMUNITY

Oblong Trays (left to right above)

		Retail
252117	Length 17 inches	$35.00
25212	Length 20 inches	45.00
252123	Length 23 inches	55.00

Community No. 9060 3-Piece Child Set
H.H. Knife, Spoon and Fork
List . . . $6.90

SERVING OR GRAVY LADLE

SUGAR SPOON

LARGE SERVING OR BERRY SPOON

Ballad
in Community Silverplate

Enjoy the charm of this period inspiration. Graceful spout and handles accent the luxury and elegance that expresses this classic Ballad design.

1958 Catalog

Berkeley Square Pattern

1936 Catalog

Bird of Paradise Pattern

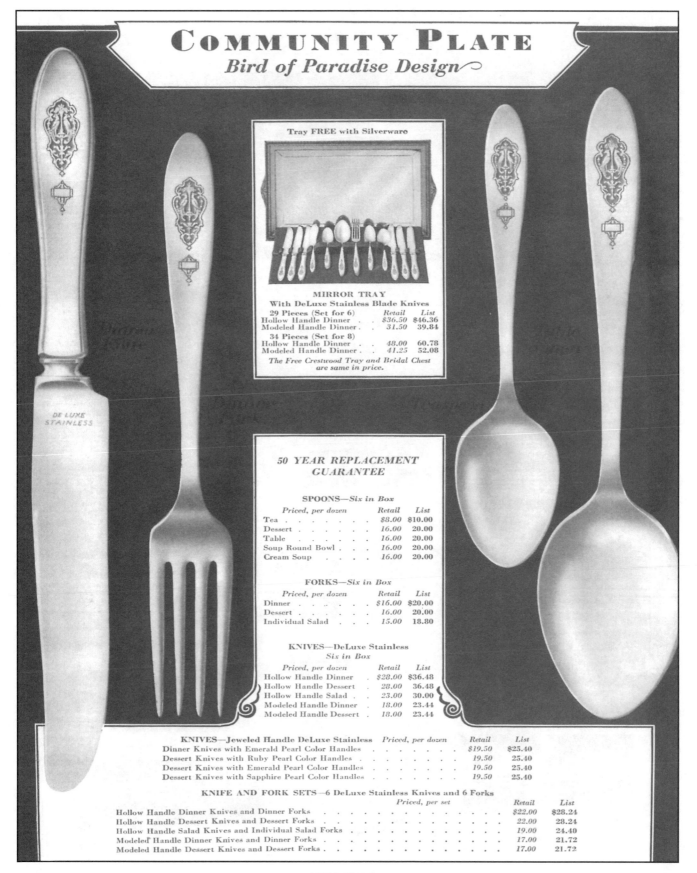

COMMUNITY PLATE
Bird of Paradise Design

Tray FREE with Silverware

MIRROR TRAY
With DeLuxe Stainless Blade Knives

29 Pieces (Set for 6)	Retail	List
Hollow Handle Dinner	$36.50	$46.36
Modeled Handle Dinner	31.50	39.84
34 Pieces (Set for 8)		
Hollow Handle Dinner	48.00	60.78
Modeled Handle Dinner	41.25	52.08

*The Free Crestwood Tray and Bridal Chest
are same in price.*

50 YEAR REPLACEMENT GUARANTEE

SPOONS—Six in Box

Priced, per dozen	Retail	List
Tea	$8.00	$10.00
Dessert	16.00	20.00
Table	16.00	20.00
Soup Round Bowl	16.00	20.00
Cream Soup	16.00	20.00

FORKS—Six in Box

Priced, per dozen	Retail	List
Dinner	$16.00	$20.00
Dessert	16.00	20.00
Individual Salad	15.00	18.80

KNIVES—DeLuxe Stainless
Six in Box

Priced, per dozen	Retail	List
Hollow Handle Dinner	$28.00	$36.48
Hollow Handle Dessert	28.00	36.48
Hollow Handle Salad	23.00	30.00
Modeled Handle Dinner	18.00	23.44
Modeled Handle Dessert	18.00	23.44

KNIVES—Jeweled Handle DeLuxe Stainless Priced, per dozen

	Retail	List
Dinner Knives with Emerald Pearl Color Handles	$19.50	$25.40
Dessert Knives with Ruby Pearl Color Handles	19.50	25.40
Dessert Knives with Emerald Pearl Color Handles	19.50	25.40
Dessert Knives with Sapphire Pearl Color Handles	19.50	25.40

KNIFE AND FORK SETS—6 DeLuxe Stainless Knives and 6 Forks

Priced, per set	Retail	List
Hollow Handle Dinner Knives and Dinner Forks	$22.00	$28.24
Hollow Handle Dessert Knives and Dessert Forks	22.00	28.24
Hollow Handle Salad Knives and Individual Salad Forks	19.00	24.40
Modeled Handle Dinner Knives and Dinner Forks	17.00	21.72
Modeled Handle Dessert Knives and Dessert Forks	17.00	21.72

DE LUXE STAINLESS

1931 Catalog

See Price Guide — Group 2

COMMUNITY PLATE
Bird of Paradise Design

Priced, each   *Retail*   *List*
Sugar Spoon $1.25 $1.57

Priced, each   *Retail*   *List*
Berry or Serving Spoon $3.50 $4.38
Small Berry or Preserve Spoon . . 3.00   3.75

Priced, set of six   *Retail*   *List*
Individual Salad or Pastry Forks $7.50 $9.40

Butter Knife, *each* $1.25 $1.57
Butter Knife and Sugar Spoon, *set* 2.50   3.12

Priced, each   *Retail*   *List*
Cold Meat or Serving Fork . . $2.50 $3.13
Small Cold Meat or Sardine Fork 2.25   2.82

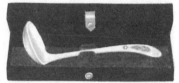

Priced, each   *Retail*   *List*
Salad Dressing or Small Ladle $2.25 $2.82
Serving or Gravy Ladle . . . 3.00   3.75
Medium Soup or Serving Ladle 8.50   10.64

Priced, set of six   *Retail*   *List*
Oyster or Seafood Forks . . $5.50 $6.88

BABY SPOONS AND FORKS
In Brightly Decorated Boxes   *Retail*   *List*
Spoon, Bent Handle *each* . . . $1.00 $1.25
Spoon, Straight Handle, *each* . . 1.00   1.25
Fork, Straight Handle *each* . . 1.00   1.25
Fork and Bent Spoon, *set* . . 2.00   2.50
Fork and Straight Spoon, *set* . . 2.00   2.50

Priced, set of six   *Retail*   *List*
Bouillon or Consomme Spoons $7.50 $9.40

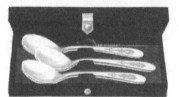

Priced, set of six   *Retail*   *List*
Cream Soup Spoons . . . $8.00 $10.00

CHILD'S SETS
In Brightly Decorated Boxes   *Retail*   *List*
With Hollow Handle Knife, set . . $4.00 $5.00
With Flat Handle Knife, set . . 3.00   3.76

Priced, set of six   *Retail*   *List*
Ind. Butter Spreaders . . . $6.50 $8.14

Priced. each   *Retail*   *List*
Pickle or Olive Fork . . $1.50 $1.88

CARVERS
De Luxe Stainless Blades
        Retail   *List*
2-Piece, Hollow Handle (7-inch Blade), set . $12.50 $16.28
2-Piece, Hollow Handle (5-inch Blade), set . 8.50   11.08
2-Pc. Mdld. Hdle. Standard Stainless (5-in. Blade), set 5.50   7.13
Large, 3-Piece Hollow Handle, set 20.00   26.06
De Luxe Knife Sharpener, each 2.75   3.58

Priced, each   *Retail*   *List*
Olive or Salted Nut Spoon $2.00 $2.50

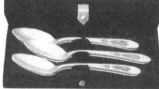

Priced, set of six   *Retail*   *List*
After Dinner Coffee Spoons . $4.00 $5.00
Five O'Clock Tea Spoons . 4.00   5.00

PIECES NOT ILLUSTRATED
Priced, each   *Retail*   *List*
Pie or Ice Cream Server, H.H., $4.50 $5.63
Cheese Server, H. H. . . , 3.00   3.75
Jam or Conserve Spoon . . 1.75   2.19
Lemon or Relish Fork . . 1.50   1.88
Pierced Bon Bon Spoon . . 2.50   3.13
Jelly Server 1.75   2.19
Cake Serving Set . . . 8.00   10.26
Cake Fork 3.00   3.76
Cake or Bread Knife . . 5.00   6.51
Game Shears . . . 11.00   14.34
Sugar Tongs 2.00   2.50

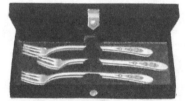

Priced, set of six   *Retail*   *List*
Orange or Grapefruit Spoons $6.00 $7.50

Priced, set of six   *Retail List*
Iced Tea or Iced Drink Spoons . $6.00 $7.50

Priced, set of six   *Retail*   *List*
Ice Cream or Sundae Spoons . $6.00 $7.50
Ice Cream or Sherbet Forks . 6.50   8.14
Individual Pie Forks . . 9.00   11.26
H. H. Tea or Butter Knives . 12.00   15.64

Priced, each   *Retail*   *List*
Pierced Pastry Server $4.50 $5.63
Pierced Round Server 3.50   4.38

1930 Catalog

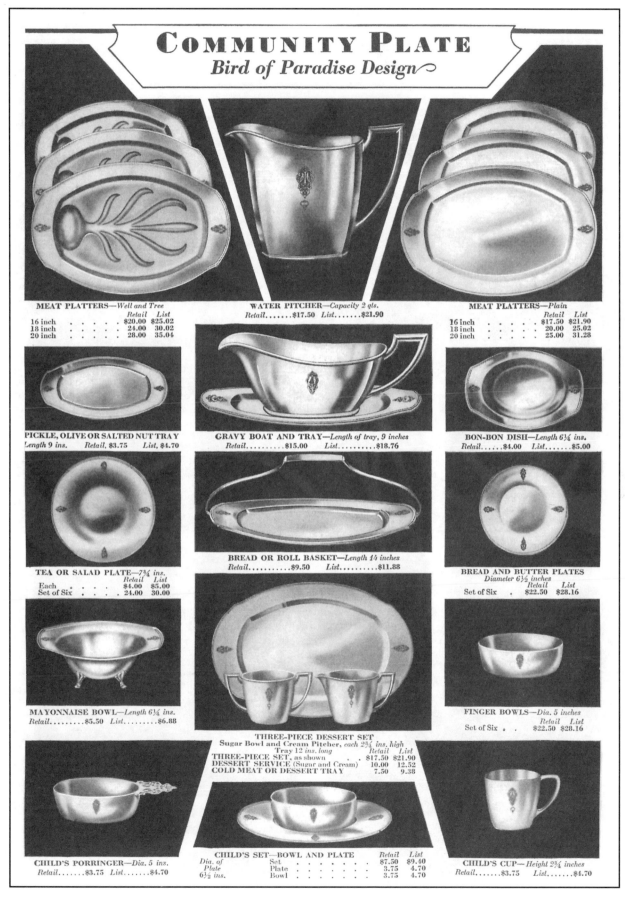

COMMUNITY PLATE
Bird of Paradise Design

MEAT PLATTERS—*Well and Tree*

	Retail	List
16 inch	$20.00	$25.02
18 inch	24.00	30.02
20 inch	28.00	35.04

WATER PITCHER—*Capacity 2 qts.*
Retail.......$17.50   List.......$21.90

MEAT PLATTERS—*Plain*

	Retail	List
16 inch	$17.50	$21.90
18 inch	20.00	25.02
20 inch	25.00	31.28

PICKLE, OLIVE OR SALTED NUT TRAY
Length 9 ins.   Retail, $3.75   List, $4.70

GRAVY BOAT AND TRAY—*Length of tray, 9 inches*
Retail.........$15.00   List.........$18.76

BON-BON DISH—*Length 6¼ ins.*
Retail.....$4.00   List.......$5.00

TEA OR SALAD PLATE—7¾ ins.

	Retail	List
Each	$4.00	$5.00
Set of Six	24.00	30.00

BREAD OR ROLL BASKET—*Length 14 inches*
Retail..........$9.50   List.........$11.88

BREAD AND BUTTER PLATES
Diameter 6½ inches

	Retail	List
Set of Six	$22.50	$28.16

MAYONNAISE BOWL—*Length 6¼ ins.*
Retail.........$5.50   List.........$6.88

THREE-PIECE DESSERT SET
Sugar Bowl and Cream Pitcher, *each 2¾ ins. high*
Tray 12 ins. long

	Retail	List
THREE-PIECE SET, as shown	$17.50	$21.90
DESSERT SERVICE (Sugar and Cream)	10.00	12.52
COLD MEAT OR DESSERT TRAY	7.50	9.38

FINGER BOWLS—*Dia. 5 inches*

	Retail	List
Set of Six	$22.50	$28.16

CHILD'S PORRINGER—*Dia. 5 ins.*
Retail......$3.75   List......$4.70

CHILD'S SET—BOWL AND PLATE

		Retail	List
Dia. of Plate 6½ ins.	Set	$7.50	$9.40
	Plate	3.75	4.70
	Bowl	3.75	4.70

CHILD'S CUP—*Height 2¾ inches*
Retail......$3.75   List......$4.70

1930 Catalog

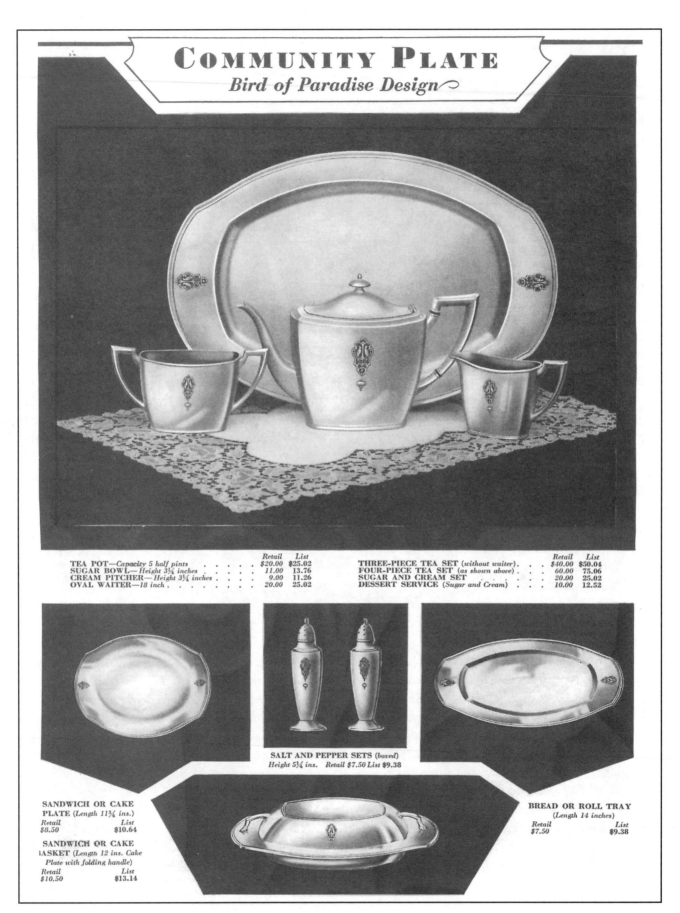

COMMUNITY PLATE
Bird of Paradise Design

	Retail	List		Retail	List
TEA POT—*Capacity 5 half pints*	$20.00	$25.02	THREE-PIECE TEA SET (*without waiter*)	$40.00	$50.04
SUGAR BOWL—*Height 3¾ inches*	11.00	13.76	FOUR-PIECE TEA SET (*as shown above*)	60.00	75.06
CREAM PITCHER—*Height 3¼ inches*	9.00	11.26	SUGAR AND CREAM SET	20.00	25.02
OVAL WAITER—*18 inch*	20.00	25.02	DESSERT SERVICE (*Sugar and Cream*)	10.00	12.52

SALT AND PEPPER SETS (*boxed*)
Height 5¼ ins.   Retail $7.50 List $9.38

**SANDWICH OR CAKE
PLATE** (*Length 11¾ ins.*)
Retail $8.50   *List* $10.64

**SANDWICH OR CAKE
BASKET** (*Length 12 ins. Cake
Plate with folding handle*)
Retail $10.50   *List* $13.14

BREAD OR ROLL TRAY
(*Length 14 inches*)
Retail $7.50   *List* $9.38

1930 Catalog

Coronation Pattern

No. 2 cake plate and server set.

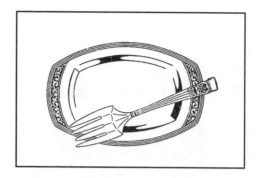

No. 1 cold meat tray and fork set.

Coronation was introduced in 1936 to commemorate the crowning of Edward VIII of England. Due to his abdication, this event never took place. In addition to being a highly successful pattern in America, it was also marketed in both England and Canada. Oneida silversmiths tell us they produced more Coronation silver than any of their other patterns. Most hollow ware pieces date from the earlier production years and were quite expensive for their day. This alone accounts for the scarcity of Coronation hollow ware. Most brides who chose Coronation flatware were never aware that matching hollow ware was made. There may have been some hollow ware pieces made of which we have no documentation. Note that there are two different oblong trays. The catalogs show two different water pitchers, either one of which would be quite a prize! The cake plate (with server) and the cold meat tray (with fork) were Oneida promotional items offered during the first few months this pattern was made. After WWII, the 1946 production of Coronation hollow ware was limited to the 5-piece tea/coffee set (coffee, tea, sugar, cream, waste), which retailed for $125.00. The only tray shown in the catalogs at this time was oblong, handled, measuring 22", priced at $50.00. The water pitcher was $27.50, the well/tree platter was $30.00, and the plain meat platter was $27.50. Also made were the covered vegetable dish, the shakers, and a small oblong waiter. Large quantities of viande flatware sets were made.

The smaller size salad forks and individual butter spreaders were possibly originally made for the viande sets, but these spreaders must have been discontinued after a few months. The smaller salad forks were sold in both viande and dinner sets, possibly due to customer preference. All individual butter spreaders are scarce, and were not included in standard sets. Most boxed sets of Coronation were sold with long bowl soups; the set containing the round bowl is hard to find and higher priced. The pickle fork in Coronation is very hard to find, and it is not understood why so few were produced. It is possible that they were marketed as a promotional item and boxed with a glass relish dish. This might also be true for the small pierced bonbon. Oneida made two different sized serving spoons, the larger of which is 1⅞" wide. There is also a large berry spoon which has ridges in the bowl. We have examined a Coronation set that was purchased in England and there are two notable differences: the round bowl cream soup had ridges in the bowl (like the sugar), and the stainless knife blade was marked Sheffield. Oneida made true luncheon sets in Coronation, but in all the years we have been dealing in silver plate, we have seen fewer than five sets. Do not confuse the viande size with that of a luncheon. There is a Coronation pierced jelly that is almost impossible to find. Some Coronation pieces are currently in production.

See Price Guide — Group 2

COMMUNITY PLATE

Leadership in Design Authority

THE NEW *Coronation* DESIGN

IN COMMUNITY PLATE SERVICE WARE

CAKE PLATE AND SERVER SET...*Regularly* $11.50... **$9.00**
For cake or pie service, sandwiches, canapes.

COLD MEAT TRAY AND FORK SET...*Regularly* $10.50... **$8.50**
For cold meat, hors d'oeuvres, curries, cold lobster

1938 Catalog

*COMMUNITY

The Finest Silverplate

*CORONATION DESIGN

Truly regal in appearance, the Coronation design suggests the impressiveness of ritual and royal splendor. The rich, massive ornamentation balances the concave flutes to lend an air of dignity and distinction. Deeply modeled decorations add effective contrast.

			Consumer
231436	4-Piece Tea and Coffee Set (Tea Pot, Coffee Pot, Sugar Bowl, and Cream Pitcher)	Each	$73.00
231425	3-Piece Coffee Set (Coffee Pot, Sugar Bowl, and Cream Pitcher)	Each	50.00
231400	3-Piece Tea Set (Tea Pot, Sugar Bowl, and Cream Pitcher)	Each	48.00

INDIVIDUAL ITEMS

			Consumer
231000	Teapot (Capacity 8 Cups)	Each	$23.00
231006	Coffeepot (Capacity 10 Cups)	Each	25.00
231012	Sugar Bowl, with Cover, Height 5¾"	Each	13.50
231018	Cream Pitcher, Gold Lined, Height 4¾"	Each	11.50
231035	Waste Bowl, Gold Lined, Height 3¼"	Each	7.00
231826	†Oblong Tray, Length 20"	Each	30.00
231828	†Oblong Tray, Length 22"	Each	35.00

†Oblong Tray length does not include handles.

ITEMS NOT ILLUSTRATED

231811	Oval Waiter, Length 18¾"	Each	$17.50
231832	Round Waiter, Diameter 14"	Each	15.00
231851	Bread or Roll Tray, Length 14½"	Each	10.00
231844	Relish Dish, Glass Lined, Diameter 14"	Each	17.50
231900	Sandwich or Cake Plate, Diameter 12"	Each	10.00
231865	Cheese and Cracker Dish, with Glass, Diameter 12"	Each	12.50
231465	Salt and Pepper Shakers, Height 4"	Per Pair	10.00
231804	Meat Platter, Plain, Length 18¾"	Each	17.50

Cons.
231031 Water Pitcher. $20.00
Capacity 2 Quarts, with Ice Guard

231032 Water Pitcher. 20.00
Capacity 2 Quarts, without Ice Guard

Consumer
231470 Gravy Boat and Tray, Capacity 12 oz. $20.00

Consumer
231818 Meat Platter, Well and Tree..... $20.00
Length 18¾"

Consumer
231040 Double Vegetable Dish, Length 14"..... $20.00

Coronation Pattern

Left to right: hollow handle pastry server, 7⁷⁄₁₆" ice tea (beverage) spoon, 6¹⁄₁₀" jelly server, 6³⁄₁₀" pickle fork. Bottom: 5⅝" pabulum (infant feeding) spoon.

Coronation Pattern

SALAD FORK

INDIVIDUAL BUTTER KNIFE

BUTTER KNIFE

5 O'CLOCK TEASPOON

SUGAR SPOON

PIERCED PASTRY SERVER

COLD MEAT OR SERVING FORK

SERVING OR TABLE SPOON

ICED DRINK SPOON

ROUND BOWL SOUP SPOON

SERVING OR GRAVY LADLE

AFTER DINNER COFFEE SPOON

PIERCED ROUND SERVER

COCKTAIL OR OYSTER FORK

OVAL BOWL SOUP (DESSERT) SPOON

Community THE FINEST SILVERPLATE

FOLLOWING ITEMS AVAILABLE IN ALL THREE COMMUNITY PATTERNS	Prices to Retail Dealers Cash Dis. 2%	Prices to the Consumer
Teaspoon...........................8 in box	$5.00 Dozen	$8.20 Dozen
Oval Bowl Soup (Dessert) Spoon...........8 in box	10.00 Dozen	16.40 Dozen
Round Bowl Soup Spoon..................8 in box	10.00 Dozen	16.40 Dozen
Cream Soup Spoon......................8 in box	10.00 Dozen	16.40 Dozen
Iced Drink Spoon.......................8 in box	10.00 Dozen	16.40 Dozen
Serving or Table Spoon..................8 in box	10.00 Dozen	16.40 Dozen
Dinner Fork...........................8 in box	10.00 Dozen	16.40 Dozen
Grille Fork............................8 in box	10.00 Dozen	16.40 Dozen
Dessert Fork..........................8 in box	10.00 Dozen	16.40 Dozen
Dinner Knife..........................8 in box	16.56 Dozen	27.60 Dozen
Grille Knife...........................8 in box	16.56 Dozen	27.60 Dozen
Dessert Knife.........................8 in box	16.56 Dozen	27.60 Dozen
(Above Knives have Hollow Handles and DeLuxe Stainless Blades)		
Salad or Pastry Fork....................8 in box	10.00 Dozen	16.40 Dozen
Cocktail or Oyster Fork..................8 in box	10.00 Dozen	16.40 Dozen
Ind. Butter or Cheese Knife...............8 in box	10.00 Dozen	16.40 Dozen
Butter Knife...........................1 in box	8.28 Dozen	1.15 Each
Sugar Spoon..........................1 in box	8.28 Dozen	1.15 Each

The following items, illustrated above, will be available later:

5 O'Clock Teaspoon
After Dinner Coffee Spoon
Cold Meat or Serving Fork

Serving or Gravy Ladle
Pierced Pastry Server
Pierced Round Server

1946 Catalog

Coronation Pattern
and Navarre, Fostoria Glass Company

These two patterns, both introduced in 1936, were designed to coordinate. The design on the handles of the silver pieces perfectly matches the central motif on the glass pieces.

Left to right: 5½" viande butter spreader, 6¾" salad fork, 6⁵⁄₁₆" viande salad fork, 4½" bonbon server.

Fostoria MADE IN U.S.A.

sparkle

YOU love to live with

Lovely *Navarre!* It's skillfully designed to harmonize with modern or period settings. And prudently priced for wise budgets. The dainty, curving flow of this flawless "Master-Etching" has a nice-to-live-with look . . . dating back to a Parisian period when courtly manners were in vogue. You'll be grateful that American craftsmanship has captured this distinction. And you'll find *Navarre*, in stemware and scores of accessory pieces, or many other Fostoria selections, at the better stores everywhere.

Coronation Pattern

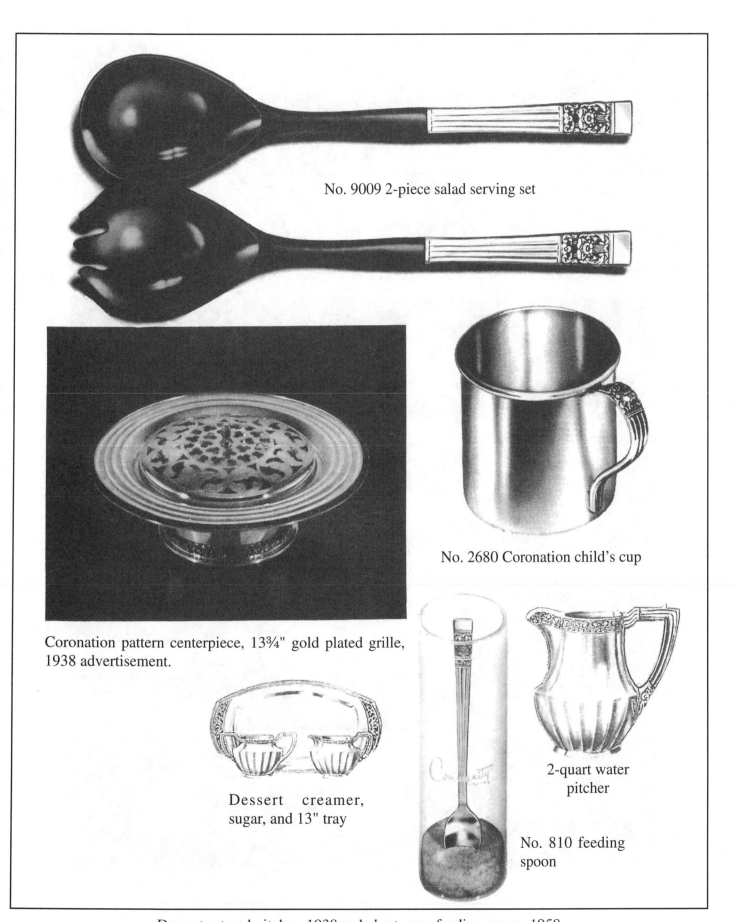

No. 9009 2-piece salad serving set

Coronation pattern centerpiece, 13¾" gold plated grille, 1938 advertisement.

No. 2680 Coronation child's cup

Dessert creamer, sugar, and 13" tray

2-quart water pitcher

No. 810 feeding spoon

Dessert set and pitcher, 1938; salad set, cup, feeding spoon, 1958.

See Price Guide — Group 2

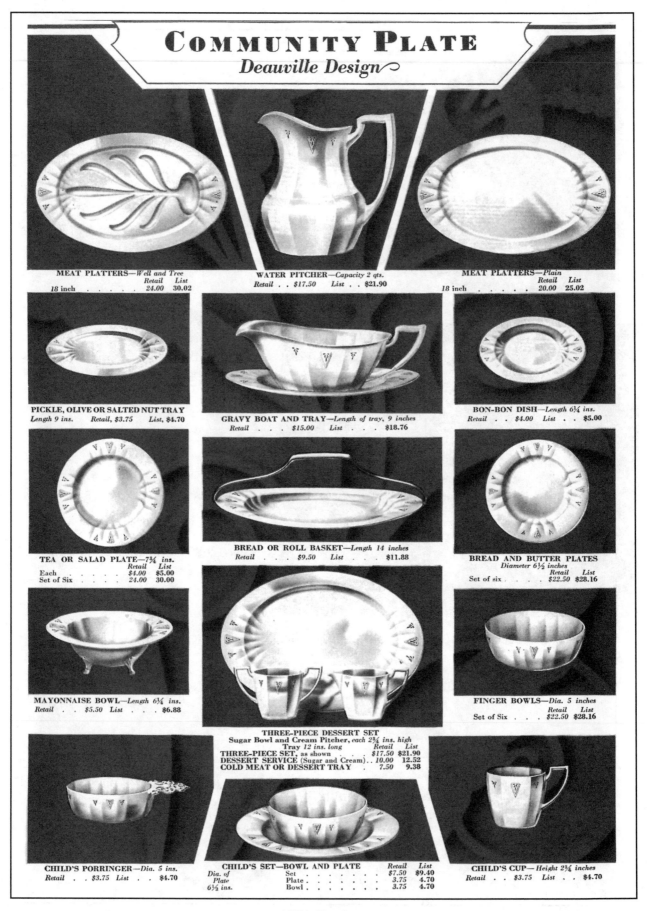

COMMUNITY PLATE
Deauville Design

MEAT PLATTERS—*Well and Tree*
	Retail	List
18 inch	24.00	30.02

WATER PITCHER—*Capacity 2 qts.*
Retail . . $17.50   List . . $21.90

MEAT PLATTERS—*Plain*
	Retail	List
18 inch	20.00	25.02

PICKLE, OLIVE OR SALTED NUT TRAY
Length 9 ins.   Retail, $3.75   List, $4.70

GRAVY BOAT AND TRAY—*Length of tray, 9 inches*
Retail . . . $15.00   List . . . $18.76

BON-BON DISH—*Length 6¼ ins.*
Retail . . $4.00   List . . $5.00

TEA OR SALAD PLATE—*7¾ ins.*
	Retail	List
Each	$4.00	$5.00
Set of Six	24.00	30.00

BREAD OR ROLL BASKET—*Length 14 inches*
Retail . . . $9.50   List . . . $11.88

BREAD AND BUTTER PLATES
Diameter 6½ inches
	Retail	List
Set of six	$22.50	$28.16

MAYONNAISE BOWL—*Length 6¼ ins.*
Retail . . $5.50   List . . . $6.88

THREE-PIECE DESSERT SET
Sugar Bowl and Cream Pitcher, *each 2¾ ins. high*
Tray *12 ins. long*
		Retail	List
THREE-PIECE SET, as shown		$17.50	$21.90
DESSERT SERVICE (Sugar and Cream)		10.00	12.52
COLD MEAT OR DESSERT TRAY		7.50	9.38

FINGER BOWLS—*Dia. 5 inches*
	Retail	List
Set of Six	$22.50	$28.16

CHILD'S PORRINGER—*Dia. 5 ins.*
Retail . . $3.75   List . . . $4.70

CHILD'S SET—BOWL AND PLATE
		Retail	List
Dia. of Plate 6½ ins.	Set	$7.50	$9.40
	Plate	3.75	4.70
	Bowl	3.75	4.70

CHILD'S CUP—*Height 2¾ inches*
Retail . . $3.75   List . . . $4.70

1931 Catalog

Deauville Pattern

COMMUNITY PLATE
Deauville Design

	Retail	List
TEA POT—*Capacity 5 half pints*	$20.00	$25.02
SUGAR BOWL—*Height 3¼ inches*	11.00	13.76
CREAM PITCHER—*Height 3¼ inches*	9.00	11.26
OVAL WAITER—*18 inch*	20.00	25.02

	Retail	List
THREE-PIECE TEA SET (*without waiter*)	$40.00	$50.04
FOUR-PIECE TEA SET (*as shown above*)	60.00	75.06
SUGAR AND CREAM SET	20.00	25.02
DESSERT SERVICE (*Sugar and Cream*)	10.00	12.52

SALT AND PEPPER SETS (*boxed*)
Height 5¼ ins. Retail $7.50 List $9.38

SANDWICH OR CAKE PLATE (*Length 11¾ ins.*)
Retail $7.50   List $9.38

SANDWICH OR CAKE BASKET (*Length 12 ins. Cake Plate with folding handle*)
Retail $10.50   List $13.14

BREAD OR ROLL TRAY (*Length 14 inches*)
Retail $7.50   List $9.38

1930 Catalog

See Price Guide — Group 2

Deauville Pattern

Deauville Design • **COMMUNITY PLATE**

Replacement Guarantee

Inspired by the sophisticated smartness of one of Europe's most exclusive watering places, the Deauville design interprets with dynamic simplicity the essence of the modern spirit. It is fresh, daring, young, in a manner truly French—yet it possesses a dignity, an assured restraint, that are the unmistakable evidences of distinction. The hostess who would key her table to the mood of today and tomorrow will find its most vivid expression in the Deauville design.

Always state design wanted

KNIFE AND FORK SETS
(6 DeLuxe Stainless Knives and 6 Forks)
(in Cameo Gift Case)

Priced, Per Set	Consumer	List
Grille Knives, H. H. and Grille Fks.	$21.00	$25.20
Dinner Knives, H.H. and Dinner Fks.	21.00	25.20
Dessert Knives, H.H. and Dessert Fks.	21.00	25.20
Dinner Knives, Mod.H. and Din. Fks.	18.00	21.60
Dessert Knives, Mod.H. and Des. Fks.	18.00	21.60

LADLES

Salad Dressing or Small	Each	1.75	2.10
Serving or Gravy	Each	2.25	2.70
Medium Soup or Serving	Each	8.00	9.60

CARVERS (DeLuxe Stainless Blades)

2-Piece, H. H. (7-in. Blade)	Per Set	10.00	12.00
2-Piece, H. H. (5-in. Blade)	Per Set	6.00	7.20
3-Piece, Large, H. H.	Per Set	17.00	20.40
Double Service, 3-Pc., H. H.	Per Set	18.00	21.60

Butter Knife	Each	1.50	1.80
Game Shears	Each	10.00	12.00
★Sugar Tongs	Each	1.75	2.10
Pie or Ice Cream Server, H. H.	Each	3.25	3.90
Pastry Server, Pierced	Each	3.00	3.60
Round Server, Pierced	Each	2.25	2.70
★Small Server (Jelly Server)	Each	1.75	2.10
Butter Knife and Sugar Spoon Set.	Each	3.00	3.60
Fruit Knives, H.H., DeLuxe Stain.	Set of 6	10.00	12.00
★Ind. Butter or Cheese Knives	Set of 6	6.50	7.80

BABY SPOONS AND FORKS
(In brightly decorated boxes)

Spoon, Bent Handle	Each	.75	.90
Spoon, Straight Handle	Each	.75	.90
Fork, Straight Handle	Each	.75	.90
Fork and Bent Spoon	Per Set	1.50	1.80
Fork and Straight Spoon	Per Set	1.50	1.80

CHILD'S SET (in brightly decorated box)

GRILLE KNIFE

GRILLE FORK

IND. BUTTER KNIFE

BABY SPOON STRT. H.

FRUIT KNIFE

PIERCED PASTRY SERVER

H. H. PIE

CARVING SET 2 PC. 7 IN.

SMALL SERVER

PIERCED ROUND SERVER

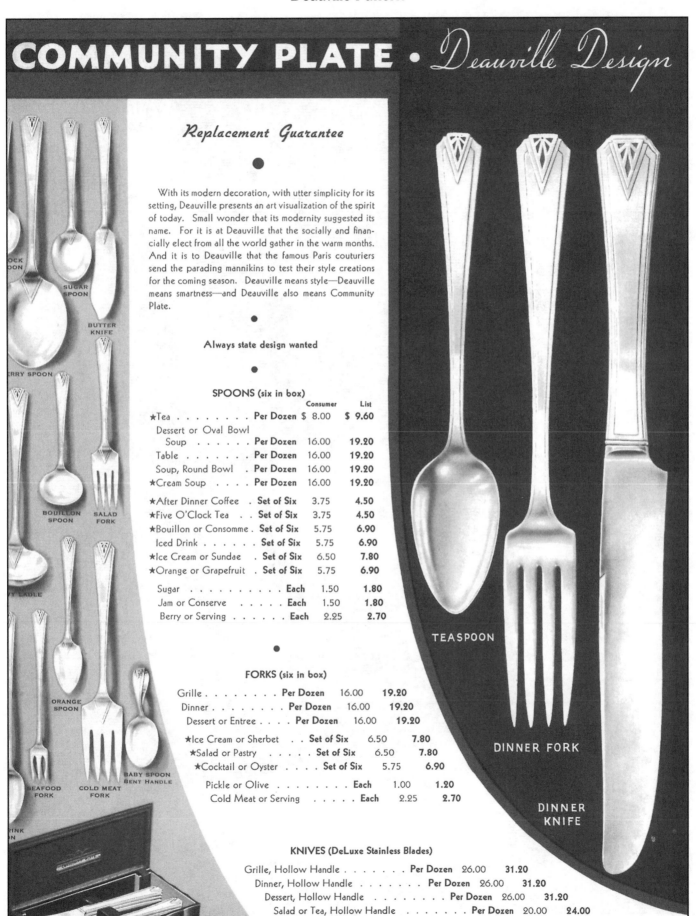

COMMUNITY PLATE · *Deauville Design*

Replacement Guarantee

●

With its modern decoration, with utter simplicity for its setting, Deauville presents an art visualization of the spirit of today. Small wonder that its modernity suggested its name. For it is at Deauville that the socially and financially elect from all the world gather in the warm months. And it is to Deauville that the famous Paris couturiers send the parading mannikins to test their style creations for the coming season. Deauville means style—Deauville means smartness—and Deauville also means Community Plate.

●

Always state design wanted

●

SPOONS (six in box)

		Consumer	List
★Tea	Per Dozen	$ 8.00	$ 9.60
Dessert or Oval Bowl Soup	Per Dozen	16.00	19.20
Table	Per Dozen	16.00	19.20
Soup, Round Bowl	Per Dozen	16.00	19.20
★Cream Soup	Per Dozen	16.00	19.20
★After Dinner Coffee	Set of Six	3.75	4.50
★Five O'Clock Tea	Set of Six	3.75	4.50
★Bouillon or Consomme	Set of Six	5.75	6.90
Iced Drink	Set of Six	5.75	6.90
★Ice Cream or Sundae	Set of Six	6.50	7.80
★Orange or Grapefruit	Set of Six	5.75	6.90
Sugar	Each	1.50	1.80
Jam or Conserve	Each	1.50	1.80
Berry or Serving	Each	2.25	2.70

●

FORKS (six in box)

Grille	Per Dozen	16.00	19.20
Dinner	Per Dozen	16.00	19.20
Dessert or Entree	Per Dozen	16.00	19.20
★Ice Cream or Sherbet	Set of Six	6.50	7.80
★Salad or Pastry	Set of Six	6.50	7.80
★Cocktail or Oyster	Set of Six	5.75	6.90
Pickle or Olive	Each	1.00	1.20
Cold Meat or Serving	Each	2.25	2.70

KNIVES (DeLuxe Stainless Blades)

Grille, Hollow Handle	Per Dozen	26.00	31.20
Dinner, Hollow Handle	Per Dozen	26.00	31.20
Dessert, Hollow Handle	Per Dozen	26.00	31.20
Salad or Tea, Hollow Handle	Per Dozen	20.00	24.00
Dinner, Modeled Handle	Per Dozen	20.00	24.00

TEASPOON

DINNER FORK

DINNER KNIFE

Community
THE FINEST SILVERPLATE

CREAM SOUP
SPOON

TEASPOON

GRILLE KNIFE

GRILLE FORK

DINNER FORK

DINNER KNIFE

*Evening Star**

This elegant new floral pattern by Community captures the essence of traditional American design—its deep-carved floral motif will harmonize perfectly with the most cherished table appointments . . . a pattern to live with—a pattern to love, for keeps.

*TRADE-MARK

Evening Star Pattern

THE FINEST SILVERPLATE

OPEN STOCK PRICES ON ALL COMMUNITY PATTERNS

AUGUST 1, 1949

SPOONS		Consumer Price	
		Set of 8	Set of 12
Tea...........................8 in box		$ 5.67	$ 8.50
Oval Bowl Soup (Dessert)......8 in box		11.33	17.00
Serving or Table...............8 in box		12.00	18.00
Round Bowl Soup.............8 in box		11.33	17.00
†Five O'Clock Tea............8 in box		5.67	8.50
†After Dinner Coffee.........8 in box		5.67	8.50
Cream Soup...................8 in box		11.33	17.00
Iced Drink...................8 in box		11.33	17.00

SERVING PIECES			Each
Butter Knife..................1 in box		—	1.50
Sugar Spoon..................1 in box		—	1.50
Cold Meat or Serving Fork......1 in box		—	2.25
Serving or Gravy Ladle........1 in box		—	2.25

†Not available in Evening Star.

FORKS		Consumer Price	
		Set of 8	Set of 12
Dinner......................8 in box		$11.33	$17.00
Grille.......................8 in box		11.33	17.00
Dessert.....................8 in box		11.33	17.00
Salad or Pastry...............8 in box		11.33	17.00
Cocktail or Oyster............8 in box		11.33	17.00

KNIVES

Ind. Butter or Cheese Spreader..8 in box		11.33	17.00

Hollow Handle, DeLuxe Stainless Blades

Dinner......................8 in box		18.60	27.90
°Grille......................8 in box		18.60	27.90
Dessert.....................8 in box		18.60	27.90

°All Community Grille Knives have DeLuxe Serra-blades.

NO FEDERAL TAX   ALWAYS SPECIFY PATTERN WANTED

All orders for both sets and open stock subject to prices prevailing at date of shipment

The Consumer's Prices listed herein are the prescribed minimum resale prices on Community in all states which have enacted Fair Trade Acts.

1949 Catalog

Flight Pattern

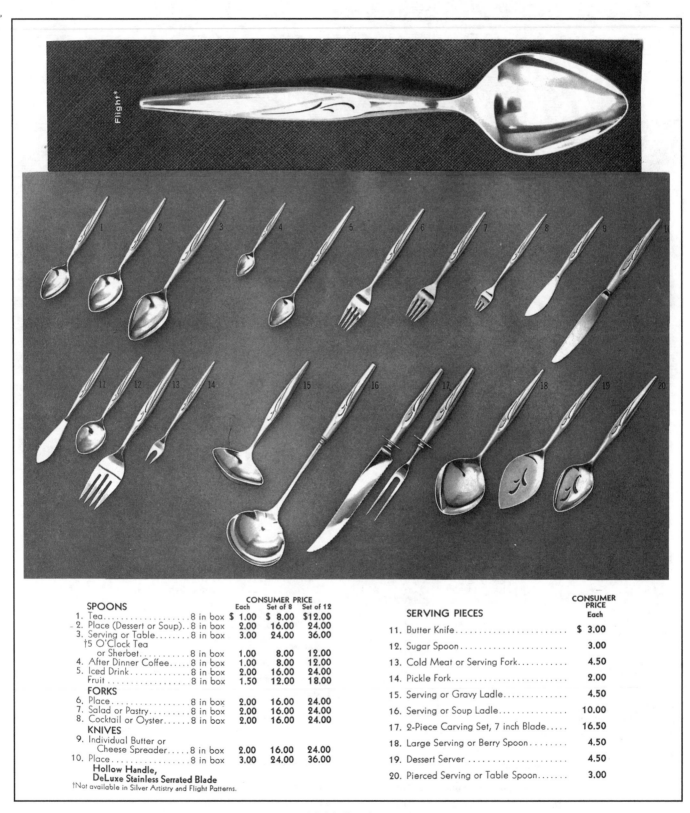

SPOONS		CONSUMER PRICE	
	Each	Set of 8	Set of 12
1. Tea....................8 in box	$ 1.00	$ 8.00	$12.00
2. Place (Dessert or Soup)..8 in box	2.00	16.00	24.00
3. Serving or Table........8 in box	3.00	24.00	36.00
†5 O'Clock Tea			
or Sherbet..........8 in box	1.00	8.00	12.00
4. After Dinner Coffee.....8 in box	1.00	8.00	12.00
5. Iced Drink.............8 in box	2.00	16.00	24.00
Fruit................8 in box	1.50	12.00	18.00
FORKS			
6. Place.................8 in box	2.00	16.00	24.00
7. Salad or Pastry........8 in box	2.00	16.00	24.00
8. Cocktail or Oyster......8 in box	2.00	16.00	24.00
KNIVES			
9. Individual Butter or			
Cheese Spreader.....8 in box	2.00	16.00	24.00
10. Place.................8 in box	3.00	24.00	36.00

**Hollow Handle,
DeLuxe Stainless Serrated Blade**
†Not available in Silver Artistry and Flight Patterns.

SERVING PIECES	CONSUMER PRICE Each
11. Butter Knife.........................	$ 3.00
12. Sugar Spoon......................	3.00
13. Cold Meat or Serving Fork..........	4.50
14. Pickle Fork......................	2.00
15. Serving or Gravy Ladle.............	4.50
16. Serving or Soup Ladle..............	10.00
17. 2-Piece Carving Set, 7 inch Blade.....	16.50
18. Large Serving or Berry Spoon........	4.50
19. Dessert Server	4.50
20. Pierced Serving or Table Spoon.......	3.00

1966 Catalog

Flower -De- Luce Pattern

1907

See Price Guide — Group 1

Flower -De- Luce Pattern

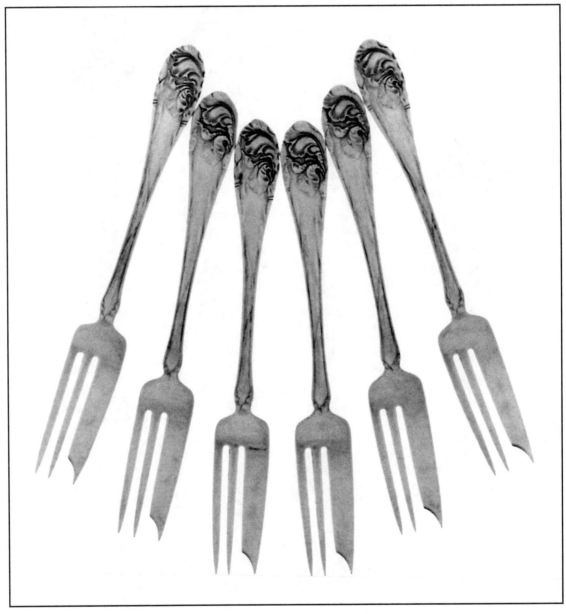

7" individual pastry forks.

Georgian Pattern

Left to right: 7⅛" dessert spoon, 6½" salad fork, 8¹⁵⁄₁₆" berry serving spoon, 5⅝" citrus/grapefruit spoon, 7" individual pastry fork with cutting tine. Patented 1912.

See Price Guide — Group 1

Grosvenor Pattern

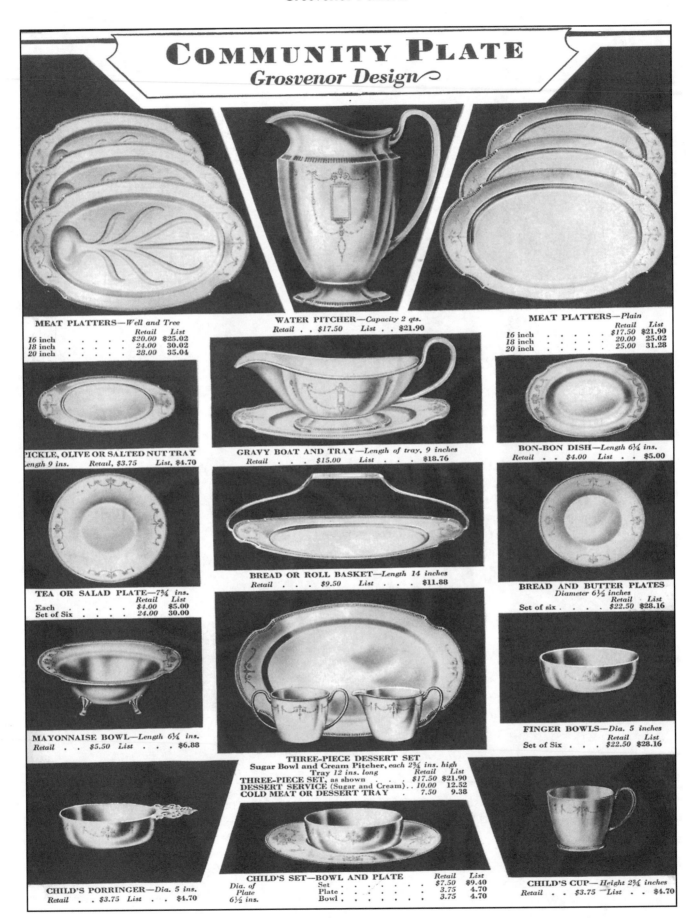

COMMUNITY PLATE
Grosvenor Design

MEAT PLATTERS—*Well and Tree*

	Retail	List
16 inch	$20.00	$25.02
18 inch	24.00	30.02
20 inch	28.00	35.04

WATER PITCHER—*Capacity 2 qts.*
Retail . . $17.50   List . . $21.90

MEAT PLATTERS—*Plain*

	Retail	List
16 inch	$17.50	$21.90
18 inch	20.00	25.02
20 inch	25.00	31.28

PICKLE, OLIVE OR SALTED NUT TRAY
Length 9 ins.   Retail, $3.75   List, $4.70

GRAVY BOAT AND TRAY—*Length of tray, 9 inches*
Retail . . . $15.00   List . . . $18.76

BON-BON DISH—*Length 6¼ ins.*
Retail . . $4.00   List . . $5.00

TEA OR SALAD PLATE—*7¾ ins.*

	Retail	List
Each	$4.00	$5.00
Set of Six	24.00	30.00

BREAD OR ROLL BASKET—*Length 14 inches*
Retail . . . $9.50   List . . . $11.88

BREAD AND BUTTER PLATES
Diameter 6½ inches

	Retail	List
Set of six	$22.50	$28.16

MAYONNAISE BOWL—*Length 6¼ ins.*
Retail . . $5.50 List . . . $6.88

THREE-PIECE DESSERT SET
Sugar Bowl and Cream Pitcher, *each 2¾ ins. high*
Tray 12 ins. long

	Retail	List
THREE-PIECE SET, as shown	$17.50	$21.90
DESSERT SERVICE (Sugar and Cream)	10.00	12.52
COLD MEAT OR DESSERT TRAY	7.50	9.38

FINGER BOWLS—*Dia. 5 inches*

	Retail	List
Set of Six	$22.50	$28.16

CHILD'S PORRINGER—*Dia. 5 ins.*
Retail . . $3.75 List . . $4.70

CHILD'S SET—BOWL AND PLATE

Dia. of Plate 6½ ins.		Retail	List
Set		$7.50	$9.40
Plate		3.75	4.70
Bowl		3.75	4.70

CHILD'S CUP—*Height 2¾ inches*
Retail . . $3.75 List . . $4.70

1931 Catalog

Grosvenor Pattern

Always state design wanted

SPOONS (six in box)

		Consumer	List
★Tea	Per Doz.	$ 8.00	$ 9.60
Dessert or Oval Bowl Soup	Per Doz.	16.00	19.20
Table	Per Doz.	16.00	19.20
Soup, Round Bowl . . .	Per Doz.	16.00	19.20
★Cream Soup	Per Doz.	16.00	19.20
★After Dinner Coffee . .	Set of 6	3.75	4.50
★Five O'Clock Tea . . .	Set of 6	3.75	4.50
★Bouillon or Consomme .	Set of 6	5.75	6.90
Iced Drink	Set of 6	5.75	6.90
★Ice Cream or Sundae . .	Set of 6	6.50	7.80
Sugar	Each	1.50	1.80
Jam or Conserve	Each	1.50	1.80
Berry or Serving	Each	2.25	2.70

FORKS (six in box)

Grille	Per Doz.	16.00	19.20
Dinner	Per Doz.	16.00	19.20
Dessert or Entree . . .	Per Doz.	16.00	19.20
★Ice Cream or Sherbet . .	Set of 6	6.50	7.80
★Salad or Pastry	Set of 6	6.50	7.80
★Cocktail or Oyster . . .	Set of 6	5.75	6.90
Pickle or Olive	Each	1.00	1.20
Cold Meat or Serving . . .	Each	2.25	2.70

KNIVES (DeLuxe Stainless Blades)

Grille, Hollow Handle .	Per Doz.	26.00	31.20
Dinner, Hollow Handle .	Per Doz.	26.00	31.20
Dessert, Hollow Handle .	Per Doz.	26.00	31.20
Salad or Tea, H. Handle .	Per Doz.	20.00	24.00
Dinner, Mod. Handle . .	Per Doz.	20.00	24.00
Dessert, Mod. Handle . .	Per Doz.	20.00	24.00

KNIFE AND FORK SETS
(6 DeLuxe Stainless Knives and 6 Forks)
(in Cameo Gift Case)

Priced, Per Set

Grille Knives, H. H. and Grille Forks	21.00	25.20
Dinner Knives, H. H. and Dinner Forks	21.00	25.20
Dessert Knives, H. H. and Dessert Forks	21.00	25.20
Dinner Knives, Mod. H. and Dinner Forks	18.00	21.60
Dessert Knives, Mod. H. and Dessert Forks	18.00	21.60

LADLES

Salad Dressing or Small	Each	1.75	2.10
Serving or Gravy	Each	2.25	2.70
Medium Soup or Serving . . .	Each	8.00	9.60

CARVERS (DeLuxe Stainless Blades)

2-Piece, H. H. (5-in. Blade) . .	Per Set	6.00	7.20

MISCELLANEOUS

Butter Knife	Each	1.50	1.80
Game Shears	Each	10.00	12.00
★Sugar Tongs	Each	1.75	2.10
Pastry Server, Pierced	Each	3.00	3.60
Round Server, Pierced	Each	2.25	2.70
★Small Server (Jelly Server)	Each	1.75	2.10
Butter Knife and Sugar Spoon Set	Each	3.00	3.60
Fruit Knives, H.H., DeLuxe Stainless	Set of 6	10.00	12.00
★Individual Butter or Cheese Knives	Set of 6	6.50	7.80

Labels on illustration: SALAD FORK, SUGAR SPOON, BUTTER KNIFE, PIERCED PASTRY SERVER, SEA FOOD FORK, CREAM SOUP SPOON, GRAVY LADLE, BERRY SPOON, ICED DRINK SPOON, SMALL SERVER, COLD MEAT FORK, PIERCED ROUND SERVER, TEASPOON, DINNER FORK, DINNER KNIFE

★Packed in DeLuxe Gift Box

Retail Dealers receive 2% Additional Dealer Discount for orders of $25.00 or more.

1936 Catalog

See Price Guide — Group 2

COMMUNITY PLATE
Grosvenor Design

	Retail	List		Retail	List
TEA POT—Capacity 5 half pints	$25.00	$31.28	THREE-PIECE TEA SET (*without waiter*)	$50.00	$62.56
SUGAR BOWL—Height 6¼ inches	15.00	18.76	FOUR-PIECE TEA SET (*as shown above*)	70.00	87.58
CREAM PITCHER—Height 6¼ inches	10.00	12.52	SUGAR AND CREAM SET	25.00	31.28
OVAL WAITER—18 inch	20.00	25.02	DESSERT SERVICE (*Sugar and Cream*)	10.00	12.52

DOUBLE VEGETABLE DISH (*Length*   Retail   List
12 ins. *Cover can be used as additional dish*) $17.50 $21.90
OPEN VEGETABLE DISH   8.75   10.96

BREAD OR ROLL TRAY
(*Length 14 inches*)
Retail, $7.50   List, $9.38

SANDWICH OR CAKE PLATE
(*Length 11¾ ins.*)—Retail, $8.50   List, $10.64
SANDWICH OR CAKE BASKET
(*Length 12 ins. Cake Plate with folding handle*)
Retail, $10.50   List, $13.14

Priced, per Pair   Retail   List
HIGH CANDLESTICKS (*Height 10¼ inches*) . $17.50 $21.90
LOW CANDLESTICKS (*Height 3¼ inches*) . 10.00   12.52

SALT AND PEPPER SHAKERS
(*Height 5¼ inches*)
Retail, $7.50   List, $9.38
Priced per Pair

1931 Catalog

Grosvenor Pattern

Priced, each   Retail   List
Sugar Spoon $1.25 $1.57

Retail   List
Butter Knife, each $1.25 $1.57
Butter Knife and Sugar Spoon, set .   2.50   3.12

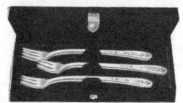

Priced, set of six   Retail   List
Oyster or Seafood Forks . . $5.50 $6.88

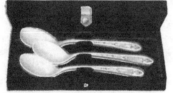

Priced, set of six   Retail   List
Cream Soup Spoons . . . $8.00 $10.00

Priced, each   Retail   List
Pickle or Olive Fork . . . $1.50 $1.88

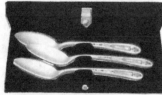

Priced, set of six   Retail   List
After Dinner Coffee Spoons . $4.00 $5.00
Five O'Clock Tea Spoons .   4.00   5.00

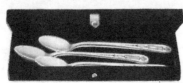

Priced, set of six   Retail   List
Iced Tea or Iced Drink Spoons . $6.00 $7.50

COMMUNITY PLATE
Grosvenor Design

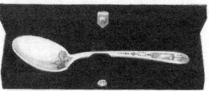

Priced, each   Retail   List
Berry or Serving Spoon $3.50 $4.38
Small Berry or Preserve Spoon . .   3.00   3.75

Priced, each   Retail   List
Cold Meat or Serving Fork . . . $2.50 $3.13
Small Cold Meat or Sardine Fork .   2.25   2.82

BABY SPOONS AND FORKS
In Brightly Decorated Boxes   Retail   List
Spoon, Bent Handle, each . . . $1.00 $1.25
Spoon, Straight Handle, each . .   1.00   1.25
Fork, Straight Handle, each . .   1.00   1.25
Fork and Bent Spoon, set . . .   2.00   2.50
Fork and Straight Spoon, set . .   2.00   2.50

CHILD'S SETS
In Brightly Decorated Boxes   Retail   List
With Hollow Handle Knife, set . . $4.00 $5.00
With Flat Handle Knife, set . .   3.00   3.76

CARVERS
De Luxe Stainless Blades
           Retail   List
2-Piece, Hollow Handle (7-inch Blade), set . $12.50 $16.28
2-Piece, Hollow Handle (5-inch Blade), set .   8.50 11.08
2-Pc. Mdld. Hdle. Standard Stainless (5-in. Blade), set   5.50   7.18
Large, 3-Piece Hollow Handle, set 20.00 26.06
De Luxe Knife Sharpener, each 2.75   3.58

PIECES NOT ILLUSTRATED
Priced, each   Retail   List
Pie or Ice Cream Server, H.H., . $4.50 $5.63
Cheese Server, H. H. . . .   3.00   3.75
Jam or Conserve Spoon . .   1.75   2.19
Lemon or Relish Fork . .   1.50   1.88
Pierced Bon Bon Spoon . .   2.50   3.13
Jelly Server 1.75   2.19
Cake Serving Set . . .   8.00 10.26
Cake Fork 3.00   3.76
Cake or Bread Knife . .   5.00   6.51
Game Shears 11.00 14.34
Sugar Tongs 2.00   2.50

Priced, set of six   Retail   List
Ice Cream or Sundae Spoons . $6.00 $7.50
Ice Cream or Sherbet Forks .   6.50   8.14
Individual Pie Forks . .   9.00 11.26
H. H. Tea or Butter Knives . 12.00 15.64

Priced, set of six   Retail   List
Individual Salad or Pastry Forks $7.50 $9.40

Priced, each   Retail   List
Salad Dressing or Small Ladle $2.25 $2.82
Serving or Gravy Ladle . . .   3.00   3.75
Medium Soup or Serving Ladle   8.50 10.64

Priced, set of six   Retail   List
Bouillon or Consomme Spoons $7.50 $9.40

Priced, set of six   Retail   List
Ind. Butter Spreaders . . . $6.50 $8.14

Priced, each   Retail   List
Olive or Salted Nut Spoon . $2.00 $2.50

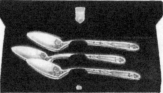

Priced, set of six   Retail   List
Orange or Grapefruit Spoons $6.00 $7.50

Priced, each   Retail   List
Pierced Pastry Server $4.50 $5.63
Pierced Round Server   3.50   4.38

1931 Catalog

THE

HAMPTON COURT PATTERN

Bright Butler Finish

A new design—adapted by Community craftsmen from a decorative motif adorning the magnificent reception room in Hampton Court Palace, England, owned by the famous Cardinal Wolsey in the reign of King Henry VIII —1491 to 1547 A. D.

DINNER KNIFE

DESSERT SPOON

DINNER FORK

TABLE SPOON

50 Year Replacement Guarantee

SPOONS—*Six in Box* *Set of Six*	KNIVES (*Plated Blades*) Six in Blue Velvet Lined Gift Box	KNIVES (*Stainless Blades*) Six in Blue Velvet Lined Gift Box
Tea $3.75	*Set of Six*	*Set of Six*
Dessert 7.25	Hollow Handle Dinner . $11.00	Hollow Handle Dinner De Luxe . $13.00
Table 7.50	Hollow Handle Dessert . 10.75	Hollow Handle Dessert De Luxe . 12.75
Soup (Round Bowl) . . . 7.50	Modeled Handle Dinner . 7.00	Modeled Handle Dinner 7.50
FORKS—*Six in Box*	Modeled Handle Dessert . . 6.75	
Dinner $7.50		
Dessert 7.25		

Circa 1928

King Cedric Design • COMMUNITY PLATE

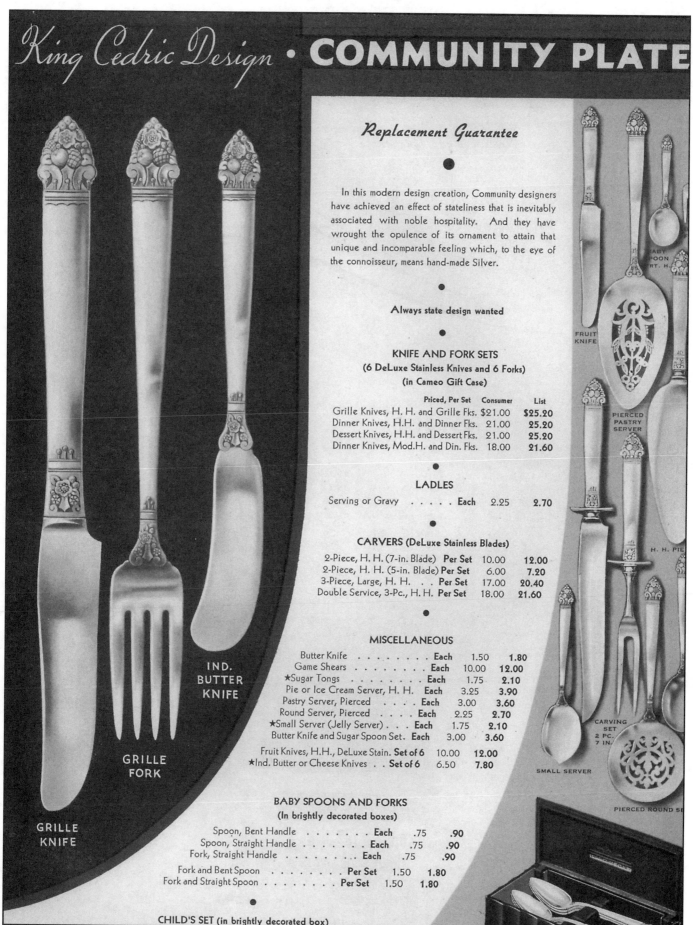

Replacement Guarantee

•

In this modern design creation, Community designers have achieved an effect of stateliness that is inevitably associated with noble hospitality. And they have wrought the opulence of its ornament to attain that unique and incomparable feeling which, to the eye of the connoisseur, means hand-made Silver.

•

Always state design wanted

•

KNIFE AND FORK SETS
(6 DeLuxe Stainless Knives and 6 Forks)
(in Cameo Gift Case)

	Priced, Per Set	Consumer	List
Grille Knives, H. H. and Grille Fks.		$21.00	$25.20
Dinner Knives, H.H. and Dinner Fks.		21.00	25.20
Dessert Knives, H.H. and Dessert Fks.		21.00	25.20
Dinner Knives, Mod.H. and Din. Fks.		18.00	21.60

•

LADLES

		Consumer	List
Serving or Gravy . . . . . Each		2.25	2.70

•

CARVERS (DeLuxe Stainless Blades)

		Consumer	List
2-Piece, H. H. (7-in. Blade) Per Set		10.00	12.00
2-Piece, H. H. (5-in. Blade) Per Set		6.00	7.20
3-Piece, Large, H. H. . . Per Set		17.00	20.40
Double Service, 3-Pc., H. H. Per Set		18.00	21.60

MISCELLANEOUS

		Consumer	List
Butter Knife . . . . Each		1.50	1.80
Game Shears . . . . Each		10.00	12.00
★Sugar Tongs . . . . Each		1.75	2.10
Pie or Ice Cream Server, H. H. Each		3.25	3.90
Pastry Server, Pierced . . . Each		3.00	3.60
Round Server, Pierced . . . Each		2.25	2.70
★Small Server (Jelly Server) . . Each		1.75	2.10
Butter Knife and Sugar Spoon Set. Each		3.00	3.60
Fruit Knives, H.H., DeLuxe Stain. Set of 6		10.00	12.00
★Ind. Butter or Cheese Knives . . Set of 6		6.50	7.80

BABY SPOONS AND FORKS
(In brightly decorated boxes)

		Consumer	List
Spoon, Bent Handle . . . . Each		.75	.90
Spoon, Straight Handle . . . . Each		.75	.90
Fork, Straight Handle . . . . Each		.75	.90
Fork and Bent Spoon . . . . Per Set		1.50	1.80
Fork and Straight Spoon . . . . Per Set		1.50	1.80

CHILD'S SET (in brightly decorated box)

IND. BUTTER KNIFE

GRILLE FORK

GRILLE KNIFE

FRUIT KNIFE

PIERCED PASTRY SERVER

H. H. PIE

CARVING SET 2 PC. 7 IN.

SMALL SERVER

PIERCED ROUND SE

COMMUNITY PLATE • *Lady Hamilton Design*

Replacement Guarantee

The magic of a new simplicity is given to the table of today's hostess in the Lady Hamilton—a simplicity that is the essence of modern distinction and the birthright of true aristocracy. It is a design exquisitely feminine, with a charm as lovely and youthful as tomorrow's bride. And perhaps its greatest appeal is that though it is as modern as the women for whose tables it is created, it mirrors the grace of a glamorous past.

Always state design wanted

SPOONS (six in box)

		Consumer	List
★Tea	Per Dozen	$ 8.00	$ 9.60
Dessert or Oval Bowl Soup	Per Dozen	16.00	19.20
Table	Per Dozen	16.00	19.20
Soup, Round Bowl .	Per Dozen	16.00	19.20
★Cream Soup	Per Dozen	16.00	19.20
★After Dinner Coffee .	Set of Six	3.75	4.50
★Five O'Clock Tea . .	Set of Six	3.75	4.50
★Bouillon or Consomme	Set of Six	5.75	6.90
Iced Drink	Set of Six	5.75	6.90
★Orange or Grapefruit	Set of Six	5.75	6.90
Sugar	Each	1.50	1.80
Berry or Serving	Each	2.25	2.70

FORKS (six in box)

Grille	Per Dozen	16.00	19.20
Dinner	Per Dozen	16.00	19.20
Dessert or Entree	Per Dozen	16.00	19.20
★Ice Cream or Sherbet .	Set of Six	6.50	7.80
★Salad or Pastry	Set of Six	6.50	7.80
★Cocktail or Oyster	Set of Six	5.75	6.90
Pickle or Olive	Each	1.00	1.20
Cold Meat or Serving	Each	2.25	2.70

KNIVES (DeLuxe Stainless Blades)

Grille, Hollow Handle	Per Dozen	26.00	31.20
Dinner, Hollow Handle	Per Dozen	26.00	31.20
Dessert, Hollow Handle	Per Dozen	26.00	31.20

SUGAR SPOON

BUTTER KNIFE

BOUILLON SPOON

SALAD FORK

ORANGE SPOON

SEAFOOD FORK

COLD MEAT FORK

BABY SPOON BENT HANDLE

TEASPOON

DINNER FORK

DINNER KNIFE

Lady Hamilton Design • COMMUNITY PLATE

Replacement Guarantee

It is fitting that, in the Lady Hamilton design, the pieces are of the long and slender type that is known to Silversmiths as "pointed antique"—a type that the beautiful and charming hostess after whom the design is named may easily have used to appoint her table for those brilliant dinners she gave more than a hundred years ago at the Court of Naples. This grace of line is enhanced by the ornament, adapted with such exquisite delicacy, from Nature.

Always state design wanted

KNIFE AND FORK SETS
(6 DeLuxe Stainless Knives and 6 Forks)
(in Cameo Gift Case)

	Priced, Per Set Consumer	List
Grille Knives, H. H. and Grille Fks.	$21.00	$25.20
Dinner Knives, H.H. and Dinner Fks.	21.00	25.20
Dessert Knives, H.H. and Dessert Fks.	21.00	25.20
Dinner Knives, Mod.H. and Din. Fks.	18.00	21.60

LADLES

Serving or Gravy	Each	2.25	2.70
Medium Soup or Serving . .	Each	8.00	9.60

CARVERS (DeLuxe Stainless Blades)

2-Piece, H. H. (7-in. Blade)	Per Set	10.00	12.00
2-Piece, H. H. (5-in. Blade)	Per Set	6.00	7.20
3-Piece, Large, H. H. . .	Per Set	17.00	20.40
Double Service, 3-Pc., H. H.	Per Set	18.00	21.60

MISCELLANEOUS

Butter Knife	Each	1.50	1.80
Game Shears	Each	10.00	12.00
★Sugar Tongs	Each	1.75	2.10
Pie or Ice Cream Server, H. H.	Each	3.25	3.90
Pastry Server, Pierced	Each	3.00	3.60
Round Server, Pierced	Each	2.25	2.70
★Small Server (Jelly Server) . .	Each	1.75	2.10
Butter Knife and Sugar Spoon Set.	Each	3.00	3.60
Fruit Knives, H.H., DeLuxe Stain.	Set of 6	10.00	12.00
★Ind. Butter or Cheese Knives . .	Set of 6	6.50	7.80

BABY SPOONS AND FORKS
(In brightly decorated boxes)

Spoon, Bent Handle	Each	.75	.90
Spoon, Straight Handle	Each	.75	.90
Fork, Straight Handle	Each	.75	.90
Fork and Bent Spoon	Per Set	1.50	1.80
Fork and Straight Spoon	Per Set	1.50	1.80

CHILD'S SET (in brightly decorated box)

IND. BUTTER KNIFE

GRILLE FORK

GRILLE KNIFE

FRUIT KNIFE

PIERCED PASTRY SERVER

H. H. PIE SER

CARVING SET 2 PC. 7 IN.

SMALL SERVER

See Price Guide — Group 2

Louis XVI Pattern

Turn over a new leaf. If you are not already carrying Community Silver, do so. Community Silver has the heaviest plate, is the best advertised, and your profit is fully protected. Shown below is the Louis XVI design. In exquisite grace and delicacy of line, it harmonizes perfectly with the period it represents — the later French Renaissance — while in rich simplicity it rivals the best examples of sterling silver.

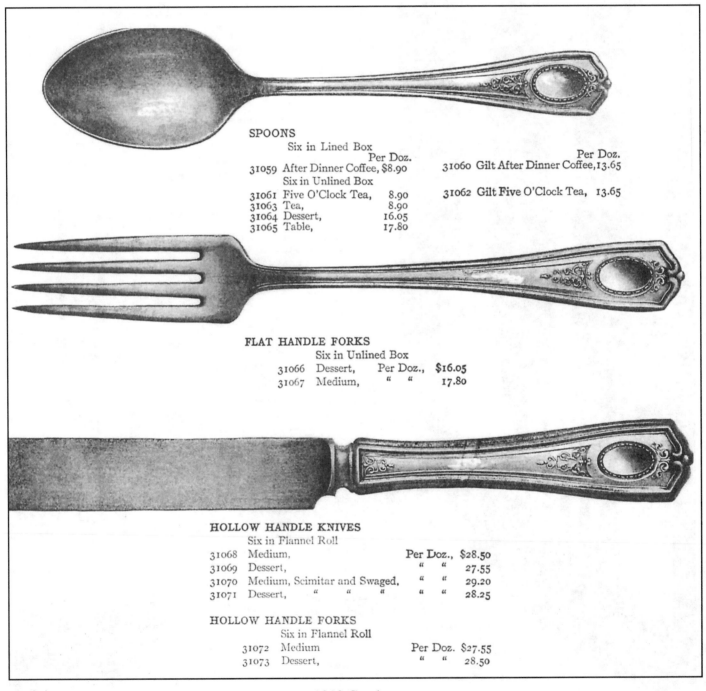

SPOONS
Six in Lined Box

		Per Doz.			Per Doz.
31059	After Dinner Coffee,	$8.90	31060	Gilt After Dinner Coffee,	13.65

Six in Unlined Box

31061	Five O'Clock Tea,	8.90	31062	Gilt Five O'Clock Tea,	13.65
31063	Tea,	8.90			
31064	Dessert,	16.05			
31065	Table,	17.80			

FLAT HANDLE FORKS
Six in Unlined Box

31066	Dessert,	Per Doz.,	$16.05
31067	Medium,	" "	17.80

HOLLOW HANDLE KNIVES
Six in Flannel Roll

31068	Medium,	Per Doz.,	$28.50
31069	Dessert,	" "	27.55
31070	Medium, Scimitar and Swaged,	" "	29.20
31071	Dessert, " " "	" "	28.25

HOLLOW HANDLE FORKS
Six in Flannel Roll

31072	Medium	Per Doz.	$27.55
31073	Dessert,	" "	28.50

1913 Catalog

Louis XVI Pattern

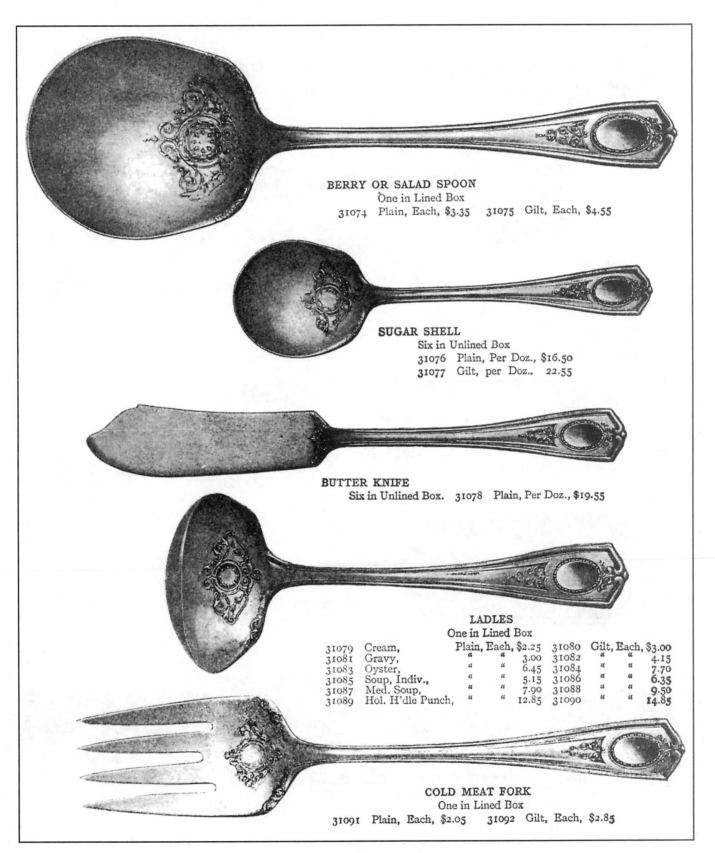

BERRY OR SALAD SPOON
One in Lined Box
31074 Plain, Each, $3.35   31075 Gilt, Each, $4.55

SUGAR SHELL
Six in Unlined Box
31076 Plain, Per Doz., $16.50
31077 Gilt, per Doz., 22.55

BUTTER KNIFE
Six in Unlined Box. 31078 Plain, Per Doz., $19.55

LADLES
One in Lined Box

31079	Cream,	Plain, Each, $2.25	31080	Gilt, Each, $3.00
31081	Gravy,	" " 3.00	31082	" " 4.15
31083	Oyster,	" " 6.45	31084	" " 7.70
31085	Soup, Indiv.,	" " 5.15	31086	" " 6.35
31087	Med. Soup,	" " 7.90	31088	" " 9.50
31089	Hol. H'dle Punch,	" " 12.85	31090	" " 14.85

COLD MEAT FORK
One in Lined Box
31091 Plain, Each, $2.05   31092 Gilt, Each, $2.85

1913 Catalog

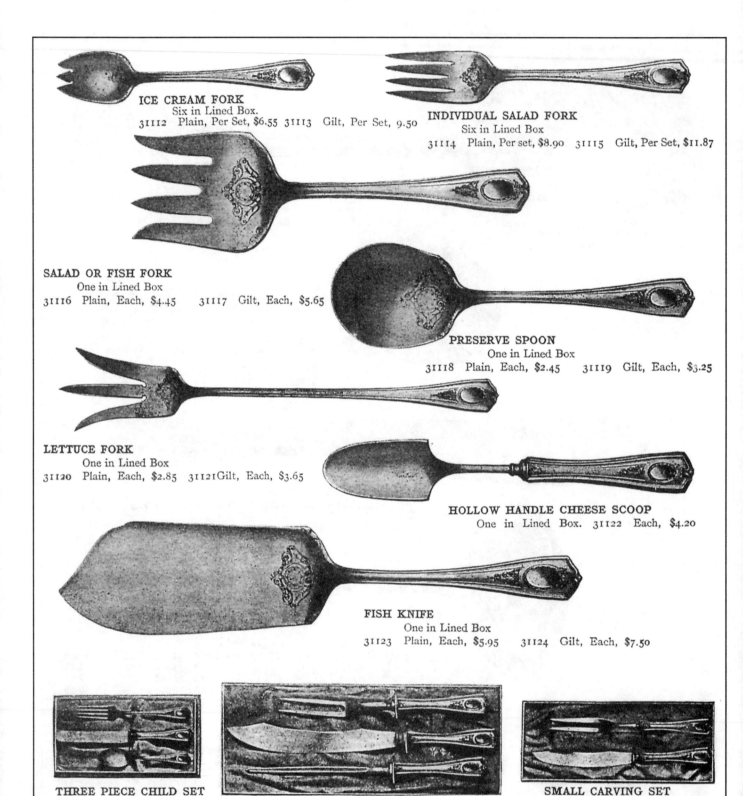

ICE CREAM FORK
Six in Lined Box.
31112 Plain, Per Set, $6.55 31113 Gilt, Per Set, 9.50

INDIVIDUAL SALAD FORK
Six in Lined Box
31114 Plain, Per set, $8.90 31115 Gilt, Per Set, $11.87

SALAD OR FISH FORK
One in Lined Box
31116 Plain, Each, $4.45 31117 Gilt, Each, $5.65

PRESERVE SPOON
One in Lined Box
31118 Plain, Each, $2.45 31119 Gilt, Each, $3.25

LETTUCE FORK
One in Lined Box
31120 Plain, Each, $2.85 31121 Gilt, Each, $3.65

HOLLOW HANDLE CHEESE SCOOP
One in Lined Box. 31122 Each, $4.20

FISH KNIFE
One in Lined Box
31123 Plain, Each, $5.95 31124 Gilt, Each, $7.50

THREE PIECE CHILD SET
One Set in Lined Box
31125 Hollow Handle Knife, Per Set $4.45
31126 Flat Nickel Knife, " " 3.05

LARGE CARVING SET
One Set in Lined Box
31127 Per Set, $19.00

SMALL CARVING SET
One Set in Lined Box
31128 Per Set, $8.75

Reproduction one-fifth size.

1913 Catalog

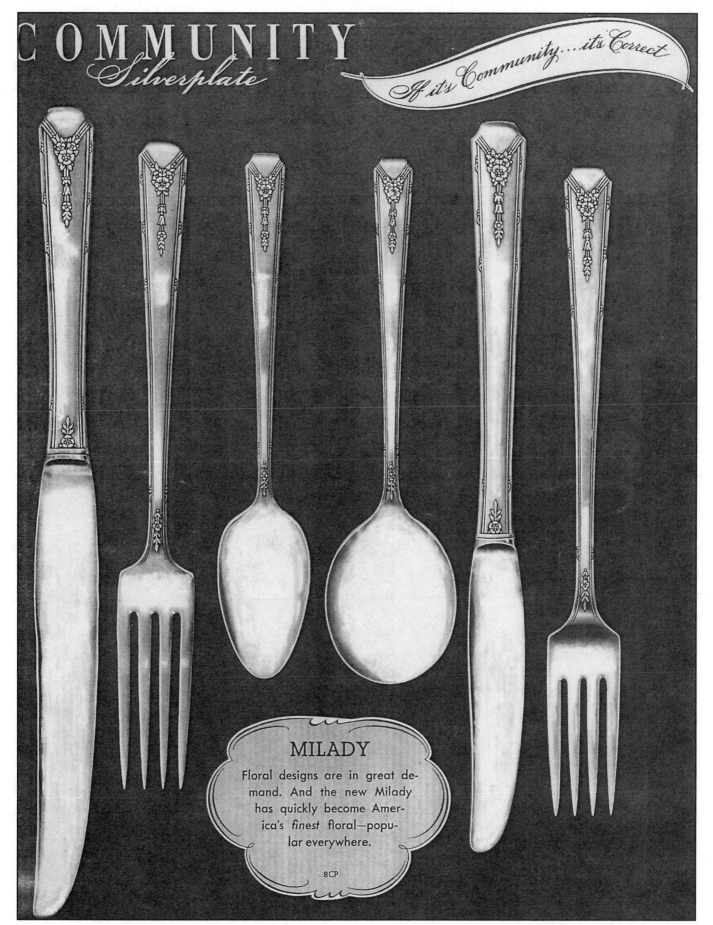

COMMUNITY
Silverplate

If it's Community...it's Correct

MILADY

Floral designs are in great demand. And the new Milady has quickly become America's *finest* floral—popular everywhere.

8CP

See Price Guide — Group 2

COMMUNITY Silverplate

If it's Community... it's Correct

GUARANTEED WITHOUT QUALIFICATION

MILADY* DESIGN

Always specify design wanted

SPOONS	Consumer Price Per Dozen	LIST PRICE
Tea	$ 6.00	$ 7.20
Oval Bowl Soup (Dessert)	12.00	14.40
Serving (Table)	12.00	14.40
Round Bowl Soup	12.00	14.40
Cream Soup	12.00	14.40
Iced Drink	12.00	14.40
After Dinner Coffee	6.00	7.20
Five O'Clock Tea	6.00	7.20

FORKS		
Grille (long handle)	12.00	14.40
Dinner (long tines)	12.00	14.40
Dessert (Breakfast or Luncheon)	12.00	14.40
Salad or Pastry	12.00	14.40
Cocktail or Oyster	12.00	14.40

KNIVES		
Ind. Butter or Cheese Knives	12.00	14.40

Hollow Handles, DeLuxe Stainless Blades

Grille (long handle)	24.00	28.80
Dinner (long blade)	24.00	28.80
Dessert (Breakfast or Luncheon)	24.00	28.80
Salad or Fruit	24.00	28.80

KNIFE AND FORK SETS
(6 DeLuxe Stainless Knives and 6 Forks)

	Per Set	
Grille Knives, Hollow Handle and Grille Forks	18.00	21.60
Dinner Knives, Hollow Handle and Dinner Forks	18.00	21.60
Dessert Knives, Hollow Handle and Dessert Forks	18.00	21.60

SERVING PIECES

	Each	
Butter Knife	1.25	1.50
Sugar Spoon	1.25	1.50
Serving Spoon	1.00	1.20
Cold Meat or Serving Fork	1.75	2.10
Serving or Gravy Ladle	1.75	2.10
Round Server, Pierced	1.75	2.10
Pastry Server, Pierced	2.75	3.30
Pie or Ice Cream Server, Hollow Handle	3.00	3.60

BABY AND CHILD ITEMS
(In Crystal Gift Cases)

	Each	
Baby Spoon, Bent Handle	1.00	1.20
Food-Master Baby Spoon	1.00	1.20
Food-Master Baby Fork	1.00	1.20
Food-Master Baby Fork and Spoon Set	1.75	2.10
3-Piece Child's Set (Spoon, Fork and H. H. Grille Style Knife, DeLuxe Stainless) Set	2.75	3.30

CARVERS (DeLuxe Stainless Blades)
(In Crystal Gift Cases)

1949 Price List

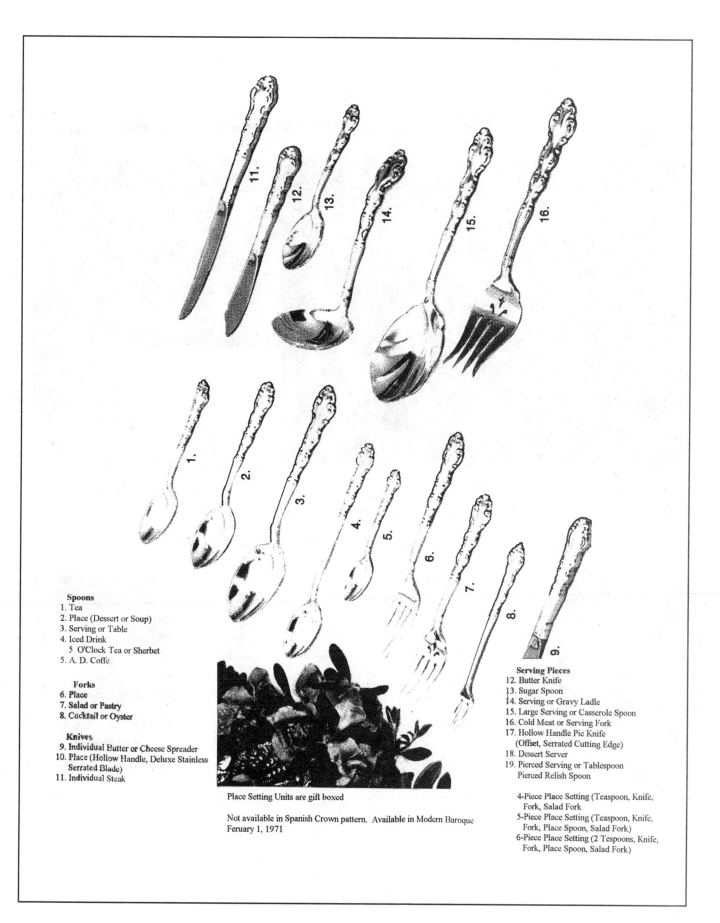

Spoons
1. Tea
2. Place (Dessert or Soup)
3. Serving or Table
4. Iced Drink
   5 O'Clock Tea or Sherbet
5. A. D. Coffe

Forks
6. Place
7. Salad or Pastry
8. Cocktail or Oyster

Knives
9. Individual Butter or Cheese Spreader
10. Place (Hollow Handle, Deluxe Stainless
    Serrated Blade)
11. Individual Steak

Serving Pieces
12. Butter Knife
13. Sugar Spoon
14. Serving or Gravy Ladle
15. Large Serving or Casserole Spoon
16. Cold Meat or Serving Fork
17. Hollow Handle Pie Knife
    (Offset, Serrated Cutting Edge)
18. Dessert Server
19. Pierced Serving or Tablespoon
    Pierced Relish Spoon

4-Piece Place Setting (Teaspoon, Knife,
  Fork, Salad Fork
5-Piece Place Setting (Teaspoon, Knife,
  Fork, Place Spoon, Salad Fork)
6-Piece Place Setting (2 Tespoons, Knife,
  Fork, Place Spoon, Salad Fork)

Place Setting Units are gift boxed

Not available in Spanish Crown pattern. Available in Modern Baroque
Feruary 1, 1971

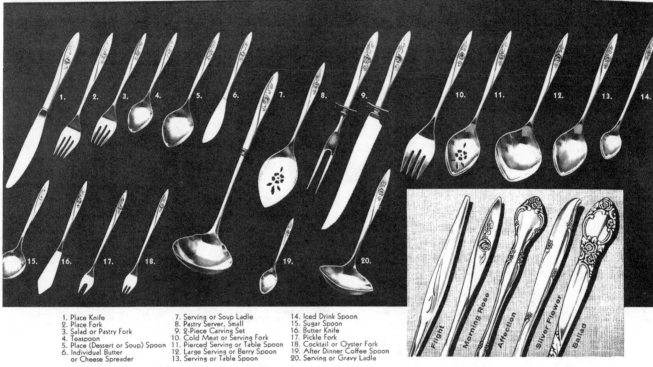

COMMUNITY SILVERPLATE BY ONEIDA SILVERSMITHS

1. Place Knife	7. Serving or Soup Ladle	14. Iced Drink Spoon
2. Place Fork	8. Pastry Server, Small	15. Sugar Spoon
3. Salad or Pastry Fork	9. 2-Piece Carving Set	16. Butter Knife
4. Teaspoon	10. Cold Meat or Serving Fork	17. Pickle Fork
5. Place (Dessert or Soup) Spoon	11. Pierced Serving or Table Spoon	18. Cocktail or Oyster Fork
6. Individual Butter	12. Large Serving or Berry Spoon	19. After Dinner Coffee Spoon
or Cheese Spreader	13. Serving or Table Spoon	20. Serving or Gravy Ladle

OPEN STOCK IN COMMUNITY PATTERNS — JUNE 15, 1963

68 55 Morning Rose Child's Cup
Consumer . . $4.75

SERVING PIECES	RETAIL PRICE Each
Butter Knife	$ 3.00
Sugar Spoon	3.00
Cold Meat or Serving Fork	4.50
Pickle Fork	2.00
§Pierced Relish Spoon	3.00
Serving or Gravy Ladle	4.50
Serving or Soup Ladle	10.00
2-Piece Carving Set, 7 inch Blade	16.50
Large Serving or Berry Spoon	4.50
‡Pastry Server	5.50
°Pastry Server, Small	3.00
Pierced Serving or Table Spoon	3.00
5-Piece Place Setting in Box (Teaspoon, Knife, Fork, Place Spoon, Salad Fork).	10.00

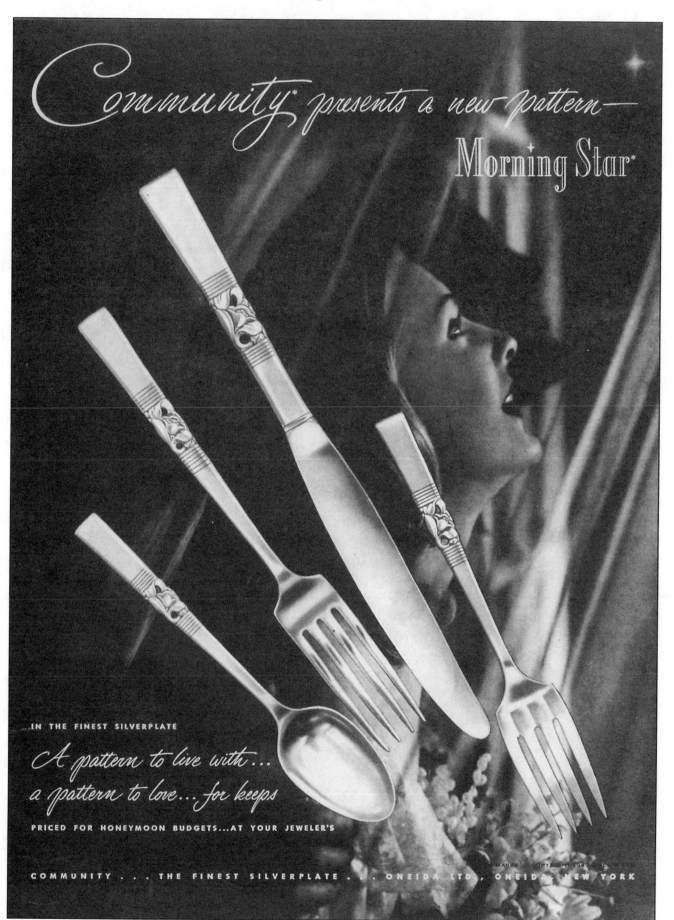

See Price Guide — Group 2

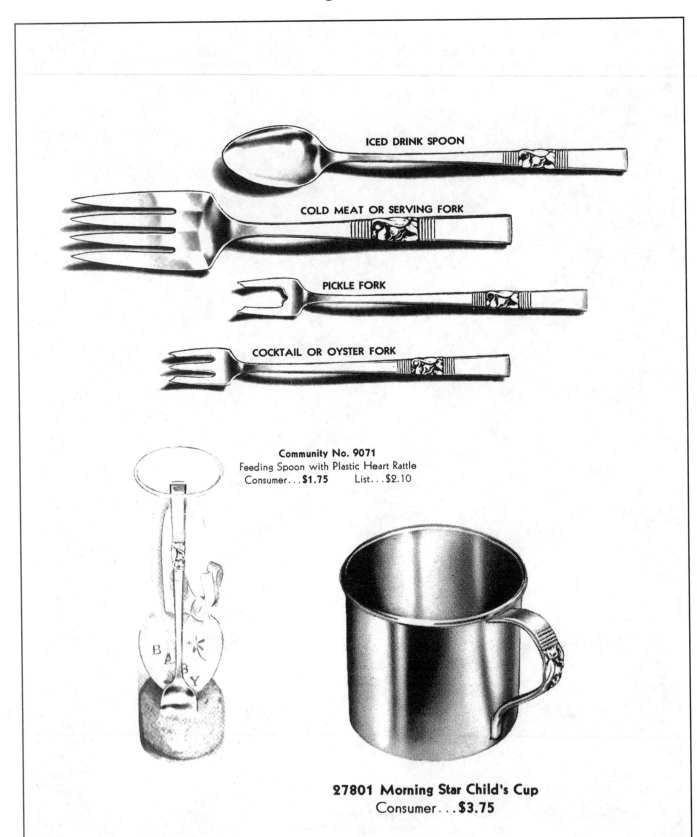

ICED DRINK SPOON

COLD MEAT OR SERVING FORK

PICKLE FORK

COCKTAIL OR OYSTER FORK

Community No. 9071
Feeding Spoon with Plastic Heart Rattle
Consumer...**$1.75**   List...$2.10

27801 Morning Star Child's Cup
Consumer...**$3.75**

1958 Catalog

THE FINEST SILVERPLATE

OPEN STOCK PRICES
ON ALL COMMUNITY PATTERNS
Always specify Pattern wanted

		Consumer Price	
		Set of 8	Set of 12
SPOONS			
Tea..........................8 in box		$ 5.67	$ 8.50
Oval Bowl Soup (Dessert).....8 in box		11.33	17.00
Serving or Table............8 in box		12.00	18.00
Round Bowl Soup..........8 in box		11.33	17.00
Cream Soup...............8 in box		11.33	17.00
Iced Drink.................8 in box		11.33	17.00
FORKS			
Dinner.....................8 in box		11.33	17.00
Grille......................8 in box		11.33	17.00
Dessert.....................8 in box		11.33	17.00
Salad or Pastry............8 in box		11.33	17.00
Cocktail or Oyster..........8 in box		11.33	17.00
KNIVES			
Individual Butter or Cheese....8 in box		11.33	17.00
Hollow Handle, DeLuxe Stainless Blades			
Dinner.....................8 in box		18.60	27.90
Grille......................8 in box		18.60	27.90
Dessert.....................8 in box		18.60	27.90
SERVING PIECES			Each
Butter Knife................1 in box		——	1.50
Sugar Spoon...............1 in box		——	1.50
Cold Meat or Serving Fork....1 in box		——	2.25
Serving or Gravy Ladle.......1 in box		——	2.25

NO FEDERAL TAX

All orders for both sets and open stock subject to prices prevailing at date of shipment

The Consumer's Prices listed herein are the prescribed minimum resale prices on Community in all states which have enacted Fair Trade Acts.

*TRADE-MARK

COMMUNITY PLATE PRESENTS

The NOBLESSE

Another
Community
Selling
Triumph

IT'S here — another harvest of profit for you from COMMUNITY —the same COMMUNITY that gave you 'Deauville'.
And now the '*NOBLESSE*' to peak your Fall sales!

Noblesse Pattern

Noblesse Design • COMMUNITY PLATE

Replacement Guarantee

To the hostess who would express upon her table her modernity of taste and sophistication, the Noblesse design offers an effect that is at once distinguished in its individuality and impressively of today.

Always state design wanted

KNIFE AND FORK SETS
(6 DeLuxe Stainless Knives and 6 Forks)
(in Cameo Gift Case)

	Priced, Per Set Consumer	List
Grille Knives, H. H. and Grille Fks.	$21.00	$25.20
Dinner Knives, H.H. and Dinner Fks.	21.00	25.20
Dessert Knives, H.H. and Dessert Fks.	21.00	25.20
Dinner Knives, Mod.H. and Din. Fks.	18.00	21.60
Dessert Knives, Mod. H. and Des. Fks.	18.00	21.60

LADLES

Salad Dressing or Small	Each	1.75	2.10
Serving or Gravy	Each	2.25	2.70
Medium Soup or Serving	Each	8.00	9.60

CARVERS (DeLuxe Stainless Blades)

2-Piece, H. H. (7-in. Blade)	Per Set	10.00	12.00
2-Piece, H. H. (5-in. Blade)	Per Set	6.00	7.20
3-Piece, Large, H. H.	Per Set	17.00	20.40
Double Service, 3-Pc., H. H.	Per Set	18.00	21.60

MISCELLANEOUS

Butter Knife	Each	1.50	1.80
Game Shears	Each	10.00	12.00
★Sugar Tongs	Each	1.75	2.10
Pie or Ice Cream Server, H. H.	Each	3.25	3.90
Pastry Server, Pierced	Each	3.00	3.60
Round Server, Pierced	Each	2.25	2.70
★Small Server (Jelly Server)	Each	1.75	2.10
Butter Knife and Sugar Spoon Set.	Each	3.00	3.60
Fruit Knives, H.H., DeLuxe Stain.	Set of 6	10.00	12.00
★Ind. Butter or Cheese Knives	Set of 6	6.50	7.80

BABY SPOONS AND FORKS
(In brightly decorated boxes)

Spoon, Bent Handle	Each	.75	.90
Spoon, Straight Handle	Each	.75	.90
Fork, Straight Handle	Each	.75	.90
Fork and Bent Spoon	Per Set	1.50	1.80

GRILLE KNIFE

GRILLE FORK

IND. BUTTER KNIFE

FRUIT KNIFE

BABY KNIFE

BABY SPOON RT. H.

PIERCED PASTRY SERVER

H. H. PIE SE

CARVING SET 2 PC. 7 IN.

SMALL SERVER

PIERCE ROUND SE

Noblesse Pattern

Water Pitcher, Capacity 2¼ quarts, Height 7¾ inches $14.75 / List Each $17.70

Sandwich or Cake Plate, Diameter 11½ inches . . . . Consumer Each $6.50 / List Each $7.80

Child's Cup, Gold Lined, Height 2½ inches . . . . Consumer Each $2.50 / List Each $3.00

	Consumer Each	List Each
Bread or Roll Basket, Length 14¾ inches	$6.50	$7.80
Relish Dish, Glass Lined, Diameter 14 inches	12.00	14.40
Oval Waiter, Length 19 inches . . .	12.50	15.00
Sugar and Cream Set	16.00	19.20
Pickle, Olive or Salted Nut Tray, Length 8¼ inches	3.00	3.60

	Consumer Each	List Each
3-Piece Dessert Service, as illustrated	$12.50	$15.00
2-Piece Dessert Set, Sugar and Creamer	7.50	9.00
Dessert Creamer, Gold Lined, Height 2½ inches . .	4.00	4.80
Dessert Sugar Bowl, Gold Lined, Height 2½ inches .	3.50	4.20
Cold Meat or Dessert Tray, Length 12¾ inches . . .	5.00	6.00

Salt and Pepper Shakers, Height 5 in. Consumer Per Pair $5.50 / List Per Pair $6.60

Bread or Roll Tray, Length 14¾ in. Consumer Each $5.00 / List Each $6.00

Sandwich or Cake Basket, Length 12¾ inches . . . . Consumer Each $8.00 / List Each $9.60

Patented 1930. Catalog date: possibly 1929.

COMMUNITY PLATE
Patrician Moderne Design

50 YEAR REPLACEMENT GUARANTEE

*The Patrician Moderne Design is packed in red and black gift boxes
the same as other Community Plate Designs*

COMPLETE LISTING PATRICIAN MODERNE FLATWARE

SPOONS—Six in Box

Priced, per dozen	Retail	List
Tea	$8.00	$10.00
Dessert	16.00	20.00
Table	16.00	20.00
Soup R. B.	16.00	20.00

Priced, set of six	Retail	List
After Dinner Coffee Spoons	$4.00	$5.00
Five O'Clock Tea Spoons	4.00	5.00
Ice Cream or Sundae Spoons	6.00	7.50
Cream Soup Spoons	8.00	10.00
Bouillon or Consomme Spoons	7.50	9.40
Iced Tea or Iced Drink Spoons	6.00	7.50
Orange or Grapefruit Spoons	6.00	7.50

Priced, each	Retail	List
Sugar Spoon	$1.25	$1.57
Jam or Conserve Spoon	1.75	2.19
Pierced Bon Bon Spoon	2.50	3.13
Berry or Serving Spoon	3.50	4.38
Small Berry or Preserve Spoon	3.00	3.75
Olive or Salted Nut Spoon	2.00	2.50

FORKS—Six in Box

Priced, per dozen	Retail	List
Dinner	$16.00	$20.00
Dessert	16.00	20.00

Priced, set of six	Retail	List
Individual Salad or Pastry Forks	$7.50	$9.40
Ice Cream or Sherbet Forks	6.50	8.14
Individual Pie Forks	9.00	11.26
Oyster or Seafood Forks	5.50	6.88

Priced, each	Retail	List
Cold Meat or Serving Fork	$2.50	$3.13
Small Cold Meat or Sardine Fork	2.25	2.82
Pickle or Olive Fork	1.50	1.88
Lemon or Relish Fork	1.50	1.88
Cake Fork	3.00	3.76

KNIVES—DeLuxe Stainless

Priced, per dozen	Retail	List
Hollow Handle Dinner	$28.00	$36.48
Hollow Handle Dessert	28.00	36.48
Hollow Handle Salad	23.00	30.00
Modeled Handle Dinner	18.00	23.44
Modeled Handle Dessert	18.00	23.44

"JEWELED" HANDLED KNIVES
With DeLuxe Stainless Blades

Priced, per dozen	Retail	List
Dinner Knives in Emerald Color	$19.50	$25.40
Dessert Knives in Ruby Color	19.50	25.40
Dessert Knives in Emerald Color	19.50	25.40
Dessert Knives in Sapphire Color	19.50	25.40

KNIVES

	Retail	List
Ind. Butter Spreaders, set of six	$6.50	$8.14
Butter Knife, each	1.25	1.57
Cake or Bread Knife, each	5.00	6.51

KNIFE AND FORK SETS
6 DeLuxe Stainless Knives and 6 Forks

Priced, per set	Retail	List
H. H. Dinner Knives and Forks	$22.00	$28.24
H. H. Dessert Knives and Forks	22.00	28.24
H. H. Salad Knives and Salad Forks	19.00	24.40
M. H. Dinner Knives and Forks	17.00	21.72
M. H. Dessert Knives and Forks	17.00	21.72

LADLES

Priced, each	Retail	List
Salad Dressing or Small Ladle	$2.25	$2.82
Serving or Gravy Ladle	3.00	3.75
Medium Soup or Serving Ladle	8.50	10.64

CARVERS—DeLuxe Stainless Blades

Priced, per set	Retail	List
2-Piece, H. H. (7-in. Blade)	$12.50	$16.28
2-Piece, H. H. (5-in. Blade)	8.50	11.08
2-Pc. Mod. H. Standard Stainless (5-in.)	5.50	7.18
Large, 3-Piece Hollow Handle, set	20.00	26.06

MISCELLANEOUS

Priced, each	Retail	List
Game Shears	$11.00	$14.34
Sugar Tongs	2.00	2.50
Pie or Ice Cream Server, H. H.	4.50	5.63
Pierced Pastry Server	4.50	5.63
Pierced Round Server	3.50	4.38
Jelly Server	1.75	2.19

SETS

	Retail	List
Butter Knife and Sugar Spoon	$2.50	$3.12
Cake Serving	8.00	10.26

BABY SPOONS AND FORKS

In Brightly Decorated Boxes	Retail	List
Spoon, Bent Handle, each	$1.00	$1.25
Spoon, Straight Handle, each	1.00	1.25
Fork, Straight Handle, each	1.00	1.25
Fork and Bent Spoon, set	2.00	2.50
Fork and Straight Spoon, set	2.00	2.50

CHILD'S SETS

In Brightly Decorated Boxes	Retail	List
With Hollow Handle Knife, set	$4.00	$5.00
With Flat Handle Knife, set	3.00	3.76

COMPLETE LISTING
PATRICIAN MODERNE HOLLOWWARE

TEA SERVICE

	Retail	List
3-Piece Tea Set *(without waiter)*	$40.00	$50.04
Tea Pot *(5 half pints)* Illustrated Below		
Sugar Bowl	20.00	25.02
Cream Pitcher	11.00	13.76
Sugar and Cream Set	9.00	11.26
4-Piece Tea Set *(including waiter)*	20.00	25.02
	60.00	75.06

Priced, each

OTHER HOLLOWWARE PIECES

	Retail	List
Dessert Service *(Sugar and Cream)*	10.00	12.52
Bread or Roll Tray	7.50	9.38
Water Pitcher *(2 quarts)*	17.50	21.90
Double Vegetable Dish	17.50	21.90
Open Vegetable Dish	8.75	10.96
Oval Waiter, *18-inch*	20.00	25.02
Cold Meat or Dessert Tray	7.50	9.38
Gravy Boat and Tray	15.00	18.76
Bread or Roll Basket	9.50	11.88
Sandwich or Cake Plate	7.50	9.38
Sandwich or Cake Basket	10.50	13.14
Meat Platter, Plain, *18-inch*	20.00	25.02
Meat Platter, Well and Tree, *18-inch*	24.00	30.02
Mayonnaise Bowl	5.50	6.88
Bon Bon Dish	4.00	5.00
Tea or Salad Plate	4.00	5.00
Pickle, Olive or Salted Nut Tray	3.75	4.70
Child's Cup	3.75	4.70
Child's Porringer	3.75	4.70
Child's Bowl	3.75	4.70
Child's Plate	3.75	4.70
Child's Set *(Bowl and Plate)*	7.50	9.40
Set of 6 Tea or Salad Plates	24.00	30.00
Set of 6 Bread and Butter Plates	22.50	28.16
Set of 6 Finger Bowls	22.50	28.16
3-Piece Dessert Set	17.50	21.90
Dessert Creamer	5.00	6.26
Dessert Sugar Bowl	5.00	6.26

Priced, per pair

	Retail	List
Salt and Pepper Shakers *(boxed)*, Height 5¼ inches	7.50	9.38

1930 Catalog

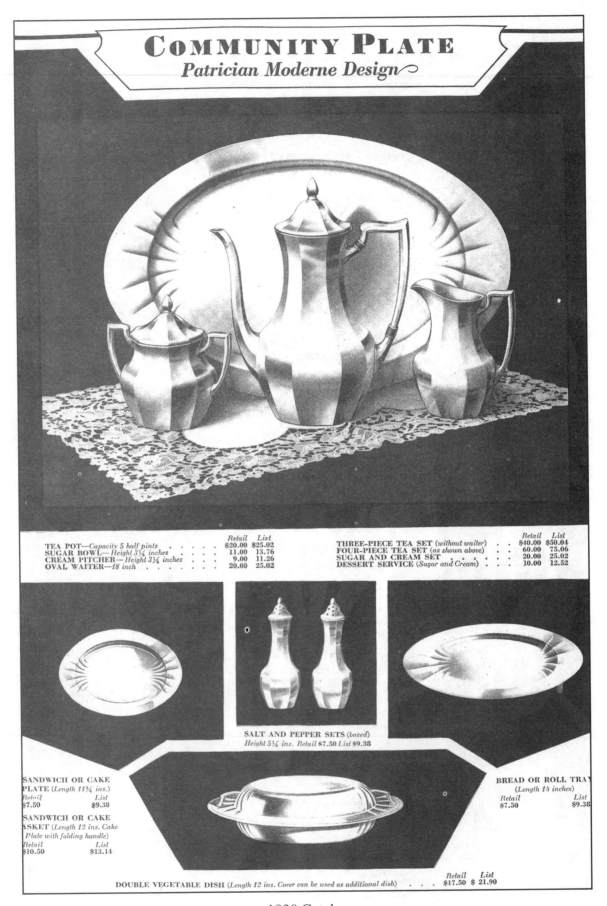

COMMUNITY PLATE
Patrician Moderne Design

	Retail	List				Retail	List
TEA POT—*Capacity 5 half pints*	$20.00	$25.02		THREE-PIECE TEA SET (*without waiter*)		$40.00	$50.04
SUGAR BOWL— *Height 3¼ inches*	11.00	13.76		FOUR-PIECE TEA SET (*as shown above*)		60.00	75.06
CREAM PITCHER— *Height 3¼ inches*	9.00	11.26		SUGAR AND CREAM SET		20.00	25.02
OVAL WAITER—*18 inch*	20.00	25.02		DESSERT SERVICE (*Sugar and Cream*)		10.00	12.52

SALT AND PEPPER SETS (*boxed*)
Height 5¼ ins. Retail $7.50 List $9.38

SANDWICH OR CAKE PLATE (*Length 11¾ ins.*)

Retail	List
$7.50	$9.38

SANDWICH OR CAKE ASKET (*Length 12 ins. Cake Plate with folding handle*)

Retail	List
$10.50	$13.14

BREAD OR ROLL TRAY (*Length 14 inches*)

Retail	List
$7.50	$9.38

	Retail	List
DOUBLE VEGETABLE DISH (*Length 12 ins. Cover can be used as additional dish*)	$17.50	$21.90

1930 Catalog

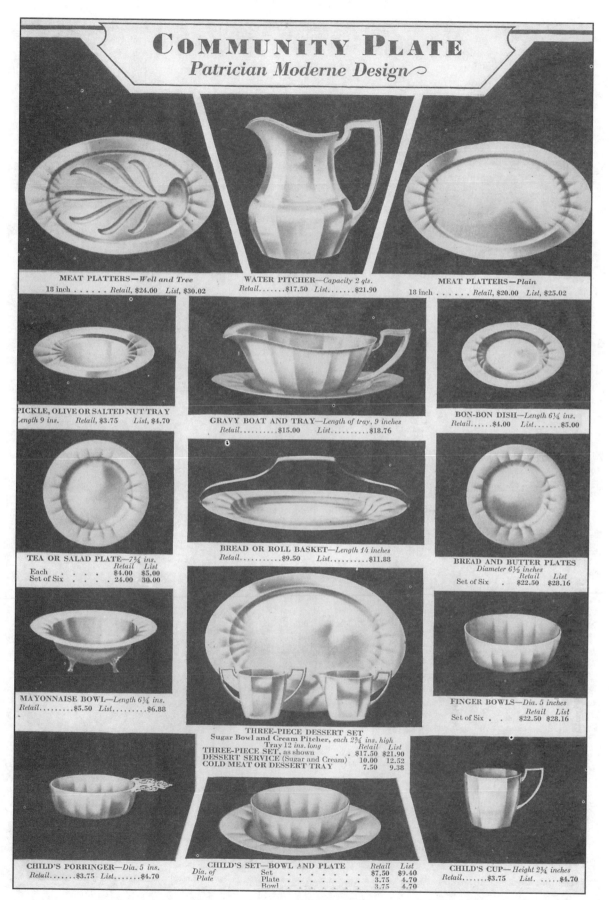

COMMUNITY PLATE
Patrician Moderne Design

MEAT PLATTERS—*Well and Tree*
18 inch . . . . . . *Retail,* $24.00 *List,* $30.02

WATER PITCHER—*Capacity 2 qts.*
Retail. . . . . . .$17.50 *List.* $21.90

MEAT PLATTERS—*Plain*
18 inch . . . . . . *Retail,* $20.00 *List,* $25.02

PICKLE, OLIVE OR SALTED NUT TRAY
Length 9 ins.   *Retail,* $3.75   *List,* $4.70

GRAVY BOAT AND TRAY—*Length of tray, 9 inches*
Retail. . . . .$15.00   *List.* $18.76

BON-BON DISH—*Length 6¼ ins.*
Retail. . . . . . .$4.00 *List.* $5.00

TEA OR SALAD PLATE—*7¾ ins.*

	Retail	List
Each	$4.00	$5.00
Set of Six	24.00	30.00

BREAD OR ROLL BASKET—*Length 14 inches*
Retail. . . . .$9.50   *List.* $11.83

BREAD AND BUTTER PLATES
Diameter 6½ inches

	Retail	List
Set of Six	$22.50	$28.16

MAYONNAISE BOWL—*Length 6¼ ins.*
Retail. . . . .$5.50 *List.* $6.88

THREE-PIECE DESSERT SET
Sugar Bowl and Cream Pitcher, each 2¾ ins. high
Tray 12 ins. long

FINGER BOWLS—*Dia. 5 inches*

	Retail	List
Set of Six	$22.50	$28.16

	Retail	List
THREE-PIECE SET, as shown	$17.50	$21.90
DESSERT SERVICE (Sugar and Cream)	10.00	12.52
COLD MEAT OR DESSERT TRAY	7.50	9.38

CHILD'S PORRINGER—*Dia. 5 ins.*
Retail. . . . . . .$3.75 *List.* $4.70

CHILD'S SET—BOWL AND PLATE

Dia. of Plate		Retail	List
	Set	$7.50	$9.40
	Plate	3.75	4.70
	Bowl	3.75	4.70

CHILD'S CUP—*Height 2¾ inches*
Retail. . . . . . .$3.75 *List.* $4.70

1930 Catalog

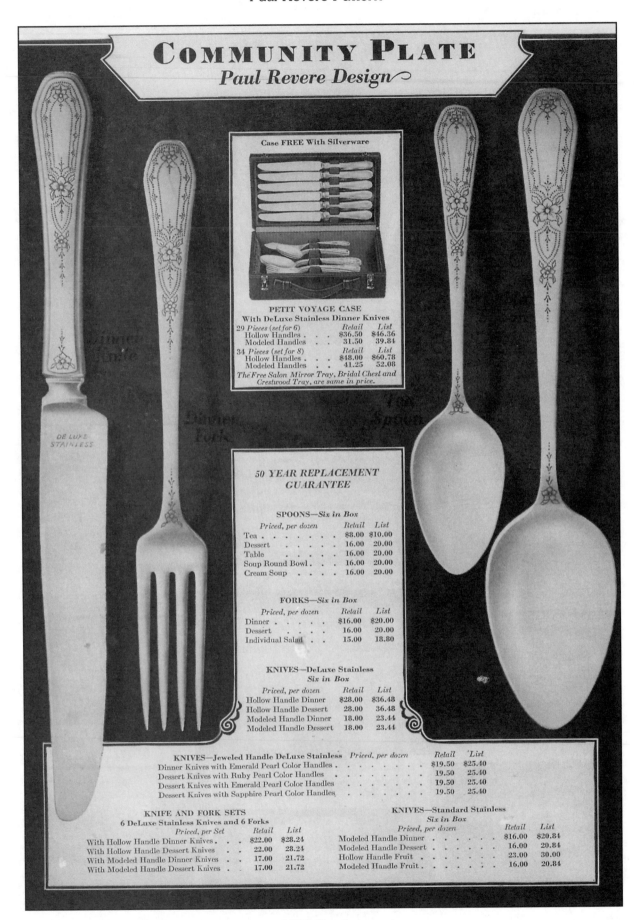

COMMUNITY PLATE
Paul Revere Design

Case FREE With Silverware

PETIT VOYAGE CASE
With DeLuxe Stainless Dinner Knives

29 Pieces (set for 6)	Retail	List
Hollow Handles	$36.50	$46.36
Modeled Handles	31.50	39.84

34 Pieces (set for 8)	Retail	List
Hollow Handles	$48.00	$60.78
Modeled Handles	41.25	52.08

The Free Salon Mirror Tray, Bridal Chest and Crestwood Tray, are same in price.

50 YEAR REPLACEMENT GUARANTEE

SPOONS—Six in Box

Priced, per dozen	Retail	List
Tea	$8.00	$10.00
Dessert	16.00	20.00
Table	16.00	20.00
Soup Round Bowl	16.00	20.00
Cream Soup	16.00	20.00

FORKS—Six in Box

Priced, per dozen	Retail	List
Dinner	$16.00	$20.00
Dessert	16.00	20.00
Individual Salad	15.00	18.80

KNIVES—DeLuxe Stainless
Six in Box

Priced, per dozen	Retail	List
Hollow Handle Dinner	$28.00	$36.48
Hollow Handle Dessert	28.00	36.48
Modeled Handle Dinner	18.00	23.44
Modeled Handle Dessert	18.00	23.44

KNIVES—Jeweled Handle DeLuxe Stainless Priced, per dozen

	Retail	List
Dinner Knives with Emerald Pearl Color Handles	$19.50	$25.40
Dessert Knives with Ruby Pearl Color Handles	19.50	25.40
Dessert Knives with Emerald Pearl Color Handles	19.50	25.40
Dessert Knives with Sapphire Pearl Color Handles	19.50	25.40

KNIFE AND FORK SETS
6 DeLuxe Stainless Knives and 6 Forks

Priced, per Set	Retail	List
With Hollow Handle Dinner Knives	$22.00	$28.24
With Hollow Handle Dessert Knives	22.00	28.24
With Modeled Handle Dinner Knives	17.00	21.72
With Modeled Handle Dessert Knives	17.00	21.72

KNIVES—Standard Stainless
Six in Box

Priced, per dozen	Retail	List
Modeled Handle Dinner	$16.00	$20.84
Modeled Handle Dessert	16.00	20.84
Hollow Handle Fruit	23.00	30.00
Modeled Handle Fruit	16.00	20.84

1930 Catalog

Paul Revere Pattern

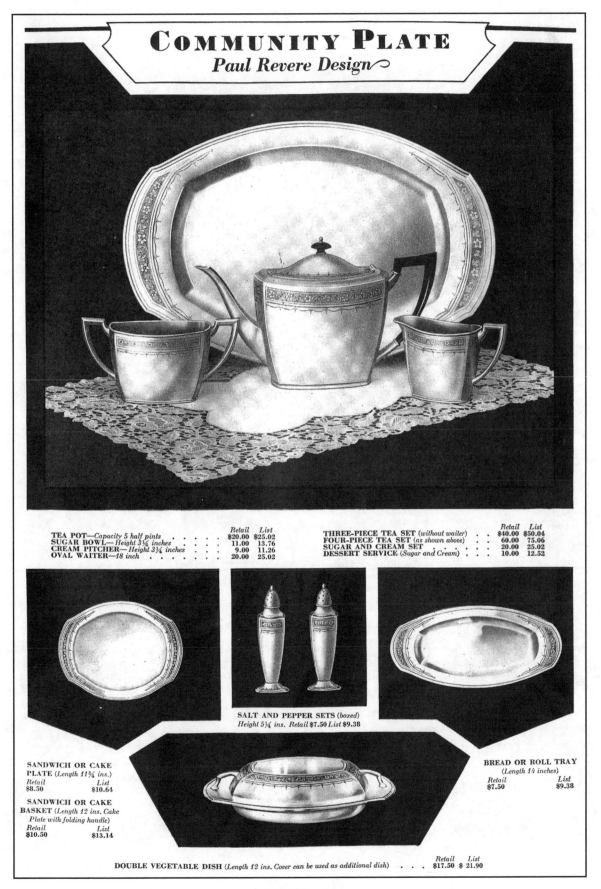

COMMUNITY PLATE
Paul Revere Design

	Retail	List		Retail	List
TEA POT—*Capacity 5 half pints*	$20.00	$25.02	THREE-PIECE TEA SET (*without waiter*)	$40.00	$50.04
SUGAR BOWL—*Height 3¼ inches*	11.00	13.76	FOUR-PIECE TEA SET (*as shown above*)	60.00	75.06
CREAM PITCHER—*Height 3¼ inches*	9.00	11.26	SUGAR AND CREAM SET	20.00	25.02
OVAL WAITER—*18 inch*	20.00	25.02	DESSERT SERVICE (*Sugar and Cream*)	10.00	12.52

SALT AND PEPPER SETS (*boxed*)
Height 5¼ ins. Retail $7.50 List $9.38

**SANDWICH OR CAKE
PLATE** (*Length 11¾ ins.*)
Retail $8.50   *List* $10.64

**SANDWICH OR CAKE
BASKET** (*Length 12 ins. Cake
Plate with folding handle*)
Retail $10.50   *List* $13.14

BREAD OR ROLL TRAY
(*Length 14 inches*)
Retail $7.50   *List* $9.38

DOUBLE VEGETABLE DISH (*Length 12 ins. Cover can be used as additional dish*) . . . *Retail* $17.50 *List* $21.90

1930 Catalog

See Price Guide — Group 2

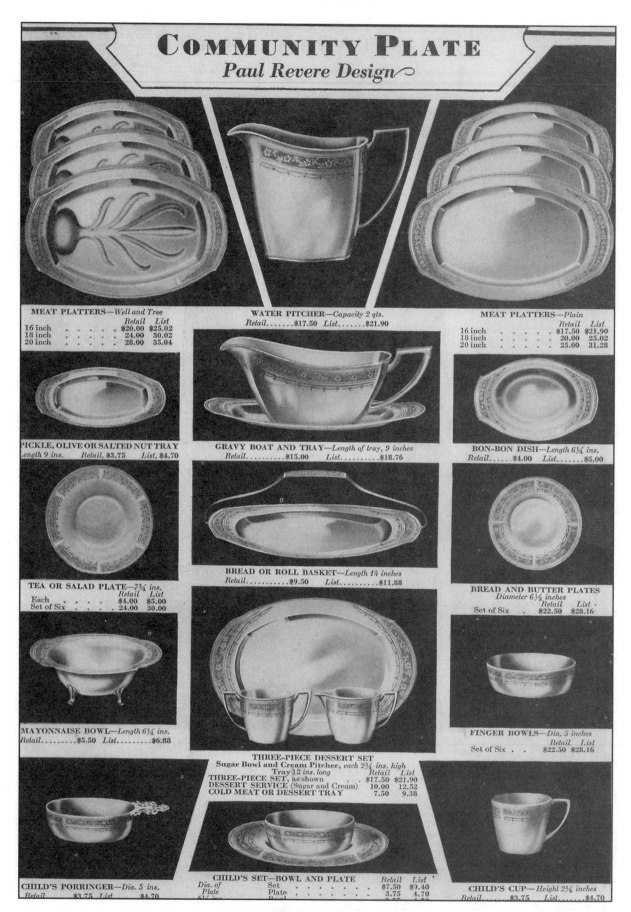

COMMUNITY PLATE
Paul Revere Design

MEAT PLATTERS—*Well and Tree*

	Retail	List
16 inch	$20.00	$25.02
18 inch	24.00	30.02
20 inch	28.00	35.04

WATER PITCHER—*Capacity 2 qts.*
Retail.......$17.50   List.......$21.90

MEAT PLATTERS—*Plain*

	Retail	List
16 inch	$17.50	$21.90
18 inch	20.00	25.02
20 inch	25.00	31.28

PICKLE, OLIVE OR SALTED NUT TRAY
Length 9 ins.   Retail, $3.75   List, $4.70

GRAVY BOAT AND TRAY—*Length of tray, 9 inches*
Retail.........$15.00   List.........$18.76

BON-BON DISH—*Length 6¼ ins.*
Retail......$4.00   List......$5.00

BREAD OR ROLL BASKET—*Length 14 inches*
Retail.........$9.50   List.........$11.88

TEA OR SALAD PLATE—*7¾ ins.*

	Retail	List
Each	$4.00	$5.00
Set of Six	24.00	30.00

BREAD AND BUTTER PLATES
Diameter 6½ inches

	Retail	List
Set of Six	$22.50	$28.16

MAYONNAISE BOWL—*Length 6¼ ins.*
Retail.........$5.50   List.........$6.88

FINGER BOWLS—*Dia. 5 inches*

	Retail	List
Set of Six	$22.50	$28.16

THREE-PIECE DESSERT SET
Sugar Bowl and Cream Pitcher, each 2¾ ins. high
Tray 12 ins. long

	Retail	List
THREE-PIECE SET, as shown	$17.50	$21.90
DESSERT SERVICE (Sugar and Cream)	10.00	12.52
COLD MEAT OR DESSERT TRAY	7.50	9.38

CHILD'S PORRINGER—*Dia. 5 ins.*
Retail $3.75   List $4.70

CHILD'S SET—BOWL AND PLATE

		Retail	List
Dia. of Plate	Set	$7.50	$9.40
	Plate	3.75	4.70

CHILD'S CUP—*Height 2¾ inches*
Retail......$3.75   List......$4.70

1930 Catalog

Royal Grandeur Pattern

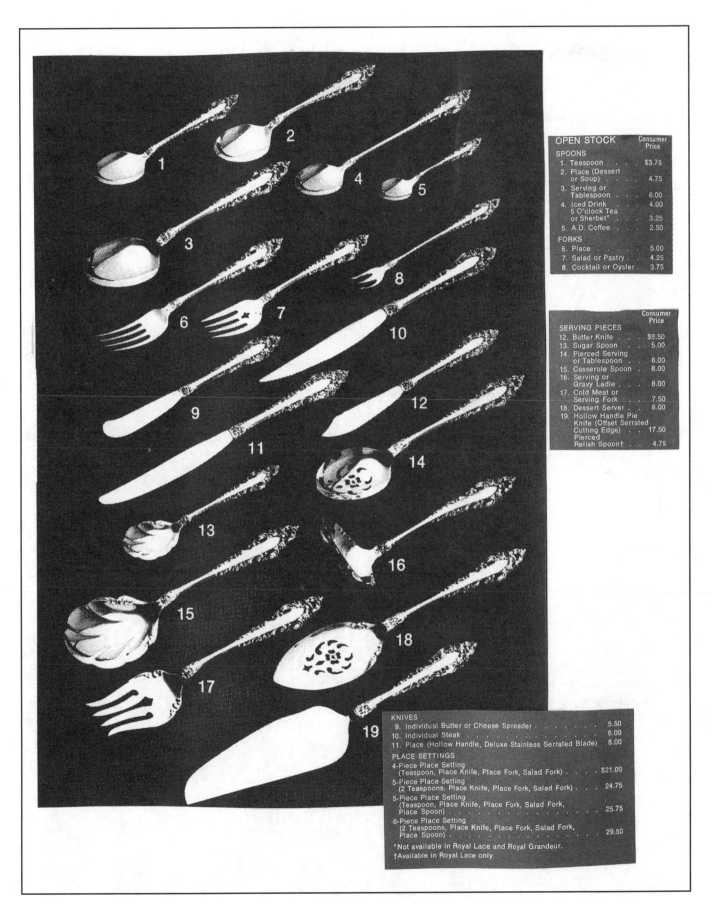

OPEN STOCK
		Consumer Price
SPOONS		
1.	Teaspoon . . .	$3.75
2.	Place (Dessert or Soup) . . .	4.75
3.	Serving or Tablespoon . .	6.00
4.	Iced Drink 5 O'clock Tea or Sherbet° . .	4.00
5.	A.D. Coffee . . .	3.25
		2.50
FORKS		
6.	Place	5.00
7.	Salad or Pastry .	4.25
8.	Cocktail or Oyster .	3.75

		Consumer Price
SERVING PIECES		
12.	Butter Knife . . .	$5.50
13.	Sugar Spoon . .	5.00
14.	Pierced Serving or Tablespoon . .	6.00
15.	Casserole Spoon .	8.00
16.	Serving or Gravy Ladle . . .	8.00
17.	Cold Meat or Serving Fork . .	7.50
18.	Dessert Server . .	8.00
19.	Hollow Handle Pie Knife (Offset Serrated Cutting Edge) . .	17.50
	Pierced Relish Spoon† . .	4.75

KNIVES
9. Individual Butter or Cheese Spreader 5.50
10. Individual Steak 8.00
11. Place (Hollow Handle, Deluxe Stainless Serrated Blade) 8.00

PLACE SETTINGS
4-Piece Place Setting
(Teaspoon, Place Knife, Place Fork, Salad Fork) . . . $21.00
5-Piece Place Setting
(2 Teaspoons, Place Knife, Place Fork, Salad Fork) . . 24.75
5-Piece Place Setting
(Teaspoon, Place Knife, Place Fork, Salad Fork, Place Spoon) 25.75
6-Piece Place Setting
(2 Teaspoons, Place Knife, Place Fork, Salad Fork, Place Spoon) 29.50

°Not available in Royal Lace and Royal Grandeur.
†Available in Royal Lace only.

1976 Catalog

See Price Guide — Group 2

Spoons	Cons. Price
1. Teaspoon	$3.50
2. Place Spoon	4.25
3. Serving or Tablespoon . . .	5.50
4. Iced Drink Spoon	4.00
5 O'Clock Tea or Sherbet Spoon°	3.25
5. A.D. Coffee Spoon	2.50

Forks	
6. Place Fork	4.75
7. Salad or Pastry Fork	4.25
8. Cocktail or Oyster Fork . . .	3.75

Knives	
9. Ind. Butter or Cheese Spreader .	5.50
10. Ind. Steak Knife	8.00
11. Place Knife	8.00

Serving Pieces	Cons. Price
12. Butter Knife	$5.00
13. Sugar Spoon	5.00
14. Pcd. Serving or Tablespoon . .	5.50
15. Casserole Spoon	8.00
16. Serving or Gravy Ladle . . .	8.00
17. Cold Meat or Serving Fork . .	7.50
18. Dessert Server	8.00
19. Hollow Handle Pie Knife . . .	15.00
Pierced Relish Spoon°° . . .	4.75

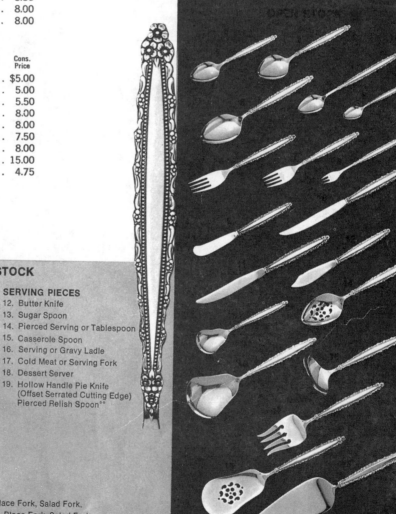

OPEN STOCK

SPOONS
1. Teaspoon
2. Place Spoon (Dessert or Soup)
3. Serving or Tablespoon
4. Iced Drink Spoon
   5 O'Clock Tea or Sherbet Spoon°
5. A.D. Coffee Spoon

FORKS
6. Place Fork
7. Salad or Pastry Fork
8. Cocktail or Oyster Fork

KNIVES
9. Individual Butter or Cheese Spreader
10. Individual Steak Knife
11. Place Knife (Hollow Handle, Deluxe
   Stainless Serrated Blade)

SERVING PIECES
12. Butter Knife
13. Sugar Spoon
14. Pierced Serving or Tablespoon
15. Casserole Spoon
16. Serving or Gravy Ladle
17. Cold Meat or Serving Fork
18. Dessert Server
19. Hollow Handle Pie Knife
   (Offset Serrated Cutting Edge)
   Pierced Relish Spoon°°

PLACE SETTINGS
4-Pc. Place Setting—Teaspoon, Place Knife, Place Fork, Salad Fork.
5-Pc. Place Setting—2 Teaspoons, Place Knife, Place Fork, Salad Fork.
5-Pc. Place Setting—Teaspoon, Place Knife, Place Fork, Salad Fork, Place Spoon.
6-Pc. Place Setting—2 Teaspoons, Place Knife, Place Fork, Salad Fork, Place Spoon.

°Not available in Royal Lace pattern. °°Available in Spanish Crown pattern only.

1974 Price List

Sheraton Pattern

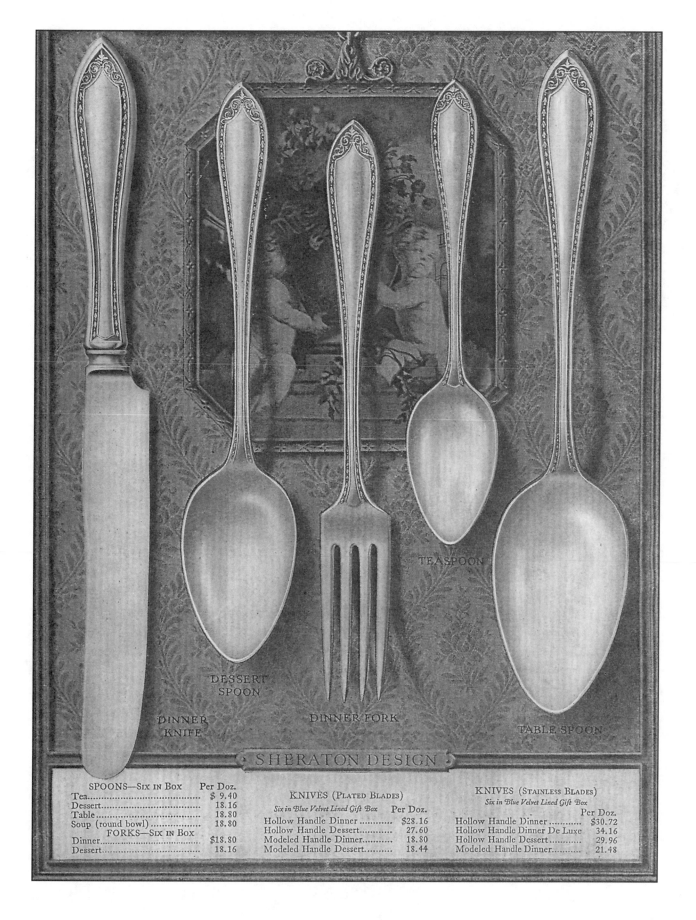

DINNER
KNIFE

DESSERT
SPOON

DINNER FORK

TEASPOON

TABLE SPOON

SHERATON DESIGN

SPOONS—Six in Box	Per Doz.	KNIVES (Plated Blades)		KNIVES (Stainless Blades)	
		Six in Blue Velvet Lined Gift Box	Per Doz.	Six in Blue Velvet Lined Gift Box	Per Doz.
Tea	$ 9.40	Hollow Handle Dinner	$28.16	Hollow Handle Dinner	$30.72
Dessert	18.16	Hollow Handle Dessert	27.60	Hollow Handle Dinner De Luxe	34.16
Table	18.80	Modeled Handle Dinner	18.80	Hollow Handle Dessert	29.96
Soup (round bowl)	18.80	Modeled Handle Dessert	18.44	Modeled Handle Dinner	21.48
FORKS—Six in Box					
Dinner	$18.80				
Dessert	18.16				

See Price Guide — Group 1

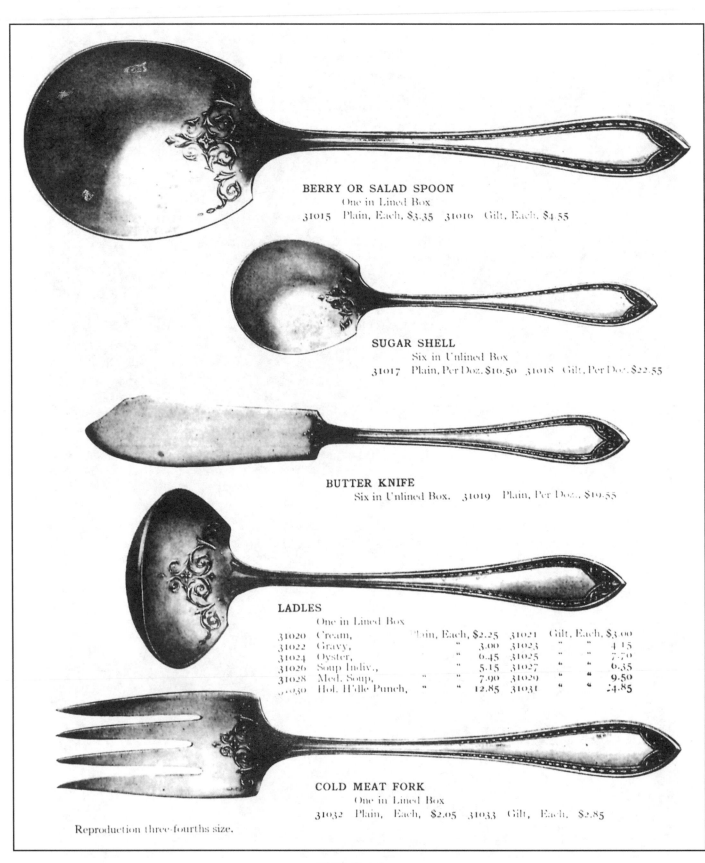

BERRY OR SALAD SPOON
  One in Lined Box
31015 Plain, Each, $3.35 31016 Gilt, Each, $4.55

SUGAR SHELL
  Six in Unlined Box
31017 Plain, Per Doz. $16.50 31018 Gilt, Per Doz. $22.55

BUTTER KNIFE
  Six in Unlined Box. 31019 Plain, Per Doz., $19.55

LADLES
  One in Lined Box

31020	Cream,	Plain, Each, $2.25	31021	Gilt, Each, $3.00
31022	Gravy,	"	3.00	31023	" "	4.15
31024	Oyster,	"	6.45	31025	" "	7.70
31026	Soup Indiv.,	"	5.15	31027	" "	6.35
31028	Med. Soup,	"	"	7.90	31029	" "	9.50
31030	Hol. H'dle Punch,	"	"	12.85	31031	" "	24.85

COLD MEAT FORK
  One in Lined Box
31032 Plain, Each, $2.05 31033 Gilt, Each, $2.85

Reproduction three-fourths size.

1913 Catalog

Silver Artistry Pattern

1958 Catalog

See Price Guide — Group 2

Silver Artistry pattern illustrated

SPOONS		CONSUMER PRICE		List Price
	Each	Set of 8	Set of 12	Per Dozen
1. Tea .... 8 in box	$1.25	$10.00	$15.00	$18.00
2. Place (Dessert or Soup) .. 8 in box	2.25	18.00	27.00	32.40
3. Serving or Table .... 8 in box	3.00.	24.00	36.00	43.20
4. Iced Drink .... 8 in box	2.25	18.00	27.00	32.40
5. Fruit ,................. 8 in box	1.50	12.00	18.00	21.60
6. †5 O'Clock Tea or Sherbet . 8 in box	1.25	10.00	15.00	18.00
7. After Dinner Coffee ...... 8 in box	1.25	10.00	15.00	18.00
FORKS				
8. Place .... 8 in box	2.25	18.00	27.00	32.40
9. Salad or Pastry .... 8 in box	2.25	18.00	27.00	32.40
10. Cocktail or Oyster .... 8 in box	2.25	18.00	27.00	32.40
KNIVES				
11. Individual Butter or Cheese Spreader ...... 8 in box	2.25	18.00	27.00	32.40
12. Place (Hollow Handle, Deluxe Stainless Serrated Blade) .... 8 in box	3.50	28.00	42.00	50.40

†Not available in Silver Sands and Flight patterns.

SERVING PIECES	Consumer Price Each	List Price Each
13. Butter Knife	$3.00	$3.60
14. Sugar Spoon	3.00	3.60
15. Serving or Gravy Ladle	4.95	5.94
16. Cold Meat or Serving Fork	4.95	5.94
17. Large Serving or Berry Spoon..	4.95	5.94
18. Dessert Server	4.50	5.40
19. Pierced Serving or Table Spoon	3.00	3.60

Price List   June 15, 1965

COMMUNITY SILVERPLATE

1965 Price List

Silver Sands Pattern

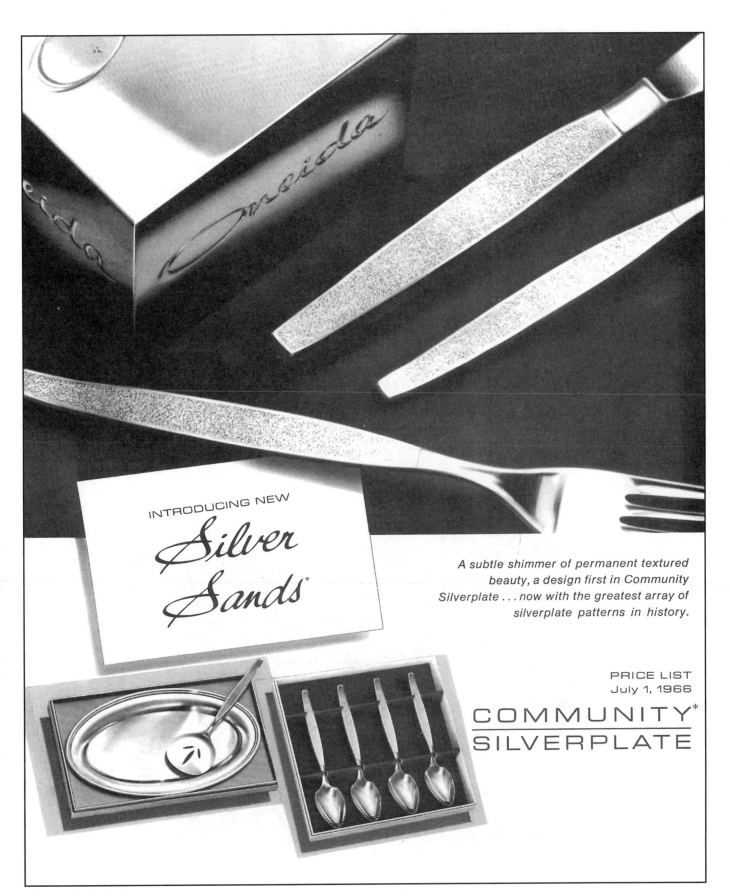

INTRODUCING NEW

*Silver Sands**

A subtle shimmer of permanent textured beauty, a design first in Community Silverplate . . . now with the greatest array of silverplate patterns in history.

PRICE LIST
July 1, 1966

COMMUNITY*
SILVERPLATE

1966 Price List

See Price Guide — Group 2

Silver Valentine Pattern

TANGIER* SILVER ARTISTRY* SPANISH CROWN* AFFECTION* SILVER VALENTINE*

*Trademarks of Oneida Ltd.

LIFETIME GUARANTEE

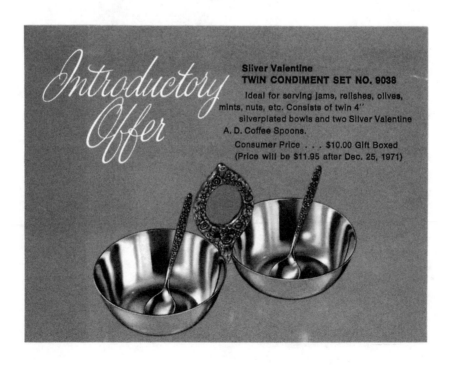

Introductory Offer

Silver Valentine
TWIN CONDIMENT SET NO. 9038

Ideal for serving jams, relishes, olives, mints, nuts, etc. Consists of twin 4'' silverplated bowls and two Silver Valentine A. D. Coffee Spoons.

Consumer Price . . . $10.00 Gift Boxed
(Price will be $11.95 after Dec. 25, 1971)

1971 Advertisement. Also made in gold plate.

South Seas Pattern
"Gifts for the Children…"

GIFTS FOR THE

CHILDREN . . .

COMMUNITY*
The Finest Silverplate

Community No. 9002 6-Piece Progress Set
Feeding Spoon, 2-Piece Baby Set, 3-Piece Child Set

IND. BUTTER OR CHEESE SPREADER

Community No. 9039 3-Piece Primary Set
Child's Cup, Spoon and Fork
(Cup $3.75 Value Subject to Federal Tax)
Consumer. . .**$5.95**   List. . .$7.14

1958 Catalog

South Seas Pattern

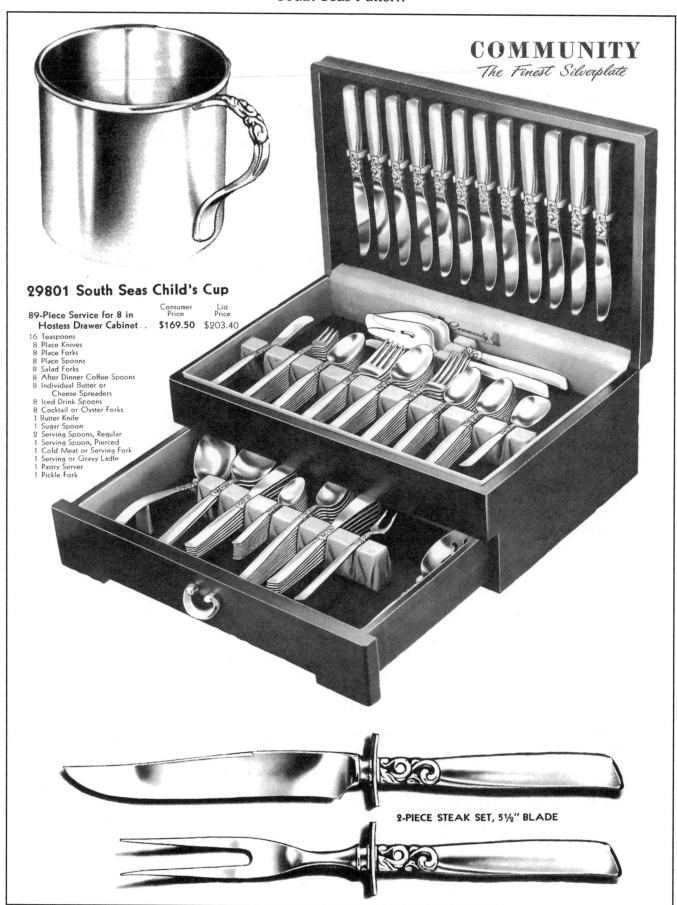

COMMUNITY
The Finest Silverplate

29801 South Seas Child's Cup

89-Piece Service for 8 in Hostess Drawer Cabinet ..	Consumer Price $169.50	List Price $203.40

16 Teaspoons
8 Place Knives
8 Place Forks
8 Place Spoons
8 Salad Forks
8 After Dinner Coffee Spoons
8 Individual Butter or
    Cheese Spreaders
8 Iced Drink Spoons
8 Cocktail or Oyster Forks
1 Butter Knife
1 Sugar Spoon
2 Serving Spoons, Regular
1 Serving Spoon, Pierced
1 Cold Meat or Serving Fork
1 Serving or Gravy Ladle
1 Pastry Server
1 Pickle Fork

2-PIECE STEAK SET, 5½" BLADE

July 1, 1957 Price List

Spanish Crown Pattern

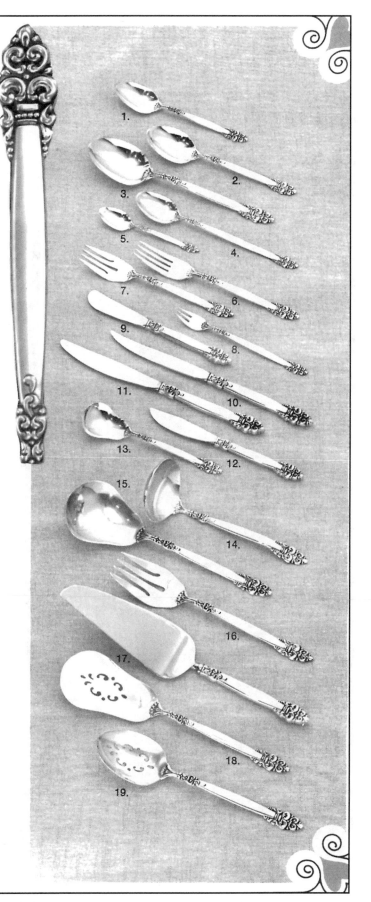

COMMUNITY*
SILVERPLATE

Spoons
1. Teaspoon $3.50
2. Place Spoon 4.25
3. Serving or Tablespoon . . . 5.50
4. Iced Drink Spoon 4.00
   5 O'Clock Tea or Sherbet Spoon° 3.25
5. A.D. Coffee Spoon 2.50

Forks
6. Place Fork 4.75
7. Salad or Pastry Fork 4.25
8. Cocktail or Oyster Fork . . . 3.75

Knives
9. Ind. Butter or Cheese Spreader . 5.50
10. Ind. Steak Knife 8.00
11. Place Knife 8.00

Serving Pieces
12. Butter Knife $5.00
13. Sugar Spoon 5.00
14. Pcd. Serving or Tablespoon . . 5.50
15. Casserole Spoon 8.00
16. Serving or Gravy Ladle . . . 8.00
17. Cold Meat or Serving Fork . . 7.50
18. Dessert Server 8.00
19. Hollow Handle Pie Knife . . . 15.00
    Pierced Relish Spoon** . . . 4.75

2-PIECE HOSTESS HELPER NO. 9022

1970 Price List

See Price Guide — Group 2

PIERCED SERVING OR TABLE SPOON

Oneida
SILVERSMITHS

Twilight*

PIE OR CAKE SERVER

SERVING OR SOUP LADLE

30801 Twilight Child's Cup
Consumer...$3.75

COMMUNITY

SILVERPLATE

Twilight, sparkling like a single jewel, classically elegant.

Community No. 801
Baby Spoon, Bent Handle

While Orchid is a very desirable pattern, many of the orchid growers collect this pattern as well as the crystal "Orchid" made by the Heisey Glass Company. Oneida silversmiths tell us that the shakers are the only hollow ware made. Illustrations on this page and the next are dated 1958.

28602 White Orchid* in Community*. . . To match

PASTRY SERVER

2-PIECE GAME SET, 7" BLADE

See Price Guide — Group 2

White Orchid Pattern

White Orchid*

White Orchid, delight-fully feminine, romantic.

28801 White Orchid Child's Cup
Consumer...**$3.75**

Community No. 9027
3-Piece Baby Set
Feeding Spoon, Baby Spoon and Fork
Consumer...**$3.75**   List...$4.50

1958 Catalog

White Orchid Pattern

2-PIECE STEAK SET, 5½" BLADE

PIERCED PASTRY SERVER

2-PIECE GAME SET, 7" BLADE

SERVING OR SOUP LADLE

PIERCED SERVING SPOON

No. 9009 2-PIECE SALAD SERVING SET

Community
THE FINEST SILVERPLATE

OPEN STOCK PRICES ON ALL COMMUNITY PATTERNS
JULY 1, 1953

		CONSUMER PRICE (Fair Traded)		
SPOONS		Each	Set of 8	Set of 12
Tea	8 in box	$ .85	$ 6.80	$10.20
Oval Bowl Soup (Dessert)	8 in box	1.70	13.60	20.40
Serving or Table	8 in box	1.70	13.60	20.40
Round Bowl Soup	8 in box	1.70	13.60	20.40
5 O'Clock Tea or Sherbet	8 in box	.85	6.80	10.20
After Dinner Coffee	8 in box	.85	6.80	10.20
Cream Soup	8 in box	1.70	13.60	20.40
Iced Drink	8 in box	1.70	13.60	20.40
FORKS				
Dinner	8 in box	1.70	13.60	20.40
Grille	8 in box	1.70	13.60	20.40
Dessert	8 in box	1.70	13.60	20.40
Salad or Pastry	8 in box	1.70	13.60	20.40
Cocktail or Oyster	8 in box	1.70	13.60	20.40
KNIVES				
Individual Butter or Cheese Spreader	8 in box	1.70	13.60	20.40
Hollow Handle, DeLuxe Stainless Blades				
°Dinner	8 in box	2.63	21.00	31.50
°Grille	8 in box	2.63	21.00	31.50
Dessert	8 in box	2.63	21.00	31.50
°Steak Set, 8 Knives	8 in box	——	21.00	——

(Available with either Dinner or Grille Style Knives)

SERVING PIECES				Each
Butter Knife	1 in box	——	——	2.50
Sugar Spoon	1 in box	——	——	2.50
Cold Meat or Serving Fork	1 in Gift Box	——	——	3.00
Pickle Fork	1 in Gift Box	——	——	1.75
Serving or Gravy Ladle	1 in Gift Box	——	——	3.00
Serving or Soup Ladle	1 in Gift Box and Protective Covering			8.00
Pie or Cake Server, H.H.	1 in Gift Box	——	——	5.50
2-Piece Steak Set, 5½" Blade	1 in Gift Box	——	——	10.00
2-Piece Game Set, 7" Blade	1 in Gift Box	——	——	13.50
Large Serving or Salad Spoon	1 in Gift Box	——	——	3.00
Pierced Round Server	1 in Gift Box	——	——	3.00
Pierced Pastry Server	1 in Gift Box	——	——	4.00
Pierced Serving Spoon	1 in Gift Box	——	——	2.00
Jelly Server	1 in Gift Box	——	——	2.00
No. 9009 2-Piece Salad Serving Set	1 in Gift Box	——	——	10.00

6-PIECE PLACE SETTING 9.42
(Knife, Fork, 2 Teaspoons, Soup Spoon, Salad Fork)

24-PIECE COMPLETING SET OF 4 . . . . . . 37.70
8 Teaspoons   4 Knives   4 Salad Forks
4 Soup Spoons   4 Forks

°All Community Dinner and Grille Knives have DeLuxe Serra-blades.

NO FEDERAL TAX

ALWAYS SPECIFY PATTERN WANTED
White Orchid, Evening Star, Coronation, Lady Hamilton, Morning Star

Prices subject to change without notice. All orders subject to prices prevailing at date of shipment and availability of merchandise. The Consumer's Prices listed herein are the prescribed minimum or stipulated resale prices on Community in all states which have enacted Fair Trade Acts.

White Orchid Pattern

OVAL BOWL SOUP SPOON
ICED DRINK SPOON
SERVING OR TABLE SPOON
SUGAR SPOON
SERVING OR GRAVY LADLE
JELLY SERVER
ROUND BOWL SOUP SPOON
CREAM SOUP SPOON
LARGE SERVING OR SALAD SPOON
5 O'CLOCK TEA OR SHERBET SPOON
TEASPOON
AFTER-DINNER COFFEE SPOON

COCKTAIL OR OYSTER FORK
BUTTER KNIFE
DINNER FORK
GRILLE FORK
DESSERT FORK
COLD MEAT OR SERVING FORK
DINNER KNIFE
DESSERT KNIFE
IND. BUTTER OR CHEESE SPREADER
GRILLE KNIFE
PIE OR CAKE SERVER
PIERCED ROUND SERVER
SALAD OR PASTRY FORK

*Trade-marks of Oneida Ltd.

1953 Catalog

Heirloom Plate

Cardinal & Adelphi Patterns

1926 Advertisement

Longchamps, Grenoble & Chateau Patterns

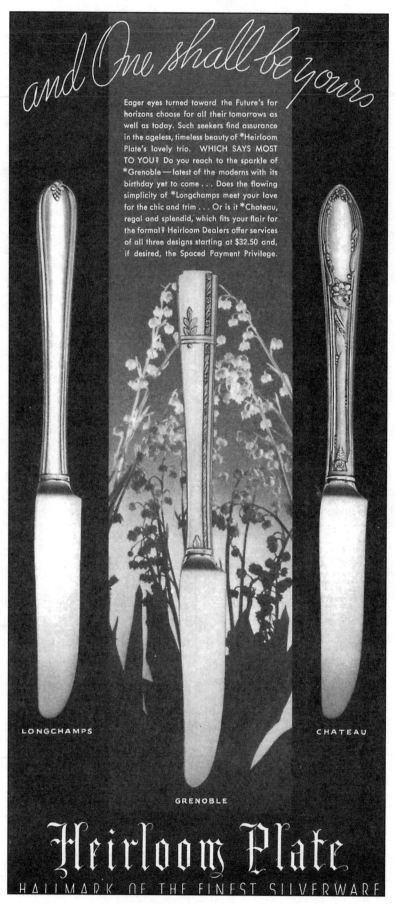

1937 Advertisement. Grenoble will also be found backstamped "Prestige."

Holmes & Edwards

American Beauty Rose Pattern

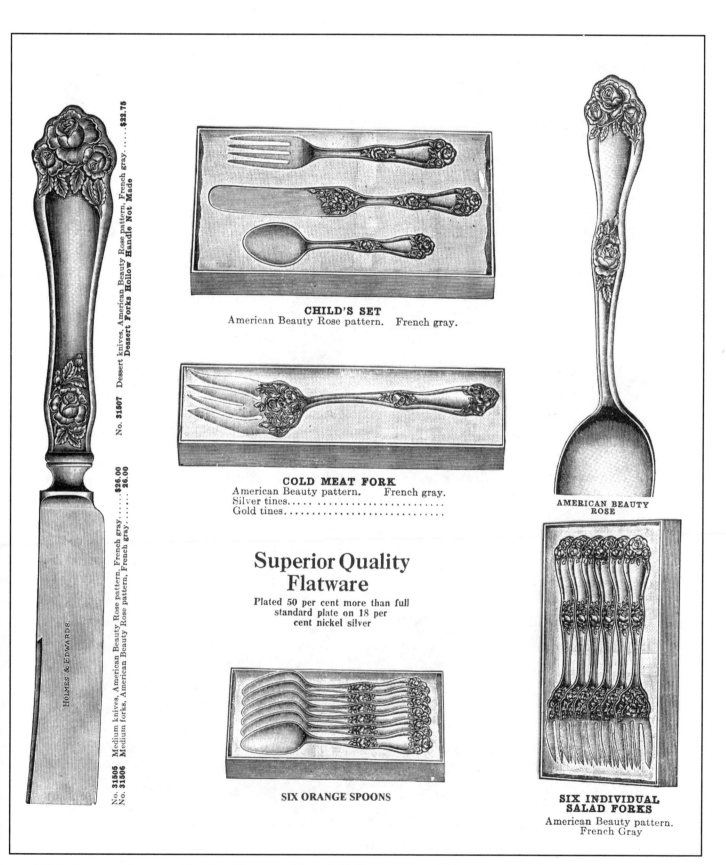

No. 31507   Dessert knives, American Beauty Rose pattern, French gray......$22.75
Dessert Forks Hollow Handle Not Made

No. 31505   Medium knives, American Beauty Rose pattern, French gray......$26.00
No. 31506   Medium forks, American Beauty Rose pattern, French gray......26.00

HOLMES & EDWARDS.

CHILD'S SET
American Beauty Rose pattern.   French gray.

COLD MEAT FORK
American Beauty pattern.   French gray.
Silver tines.............................
Gold tines...............................

Superior Quality Flatware
Plated 50 per cent more than full
standard plate on 18 per
cent nickel silver

SIX ORANGE SPOONS

AMERICAN BEAUTY ROSE

SIX INDIVIDUAL SALAD FORKS
American Beauty pattern.
French Gray

1913 Catalog. Superior Quality Flatware. Plated 50% more than full standard plate on 18% nickel silver.

109   See Price Guide — Group 1

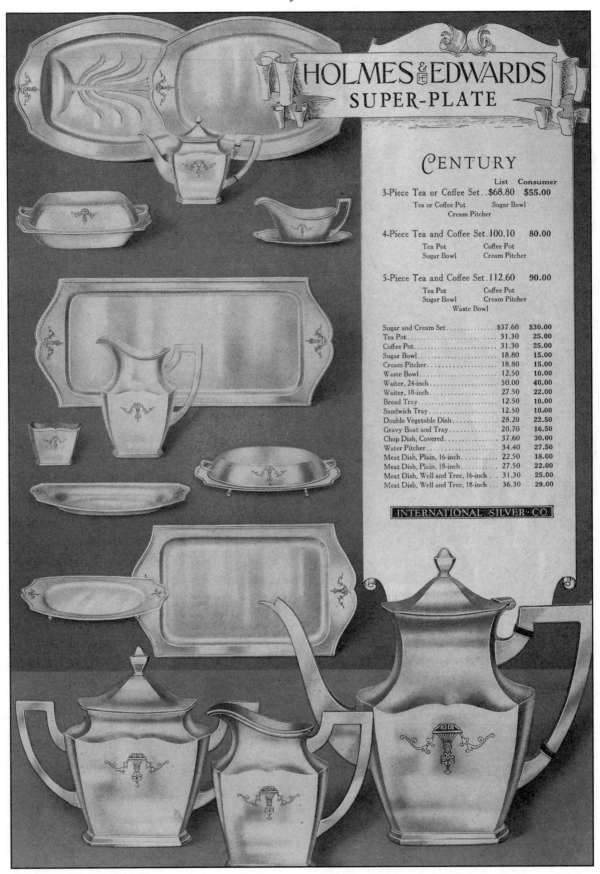

CENTURY

	List	Consumer
3-Piece Tea or Coffee Set	$68.80	$55.00

Tea or Coffee Pot   Sugar Bowl
Cream Pitcher

4-Piece Tea and Coffee Set	100.10	80.00

Tea Pot   Coffee Pot
Sugar Bowl   Cream Pitcher

5-Piece Tea and Coffee Set	112.60	90.00

Tea Pot   Coffee Pot
Sugar Bowl   Cream Pitcher
Waste Bowl

Sugar and Cream Set	$37.60	$30.00
Tea Pot	31.30	25.00
Coffee Pot	31.30	25.00
Sugar Bowl	18.80	15.00
Cream Pitcher	18.80	15.00
Waste Bowl	12.50	10.00
Waiter, 24-inch	50.00	40.00
Waiter, 18-inch	27.50	22.00
Bread Tray	12.50	10.00
Sandwich Tray	12.50	10.00
Double Vegetable Dish	28.20	22.50
Gravy Boat and Tray	20.70	16.50
Chop Dish, Covered	37.60	30.00
Water Pitcher	34.40	27.50
Meat Dish, Plain, 16-inch	22.50	18.00
Meat Dish, Plain, 18-inch	27.50	22.00
Meat Dish, Well and Tree, 16-inch	31.30	25.00
Meat Dish, Well and Tree, 18-inch	36.30	29.00

HOLMES & EDWARDS SUPER-PLATE

INTERNATIONAL SILVER CO.

1930 Catalog

Century Pattern

HOLMES & EDWARDS
SOMETHING MORE THAN PLATE — INLAID

CENTURY

	Plain Box	List Doz.	Consumer
Tea Spoons...............Inlaid	$8.34	doz.	$7.50
Dessert or Oval Soup Spoons...Inlaid	16.68	doz.	15.00
Table or Serving Spoons....Inlaid	16.68	doz.	15.00
Round Bowl Soup Spoons.....Inlaid	16.68	doz.	15.00
Breakfast or Luncheon Forks..Inlaid	16.68	doz.	15.00
Dinner Forks.............Inlaid	16.68	doz.	15.00

SPOONS IN SUPER CASES

Baby (Bent Handle)............doz.	13.26	each	1.00
Baby (Short Handle) ....doz.	13.26	each	1.00
Berry, Salad or Serving........doz.	46.80	each	3.50
Bouillon....................doz.	16.14	six	7.25
Coffee (Demi Tasse)...........doz.	8.34	six	3.75
Cream Soup or Cereal.........doz.	16.68	six	7.50
Five o'Clock Tea, Sherbet or Child's, Plain Box..........doz.	8.34	six	3.75
Iced Drink or Parfait..........doz.	13.38	six	6.00
Olive......................doz.	23.28	each	1.75
Orange or Grape Fruit.........doz.	12.80	six	5.75
Preserve...................doz.	36.78	each	2.75
Sugar.....................doz.	16.52	each	1.25

FORKS IN SUPER CASES

Baby (Short Handle)...........doz.	13.26	each	1.00
Cold Meat, Salad or Serving.....doz.	33.28	each	2.50
Cold Meat (Small) ....doz.	26.78	each	2.00
Five o'Clock Tea or Child's, Plain Box......................doz.	13.26	six	6.00
Ice Cream..................doz.	13.88	six	6.25
Oyster or Sea Food...........doz.	11.68	six	5.25
Pie or Pastry, Individual.......doz.	18.90	six	8.50
Pickle.....................doz.	20.02	each	1.50
Salad, Individual.............doz.	16.68	six	7.50

KNIVES AND LADLES IN SUPER CASES

Butter Knife................doz.	16.52	each	1.25
Butter Spreaders............doz.	13.92	six	6.25
Gravy Ladle................doz.	36.78	each	2.75
Soup Ladle.................doz.	106.84	each	8.00
Whipped Cream Ladle.........doz.	30.00	each	2.25

SPECIAL SERVING PIECES IN SUPER CASES

Cake Server................doz.	26.78	each	2.00
Flat Server, Pierced..........doz.	56.80	each	4.25
Jelly Server................doz.	23.52	each	1.75
Sugar Tongs................doz.	26.78	each	2.00
Tomato or Egg Server.........doz.	43.54	each	3.25

SOLID HANDLE CUTLERY, FRENCH BLADES

Dinner Knives, Stainless........doz.	17.64	doz.	14.00
Dinner Knives, Plated..........doz.	12.60	doz.	10.00
Breakfast or Luncheon Knives, Stainless....................doz.	17.64	doz.	14.00
Breakfast or Luncheon Knives, Plated....................doz.	12.60	doz.	10.00
Breakfast Forks, Solid Handles, Super Case................doz.	12.60	doz.	10.00
Tea, Salad or Child's Knives, Plated doz.	12.60	doz.	10.00
Fruit Knives, Stainless, Super Case doz.	15.72	doz.	12.50

HOLLOW HANDLE CUTLERY, FRENCH BLADES

Dinner Knives, Mirror Stainless ..doz.	35.40	six	14.00
Dinner Knives, Stainless........doz.	30.24	six	12.00
Breakfast Knives, Mirror Stainless doz.	35.40	six	14.00
Breakfast Knives, Stainless......doz.	30.24	six	12.00
Tea, Salad or Child's Knives, Plated doz.	27.70	six	11.00
Fruit Knives, Stainless, Super Case doz.	27.70	six	11.00
Butter Spreaders, Super Case....doz.	23.40	six	10.50
Cheese Server, Super Case......doz.	36.78	each	2.75
Pie Server, Super Case.........doz.	60.30	each	4.50

HOLLOW HANDLE CARVING SETS STAINLESS STEEL BLADES
Blades: Large 8″, Medium 7″, Small 6″

3-Piece Beef (Large), Super Case..set	22.74	set	18.00
3-Piece Game (Medium), Super Case set	19.60	set	15.60
2-Piece Game (Medium), Super Case set	15.44	set	12.25
3-Piece Steak (Small), Super Case .set	14.18	set	11.25
2-Piece Steak (Small), Super Case..set	10.12	set	8.00
Poultry and Game Shears, Plain Box....................each	12.52	each	10.00

SOLID HANDLE

2-Piece Steak (Small), Stainless Blade, 6-inch, Super Case......set	6.26	set	5.00

TWO-PIECE SETS IN SUPER CASES

Sugar Spoon and Butter Knife....doz.	33.28	set	2.50
Baby Spoon and Fork (Short Handle)..................doz.	26.78	set	2.00
H. H. Salad Set, Olivewood Tines and Bowl..................doz.	100.34	set	7.50

THREE-PIECE CHILD'S SETS IN SUPER CASES

With Solid Handle Knife.........doz.	37.78	set	2.50
With Hollow Handle Knife........doz.	53.30	set	4.00
With Flat Knife...............doz.	40.04	set	3.00

Pieces illustrated are

Dinner Knife	Individual Salad Fork
Tea Spoon	Dinner Fork

Illustrations Full Size

INTERNATIONAL SILVER CO.

1930 Catalog

Holmes & Edwards

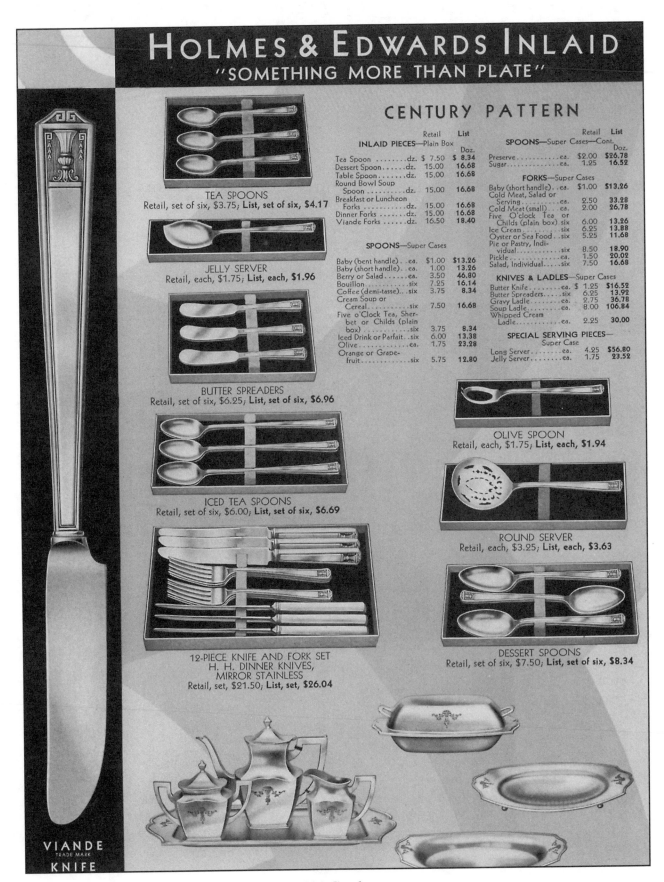

HOLMES & EDWARDS INLAID
"SOMETHING MORE THAN PLATE"

CENTURY PATTERN

TEA SPOONS
Retail, set of six, $3.75; List, set of six, $4.17

JELLY SERVER
Retail, each, $1.75; List, each, $1.96

BUTTER SPREADERS
Retail, set of six, $6.25; List, set of six, $6.96

ICED TEA SPOONS
Retail, set of six, $6.00; List, set of six, $6.69

12-PIECE KNIFE AND FORK SET
H. H. DINNER KNIVES,
MIRROR STAINLESS
Retail, set, $21.50; List, set, $26.04

INLAID PIECES—Plain Box	Retail Doz.	List Doz.
Tea Spoon ....dz.	$ 7.50	$ 8.34
Dessert Spoon......dz.	15.00	16.68
Table Spoon.......dz.	15.00	16.68
Round Bowl Soup Spoon ....dz.	15.00	16.68
Breakfast or Luncheon Forks ....dz.	15.00	16.68
Dinner Forks ....dz.	15.00	16.68
Viande Forks ......dz.	16.50	18.40

SPOONS—Super Cases	Retail	List Doz.
Baby (bent handle).. ea.	$1.00	$13.26
Baby (short handle).. ea.	1.00	13.26
Berry or Salad......ea.	3.50	46.80
Bouillon ....six	7.25	16.14
Coffee (demi-tasse)..six	3.75	8.34
Cream Soup or Cereal............six	7.50	16.68
Five o'Clock Tea, Sherbet or Childs (plain box) ....six	3.75	8.34
Iced Drink or Parfait..six	6.00	13.38
Olive..............ea.	1.75	23.28
Orange or Grapefruit.............six	5.75	12.80

SPOONS—Super Cases—Cont.	Retail	List Doz.
Preserve............ea.	$2.00	$26.78
Sugar...............ea.	1.25	16.52

FORKS—Super Cases	Retail	List Doz.
Baby (short handle)..ea.	$1.00	$13.26
Cold Meat, Salad or Serving..........ea.	2.50	33.28
Cold Meat (small)...ea.	2.00	26.78
Five O'clock Tea or Childs (plain box).six	6.00	13.26
Ice Cream..........six	6.25	13.88
Oyster or Sea Food..six	5.25	11.68
Pie or Pastry, Individual..............six	8.50	18.90
Pickle.............ea.	1.50	20.02
Salad, Individual.....six	7.50	16.68

KNIVES & LADLES—Super Cases	Retail	List Doz.
Butter Knife........ea.	$ 1.25	$16.52
Butter Spreaders.....six	6.25	13.92
Gravy Ladle........ea.	2.75	36.78
Soup Ladle.........ea.	8.00	106.84
Whipped Cream Ladle.............ea.	2.25	30.00

SPECIAL SERVING PIECES—Super Case	Retail	List Doz.
Long Server.........ea.	4.25	$56.80
Jelly Server.........ea.	1.75	23.52

OLIVE SPOON
Retail, each, $1.75; List, each, $1.94

ROUND SERVER
Retail, each, $3.25; List, each, $3.63

DESSERT SPOONS
Retail, set of six, $7.50; List, set of six, $8.34

VIANDE TRADE MARK **KNIFE**

1931 Catalog

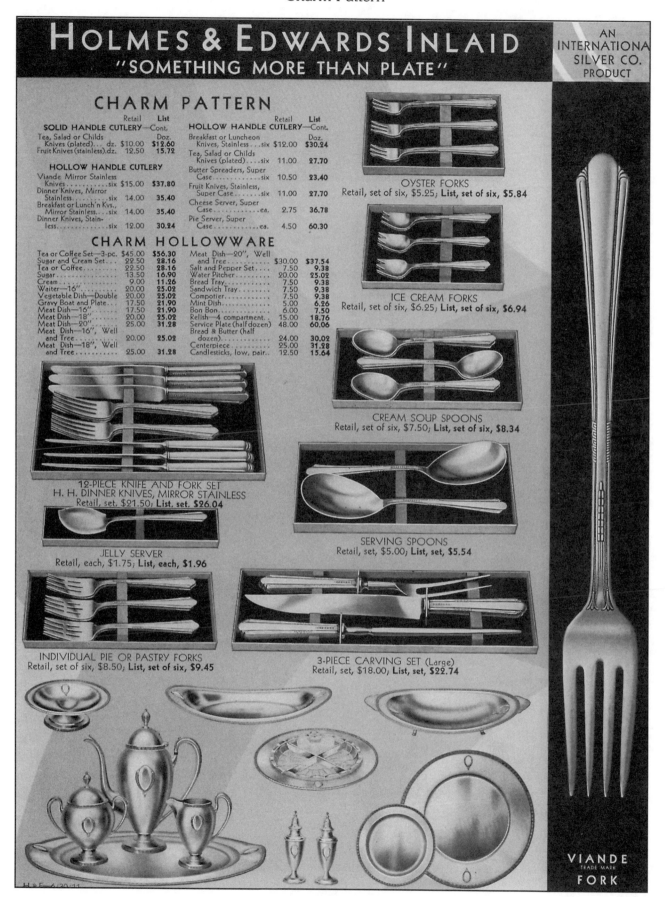

HOLMES & EDWARDS INLAID
"SOMETHING MORE THAN PLATE"

AN INTERNATIONAL SILVER CO. PRODUCT

CHARM PATTERN

SOLID HANDLE CUTLERY—Cont.	Retail	List
Tea, Salad or Childs Knives (plated)... dz.	$10.00	Doz. $12.60
Fruit Knives (stainless).dz.	12.50	15.72

HOLLOW HANDLE CUTLERY

	Retail	List
Viande Mirror Stainless Knives...........six	$15.00	$37.80
Dinner Knives, Mirror Stainless...........six	14.00	35.40
Breakfast or Lunch'n Kvs., Mirror Stainless....six	14.00	35.40
Dinner Knives, Stainless...............six	12.00	30.24

HOLLOW HANDLE CUTLERY—Cont.	Retail	List
Breakfast or Luncheon Knives, Stainless...six	$12.00	Doz. $30.24
Tea, Salad or Childs Knives (plated)....six	11.00	27.70
Butter Spreaders, Super Case............six	10.50	23.40
Fruit Knives, Stainless, Super Case.......six	11.00	27.70
Cheese Server, Super Case.............ea.	2.75	36.78
Pie Server, Super Case.............ea.	4.50	60.30

CHARM HOLLOWWARE

	Retail	List
Tea or Coffee Set—3-pc.	$45.00	$56.30
Sugar and Cream Set...	22.50	28.16
Tea or Coffee.........	22.50	28.16
Sugar...............	13.50	16.90
Cream..............	9.00	11.26
Waiter—16".........	20.00	25.02
Vegetable Dish—Double	20.00	25.02
Gravy Boat and Plate...	17.50	21.90
Meat Dish—16"......	17.50	21.90
Meat Dish—18"......	20.00	25.02
Meat Dish—20"......	25.00	31.28
Meat Dish—16", Well and Tree...........	20.00	25.02
Meat Dish—18", Well and Tree...........	25.00	31.28

	Retail	List
Meat Dish—20", Well and Tree..........	$30.00	$37.54
Salt and Pepper Set....	7.50	9.38
Water Pitcher........	20.00	25.02
Bread Tray..........	7.50	9.38
Sandwich Tray........	7.50	9.38
Compotier..........	7.50	9.38
Mint Dish...........	5.00	6.26
Bon Bon............	6.00	7.50
Relish—4 compartment.	15.00	18.76
Service Plate (half dozen)	48.00	60.06
Bread & Butter (half dozen)...........	24.00	30.02
Centerpiece.........	25.00	31.28
Candlesticks, low, pair..	12.50	15.64

OYSTER FORKS
Retail, set of six, $5.25; List, set of six, $5.84

ICE CREAM FORKS
Retail, set of six, $6.25; List, set of six, $6.94

CREAM SOUP SPOONS
Retail, set of six, $7.50; List, set of six, $8.34

SERVING SPOONS
Retail, set, $5.00; List, set, $5.54

12-PIECE KNIFE AND FORK SET
H. H. DINNER KNIVES, MIRROR STAINLESS
Retail, set, $21.50; List, set, $26.04

JELLY SERVER
Retail, each, $1.75; List, each, $1.96

INDIVIDUAL PIE OR PASTRY FORKS
Retail, set of six, $8.50; List, set of six, $9.45

3-PIECE CARVING SET (Large)
Retail, set, $18.00; List, set, $22.74

VIANDE FORK

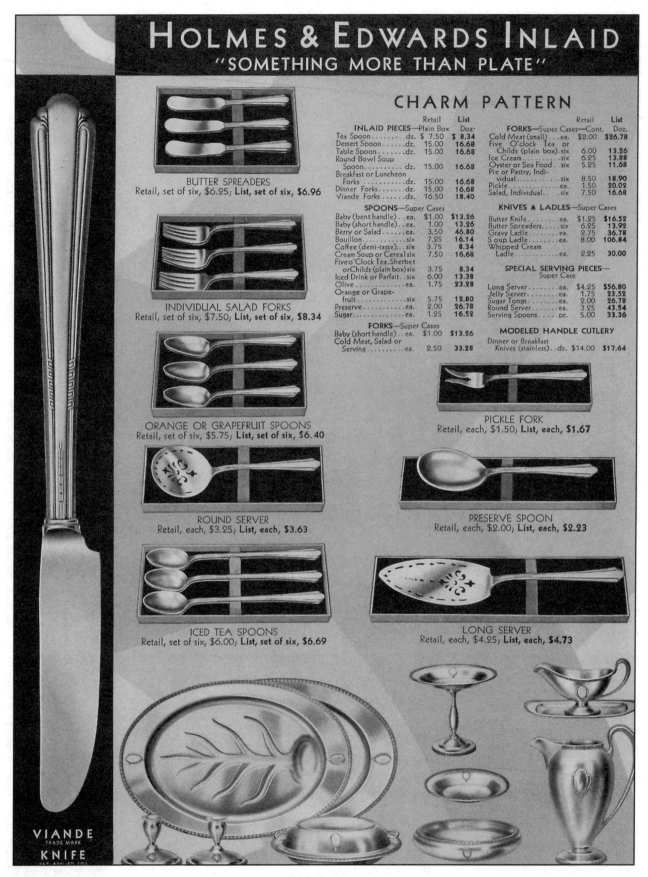

HOLMES & EDWARDS INLAID
"SOMETHING MORE THAN PLATE"

CHARM PATTERN

BUTTER SPREADERS
Retail, set of six, $6.25; List, set of six, $6.96

INDIVIDUAL SALAD FORKS
Retail, set of six, $7.50; List, set of six, $8.34

ORANGE OR GRAPEFRUIT SPOONS
Retail, set of six, $5.75; List, set of six, $6.40

ROUND SERVER
Retail, each, $3.25; List, each, $3.63

ICED TEA SPOONS
Retail, set of six, $6.00; List, set of six, $6.69

PICKLE FORK
Retail, each, $1.50; List, each, $1.67

PRESERVE SPOON
Retail, each, $2.00; List, each, $2.23

LONG SERVER
Retail, each, $4.25; List, each, $4.73

		Retail Plain Box	List Doz.
INLAID PIECES—Plain Box			
Tea Spoon	dz.	$7.50	$8.34
Dessert Spoon	dz.	15.00	16.68
Table Spoon	dz.	15.00	16.68
Round Bowl Soup Spoon	dz.	15.00	16.68
Breakfast or Luncheon Forks	dz.	15.00	16.68
Dinner Forks	dz.	15.00	16.68
Viande Forks	dz.	16.50	18.40
SPOONS—Super Cases			
Baby (bent handle)	ea.	$1.00	$13.26
Baby (short handle)	ea.	1.00	13.26
Berry or Salad	ea.	3.50	46.80
Bouillon	six	7.25	16.14
Coffee (demi-tasse)	six	3.75	8.34
Cream Soup or Cereal	six	7.50	16.68
Five o'Clock Tea, Sherbet or Childs (plain box)	six	3.75	8.34
Iced Drink or Parfait	six	6.00	13.38
Olive	ea.	1.75	23.28
Orange or Grapefruit	six	5.75	12.80
Preserve	ea.	2.00	26.78
Sugar	ea.	1.25	16.52
FORKS—Super Cases			
Baby (short handle)	ea.	$1.00	$13.26
Cold Meat, Salad or Serving	ea.	2.50	33.28

		Retail	List Doz.
FORKS—Super Cases—Cont.			
Cold Meat (small)	ea.	$2.00	$26.78
Five O'clock Tea or Childs (plain box)	six	6.00	13.26
Ice Cream	six	6.25	13.88
Oyster or Sea Food	six	5.25	11.68
Pie or Pastry, Individual	six	8.50	18.90
Pickle	ea.	1.50	20.02
Salad, Individual	six	7.50	16.68
KNIVES & LADLES—Super Cases			
Butter Knife	ea.	$1.25	$16.52
Butter Spreaders	six	6.25	13.92
Gravy Ladle	ea.	2.75	36.78
Soup Ladle	ea.	8.00	106.84
Whipped Cream Ladle	ea.	2.25	30.00
SPECIAL SERVING PIECES—Super Case			
Long Server	ea.	$4.25	$56.80
Jelly Server	ea.	1.75	23.52
Sugar Tongs	ea.	2.00	26.78
Round Server	ea.	3.25	43.54
Serving Spoons	pr.	5.00	33.36
MODELED HANDLE CUTLERY			
Dinner or Breakfast Knives (stainless)	dz.	$14.00	$17.64

VIANDE
TRADE MARK
KNIFE

1931 Catalog

Introduced in 1938. Left to right: 9¹⁄₁₀" hollow handle dinner knife, 7⁷⁄₁₀" ice tea spoon, 6²⁄₅" jelly server, 6⁹⁄₁₀" individual salad fork, 9" cold meat fork server. Bottom: 6¹⁄₁₀" sugar spoon.

See Price Guide — Group 2

De Sancy Pattern

Dolly Madison Pattern

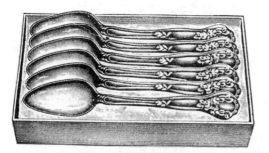

SIX ORANGE SPOONS

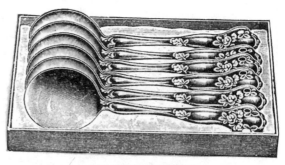

SIX SOUP SPOONS

DOLLY MADISON

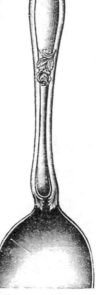

SIX INDIVIDUAL SALAD FORKS
Dolly Madison pattern.   Gray finish.

CHILD'S EDUCATOR SET
Dolly Madison pattern.
Gray finish
One short handle spoon
and fork.

CHILD'S SET
Dolly Madison pattern.   Gray finish.

Superior Quality Flat-
ware. Plated 50% more
than full standard plate on
18% nickel silver.

Dolly Madison Pattern

Medium knives, Dolly Madison pattern, French gray
Medium forks, Dolly Madison pattern, French gray

Dessert knives, Dolly Madison pattern, French gray
Dessert Forks Hollow Handle Not Made

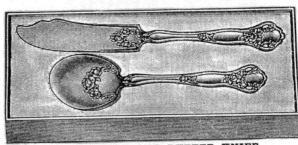

BERRY SPOON
Dolly Madison pattern.   Gray finish.
Silver bowl.........................
Gold bowl...............................

SUGAR SHELL AND BUTTER KNIFE
Dolly Madison pattern.   Gray finish.
Silver bowls.........................
Gold bowls...........................

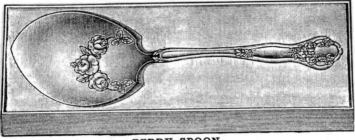

COLD MEAT FORK
Dolly Madison pattern.   Gray finish.

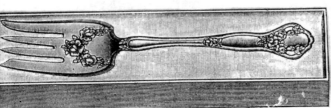

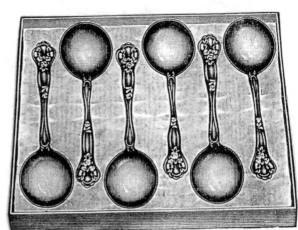

SIX BOUILLON SPOONS
Dolly Madison pattern.   Gray finish.

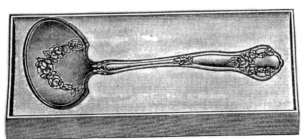

CREAM LADLE
Dolly Madison pattern.   French gray.
Silver bowl   Gold bowl

1913 Catalog
Nickel silver, hollow handle, quadruple silver, plated knives and forks

Lafayette Pattern

Superior Quality Flatware. Plated 50% more than full standard plate on 18% nickel silver.

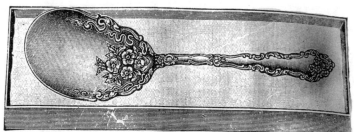

BERRY SPOON

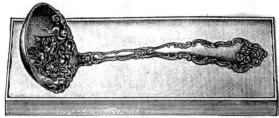

CREAM LADLE
Lafayette pattern.   French gray.

Medium knives, La Fayette pattern, French gray
Medium forks, La Fayette pattern, French gray

Dessert knives, La Fayette pattern, French gray
Dessert Forks Hollow Handle Not Made

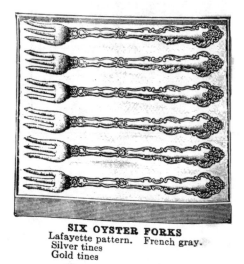

SIX OYSTER FORKS
Lafayette pattern.   French gray.
Silver tines
Gold tines

PIE KNIFE
Orient Pattern

Introduced 1908. 1913 Catalog.

See Price Guide — Group 1

Lovely Lady Pattern

Patented 1937. Sterling inlaid silverplate. Left to right: 4½" sauce ladle, 7⅝" pierced tomato server, 5⅞" gravy ladle, 8⅞" berry spoon.

May Queen Pattern

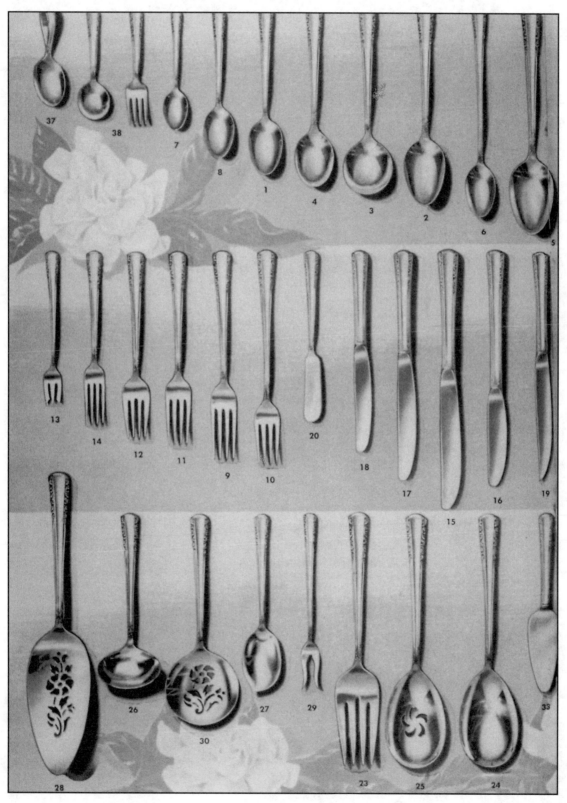

1953 Catalog

See Price Guide — Group 2

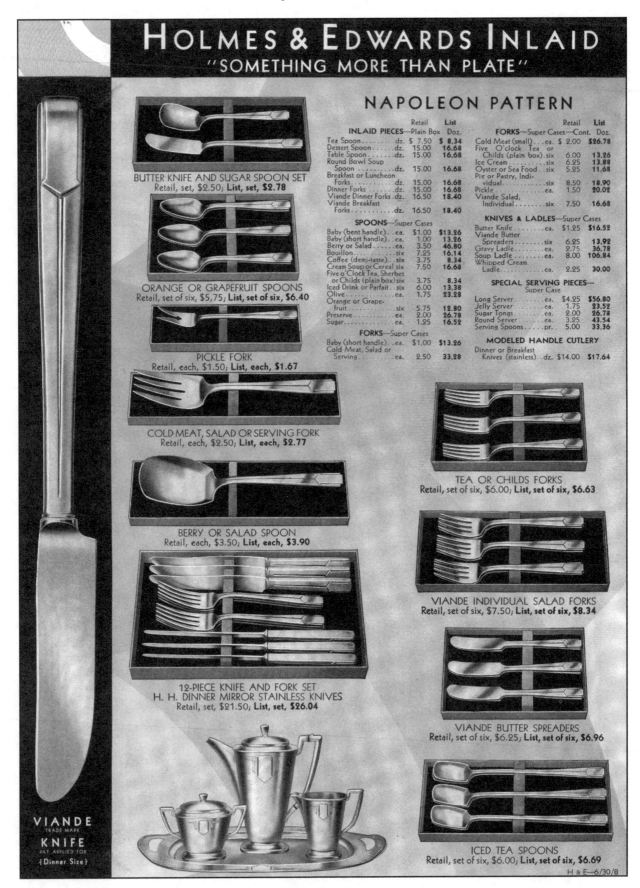

HOLMES & EDWARDS INLAID
"SOMETHING MORE THAN PLATE"

NAPOLEON PATTERN

INLAID PIECES—Plain Box	Retail	List Doz.
Tea Spoon..........dz.	$ 7.50	$ 8.34
Dessert Spoon......dz.	15.00	16.68
Table Spoon........dz.	15.00	16.68
Round Bowl Soup Spoon ....dz.	15.00	16.68
Breakfast or Luncheon Forks............dz.	15.00	16.68
Dinner Forks........dz.	15.00	16.68
Viande Dinner Forks..dz.	16.50	18.40
Viande Breakfast Forks..........dz.	16.50	18.40

SPOONS—Super Cases	Retail	List
Baby (bent handle)...ea.	$1.00	$13.26
Baby (short handle)...ea.	1.00	13.26
Berry or Salad.......ea.	3.50	46.80
Bouillon.............six	7.25	16.14
Coffee (demi-tasse)..six	3.75	8.34
Cream Soup or Cereal six	7.50	16.68
Five o'Clock Tea, Sherbet or Childs (plain box) six	3.75	8.34
Iced Drink or Parfait..six	6.00	13.38
Olive................ea.	1.75	23.28
Orange or Grape-fruit..............six	5.75	12.80
Preserve.............ea.	2.00	26.78
Sugar................ea.	1.25	16.52

FORKS—Super Cases	Retail	List
Baby (short handle)...ea.	$1.00	$13.26
Cold Meat, Salad or Serving.............ea.	2.50	33.28

FORKS—Super Cases—Cont.	Retail	List Doz.
Cold Meat (small)...ea.	$ 2.00	$26.78
Five O'clock Tea or Childs (plain box).six	6.00	13.26
Ice Cream...........six	6.25	13.88
Oyster or Sea Food..six	5.25	11.68
Pie or Pastry, Indi-vidual..............six	8.50	18.90
Pickle...............ea.	1.50	20.02
Viande Salad, Individual..........six	7.50	16.68

KNIVES & LADLES—Super Cases	Retail	List
Butter Knife.........ea.	$1.25	$16.52
Viande Butter Spreaders........six	6.25	13.92
Gravy Ladle.........ea.	2.75	36.78
Soup Ladle..........ea.	8.00	106.84
Whipped Cream Ladle.............ea.	2.25	30.00

SPECIAL SERVING PIECES—Super Case	Retail	List
Long Server.........ea.	$4.25	$56.80
Jelly Server.........ea.	1.75	23.52
Sugar Tongs.........ea.	2.00	26.78
Round Server........ea.	3.25	43.54
Serving Spoons.....pr.	5.00	33.36

MODELED HANDLE CUTLERY	Retail	List
Dinner or Breakfast Knives (stainless)..dz.	$14.00	$17.64

BUTTER KNIFE AND SUGAR SPOON SET
Retail, set, $2.50; List, set, $2.78

ORANGE OR GRAPEFRUIT SPOONS
Retail, set of six, $5.75; List, set of six, $6.40

PICKLE FORK
Retail, each, $1.50; List, each, $1.67

COLD MEAT, SALAD OR SERVING FORK
Retail, each, $2.50; List, each, $2.77

BERRY OR SALAD SPOON
Retail, each, $3.50; List, each, $3.90

12-PIECE KNIFE AND FORK SET
H. H. DINNER MIRROR STAINLESS KNIVES
Retail, set, $21.50; List, set, $26.04

TEA OR CHILDS FORKS
Retail, set of six, $6.00; List, set of six, $6.63

VIANDE INDIVIDUAL SALAD FORKS
Retail, set of six, $7.50; List, set of six, $8.34

VIANDE BUTTER SPREADERS
Retail, set of six, $6.25; List, set of six, $6.96

ICED TEA SPOONS
Retail, set of six, $6.00; List, set of six, $6.69

H & E—6/30/8

VIANDE
TRADE MARK
KNIFE
PAT. APPLIED FOR
{Dinner Size}

1931 Catalog

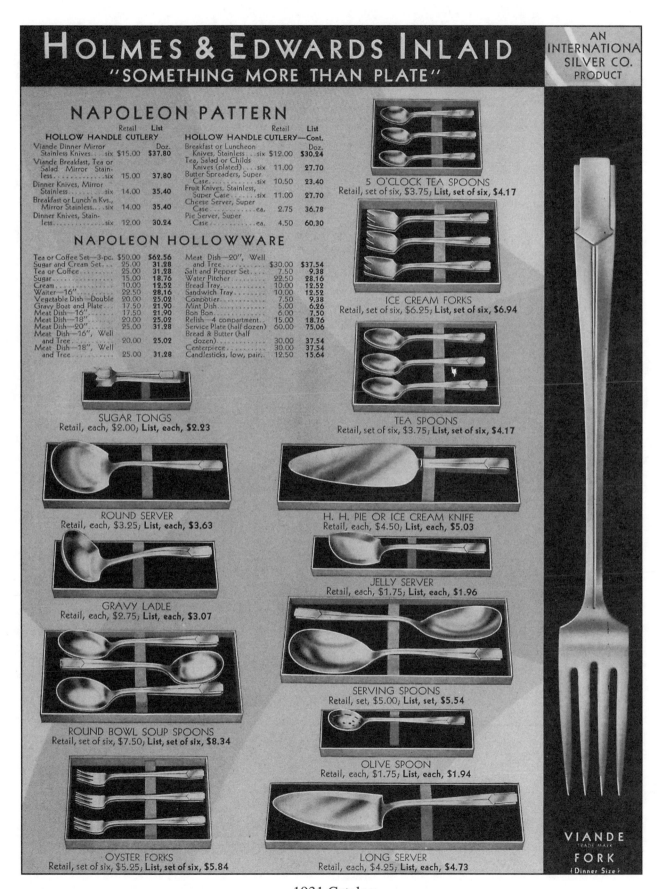

HOLMES & EDWARDS INLAID
"SOMETHING MORE THAN PLATE"

AN INTERNATIONAL SILVER CO. PRODUCT

Holmes & Edwards

NAPOLEON PATTERN

HOLLOW HANDLE CUTLERY	Retail	List
		Doz.
Viande Dinner Mirror Stainless Knives....six	$15.00	$37.80
Viande Breakfast, Tea or Salad Mirror Stainless.....six	15.00	37.80
Dinner Knives, Mirror Stainless.....six	14.00	35.40
Breakfast or Lunch'n Kvs., Mirror Stainless....six	14.00	35.40
Dinner Knives, Stainless....six	12.00	30.24

HOLLOW HANDLE CUTLERY—Cont.	Retail	List
		Doz.
Breakfast or Luncheon Knives, Stainless....six	$12.00	$30.24
Tea, Salad or Childs Knives (plated)....six	11.00	27.70
Butter Spreaders, Super. Case....six	10.50	23.40
Fruit Knives, Stainless, Super Case....six	11.00	27.70
Cheese Server, Super Case....ea.	2.75	36.78
Pie Server, Super Case....ea.	4.50	60.30

NAPOLEON HOLLOWWARE

	Retail	List		Retail	List
Tea or Coffee Set—3-pc.	$50.00	$62.56	Meat Dish—20", Well and Tree	$30.00	$37.54
Sugar and Cream Set	25.00	31.28	Salt and Pepper Set	7.50	9.38
Tea or Coffee	25.00	31.28	Water Pitcher	22.50	28.16
Sugar	15.00	18.76	Bread Tray	10.00	12.52
Cream	10.00	12.52	Sandwich Tray	10.00	12.52
Waiter—16"	22.50	28.16	Combotier	7.50	9.38
Vegetable Dish—Double	20.00	25.02	Mint Dish	5.00	6.26
Gravy Boat and Plate	17.50	21.90	Bon Bon	6.00	7.50
Meat Dish—16"	17.50	21.90	Relish—4 compartment	15.00	18.76
Meat Dish—18"	20.00	25.02	Service Plate (half dozen)	60.00	75.06
Meat Dish—20"	25.00	31.28	Bread & Butter (half dozen)	30.00	37.54
Meat Dish—16", Well and Tree	20.00	25.02	Centerpiece	30.00	37.54
Meat Dish—18", Well and Tree	25.00	31.28	Candlesticks, low, pair	12.50	15.64

SUGAR TONGS
Retail, each, $2.00; List, each, $2.23

ROUND SERVER
Retail, each, $3.25; List, each, $3.63

GRAVY LADLE
Retail, each, $2.75; List, each, $3.07

ROUND BOWL SOUP SPOONS
Retail, set of six, $7.50; List, set of six, $8.34

OYSTER FORKS
Retail, set of six, $5.25; List, set of six, $5.84

5 O'CLOCK TEA SPOONS
Retail, set of six, $3.75; List, set of six, $4.17

ICE CREAM FORKS
Retail, set of six, $6.25; List, set of six, $6.94

TEA SPOONS
Retail, set of six, $3.75; List, set of six, $4.17

H. H. PIE OR ICE CREAM KNIFE
Retail, each, $4.50; List, each, $5.03

JELLY SERVER
Retail, each, $1.75; List, each, $1.96

SERVING SPOONS
Retail, set, $5.00; List, set, $5.54

OLIVE SPOON
Retail, each, $1.75; List, each, $1.94

LONG SERVER
Retail, each, $4.25; List, each, $4.73

VIANDE FORK
(Dinner Size)

1931 Catalog

Orient Pattern

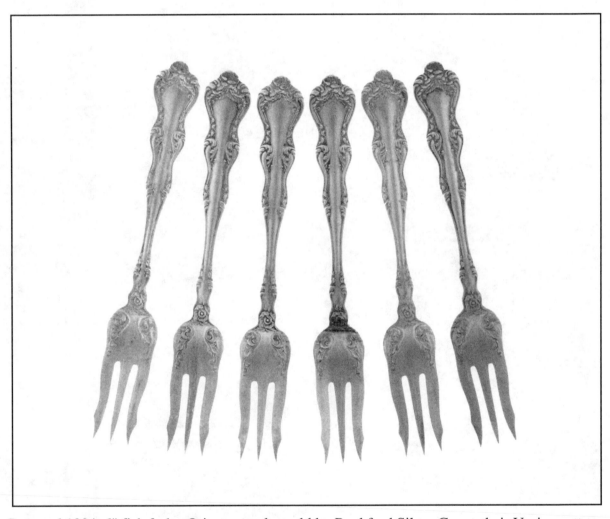

Patented 1904. 6" fish forks. Orient was also sold by Rockford Silver Co. as their Venice pattern.

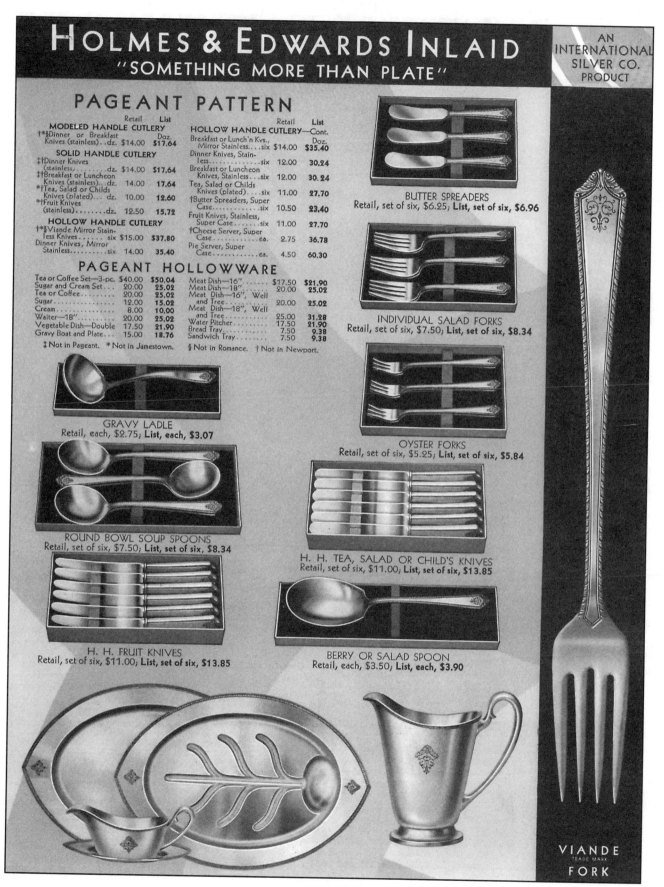

HOLMES & EDWARDS INLAID
"SOMETHING MORE THAN PLATE"

AN INTERNATIONAL SILVER CO. PRODUCT

PAGEANT PATTERN

	Retail	List
MODELED HANDLE CUTLERY		Doz.
†*§Dinner or Breakfast Knives (stainless)..dz.	$14.00	$17.64
SOLID HANDLE CUTLERY		
‡†Dinner Knives (stainless)........dz.	14.00	17.64
‡†Breakfast or Luncheon Knives (stainless)..dz.	14.00	17.64
*†Tea, Salad or Childs Knives (plated)...dz.	10.00	12.60
†Fruit Knives (stainless)........dz.	12.50	15.72
HOLLOW HANDLE CUTLERY		
†*§Viande Mirror Stainless Knives......six	$15.00	$37.80
Dinner Knives, Mirror Stainless........six	14.00	35.40

	Retail	List
HOLLOW HANDLE CUTLERY—Cont.		
Breakfast or Lunch'n Kvs., Mirror Stainless....six	$14.00	Doz. $35.40
Dinner Knives, Stainless........six	12.00	30.24
Breakfast or Luncheon Knives, Stainless...six	12.00	30.24
Tea, Salad or Childs Knives (plated)....six	11.00	27.70
†Butter Spreaders, Super Case.............six	10.50	23.40
Fruit Knives, Stainless, Super Case......six	11.00	27.70
†Cheese Server, Super Case.............ea.	2.75	36.78
Pie Server, Super Case.............ea.	4.50	60.30

PAGEANT HOLLOWWARE

	Retail	List		Retail	List
Tea or Coffee Set—3-pc.	$40.00	$50.04	Meat Dish—16"....	$17.50	$21.90
Sugar and Cream Set...	20.00	25.02	Meat Dish—18"....	20.00	25.02
Tea or Coffee........	20.00	25.02	Meat Dish—16", Well and Tree........	20.00	25.02
Sugar...............	12.00	15.02	Meat Dish—18", Well and Tree........	25.00	31.28
Cream..............	8.00	10.00	Water Pitcher......	17.50	21.90
Waiter—18"........	20.00	25.02	Bread Tray.........	7.50	9.38
Vegetable Dish—Double	17.50	21.90	Sandwich Tray......	7.50	9.38
Gravy Boat and Plate..	15.00	18.76			

‡ Not in Pageant. * Not in Jamestown. § Not in Romance. † Not in Newport.

BUTTER SPREADERS
Retail, set of six, $6.25; List, set of six, $6.96

INDIVIDUAL SALAD FORKS
Retail, set of six, $7.50; List, set of six, $8.34

OYSTER FORKS
Retail, set of six, $5.25; List, set of six, $5.84

GRAVY LADLE
Retail, each, $2.75; List, each, $3.07

ROUND BOWL SOUP SPOONS
Retail, set of six, $7.50; List, set of six, $8.34

H. H. TEA, SALAD OR CHILD'S KNIVES
Retail, set of six, $11.00; List, set of six, $13.85

H. H. FRUIT KNIVES
Retail, set of six, $11.00; List, set of six, $13.85

BERRY OR SALAD SPOON
Retail, each, $3.50; List, each, $3.90

VIANDE TRADE MARK
FORK

1931 Catalog

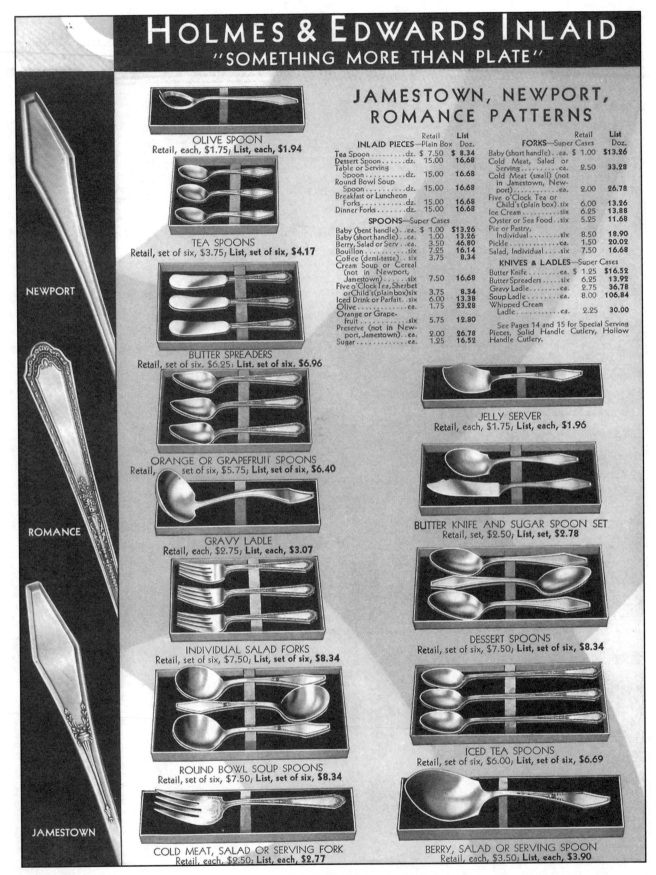

HOLMES & EDWARDS INLAID
"SOMETHING MORE THAN PLATE"

NEWPORT

ROMANCE

JAMESTOWN

OLIVE SPOON
Retail, each, $1.75; List, each, $1.94

TEA SPOONS
Retail, set of six, $3.75; List, set of six, $4.17

BUTTER SPREADERS
Retail, set of six, $6.25; List, set of six, $6.96

ORANGE OR GRAPEFRUIT SPOONS
Retail, set of six, $5.75; List, set of six, $6.40

GRAVY LADLE
Retail, each, $2.75; List, each, $3.07

INDIVIDUAL SALAD FORKS
Retail, set of six, $7.50; List, set of six, $8.34

ROUND BOWL SOUP SPOONS
Retail, set of six, $7.50; List, set of six, $8.34

COLD MEAT, SALAD OR SERVING FORK
Retail, each, $2.50; List, each, $2.77

JAMESTOWN, NEWPORT, ROMANCE PATTERNS

INLAID PIECES—Plain Box	Retail	List Doz.
Tea Spoon.........dz.	$ 7.50	$ 8.34
Dessert Spoon......dz.	15.00	16.68
Table or Serving Spoon.........dz.	15.00	16.68
Round Bowl Soup Spoon.........dz.	15.00	16.68
Breakfast or Luncheon Forks.........dz.	15.00	16.68
Dinner Forks.......dz.	15.00	16.68

SPOONS—Super Cases	Retail	List
Baby (bent handle)...ea.	$ 1.00	$13.26
Baby (short handle)...ea.	1.00	13.26
Berry, Salad or Serv...ea.	3.50	46.80
Bouillon.........six	7.25	16.14
Coffee (demi-tasse)..six	3.75	8.34
Cream Soup or Cereal (not in Newport, Jamestown).....six	7.50	16.68
Five o'Clock Tea, Sherbet or Child's(plain box)six	3.75	8.34
Iced Drink or Parfait..six	6.00	13.38
Olive.........ea.	1.75	23.28
Orange or Grapefruit.........six	5.75	12.80
Preserve (not in Newport, Jamestown)..ea.	2.00	26.78
Sugar.........ea.	1.25	16.52

FORKS—Super Cases	Retail	List Doz.
Baby (short handle)..ea.	$ 1.00	$13.26
Cold Meat, Salad or Serving.........ea.	2.50	33.28
Cold Meat (small) (not in Jamestown, Newport).........ea.	2.00	26.78
Five o'Clock Tea or Child's (plain box).six	6.00	13.26
Ice Cream.........six	6.25	13.88
Oyster or Sea Food..six	5.25	11.68
Pie or Pastry, Individual.........six	8.50	18.90
Pickle.........ea.	1.50	20.02
Salad, Individual....six	7.50	16.68

KNIVES & LADLES—Super Cases	Retail	List
Butter Knife.........ea.	$ 1.25	$16.52
Butter Spreaders.....six	6.25	13.92
Gravy Ladle.........ea.	2.75	36.78
Soup Ladle.........ea.	8.00	106.84
Whipped Cream Ladle.........ea.	2.25	30.00

See Pages 14 and 15 for Special Serving Pieces, Solid Handle Cutlery, Hollow Handle Cutlery.

JELLY SERVER
Retail, each, $1.75; List, each, $1.96

BUTTER KNIFE AND SUGAR SPOON SET
Retail, set, $2.50; List, set, $2.78

DESSERT SPOONS
Retail, set of six, $7.50; List, set of six, $8.34

ICED TEA SPOONS
Retail, set of six, $6.00; List, set of six, $6.69

BERRY, SALAD OR SERVING SPOON
Retail, each, $3.50; List, each, $3.90

1931 Catalog

Spring Garden Pattern

Bread Tray $10.00. *A remarkably lovely, truly versatile piece . . . can be used as fruit dish, sandwich tray, for flowers, many other ways.*

HOLMES & EDWARDS
STERLING INLAID°
SILVERPLATE

HERE   HERE
It's Sterling Inlaid

Gravy Boat & Tray $15.00. *A masterpiece of design. Distinctive, low silhouette sweeps up at the lip for perfect balance, perfect pouring. Tray has many uses.*

Covered Vegetable Dish $17.50. *Something new in fine silverware design: instead of the conventional straight line, the lines of this lovely dish sweep up in a graceful curve. Oval serving dish (not illustrated) $10.00.*

Well and Tree Dish $22.50. *Rich Spring Garden ornamentation, unusually graceful outline, make this essential piece a royal setting for all meats, poultry and fish.*

18″ Meat Platter $17.50. *One of the most useful service pieces of all . . . and the handsomest. Important: all prices for service pieces include Federal Tax.*

Have you seen Spring Garden flatware? This latest and loveliest pattern in famous Sterling Inlaid silverplate, comes in a 52 piece service for 8 at only $68.50 with chest. There are three other enchanting Holmes & Edwards patterns, Youth, Danish Princess, Lovely Lady. All are made in the U. S. A.

1949 Catalog

Spring Garden Pattern

3 piece Tea or Coffee Service $125. with Footed Waiter $147.50. *Inspired design perfectly executed for the ultimate in silverplate. Here is attention to small details (note the covered spout on the cream pitcher) and massive richness of ornamentation found usually on only the most expensive solid silver. "It looks like hand-chasing" experts say of the glorious Spring Garden decoration. Truly, a unique value!*

HOLMES & EDWARDS

STERLING INLAID°

SILVERPLATE

HERE   HERE

It's Sterling Inlaid

NOW! Spring Garden

has its own magnificent tea set and service pieces.

Spring Garden! This season's gayest, loveliest silverplate design, first captured for you in exquisite flatware, is now yours in the loveliest holloware imaginable.

There is a breathtakingly beautiful tea set...its wealth of detail, weight, richness of ornamentation, rivaling in appearance the finest examples of hand-worked silver. There are service pieces for your every dining need...each a triumph of designers' art and silversmiths' craft.

And here is the most delightful news of all. You will find these Spring Garden pieces priced within the reach of even the most modest budget.

Two blocks of sterling inlaid at backs of bowls and handles promise longer, lovelier silver life.

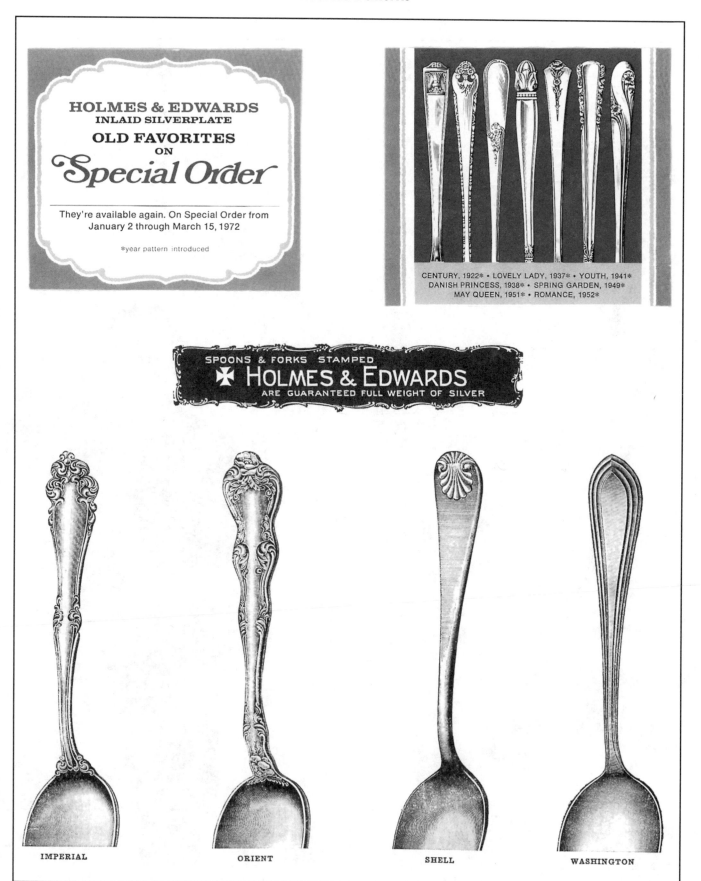

HOLMES & EDWARDS
INLAID SILVERPLATE
OLD FAVORITES
ON
Special Order

They're available again. On Special Order from
January 2 through March 15, 1972

*year pattern introduced

CENTURY, 1922* • LOVELY LADY, 1937* • YOUTH, 1941*
DANISH PRINCESS, 1938* • SPRING GARDEN, 1949*
MAY QUEEN, 1951* • ROMANCE, 1952*

SPOONS & FORKS STAMPED
HOLMES & EDWARDS
ARE GUARANTEED FULL WEIGHT OF SILVER

IMPERIAL   ORIENT   SHELL   WASHINGTON

1972 Special Order of Old Favorites

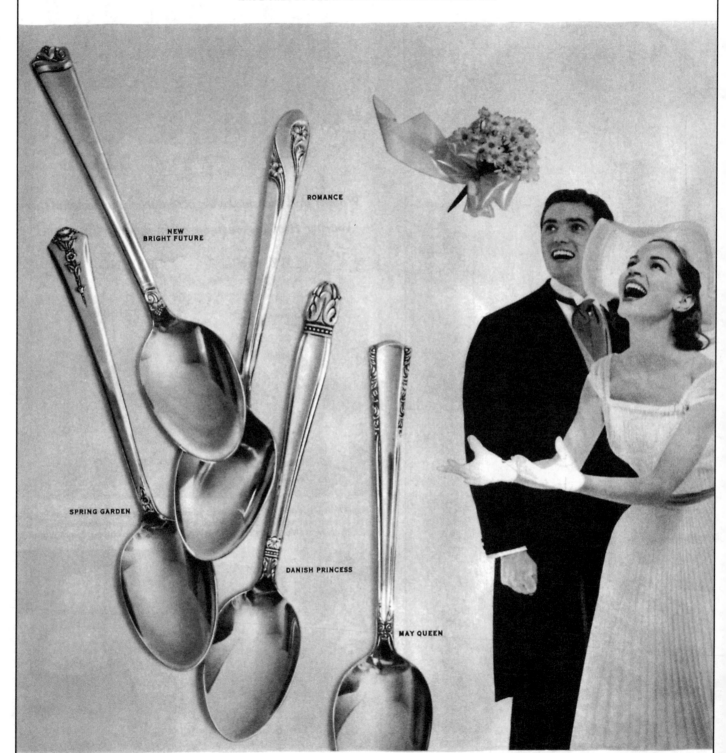

HOLMES & EDWARDS
STERLING INLAID SILVERPLATE
MADE ONLY BY THE INTERNATIONAL SILVER COMPANY

NEW
BRIGHT FUTURE

ROMANCE

SPRING GARDEN

DANISH PRINCESS

MAY QUEEN

It costs a little more . . . but think of the extra *years* of silver beauty. 52-piece set for 8, and chest, $84.50.

1953 Advertisement

Presenting...the loveliest new silverplate in years!

NATIONAL SILVER

Guildcraft

MASTERPIECES OF SILVERPLATE

"Concerto"...an inspired interpretation of the regal shell motif, from National Silver's magnificent new Guildcraft collection.

To you who treasure beauty above all things, National Silver dedicates its Guildcraft "originals"!

For here—at long last—is silverplat in the grand manner...impressively beautiful, exquisitely wrought, faultlessly correct! Every pattern will be masterpiece of priceless distinction... to live with for years, delighting always in its timeless charm and grace.

A complete selection of Guildcraft silverware will be ready for you as soon as conditions permit. Look for it! Whether you choose graceful, romanti "Concerto" (shown below) or one of the many other superb Guildcraft patterns to come, you are assured of silver whos perfect proportions, authenticity of design and luxurious weight are a lasting tribute to your discerning taste

Nobility Plate

Caprice Pattern

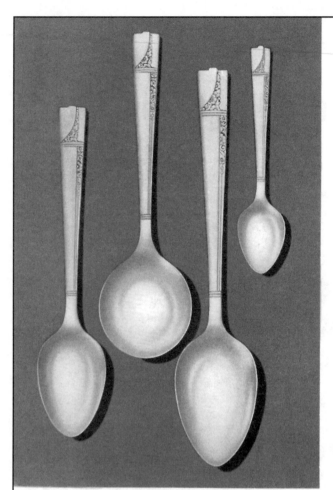

Teaspoons

Teaspoons have so many uses, you'll need at least two for each place setting. Use them for coffee, tea, hot chocolate and other beverages in cups; for desserts; for soft-boiled eggs, some vegetables, grapefruit, oranges, fruit cocktail.

Cream Soup Spoons

Use for *soup in cups* or *bowls*, and for cereals.

Dessert Spoons

Use for desserts . . . for *soup in soup plates* . . . They are especially useful as junior size serving spoons.

After Dinner Coffee Spoons

Use for after dinner coffee served in demi-tasse cups.

Nobility Plate

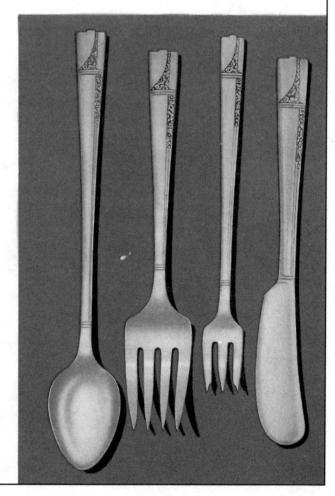

Iced Drink Spoons

Use for iced tea, iced coffee, iced chocolate, root beer or cola with ice cream, parfaits, or any beverages served in tall glasses.

Salad Forks

Use for salads, cake, pie and other pastries.

Seafood Forks

Use for clams, oysters, crab, lobster or any cold seafood cocktail served as a first course at luncheon or dinner.

Butter Spreaders

Use on individual bread and butter plates to spread butter, cheese, jelly or jam on rolls, biscuits, toast, pancakes, waffles and crackers.

1939 Catalog

Caprice Pattern

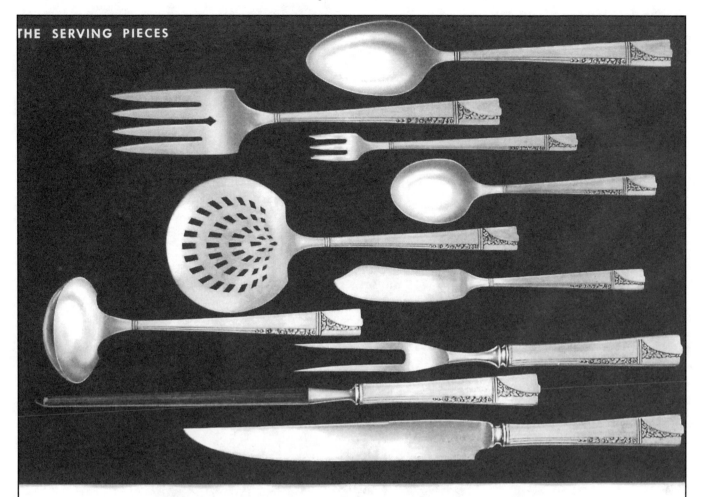

THE SERVING PIECES

Nobility Plate

Tablespoon (Serving Spoon)

Use the tablespoon alone when the food on the serving dish can be handled neatly and easily without the help of a serving fork. (Vegetables, fruits, etc.)

Cold Meat Fork (Serving Fork)

Perfect for cold sliced meats, and as a partner for the tablespoon in serving meat or fish, bulky vegetables such as broccoli, asparagus or food on toast.

Pickle or Olive Fork

For serving pickles and olives, and of course you'll need one for serving individual pats of butter.

Sugar Spoon

Although the sugar spoon's most important use is in the sugar bowl, it comes in handy for serving jams, jellies, and all relishes.

Pierced Round Server

For serving eggs, potato cakes, tomatoes, griddle cakes, egg plant, etc., and for pastries of all kinds. The pierced round server and the serving fork make a perfect set to serve salads.

Butter Knife

Use as a server for butter, cheese and peanut butter.

Gravy Ladle

Use for serving gravies, sauces, and dressings.

Carving Set

On most occasions carving is done at the table. The Nobility Three-Piece Carving Set makes carving a pleasure for it contains a fork with long tines to get a firm hold on the meat, a knife with a long keen cutting edge, and a steel for keeping it sharp.

See Price Guide — Group 2

Royal Rose Pattern

Left to right: 8⁹⁄₁₆" cold meat fork, 7¹¹⁄₁₆" dinner fork, 6³⁄₈" salad fork, 6¼" cream soup, 6¹⁄₁₆" sugar spoon. Bottom: 7⁵⁄₁₆" tomato server.

Paragon Extra-Triple

Angelica Pattern

9¾" hollow handle dinner knife and 8⅜" cold meat fork. Introduced in 1913, this pattern will also be found marked R. C. Co. and Cambridge Silver Plate. Paragon was sold by Sears Roebuck and Co.

See Price Guide — Group 1

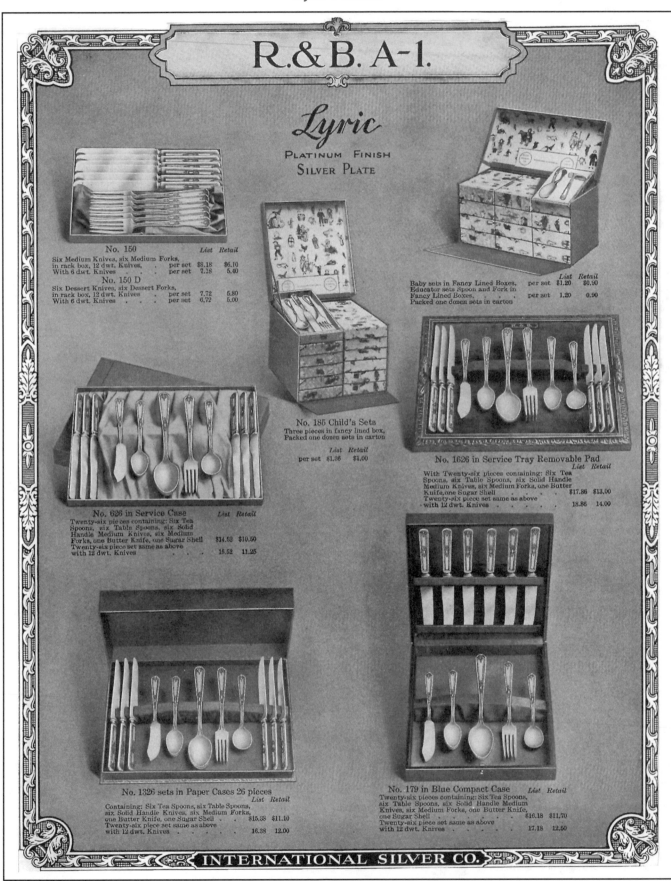

R.&B. A-1.

Lyric

PLATINUM FINISH
SILVER PLATE

No. 150
Six Medium Knives, six Medium Forks,
in rack box, 12 dwt. Knives, . . per set $8.18 $6.10
With 6 dwt. Knives . . . per set 7.18 5.40

No. 150 D
Six Dessert Knives, six Dessert Forks,
in rack box, 12 dwt. Knives . . per set 7.72 5.80
With 6 dwt. Knives . . . . per set 6.72 5.00

Baby sets in Fancy Lined Boxes, per set $1.20 $0.90
Educator sets Spoon and Fork in
Fancy Lined Boxes, . . per set 1.20 0.90
Packed one dozen sets in carton

No. 185 Child's Sets
Three pieces in fancy lined box,
Packed one dozen sets in carton
List Retail
per set $1.36 $1.00

No. 1626 in Service Tray Removable Pad
List Retail
With Twenty-six pieces containing: Six Tea
Spoons, six Table Spoons, six Medium
Medium Knives, six Medium Forks, one Butter
Knife, one Sugar Shell . . . $17.86 $13.00
Twenty-six piece set same as above
with 12 dwt. Knives . . . 18.86 14.00

No. 626 in Service Case
List Retail
Twenty-six pieces containing: Six Tea
Spoons, six Table Spoons, six Solid
Handle Medium Knives, six Medium
Forks, one Butter Knife, one Sugar Shell $14.52 $10.50
Twenty-six piece set same as above
with 12 dwt. Knives . . . 15.52 11.25

No. 1326 sets in Paper Cases 26 pieces
List Retail
Containing: Six Tea Spoons, six Table Spoons,
six Solid Handle Knives, six Medium Forks,
one Butter Knife, one Sugar Shell . $15.38 $11.10
Twenty-six piece set same as above
with 12 dwt. Knives . . . 16.38 12.00

No. 179 in Blue Compact Case *List Retail*
Twenty-six pieces containing: Six Tea Spoons,
six Table Spoons, six Solid Handle Medium
Knives, six Medium Forks, one Butter Knife,
one Sugar Shell . . . $16.18 $11.70
Twenty-six piece set same as above
with 12 dwt. Knives . . . 17.18 12.50

INTERNATIONAL SILVER CO.

1930 Catalog

R. & B. A-1 (International Silver Co.)

R. & B. A-1.

Lyric
PLATINUM FINISH
SILVER PLATE

All staple pieces are stamped R. & B. A-1, and guaranteed to be plated EXTRA PLATE which is 25% heavier than standard plate. EXTRA PLATE tea spoons will strip 50 dwts. of silver to the gross; other staple pieces in proportion.

Baby Spoon
One in lined box . . . . each $ .60 $ .45

Berry Spoon
One in lined box . . . . each $1.58 $1.16

Butter Spreaders
		List	Retail
One dozen in unlined box	. . per doz.	$5.98	$4.30
Half dozen in lined box	. . per doz.	6.38	4.60

Orange Spoons
		List	Retail
One dozen in unlined box	. . per doz.	$5.96	$4.30
Half dozen in lined box	. . per doz.	6.24	4.50

Ladles
One each in lined box
		List	Retail
Cream, Plain	. . each	$1.08	$ .80
Gravy, Plain	. . each	1.34	1.00
Medium Soup	. . each	3.74	2.70

Cold Meat Fork
One in lined box . . . . each $1.18 $ .85

No. 183 Butter Knife and Sugar Shell   List   Retail
Two pieces in lined box . . . . per set $1.36 $1.00
Butter Knife, Bent Handle
One dozen in unlined box . . . . per doz. 6.96   5.00
One each in lined box . . . . each .78   .55
Sugar Shell
One dozen in unlined box . . . . per doz. 6.24   4.50
One each in lined box . . . . each .70   .50

Individual Salad Forks
		List	Retail
One dozen in unlined box	. . per doz.	$8.06	$5.80
Half dozen in lined box	. . per doz.	8.62	6.20

Tea Spoon
Actual
Size

PIECES NOT ILLUSTRATED

Spoons
	List	Retail
Tea, one dozen in unlined box, per dozen	$3.48	$2.50
Dessert, one dozen in unlined box, per dozen	6.24	4.50
Table, one dozen in unlined box, per dozen	6.96	5.00
Bouillon, one dozen in unlined box, per dozen	6.10	4.40
Bouillon, half dozen in lined box, per dozen	6.66	4.80
Coffee, one dozen in unlined box, per dozen	3.24	2.34
Coffee, half dozen in lined box, per dozen	3.52	2.54
Iced Tea, one dozen in unlined box, per dozen	5.28	3.80
Soup, one dozen in unlined box, per dozen	6.52	4.70
Soup, half dozen in lined box, per dozen	7.08	5.10

Forks
	List	Retail
Medium, one dozen in unlined box, per dozen	$6.96	$5.00
Dessert, one dozen in unlined box, per dozen	6.24	4.50
Oyster, half dozen in lined box, per dozen	6.40	4.60
Oyster, one dozen in unlined box, per dozen	5.84	4.20
Pickle, long, one dozen in unlined box, per dozen	8.04	5.80
Pickle, long, one in lined box, per dozen	9.00	6.50

Solid Handle Steel Knives Silver Plated   List   Retail
	List	Retail
Medium, R. & B. 6 dwt., per dozen	7.40	5.70
Dessert, R. & B. 6 dwt., per dozen	7.20	5.50
Medium, R. & B. 12 dwt., per dozen	9.40	7.20
Dessert, R. & B. 12 dwt., per dozen	9.20	7.00
Solid Handle Steel Fruit Knives. Packed ½ dozen in box, per dozen	5.90	4.30
Hollow Handle Breakfast Knives. Packed ½ dozen in lined box, per dozen	23.40	18.00
Hollow Handle Breakfast Knives, Stainless. Packed ½ dozen in lined box, per dozen	27.30	21.00

Miscellaneous
	List	Retail
Sugar Tongs, one in lined box, each	1.46	1.05
Dessert Servers, one in lined box, each	1.90	1.40

INTERNATIONAL SILVER CO.

Reed & Barton

Lydia Pattern

Circa 1895. 6½" hollow handle fruit knives

Left to right: 7" butter knife, 8¹⁄₁₀" large cold meat fork, 6¾" small cold meat fork, 6¹⁄₁₀" jelly server. Tiger Lily was introduced in 1901. It was a heavy, large complete line. When fancy patterns became unpopular, the pattern was discontinued. Reed & Barton brought this pattern back after WWII under the name "Festivity." Collectors prefer to call the pattern Tiger Lily.

Tiger Lily backstamp   Festivity backstamp

Rockford Silverplate Company

Rosemary Pattern

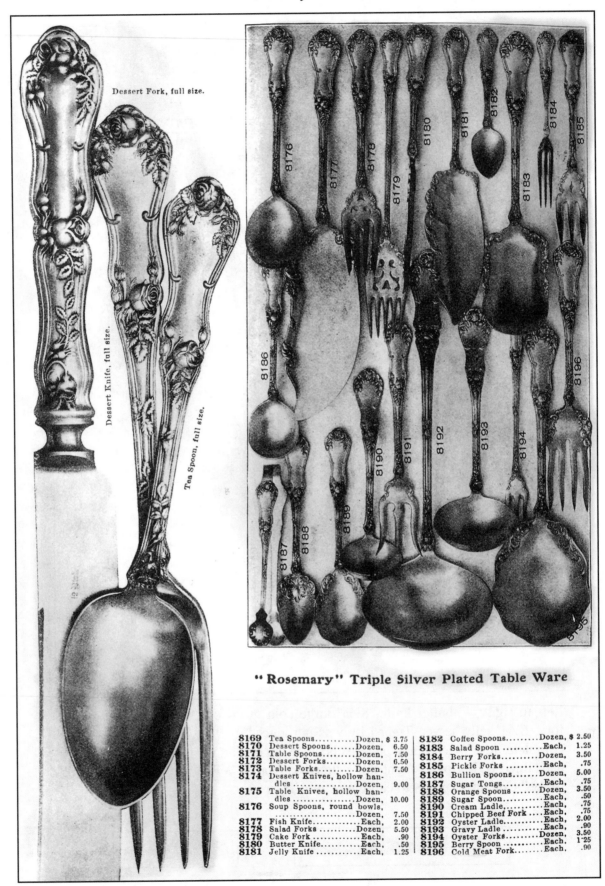

Dessert Fork, full size.

Dessert Knife, full size.

Tea Spoon, full size.

"Rosemary" Triple Silver Plated Table Ware

8169	Tea Spoons............Dozen,	$ 3.75		8182	Coffee Spoons.........Dozen,	$ 2.50
8170	Dessert Spoons......Dozen,	6.50		8183	Salad Spoon ....Each,	1.25
8171	Table Spoons........Dozen,	7.50		8184	Berry Forks...........Dozen,	3.50
8172	Dessert Forks.......Dozen,	6.50		8185	Pickle Forks ....Each,	.75
8173	Table Forks...........Dozen,	7.50		8186	Bullion Spoons.......Dozen,	5.00
8174	Dessert Knives, hollow handles ....Dozen,	9.00		8187	Sugar Tongs...........Each,	.75
8175	Table Knives, hollow handles ....Dozen,	10.00		8188	Orange Spoons ....Dozen,	3.50
				8189	Sugar Spoon ....Each,	.50
8176	Soup Spoons, round bowls, ...Dozen,	7.50		8190	Cream Ladle,..........Each,	.75
				8191	Chipped Beef Fork ....Each,	.75
8177	Fish Knife ....Each,	2.00		8192	Oyster Ladle...........Each,	2.00
8178	Salad Forks...........Dozen,	5.50		8193	Gravy Ladle...........Each,	.90
8179	Cake Fork ....Each,	.90		8194	Oyster Forks.........Dozen,	3.50
8180	Butter Knife..........Each,	.50		8195	Berry Spoon ....Each,	1.25
8181	Jelly Knife ....Each,	1.25		8196	Cold Meat Fork........Each,	.90

1905 Catalog

Rogers & Bros. (Star Mark, A-1)
Crest Pattern

★ ROGERS & BRO.

PIE SERVER—HOLLOW HANDLE
Crest Pattern.   Gray Finish
No. **32440**   Silver blade..............................each   **$4.20**

SIX SOUP SPOONS
Crest Pattern.   Gray Finish
No. **32445**   Silver bowls..............per set   **$5.95**

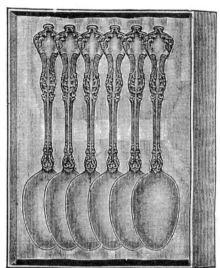

SIX TEA SPOONS
Crest pattern.   Gray finish.
No. **32487**   Silver bowls....per set **$3.45**

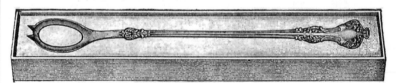

OLIVE SPOON
Crest Pattern.   Gray Finish
No. **32444**   Silver bowl.................each   **$0.95**

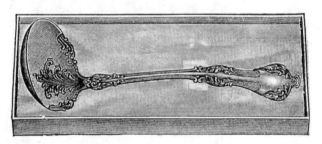

Crest pattern. Gray finish.			
No. **32468**	Cream Ladle.	Silver bowl.............each	**$1.45**
No. **32469**	Cream Ladle.	Gold bowl...............each	2.05
No. **32470**	Gravy Ladle.	Silver bowl.............each	1.90
No. **32471**	Gravy Ladle.	Gold bowl...............each	2.80
No. **32472**	Oyster Ladle.	Silver bowl.............each	4.10
No. **32473**	Oyster Ladle.	Gold bowl...............each	5.10
No. **32474**	Medium Ladle.	Silver bowl.............each	5.00
No. **32475**	Medium Ladle.	Gold bowl...............each	6.25

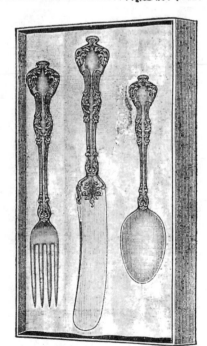

CHILD'S SET
Crest pattern.   Gray finish.

1913 Catalog. Patented 1906

★ ROGERS & BRO.

No. 31498   Medium knives, Crest pattern, gray finish.....................$26.00
No. 31499   Medium forks, Crest pattern, gray finish..................... 26.00

No. 31500   Dessert knives, Crest pattern, gray finish.....................$22.50
No. 31501   Dessert forks, Crest pattern, gray finish..................... 22.50

SUGAR SHELL
Crest Pattern.   Gray Finish
No. 32423   Silver bowl..............each   **$1.10**
No. 32424   Gold bowl..............each   1.50

SIX BOUILLON SPOONS
Crest pattern.   Gray finish.

BUTTER KNIFE—Crest Pattern.   Gray Finish
No. 32413   Silver blade................each   **$1.25**
No. 32414   Gold blade.................each   1.70

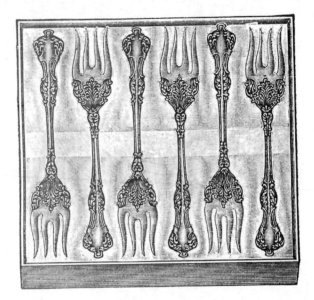

SIX INDIVIDUAL SALAD FORKS
Crest pattern.   Gray finish.
No. 32508   Silver tines.................per set **$5.95**
No. 32509   Gold tines....................per set   8.45

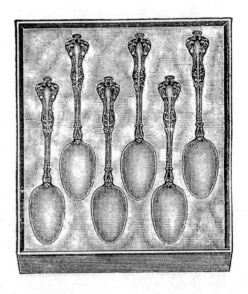

SIX COFFEE SPOONS—Crest Pattern.   Gray Finish
No. 32425   Silver bowl...............per set **$2.55**
No. 32426   Gold bowl...............per set   4.80

1913 Catalog

★ ROGERS & BRO.

BREADKNIFE
Hollow handle.
Crest pattern.
Gray finish.
Length, 14½ inches.

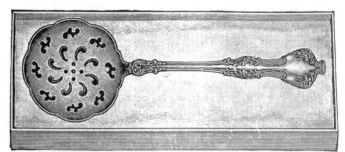

CUCUMBER SERVER—Crest Pattern. Gray Finish
No. 32427　Silver bowl..................each　**$2.50**
No. 32428　Gold bowl...................each　**3.15**

FOOD PUSHER
Crest pattern.
French gray.
No. **32491**　Silver
blade, each **$0.80**

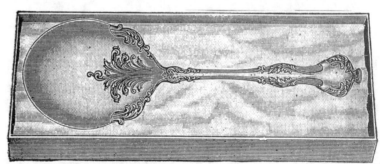

BERRY SPOON—Crest Pattern.　Gray Finish
No. 32401　Silver Bowl....................................each　**$2.50**
No. 32402　Gold bowl.....................................each　**3.45**

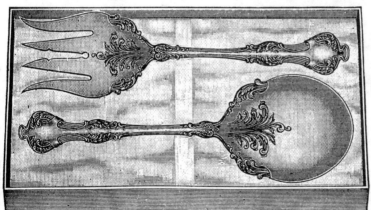

SALAD SET.　Crest pattern.　Gray finish.
One salad spoon, one salad fork.
No. **32510**　Silver bowl and tines.........................per set　**$5.65**
No. **32511**　Gold bowl and tines..........................per set　**7.50**

BABY SPOON
Crest pattern.　Gray finish.
No. **32498**　Silver bowl................each **$0.80**
No. **32499**　Gold bowl.................each　**1.10**

Empire Pattern

★ **ROGERS & BRO. A-1**
TRADE MARK

EMPIRE
PLATINUM FINISH
SILVER PLATE

Every article bearing this celebrated Trade Mark ★ROGERS & BRO. A-1 is Heavily Silver Plated on highest grade Nickel Silver Base and guaranteed, with ordinary care, to last a lifetime. This well known Brand has had a continuous sale for more than 70 years.

Furnished in the complete line
A-1 XII Sectional Plate

			Prices Per doz.	
			List	Retail
Tea Spoons	½ doz. in unlined box		$ 6.56	$ 5.00
Desst. "	½ " " " "		11.76	9.00
Table "	½ " " " "		13.12	10.00
Soup Spns. Round Bowl				
	½ doz. in unlined box		13.12	10.00
Soup Spns. Round Bowl				
	½ doz. in Blue Velvet Lined Box		13.74	11.00
Dinner Forks	½ doz. in unlined box		13.12	10.00
Desst. Forks	" " " " "		11.76	9.00

Hollow Handle Cutlery
Knives packed 6 in.
Blue Velvet Lined Box

Dinner Kns.	Plated French Blades	24.76	20.00
Dinner Kns.	French Stainless Blades	28.60	22.00
Dessert Kns.	Plated French Blades	24.14	19.00
Dessert Kns.	French Stainless Blades	27.98	21.00
Breakfast Kns.	Plated French Blades	24.44	20.00
Breakfast Kns.	French Stainless Blades	28.30	22.00

Six Each Knives and Forks	Prices Per Set	
in Blue Velvet Lined Box	List	Retail
Set No. 163½ Dinner French Blades	$18.94	15.00
No. 164½ Bkft. " "	18.10	14.50
No. 165½ Dessert "	18.00	14.00

Above sets with Knives, Stainless Blades $1.92 list per set extra. Retail $1.00 per set extra.

Carving Sets 3 Pc. Stainless Steel Blades	19.56	16.00
Bird Sets 2 Pc. Stainless Steel Blades	9.78	7.50

Solid Handle Cutlery

	Prices Per doz.	
	List	Retail
#12 Dinner Kns. Plated French Blades	9.88	8.00
#12 Dinner Kns. Stainless French Blades	17.48	14.00
#12 Dessert Kns. Plated Blades	9.63	8.00
#12 Bkft. Kns. Scimeter Swaged Blades		
Plated	10.00	8.00

Pieces not illustrated on following page

	List	Retail
Orange Spoons set of six in		
Blue Velvet Lined Box per set	$4.16	3.25
Bouillon Spoons set of six in		
Blue Velvet Lined Box per set	6.24	4.50
Oyster Forks set of six in		
Blue Velvet Lined Box per set	4.38	3.50
Jelly Knife in Blue Velvet Lined Box		
each	2.08	1.75

Illustrations Actual Size

Dinner Fork

Tea Spoon

H. H. Dinner Knife

S. H. Dinner Knife

INTERNATIONAL SILVER CO.

1930 Catalog

STAR ★ BRAND

★ ROGERS & BRO.

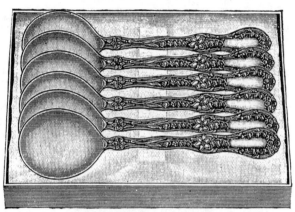

SUGAR TONGS
Florette pattern. Gray finish.

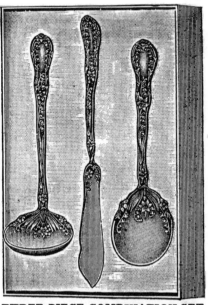

THREE-PIECE COMBINATION SET
Florette pattern. Gray finish.
One cream ladle, one butter knife.
one sugar shell.

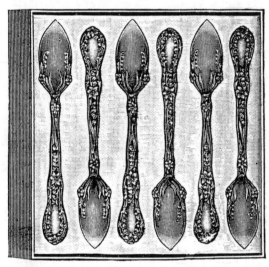

SIX SOUP SPOONS
Florette Pattern. Gray Finish

No. 32447 Silver bowls.................per set **$5.95**

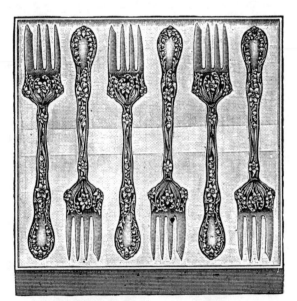

SIX ORANGE SPOONS

No. 32483 Silver bowl........ ....per set **$3.75**
No. 32484 Gold bowl................... per set   6.25

SIX INDIVIDUAL SALAD FORKS
Florette pattern. Gray finish.

No. 32506 Silver tines.................per set **$5.95**
No. 32507 Gold tines....................per set   8.45

1913 Catalog. Patented 1909

ROGERS & BRO.

FINE SILVER PLATED FLATWARE

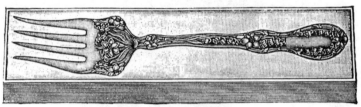

COLD MEAT FORK
Florette Pattern.   Gray Finish

Silver tines. . . . . .each **$1.60**
Gold tines. . . . . .each **2.20**

BABY SPOON
Florette pattern.   Gray finish.

Silver bowl. . . . . .each **$0.80**
Gold bowl. .each **1.10**

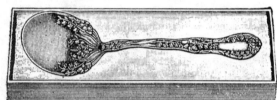

SUGAR SHELL—Florette Pattern.   Gray Finish.

Silver bowl. . . . . .each **$1.10**
Gold bowl. . . . . .each **1.50**

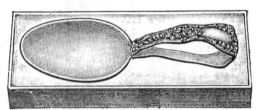

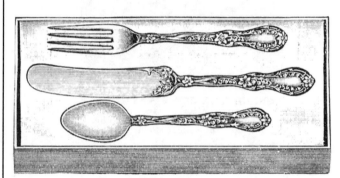

CHILD'S SET
Florette pattern.   Gray finish.

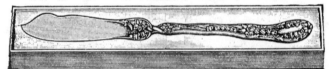

BUTTER KNIFE—Florette Pattern.   Gray Finish

Silver blade. . . . . .each **$1.25**
Gold blade. . . . . .each **1.70**

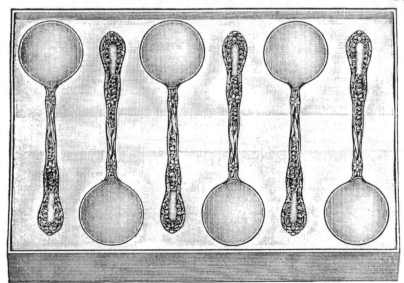

SIX BOUILLON SPOONS
Florette pattern.   French gray.

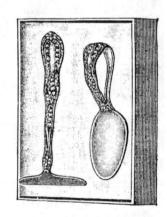

BABY SET
Florette pattern.   Gray finish.
One baby spoon, one food pusher.

1913 Catalog

Florette Pattern

 **Rogers & Bro.**

No. **31486** Medium knives, Florette pattern, gray finish......................$26.00
No. **31487** Medium forks, Florette pattern, gray finish..................... 26.00

No. **31488** Dessert knives, Florette pattern, gray finish..............$22.50
No. **31489** Dessert forks, Florette pattern, gray finish............... 22.50

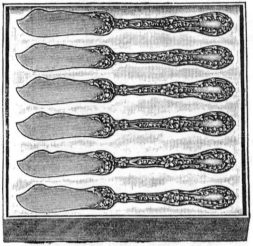

SIX BUTTER SPREADERS
Florette pattern. Gray finish.
No. **32486** Silver blades....per set **$5.30**

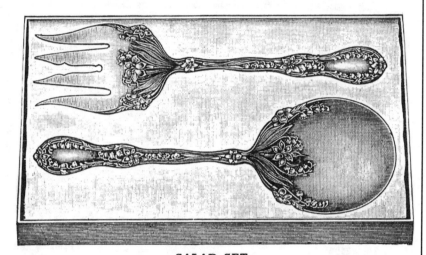

SALAD SET
Florette pattern. Gray finish.
One salad spoon, one salad fork.
No. **32512** Silver bowl and tines............................per set **$5.65**
No. **32513** Gold bowl and tines..............................per set **7.50**

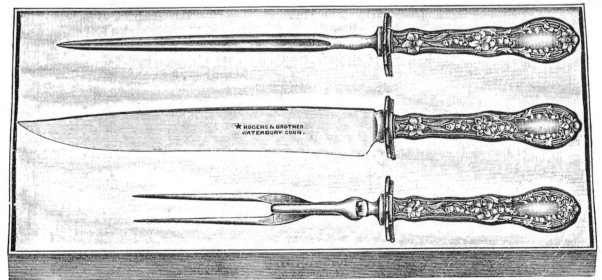

THREE-PIECE CARVING SET
Hollow handles. Florette pattern. Gray finish.
No. **32502** Per set..**$17.35**

1913 Catalog. Patented 1909

See Price Guide — Group 1

★ ROGERS & BRO.

FINE SILVER PLATED FLATWARE

Ivy Pattern

Mystic Pattern

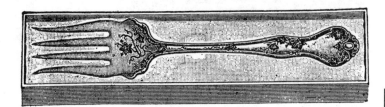

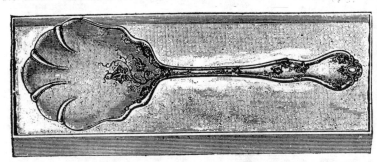

COLD MEAT FORK
Ivy Pattern.   Gray Finish

No. 32437	Silver tines.........................each	$1.60
No. 32438	Gold tines ....each	2.20

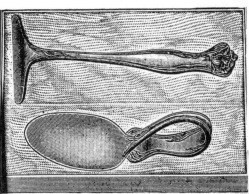

BABY SET
Mystic pattern.   Gray finish.
One baby spoon, one food pusher

BERRY SPOON—Ivy Pattern.   Gray Finish

No. 32405	Silver bowl........................each	$2.50
No. 32406	Gold bowl.........................each	3.45

STAR ★ BRAND

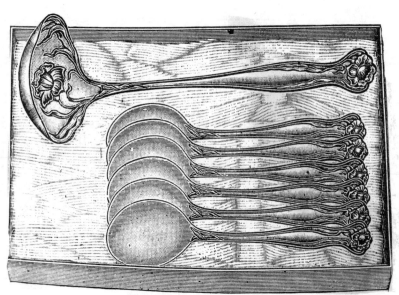

PICKLE FORK
Mystic Pattern.

(LONG)
Gray Finish

SEVEN PIECE SOUP SET
Mystic pattern.   Gray finish.
Six soup spoons, one oyster ladle.

1913 Catalog

★ ROGERS & BRO. A-1
TRADE MARK

Majestic
PLATINUM FINISH
SILVER PLATE

A Beautiful New Pattern

Every article bearing this celebrated Trade Mark ★ROGERS & BRO. A-1 is Heavily Silver Plated on highest grade Nickel Silver Base and guaranteed, with ordinary care, to last a lifetime. This well known Brand has had a continuous sale for more than 70 years.

Furnished in the complete line
A-1   XII Sectional Plate

			Prices Per doz.	
			List	Retail
Tea Spoons	½ doz. in unlined box		$ 6.56	$ 5.00
Desst. "	½ " " " "		11.76	9.00
Table "	½ " " " "		13.12	10.00
Soup Spns. Round Bowl				
	½ doz. in unlined box		13.12	10.00
Soup Spns. Round Bowl				
	½ doz. in Blue Velvet Lined Box		13.74	11.00
Dinner Forks	½ doz. in unlined box		13.12	10.00
Desst. Forks	" " " " "		11.76	9.00

Hollow Handle Cutlery
Knives packed 6 in
Blue Velvet Lined Box

Dinner Kns.	Plated French Blades	24.76	20.00
Dinner Kns.	French Stainless Blades	28.60	22.00
Dessert Kns.	Plated French Blades	24.14	19.00
Dessert Kns.	French Stainless Blades	27.98	21.00
Breakfast Kns.	Plated French Blades	24.44	20.00
Breakfast Kns.	French Stainless Blades	28.30	22.00

Six Each Knives and Forks		Prices Per Set	
in Blue Velvet Lined Box		List	Retail
Set No. 163½ Dinner French Blades		$18.94	15.00
No. 164½ Bkft. " "		18.10	14.50
No. 165½ Dessert " "		18.00	14.00

Above sets with Knives, Stainless Blades $1.92 list per set extra, Retail $1.00 per set extra.

Carving Sets 3 Pc. Stainless Steel Blades	19.56	16.00
Bird Sets 2 Pc. Stainless Steel Blades	9.78	7.50

Solid Handle Cutlery

	Prices Per doz.	
	List	Retail
#12 Dinner Kns. Plated French Blades	9.83	8.00
#12 Dinner Kns. Stainless French Blades	17.48	14.00
#12 Dessert Kns. Plated Blades	9.68	8.00
#12 Bkft. Kns. Scimeter Swaged Blades		
Plated	10.00	8.00

Pieces not illustrated on following page

	List	Retail
Oyster Forks, Set of Six in		
Blue Velvet Lined Box, per set	$4.38	$3.50
Sugar Tong, one in Blue Velvet		
Lined Box, each	2.08	1.75
Baby Spoon, Bent Handle,		
one in Blue Velvet Lined Box, each	.88	.75
Baby Set, Spoon and Food Pusher,		
per set	1.74	1.50
Iced Tea Spoons, Set of Six, per set	4.50	3.50
Dessert Server, one in		
Blue Velvet Lined Box, each	6.95	3.00

Tea Spoon

Dinner Fork

H. H. Dinner Knife

Illustrations Actual Size

S. H. Dinner Knife

INTERNATIONAL SILVER CO.

1930 Catalog

Mystic Pattern

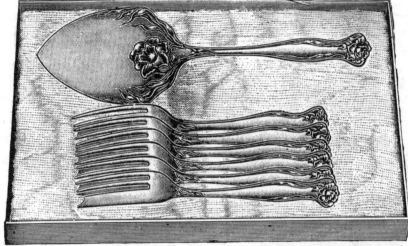

★ ROGERS & BRO.

STAR ★ BRAND

SEVEN PIECE PIE SET. Mystic pattern

New Century Pattern

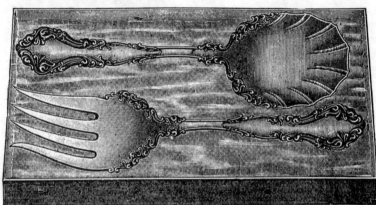

SALAD SET
New Century pattern. Gray finish.
One salad spoon, one salad fork

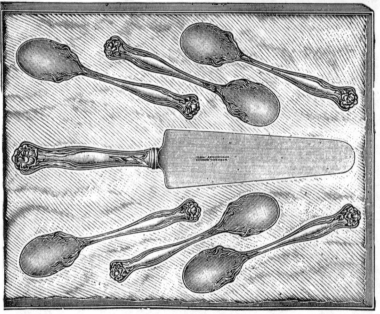

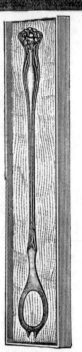

SEVEN PIECE ICE CREAM SET. Mystic pattern. Gray finish.
Six ice cream forks, one ice cream server.

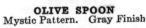

OLIVE SPOON
Mystic Pattern. Gray Finish

1913 Catalog

★ **ROGERS & BRO. A-1**
TRADE MARK

Paisley
PLATINUM FINISH
SILVER PLATE

Every article bearing this celebrated Trade Mark ✶ROGERS & BRO. A-1 is Heavily Silver Plated on highest grade Nickel Silver Base and guaranteed, with ordinary care, to last a lifetime. This well known Brand has had a continuous sale for more than 70 years.

Furnished in the complete line
A-1 XII Sectional Plate

			Prices Per doz.	
			List	Retail
Tea Spoons	½ doz. in unlined box		$ 6.56	$ 5.00
Desst. "	½ " " " "		11.76	9.00
Table "	½ " " " "		13.12	10.00
Soup Spns. Round Bowl				
	½ doz. in unlined box		13.12	10.00
Soup Spns. Round Bowl				
	½ doz. in Blue Velvet Lined Box		13.74	11.00
Dinner Forks	½ doz. in unlined box		13.12	10.00
Desst. Forks	" " " "		11.76	9.00

Hollow Handle Cutlery
Knives packed 6 in
Blue Velvet Lined Box

Dinner Kns.	Plated French Blades	24.76	20.00
Dinner Kns.	French Stainless Blades	28.60	22.00
Dessert Kns.	Plated French Blades	24.14	19.00
Dessert Kns.	French Stainless Blades	27.98	21.00
Breakfast Kns.	Plated French Blades	24.44	20.00
Breakfast Kns.	French Stainless Blades	26.30	22.00

Six Each Knives and Forks	Prices Per Set	
in Blue Velvet Lined Box	List	Retail
Set No. 163½ Dinner French Blades	$18.94	15.00
No. 164½ Bkft. " "	18.10	14.50
No. 165½ Dessert " "	18.00	14.00

Above sets with Knives, Stainless Blades $1.92 list per set extra. Retail $1.00 per set extra.

Carving Sets 3 Pc. Stainless Steel Blades	19.56	16.00
Bird Sets	2 Pc. Stainless Steel Blades	9.78	7.50

Solid Handle Cutlery

	Prices Per doz.	
	List	Retail
#12 Dinner Kns. Plated French Blades	9.88	8.00
#12 Dinner Kns. Stainless French Blades	17.48	14.00
#12 Dessert Kns. Plated Blades	9.68	8.00
#12 Bkft. Kns. Scimeter Swaged Blades		
Plated	10.00	8.00

Pieces not illustrated on following page

	List	Retail
Orange Spoons set of six in		
Blue Velvet Lined Box per set	$4.16	3.25
Bouillon Spoons set of six in		
Blue Velvet Lined Box per set	6.24	4.50
Oyster Forks set of six in		
Blue Velvet Lined Box per set	4.38	3.50
Jelly Knife in Blue Velvet Lined Box		
each	2.08	1.75

Illustrations Actual Size

Tea Spoon

Dinner Fork

H. H. Dinner Knife

S. H. Dinner Knife

INTERNATIONAL SILVER CO.

1930 Catalog

★ ROGERS & BRO. FINE SILVER PLATED FLATWARE

No. 31490 Medium Knives, Verona Pattern, bright finish
No. 31491 Medium Forks, Verona Pattern, bright finish

No. 31492 Dessert Knives, Verona Pattern, bright finish
No. 31493 Dessert Forks, Verona Pattern, bright finish

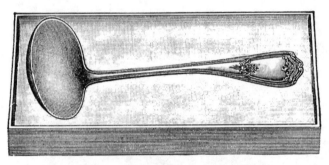

No. 32460	Cream Ladle,	Silver Bowl
No. 32461	Cream Ladle,	Gold Bowl
No. 32462	Gravy Ladle,	Silver Bowl
No. 32463	Gravy Ladle,	Gold Bowl
No. 32464	Oyster Ladle,	Silver Bowl
No. 32465	Oyster Ladle,	Gold Bowl
No. 32466	Medium Ladle,	Silver Bowl
No. 32467	Medium Ladle,	Gold Bowl

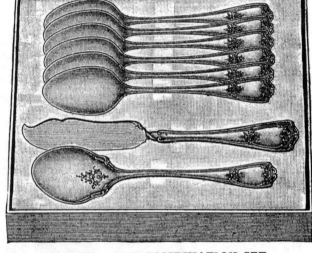

EIGHT-PIECE COMBINATION SET
Verona pattern.   Bright finish.

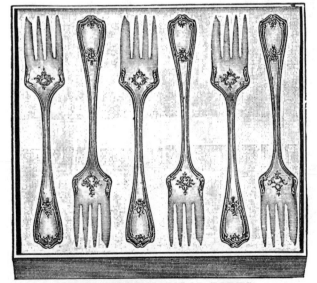

SIX INDIVIDUAL SALAD FORKS
Verona pattern.   Bright finish.

| No. 32504 | Silver tines................per set | **$5.95** |
| No. 32505 | Gold tines................per set | **8.45** |

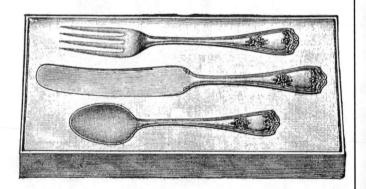

CHILD'S SET
Verona pattern.   Bright finish.

1913 Catalog. Patented 1910

★ ROGERS & BRO. STAR ★ BRAND

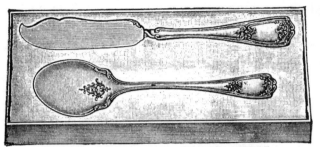

BUTTER KNIFE AND SUGAR SHELL
Verona Pattern.   Bright Finish
No. 32409   Silver bowl.....................per set   **$2.30**
No. 32410   Gold bowl.....................per set   **2.70**

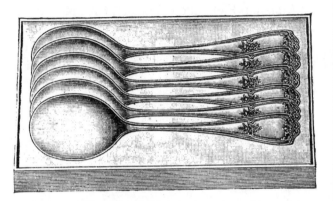

SIX SOUP SPOONS
Verona Pattern.   Gray Finish
No. 32446   Silver bowls...............per set   **$5.95**

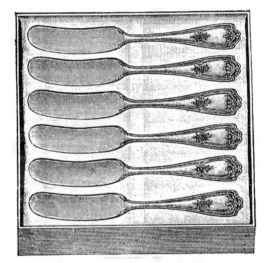

SIX BUTTER SPREADERS
Verona pattern.   Bright finish.

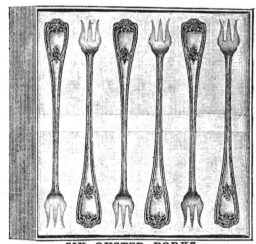

SIX OYSTER FORKS
Verona Pattern.   Gray Finish

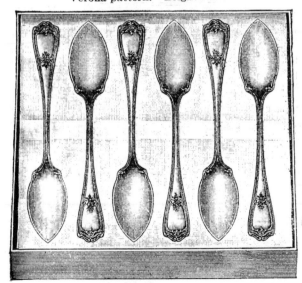

SIX ORANGE SPOONS
Verona pattern.   Bright finish.
No. 32480   Silver bowl.................per set   **$3.75**
No. 32481   Gold bowl.................per set   **6.25**

COLD MEAT FORK
Verona Pattern.   Bright Finish
Silver tines...................................each   **$1.60**
Gold tines...................................each   **2.20**

Rogers & Hamilton Company

Aldine Pattern

Aldine was manufactured by the Rogers & Hamilton Company, Waterbury, Connecticut, and patented in 1895. The illustrations shown here are from a catalog of Marshall Field and Company, Chicago, Illinois. Other firms, including Montgomery Ward and Co., marketed Aldine. Pieces will be found marked "Aurora Silver Plate." Rogers & Hamilton advertised Aldine as highest grade plated ware. The pie knife illustrated is 9½" long and sold for $1.50 in 1898. Note that the illustrated individual salad or pie fork is the same piece. It is possible that another salad fork was later produced.

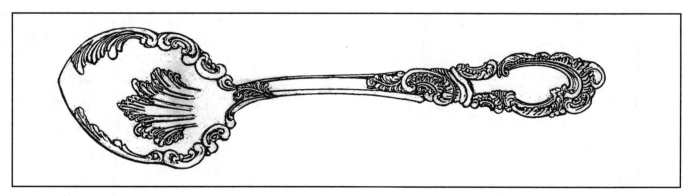

Sugar Shell (actual size)

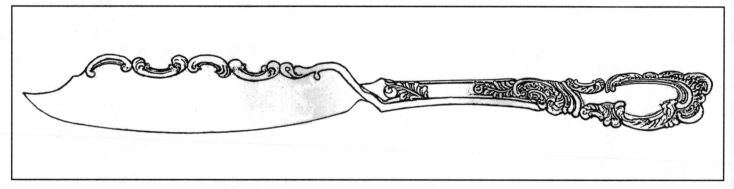

Butter Knife, twist handle (actual size)

Aldine Pattern

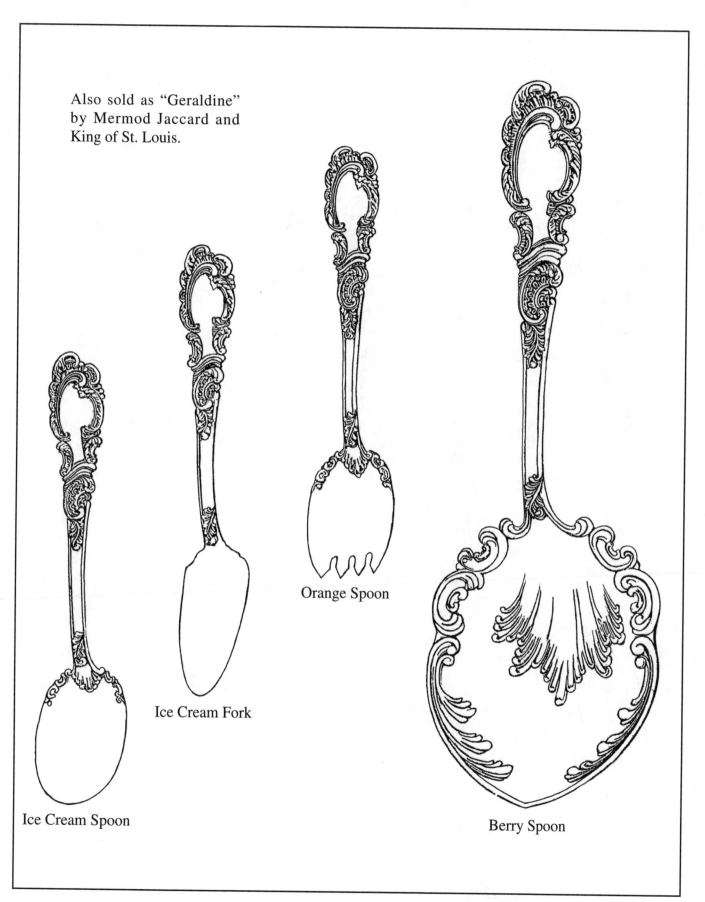

Also sold as "Geraldine" by Mermod Jaccard and King of St. Louis.

Orange Spoon

Ice Cream Fork

Ice Cream Spoon

Berry Spoon

Items shown actual size

See Price Guide — Group 1

Aldine Pattern

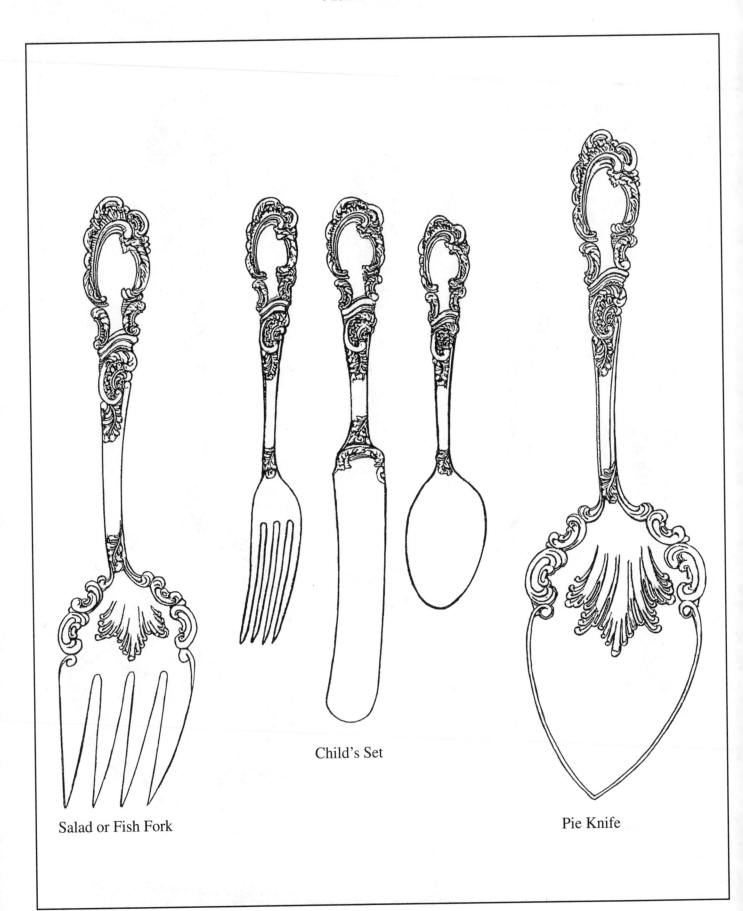

Salad or Fish Fork

Child's Set

Pie Knife

Items shown reduced size.

156

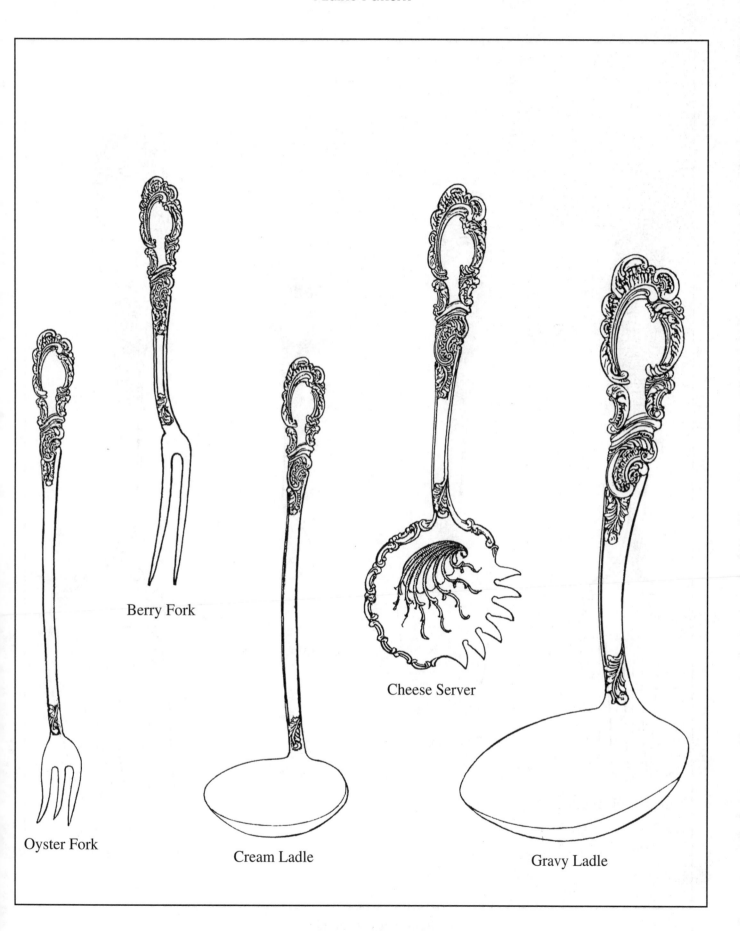

Oyster Fork

Berry Fork

Cream Ladle

Cheese Server

Gravy Ladle

Aldine Pattern

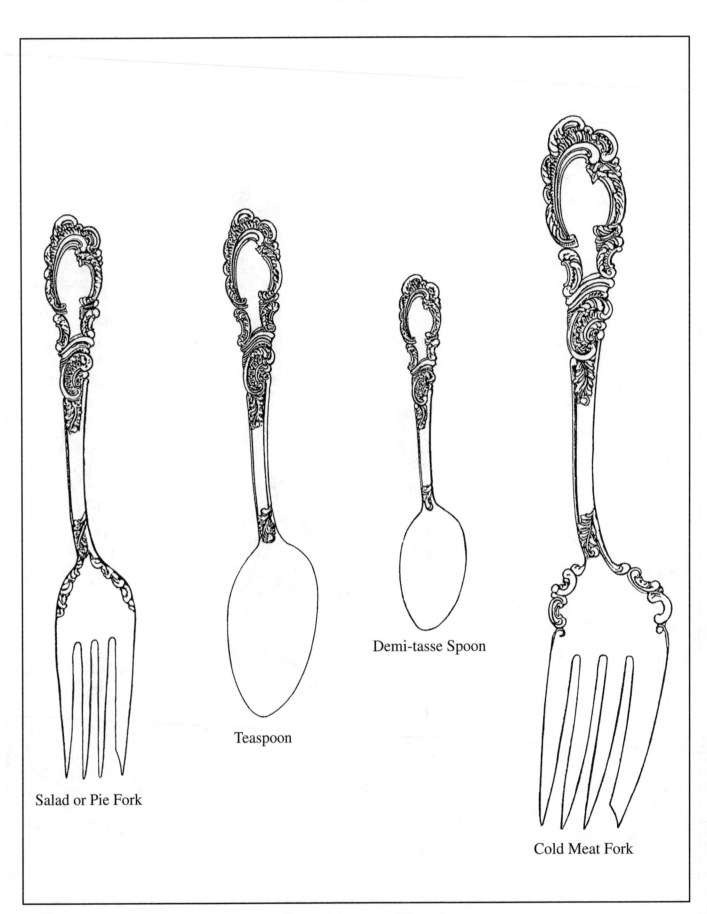

Salad or Pie Fork

Teaspoon

Demi-tasse Spoon

Cold Meat Fork

Items shown actual size.

This pattern was patented in 1896. Highly collectible because of its beauty, some items, like the hollow handle knives, are very difficult to find. Many items will be found with gilded bowls. Shown: $5^{11}/_{16}$" grapefruit/orange spoons and $7\frac{1}{2}$" cream soup spoons.

1847 Rogers Bros.

Adoration Pattern

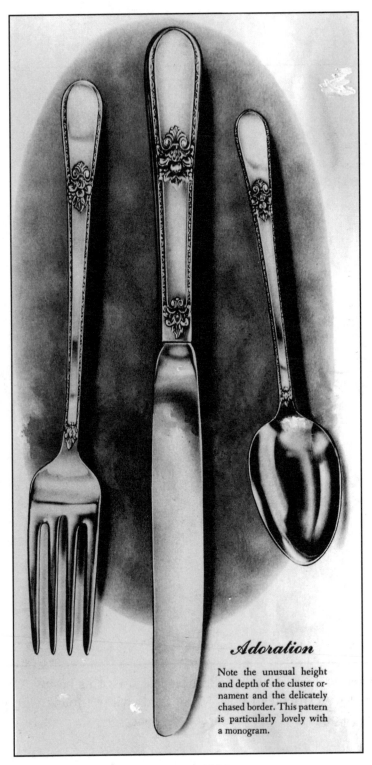

Adoration

Note the unusual height and depth of the cluster ornament and the delicately chased border. This pattern is particularly lovely with a monogram.

Patented 1939

ADORATION was introduced around 1937. It was made in many different pieces. It is relatively scarce.

No. 5321
10 oz. Goblet
Height 7½"

No. 5321
6 oz. Saucer Champagne
or Tall Sherbet
Height 6"

No. 5321
3½ oz. Liquor Cocktail
Height 5½"

No. 5321
3 oz. Wine
Height 6¼"

No. 5321
1 oz. Cordial
Height 4½"

No. 5321
4½ oz. Oyster Cocktail
Height 3½"

No. 5321
5 oz. Footed Orange Juice
Height 4½"

No. 5321
13 oz. Footed Ice Tea
Height 6¼"

No. 5321
6 oz. Ice Cream
Height 3½"

No. 30½
8½ in. Salad Plate
(Also made in 7½" Dessert Size)
(Also made in 6½" Bread &
Butter Plate)

This Duncan & Miller etching was designed to match 1847 Rogers Bros. Adoration silver pattern.

1847 ROGERS BROS.
ORIGINAL AND GENUINE ROGERS SILVERPLATE

AN INTERNATIONAL SILVER CO. PRODUCT

AMBASSADOR PATTERN (CONT'D)

84105   ICE CREAM FORKS
Retail, set of six, $6.25; List, set of six, $7.68

84204   JELLY SERVER
Retail, each, $1.75; List, each, $2.14

84301   BUTTER KNIFE AND SUGAR SPOON SET
Retail, set, $2.50; List, set, $3.06

84201   BUTTER KNIFE OR SERVER
Retail, each, $1.25; List, each, $1.52

84017   SUGAR SPOON
Retail, each, $1.25; List, each, $1.52

84227   GRAVY LADLE
Retail, each, $2.75; List, each, $3.38

84226   SAUCE LADLE, small
Retail, each, $2.25; List, each, $2.76

84253   LONG SERVER
Retail, each, $4.25; List, each, $5.22

84252   ROUND SERVER
Retail, each, $3.25; List, each, $3.98

84254   PIE OR ICE CREAM KNIFE
Retail, each, $4.50; List, each, $5.52

84108   PICKLE FORK
Retail, each, $1.50; List, each, $1.84

84103   SERVING FORK, large
Retail, each, $2.50; List, each, $3.06

84104   SERVING FORK, small
Retail, each, $2.00; List, each, $2.46

84003   BERRY OR SALAD SPOON
Retail, each, $3.50; List, each, $4.30

84004   BERRY SPOON, small
Retail, each, $2.00; List, each, $2.46

84277   SUGAR TONGS
Retail, each, $2.00; List, each, $2.46

84019   SERVING SPOONS
Retail, set of two, $5.00; List, set of two, $6.14

VIANDE
TRADE MARK
FORK
{Dinner Size}

1931 Catalog

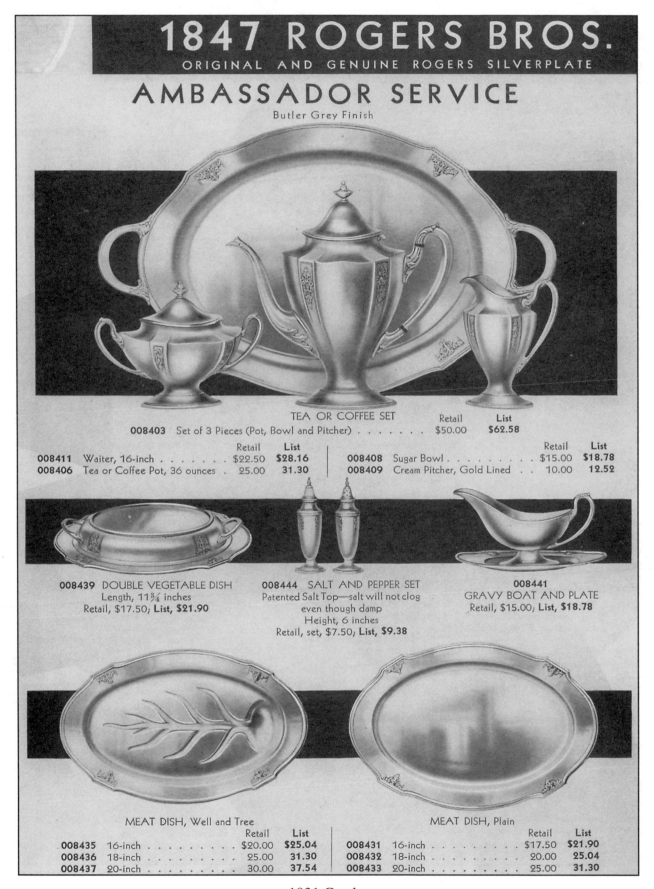

1847 ROGERS BROS.
ORIGINAL AND GENUINE ROGERS SILVERPLATE

AMBASSADOR SERVICE
Butler Grey Finish

TEA OR COFFEE SET

		Retail	List
008403	Set of 3 Pieces (Pot, Bowl and Pitcher)	$50.00	$62.58

		Retail	List				Retail	List
008411	Waiter, 16-inch	$22.50	$28.16		008408	Sugar Bowl	$15.00	$18.78
008406	Tea or Coffee Pot, 36 ounces .	25.00	31.30		008409	Cream Pitcher, Gold Lined . .	10.00	12.52

008439 DOUBLE VEGETABLE DISH
Length, 11¾ inches
Retail, $17.50; List, $21.90

008444 SALT AND PEPPER SET
Patented Salt Top—salt will not clog
even though damp
Height, 6 inches
Retail, set, $7.50; List, $9.38

008441
GRAVY BOAT AND PLATE
Retail, $15.00; List, **$18.78**

MEAT DISH, Well and Tree

		Retail	List
008435	16-inch	$20.00	$25.04
008436	18-inch	25.00	31.30
008437	20-inch	30.00	37.54

MEAT DISH, Plain

		Retail	List
008431	16-inch	$17.50	$21.90
008432	18-inch	20.00	25.04
008433	20-inch	25.00	31.30

1931 Catalog

See Price Guide — Group 2

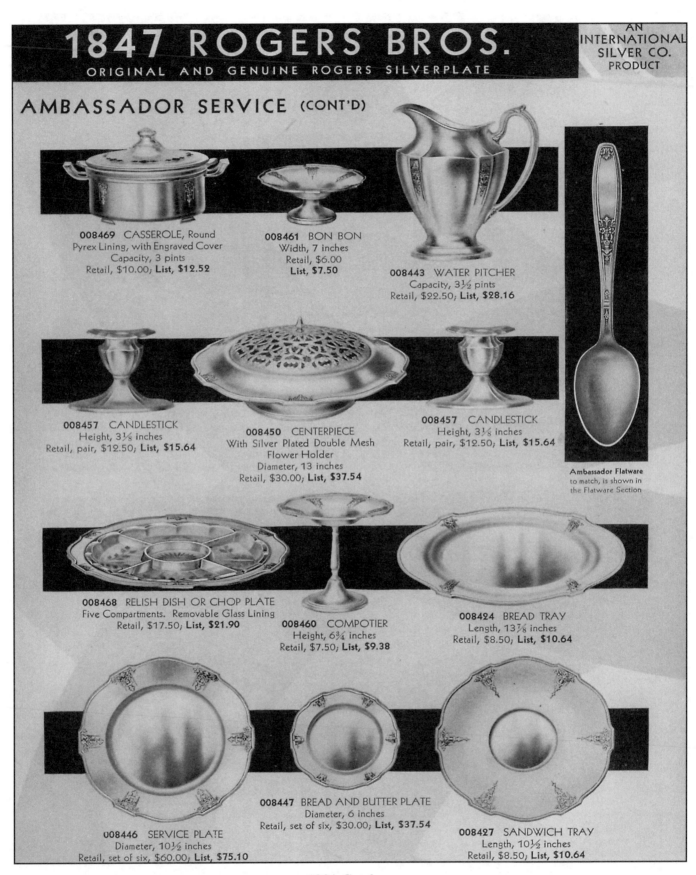

1847 ROGERS BROS.
ORIGINAL AND GENUINE ROGERS SILVERPLATE

AN INTERNATIONAL SILVER CO. PRODUCT

AMBASSADOR SERVICE (CONT'D)

008469 CASSEROLE, Round
Pyrex Lining, with Engraved Cover
Capacity, 3 pints
Retail, $10.00; **List, $12.52**

008461 BON BON
Width, 7 inches
Retail, $6.00
List, $7.50

008443 WATER PITCHER
Capacity, 3½ pints
Retail, $22.50; **List, $28.16**

008457 CANDLESTICK
Height, 3⅛ inches
Retail, pair, $12.50; **List, $15.64**

008450 CENTERPIECE
With Silver Plated Double Mesh
Flower Holder
Diameter, 13 inches
Retail, $30.00; **List, $37.54**

008457 CANDLESTICK
Height, 3⅛ inches
Retail, pair, $12.50; **List, $15.64**

Ambassador Flatware
to match, is shown in
the Flatware Section

008468 RELISH DISH OR CHOP PLATE
Five Compartments. Removable Glass Lining
Retail, $17.50; **List, $21.90**

008460 COMPOTIER
Height, 6¾ inches
Retail, $7.50; **List, $9.38**

008424 BREAD TRAY
Length, 13⅞ inches
Retail, $8.50; **List, $10.64**

008446 SERVICE PLATE
Diameter, 10½ inches
Retail, set of six, $60.00; **List, $75.10**

008447 BREAD AND BUTTER PLATE
Diameter, 6 inches
Retail, set of six, $30.00; **List, $37.54**

008427 SANDWICH TRAY
Length, 10½ inches
Retail, $8.50; **List, $10.64**

1931 Catalog

008403 TEA OR COFFEE SET
Three Pieces
Coffee Pot, Sugar Bowl and Cream
Pitcher
List, set, $81.36; Consumer, set, $65.00

008411 WAITER, 16 inch, oval
(not illustrated)
List, each, $31.30
Consumer, each, $25.00

008446 SERVICE PLATE, 10½ in.
List, each, $12.52; Consumer, $10.00

008447 BREAD AND BUTTER PLATE
Diameter, 6 inches
List, each, $6.26; Consumer, each, $5.00

008444 SALT AND PEPPER SET
Height, 6¼ inches
List, set, $12.52; Consumer, set, $10.00

008453 CANDLESTICKS
Height, 10 inches
List, pair, $31.30; Consumer, pair, $25.00

008440 DOUBLE VEGETABLE DISH
Lock Handle
Length, 11¾ inches
List, each, $31.30; Consumer, each, $25.00

AMBASSADOR PATTERN

Chased
Butler Grey Finish

*Matching the Spoons, Forks and Knives
in the Ambassador Pattern*

MEAT DISHES, Plain

		List	Consumer
008430	14 inch....	$18.78	$15.00
008431	16 inch....	25.04	20.00
008432	18 inch....	31.30	25.00
008433	20 inch....	37.54	30.00

MEAT DISHES, Well and Tree

008436	18 inch....	$40.68	$32.50
008437	20 inch....	46.94	37.50
008438	22 inch....	65.70	52.50

008441 GRAVY BOAT AND PLATE
Capacity, 16 ounces
List, set, $25.04; Consumer, set, $20.00

008450 CENTERPIECE, Gold Lined
Diameter, 13 inches
With Silver Plated Double Mesh
List, each, $50.06; Consumer, each, $40.00

008443 WATER PITCHER
Capacity, 3½ pints
List, each, $37.54; Consumer, each, $30.00

008424 BREAD TRAY
Length, 13⅞ inches
List, each, $15.64
Consumer, each, $12.50

TEA POT, COFFEE POT, SUGAR BOWL, CREAM PITCHER AND WASTE BOWL

		List	Consumer
008405	Set of Five Pieces................	$125.16	$100.00
008404	Set of Four Pieces................	112.64	90.00
008403	Set of Three Pieces..............	81.36	65.00
008406	Coffee Pot (or Chocolate), 36 ounces	31.30	25.00
008407	Tea Pot, 24 ounces..............	31.30	25.00

		List	Consumer
008408	Sugar Bowl......................	$25.04	$20.00
008409	Cream Pitcher, Gold Lined........	25.04	20.00
008410	Waste Bowl, Gold Lined.........	12.52	10.00
008412	Waiter, 22 inch, oval (not illustrated)	50.06	40.00
008411	Waiter, 16 inch, oval (not illustrated)	31.30	25.00

1931 Catalog

See Price Guide — Group 2

Ancestral Pattern

86105 ICE CREAM FORKS
List set of six, $7.68; Consumer, set of six, $6.25

86108 PICKLE FORK
List, each, $1.84; Consumer, each, $1.50

86204 JELLY SERVER
List, each, $2.15; Consumer, each, $1.75

CHILD'S SETS
86352 Spoon, Fork and Flat Handle Knife
List, set, $3.68; Consumer, set, $3.00
86353 Spoon, Fork and Hollow Handle Knife
List, set, $4.38; Consumer, set, $3.50
86356 Spoon, Fork and Solid Handle Knife
List, set, $3.07; Consumer, set, $2.50

86252 CUCUMBER OR TOMATO SERVER
List, each, $3.99; Consumer, each, $3.25

86003 BERRY OR SALAD SPOON
List, each, $4.30; Consumer, each, $3.50
86004 BERRY SPOON, SMALL, OR PRESERVE
List, each, $3.38; Consumer, each, $2.75

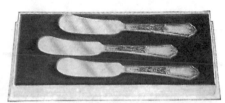

86202 BUTTER SPREADERS
List, set of six, $7.68; Consumer, set of six, $6.25

86001 BABY SPOON, BENT HANDLE
List, each, $1.23; Consumer, each, $1.00
86002 BABY SPOON, SHORT HANDLE
List, each, $1.23; Consumer, each, $1.00

BABY SETS
86304 Baby Spoon and Fork, Short Handles
List, set, $2.46; Consumer, set, $2.00
86303 Baby Spoon and Food Pusher
List, set, $2.46; Consumer, set, $2.00

86111 SALAD FORKS, INDIVIDUAL
List, set of six, $9.18; Consumer, set of six, $7.50

86103 COLD MEAT FORK
List, each, $3.07; Consumer, each, $2.50
86104 COLD MEAT FORK, SMALL
List, each, $2.46; Consumer, each, $2.00

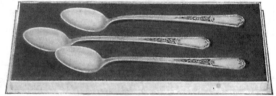

86012 ICED TEA SPOONS
List, set of six, $7.36; Consumer, set of six, $6.00

.1847 ROGERS BROS.
SILVERPLATE

1930 Catalog

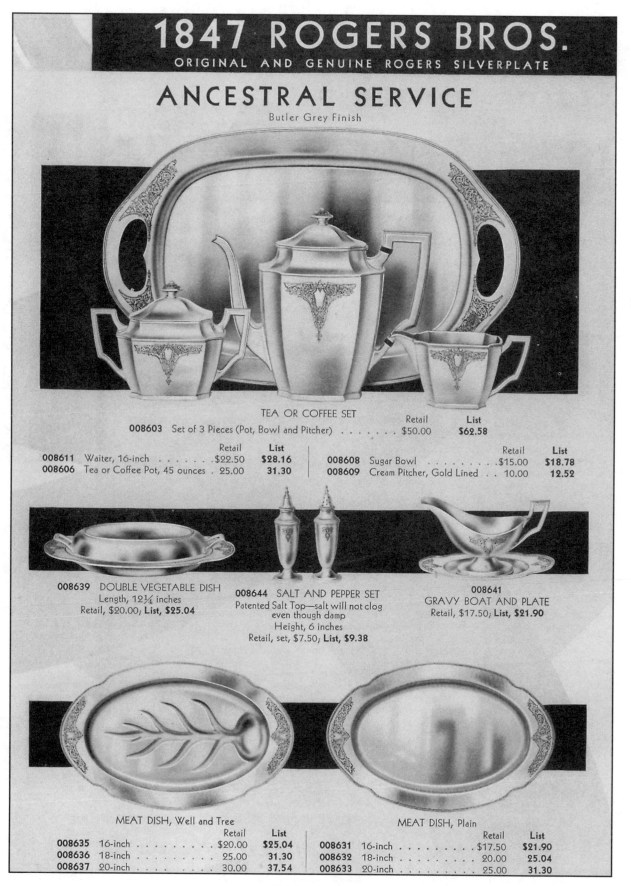

1847 ROGERS BROS.
ORIGINAL AND GENUINE ROGERS SILVERPLATE

ANCESTRAL SERVICE
Butler Grey Finish

TEA OR COFFEE SET

		Retail	List
008603	Set of 3 Pieces (Pot, Bowl and Pitcher)	$50.00	$62.58

		Retail	List
008611	Waiter, 16-inch	$22.50	$28.16
008606	Tea or Coffee Pot, 45 ounces .	25.00	31.30

		Retail	List
008608	Sugar Bowl	$15.00	$18.78
008609	Cream Pitcher, Gold Lined . .	10.00	12.52

008639 DOUBLE VEGETABLE DISH
Length, 12¼ inches
Retail, $20.00; **List, $25.04**

008644 SALT AND PEPPER SET
Patented Salt Top—salt will not clog
even though damp
Height, 6 inches
Retail, set, $7.50; **List, $9.38**

008641
GRAVY BOAT AND PLATE
Retail, $17.50; **List, $21.90**

MEAT DISH, Well and Tree

		Retail	List
008635	16-inch	$20.00	$25.04
008636	18-inch	25.00	31.30
008637	20-inch	30.00	37.54

MEAT DISH, Plain

		Retail	List
008631	16-inch	$17.50	$21.90
008632	18-inch	20.00	25.04
008633	20-inch	25.00	31.30

1931 Catalog

See Price Guide — Group 2

1847 ROGERS BROS.
ORIGINAL AND GENUINE ROGERS SILVERPLATE

ANCESTRAL SERVICE (CONT'D)

008669 CASSEROLE, Round
Pyrex Lining, with Engraved Cover
Capacity, 3 pints
Retail, $10.00; **List, $12.52**

008661 BON BON
Width, 7 inches
Retail, $6.00
List, $7.50

008643 WATER PITCHER
Capacity, 4½ pints
Retail, $22.50; **List, $28.16**

008657 CANDLESTICK
Height, 3¾ inches
Retail, pair, $12.50; **List, $15.64**

008650 CENTERPIECE
With Silver Plated Double Mesh
Flower Holder
Diameter, 12½ inches
Retail, $30.00; **List, $37.54**

008657 CANDLESTICK
Height, 3¾ inches
Retail, pair, $12.50; **List, $15.64**

Ancestral Flatware
to match, is shown in
the Flatware Section

008668 RELISH DISH OR CHOP PLATE
Five Compartments. Removable Glass Lining
Retail, $17.50; **List, $21.90**

008660 COMPOTIER
Height, 7 inches
Retail, $7.50; **List, $9.38**

008624 BREAD TRAY
Length, 12¾ inches
Retail, $10.00; **List, $12.52**

008627 SANDWICH TRAY
Length, 12¾ inches
Retail, $10.00; **List, $12.52**

008647 BREAD AND BUTTER PLATE
Diameter, 6½ inches
Retail, set of six, $30.00; **List, $37.54**

008646 SERVICE PLATE
Diameter, 10½ inches
Retail, set of six, $60.00; **List, $75.10**

1931 Catalog

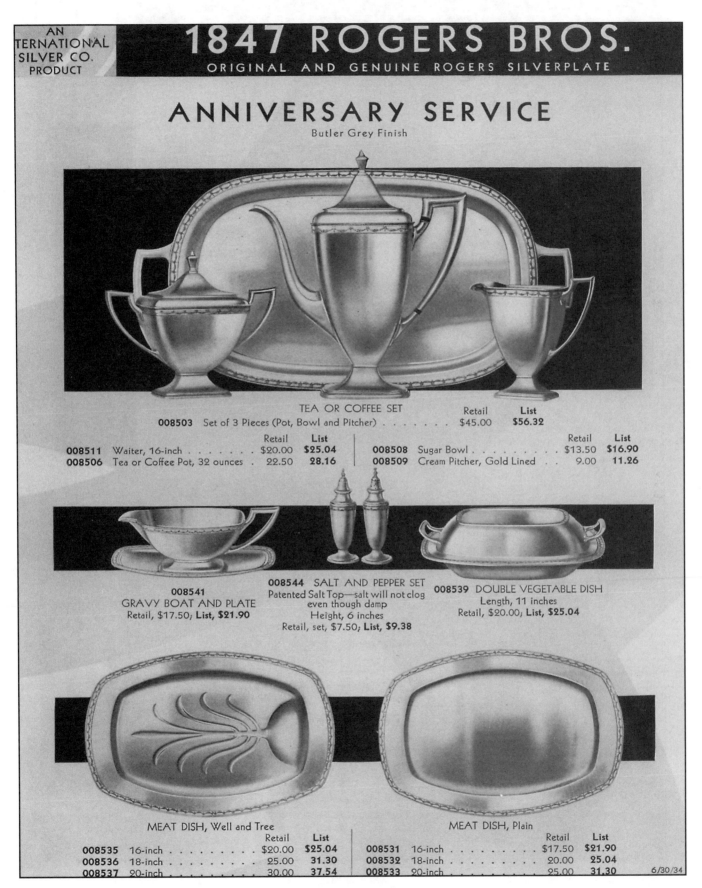

AN
TERNATIONAL
SILVER CO.
PRODUCT

1847 ROGERS BROS.
ORIGINAL AND GENUINE ROGERS SILVERPLATE

ANNIVERSARY SERVICE
Butler Grey Finish

TEA OR COFFEE SET

		Retail	List
008503	Set of 3 Pieces (Pot, Bowl and Pitcher)	$45.00	$56.32

		Retail	List			Retail	List
008511	Waiter, 16-inch	$20.00	$25.04	008508	Sugar Bowl	$13.50	$16.90
008506	Tea or Coffee Pot, 32 ounces	22.50	28.16	008509	Cream Pitcher, Gold Lined	9.00	11.26

008541
GRAVY BOAT AND PLATE
Retail, $17.50; List, $21.90

008544 SALT AND PEPPER SET
Patented Salt Top—salt will not clog
even though damp
Height, 6 inches
Retail, set, $7.50; List, $9.38

008539 DOUBLE VEGETABLE DISH
Length, 11 inches
Retail, $20.00; List, $25.04

MEAT DISH, Well and Tree

		Retail	List
008535	16-inch	$20.00	$25.04
008536	18-inch	25.00	31.30
008537	20-inch	30.00	37.54

MEAT DISH, Plain

		Retail	List
008531	16-inch	$17.50	$21.90
008532	18-inch	20.00	25.04
008533	20-inch	25.00	31.30

6/30/34

1931 Catalog

See Price Guide — Group 2

1847 ROGERS BROS.
ORIGINAL AND GENUINE ROGERS SILVERPLATE

AN INTERNATIONAL SILVER CO. PRODUCT

ANNIVERSARY PATTERN (CONT'D)

85105 ICE CREAM FORKS
Retail, set of six, $6.25; List, set of six, $7.68

85204 JELLY SERVER
Retail, each, $1.75; List, each, $2.14

85301 BUTTER KNIFE AND SUGAR SPOON SET
Retail, set, $2.50; List, set, $3.06
85201 BUTTER KNIFE OR SERVER
Retail, each, $1.25; List, each, $1.52
85017 SUGAR SPOON
Retail, each, $1.25; List, each, $1.52

85227 GRAVY LADLE
Retail, each, $2.75; List, each, $3.38
85226 SAUCE LADLE, small
Retail, each, $2.25; List, each, $2.76

85253 LONG SERVER
Retail, each, $4.25; List, each, $5.22

85252 ROUND SERVER
Retail, each, $3.25; List, each, $3.98

85254 PIE OR ICE CREAM KNIFE
Retail, each, $4.50; List, each, $5.52

85108 PICKLE FORK
Retail, each, $1.50; List, each, $1.84

85103 SERVING FORK, large
Retail, each, $2.50; List, each, $3.06
85104 SERVING FORK, small
Retail, each, $2.00; List, each, $2.46

85003 BERRY OR SALAD SPOON
Retail, each, $3.50; List, each, $4.30
85004 BERRY SPOON, small
Retail, each, $2.00; List, each $2.46

85277 SUGAR TONGS
Retail, each, $2.00; List, each, $2.46

85019 SERVING SPOONS
Retail, set of two, $5.00; List, set of two, $6.14

VIANDE
TRADE MARK
FORK
{Dinner Size}

6/30/19

1931 Catalog

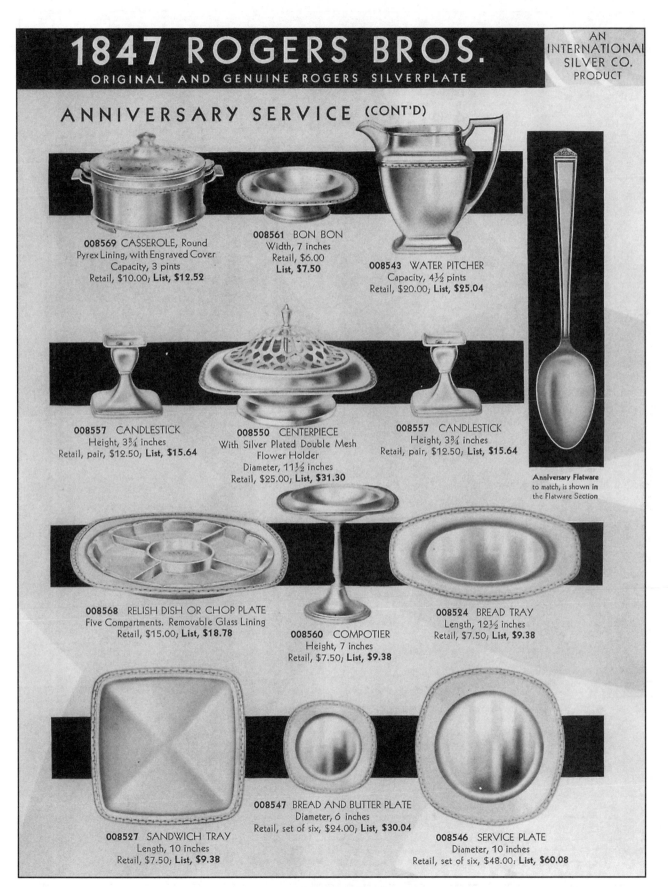

1847 ROGERS BROS.
ORIGINAL AND GENUINE ROGERS SILVERPLATE

AN INTERNATIONAL SILVER CO. PRODUCT

ANNIVERSARY SERVICE (CONT'D)

008569 CASSEROLE, Round
Pyrex Lining, with Engraved Cover
Capacity, 3 pints
Retail, $10.00; **List, $12.52**

008561 BON BON
Width, 7 inches
Retail, $6.00
List, $7.50

008543 WATER PITCHER
Capacity, 4½ pints
Retail, $20.00; **List, $25.04**

008557 CANDLESTICK
Height, 3¾ inches
Retail, pair, $12.50; **List, $15.64**

008550 CENTERPIECE
With Silver Plated Double Mesh
Flower Holder
Diameter, 11½ inches
Retail, $25.00; **List, $31.30**

008557 CANDLESTICK
Height, 3¾ inches
Retail, pair, $12.50; **List, $15.64**

Anniversary Flatware
to match, is shown in
the Flatware Section

008568 RELISH DISH OR CHOP PLATE
Five Compartments. Removable Glass Lining
Retail, $15.00; **List, $18.78**

008560 COMPOTIER
Height, 7 inches
Retail, $7.50; **List, $9.38**

008524 BREAD TRAY
Length, 12½ inches
Retail, $7.50; **List, $9.38**

008527 SANDWICH TRAY
Length, 10 inches
Retail, $7.50; **List, $9.38**

008547 BREAD AND BUTTER PLATE
Diameter, 6 inches
Retail, set of six, $24.00; **List, $30.04**

008546 SERVICE PLATE
Diameter, 10 inches
Retail, set of six, $48.00; **List, $60.08**

1931 Catalog

See Price Guide — Group 2

ARGOSY PATTERN

A delicate balance, joined with subtle, ornamental tracery, is the secret of the gay charm of the ARGOSY pattern

Six in Box

		Per Dozen	
		List	Consumer
8701	Tea Spoons..............	$9.18	$7.50
8702	Dessert or Oval Soup Spoons	18.36	15.00
8703	Table or Serving Spoons...	18.36	15.00
8704	Soup Spoons, Round Bowl.	18.36	15.00
87006	Cream Soup or Cereal Spoons, Gift Box.......	18.36	15.00
87005	Bouillon Spoons, Gift Box..	17.74	14.50
8705	Dinner Forks.............	18.36	15.00
8706	Dessert or Luncheon Forks	18.36	15.00

Solid Handle Knives
With Stainless Blades

87472s	Dinner Knives..........	$18.28	$14.00
87474s	Dessert or Luncheon Knives	18.28	14.00
87475s	Fruit Knives	16.32	12.50

The above knives have French shape blades

87008   COFFEE SPOONS
List, set of six, $4.59; Consumer, set of six, $3.75

87013   OLIVE SPOON
List, each, $2.15; Consumer, each, $1.75

87106   OYSTER OR COCKTAIL FORKS
List, set of six, $6.45; Consumer, set of six, $5.25

87227   GRAVY LADLE
List, each, $3.38; Consumer, each, $2.75

87226   MAYONNAISE OR SAUCE LADLE
List, each, $2.76; Consumer, each, $2.25

87254M   PIE OR ICE CREAM SERVER, Mirror Finish Stainless Blade
List, each, $5.52; Consumer, each, $4.50

Hollow Handle Knives
With Stainless Blades

		Per Dozen	
		List	Consumer
87402M	Dinner Knives, Mirror Finish..................	$36.50	$28.00
87402s	Dinner Knives	31.30	24.00
87404M	Dessert or Luncheon Knives, Mirror Finish	36.50	28.00
87404s	Dessert or Luncheon Knives	31.30	24.00

The above knives have French shape blades

87406s	Fruit Knives	28.70	22.00
87208s	Tea or Salad Knives......	28.70	22.00

87017   SUGAR SPOON
List, each, $1.53; Consumer, each, $1.25

87301   BUTTER KNIFE AND SUGAR SPOON
List, set, $3.06; Consumer, set, $2.50

87201   BUTTER KNIFE
List, each, $1.53; Consumer, each, $1.25

87014   ORANGE OR GRAPE FRUIT SPOONS
List, set of six, $7.05; Consumer, set of six, $5.75

87253   DESSERT SERVER
List, each, $5.22; Consumer, each, $4.25

.1847 ROGERS BROS.
SILVERPLATE

1930 Catalog

008703 TEA OR COFFEE SET
Three Pieces
Coffee Pot, Sugar Bowl and Cream
Pitcher
List, set, $81.36; Consumer, set, $65.00

008711 WAITER, 16 inch, oval
(not illustrated)
List, each, $31.30; Consumer, each, $25.00

008746 SERVICE PLATE, 10½ in.
List, each, $12.52; Consumer, each, $10.00

008747 BREAD AND BUTTER PLATE
Diameter, 6½ inches
List, each, $6.26; Consumer, each, $5.00

008744 SALT AND PEPPER SET
Height, 5½ inches
List, set, $12.52; Consumer, set, $10.00

008753 CANDLESTICKS
Height, 10 inches
List, pair, $31.30; Consumer, pair, $25.00

008739 DOUBLE VEGETABLE DISH
Side Handles
Length, 12¼ inches
List, each, $31.30
Consumer, each, $25.00

ARGOSY PATTERN

**Chased
Butler Grey Finish**

*Matching the Spoons, Forks and Knives
in the Argosy Pattern*

MEAT DISHES, Plain

		List	Consumer
008731	16 inch	$25.04	$20.00
008732	18 inch	31.30	25.00
008733	20 inch	37.54	30.00

MEAT DISHES, Well and Tree

008735	16 inch	$34.42	$27.50
008736	18 inch	40.68	32.50
008737	20 inch	46.94	37.50

008741 GRAVY BOAT AND PLATE
Capacity, 10 ounces
List, set, $25.04; Consumer, set, $20.00

008750 CENTERPIECE, Gold Lined
Diameter, 13 inches
With Silver Plated Double Mesh
List, each, $50.06; Consumer, each, $40.00

008743 WATER PITCHER
Capacity, 4½ pints
List, each, $37.54; Consumer, each, $30.00

008724 BREAD TRAY
Length, 18¾ inches
List, each, $15.64
Consumer, each, $12.50

TEA POT, COFFEE POT, SUGAR BOWL, CREAM PITCHER AND WASTE BOWL

		List	Consumer
008705	Set of Five Pieces	$125.16	$100.00
008704	Set of Four Pieces	112.64	90.00
008703	Set of Three Pieces	81.36	65.00
008706	Coffee Pot (or Chocolate), 32 ounces	31.30	25.00
008707	Tea Pot, 32 ounces	31.30	25.00

		List	Consumer
008708	Sugar Bowl	$25.04	$20.00
008709	Cream Pitcher, Gold Lined	25.04	20.00
008710	Waste Bowl, Gold Lined	12.52	10.00
008712	Waiter, 22 inch, oval (not illustrated)	50.06	40.00
008711	Waiter, 16 inch, oval (not illustrated)	31.30	25.00

.1847 ROGERS BROS.
SILVERPLATE

1931 Catalog

See Price Guide — Group 2

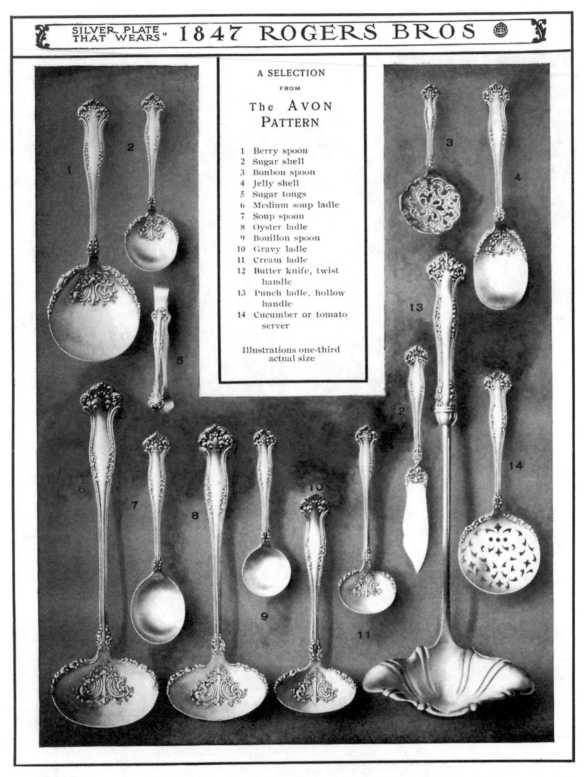

SILVER PLATE THAT WEARS" 1847 ROGERS BROS

A SELECTION FROM

The AVON PATTERN

1 Berry spoon
2 Sugar shell
3 Bonbon spoon
4 Jelly shell
5 Sugar tongs
6 Medium soup ladle
7 Soup spoon
8 Oyster ladle
9 Bouillon spoon
10 Gravy ladle
11 Cream ladle
12 Butter knife, twist handle
13 Punch ladle, hollow handle
14 Cucumber or tomato server

Illustrations one-third actual size

Avon is a beautiful art nouveau pattern that was patented in 1901. Large quantities were manufactured and can still be found. The bonbon is unusual and rare; it reflects the style of a sterling bonbon. The pierced cucumber/tomato is very desirable, as is the hollow-handle punch ladle. The medium ladle is a soup tureen ladle. The jelly spoon is hard to find. It has a more elongated bowl than a small berry. The roast holder is another scarce item. All illustrations shown here are dated 1906. In the back of this 1847 Rogers Bros. section are found more Avon pieces. Avon was also marketed as "Carvel" by the retail jewelry firm Mermod, Jaccard, and King of St. Louis.

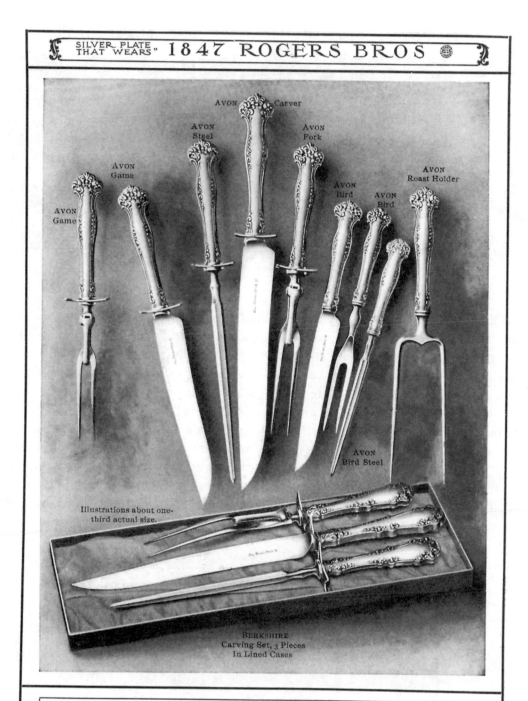

This is the season when Carving Sets have their most important duties to perform. Besides the patterns here shown, there are others—some new, others that have been popular for years. All "1847 Rogers Bros." carvers have hollow handles, nickel silver, silver soldered, with blades of the finest crucible steel. The plate is of the highest grade.

1847 Rogers Bros. Butter Knife and Sugar Shell.

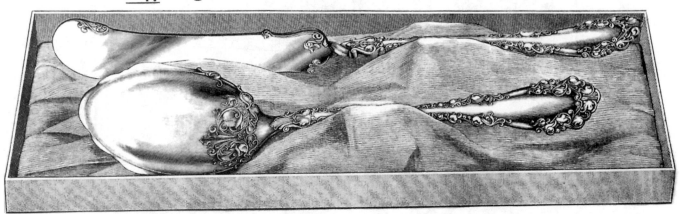

Berkshire was a major pattern in the 1847 Rogers Bros. line. It was introduced in 1897 and is today a highly collectible pattern. It does not command the prices of Charter Oak or Vintage. Most of the catalog pages we show are dated 1906. The crumb knife, fish knife, and cheese scoop are outstanding. The pickle fork and individual ice cream spoons are desirable items that are hard, but not impossible, to find.

We know that there are at least four large forks in Berkshire. The fish fork we show may be the No. 4 that is shown on an old price list. We have not seen illustrations of all the known Berkshire serving pieces. Some boxed dinner sets had knives that were either the Arabesque pattern or completely plain. At the end of the 1847 Rogers Bros. section, we show some miscellaneous catalog sheets; several Berkshire pieces are pictured there. There are possibly four different fruit knives, but we have illustrated only the No. 1 and No. 2. We cannot be certain that hollow ware was made in Berkshire, but note the 1898 *McClure's Magazine* illustration that shows Berkshire flatware with hollow ware of a similar design.

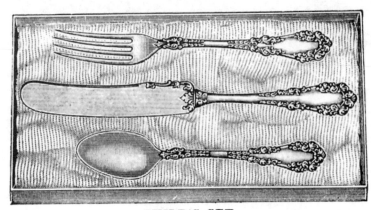

CHILD'S SET

1847 ROGERS BROS

"SILVER PLATE THAT WEARS"

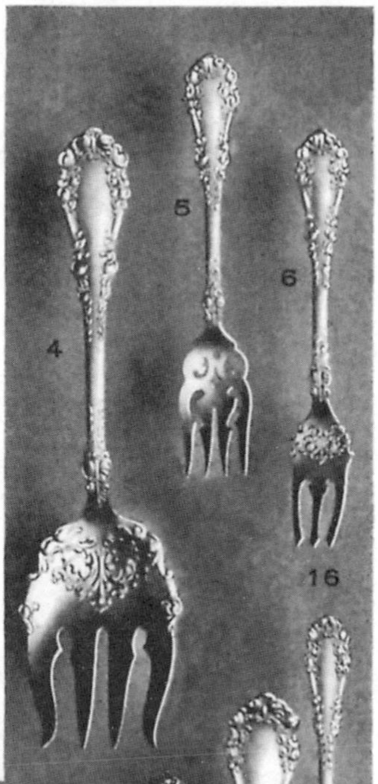

A SELECTION

FROM

The BERKSHIRE PATTERN

1 Fish knife, individual
2 Fish fork, individual
3 Pie knife
4 Fish fork
5 Salad fork, individual
6 Pickle fork
7 Fish knife
8 Cold meat fork
9 Iced tea spoon
10 Beef fork
11 Child's set, knife, fork
     and spoon
12 Ice cream spoon
13 Cheese scoop, hollow
     handle
14 Fruit or berry fork
15 Crumb knife
16 Oyster fork

Illustrations one-third
actual size

Patterns come and go. The popularity of some is very fleeting. The "Berkshire" has proved the exception to the rule. The demand for this design has been phenomenal. It has increased rather than diminished. Artistic and graceful, it has not made the mistake of being too "fancy." It is, above all, the one pattern no dealer should be without.

1906 Catalog

See Price Guide — Group 1

Berkshire Pattern

"Silver plate that wears"

Left to right: 9¹¹⁄₁₆" oyster/soup ladle, 6¼" sauce ladle, 4⅜" demi-tasse spoon, 6¹⁄₁₆" salad fork.

Berkshire Pattern

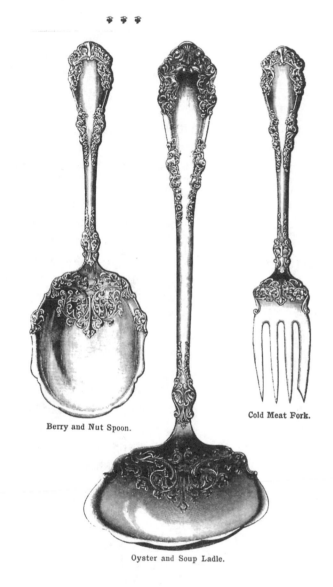

1847 Rogers Bros. Berry and Nut Spoon.

This Berry and Nut Spoon is one of 1847 Rogers Bros. most popular pieces. Extra silver-plated on nickel silver, 8¾ inches long. Burnished handle and satin finished bowl. We offer the beautiful Berkshire pattern, in a neat, lined case.

Oyster and Soup Ladle.

This Ladle is one of the most attractive and useful articles offered on the page. 1847 Rogers Bros. extra silver-plated, bright handle, satin finished bowl, 10 inches long, and Berkshire pattern.

Cold Meat Fork.

The Fork is extra silver-plated, 8½ inches long, and especially designed for serving either cold meat or cake. 1847 Rogers Bros. latest style, Berkshire pattern, and very popular with the best trade.

Berry and Nut Spoon.

Cold Meat Fork.

Oyster and Soup Ladle.

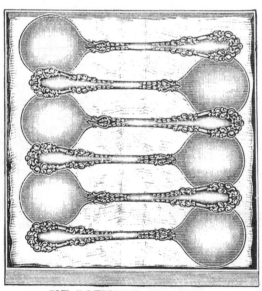

SIX BOUILLON SPOONS
Berkshire pattern, bright finish

BEEF FORK
Berkshire pattern
bright finish

PUT UP IN FANCY LINED BOXES

See Price Guide — Group 1

Charter Oak Pattern

Charter Oak, one of the most desirable of the fancy silver plated patterns, was introduced in 1906. It is such a fun pattern to collect! The large pieces are unbelievably beautiful; the punch ladle and fish knife are real knockouts. Salad forks are hard, but not impossible, to find. Ice tea/beverage spoons are very rare. Solid-handled knives are hard to find, and there is little demand for them because they are not as attractive as the hollow-handled ones. Round bowl soups are harder to find than bouillons. Any unusual piece, such as a cheese scoop, bread knife, or sugar tongs, is a real prize. Many of the pieces seen in the Vintage pattern were also produced in Charter Oak, so collectors should study the Vintage pieces to learn what was possibly manufactured.

Many hollow-handled knives have worn or pitted blades which can be replaced with stainless steel blunt-end blades. Some collectors have had the luncheon knives made into individual steak knives.

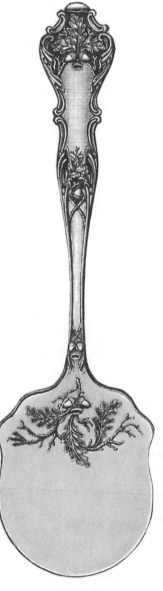

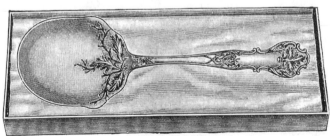

BUTTER KNIFE
Charter Oak pattern, gray finish

BERRY SPOON
Charter Oak pattern, gray finish

SUGAR SHELL
Charter Oak pattern, gray

See Price Guide — Group 1

CHEESE SCOOP
Vintage pattern, gray finish, hollow handle
No. **31789** Silver blade...................... each **$3.60**

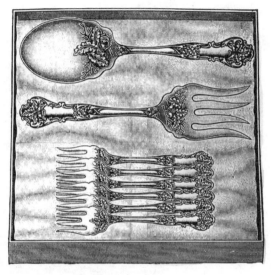

SALAD SET
Charter Oak pattern, gray finish. Six individual salad forks, one each serving salad spoon and fork.
No. **31836** Silver tines and bowl.......... per set **$18.00**

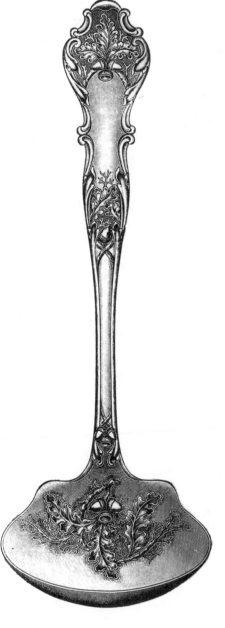

No. **33242 Gravy Ladle.** Silver bowl
No. **33243 Cravy Ladle.** Gold bowl
No. **33244 Oyster Ladle.** Silver bowl
No. **33245 Oyster Ladle.** Gold bowl

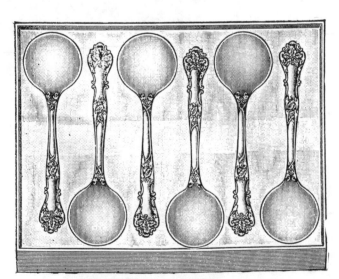

SIX BOUILLON SPOONS
Charter Oak pattern, gray finish
No. **31824** Silver bowls................per set **$8.10**

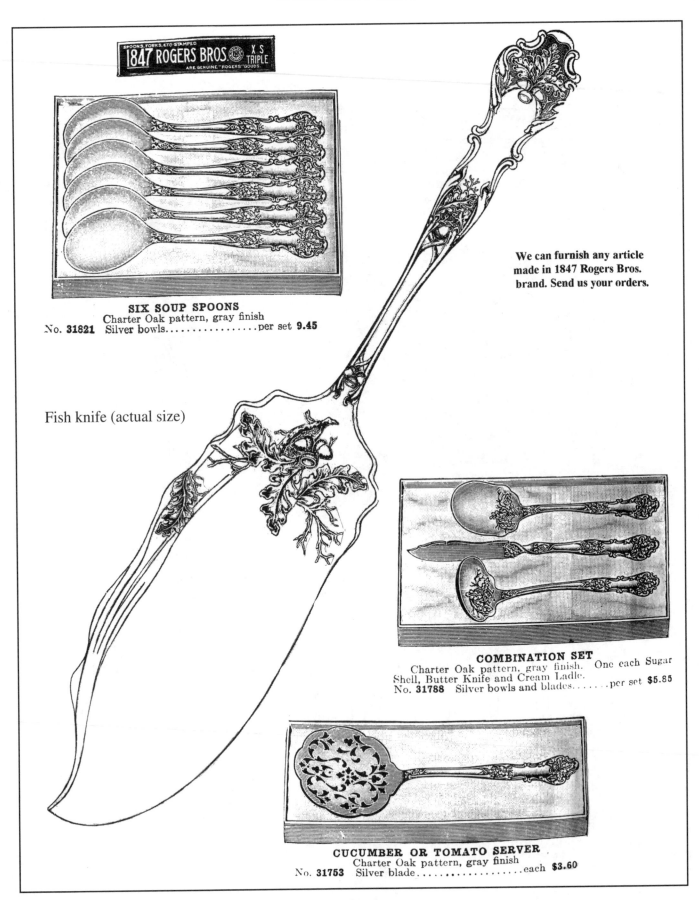

1847 ROGERS BROS. XS TRIPLE
SPOONS, FORKS, ETC. STAMPED
ARE GENUINE "ROGERS" GOODS

SIX SOUP SPOONS
Charter Oak pattern, gray finish
No. **31821** Silver bowls................per set **9.45**

Fish knife (actual size)

We can furnish any article
made in 1847 Rogers Bros.
brand. Send us your orders.

COMBINATION SET
Charter Oak pattern, gray finish. One each Sugar
Shell, Butter Knife and Cream Ladle.
No. **31788** Silver bowls and blades......per set **$5.85**

CUCUMBER OR TOMATO SERVER
Charter Oak pattern, gray finish
No. **31753** Silver blade................each **$3.60**

1913 Catalog

Charter Oak Pattern

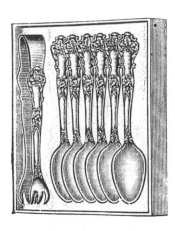

COFFEE SET

Charter Oak pattern, gray finish. One Sugar Tongs, six Coffee Spoons.

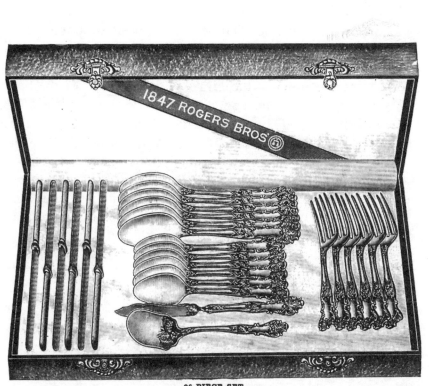

26-PIECE SET

Charter Oak pattern, gray finish. Six plain 16 dwt. medium knives, six each XS triple plated medium forks, tea spoons and table spoons, one sugar shell, one butter knife. Put up in fancy lined leatherette case.

No. **31837** Complete set..$33.12

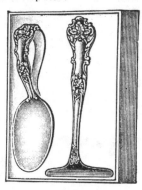

BABY SET

Charter Oak pattern, gray finish. One Baby Spoon, one Food Pusher.
No. **31830** Per set..**$2.25**

Scimiter swadged blade. First Quality silver plated. Put up 6 in flannel roll.

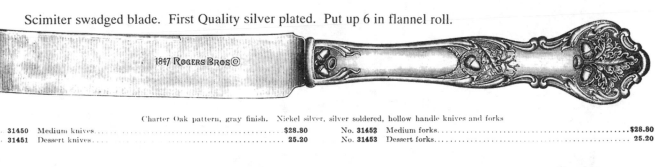

Charter Oak pattern, gray finish. Nickel silver, silver soldered, hollow handle knives and forks

31450	Medium knives.........................$28.80	No. 31452	Medium forks.........................$28.80
31451	Dessert knives............25.20	No. 31453	Dessert forks.........................25.20

Charter Oak pattern, gray finish. Spoon handle forks.

D. 31454	Medium Forks, XS triple plated.........$17.10	No. 31456	Dessert forks, XS triple plated.........$15.30
D. 31455	Medium forks, XS quintuple plated.........23.40	No. 31457	Dessert forks, XS quintuple plated.........19.80

1913 Catalog

See Price Guide — Group 1

Columbia Pattern

This beautiful pattern features a stylized dolphin on the handles. Like the antique glassware bowls and candlesticks, the dolphin has scales. Note the Columbia dolphin has a dragon-like tongue and the tail wraps around the handles of the silverware. This pattern was designed for the Columbian Exposition held in Chicago in 1893. The nations of the world joined with America to celebrate the 400th anniversary of Columbus's discovery. This pattern was possibly 1847 Rogers Bros. first attempt to make a large full-line pattern. The essential individual place pieces that are hard to find are salad forks, butter spreaders, and round bowl soups. We have not seen an ice tea spoon. In this time period ice was expensive and melted rapidly in warm weather, so iced drinks were served on a limited basis. Some pieces, such as nut picks and berry forks, were always sold in boxed sets of six. Unlike most berry forks, those of Columbia have only two tines. There seems to be an ample supply of youth forks and spoons, but not youth knives. Many of the salad pieces had gilded bowls. In our photograph of the gilded fork, one can see the beautiful additional engraving in the bowl part. Some collectors call these salad pieces a "ragout" set but we have not found documentation that confirms this. Most hollow handle knives have unsightly blades but these can be replaced with stainless steel blunt-end blades. The hollow-handled forks are especially attractive and fun to use. They were produced in both the dinner and luncheon sizes.

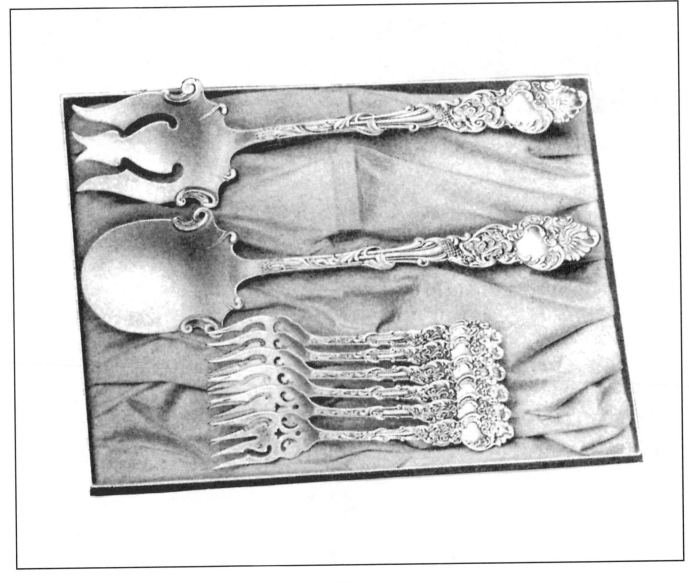

184

Columbia Pattern

Left to right:7½" hollow handle fruit knife, 5¹³⁄₁₆" citrus spoon, 5⅞" teaspoon, 7½" dinner fork, 8" hollow handle dinner fork. Bottom: 4½" demi-tasse spoon.

See Price Guide — Group 1

Columbia Pattern

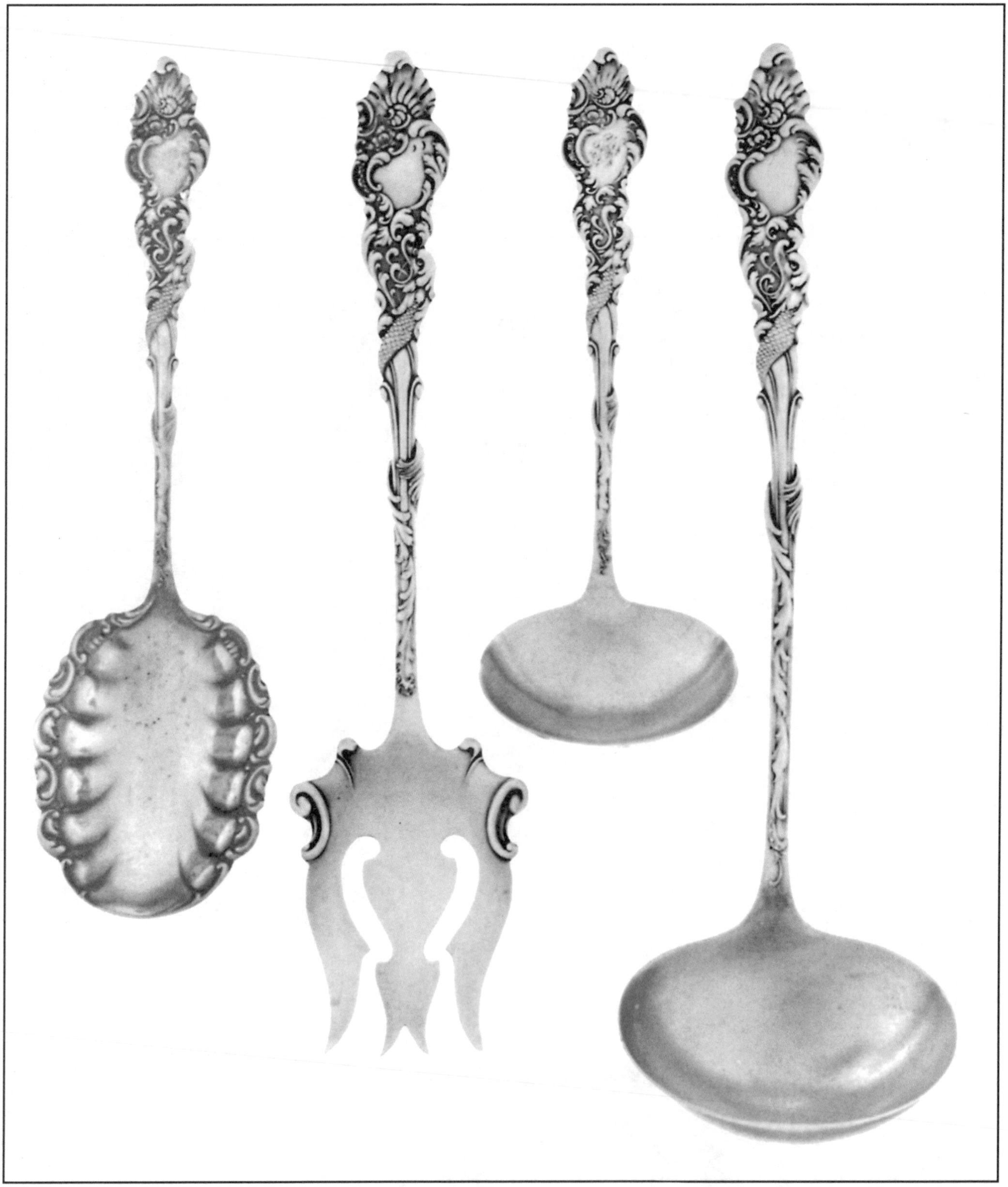

Left to right: 8 5/16" berry spoon, 10 3/8" salad fork, 7 3/4" gravy ladle, 11 1/8" medium ladle.

Patented 1914. Left to right: hollow handle dinner knife, gravy ladle, dinner fork, salad fork, cold meat serving fork. Bottom: sugar spoon.

See Price Guide — Group 1

Butter Dish **$3.95**

Length, 7¼ inches

The handsomely carved finial, in all 1847 Rogers Bros. patterns, offers an elaborate contrast to an otherwise plain silver cover. The deep dish is Duncan & Miller clear crystal tear-drop pattern—each piece hand made for enduring charm. Ample for ¼-pound print of butter and just as useful for pickles, olives, jellies, jams and relishes of all kinds.

Furnished in all six 1847 Rogers Bros. patterns: *Heritage, Daffodil, Remembrance, Eternally Yours, First Love* and *Adoration*.

Packed six to a carton.

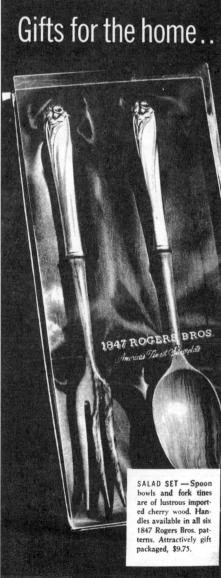

Gifts for the home..

1847 ROGERS BROS.
America's Finest Silverplate

SALAD SET — Spoon bowls and fork tines are of lustrous imported cherry wood. Handles available in all six 1847 Rogers Bros. patterns. Attractively gift packaged, $9.75.

Daffodil was introduced in 1950 as a full line of accessory pieces including three sizes of carving sets. The hollow handle soup ladle retailed for $7.50, while the hollow punch ladle was twice that amount. The salad set with cherry wood sold for $9.75, an expensive item for the time. The sugar tongs and jelly server are both hard to find. Note that Daffodil has two sizes of round bowl soup spoons. The silver butter cover and cheese server are rare. It appears that not many of the cheese pieces were made. The pierced berry/serving spoon is a choice item. Many collections do not contain this piece.

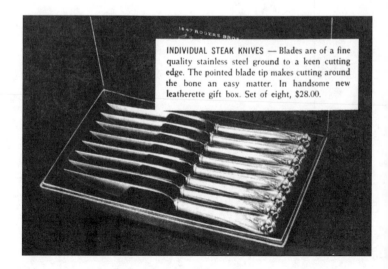

INDIVIDUAL STEAK KNIVES — Blades are of a fine quality stainless steel ground to a keen cutting edge. The pointed blade tip makes cutting around the bone an easy matter. In handsome new leatherette gift box. Set of eight, $28.00.

Daffodil
1847 ROGERS BROS.

No. 9917 Water Pitcher ....Retail, $37.50
Cap., 2 qts.; Ht. 9¼ in.

No. 9916 Candelabrum Retail, $15.00
Height 6½ inches
Spread 9¼ inches

	Retail
No. 9900/5 *Daffodil* Tea and Coffee Service, 5 pcs.	$160.00
(Coffee-Pot, Tea Pot, Sugar Bowl, Cream Pitcher, Waste Bowl)	
No. 9906 Kettle, Cap. 50 ounces, ht. 14 in.	90.00
No. 9992 Waiter, Chased, Length 22½ in.	60.00
No. 9900/3 *Daffodil* Coffee Service, 3 pieces	97.50
(Coffee Pot, Sugar Bowl, Cream Pitcher)	
No. 9990 Waiter, Chased, Length 20 inches	42.50

	Retail			Retail
No. 9901 Coffee Pot, 11 Cups,		No. 9903 Sugar Bowl, Covered	$27.50
Height 11 inches $45.00		No. 9904 Cream Pitcher,	
No. 9902 Tea Pot, 10 Cups,		Gold Lined	25.00
Height 8 inches 45.00		No. 9905 Waste Bowl,	
		Gold Lined	17.50

Retail Prices subject to Federal Tax.

No. 9914 Center Bowl $15.00
No. 9914/12 Footed Vege-
table Dish with Cover
Length, 11½ in. 22.50

No. 9926 Buffet Tray Retail, $12.50
Size, 12 x 12 in.

No. 9919 Bread Tray ....Retail, $10.00
Length, 13 inches

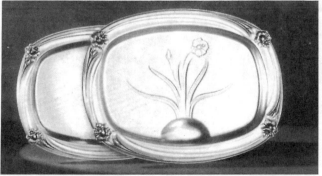

No. 9909 Meat Dish ....Retail, $15.00
Capacity, 16½ inches
No. 9910 Well and Tree Platter ....Retail, $22.50
Length, 18 inches

No. 9913 Gravy Set ....Retail, $15.00
Capacity of Boat, 12 ounces
No. 9912 Double Vegetable Dish ....Retail, $17.50
Length, 11½ inches

1958 Catalog

See Price Guide — Group 2

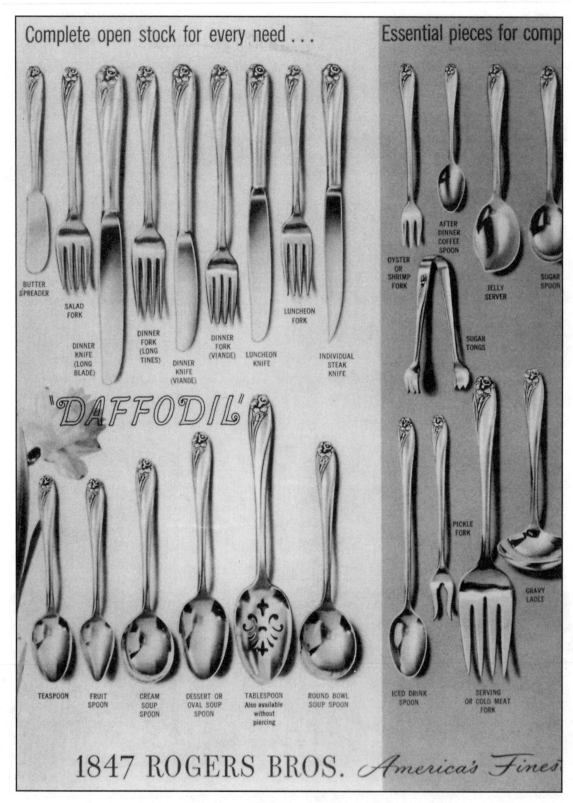

1953 Catalog

Daffodil Pattern

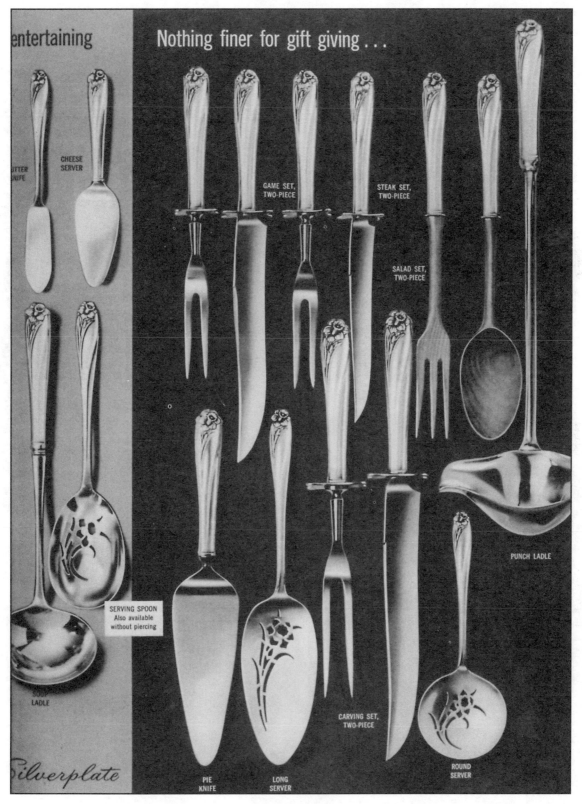

entertaining

Nothing finer for gift giving . . .

BUTTER KNIFE

CHEESE SERVER

GAME SET, TWO-PIECE

STEAK SET, TWO-PIECE

SALAD SET, TWO-PIECE

SERVING SPOON
Also available without piercing

SOUP LADLE

PIE KNIFE

LONG SERVER

CARVING SET, TWO-PIECE

PUNCH LADLE

ROUND SERVER

Silverplate

1953 Catalog

191

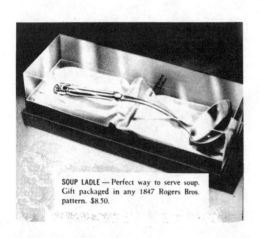

SOUP LADLE — Perfect way to serve soup. Gift packaged in any 1847 Rogers Bros. pattern. $8.50.

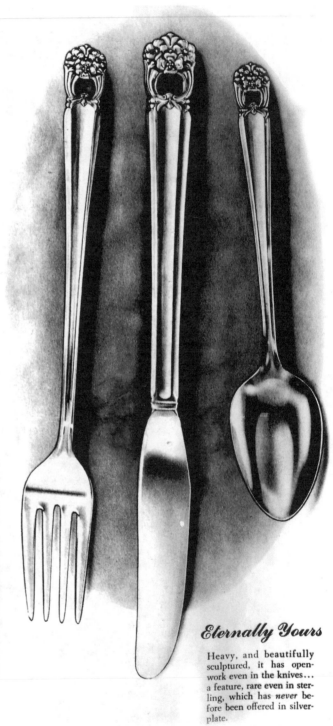

HOSTESS GIFT SET Complements all standard services. Cold Meat Fork, Gravy Ladle, Serving Spoon, Hollow Handle Pie or Cake Server, Round Server and Pickle Fork gift packaged in any 1847 Rogers Bros. pattern. $19.95.

Eternally Yours

Heavy, and beautifully sculptured, it has openwork even in the knives... a feature, rare even in sterling, which has *never* before been offered in silverplate.

America's Finest Silverplate

1953 Catalog

Eternally Yours Pattern

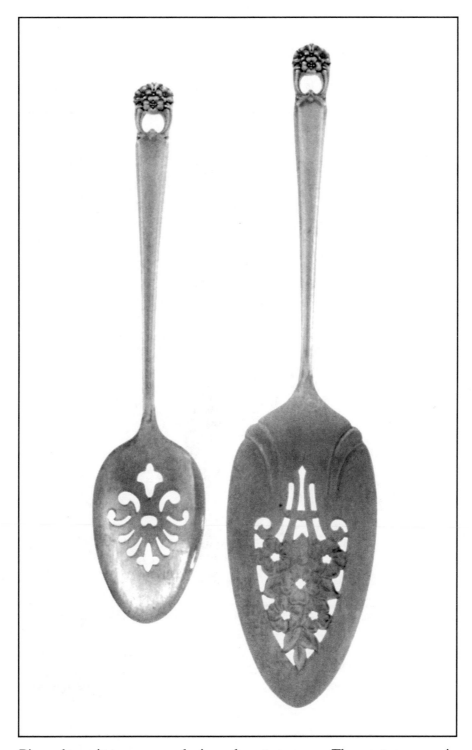

Pierced serving spoon and pierced pastry server. The pastry server is not easy to find.

See Price Guide — Group 2

Eternally Yours Pattern

Left to right: 4¹³⁄₁₆" spoon (not a baby spoon, not marked "Eternally Yours," use unknown), 6" citrus/orange spoon, 7¼" hollow-handled youth knife, 9" pierced berry serving spoon (rare).

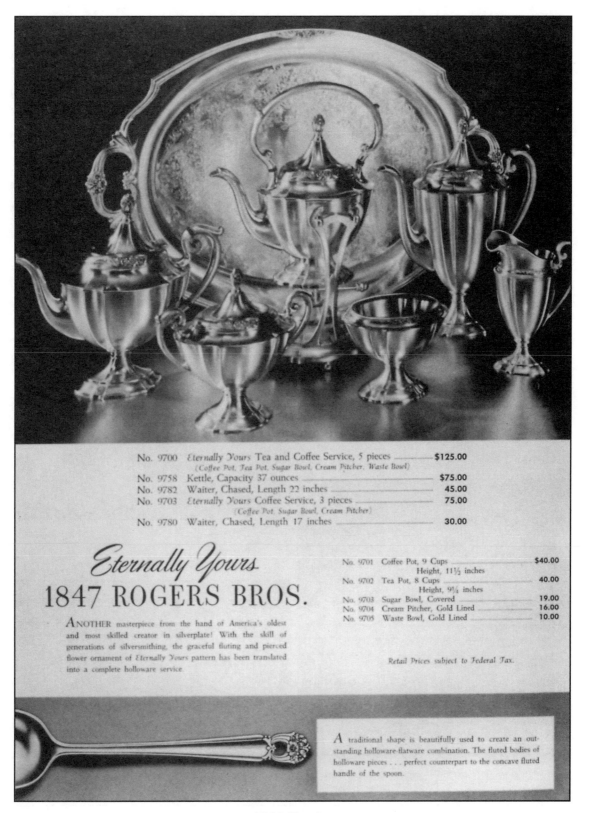

No. 9700   *Eternally Yours* Tea and Coffee Service, 5 pieces _____ $125.00
            (Coffee Pot, Tea Pot, Sugar Bowl, Cream Pitcher, Waste Bowl)
No. 9758   Kettle, Capacity 37 ounces _____ $75.00
No. 9782   Waiter, Chased, Length 22 inches _____ 45.00
No. 9703   *Eternally Yours* Coffee Service, 3 pieces _____ 75.00
            (Coffee Pot, Sugar Bowl, Cream Pitcher)
No. 9780   Waiter, Chased, Length 17 inches _____ 30.00

Eternally Yours
1847 ROGERS BROS.

ANOTHER masterpiece from the hand of America's oldest
and most skilled creator in silverplate! With the skill of
generations of silversmithing, the graceful fluting and pierced
flower ornament of *Eternally Yours* pattern has been translated
into a complete holloware service.

No. 9701   Coffee Pot, 9 Cups _____ $40.00
            Height, 11½ inches
No. 9702   Tea Pot, 8 Cups _____ 40.00
            Height, 9¼ inches
No. 9703   Sugar Bowl, Covered _____ 19.00
No. 9704   Cream Pitcher, Gold Lined _____ 16.00
No. 9705   Waste Bowl, Gold Lined _____ 10.00

Retail Prices subject to Federal Tax.

A traditional shape is beautifully used to create an outstanding holloware-flatware combination. The fluted bodies of
holloware pieces . . . perfect counterpart to the concave fluted
handle of the spoon.

1953 Catalog

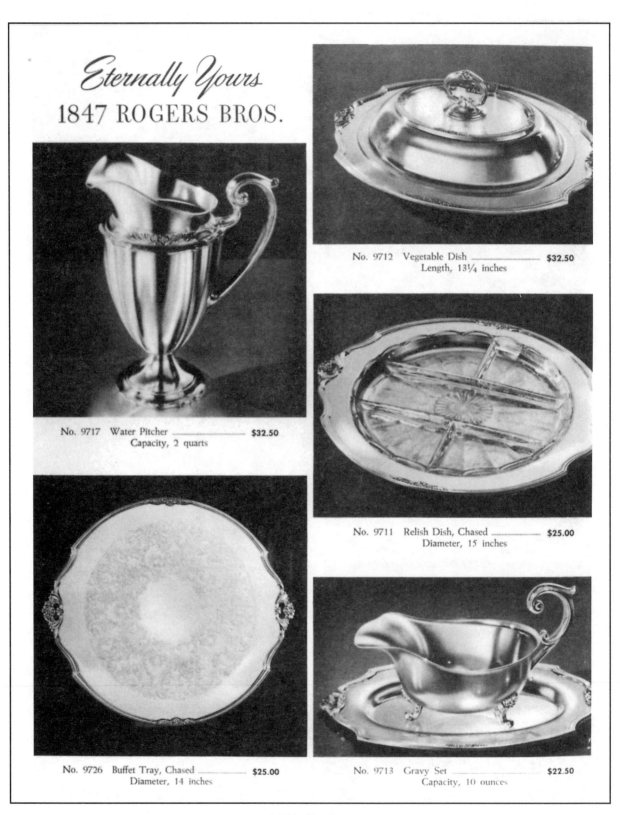

Eternally Yours
1847 ROGERS BROS.

No. 9717   Water Pitcher _____ $32.50
Capacity, 2 quarts

No. 9712   Vegetable Dish _____ $32.50
Length, 13¼ inches

No. 9711   Relish Dish, Chased _____ $25.00
Diameter, 15 inches

No. 9726   Buffet Tray, Chased _____ $25.00
Diameter, 14 inches

No. 9713   Gravy Set _____ $22.50
Capacity, 10 ounces

1953 Catalog

Eternally Yours

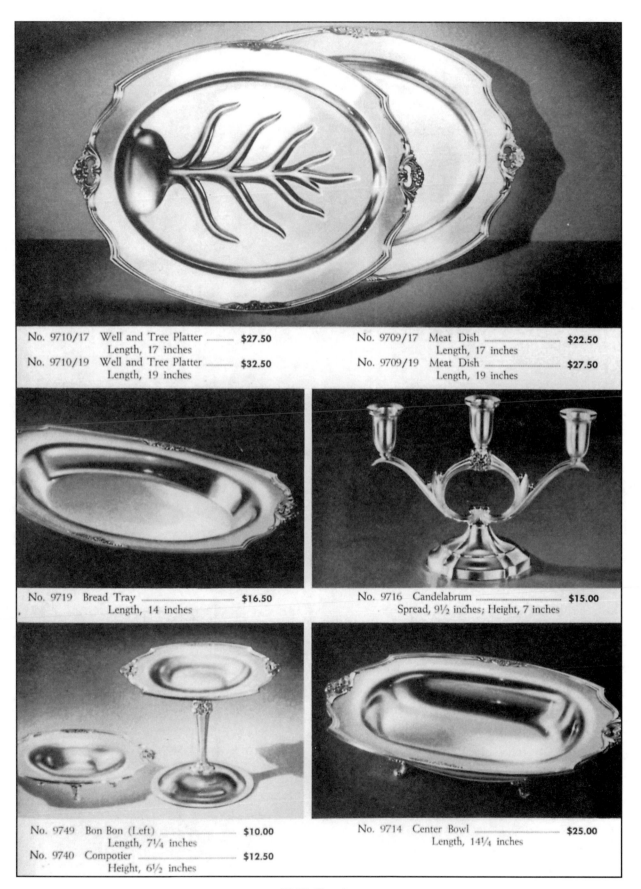

No. 9710/17	Well and Tree Platter	**$27.50**	No. 9709/17 Meat Dish	**$22.50**
	Length, 17 inches		Length, 17 inches	
No. 9710/19	Well and Tree Platter	**$32.50**	No. 9709/19 Meat Dish	**$27.50**
	Length, 19 inches		Length, 19 inches	

No. 9719 Bread Tray ———— **$16.50**
Length, 14 inches

No. 9716 Candelabrum ———— **$15.00**
Spread, 9½ inches; Height, 7 inches

No. 9749 Bon Bon (Left) ———— **$10.00**
Length, 7¼ inches

No. 9740 Compotier ———— **$12.50**
Height, 6½ inches

No. 9714 Center Bowl ———— **$25.00**
Length, 14¼ inches

1953 Catalog

.1847 ROGERS BROS.

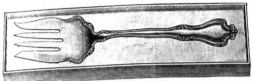

COLD MEAT FORK
Faneuil pattern, bright finish

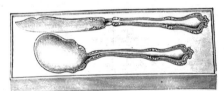

BUTTER KNIFE AND SUGAR SHELL
Faneuil pattern, bright finish

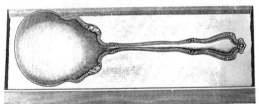

BERRY SPOON
Faneuil pattern, bright finish

So recognized is the leadership of 1847 ROGERS BROS. Silverplate in the field of fine silverware, that others often seek to suggest its quality by similar sounding names... But sateen is not satin. Those who go part way in name, seldom go all the way in quality and craftsmanship.

The *complete* trade mark enchased on every piece thus: 1847 ROGERS BROS. insures your complete satisfaction through a lifetime of silver service. ... There is but *one* 1847 ROGERS BROS. Silverplate. In service for 80 years, it is guaranteed without time-limit.

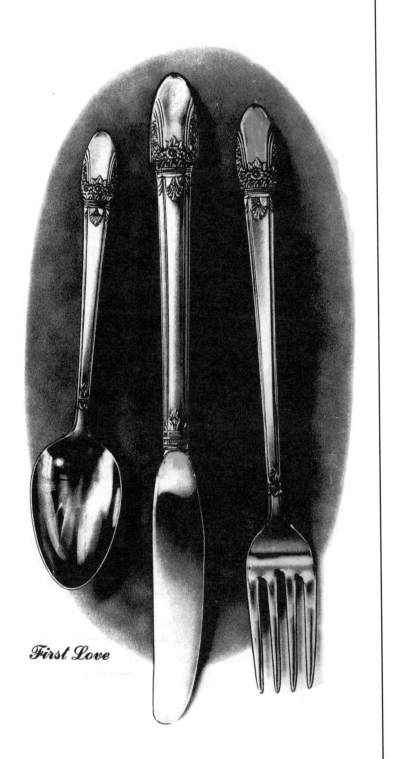

First Love

First Love, right, was the all-time bestseller for 1847 Rogers Bros.

Left to right: 9" salad spoon, 6" sugar spoon, 9" salad fork, 6¼" chipped beef fork. These pieces with the fancy bowl are from early production of First Love. They are not marked with the pattern name. All are rare except the chipped beef fork.

First Love Pattern

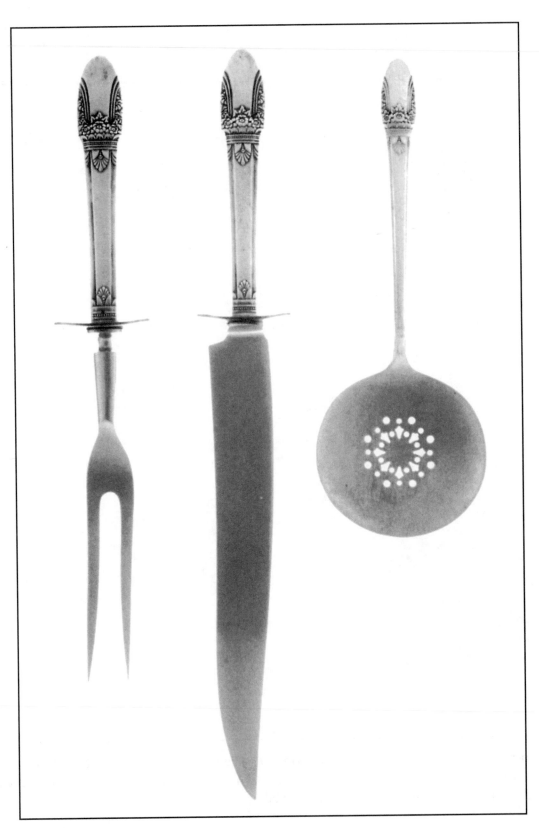

Left to right: 9¾" hollow handled carving fork, 11⅝" hollow handled carving knife, 7⁹⁄₁₆" round server.

KIDDIE KIT with plate molded of Monsanto Lustrex, without cup, $2.95 set, retail. With cup, $6.75 set, retail (plus Federal Tax on cup only.)

1948 Catalog

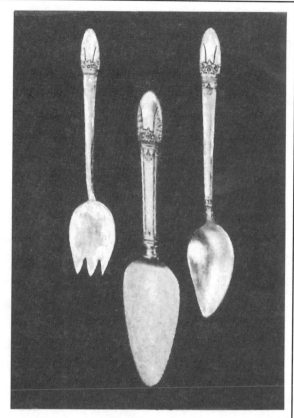

1937 Advertisement. Ice cream fork, cheese knife, citrus spoon

STEP-UP SET, $6.75 retail. *Includes:* Baby Feeding Spoon, 2-pc. Educator Set and 3-pc. Youngster Set in attractive gift case with moulded transparent cover—*First Love* pattern only.

1948 Catalog

THREE PIECE YOUNGSTER SET—*First Love* pattern, $4.50, retail.

1948 Catalog

See Price Guide — Group 2

First Love Pattern

Patented 1937. Three-toed gravy boat

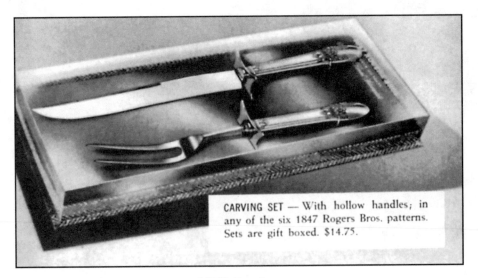

CARVING SET — With hollow handles; in any of the six 1847 Rogers Bros. patterns. Sets are gift boxed. $14.75.

1953 Catalog

Left to right: 8½" pierced tablespoon, 8⅜" tablespoon, 10⅝" pierced pastry server, 9" berry serving spoon.

See Price Guide — Group 2

Etching Pattern
Duncan & Miller

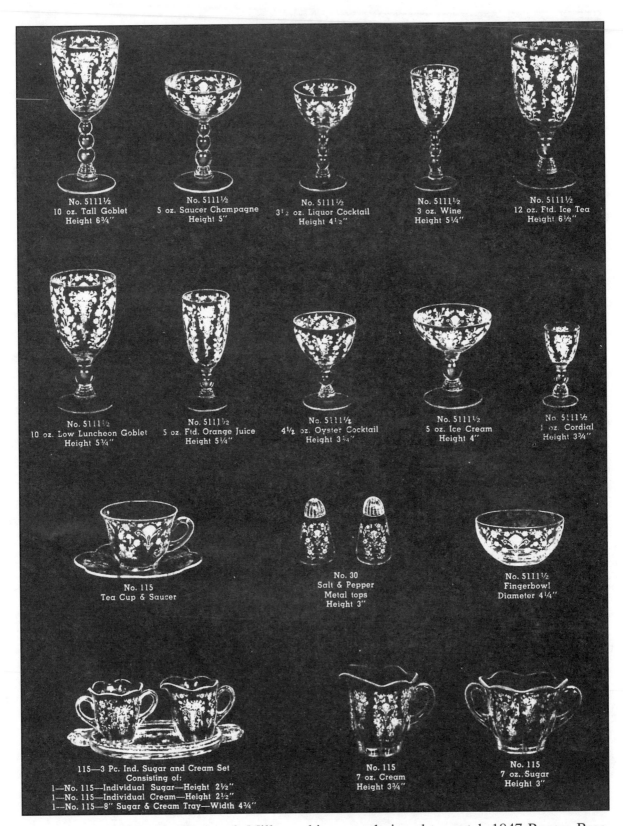

No. 5111½
10 oz. Tall Goblet
Height 6¾"

No. 5111½
5 oz. Saucer Champagne
Height 5"

No. 5111½
3½ oz. Liquor Cocktail
Height 4½"

No. 5111½
3 oz. Wine
Height 5¼"

No. 5111½
12 oz. Ftd. Ice Tea
Height 6½"

No. 5111½
10 oz. Low Luncheon Goblet
Height 5¾"

No. 5111½
5 oz. Ftd. Orange Juice
Height 5¼"

No. 5111½
4½ oz. Oyster Cocktail
Height 3¾"

No. 5111½
5 oz. Ice Cream
Height 4"

No. 5111½
1 oz. Cordial
Height 3¾"

No. 115
Tea Cup & Saucer

No. 30
Salt & Pepper
Metal tops
Height 3"

No. 5111½
Fingerbowl
Diameter 4¼"

115—3 Pc. Ind. Sugar and Cream Set
Consisting of:
1—No. 115—Individual Sugar—Height 2½"
1—No. 115—Individual Cream—Height 2½"
1—No. 115—8" Sugar & Cream Tray—Width 4¾"

No. 115
7 oz. Cream
Height 3¾"

No. 115
7 oz. Sugar
Height 3"

Introduced in 1937, this Duncan & Miller etching was designed to match 1847 Rogers Bros. First Love silver pattern.

new, new **Flair**

so modern...it sets a new tradition

Here at last is modern silverware that makes no compromise with yesterday. New, new Flair, in 1847 Rogers Bros.

Flair breaks sharply with old traditions of style and ornament. Each piece is styled to suit the new demands of modern living.

Excitingly new in design! Its great beauty of form seems to come from within...from the beauty of the gleaming silver itself.

Choose Flair joyfully for your home today, confident that it will be right and beautiful for generations. 52-piece service for eight, $89.75. Budget terms. No Fed. tax.

1847

1847 ROGERS BROS.

AMERICA'S FINEST SILVERPLATE

A PRODUCT OF THE INTERNATIONAL SILVER COMPANY

New balanced place setting. Flair is the first modern silverplate pattern to beautify your table with a truly balanced place setting.

New Flair holloware brings you modern beauty and versatility. Footed Platter, $22.50.* Double Serving Dish, $22.50.* Roll Tray.

1955 Catalog

Flair Pattern

No. H-32 THREE PIECE RELISH SET

H-2 TWO-PIECE EDUCATOR SET — Miniature Fork and Spoon Set helps baby learn to feed himself. Retail, $2.75

Flair

1847 ROGERS BROS.

H-59 CHILD'S CUP — Choice of plain handle or handle to match any 1847 Rogers Bros. pattern. Contoured cup (left) in *Flair* pattern only. Retail, $4.00 plus 10% Federal Tax

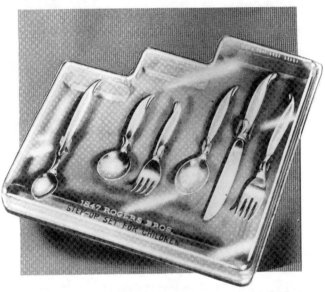

H-6 Step-Up Set. Matched silverware for all baby's needs from birth to ten years includes Infant Feeding Spoon, 2-pc. Educator Set and 3-pc. Youngster Set.

Party knife in Flair pattern only. Multi-purpose knife with hollow handle and 8½" stainless steel serrated blade makes "cutting the cake" a festive ceremony. Gift boxed.

1967 Catalog

Flair Pattern

	Retail
No. 9500/3 *Flair* Hot Beverage Service, 3 pieces	$65.00
Consisting of: No. 9501 Hot Beverage Server, 10 cups, Ht. 10¼ in.	37.50
No. 9503 Sugar Bowl, Covered	13.00
No. 9504 Cream Pitcher	14.50
No. 9580 Serving Tray, Length 18 inches	17.50

Retail Prices subject to Federal Tax.

No. 9517 Beverage Pitcher .... Retail, $30.00
Capacity, 1½ quarts

No. 9516 Candelabrum .... Retail, $17.50
3-Light, Height 7¾ inches

1967 Catalog

See Price Guide — Group 2

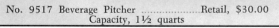

Flair Pattern

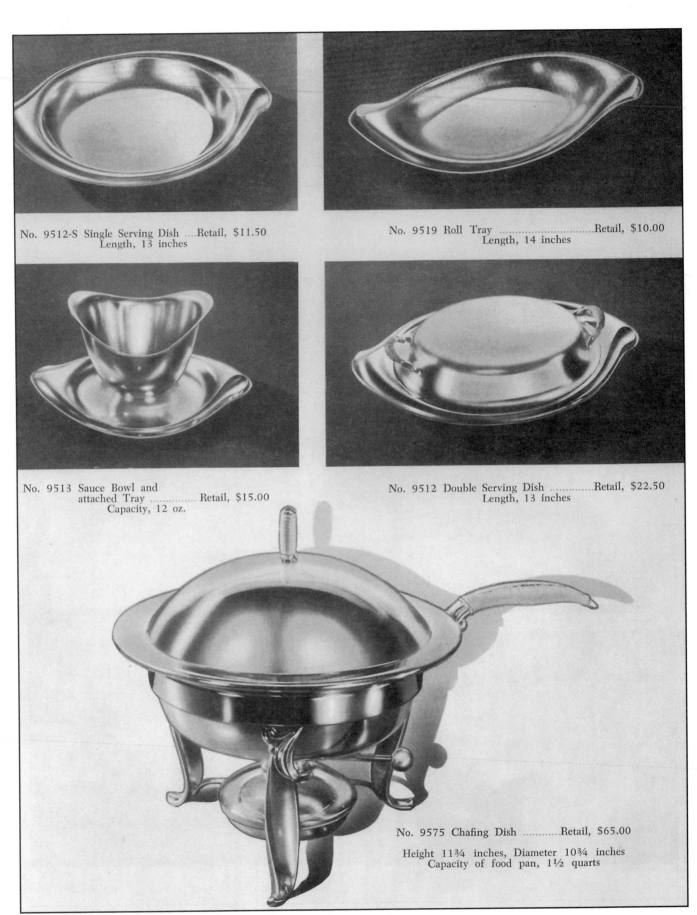

No. 9512-S Single Serving Dish ....Retail, $11.50
Length, 13 inches

No. 9519 Roll Tray ....Retail, $10.00
Length, 14 inches

No. 9513 Sauce Bowl and
attached Tray .... Retail, $15.00
Capacity, 12 oz.

No. 9512 Double Serving Dish ....Retail, $22.50
Length, 13 inches

No. 9575 Chafing Dish ....Retail, $65.00

Height 11¾ inches, Diameter 10¾ inches
Capacity of food pan, 1½ quarts

1967 Catalog

No. 9514 Center Bowl ....Retail, $20.00
Length, 13½ inches

No. 9511 Relish Dish ....Retail, $9.00
Length, 12 in. 3-Comp. Glass Lining

No. 9529 Utility Tray ....Retail, $7.50
Length, 12 inches

No. 9510 Footed Platter with Well ....Retail, $22.50
Length, 18 inches

No. 9526 Buffet Tray ....Retail, $17.50
Length, 18 inches

Retail
No. 9531/2 Sugar and Cream $22.50
No. 9529 Tray, Length 12 inches 7.50

No. 9548 Tid-Bit Dish ....Retail, $5.00
Length, 7 inches

1967 Catalog

See Price Guide — Group 2

Flair Pattern

Top, left to right: pierced serving spoon, salad spoon and fork with olive wood. Bottom: youth knife and fork.

1847 ROGERS BROS.®

AMERICA'S FINEST SILVERPLATE

RETAIL PRICE LIST FOR ALL PATTERNS

Effective July 1, 1966. Retail prices shown are those quoted to consumers on direct inquiry and subject to change without notice. All goods billed at prices prevailing on date of shipment. Retail Prices shown are the prescribed minimum in those states having a Fair Trade Law.

PLACE SETTING PIECES

	One Retail	List	Eight Retail	List	Twelve Retail	List
A Teaspoons	$1.25	$1.50	$10.00	$12.00	$15.00	$18.00
B Forks	2.25	2.70	18.00	21.60	27.00	32.40
C Knives	3.50	4.20	28.00	33.60	42.00	50.40
D Salad Forks	2.25	2.70	18.00	21.60	27.00	32.40
E Service Spoons (Soup or Dessert)	2.25	2.70	18.00	21.60	27.00	32.40
F Spreaders, Butter or Cheese	2.25	2.70	18.00	21.60	27.00	32.40
G A.D. Coffee Spoons	1.25	1.50	10.00	12.00	15.00	18.00
H Cocktail Forks	2.25	2.70	18.00	21.60	27.00	32.40
I Iced Drink Spoons	2.25	2.70	18.00	21.60	27.00	32.40

SERVING PIECES

	Retail Each	List
J Butter Knife	$3.00	$3.60
K Sugar Spoon	3.00	3.60
L Cold Meat or Serving Fork	4.95	5.94
M Large Pastry Server	5.95	7.14
N Gravy Ladle	4.95	5.94
O Pie or Cake Server, H. H.	6.95	8.34
P Pierced Relish Spoon	3.00	3.60
Q Pickle or Lemon Fork	3.00	3.60
R Pierced Tablespoon	3.00	3.60
S Salad or Serving Spoon	4.95	5.94
T Regular Tablespoon	3.00	3.60
Punch Ladle, H. H.†	17.50	21.00
Soup Ladle, H. H.*	10.00	12.00

* not available in Garland or Magic Rose
† available in Heritage only

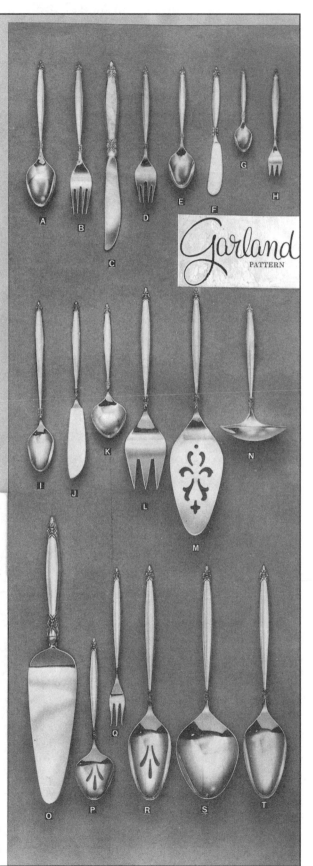

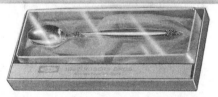

H-1 Infant Feeding Spoon. Long handle spoon with specially designed small shallow bowl for feeding solid food to baby. Retail **$1.75** List $1.92

H-6 Step-Up Set. Matched silverware for all baby's needs from birth to ten years includes Infant Feeding Spoon, 2-pc. Educator Set and 3-pc. Youngster Set.
Retail **$9.50** List $10.46

Garland (1966), Silver Lace (1969), Esperanto (1968),
Grand Heritage (1968), Reflection, King Frederik & Love

LEFT to RIGHT . . .
Garland*
Reflection*
Silver Lace*
Esperanto*
King Frederik*
(Made in U.S.A.)
Grand Heritage*
New! Love*

Heraldic Pattern

Heraldic is a wonderful hand-hammered and chased pattern that was designed in keeping with the Arts and Crafts movement. It was a very popular 1847 Rogers Bros. pattern produced in tremendous quantity. Numerous coffee/tea services have appeared through the years. The flatware pieces shown here, dated 1930 – 1931, are a small example of what was produced. Heraldic was nearing the end of its active period by the early 1930s with styles moving away from the hammered look. Heraldic's patent date is 1916.

See Price Guide — Group 2

Heraldic Pattern

Six in Box

		Per Dozen	
		List	Consumer
8101	Tea Spoons.................	$9.18	$7.50
8102	Dessert or Oval Soup Spoons	18.36	15.00
8103	Table or Serving Spoons...	18.36	15.00
8104	Soup Spoons, Round Bowl..	18.36	15.00
81005	Bouillon Spoons, Gift Box..	17.74	14.50
8105	Dinner Forks...........	18.36	15.00
8106	Dessert or Luncheon Forks..	18.36	15.00

Solid Handle Knives
With Stainless Blades

81472s	Dinner Knives...........	$18.28	$14.00

The above knives have French shape blades

81475s	Fruit Knives.............	16.32	12.50

Hollow Handle Knives
With Stainless Blades

		Per Dozen	
		List	Consumer
81402M	Dinner Knives, Mirror Finish....................	$36.50	$28.00
81402s	Dinner Knives...........	31.30	24.00
81404M	Dessert or Luncheon Knives, Mirror Finish...........	36.50	28.00
81404s	Dessert or Luncheon Knives	31.30	24.00

The above knives have French shape blades

81406s	Fruit Knives.............	28.70	22.00
81208s	Tea or Salad Knives......	28.70	22.00

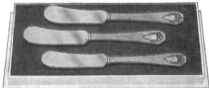

81202   BUTTER SPREADERS
List, set of six, $7.68; Consumer, set of six, $6.25

81227   GRAVY LADLE
List, each, $3.38; Consumer, each, $2.75

81226   MAYONNAISE OR SAUCE LADLE
List, each, $2.76; Consumer, each, $2.25

81103   COLD MEAT FORK
List, each, $3.07; Consumer, each, $2.50

81003   BERRY OR SALAD SPOON
List, each, $4.30; Consumer, each, $3.50

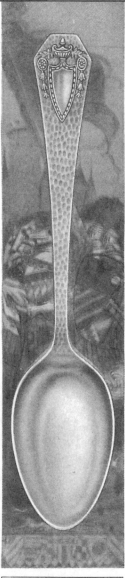

HERALDIC *pattern— a revival of the antique, hand-hammered effect, with a decorative crest to relieve severity*

81017   SUGAR SPOON
List, each, $1.53; Consumer, each, $1.25

81111   SALAD FORKS, INDIVIDUAL
List, set of six, $9.18; Consumer, set of six, $7.50

81201   BUTTER KNIFE
List, each, $1.53; Consumer, each, $1.25

81014   ORANGE OR GRAPE FRUIT SPOONS
List, set of six, $7.05; Consumer, set of six, $5.75

81254M   PIE OR ICE CREAM SERVER, Mirror Finish Stainless Blade
List, each, $5.52; Consumer, each, $4.50

81253   DESSERT SERVER
List, each, $5.22; Consumer, each, $4.25

.1847 ROGERS BROS.
SILVERPLATE

1930 Catalog

008103 TEA OR COFFEE SET
Three Pieces
Coffee Pot, Sugar Bowl and Cream
Pitcher
List, set, $81.36; Consumer, set, $65.00

008111 WAITER, 16 inch, oblong
(not illustrated)
List, each, $31.30; Consumer, $25.00

008146 SERVICE PLATE, 11 in.
List, each, $12.52; Consumer, $10.00

008147 BREAD AND BUTTER PLATE
Diameter, 7 inches
List, each, $6.26; Consumer, each, $5.00

008144 SALT AND PEPPER SET
Height, 6¼ inches
List, set, $12.52; Consumer, set, $10.00

008153 CANDLESTICKS
Height, 9¼ inches
List, pair, $31.30; Consumer, pair, $25.00

008140 DOUBLE VEGETABLE DISH
Lock Handle
Length, 10½ inches
List, each, $31.30; Consumer, each, $25.00

HERALDIC PATTERN

**Hand Hammered and Chased
Butler Grey Finish**

*Matching the Spoons, Forks and Knives
in the Heraldic Pattern*

For price guide see pattern group II

MEAT DISHES, Plain

		List	Consumer
008131	16 inch....	$25.04	$20.00
008133	20 inch....	37.54	30.00
008134	22 inch....	56.32	45.00

MEAT DISHES, Well and Tree

008135	16 inch....	$34.42	$27.50
008137	20 inch....	46.94	37.50
008138	22 inch....	65.70	52.50

008141 GRAVY BOAT AND PLATE
Capacity, 7 ounces
List, set, $25.04; Consumer, set, $20.00

008150 CENTERPIECE, Gold Lined
Diameter, 13 inches
With Silver Plated Double Mesh
List, each, $50.06; Consumer, each, $40.00

008143 WATER PITCHER
Capacity, 3 pints
List, each, $37.54; Consumer, each, $30.00

008124 BREAD TRAY
Length, 12 inches
List, each, $15.64
Consumer, each, $12.50

TEA POT, COFFEE POT, SUGAR BOWL, CREAM PITCHER AND WASTE BOWL

		List	Consumer			List	Consumer
008105	Set of Five Pieces..............	$125.16	$100.00	008108	Sugar Bowl..................	$25.04	$20.00
008104	Set of Four Pieces.............	112.64	90.00	008109	Cream Pitcher, Gold Lined.......	25.04	20.00
008103	Set of Three Pieces.............	81.36	65.00	008110	Waste Bowl, Gold Lined.........	12.52	10.00
008106	Coffee Pot (or Chocolate), 32 ounces	31.30	25.00	008112	Waiter, 22 inch, oblong (not illus.)	50.06	40.00
008107	Tea Pot, 32 ounces..............	31.30	25.00	008111	Waiter, 16 inch, oblong (not illus.)	31.30	25.00

.1847 ROGERS BROS.
S I L V E R P L A T E

1931 Catalog

Heritage Pattern

Heritage was patented in 1953. It is a highly collectible pattern that was made in large quantities; therefore, a set can be easily assembled. Of the place pieces, the demi-tasse, fruit, and round bowl soup spoons are hard to find. Serving pieces that might be a challenge to find include the cheese server, carving set, and sugar tongs. The punch ladle was made in quantity. There is a bonbon spoon (not illustrated), shaped like a shovel, that comes both plain and pierced. Notice the retail prices of Heritage hollow ware; some were quite expensive. The coffee urn, ice bowl, and soup tureen are considered rare. Items shown on this page are dated 1967.

HERITAGE — 1847 Rogers Bros. Silverplate

Retail

No. 9451 Coffee Urn, Capacity, 50 cups, Height 18½ inches. Adjustable alcohol burner **$175.00**

HERITAGE—1847 Rogers Bros. Silverplate

Retail

No. 9464 Height, 5 inches pair **$16.50**

No. 9450 Soup Tureen
Retail, $50.00
Diameter 12 inches
Height 9 inches, Capacity 3 quarts
No. 9450 L Soup Ladle Retail, $8.50

No. 9427 Vacuum Ice Bowl
Retail, $50.00
Diameter 9½ inches
Height 9 inches
Genuine Thermos Liner

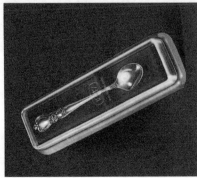

H-1 Infant Feeding Spoon. Long handle spoon with specially designed small shallow bowl for feeding solid food to baby.

H-7 Companion Set. Matching Fork, Spoon and Cup for baby just learning to eat by himself.

Retail **$7.50**

1958 Catalog

See Price Guide — Group 2

Heritage Pattern

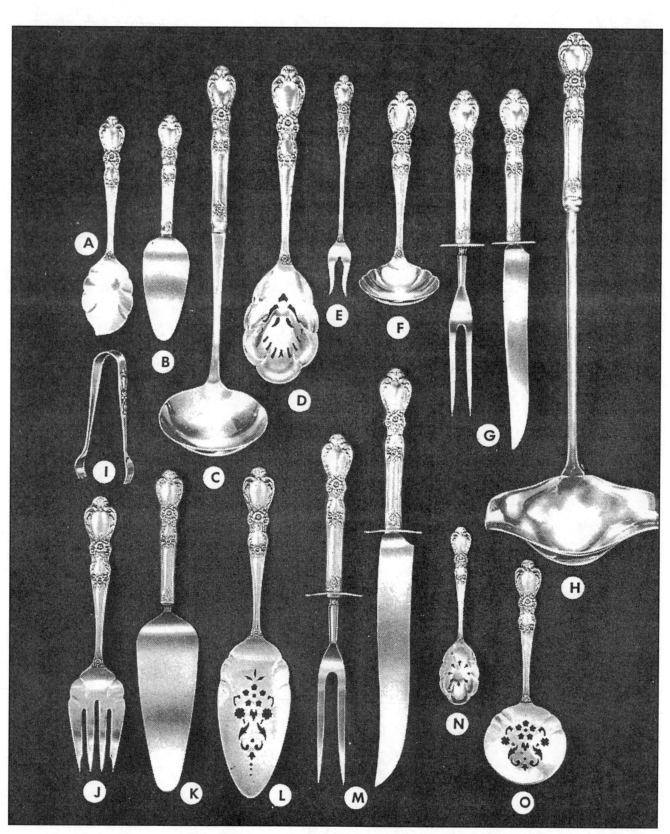

1963 Catalog. See opposite page for descriptions and prices.

Heritage Pattern

A. Jelly server. For jellies, jams, relishes, cottage and cut cheese. $2.00 each.

B. Cheese server. Hollow handle, designed solely for cutting and serving cheese. $4.00 each.

C. Soup ladle. Hollow handle, handsome accessory for regal entertaining. Also used for punch. $8.50 each.

D. Serving Spoon. Larger than tablespoon for salads, vegetables, baked beans, macaroni. Available without piercing for berries. $3.25 each.

E. Pickle fork. Multi-use piece for use with pickles, olives, lemon slices, butter pats. $2.00 each.

F. Gravy ladle. Indispensable for serving gravies, stew, creamed dishes, soup, whipped cream and dessert sauces. $3.25 each.

G. Steak set (2 pieces). For carving and serving steak, small roasts, and poultry. $9.75 each.

H. Punch ladle. Hollow handle, gracefully styled with double lip for pouring convenience. $14.75 each.

I. Sugar tongs. Correct accessory for serving sugar cubes. Can be used with bonbons and chocolates. $2.50 each.

J. Serving or cold meat fork. Necessary for serving salads, fish, bacon, and chops. $3.25 each.

K. Pie knife. Hollow handle, suitable for serving all pastries, waffles, hot cakes, fish, and cutlets. $5.00 each.

L. Long server. Convenient for use with pies, cakes, frozen desserts. $4.50 each.

M. Carving set (2 pieces). A requisite for carving and serving large birds, roasts, and hams. $14.75 each.

N. Pierced relish spoon. Designed for relish service but can be used for olives, pickles, and cottage cheese. $2.00 each.

O. Round server. For convenient service with hard to balance food like broccoli, croquettes, eggs, sliced tomatoes, and cucumbers. $3.25 each.

HERITAGE — 1847 Rogers Bros. Silverplate

No. 9479/L Lazy Susan. Diameter, 15½ inches. 5 removable glass liners. Silverplated cover on center dish. Revolving Base

Retail

$50.00

HERITAGE — 1847 Rogers Bros. Silverplate — Oval Tray, Chased
No. 9482   Length, 24 inches, Overall length, 28 inches .... Retail $70.00

HERITAGE — 1847 Rogers Bros. Silverplate — Tray, Chased
No. 9473   Diameter, 17 inches .... Retail $30.00
No. 9472   Diameter, 15 inches .... Retail 25.00

1967 Catalog

No. 9417 Water Pitcher ....Retail, $37.50
Capacity, 2 quarts

HERITAGE . . . 1847 Rogers Bros.
9484 Food Warmer, 3 qts. **$115.00**

Heritage
1847 ROGERS BROS.

Cigarette Box ....Retail; $4.95
Length, 5 inches. Choice of handle to match
1847 Rogers Bros. patterns except *Flair*.
Genuine hand-made Duncan & Miller clear
crystal bottom.

Retail Prices subject to Federal Tax.

No. 9445   Punch Bowl, Cap. 12 qts., Diam. 17 in. ......Retail, $80.00
No. 9474   Tray, Diam. 22½ in. ....Retail, $60.00
No. 9446   Punch Cup ....Retail, $ 8.00
No. 9447   Ladle (no tax) ....Retail, $17.50

No. 9453 Buffet Dish ....Retail, $50.00
Length 13¼ inches, Width 10¼ inches

No. 9411 Relish Dish ....Retail, $25.00
Length 16½ inches, 4 comp. glass lining

1958 Catalog

See Price Guide — Group 2

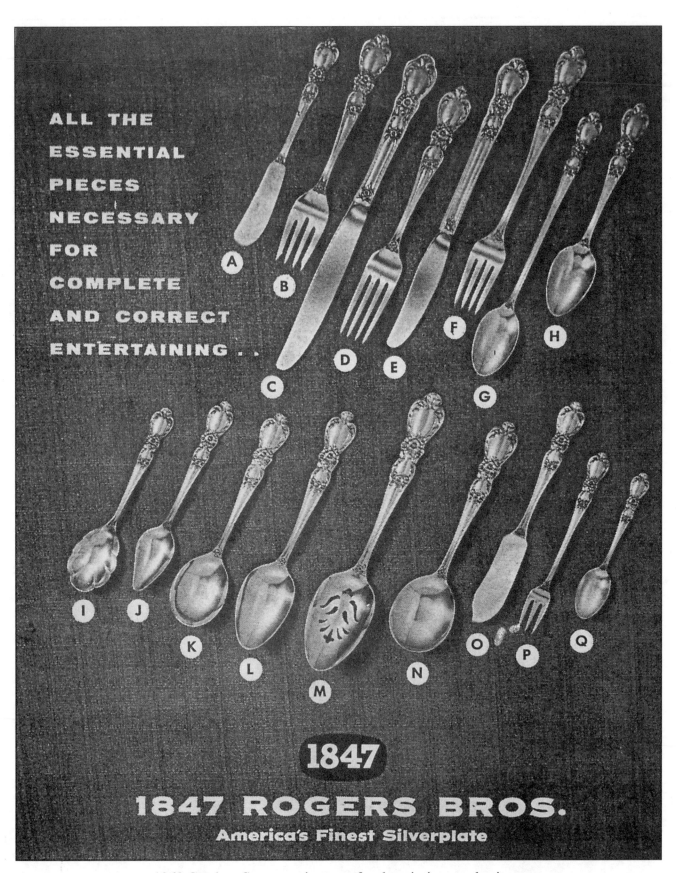

ALL THE
ESSENTIAL
PIECES
NECESSARY
FOR
COMPLETE
AND CORRECT
ENTERTAINING..

1847

1847 ROGERS BROS.
America's Finest Silverplate

1963 Catalog. See opposite page for descriptions and prices.

Heritage Pattern

A. Butter spreader. Used with bread and butter plate for butter, cheese, jelly, and jam. $1.63 each.

B. Salad fork. In addition to salad, suitable for pastries, sliced desserts, and sandwiches. $1.63 each.

C. Dinner knife (long blade). Also used for breakfast, luncheon, formal and informal dinners. $2.67 each.

D. Dinner fork (long tines). Companion to dinner knife. Can be used with tablespoon for serving vegetables. $1.63 each.

E. Dinner knife (viand). Popular place knife with long handle and short blade. $2.67 each.

F. Dinner fork (viand). Used with viand knife for meat course at dinner, breakfast, or lunch. $1.63 each.

G. Iced drink spoon. Long handle for all iced beverages and tall-glass ice cream desserts. $1.63 each.

H. Teaspoon. Exceptionally versatile for beverages, frozen desserts, cereal, and liquid vegetables. 82¢ each.

I. Sugar spoon. Necessary for granulated or powdered sugar. Adaptable for relishes and jellies. $1.50 each.

J. Fruit spoon. An individualized piece for oranges, grapefruit, melons. $1.00 each.

K. Cream soup spoon. For hot or cold soup served in soup plate or bouillon cups. Practical for cereal and dessert. $1.63 each.

L. Dessert or oval soup spoon. Proper with dessert served on a plate or soup in a soup plate. A small serving spoon. $1.63 each.

M. Tablespoon. No limit to its service. For vegetables, casseroles, salads, puddings. Available with piercing for moist vegetables. $2.00 each.

N. Round bowl soup spoon. Preferred for use with low soup plate; dessert served on a plate. $1.63 each.

O. Butter knife. Essential for correct butter service when individual butter spreaders are not used. $1.50 each.

P. Cocktail fork. Place setting piece used exclusively with oysters, shrimps, and other seafood cocktails. $1.63 each.

Q. After dinner coffee spoon. For demitasse, old-fashioned cocktails, tiny bowls of horseradish, mustard, or salted nuts. 83¢ each.

No. 9475 Chafing Dish .... Retail, $75.00
  Height 10½ inches, Diameter 12 inches—Capacity 1½ Quarts—Removable Ebony Handle
No. 9473 Tray, Chased, Diameter 17 inches .... Retail, $27.50
No. 9475/S Chafing Dish Spoon, Length 12¾ inches .... Retail, $6.00

Retail Prices subject to Federal Tax.

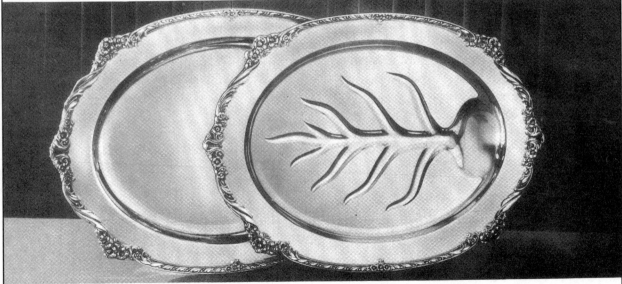

No. 9409 Meat Dish ....Retail, $30.00   No. 9410 Well and Tree Platter ....Retail, $35.00
Length, 19 inches   Length, 19 inches

Heritage Pattern

1967 Catalog

Heritage Pattern

No. 9421 Sandwich Tray ....Retail, $17
Diameter, 12 inches

No. 9416 Candelabrum, Ht. 17 inches ....Retail, $37.50 each

No. 9415 Candlestick, Ht. 10¼ inches ..Retail, $27.50 pair

Butter Dish ....Retail, $3.95
Length 7¼ inches. Choice of handle to match
1847 Rogers Bros. patterns except *Flair*. Genuine hand-made Duncan & Miller clear crystal
bottom.

No. 9414 Center Bowl ....Retail, $27.50
Diameter, 12 inches

No. 9464 Open Salt & Pepper ....Retail, $15.00 pr.
Ht. of Pepper 5 in.; Diam. of Salt 3½ in.
No. 9464R Salt & Pepper Shakers ....Retail, $15.00 pr.

No. 9419 Bread Tray ....Retail, $17.50
Length, 14 inches

No. 9495 Shell Dish ....Retail, $15.00
Length, 10½ inches

1967 Catalog

See Price Guide — Group 2

Retail

No. 9400/5 *Heritage* Tea and Coffee Service,
5 pieces $160.00
(*Coffee Pot, Tea Pot, Sugar Bowl, Cream Pitcher, Waste Bowl*)
No. 9400/3 *Heritage* Coffee Service, 3 pieces   97.50
(*Coffee Pot, Sugar Bowl, Cream Pitcher*)
No. 9490   Waiter, Chased, Length 20 inches   42.50
No. 9492   Waiter, Chased, Length 24 inches   60.00
No. 9493   Waiter, Chased, Length 27 inches
(for 6-piece Service) 75.00

Retail

No. 9401   Coffee Pot, 11 cups,
Height 10½ inches $45.00
No. 9402   Tea Pot, 10 cups,
Height 8¼ inches 45.00
No. 9403   Sugar Bowl, Covered 27.50
No. 9404   Cream Pitcher, Gold Lined ..   25.00
No. 9405   Waste Bowl, Gold Lined 17.50
No. 9406   Kettle, Capacity 60 oz.,
Height 14¼ in. 90.00

No. 9413 Gravy Set ......Retail, $35.00
Capacity of boat, 16 ounces

No. 9412 Double Vegetable Dish ....Retail, $35.00
Length, 13¼ inches

1967 Catalog

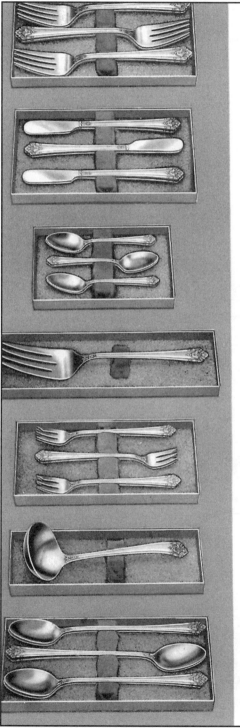

90114
SALAD FORKS
Retail, set of six, $6.50
List, set of six, $7.80

90209
BUTTER SPREADERS
Retail, set of six, $6.50
List, set of six, $7.80

90008
AFTER DINNER COFFEE SPOONS
Retail, set of six, $3.75
List, set of six, $4.50

90103
SERVING OR COLD MEAT FORK, Large
Retail, each, $2.25
List, each, $2.70

90106
OYSTER OR COCKTAIL FORKS
Retail, set of six, $6.00
List, set of six, $7.20

90227
GRAVY LADLE
Retail, each, $2.25
List, each, $2.70

90226
SAUCE LADLE, Small
Retail, each, $1.75
List, each, $2.10

90012
ICED TEA SPOONS
Retail, set of six, $6.00
List, set of six, $7.20

(Not Illustrated)	Retail Each	List
90201 Butter Knife or Server...	$1.50	**$1.80**
90204 Jelly Server...........	1.75	**2.10**
90253 Long Server..........	3.50	**4.20**
90108 Pickle Fork...........	1.25	**1.50**
90254 Pie or Ice Cream Knife ..	3.50	**4.20**
90252 Round Server.........	2.25	**2.70**
90019 Serving or Berry Spoon..	2.25	**2.70**
90017 Sugar Spoon	1.50	**1.80**
90277 Sugar Tongs.	1.75	**2.10**

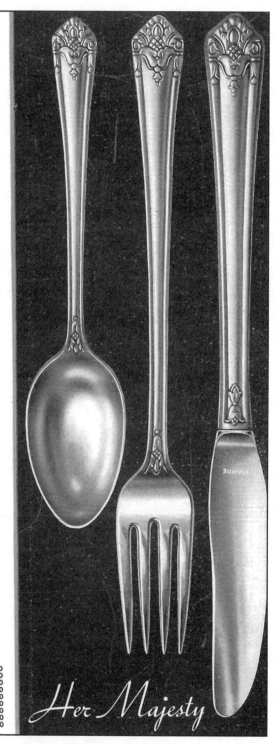

Her Majesty

1847 ROGERS BROS.
HER MAJESTY SERVICE

1936

009069
CASSEROLE, Round
Pyrex Lining, with Engraved Cover
Capacity, 3 pints
$10.00

DESSERT SET

009079.	3 pieces	$21.00
009081.	Dessert Sugar Bowl.	7.50
009082.	Dessert Cream Pitcher	7.50
009083.	Dessert Tray, 10½ inch............	6.00

009043
WATER PITCHER
Capacity, 2 quarts
$21.00

009056
CANDELABRUM
Two-Light. Width, 10½ inches
$9.00 Each

009050
CENTERPIECE
With Silver Plated Double Mesh Flower
Holder. Diameter, 12¼ inches
$18.00

009057
CANDLESTICK
Height, 4 inches
$10.00 Pair

A complete matching
Flatware Service is
made in Her Majesty
Pattern.

009068
RELISH DISH OR CHOP PLATE
Diameter, 14 inches
Five Compartments. Removable Glass
Lining
$15.00

009060
COMPOTIER
Height, 6¾ inches
$7.50

009024
BREAD TRAY
Length, 14 inches
$8.00

009027
SANDWICH TRAY
Length, 13 inches
$9.00

009061
BON BON
Width, 7 inches
$5.00

009046
SERVICE PLATE
Diameter, 11 inches
$7.50 Each

009047
BREAD AND BUTTER
PLATE
Diameter, 6¾ inches
$4.00 Each

1936 Catalog

THE GLEAMING COURTLY BEAUTY SUGGESTS THE ELEGANCE OF HAND-WROUGHT SILVER OF THE GEORGIAN PERIOD
LUSTER FINISH

TEA AND COFFEE SET

009005. Set of 5 Pieces (Coffee Pot, Tea Pot, Sugar Bowl, Cream Pitcher and Waste Bowl) .. **$72.00**
009003. Tea or Coffee Set, 3 Pieces (Coffee Pot, Sugar Bowl and Cream Pitcher) **44.00**

009006.	Tea or Coffee Pot, 9 cups............	$21.00	009010.	Waste Bowl, Gold Lined	$ 7.00
009007.	Tea Pot, 9 cups....................	21.00	009012.	Waiter, 22-inch (for 5-Piece Set)....	36.00
009008.	Sugar Bowl, Co ered	12.00	009011.	Waiter, 16-inch (for 3-Piece Set).....	21.00
009009.	Cream Pitcher, Gold Lined..........	11.00			

009039	**009044**	**009041**
DOUBLE VEGETABLE DISH	**SALT AND PEPPER SET**	**GRAVY BOAT AND PLATE**
Length, 12 inches	Patented Salt Top—salt will not clog	Capacity, 10 ounces
$18.00	even though damp	**$16.00**
	Height, 6 inches	
	$7.00	

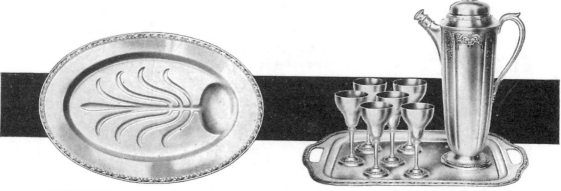

MEAT DISH		MEAT DISH		BEVERAGE SET		
Well and Tree		Plain		009077.	Set of 8 Pieces (Mixer, Serv- ing Tray and 6 Cups) ...	$64.00
009035. 16-inch.....	$16.00	009031. 16-inch.....	$15.00	009074.	Mixer, Capacity 1½ quarts	24.00
009036. 18-inch.....	21.00	009032. 18-inch.....	18.00	009075.	Cocktail Cups, Gold Lined. each	4.00
009037. 20-inch.....	27.00	009033. 20-inch.....	24.00	009076.	Serving Tray, 16 inch.....	16.00

1936 Catalog

King Frederik Pattern

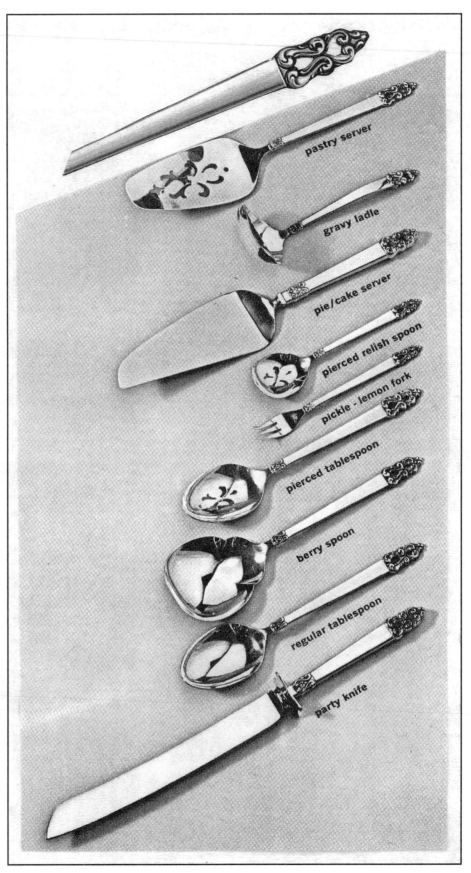

pastry server

gravy ladle

pie/cake server

pierced relish spoon

pickle - lemon fork

pierced tablespoon

berry spoon

regular tablespoon

party knife

1970

LEGACY PATTERN

Six in Box

		Per Dozen	
		List	Consumer
8801	Tea Spoons..............	$9.18	$7.50
8802	Dessert or Oval Soup Spoons	18.36	15.00
8803	Table or Serving Spoons...	18.36	15.00
8804	Soup Spoons, Round Bowl.	18.36	15.00
88006	Cream Soup or Cereal Spoons, Gift Box	18.36	15.00
88005	Bouillon Spoons, Gift Box..	17.74	14.50
8805	Dinner Forks.............	18.36	15.00
8806	Dessert or Luncheon Forks.	18.36	15.00

Solid Handle Knives
With Stainless Blades

		List	Consumer
88472s	Dinner Knives............	$18.28	$14.00
88474s	Dessert or Luncheon Knives	18.28	14.00
88475s	Fruit Knives.............	16.32	12.50

The above knives have French shape blades

88008 COFFEE SPOONS
List, set of six, $4.59; Consumer, set of six, $3.75

88013 OLIVE SPOON
List, each, $2.15; Consumer, each, $1.75

88106 OYSTER OR COCKTAIL FORKS
List, set of six, $6.45; Consumer, set of six, $5.25

88227 GRAVY LADLE
List, each, $3.38; Consumer, each, $2.75

88226 MAYONNAISE OR SAUCE LADLE
List, each, $2.76; Consumer, each, $2.25

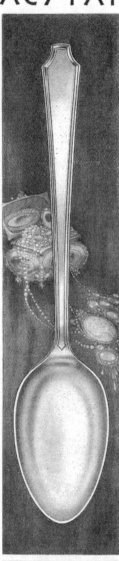

LEGACY pattern — moded for today and tomorrow, but bequeathed with the artistry of four generations

Hollow Handle Knives
With Stainless Blades

		Per Dozen	
		List	Consumer
88402M	Dinner Knives, Mirror Finish....................	$36.50	$28.00
88402s	Dinner Knives............	31.30	24.00
88404M	Dessert or Luncheon Knives, Mirror Finish..........	36.50	28.00
88404s	Dessert or Luncheon Knives	31.30	24.00

The above knives have French shape blades

| 88406s | Fruit Knives............. | 28.70 | 22.00 |
| 88208s | Tea or Salad Knives ...... | 28.70 | 22.00 |

88017 SUGAR SPOON
List, each, $1.53; Consumer, each, $1.25

88301 BUTTER KNIFE AND SUGAR SPOON
List, set, $3.06; Consumer, set, $2.50

88201 BUTTER KNIFE
List, each, $1.53; Consumer, each, $1.25

88014 ORANGE OR GRAPE FRUIT SPOONS
List, set of six, $7.05; Consumer, set of six, $5.75

88254M PIE OR ICE CREAM SERVER, Mirror Finish Stainless Blade
List, each, $5.52; Consumer, each, $4.50

88253 DESSERT SERVER
List, each, $5.22; Consumer, each, $4.25

.1847 ROGERS BROS.
SILVERPLATE

008803 TEA OR COFFEE SET
Three Pieces
Coffee Pot, Sugar Bowl and Cream
Pitcher
List, set, $81.36; Consumer, set, $65.00

008811 WAITER, 16 inch, oblong
(not illustrated)
List, each, $31.30; Consumer, each, $25.00

008846 SERVICE PLATE, 10¾ in.
List, each, $12.52; Consumer, each, $10.00

008847 BREAD AND BUTTER PLATE
Diameter, 6½ inches
List, each, $6.26; Consumer, each, $5.00

008844 SALT AND PEPPER SET
Height, 4⅞ inches
List, set, $12.52; Consumer, set, $10.00

008841 GRAVY BOAT AND PLATE
Capacity, 16 ounces
List, set, $25.04; Consumer, set, $20.00

MEAT DISHES, Plain

		List	Consumer
008831	16 inch	$25.04	$20.00
008832	18 inch	31.30	25.00
008833	20 inch	37.54	30.00

MEAT DISHES, Well and Tree

008835	16 inch	$34.42	$27.50
008836	18 inch	40.68	32.50
008837	20 inch	46.94	37.50

LEGACY PATTERN

Light Butler Finish
Macassar Ebony Trim

*Matching the Spoons, Forks and Knives
in the Legacy Pattern*

008843 WATER PITCHER
Capacity, 4 pints
List, each, $37.54; Consumer, each, $30.00

008824 BREAD TRAY
Length, 12¼ inches
List, each, $15.64; Consumer, each, $12.50

008850 CENTERPIECE
Width, 14 inches
Flower Holder
with Silver Plated Double Mesh
List, each, $50.06; Consumer, each, $40.00

008853 CANDLESTICKS
Height, 10 inches
List, pair, $31.30; Consumer, pair, $25.00

008839 DOUBLE VEGETABLE DISH
Side Handles
Length, 12½ inches
List, each, $31.30; Consumer, each, $25.00

TEA POT, COFFEE POT, SUGAR BOWL, CREAM PITCHER, WASTE BOWL AND WAITER

		List	Consumer			List	Consumer
008805	Set of Five Pieces	$125.16	$100.00	008808	Sugar Bowl	$25.04	$20.00
008804	Set of Four Pieces	112.64	90.00	008809	Cream Pitcher, Gold Lined	25.04	20.00
008803	Set of Three Pieces	81.36	65.00	008810	Waste Bowl, Gold Lined	12.52	10.00
008806	Coffee Pot (or Chocolate), 32 ounces	31.30	25.00	008812	Waiter, 22 inch, oblong	50.06	40.00
008807	Tea Pot, 32 ounces	31.30	25.00	008811	Waiter, 16 inch, oblong (not illus.)	31.30	25.00

.1847 ROGERS BROS.
SILVERPLATE

1931 Catalog

1847 Rogers Bros.

1847 ROGERS BROS.
ORIGINAL AND GENUINE ROGERS SILVERPLATE

AN INTERNATIONA SILVER CO. PRODUCT

LEGACY PATTERN (CONT'D)

88105   ICE CREAM FORKS
Retail, set of six, $6.25; **List, set of six, $7.68**

88204   JELLY SERVER
Retail, each, $1.75; **List, each, $2.14**

88301   BUTTER KNIFE AND SUGAR SPOON SET
Retail, set, $2.50; **List, set, $3.06**
88201   BUTTER KNIFE OR SERVER
Retail, each, $1.25; **List, each, $1.52**
88017   SUGAR SPOON
Retail, each, $1.25; **List, each, $1.52**

88227   GRAVY LADLE
Retail, each, $2.75; **List, each, $3.38**
88226   SAUCE LADLE, small
Retail, each, $2.25; **List, each, $2.76**

88253   LONG SERVER
Retail, each, $4.25; **List, each, $5.22**

88252   ROUND SERVER
Retail, each, $3.25; **List, each, $3.98**

88254   PIE OR ICE CREAM KNIFE
Retail, each, $4.50; **List, each, $5.52**

88108   PICKLE FORK
Retail, each, $1.50; **List, each, $1.84**

88103   SERVING FORK, large
Retail, each, $2.50; **List, each, $3.06**
88104   SERVING FORK, small
Retail, each, $2.00; **List, each, $2.46**

88003   BERRY OR SALAD SPOON
Retail, each, $3.50; **List, each, $4.30**
88004   BERRY SPOON, small
Retail, each, $2.00; **List, each, $2.46**

88277   SUGAR TONGS
Retail, each, $2.00; **List, each, $2.46**

88019   SERVING SPOONS
Retail, set of two, $5.00; **List, set of two, $6.14**

VIANDE
TRADE MARK
FORK
Dinner Size

1931 Catalog

See Price Guide — Group 2

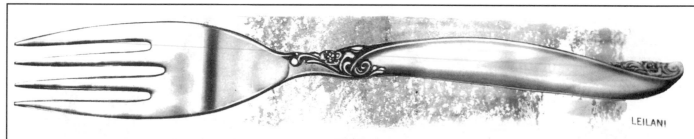

Leilani

LEILANI
1847 Rogers Bros. Silverplate
Retail

No. 9100/4 4-pieces
(Carafe, sugar
bowl, cream
pitcher, warmer) $79.75
No. 9190 Tray,
Length, 18½
inches 30.00
No. 9101 Carafe,
10 cups, Height,
8½ inches 29.75
No. 9103 Sugar Bowl,
Covered 18.50
No. 9104 Cream
Pitcher 16.50
No. 9108 Warmer
with glass candle
cup. Height,
2⅞ inches 15.00

1847 Rogers Bros. Cold Meat Fork.

The Fork is extra silver-plated, 6½ inches long, and especially designed for serving either cold meat or cake. Gold-plated tines, latest style and very popular.

Lotus

1895

Love Pattern

1847 ROGERS BROS
SILVERPLATE

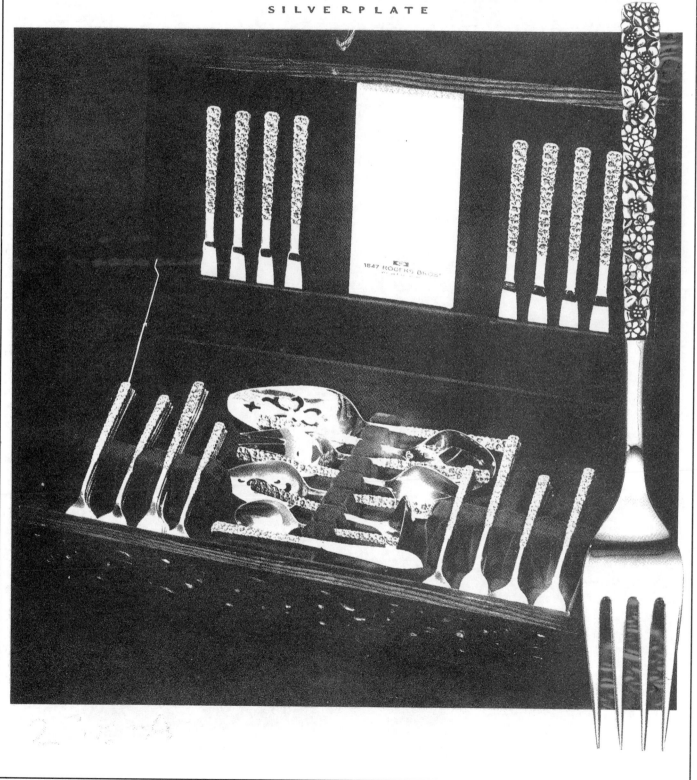

1973

235

Beautiful Silverplated Holloware
1847 ROGERS BROS.®

NEW!

Magic ROSE

*Tea and Coffee Service**

1847 ROGERS BROS. SILVERPLATE

		Retail
No. 9600/4	4-Pieces (coffee pot, tea pot, sugar bowl, cream pitcher)	$155.00
No. 9681	Waiter, chased, length 20"	55.00
No. 9600/3	3-Pieces (coffee pot, sugar bowl, cream pitcher)	105.00
No. 9601	Coffee Pot, 10 cups. Height 11½"	50.00
No. 9602	Tea Pot, 9 cups. Height 9"	50.00
No. 9603	Sugar Bowl, covered	27.50
No. 9604	Cream Pitcher, gold lined	27.50

*Available October 15, 1964

MAGIC ROSE—1847 Rogers Bros. Silverplate
No. 9612   Length, 12½ inches .... Retail $38.50

Magic Rose Pattern

1847 ROGERS BROS.®

America's Finest Silverplate

RETAIL PRICE LIST FOR ALL PATTERNS

Effective July 1, 1965. Retail prices shown are those quoted to consumers on direct inquiry and subject to change without notice. All goods billed at prices prevailing on date of shipment. There is no Federal Tax on silverplated flatware. Retail Prices shown are minimum in those states having a Fair Trade Law.

PLACE SETTING PIECES

		One Retail	Eight Retail	Twelve Retail
A	Teaspoons	$1.25	$10.00	$15.00
B	Forks	2.25	18.00	27.00
C	Knives	3.50	28.00	42.00
D	Salad Forks	2.25	18.00	27.00
	*Dessert or Oval Soup Spoons†	2.25	18.00	27.00
	*Round Bowl Soup Spoons†	2.25	18.00	27.00
E	Service Spoons (Soup or Dessert)‡	2.25	18.00	27.00
F	Spreaders, Butter or Cheese	2.25	18.00	27.00
G	A.D. Coffee Spoons	1.25	10.00	15.00
H	Cocktail Forks	2.25	18.00	27.00
I	Iced Drink Spoons	2.25	18.00	27.00

SERVING PIECES

		Retail Each
J	Butter Knife	$ 3.00
K	Sugar Spoon	3.00
L	Cold Meat or Serving Fork	4.95
M	Gravy Ladle	4.95
N	Pickle or Lemon Fork	3.00
O	Pie or Pastry Server, H.H.	6.95
P	Pierced Relish Spoon	3.00
Q	Pierced Tablespoon	3.00
	*Punch Ladle, H.H.†	17.50
R	Salad or Serving Spoon	4.95
	Soup Ladle, H.H.°	10.00
S	Plain Tablespoon	3.00

*item not illustrated   ‡not available in Heritage
†available in Heritage only   °not available in Garland or Magic Rose

MAGIC ROSE – 1847 Rogers Bros. Silverplate
No. 9613   Capacity; 12 ozs. .... Retail $35.00

**MAGIC ROSE – 1847 Rogers Bros. Silverplate –
Bowl, Footed**
No. 9635   Diameter, 12 inches .... Retail $35.00

See Price Guide — Group 2

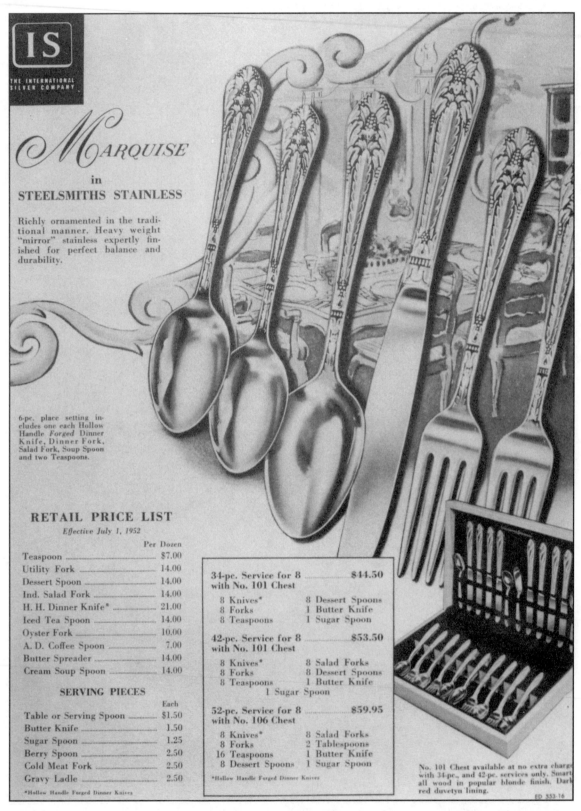

1953 International Silver catalog illustration. Marquise, an 1847 Rogers Bros. silver pattern that was reintroduced in stainless after WWII.

Marquise Pattern

CRAFTED IN THE MANNER OF OLD ENGLISH AND FRENCH SILVER . . . YET COMPLETELY A PATTERN OF TO-DAY
LUSTER FINISH

TEA AND COFFEE SET

009105.   Set of 5 Pieces (Coffee Pot, Tea Pot, Sugar Bowl, Cream Pitcher, and Waste Bowl) $82.00
009103.   Tea or Coffee Set, 3 Pieces (Coffee Pot, Sugar Bowl, and Cream Pitcher) 50.00

009106.	Tea or Coffee Pot, 9 cups	$25.00	009110.	Waste Bowl, Gold Lined	$ 7.00
009107.	Tea Pot, 8 cups	25.00	009112.	Waiter, 22-inch (for 5-Piece Set)	45.00
009108.	Sugar Bowl, Covered	13.00	009111.	Waiter, 16-inch (for 3-Piece Set)	27.00
009109.	Cream Pitcher, Gold Lined	12.00			

009139
DOUBLE VEGETABLE DISH
Length, 14 inches
$20.00

009145
SALT AND PEPPER SET
Salt Spoon furnished with Open Salt
$9.00

009144
SALT AND PEPPER SET
Regular Style
Height, 5¾ inches
$9.00

009141
GRAVY BOAT AND PLATE
Capacity, 10 ounces
$18.00

MEAT DISH
Well and Tree

009135.	16-inch	$19.00
009136.	18-inch	24.00
009137.	20-inch	30.00

MEAT DISH
Plain

009131.	16-inch	$18.00
009132.	18-inch	21.00
009133.	20-inch	27.00

BEVERAGE SET

009177.	Set of 8 Pieces (Mixer, Serving Tray and 6 Cups)	$78.00
009174.	Mixer, Capacity 2 quarts	24.00
009175.	Cocktail Cups, Gold Lined, each	4.50
009176.	Serving Tray, Length, 16 inches	27.00

1936 Catalog

See Price Guide — Group 2

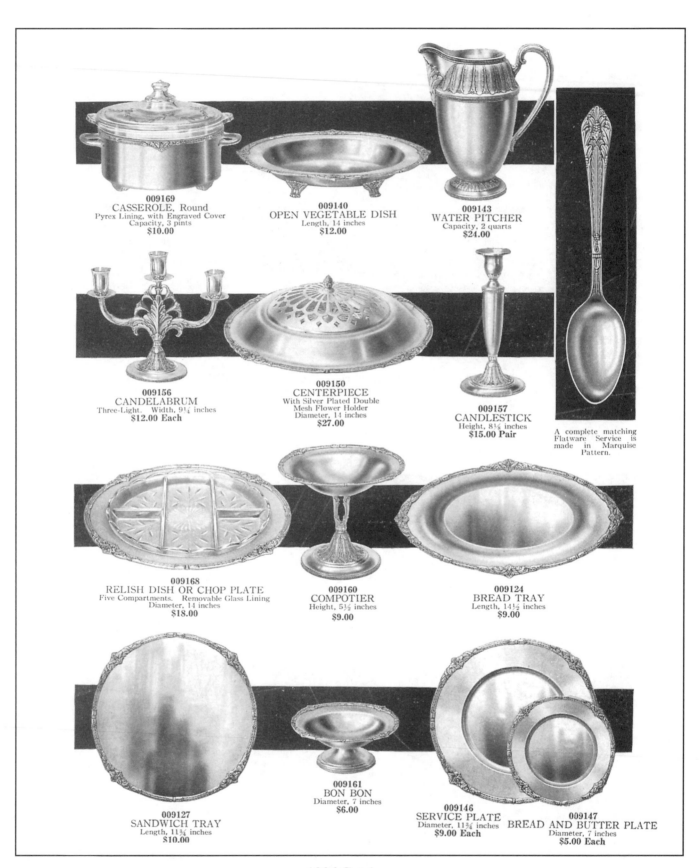

009169
CASSEROLE, Round
Pyrex Lining, with Engraved Cover
Capacity, 3 pints
$10.00

009140
OPEN VEGETABLE DISH
Length, 14 inches
$12.00

009143
WATER PITCHER
Capacity, 2 quarts
$24.00

009156
CANDELABRUM
Three-Light.   Width, 9¼ inches
$12.00 Each

009150
CENTERPIECE
With Silver Plated Double
Mesh Flower Holder
Diameter, 14 inches
$27.00

009157
CANDLESTICK
Height, 8½ inches
$15.00 Pair

A complete matching
Flatware Service is
made in Marquise
Pattern.

009168
RELISH DISH OR CHOP PLATE
Five Compartments.   Removable Glass Lining
Diameter, 14 inches
$18.00

009160
COMPOTIER
Height, 5½ inches
$9.00

009124
BREAD TRAY
Length, 14½ inches
$9.00

009127
SANDWICH TRAY
Length, 11¾ inches
$10.00

009161
BON BON
Diameter, 7 inches
$6.00

009146
SERVICE PLATE
Diameter, 11¾ inches
$9.00 Each

009147
BREAD AND BUTTER PLATE
Diameter, 7 inches
$5.00 Each

1936 Catalog

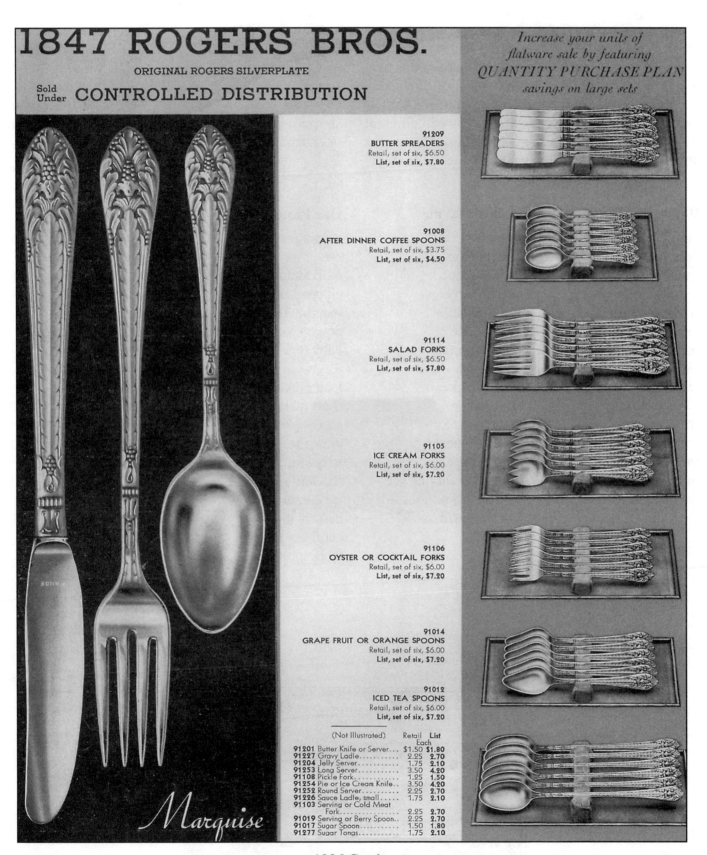

1847 ROGERS BROS.

ORIGINAL ROGERS SILVERPLATE

Sold Under **CONTROLLED DISTRIBUTION**

Increase your units of flatware sale by featuring QUANTITY PURCHASE PLAN *savings on large sets*

91209
BUTTER SPREADERS
Retail, set of six, $6.50
List, set of six, $7.80

91008
AFTER DINNER COFFEE SPOONS
Retail, set of six, $3.75
List, set of six, $4.50

91114
SALAD FORKS
Retail, set of six, $6.50
List, set of six, $7.80

91105
ICE CREAM FORKS
Retail, set of six, $6.00
List, set of six, $7.20

91106
OYSTER OR COCKTAIL FORKS
Retail, set of six, $6.00
List, set of six, $7.20

91014
GRAPE FRUIT OR ORANGE SPOONS
Retail, set of six, $6.00
List, set of six, $7.20

91012
ICED TEA SPOONS
Retail, set of six, $6.00
List, set of six, $7.20

(Not Illustrated)	Retail Each	List
91201 Butter Knife or Server...	$1.50	$1.80
91227 Gravy Ladle............	2.25	2.70
91204 Jelly Server............	1.75	2.10
91253 Long Server............	3.50	4.20
91108 Pickle Fork............	1.25	1.50
91254 Pie or Ice Cream Knife..	3.50	4.20
91252 Round Server...........	2.25	2.70
91226 Sauce Ladle, small.....	1.75	2.10
91103 Serving or Cold Meat Fork..............	2.25	2.70
91019 Serving or Berry Spoon.	2.25	2.70
91017 Sugar Spoon...........	1.50	1.80
91277 Sugar Tongs...........	1.75	2.10

Marquise

1936 Catalog

Old Colony Pattern

The popular Old Colony pattern was introduced in 1910. It became an instant success and was made in great quantities. Among patterns produced in this time period, it is possibly the easiest found and, fortunately for collectors, was an extremely large line. The hollow handle knife sharpener listed below is different from the one shown in the carving set. The master butter knife and the individual fish knife are from the same die; a slight curve was put into the handle of the butter knife. The baked potato fork is a larger version of the sandwich fork. Most of the larger Old Colony serving pieces were made in both hollow handle and one-piece styles. Many pieces were made that are not shown here, but have been verified either in catalogs or collections. A list of these pieces is as follows:

Hollow Handle	**Hollow Handle**	**One Piece**	**One Piece**
individual fish fork	ice tea spoon	asparagus fork	soup spoon
dessert fork	berry spoon	cake fork	egg spoon
lettuce fork	cheese scoop	individual fork	ice tea spoon
serving fork	cheese server	chipped beef fork	open-bowl olive
cold meat fork	medium ladle	individual fish fork	spoon
fish fork server	punch ladle	dessert fork	short handle baby
fish knife server	butter spreader	baby fork	spoon
ice cream knife	butter pick	ice cream fork	curved handle baby
cake knife No. 2	lobster pick	long pickle fork	spoon
cheese knife	nut cracker	short pickle fork	punch ladle
crumb knife	poultry shears	sandwich fork	mayonnaise ladle
breakfast knife	bottle opener	pie knife	pierced sugar sifter
fruit knife No. 1	knife sharpener	jelly knife	sugar tongs
fruit knife No. 2	bird/game carving set	fish knife server	butter pick
sawback	salad spoon and fork	ice cream spoon	nut pick
individual fish knife	servers with wood	dessert spoon	cheese scoop
		demi-tasse spoon	food pusher
		table spoon	

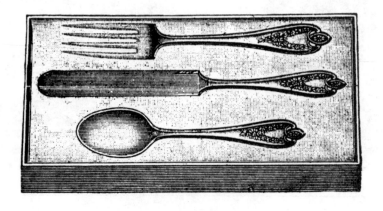

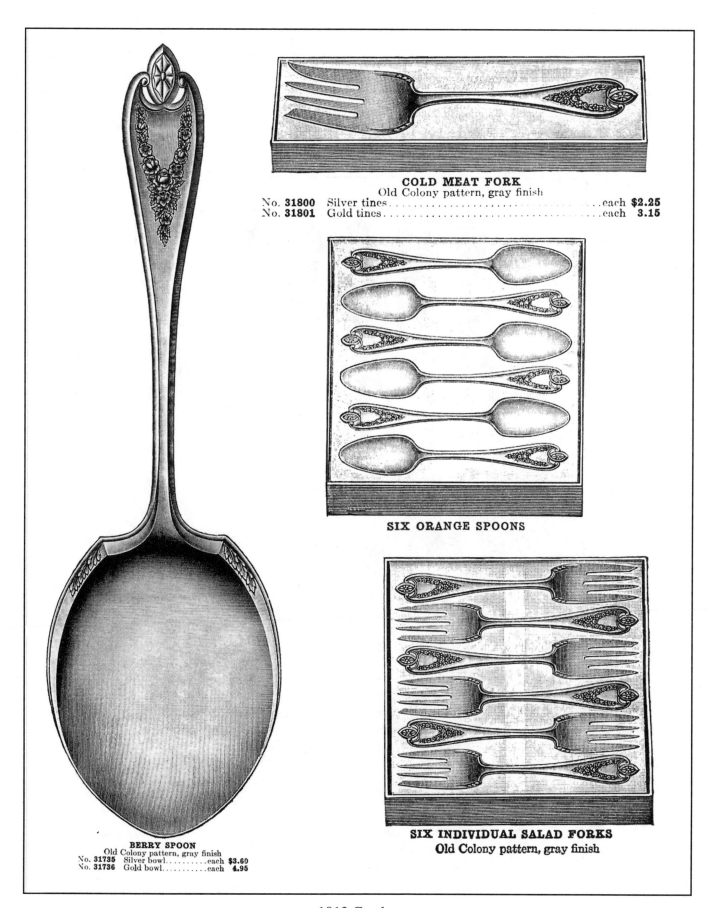

COLD MEAT FORK
Old Colony pattern, gray finish

No. **31800** Silver tines.....................................each **$2.25**
No. **31801** Gold tines......................................each **3.15**

SIX ORANGE SPOONS

SIX INDIVIDUAL SALAD FORKS
Old Colony pattern, gray finish

BERRY SPOON
Old Colony pattern, gray finish
No. **31735** Silver bowl.........each **$3.60**
No. **31736** Gold bowl..........each **4.95**

Old Colony Pattern

7⅘" hollow handle dinner forks

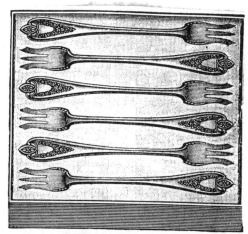

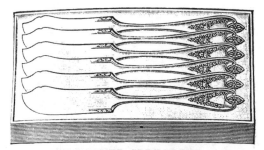

SIX BUTTER SPREADERS
Old Colony pattern, gray finish

SIX OYSTER FORKS

Old Colony pattern, gray finish. Nickel silver, silver soldered hollow handle knives and forks

No. 31434 Medium knives $28.80
No. 31435 Dessert knives 25.20

No. 31436 Medium forks..$28.80
No. 31437 Dessert forks 25.20

Scimitar swadged blade. First quality plated. Put up 6 in flannel roll.

Old Colony pattern, gray finish. Spoon handle forks.

No. 31438 Medium forks, XS triple plated $17.10
No. 31439 Medium forks, XS quintuple plated.... 23.40

No. 31440 Dessert forks, XS triple plated $15.30
No. 31441 Dessert forks, XS quintuple plated 19.80

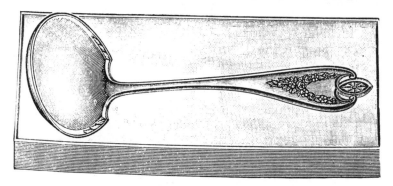

LADLES
Old Colony pattern, gray finish

No. 31775 **Cream Ladle, silver bowl**

No. 31777 **Gravy Ladle, silver bowl**

No. 31780 **Oyster Ladle, gold bowl**

No. 31782 **Medium Ladle, gold bowl**

Old Colony Pattern

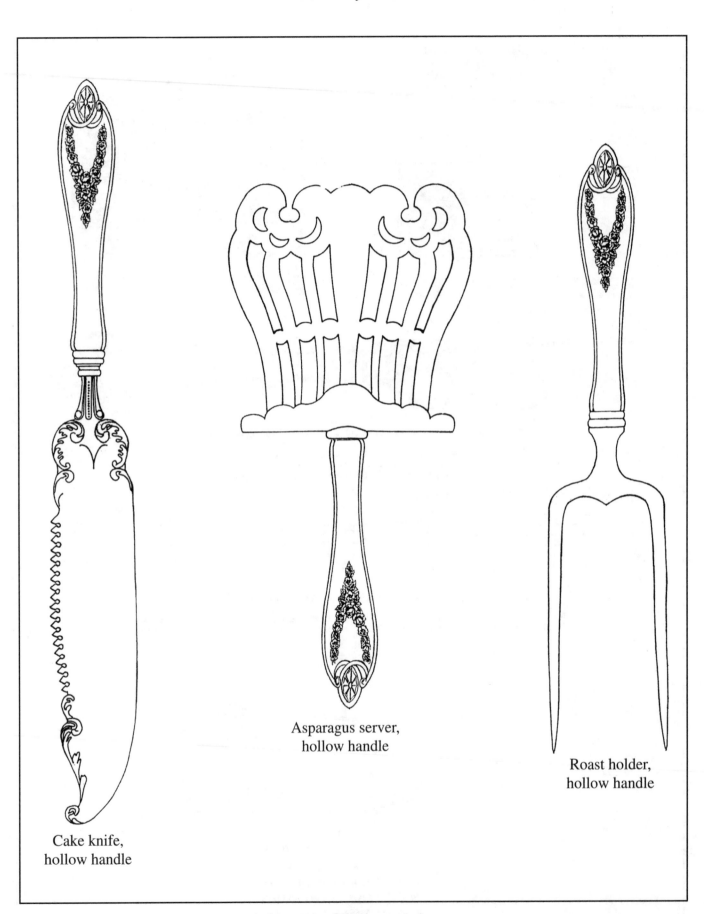

Cake knife,
hollow handle

Asparagus server,
hollow handle

Roast holder,
hollow handle

Items not shown actual size

Old Colony Pattern

Asparagus tongs,
hollow handle

Asparagus fork,
hollow handle

Pie knife,
hollow handle

Items not shown actual size

See Price Guide — Group 1

Old Colony Pattern

Left to right: 9⁷⁄₁₆" solid handle dinner knife, 7¹¹⁄₁₆" solid handle dinner fork, 6⁷⁄₁₆" individual pastry fork.

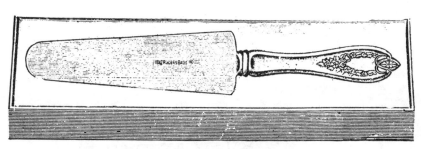

PIE SERVER—HOLLOW HANDLE
Old Colony pattern, gray finish
No. **31756** Silver blade..**$5.40**

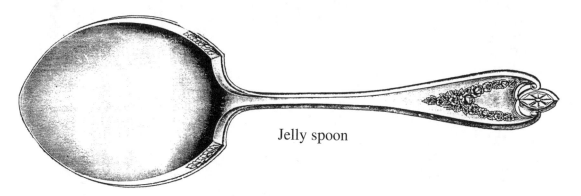

Jelly spoon

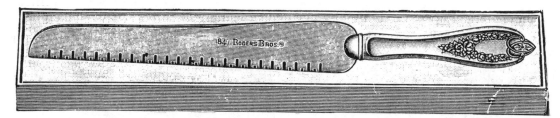

Bread knife, hollow handle

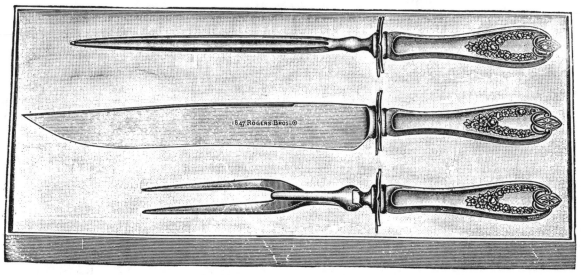

3-piece roast carving set

1913 Catalog

See Price Guide — Group 1

Old Colony Pattern

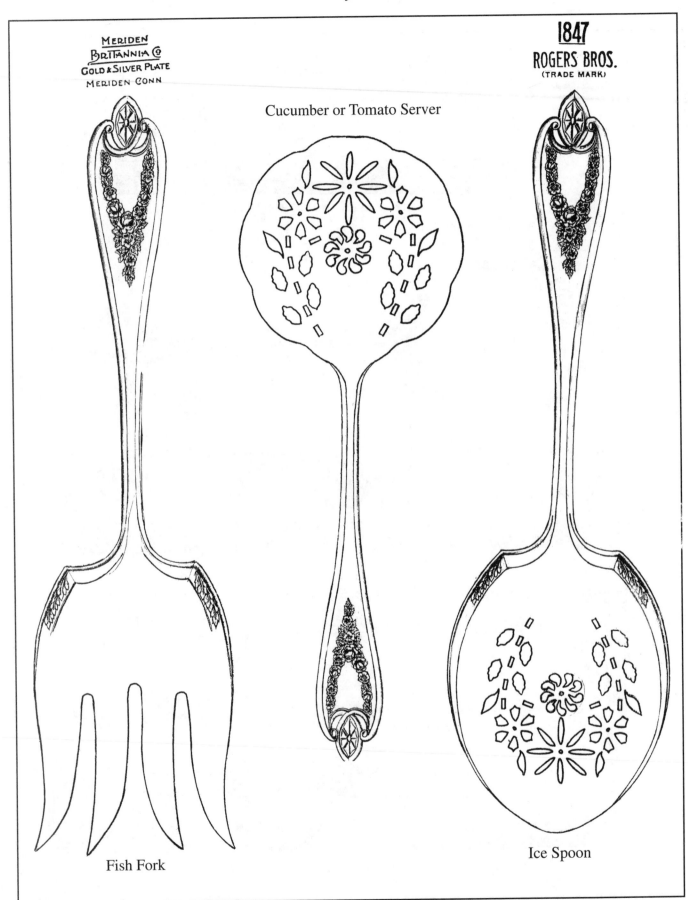

MERIDEN
BRITANNIA CO
GOLD & SILVER PLATE
MERIDEN CONN

Cucumber or Tomato Server

1847
ROGERS BROS.
(TRADE MARK)

Fish Fork

Ice Spoon

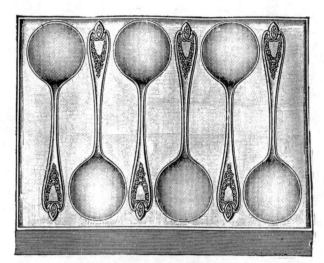

SIX BOUILLON SPOONS
Old Colony pattern, gray finish
No. **31826**   Silver bowls.................per set **$8.10**

Celebrated Silver Plated Flatware

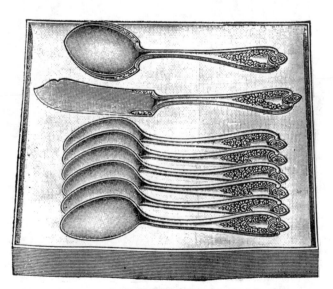

SUGAR SHELL
Old Colony pattern, gray finish

8-PIECE SET
Old Colony pattern, gray finish. Six Tea Spoons, one
Sugar Shell, one Butter Knife.
No. **31827**   Silver bowls and blades. .   . . . .per set **$8.10**

BUTTER KNIFE

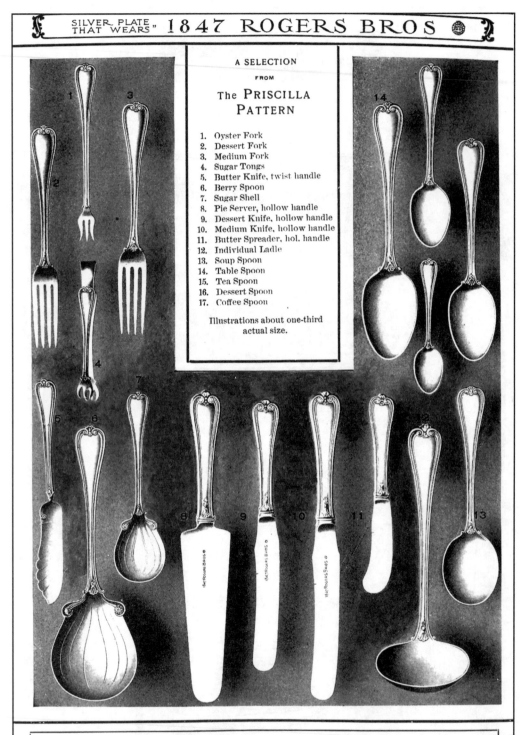

SILVER PLATE THAT WEARS " 1847 ROGERS BROS

A SELECTION

FROM

The PRISCILLA PATTERN

1. Oyster Fork
2. Dessert Fork
3. Medium Fork
4. Sugar Tongs
5. Butter Knife, twist handle
6. Berry Spoon
7. Sugar Shell
8. Pie Server, hollow handle
9. Dessert Knife, hollow handle
10. Medium Knife, hollow handle
11. Butter Spreader, hol. handle
12. Individual Ladle
13. Soup Spoon
14. Table Spoon
15. Tea Spoon
16. Dessert Spoon
17. Coffee Spoon

Illustrations about one-third
actual size.

Our latest pattern, the "Priscilla," was first shown in the early summer, but we have said little about it as we have found it impossible to keep pace with the demand. We illustrate on this page the line as far as completed in order that the dealer may be thoroughly posted regarding our goods. We do not urge orders at this time.

Priscilla was introduced in 1900. It was a pattern far too plain for its time and could not compete with the fancier patterns. For this reason it is seldom seen. Note the knife blades are different than other 1847 Rogers Bros. patterns. The bowls of the sugar shell and berry spoon are especially attractive. This catalog is dated 1905.

REFLECTION—1847 Rogers Bros. Silverplate—
Covered Casserole, Footed
Capacity, 2 qts. Diameter, 12 inches. Removable Pyrex liner
Retail **$45.00**

Dinner Fork, Reflection pattern,
patented 1959

Pie Knife, Romanesque pattern, patented 1898

Reflection Pattern

REFLECTION

PLACE SETTING PIECES

		One Retail
A.	Teaspoons	$1.00
B.	Forks	2.00
C.	Knives	3.25
D.	Salad Forks	2.00
	*Dessert or Oval Soup Spoons†..	2.00
	*Round Bowl Soup Spoons†	2.00
E.	Service Spoons‡	2.00
F.	Spreaders, Butter or Cheese	2.00
G.	A.D. Coffee Spoons	1.00
H.	Cocktail Forks	2.00
I.	Iced Drink Spoons	2.00

SOLD BY LEADING SILVERWARE DEALERS. IF YOUR DEALER CANNOT SUPPLY YOU, ASK HIM TO ORDER OR SEND FOR TRIAL BOTTLE USING COUPON ON REVERSE SIDE.

SERVING PIECES

		Retail Each
J.	Butter Knife	$ 3.00
K.	Sugar Spoon	3.00
L.	Cold Meat or Serving Fork	4.95
M.	Gravy Ladle	4.95
	*Pastry Server, Small §	3.00
N.	Pickle or Lemon Fork	3.00
O.	Pie or Pastry Server, H.H.	6.95
P.	Pierced Relish Spoon	3.00
Q.	Pierced Tablespoon	3.00
	*Punch Ladle, H.H.†	17.50
R.	Salad or Serving Spoon	4.95
S.	Soup Ladle, H.H.°	10.00
T.	Plain Tablespoon	3.00

*item not illustrated
†available Heritage only
‡not available in Heritage

°not available in Leilani or Magic Rose
§available in Heritage and Leilani only
°available in Heritage and Leilani only

RETAIL PRICE LIST FOR ALL PATTERNS

Effective June 1, 1963. Retail prices shown are those quoted to consumers on direct inquiry and subject to change without notice. All goods billed at prices prevailing on date of shipment. There is no Federal Tax on silver-plated flatware.

Reflection Pattern

Tea and Coffee Services

REFLECTION TEA AND COFFEE SERVICE
1847 Rogers Bros Silverplate

Retail

No. 9200/4 4-pieces (coffee pot, tea pot,
sugar bowl cream pitcher) $130.00
No. 9281 Waiter, Chased, Length, 20½
inches 47.50
No. 9201 Coffee Pot, 9 cups. Height,
10¼ inches 42.50

Retail

No. 9202 Tea Pot, 9 cups, Height 8¾
inches $42.50
No. 9203 Sugar Bowl, Covered 22.50
No. 9204 Cream Pitcher, Gold Lined .. 22.50

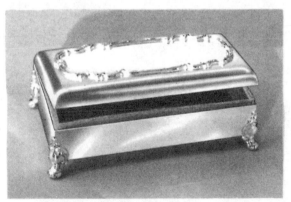

REFLECTION — 1847 Rogers Bros. Silverplate

Retail

No. 9220/F Cigarette Box, footed. Hinged
cover. Cedar lining for king and regular
sizes. Length 6½ inches, width 3½ inches,
height 2 inches $23.00
No. 9222/F Jewelry Box, footed. Same as
above except with velvet lining $23.00

REFLECTION—1847 Rogers Bros. Silverplate

No. 9243 All Purpose Dish with Base, Length,
14½ inches, Width, 10½ inches ...... Retail $30.00

1963 Catalog

See Price Guide — Group 2

REFLECTION
1847 Rogers Bros. Silverplate

No. 9217   Footed, Ice guard, Retail
Capacity, 2 qts. **$40.00**

REFLECTION
1847 Rogers Bros. Silverplate

No. 9239   Instant Coffee Jar   Retail
and Spoon Set. Clear glass jar
with silverplated cover and matching spoon .... **$ 5.00**

REFLECTION — 1847 Rogers Bros. Silverplate
Retail

No. 9250   Wine Cooler. Height 10⅞ inches,
Diameter at top, 10½ inches. Aluminum
liner for flowers included **$80.00**

REFLECTION - 1847 Rogers Bros. Silverplate - Oval Waiter, Chased
Retail

No. 9280 Length, 17 inches, Overall length, 21 inches... **$37.50**
No. 9281 Length, 20 inches, Overall length, 24 inches...   **50.00**

REFLECTION — 1847 Rogers Bros. Silverplate
Retail

No. 9295   Shell Dish, Length, 10 inches ...   **$20.00**

Reflection Pattern

.1847 ROGERS BROS.
SILVERPLATE

REFLECTION — 1847 Rogers Bros. Silverplate
Center Bowl, Footed

		Retail
No. 9214	Diameter, 12 inches	$32.50

REFLECTION — 1847 Rogers Bros. Silverplate

No. 9215	Candlestick, Height, 9⅛ inches	Retail
	pair	$37.50
No. 9216	Candelabrum, Height, 12 inches	
	Spread, 12½ inches .... each	45.00

REFLECTION — 1847 Rogers Bros. Silverplate

		Retail
No. 9212	Length, 12½ inches	$37.50

REFLECTION
1847 Rogers Bros. Silverplate
No. 9264   Height, 3½ inches,   Retail
glass lined ....pair $11.00

Reflection

Remembrance was the pattern chosen to celebrate one hundred years of the 1847 Rogers Bros. line of silverplate. It was introduced with much fanfare and heavy advertising. Soldiers had returned from WWII and hundreds of thousands were getting married. These newlyweds would need a set of silverplate and International was determined to be the firm that sold them their first set. A set was boxed in either eight or twelve place settings. The soups in the set were usually long bowl and the standard serving pieces were the butter knife and the sugar spoon.

A tremendous amount of Remembrance was manufactured in the late 1940s and early 1950s, so this pattern is easy to find. There are a few items that were not made in quantity, and there are various reasons for this. Some items proved too costly for young married couples: others just didn't have marketing appeal. These are usually pieces that a bride decided she would never use. Why purchase a punch ladle when the couple had no punch bowl? Not many homes had soup tureens, so the soup ladle in Remembrance and other patterns of this time period were not produced in quantity.

Any 1847 Rogers Bros. napkin ring is rare and the Remembrance one is no exception. The one photographed was found in a Houston convent. The family of the sister had given her a place setting plus the napkin ring on the occasion of her final vows. The dining hall tables in this convent were always kept set and ready for the next meal. Each sister had her own napkin ring and dinner fork that were engraved with her religious name.

The olive or cherry wood salad set, tongs, and pierced berry/salad serving spoon are not easy to find. Beverage and citrus spoons are common. Many of the hollow ware pieces were expensive: some exceeded the price of a flatware set. Hollow ware pieces that are seen the most in Remembrance are bread tray, covered vegetable dish, chased buffet tray, 16½" oval tray, and water pitcher. Scarce hollow ware includes the partitioned dinner dish with proper covers, punch bowl, candelabrum, gravy set, and the small creamer/sugar set. It is uncertain whether the coffee urn, soup tureen, ice bowl, and food warmer were ever made in Remembrance (see the Heritage pattern for illustration of these pieces).

The pieces photographed are from the collection of Fred and Frances Bones. The pieces that have been difficult for them to find are the platter spoon, butter cover, punch ladle, and soup ladle.

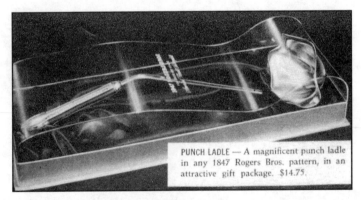

PUNCH LADLE — A magnificent punch ladle in any 1847 Rogers Bros. pattern, in an attractive gift package. $14.75.

All 1847 Rogers Bros. punch ladles were packaged in a covered plastic container.

1847 Rogers Bros. For 101 Years

Remembrance
1847 ROGERS BROS.

WHAT YOU SHOULD KNOW ABOUT 1847 ROGERS BROS.

1. 1847 Rogers Bros. is made by The International Silver Company.
2. 1847 Rogers Bros. is America's Finest Silverplate, having earned its reputation through more than 100 years of American life and progress.
3. 1847 Rogers Bros. is heavily plated with pure silver in accordance with the highest standards of durability and beauty.
4. In addition to the heavy over-all plate mentioned above, we reinforce the points of wear with an extra plating of silver on most used spoons and forks.
5. Only the finest quality nickel silver is used as a base metal.
6. Only the finest grade mirror finished stainless steel is used for forged knife blades.
7. Each pattern is designed for perfect balance.
8. 1847 Rogers Bros. patterns have raised designs not usually found in silverplate.
9. Only the most skilled and experienced craftsmen work on 1847 Rogers Bros. Silverplate.

Remembrance

Clean lined and graceful in the spirit of today. Romantic in the delicate, old-fashioned charm of its tiny flowers and scrolls and fine cut beading.

TWO PIECE EDUCATOR SET in gift box, $1.75 set, retail (*Remembrance* pattern illustrated.)

1948 Catalog

See Price Guide — Group 2

Remembrance Pattern

Left to right: 6¾" individual salad fork, 6½" hollow handle cheese server, 5½" individual cocktail fork, 4½" demi-tasse spoon, 6⅛" individual butter knife. Bottom: 2⁵⁄₁₆" napkin ring stamped "Remembrance," 1847 Rogers Bros. Silver soldered E. P. N. S., very rare.

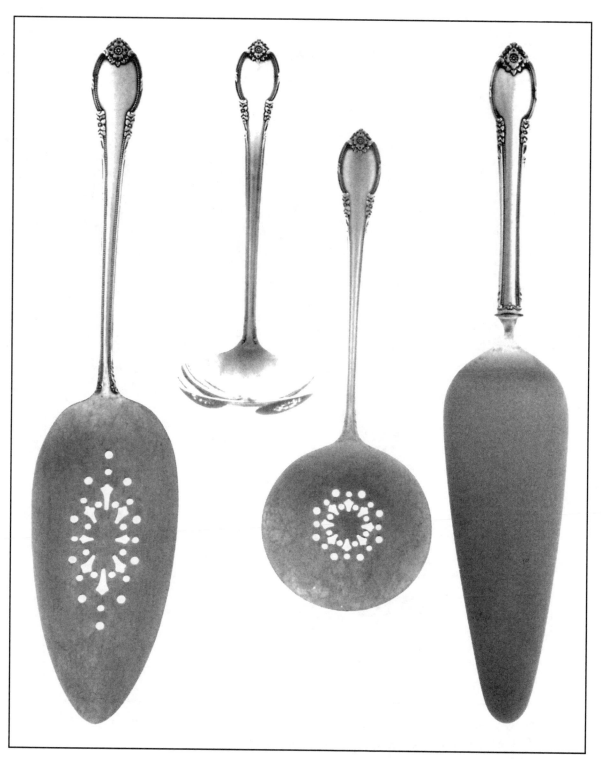

Left to right: 10⅝" pierced long server (pies, cakes), 6" gravy ladle, 7⁹⁄₁₆" round server (tomatoes, cucumbers), 10⅝" hollow handle pie knife (pastries).

Remembrance Pattern

Left to right: 8½" hollow handle dinner knife, 7¹³⁄₁₆" iced drink spoon, 4¼" child/baby fork, 6¼" youth fork, 7⁸⁄₁₆" dinner fork.

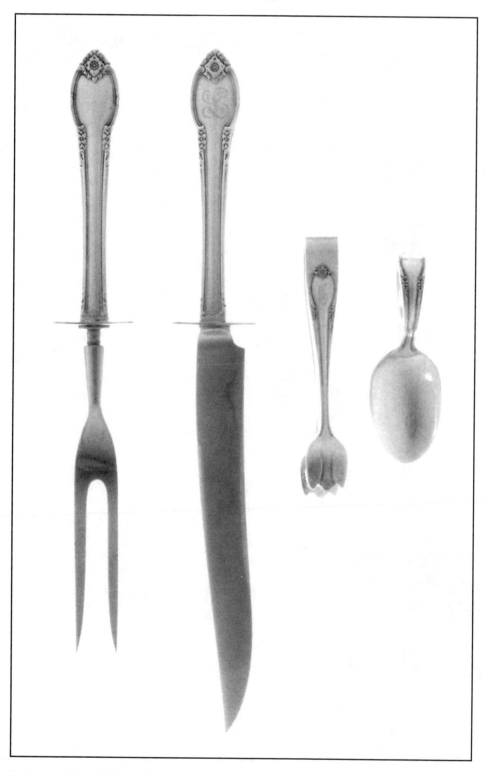

Left to right: 9⅜" hollow handle carving fork, 10⅝" hollow handle carving knife, 4⅛" sugar tongs, 3⁵⁄₁₆" bent handle baby spoon.

See Price Guide — Group 2

Remembrance Pattern

Left to right: 9" pierced berry spoon, 9" berry/salad spoon, 8½" pierced serving spoon, 8⅞" cold meat fork.

Remembrance Pattern

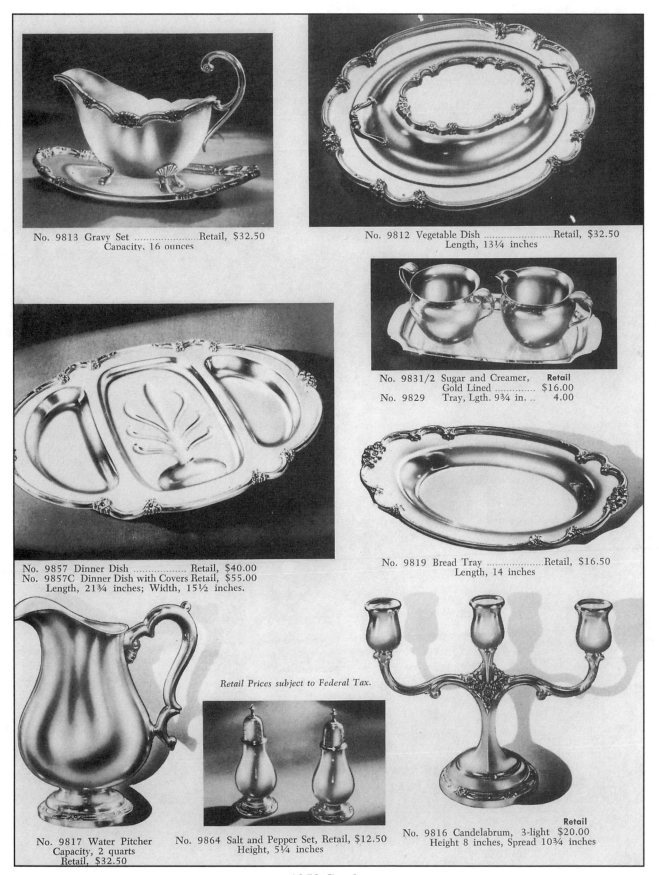

No. 9813 Gravy Set .... Retail, $32.50
Capacity, 16 ounces

No. 9812 Vegetable Dish .... Retail, $32.50
Length, 13¼ inches

	Retail
No. 9831/2 Sugar and Creamer, Gold Lined	$16.00
No. 9829 Tray, Lgth. 9¾ in. ..	4.00

No. 9857 Dinner Dish .... Retail, $40.00
No. 9857C Dinner Dish with Covers Retail, $55.00
Length, 21¾ inches; Width, 15½ inches.

No. 9819 Bread Tray .... Retail, $16.50
Length, 14 inches

Retail Prices subject to Federal Tax.

No. 9817 Water Pitcher
Capacity, 2 quarts
Retail, $32.50

No. 9864 Salt and Pepper Set, Retail, $12.50
Height, 5¼ inches

No. 9816 Candelabrum, 3-light **Retail** $20.00
Height 8 inches, Spread 10¾ inches

1958 Catalog

See Price Guide — Group 2

Remembrance Pattern

	Retail		Retail
No. 9800/5 *Remembrance* Tea and Coffee Service, 5 pcs. $125.00		No. 9800/3 Coffee Service, 3 pcs. $75.00	
(Coffee Pot, Tea Pot, Sugar Bowl, Cream Pitcher, Waste Bowl)		(Coffee Pot, Sugar Bowl, Cream Pitcher)	
No. 9892 Waiter, Chased, Length 23½ inches 60.00		No. 9890 Waiter, 20 inches 42.50	

No. 9801 Coffee Pot, 10 Cups $40.00
          Height, 11 inches
No. 9802 Tea Pot, 9 Cups 40.00
          Height, 9¼ inches

No. 9803 Sugar Bowl, Covered $19.00
No. 9804 Cream Pitcher, Gold Lined 16.00
No. 9805 Waste Bowl, Gold Lined 10.00

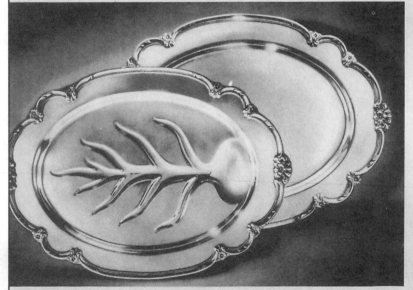

No. 9810 Well and Tree Platter ....Retail, $32.50
          Length, 19 inches
No. 9809 Meat Dish ....Retail, $27.50
          Length, 19 inches

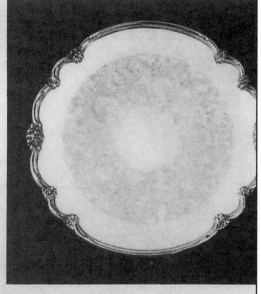

No. 9826 Buffet Tray, Chased ......Retail, $25.00
          Diameter, 14 inches

1958 Catalog

Remembrance Pattern — Etching

No. 5115
10 oz. Goblet
Height 7¼"

No. 5115
12 oz. Ftd. Ice Tea
Height 5¾"

No. 5115
3½ oz. Wine
Height 6"

No. 5115
5 oz. Saucer Champagne
Height 5½"

No. 5115
3 oz. Liquor Cocktail
Height 5¼"

No. 5115
5 oz. Ftd. Orange Juice
Height 4¼"

No. 5115
4 oz. Ftd. Oyster Cocktail
Height 3¼"

No. 5115
1 oz. Cordial
Height 4¼"

This Duncan & Miller etching was designed to match the 1847 Rogers Bros. Remembrance silver pattern.

Sharon Pattern

The Sharon pattern was introduced in 1910. It had to compete with Charter Oak and Vintage so it was never really popular. Hollow handle knives and salad forks are hard to find, but not impossible. Ice tea spoons should be considered rare. The serving pieces are worthy of collection and can be mixed with almost any silver pattern.

Eight-piece set

Berry spoon

Six oyster forks

Gravy ladle

Sugar shell

1913 Catalog

Sharon Pattern

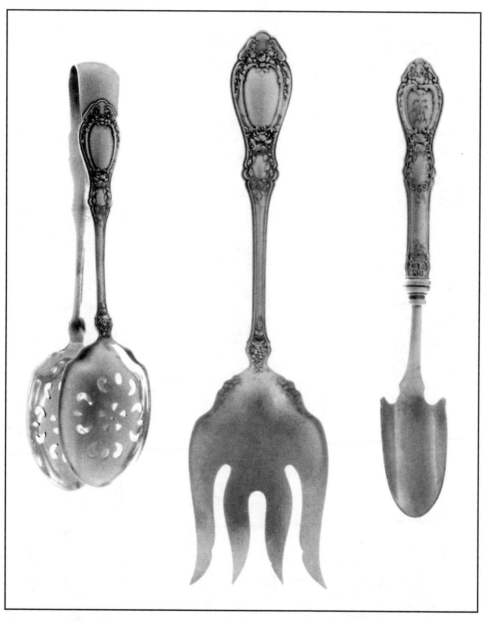

Left to right: 6⁷/₁₀" ice tongs, 8⁷/₁₀" fish serving fork, 7⅕" hollow handle cheese scoop.

See Price Guide — Group 1

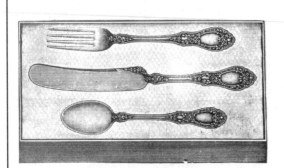

CHILD'S SET

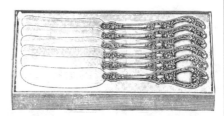

SIX BUTTER SPREADERS

COLD MEAT FORK

BUTTER KNIFE

LONG PICKLE FORK

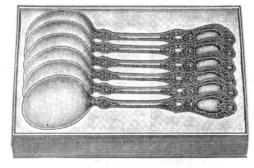

SIX SOUP SPOONS

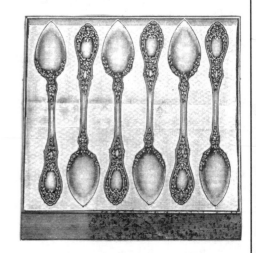

SIX ORANGE SPOONS

1913 Catalog

Shell Pattern

1847 Rogers Bros. Fruit Knives.

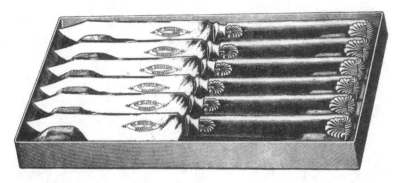

This Offer consists of a Set of six **1847** Rogers Bros. Fruit Knives, of solid steel, and heavily silver-plated. We offer the popular Shell pattern. They are handsomely burnished, strong and durable, and enclosed in a satin-lined case. The Set is a necessity in every household.

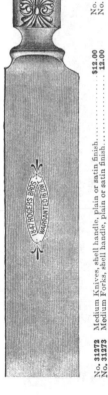

Dessert Knives, shell handle, plain or satin finish.........$11.67
Dessert Forks, shell handle, plain or satin finish......... 11.67

No. 31274
No. 31275

$12.00
12.00

Medium Knives, shell handle, plain or satin finish.........
Medium Forks, shell handle, plain or satin finish.........

No. 31272
No. 31273

1847 Rogers Bros. Housekeepers' Outfit.

We offer a choice of the popular Shell, Berkshire, Windsor or Vesta patterns. The Outfit consists of 12 Teaspoons, 6 Dessert Spoons, 3 Table Spoons, 6 Medium Knives, 6 Medium Forks, 1 Sugar Shell, 1 Butter Knife, 1 Salt Shaker, 1 Pepper Shaker.

Given for three new subscriptions and **$5.25 extra. Price $10.**
Sent by express, charges paid by receiver. Shipping weight 7 lbs.

1847 Rogers Bros. Nut Pick Set.

There are but few Offers in our List which possess the value of this beautiful Set. The six Nut Picks are nickel silver and the Nut Crack is of solid steel, all heavily silver-plated. The Set is finished in a first-class manner, and enclosed in a satin-lined Case.

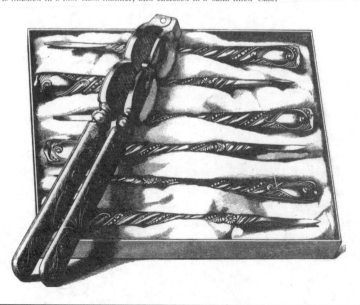

Introduced in 1860

See Price Guide — Group 1

1930 Catalog. Silhouette was created by International staff designer Leslie A. Brown.

1847 ROGERS BROS.
ORIGINAL AND GENUINE ROGERS SILVERPLATE

AN INTERNATION SILVER CO PRODUCT

NEW VIANDE PIECES
(Trade Mark)

Now the Viande Knife and Fork, Dinner Size, are joined by four other new and practical Viande pieces in the Silhouette pattern.

Their short tines and blades and long handles immediately mark them as modern as a Paris gown, fit to compete in smartness with everything else on the table—gay china, colored linens and tinted glassware. Modern women demand this modern silverware

Illustrated actual size are, left to right:

Viande Knife and Fork, Dinner Size; Viande Butter Spreader; Viande Salad Fork, Viande Fork, Luncheon Size; Viande Luncheon or Salad Knife

Silhouette		Set of Six Retail	List	Silhouette		Set of Six Retail	List
89407v	VIANDE Knives, Mirror Stainless Blades, Dinner Size	$15.00	$19.56	89114v	VIANDE Salad Forks	$7.50	$9.18
8907v	VIANDE Forks, Dinner Size	8.25	10.12	8908v	VIANDE Forks, Luncheon Size . . .	8.25	10.12
89209v	VIANDE Butter Spreaders	6.25	7.68	89408v	VIANDE Knives, Mirror Stainless Blades, Luncheon or Salad	15.00	19.56

30/9

See Price Guide — Group 2

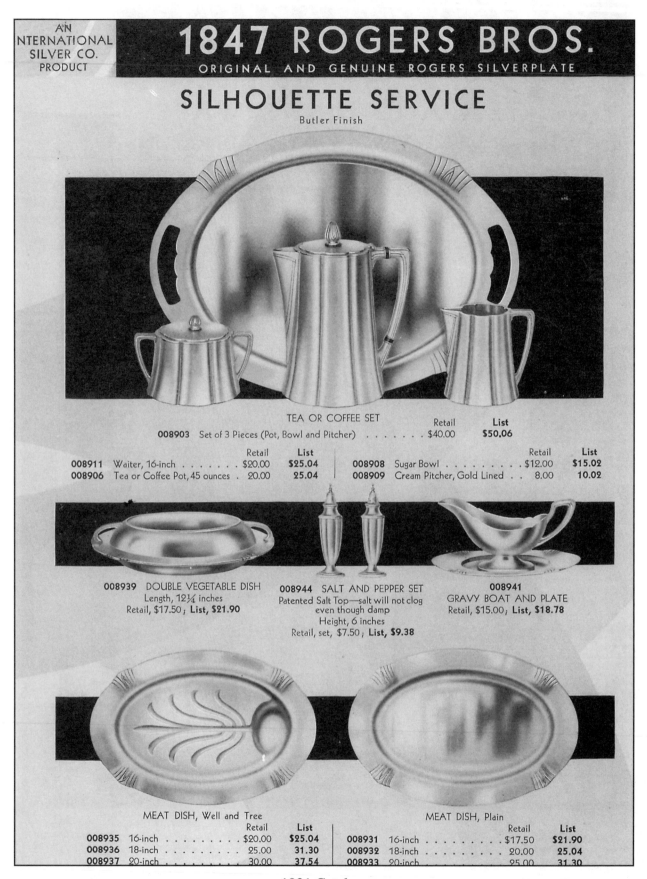

AN INTERNATIONAL SILVER CO. PRODUCT

1847 ROGERS BROS.
ORIGINAL AND GENUINE ROGERS SILVERPLATE

SILHOUETTE SERVICE
Butler Finish

TEA OR COFFEE SET

		Retail	List
008903	Set of 3 Pieces (Pot, Bowl and Pitcher)	$40.00	$50.06

		Retail	List				Retail	List
008911	Waiter, 16-inch	$20.00	$25.04		008908	Sugar Bowl	$12.00	$15.02
008906	Tea or Coffee Pot, 45 ounces	20.00	25.04		008909	Cream Pitcher, Gold Lined	8.00	10.02

008939 DOUBLE VEGETABLE DISH
Length, 12¼ inches
Retail, $17.50; List, $21.90

008944 SALT AND PEPPER SET
Patented Salt Top—salt will not clog
even though damp
Height, 6 inches
Retail, set, $7.50; List, $9.38

008941
GRAVY BOAT AND PLATE
Retail, $15.00; List, $18.78

MEAT DISH, Well and Tree		Retail	List		MEAT DISH, Plain		Retail	List
008935	16-inch	$20.00	$25.04		008931	16-inch	$17.50	$21.90
008936	18-inch	25.00	31.30		008932	18-inch	20.00	25.04
008937	20-inch	30.00	37.54		008933	20-inch	25.00	31.30

1931 Catalog

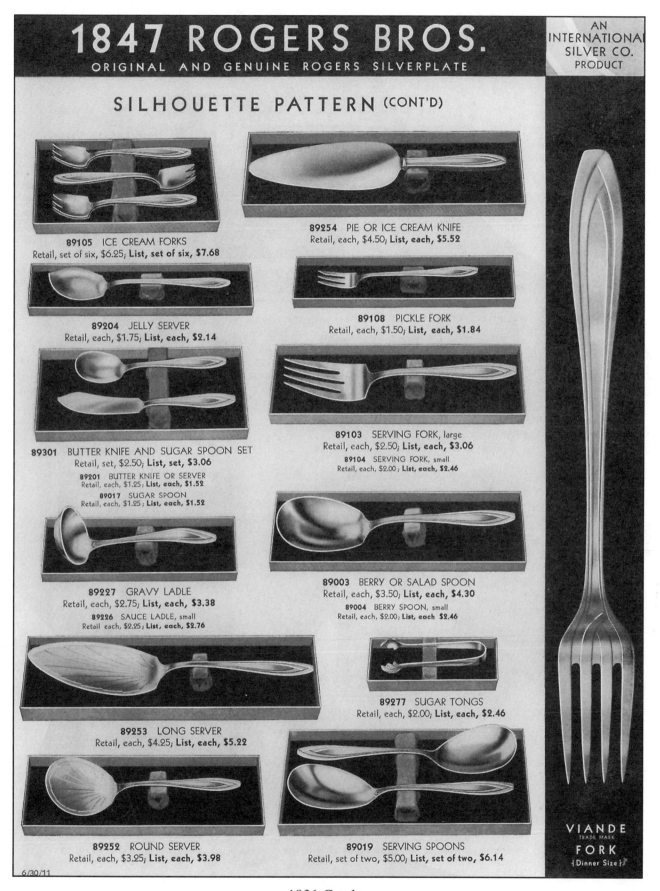

1847 ROGERS BROS.
ORIGINAL AND GENUINE ROGERS SILVERPLATE

AN INTERNATIONAL SILVER CO. PRODUCT

SILHOUETTE PATTERN (CONT'D)

89105   ICE CREAM FORKS
Retail, set of six, $6.25; List, set of six, $7.68

89254   PIE OR ICE CREAM KNIFE
Retail, each, $4.50; List, each, $5.52

89204   JELLY SERVER
Retail, each, $1.75; List, each, $2.14

89108   PICKLE FORK
Retail, each, $1.50; List, each, $1.84

89301   BUTTER KNIFE AND SUGAR SPOON SET
Retail, set, $2.50; List, set, $3.06
89201   BUTTER KNIFE OR SERVER
Retail, each, $1.25; List, each, $1.52
89017   SUGAR SPOON
Retail, each, $1.25; List, each, $1.52

89103   SERVING FORK, large
Retail, each, $2.50; List, each, $3.06
89104   SERVING FORK, small
Retail, each, $2.00; List, each, $2.46

89227   GRAVY LADLE
Retail, each, $2.75; List, each, $3.38
89226   SAUCE LADLE, small
Retail each, $2.25; List, each, $2.76

89003   BERRY OR SALAD SPOON
Retail, each, $3.50; List, each, $4.30
89004   BERRY SPOON, small
Retail, each, $2.00; List, each $2.46

89277   SUGAR TONGS
Retail, each, $2.00; List, each, $2.46

89253   LONG SERVER
Retail, each, $4.25; List, each, $5.22

89252   ROUND SERVER
Retail, each, $3.25; List, each, $3.98

89019   SERVING SPOONS
Retail, set of two, $5.00; List, set of two, $6.14

VIANDE
TRADE MARK
FORK
(Dinner Size)

6/30/11

1931 Catalog

See Price Guide — Group 2

SILHOUETTE SERVICE (CONT'D)

008969 CASSEROLE, Round
Pyrex Lining, with Engraved Cover
Capacity, 3 pints
Retail, $10.00; **List, $12.52**

008961 BON BON
Width, 7 inches
Retail, $6.00
List, $7.50

008943 WATER PITCHER
Capacity, 4½ pints
Retail, $17.50; **List, $21.90**

008957 CANDLESTICK
Height, 3¾ inches
Retail, pair, $12.50; **List, $15.64**

008950 CENTERPIECE
With Silver Plated Double Mesh
Flower Holder
Diameter, 12½ inches
Retail, $25.00; **List, $31.30**

008957 CANDLESTICK
Height, 3¾ inches
Retail, pair, $12.50; **List, $15.64**

Silhouette Flatware
to match, is shown in
the Flatware Section

008968 RELISH DISH OR CHOP PLATE
Five Compartments. Removable Glass Lining
Retail, $15.00; **List, $18.78**

008960 COMPOTIER
Height, 6⅜ inches
Retail, $7.50; **List, $9.38**

008924 BREAD TRAY
Length, 13¾ inches
Retail, $7.50; **List, $9.38**

008927 SANDWICH TRAY
Length, 13¼ inches
Retail, $7.50; **List, $9.38**

008947 BREAD AND BUTTER PLATE
Diameter, 6¾ inches
Retail, set of six, $24.00; **List, $30.04**

008946 SERVICE PLATE
Diameter, 11 inches
Retail, set of six, $48.00; **List, $60.08**

1931 Catalog

Silver Renaissance Pattern

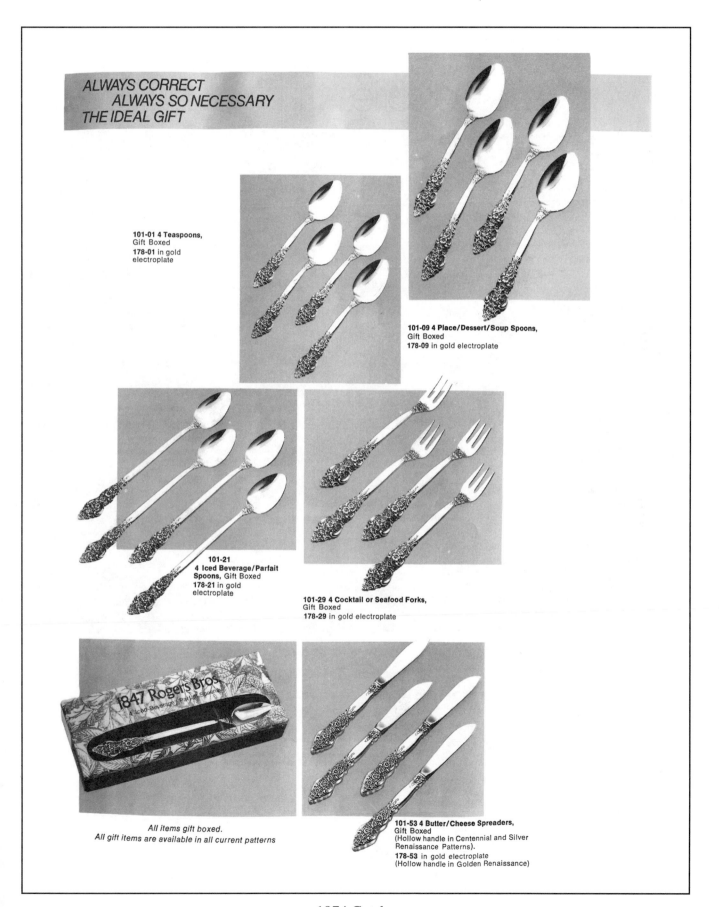

ALWAYS CORRECT
ALWAYS SO NECESSARY
THE IDEAL GIFT

101-01 4 Teaspoons,
Gift Boxed
178-01 in gold
electroplate

101-09 4 Place/Dessert/Soup Spoons,
Gift Boxed
178-09 in gold electroplate

101-21
4 Iced Beverage/Parfait
Spoons, Gift Boxed
178-21 in gold
electroplate

101-29 4 Cocktail or Seafood Forks,
Gift Boxed
178-29 in gold electroplate

All items gift boxed.
All gift items are available in all current patterns

101-53 4 Butter/Cheese Spreaders,
Gift Boxed
(Hollow handle in Centennial and Silver
Renaissance Patterns).
178-53 in gold electroplate
(Hollow handle in Golden Renaissance)

1974 Catalog

277

See Price Guide — Group 2

REFRESHING BEAUTY IN SILVERPLATE

Springtime

A design of modern simplicity, *Springtime* repeats the delicate beauty and "hand-cut" look of its matching flatware. A dainty floral motif is wrought deep into smooth contours to give each piece a touch of feminine grace for brilliant adaptability with traditional or sophisticated modern decor.

		Retail
No. 9300/4	*Springtime* Tea and Coffee Service, 4 pieces	$100.00
(*Coffee Pot, Tea Pot, Sugar Bowl, Cream Pitcher*)		
No. 9390	Waiter, 18 in. (overall length, 22½ in.)	30.00
No. 9301	Coffee Pot, 10 Cups, Height 11 in.	35.00
No. 9302	Tea Pot, 10 Cups, Hgt. 8 in.	30.00
No. 9303	Sugar Bowl, Hinged Cover	20.00
No. 9304	Cream Pitcher, Gold Lined	15.00

Retail Prices subject to Federal Tax

1967 Catalog

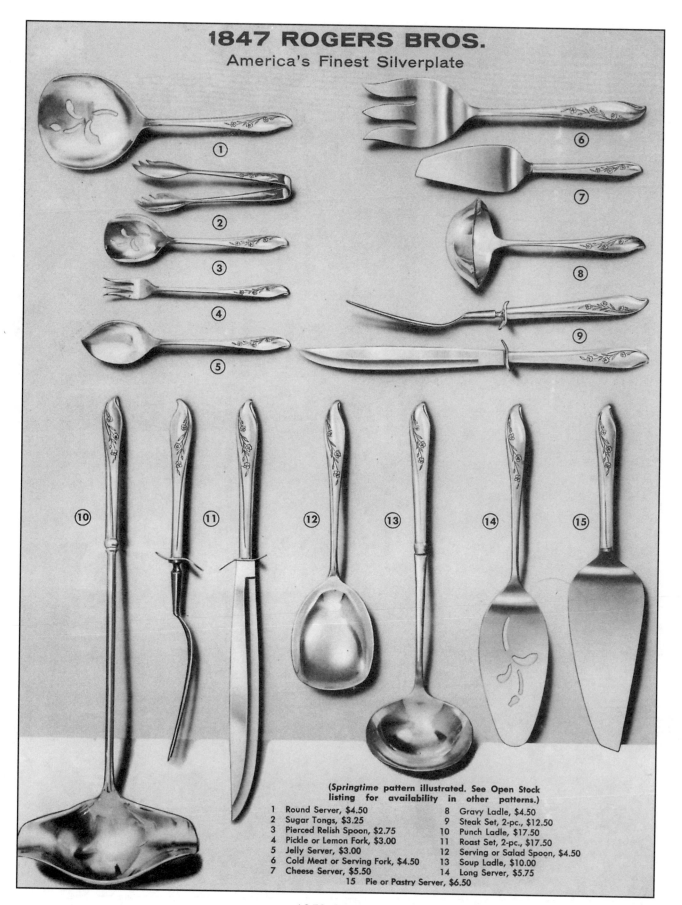

1847 ROGERS BROS.
America's Finest Silverplate

(*Springtime* pattern illustrated. See Open Stock listing for availability in other patterns.)

1	Round Server, $4.50	8	Gravy Ladle, $4.50
2	Sugar Tongs, $3.25	9	Steak Set, 2-pc., $12.50
3	Pierced Relish Spoon, $2.75	10	Punch Ladle, $17.50
4	Pickle or Lemon Fork, $3.00	11	Roast Set, 2-pc., $17.50
5	Jelly Server, $3.00	12	Serving or Salad Spoon, $4.50
6	Cold Meat or Serving Fork, $4.50	13	Soup Ladle, $10.00
7	Cheese Server, $5.50	14	Long Server, $5.75
	15 Pie or Pastry Server, $6.50		

1958 Catalog

See Price Guide — Group 2

No. 9313 Sauce Set .... Retail, $20.00
Cap. 16 ounces

No. 9300/3 Coffee Service, 3 pieces .... Retail, $70.00
(Coffee Pot, Sugar Bowl, Cream Pitcher)

No. 9372   Round Tray .... Retail, $15.00
Diameter, 14 inches

No. 9312 Double Vegetable Dish ......Retail, $22.50
Diam. 10½ inches

No. 9319 Bread Tray .... Retail, $10.00
Length 12½ inches

No. 9326   Buffet Tray .... Retail, $15.00
Diameter 14 inches

1967 Catalog

Springtime Pattern

No. 9317 Beverage Pitcher ....Retail, $30.00
Cap. 1½ quarts

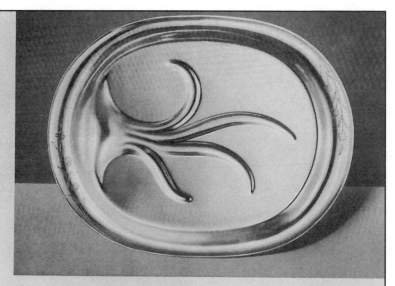

No. 9310 Well and Tree Platter ....Retail, $27.50
Length 18 inches

No. 9335 Bowl ....Retail, $10.00
Diam. 10½ inches

No. 9309 Meat Dish ....Retail, $20.00
Length 18 inches

No. 9348 Bon Bon ....Retail, $5.00
Diam. 6½ inches

No. 9364 Salt & Pepper Set
Hgt. 3½ in., Glass Lining
Retail, $7.50

No. 9387 Butter Dish Retail, $9.00
Lgth. 7½ in., China Lining

Retail Prices subject to Federal Tax

1967 Catalog

See Price Guide — Group 2

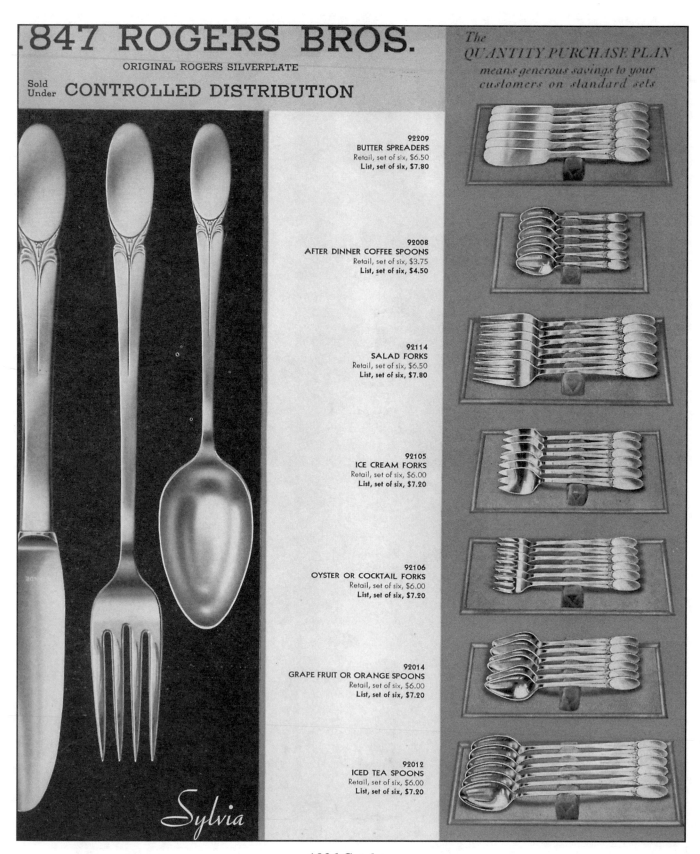

1847 ROGERS BROS.

ORIGINAL ROGERS SILVERPLATE

Sold Under **CONTROLLED DISTRIBUTION**

Sylvia

The **QUANTITY PURCHASE PLAN**
means generous savings to your customers on standard sets

92209
BUTTER SPREADERS
Retail, set of six, $6.50
List, set of six, $7.80

92008
AFTER DINNER COFFEE SPOONS
Retail, set of six, $3.75
List, set of six, $4.50

92114
SALAD FORKS
Retail, set of six, $6.50
List, set of six, $7.80

92105
ICE CREAM FORKS
Retail, set of six, $6.00
List, set of six, $7.20

92106
OYSTER OR COCKTAIL FORKS
Retail, set of six, $6.00
List, set of six, $7.20

92014
GRAPE FRUIT OR ORANGE SPOONS
Retail, set of six, $6.00
List, set of six, $7.20

92012
ICED TEA SPOONS
Retail, set of six, $6.00
List, set of six, $7.20

1936 Catalog

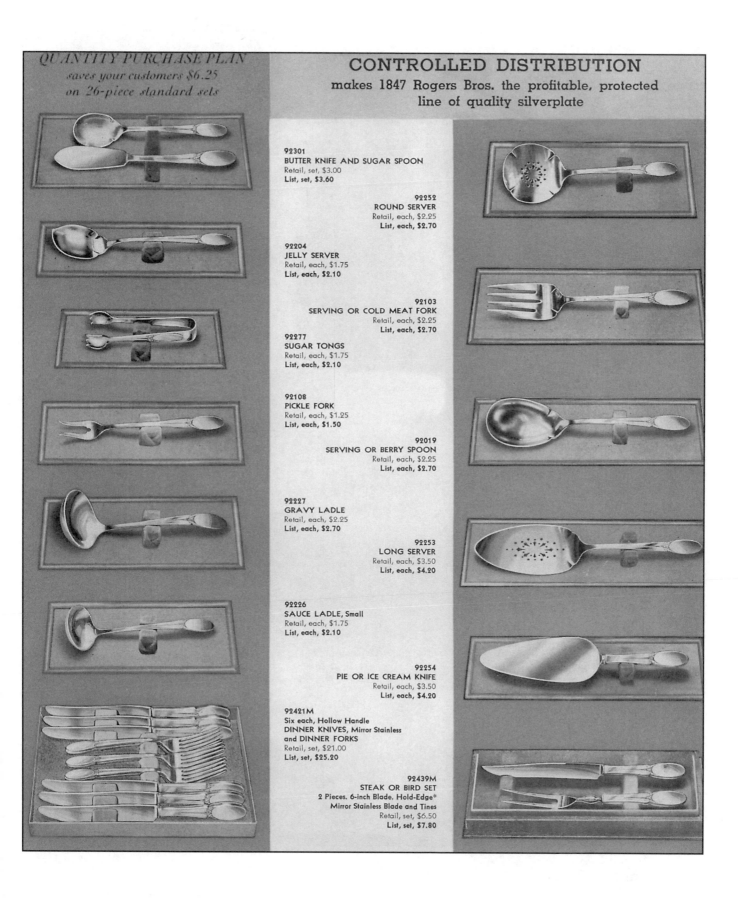

QUANTITY PURCHASE PLAN
saves your customers $6.25
on 26-piece standard sets

CONTROLLED DISTRIBUTION
makes 1847 Rogers Bros. the profitable, protected line of quality silverplate

92301
BUTTER KNIFE AND SUGAR SPOON
Retail, set, $3.00
List, set, $3.60

92252
ROUND SERVER
Retail, each, $2.25
List, each, $2.70

92204
JELLY SERVER
Retail, each, $1.75
List, each, $2.10

92103
SERVING OR COLD MEAT FORK
Retail, each, $2.25
List, each, $2.70

92277
SUGAR TONGS
Retail, each, $1.75
List, each, $2.10

92108
PICKLE FORK
Retail, each, $1.25
List, each, $1.50

92019
SERVING OR BERRY SPOON
Retail, each, $2.25
List, each, $2.70

92227
GRAVY LADLE
Retail, each, $2.25
List, each, $2.70

92253
LONG SERVER
Retail, each, $3.50
List, each, $4.20

92226
SAUCE LADLE, Small
Retail, each, $1.75
List, each, $2.10

92254
PIE OR ICE CREAM KNIFE
Retail, each, $3.50
List, each, $4.20

92421M
Six each, Hollow Handle
DINNER KNIVES, Mirror Stainless
and DINNER FORKS
Retail, set, $21.00
List, set, $25.20

92439M
STEAK OR BIRD SET
2 Pieces. 6-inch Blade. Hold-Edge*
Mirror Stainless Blade and Tines
Retail, set, $6.50
List, set, $7.80

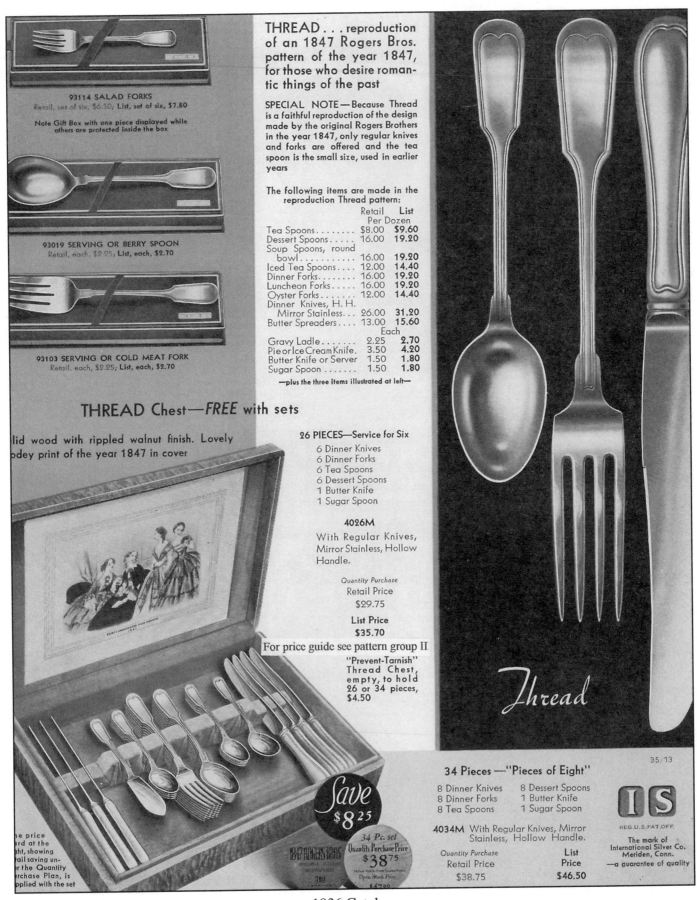

93114 SALAD FORKS
Retail, set of six, $6.50; List, set of six, $7.80

Note Gift Box with one piece displayed while others are protected inside the box

93019 SERVING OR BERRY SPOON
Retail, each, $2.25; List, each, $2.70

93103 SERVING OR COLD MEAT FORK
Retail, each, $2.25; List, each, $2.70

THREAD Chest—*FREE* with sets

lid wood with rippled walnut finish. Lovely odey print of the year 1847 in cover

THREAD . . . reproduction of an 1847 Rogers Bros. pattern of the year 1847, for those who desire romantic things of the past

SPECIAL NOTE—Because Thread is a faithful reproduction of the design made by the original Rogers Brothers in the year 1847, only regular knives and forks are offered and the tea spoon is the small size, used in earlier years

The following items are made in the reproduction Thread pattern:

	Retail	List
	Per Dozen	
Tea Spoons	$8.00	$9.60
Dessert Spoons	16.00	19.20
Soup Spoons, round bowl	16.00	19.20
Iced Tea Spoons	12.00	14.40
Dinner Forks	16.00	19.20
Luncheon Forks	16.00	19.20
Oyster Forks	12.00	14.40
Dinner Knives, H. H. Mirror Stainless	26.00	31.20
Butter Spreaders	13.00	15.60
	Each	
Gravy Ladle	2.25	2.70
Pie or Ice Cream Knife	3.50	4.20
Butter Knife or Server	1.50	1.80
Sugar Spoon	1.50	1.80

—plus the three items illustrated at left—

26 PIECES—Service for Six

6 Dinner Knives
6 Dinner Forks
6 Tea Spoons
6 Dessert Spoons
1 Butter Knife
1 Sugar Spoon

4026M

With Regular Knives, Mirror Stainless, Hollow Handle.

Quantity Purchase
Retail Price
$29.75

List Price
$35.70

For price guide see pattern group II

"Prevent-Tarnish" Thread Chest, empty, to hold 26 or 34 pieces, $4.50

Save $8.25

34 Pc. set
Quantity Purchase Price
$38.75

34 Pieces —"Pieces of Eight"

8 Dinner Knives	8 Dessert Spoons
8 Dinner Forks	1 Butter Knife
8 Tea Spoons	1 Sugar Spoon

4034M With Regular Knives, Mirror Stainless, Hollow Handle.

Quantity Purchase Retail Price	List Price
$38.75	$46.50

35/13

IS
REG. U.S. PAT. OFF.

The mark of International Silver Co. Meriden, Conn. —a guarantee of quality

Thread

e price rd at the ght, showing ail saving un- r the Quantity urchase Plan, is pplied with the set

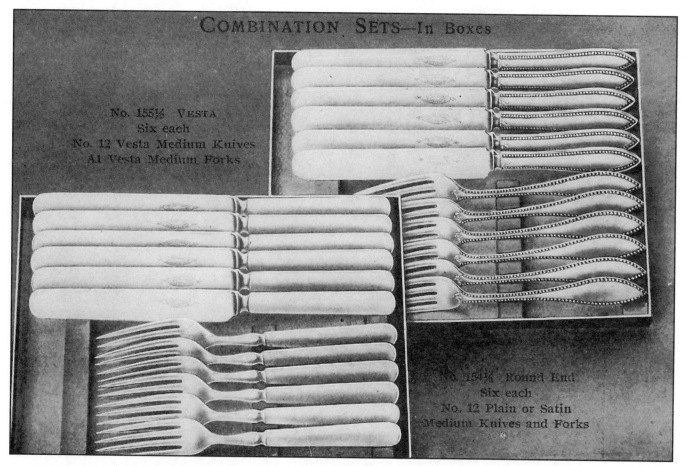

COMBINATION SETS—In Boxes

No. 155½ VESTA
Six each
No. 12 Vesta Medium Knives
A1 Vesta Medium Forks

No. 154½ Round End
Six each
No. 12 Plain or Satin
Medium Knives and Forks

This 1895 introduction is characterized by wonderful little beads that edge all the pieces. We have found that most Vesta collectors started their collections with a few inherited pieces. The dinner knives shown here are solid handle, and were made in one piece. The hollow handle knife is shown with Table Cutlery in the miscellaneous section at the back of the 1847 Rogers Bros. section. This piece is hard to find. The Vesta berry serving spoon is beautiful, and the bowl is decorative. Other Vesta pieces shown in the miscellaneous section are nut crack (rare) with two different fruit knives; sugar shell; and sugar tongs. In addition, under Ladles, items shown are oyster; gravy; cream; frappe (double lip); and oyster. These are dated 1906 – 1907. It is doubtful that much Vesta was produced after 1910.

McClure's Magazine, 1898

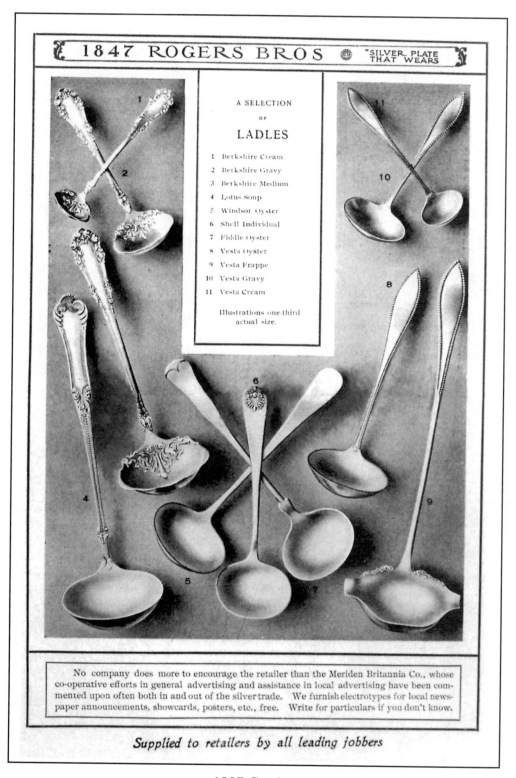

1847 ROGERS BROS ⊕ "SILVER PLATE THAT WEARS"

A SELECTION
OF
LADLES

1 Berkshire Cream
2 Berkshire Gravy
3 Berkshire Medium
4 Lotus Soup
5 Windsor Oyster
6 Shell Individual
7 Fiddle Oyster
8 Vesta Oyster
9 Vesta Frappe
10 Vesta Gravy
11 Vesta Cream

Illustrations one-third
actual size.

No company does more to encourage the retailer than the Meriden Britannia Co., whose co-operative efforts in general advertising and assistance in local advertising have been commented upon often both in and out of the silver trade. We furnish electrotypes for local newspaper announcements, showcards, posters, etc., free. Write for particulars if you don't know.

Supplied to retailers by all leading jobbers

1907 Catalog

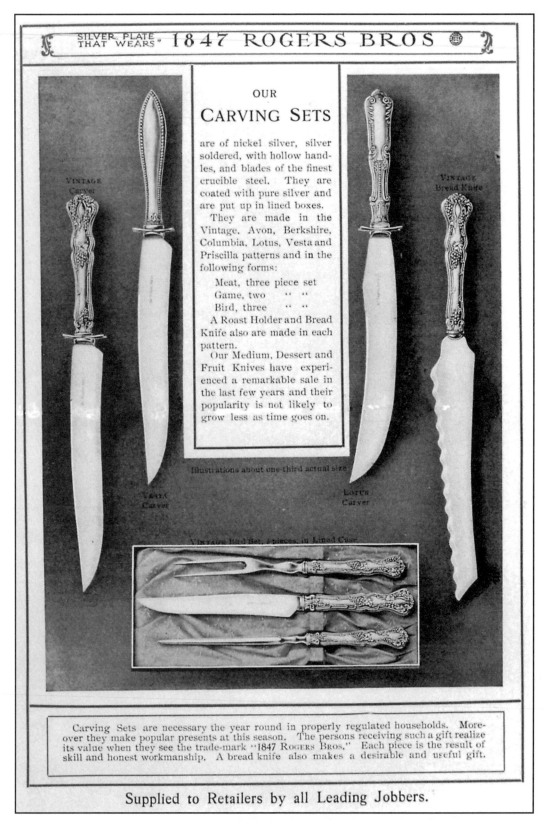

OUR CARVING SETS

are of nickel silver, silver soldered, with hollow handles, and blades of the finest crucible steel. They are coated with pure silver and are put up in lined boxes.

They are made in the Vintage, Avon, Berkshire, Columbia, Lotus, Vesta and Priscilla patterns and in the following forms:

Meat, three piece set
Game, two " "
Bird, three " "

A Roast Holder and Bread Knife also are made in each pattern.

Our Medium, Dessert and Fruit Knives have experienced a remarkable sale in the last few years and their popularity is not likely to grow less as time goes on.

Illustrations about one-third actual size

VINTAGE Carver

VESTA Carver

VINTAGE Bread Knife

LOTUS Carver

VINTAGE Bird Set, 3 pieces, in lined Case

Carving Sets are necessary the year round in properly regulated households. Moreover they make popular presents at this season. The persons receiving such a gift realize its value when they see the trade-mark "1847 ROGERS BROS." Each piece is the result of skill and honest workmanship. A bread knife also makes a desirable and useful gift.

Supplied to Retailers by all Leading Jobbers.

1907 Catalog

Avon, Berkshire, Columbia & Shell Patterns

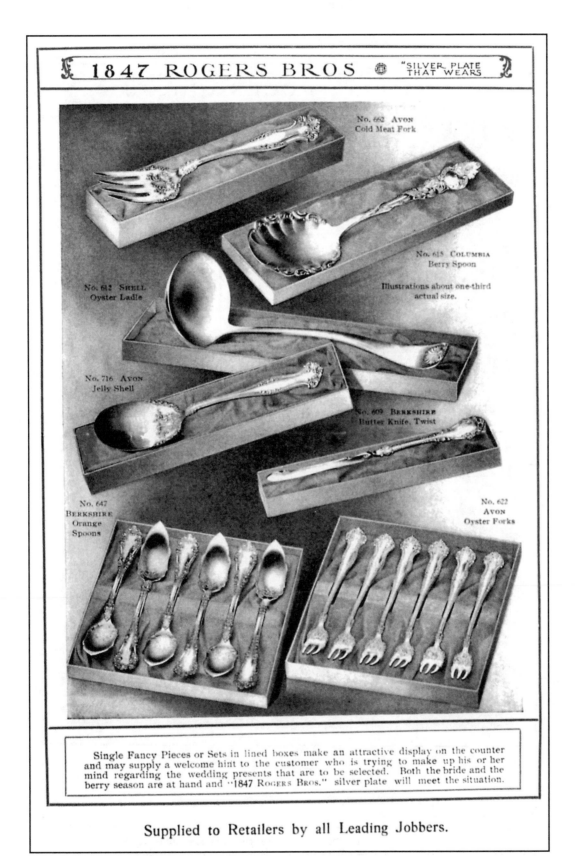

1907 Catalog

See Price Guide — Group 1

Vintage, Columbia, Avon, Berkshire, Lotus,
Shell, Windsor, Vesta & Vintage Patterns

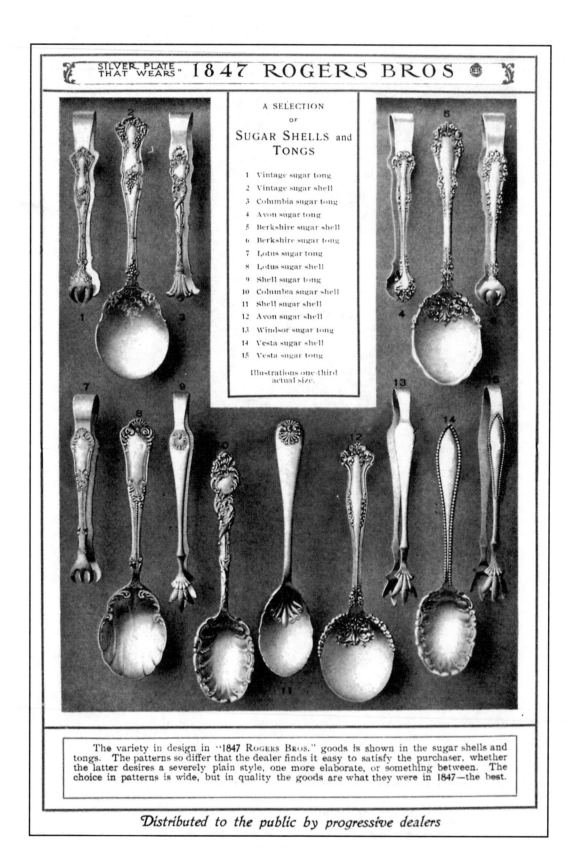

SILVER PLATE THAT WEARS" 1847 ROGERS BROS

A SELECTION
OF
SUGAR SHELLS and
TONGS

1   Vintage sugar tong
2   Vintage sugar shell
3   Columbia sugar tong
4   Avon sugar tong
5   Berkshire sugar shell
6   Berkshire sugar tong
7   Lotus sugar tong
8   Lotus sugar shell
9   Shell sugar tong
10 Columbia sugar shell
11 Shell sugar shell
12 Avon sugar shell
13 Windsor sugar tong
14 Vesta sugar shell
15 Vesta sugar tong

Illustrations one-third
actual size.

The variety in design in "1847 ROGERS BROS." goods is shown in the sugar shells and tongs. The patterns so differ that the dealer finds it easy to satisfy the purchaser, whether the latter desires a severely plain style, one more elaborate, or something between. The choice in patterns is wide, but in quality the goods are what they were in 1847—the best.

Distributed to the public by progressive dealers

1906 Catalog

Vintage Pattern

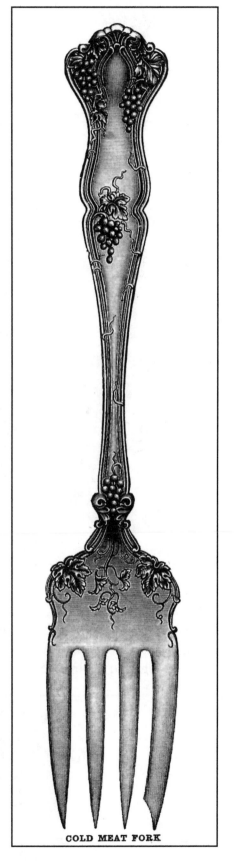

COLD MEAT FORK

Vintage was introduced in 1904 and was an instant success. There is no "Vintage" pattern other than this one from 1847 Rogers Bros. Other grape patterns have been called Vintage but they are not *the* Vintage. This pattern quickly became one of the most popular designs ever offered. The employment of grape clusters, leaves, and tendrils makes a handsome design indeed. Meriden Britannia Company advertised that "the Vintage has been adapted to all pieces usually made in the 1847 Rogers Bros. line." The number of items produced peaked at about 100. Like any large pattern, the number of open stock (catalog listed) pieces varied through the years.

The individual pastry fork, fish knife, and fish forks are very difficult to find. They came in sets of six and we believe that production and demand for the fish pieces were especially limited. The 6³⁄₁₆" pastry fork shown was advertised in 1907 as a fish fork, proving that at times 1847 Rogers Bros. changed item names. We have found very few Vintage collections that sport the fish knives and forks. Hollow handle forks are beautiful but they were more costly than regular dinner forks, so their production in no way equaled the latter. Because hollow handle luncheon forks were less expensive, more were sold and are easier to find today. The 5⅞" individual salad fork (tines turn outward) was possibly produced from 1904 to at least 1913. See our illustration for that year. This fork is slightly different from the one that the late Suzie MacLaclan featured in her 1971 book *The Collector's Handbook for Grape Nuts*. Notice the 1913 salad fork set shown has almost round holes where the tines join the body.

The 9¼" fish serving fork (not illustrated) is the same shape and design as this No. 31804/5 individual salad fork. It is possible that in the early years of Vintage this No. 31804/5 fork was marketed as a fish fork. It is especially difficult to find this piece and its larger counterpart. To complicate matters, the Vintage has another salad fork, 5⅞" to over 6", with basically straight tines of equal size. It was possibly a later addition to the pattern. It has been documented that this item was sold singly boxed as a pickle fork. For this reason there should be more of this type available today.

It is possible that a salad serving fork was made in the same style as the individual one that is 5⅞" to 6". We have not seen documentation of this but many patterns of this period had three different salad serving forks. If this piece exists, we conclude it was of very limited production. The ice cream forks are highly desirable. They are 5⁵⁄₁₆" and were produced at a later date than the 5⁷⁄₁₆" ice cream spoons. The fork is illustrated here. It was No. 31825 in the 1913 catalog. For years Vintage collectors have speculated about what is or is not a salad, pastry, or pickle fork, and dedicated collectors can endlessly discuss, measure, and speculate about this matter. This is the thread that binds collectors together.

See Price Guide — Group 1

Vintage Pattern

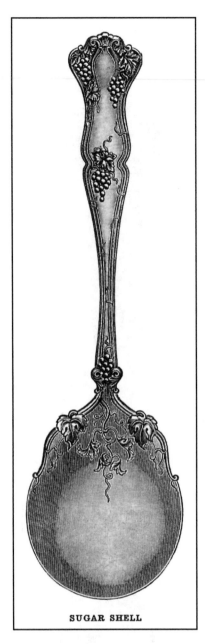

SUGAR SHELL

Any Vintage piece with a stainless blade is a piece that has a replacement. Stainless was not available during the period that Vintage was manufactured. Replacement blades should be blunt end. Any other type is out of period. Many hollow handle knives were discarded when the blades became unsightly; this is why forks are more easily found. Note that our price suggestions are only for knives with blades in very good condition.

Solid handle knives and forks were produced for several years. These pieces were forged in one piece and unfortunately the knife blades cannot be replaced. The price of these solid pieces was about one half of the hollow style. The demand for solids is minimal and current prices reflect this. Some Vintage fruit knives have a swaged blade, unique shape that 1847 Rogers Bros. apparently favored. Do not confuse the hollow handle individual butter spreaders with the knife that was sold in the child/youth set. This piece is 7⁹⁄₁₆", the butter measures 6¼". Vintage also had a solid handle fruit knife which measures 6⅛". The handle is identical in design to the solid handle dinner and dessert knives. Many years ago we owned a boxed set of six. This is another controversial item, and the confusion centers around another grape solid handle fruit knife that is also stamped "1847 Rogers Bros." on the blade. This knife was also boxed in sixes with matching nut picks, but the grape design is not that of Vintage. The end of the handle is pointed and there is a distinct bow knot in this area.

The 8¾" berry serving spoon is very attractive and was made in quantity. The ice spoon is from the same mold but has piercing to let the liquids drain. 1847 Rogers Bros. did indeed market berry spoons as nut spoons (see our 1906 Silver Standard catalog page at the back of this section). The 9" salad serving spoon (not shown) is hard to find. The salad serving spoon has an elongated bowl that has less grape motif than the berry spoon. There is yet another Vintage salad serving spoon which may have been a later introduction. Also with an elongated bowl, this grape motif is more elaborate. Producing three or even four different berry/salad serving spoons would have been in keeping with competitive patterns. Several of the Wm. A. Rogers highly decorative patterns that were in competition with Vintage are known to have four different large salad spoons.

Today it takes real effort to assemble a sizable Vintage collection. Twenty-five or thirty years ago there were large quantities of Vintage available at markets and antiques shows. The early collectors had a wide choice of the common pieces such as teaspoons, long bowl soups, and regular dinner forks. Now collectors are still finding these pieces but many are in less that perfect condition and need restoration. Collectors owe a great deal to Samuel Stohr and the International Silver Co. for designing and marketing this great silver pattern.

Vintage Pattern

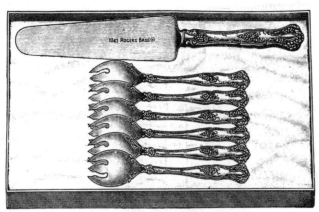

ICE CREAM SET
Vintage pattern, gray finish. Six ice cream forks, one server.
No. **31835** Silver bowls and blade................per set **$13.05**

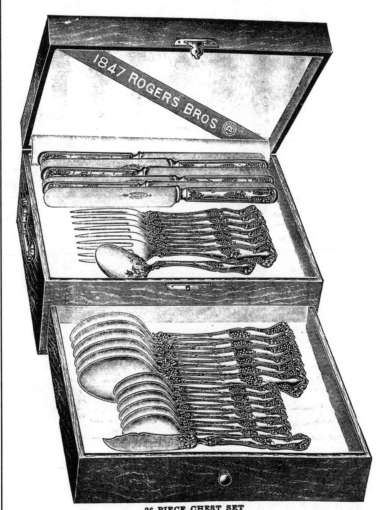

26-PIECE CHEST SET
Vintage pattern, gray finish. Six solid handle medium knives, six XS triple plate
medium forks, six tea spoons, six table spoons, one sugar shell, one butter knife. Put up
in lined oak chest with deck drawer and side handles.
No. **31834** Complete set........ ....**$36.55**

1913 Catalog

See Price Guide — Group 1

Vintage Pattern

Left to right: 8¾" ice spoon, 9¾" solid handle dinner knife, 7⅞" ice tea/beverage spoon, 8¾" berry spoon. Bottom: 5½" 5 o'clock coffee spoon.

Vintage Pattern

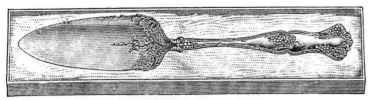

JELLY KNIFE

Vintage pattern, gray finish
No. 31751 Silver blade.........each $2.70
No. 31752 Gold blade.........each   3.60

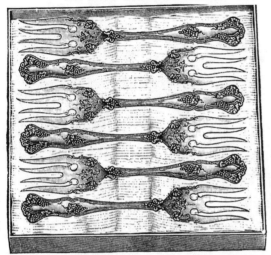

SIX INDIVIDUAL SALAD FORKS

Vintage pattern, gray finish
No. 31804 Silver tines..........per set $ 8.55
No. 31805 Gold tines...........per set   12.15

COMBINATION SET

Vintage pattern, gray finish.   One each Sugar Shell,
Butter Knife and Cream Ladle.
No. 31787 Silver bowls and blade............per set $5.85

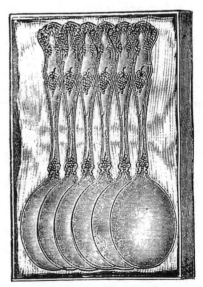

SIX SOUP SPOONS

Vintage pattern, gray finish

No. 31823   Silver bowls

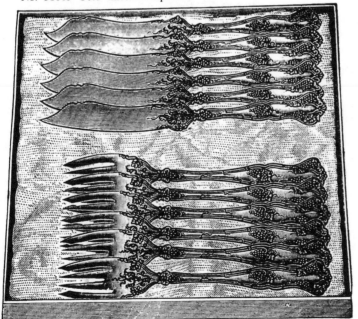

FISH SET

Vintage pattern, gray finish. Six individual fish forks, six
individual fish knives.
No. 31838 Silver blades and tines...........per set $20.70

1913 Catalog

See Price Guide — Group 1

Vintage Pattern

No. 1. This is the medium sized table fork. It is a very graceful shape, heavy and well balanced. Half dozen for $3.00.

No. 2. This is soup or "oyster" ladle. It is plenty big but not too big as to be hard to handle. $2.00.

No. 3. Here is the gravy ladle. It is a duplicate of the soup ladle, on a smaller scale. $1.20.

No. 4. This is the individual butter spreader. It's nice to have one of these by your plate. Half dozen for $2.50.

No. 5. Here's the "medium" table knife. It's a beauty. Half dozen for $4.50.

No. 6. A pie knife, or pie server. Not a piece you will find on every table. $2.00.

No. 7. Cold meat fork. There's no more useful piece of silverware made. $1.00.

No. 8 and 8A. Baby set, food pusher, and spoon. Can you think of a nicer gift? 90¢.

No. 9. Here's the Vintage sugar shell. It's a good size and very pretty. 65¢.

No. 10. Tongs for lump sugar. A dainty little piece of silverware and very desirable and convenient if you use loaf sugar. Regulation size. $1.00.

No. 11. Here's the table spoon. Surely you want at least a pair of these. These are beauties. 75¢.

No. 12. Dessert spoon. Just the right size for cereals as well as for desserts. 65¢.

Nos. 13 – 15. A child's set — knife, fork, and spoon. When the little boy or girl outgrows the baby spoon and pusher, this set is next. $1.50.

No. 16. The teaspoon. Priscilla subscribers all over the country own thousands of them. Half dozen $2.00.

No. 17. A great convenience — a berry spoon. Just as good for desserts in winter as for fruits in summer. $1.50.

No. 18. This is the butter knife, or server. It is the twist style, and exceedingly attractive. 75¢.

1911 Advertisement, *The Modern Priscilla.*

Vintage Pattern

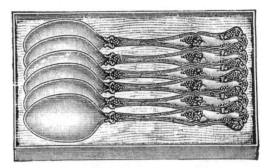

Six Tea Spoons
Vintage pattern, gray finish. No. 31832
silver bowls, $4.75 per set.

Individual pastry fork, 6³⁄₁₆"

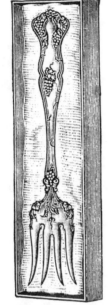

Beef Fork
Vintage pattern, gray finish, No. 31810, silver tines, $1.89 each. No. 31811, gold tines, $2.50 each.

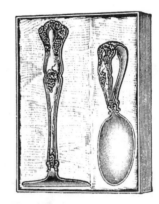

Baby Set
Vintage pattern, gray finish. One baby spoon, one food pusher. No. 31829, $2.25 per set.

Long Pickle Fork
Vintage pattern, gray finish. No. 31812, silver tines, $2.05 each.

Pie Knife

1913 Catalog

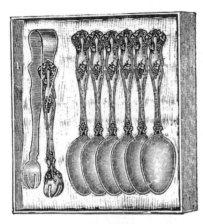

COFFEE SET
Vintage pattern, gray finish.
One Sugar Tongs, six Coffee

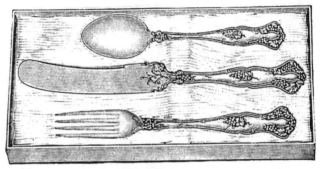

CHILD'S SET

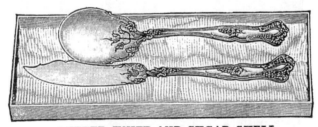

BUTTER KNIFE AND SUGAR SHELL
Vintage pattern, gray finish
No. 31745   Silver bowl and blade.....................per set $3.30

Vintage pattern, gray finish. Nickel silver, silver soldered, hollow handle knives and forks

No. 31442 Medium knives.....$28.80	No. 31444 Medium forks.....$28.80
No. 31443 Dessert knives.....25.20	No. 31445 Dessert forks.....25.20

Scimeter swadged blade. First quality silver plated. Put up 6 in flannel roll.

Vintage pattern, gray finish.   Spoon handle forks

No. 31446 Medium forks, XS triple plated.....$17.10	No. 31448 Dessert forks, XS triple plated.....$15.30
No. 31447 Medium forks, XS quintuple plated.....23.40	No. 31449 Dessert forks, XS quintuple plated.....19.80

1913 Catalog

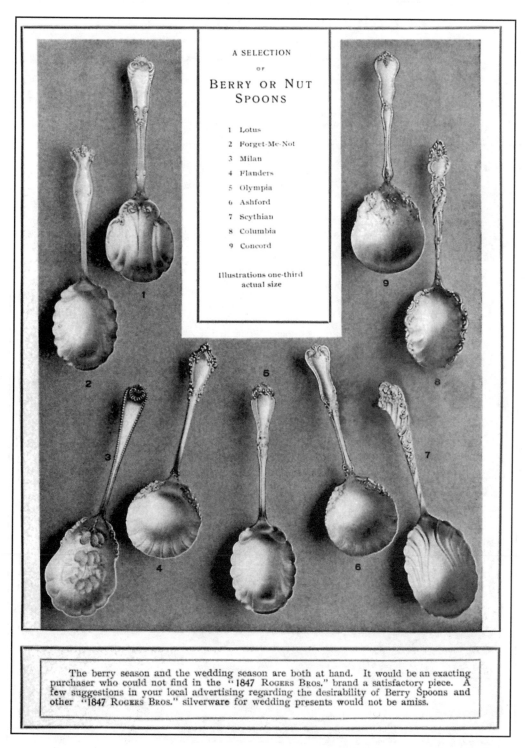

A SELECTION
OF
BERRY OR NUT
SPOONS

1 Lotus
2 Forget-Me-Not
3 Milan
4 Flanders
5 Olympia
6 Ashford
7 Scythian
8 Columbia
9 Concord

Illustrations one-third
actual size

The berry season and the wedding season are both at hand. It would be an exacting purchaser who could not find in the "1847 ROGERS BROS." brand a satisfactory piece. A few suggestions in your local advertising regarding the desirability of Berry Spoons and other "1847 ROGERS BROS." silverware for wedding presents would not be amiss.

This 1906 catalog page illustrates nine beautiful large berry spoons. Americans ate quantities of berries and fruits in the pre-WWI days. Almost all American glass and china patterns had berry sets which consisted of one large serving and six small individual bowls. Silver manufacturers produced large berry serving spoons in addition to tiny berry forks that complimented the berry bowls. Some of the patterns shown here were never full lines. They are Concord; Forget-Me-Not; Ashford; Scythian; Olympia; and Milan. Do not confuse Milan with the Shell pattern. Also note the exquisite berries in the bowl of this piece. The Flanders pattern may not be full line, but pieces other than the berry spoon are know. 1907 Catalog.

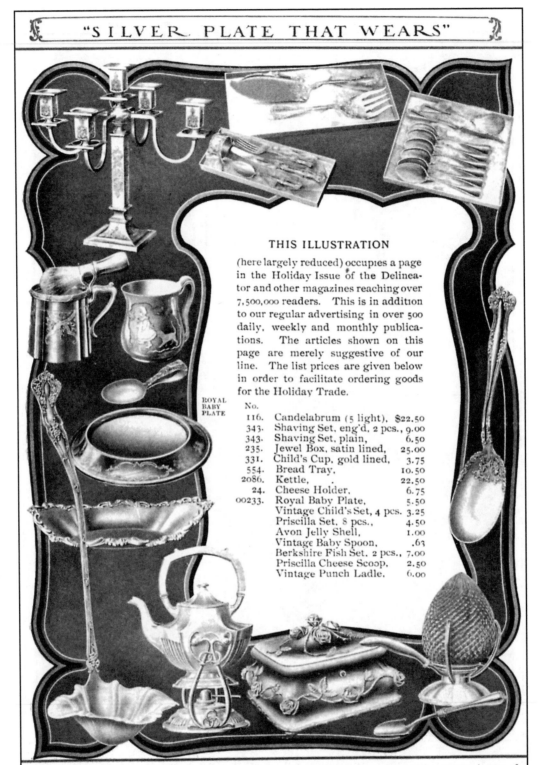

"SILVER PLATE THAT WEARS"

ROYAL
BABY
PLATE

THIS ILLUSTRATION

(here largely reduced) occupies a page
in the Holiday Issue of the Delineator and other magazines reaching over
7,500,000 readers. This is in addition
to our regular advertising in over 500
daily, weekly and monthly publica-
tions. The articles shown on this
page are merely suggestive of our
line. The list prices are given below
in order to facilitate ordering goods
for the Holiday Trade.

No.		
116.	Candelabrum (5 light),	$22.50
343.	Shaving Set, eng'd, 2 pcs.,	9.00
343.	Shaving Set, plain,	6.50
235.	Jewel Box, satin lined,	25.00
331.	Child's Cup, gold lined,	3.75
554.	Bread Tray,	10.50
2086.	Kettle,	22.50
24.	Cheese Holder,	6.75
00233.	Royal Baby Plate,	5.50
	Vintage Child's Set, 4 pcs.	3.25
	Priscilla Set, 8 pcs.,	4.50
	Avon Jelly Shell,	1.00
	Vintage Baby Spoon,	.63
	Berkshire Fish Set, 2 pcs.,	7.00
	Priscilla Cheese Scoop,	2.50
	Vintage Punch Ladle,	6.00

The Delineator will announce its Holiday Issue (mentioning its leading advertisers) in 510 of
the most prominent daily newspapers. The makers of "1847 ROGERS BROS." are the only silverware concern referred to by the Delineator.

Distributed to the public by progressive dealers

1906 Catalog

Avon, Lotus, Vesta, Berkshire, Vintage & Columbia Patterns

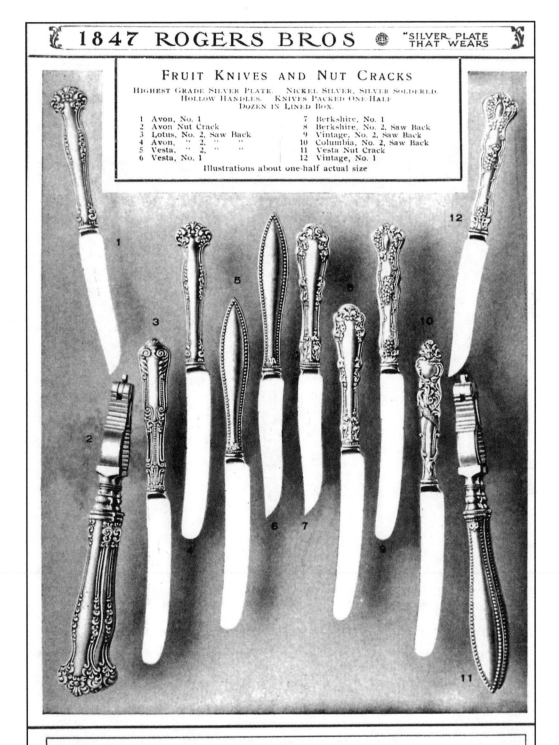

See Price Guide — Group 1

1906 Catalog

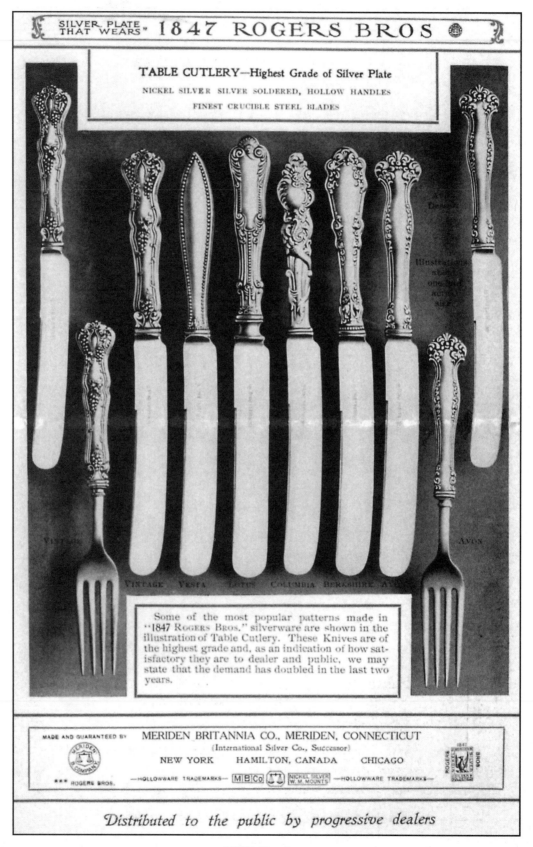

1907 Catalog

Various Patterns

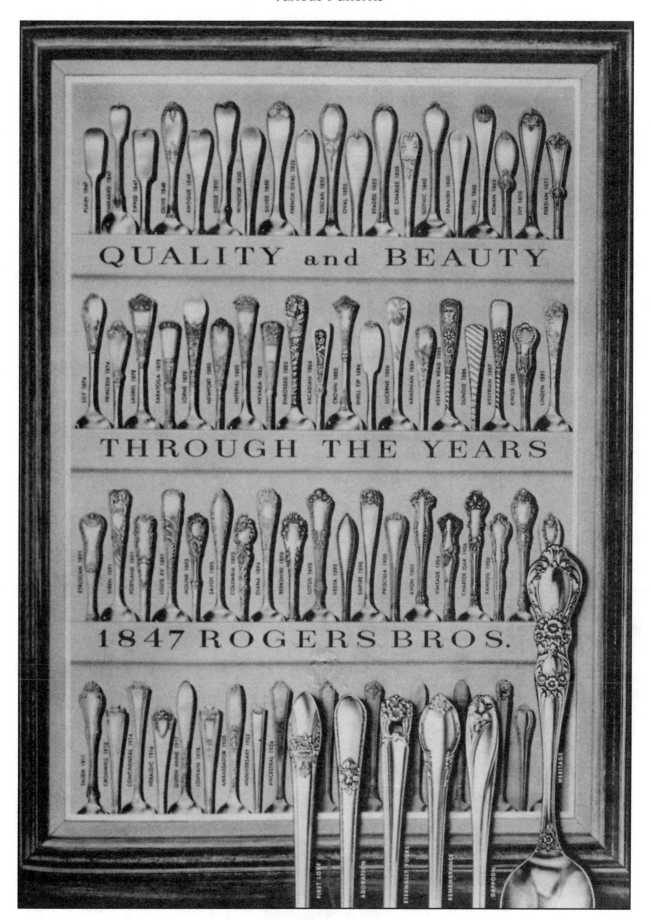

1881 Rogers A-1

Enchantment Pattern

1953 Advertisement

Greylock Pattern

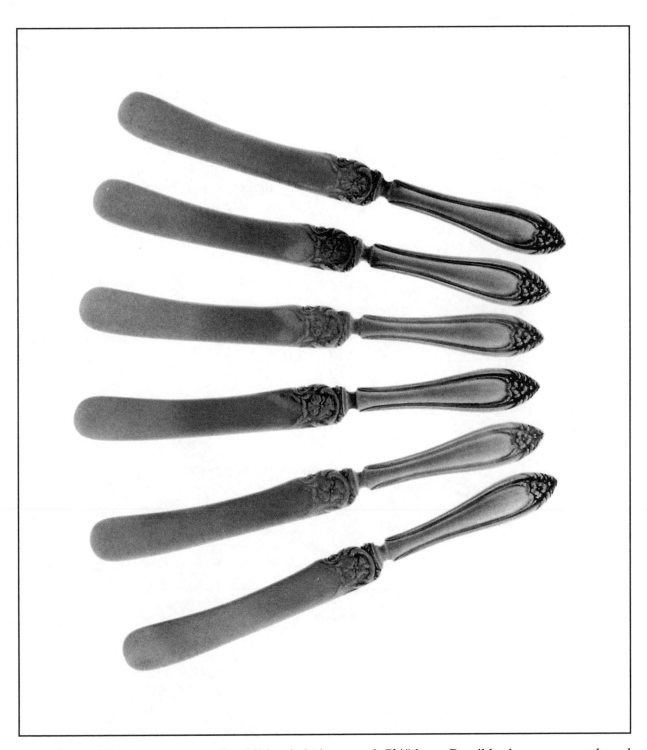

These beautiful knives are actually children's knives, each 7⅕" long. Possibly they were purchased either as individual butter spreaders or breakfast knives. They are solid handled pieces.

See Price Guide — Group 1

La Vigne Pattern

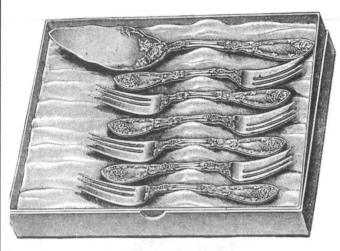

SEVEN PIECE SET
La Vigne Pattern.   French Gray.

LA VIGNE PATTERN
French Gray

The La Vigne is an exciting grape pattern to collect. All the grape patterns that were so popular in the early 1900s were named after wines. La Vigne is a large pattern with wonderful extras, such as the baby cup and napkin ring. The tongs are outstanding and highly prized. Note that the "claws" are a cluster of grapes. We illustrate both the solid and hollow handle knives. One outstanding La Vigne item is the tea strainer (not shown). Through the years we have seen numerous strainers offered for sale, so this is not an impossible item to find.

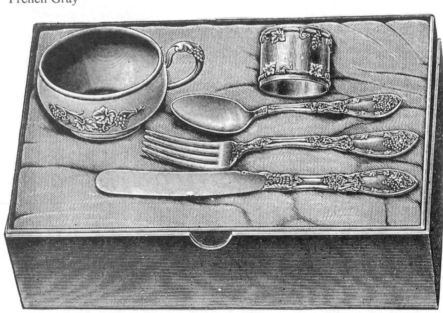

CHILD'S SET
Five Pieces. La Vigne Pattern. French Gray.

1913 Catalog

La Vigne Pattern

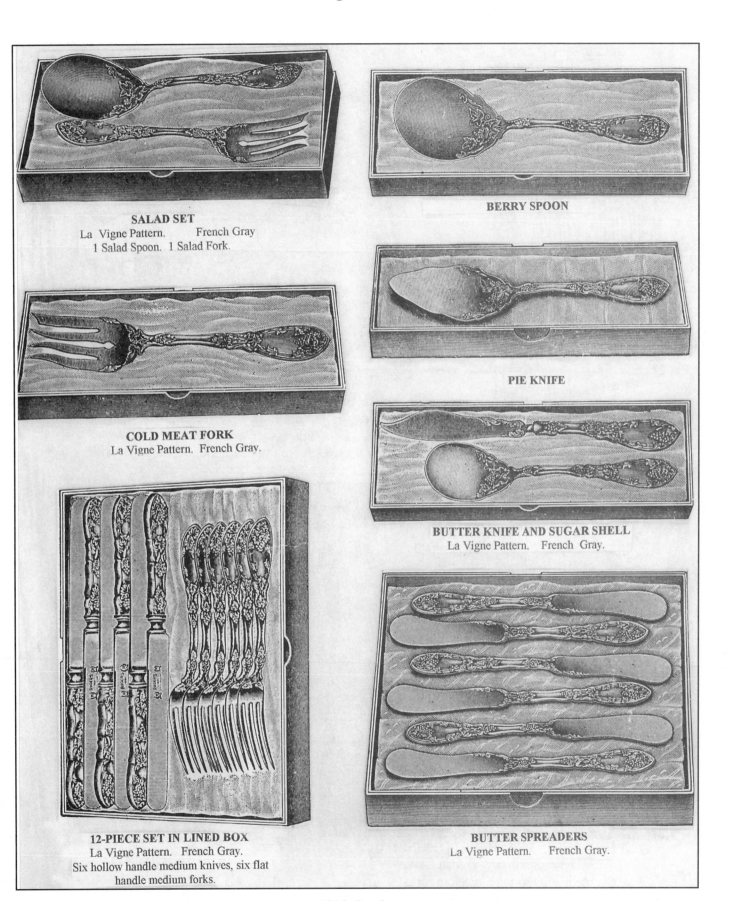

SALAD SET
La Vigne Pattern.   French Gray
1 Salad Spoon. 1 Salad Fork.

BERRY SPOON

COLD MEAT FORK
La Vigne Pattern. French Gray.

PIE KNIFE

BUTTER KNIFE AND SUGAR SHELL
La Vigne Pattern.   French Gray.

12-PIECE SET IN LINED BOX
La Vigne Pattern.   French Gray.
Six hollow handle medium knives, six flat
handle medium forks.

BUTTER SPREADERS
La Vigne Pattern.   French Gray.

1913 Catalog

See Price Guide — Group 1

La Vigne Pattern

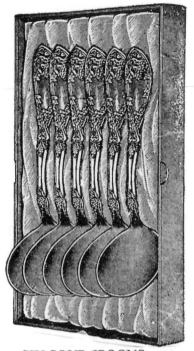

SIX SOUP SPOONS
La Vigne Pattern. French Gray.

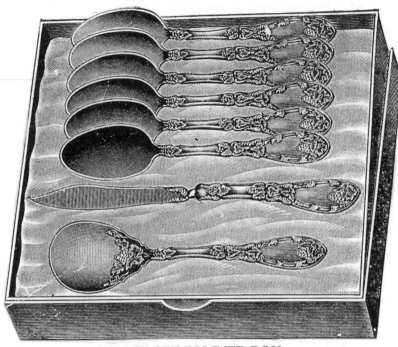

8-PIECE SET IN LINED BOX
La Vigne Pattern. French Gray.
Six tea spoons, one butter knife, one sugar shell.

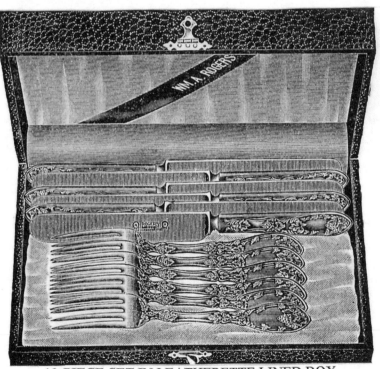

12-PIECE SET IN LEATHERETTE LINED BOX
La Vigne Pattern. French Gray.
Six medium knives, six medium forks.

SUGAR TONGS
La Vigne Pattern.   French Gray.

1913 Catalog

Plantation Pattern

"Romantic", says
JANE WYMAN
starring in
JOHNNY BELINDA
A Warner Bros. Picture

Newest, most youthful pattern in all its shining world,

Plantation reflects for your future, the gracious splendor of the past.

Its design soars high as fluted columns . . . its rich detail

is deep as the heart of a rose. Ask your jeweler to show you

this lovely new pattern in the service that gives you

More For Your "SILVER" Dollar—for instance the 42-Piece Service

for eight is $39.75. Five-Piece Place Settings are $4.50.

*Trade-mark   Copyright 1948 Oneida Ltd

1881
ROGERS
silverplate
by ONEIDA LTD.
silversmiths

Plantation

1948 Advertisement

Simeon L. & George H. Rogers Company

Thor & Encore Patterns

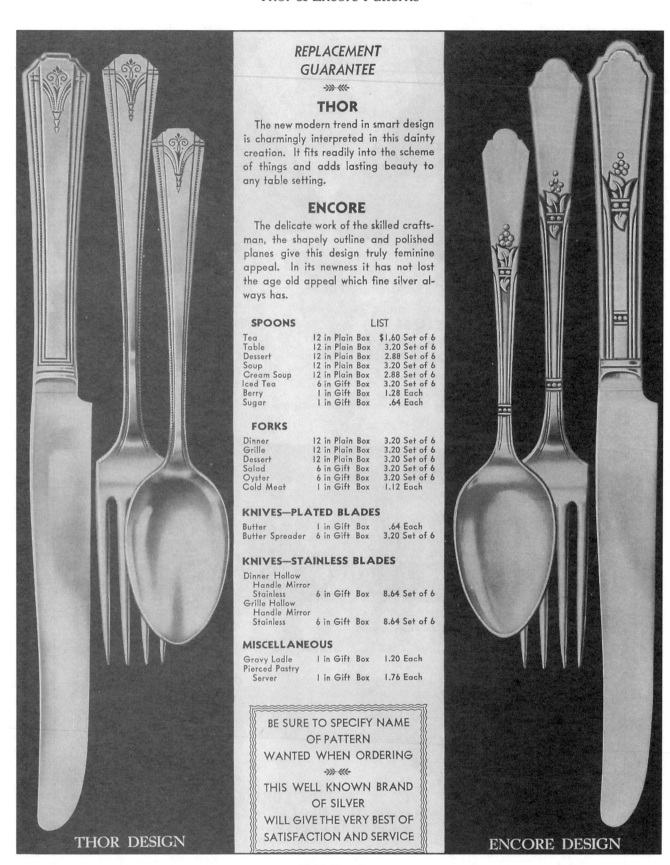

THOR

The new modern trend in smart design is charmingly interpreted in this dainty creation. It fits readily into the scheme of things and adds lasting beauty to any table setting.

ENCORE

The delicate work of the skilled craftsman, the shapely outline and polished planes give this design truly feminine appeal. In its newness it has not lost the age old appeal which fine silver always has.

SPOONS		LIST	
Tea	12 in Plain Box	$1.60	Set of 6
Table	12 in Plain Box	3.20	Set of 6
Dessert	12 in Plain Box	2.88	Set of 6
Soup	12 in Plain Box	3.20	Set of 6
Cream Soup	12 in Plain Box	2.88	Set of 6
Iced Tea	6 in Gift Box	3.20	Set of 6
Berry	1 in Gift Box	1.28	Each
Sugar	1 in Gift Box	.64	Each

FORKS			
Dinner	12 in Plain Box	3.20	Set of 6
Grille	12 in Plain Box	3.20	Set of 6
Dessert	12 in Plain Box	3.20	Set of 6
Salad	6 in Gift Box	3.20	Set of 6
Oyster	6 in Gift Box	3.20	Set of 6
Cold Meat	1 in Gift Box	1.12	Each

KNIVES—PLATED BLADES			
Butter	1 in Gift Box	.64	Each
Butter Spreader	6 in Gift Box	3.20	Set of 6

KNIVES—STAINLESS BLADES			
Dinner Hollow Handle Mirror Stainless	6 in Gift Box	8.64	Set of 6
Grille Hollow Handle Mirror Stainless	6 in Gift Box	8.64	Set of 6

MISCELLANEOUS			
Gravy Ladle	1 in Gift Box	1.20	Each
Pierced Pastry Server	1 in Gift Box	1.76	Each

THOR DESIGN

ENCORE DESIGN

1936 Catalog

Patented 1905. Left to right: 8¾" lettuce fork, 8⁵⁄₁₆" tablespoon, 9⅛" gilded bowl berry spoon, engraved "1883 – 1908," 8¹³⁄₁₆" salad serving fork.

Violet Pattern

Patented 1905. Left to right: 5⅞" individual cocktail fork, 5¹⁵⁄₁₆" teaspoon,
6⁹⁄₁₆" chipped beef fork, 7½" dinner fork, 9¾" hollow handle dinner knife.

E.H.H. Smith Silver Company

Antique Egyptian Pattern

This beautiful pattern was designed for the Cafe de L' Opera in New York. Only the demi-tasse spoon is readily found today. Numerous jewelry stores gave away this item as a premium. The pieces shown here, a service of six, turned up in the Rio Grande River valley in Texas. Patented in 1909, it is found with several different backstamps. It is unknown exactly how extensive the line is. Such wonderful extras as the grape shears, butter picks, muddlers, and nut-cracks are known to exist. Smith Silver Company was located in Bridgeport, Conn., with sales representatives in the Silversmiths' Building in both New York and Chicago. The design on the back of this pattern is outstanding. In the late 1960s to early 1970s the demi-spoon was produced and marketed as "scarab." See advertisement below.

3-Piece Jelly Dish
07 44 With Scarab Design Spoon,
Removable Glass Liner,
dia. 5½'' $3.50

313

See Price Guide — Group 1

Antique Egyptian Pattern

Left to right: underside of 7⁵⁄₁₆" soup spoon, top of soup spoon, underside of 7½" dinner fork, top of dinner fork, 10" hollow handle dinner knife. Bottom: 4½" demi-tasse spoon, 6" teaspoon.

Collection of Lydia Bones Thompson.

Patented 1906. 7½" pastry forks. Sweetpea will also be found with the Paragon backstamp.

Verdi Pattern

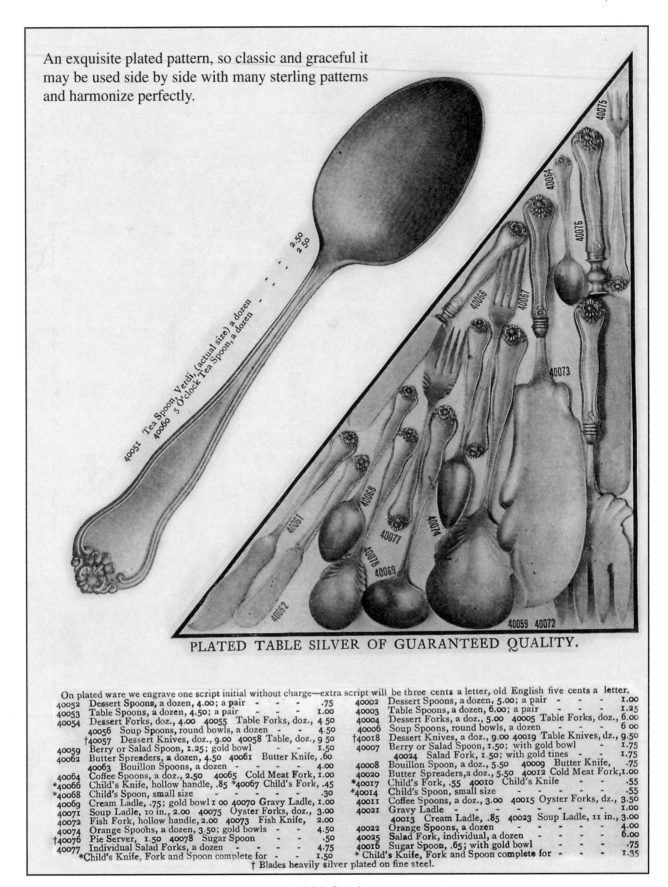

An exquisite plated pattern, so classic and graceful it may be used side by side with many sterling patterns and harmonize perfectly.

PLATED TABLE SILVER OF GUARANTEED QUALITY.

On plated ware we engrave one script initial without charge—extra script will be three cents a letter, old English five cents a letter.

40052	Dessert Spoons, a dozen, 4.00; a pair - - - .75	40002	Dessert Spoons, a dozen, 5.00; a pair - - - 1.00
40053	Table Spoons, a dozen, 4.50; a pair - - - 1.00	40003	Table Spoons, a dozen, 6.00; a pair - - - 1.25
40054	Dessert Forks, doz., 4.00 40055 Table Forks, doz., 4 50	40004	Dessert Forks, a doz., 5.00 40005 Table Forks, doz., 6.00
	40056 Soup Spoons, round bowls, a dozen - - 4.50	40006	Soup Spoons, round bowls, a dozen - - 6 00
†40057	Dessert Knives, doz., 9.00 40058 Table, doz., 9 50	†40018	Dessert Knives, a doz., 9.00 40019 Table Knives, dz., 9.50
40059	Berry or Salad Spoon, 1.25; gold bowl - - 1.50	40007	Berry or Salad Spoon, 1.50; with gold bowl - 1.75
40062	Butter Spreaders, a dozen, 4.50 40061 Butter Knife, .60		40024 Salad Fork, 1.50; with gold tines - - 1.75
	40063 Bouillon Spoons, a dozen - - - 4.00	40008	Bouillon Spoon, a doz., 5.50 40009 Butter Knife, .75
40064	Coffee Spoons, a doz., 2.50 40065 Cold Meat Fork, 1.00	40020	Butter Spreaders, a doz., 5.50 40012 Cold Meat Fork, 1.00
*40066	Child's Knife, hollow handle, .85 *40067 Child's Fork, .45	*40017	Child's Fork, .55 40010 Child's Knife - - .55
*40068	Child's Spoon, small size - - - .30	*40014	Child's Spoon, small size - - - .55
40069	Cream Ladle, .75; gold bowl 1 00 40070 Gravy Ladle, 1.00	40011	Coffee Spoons, a doz., 3.00 40015 Oyster Forks, dz., 3.50
40071	Soup Ladle, 10 in., 2.00 40075 Oyster Forks, doz., 3.00	40021	Gravy Ladle - - - - 1.00
40072	Fish Fork, hollow handle, 2.00 40073 Fish Knife, 2.00		40013 Cream Ladle, .85 40023 Soup Ladle, 11 in., 3.00
40074	Orange Spoons, a dozen, 3.50; gold bowls - 4.50	40022	Orange Spoons, a dozen - - - 4.00
†40076	Pie Server, 1.50 40078 Sugar Spoon - - .50	40025	Salad Fork, individual, a dozen - - 6.00
40077	Individual Salad Forks, a dozen - - 4.75	40016	Sugar Spoon, .65; with gold bowl - - - .75
	*Child's Knife, Fork and Spoon complete for - 1.50		* Child's Knife, Fork and Spoon complete for - 1.35

† Blades heavily silver plated on fine steel.

1905 Catalog

Holly, Oak & Iris Pattern

Three patterns being reproduced in Mexico. Marked "ALPACA PLATEDO" (Mexico). Left to right: 11⅝" Holly Pattern (patented 1904) platter spoon, 11" Oak Pattern (patented 1906) fish knife, 11⅝6" Iris Pattern (patented 1910) platter spoon. All three will be found back stamped "Paragon Silver Plate."

See Price Guide — Group 1

Stratford Sectional Silverplate Company

Carmen Pattern

Sugar Spoon and
Butter Knife
In Lined Box
List, $1.60 set
Consumer, **$1.50 set**

Iced Drink or
Parfait Spoons
In Lined Box
List, $4.05 six
Consumer
$3.25 six

Jelly Server
In Lined Box
List, $1.63 each
Consumer, **$1.50 each**

Berry, Salad or
Serving Spoon
In Lined Box
List, $2.39 each
Consumer, **$2.00 each**

Baby Spoon
(Bent Handle)
In Lined Box
List, $0.74 each
Consumer, **$0.65 each**

Gravy Ladle
In Lined Box
List, $1.83 each
Consumer
$1.50 each

Cold Meat, Salad
or Serving Fork
In Lined Box
List, $1.48 each
Consumer, **$1.25 each**

Cream Ladle
In Lined Box
List, $1.31 each
Consumer
$1.00 each

Butter Spreaders
In Lined Box
List, $5.22 six
Consumer, **$4.40 six**

Knife and Fork Set
(Dinner Set)
Solid Handle Knives, Flat Forks
List, $9.16 set
Consumer, **$7.10 set**
S. H. Stainless, *List,* $12.44 set
S. H. Stainless, Consumer, **$9.50 set**

Carmen Tea Spoon
Actual Size

Oyster or Seafood Forks
In Lined Box
List, $3.78 six
Consumer, **$3.20 six**

STAPLES IN PLAIN BOXES

	List		Consumer
Tea Spoons...................doz.	$4.16	doz.	$3.50
Dessert or Oval Soup Spoons...doz.	8.32	doz.	7.00
Table or Serving Spoons.......doz.	8.32	doz.	7.00
Dinner Forks.................doz.	8.32	doz.	7.00
Breakfast or Luncheon Forks...doz.	8.32	doz.	7.00

SPOONS IN LINED BOXES

Baby (Bent Handle)...........doz.	8.88	each	0.65
Baby (Short Handle)..........doz.	8.88	each	.65
Berry, Salad or Serving.......doz.	28.70	each	2.00
Bouillon....................doz.	9.12	six	3.50
Coffee......................doz.	4.70	six	1.85
Coffee, Plain Box.............doz.	4.16	six	1.75
Five o'Clock Tea..............doz.	4.70	six	1.85
Five o'Clock Tea, Plain Box....doz.	4.16	doz.	3.50
Iced Drink or Parfait..........doz.	8.10	six	3.25
Iced Drink or Parfait, Plain Box..doz.	7.60	six	3.15
Orange or Grape Fruit.........doz.	7.18	six	3.00
Round Bowl Soup.............doz.	8.88	six	3.60
Round Bowl Soup, Plain Box...doz.	8.32	doz.	7.00

FORKS IN LINED BOXES

Baby (Short Handle)..........doz.	8.88	each	0.65
Tea........................doz.	7.82	six	3.35
Tea, Plain Box................doz.	7.42	doz.	6.50
Cold Meat, Salad or Serving....doz.	17.74	each	1.25

	List		Consumer
Oyster or Seafood.............doz.	$7.56	six	$3.20
Salad, Individual.............doz.	11.48	six	4.80

SERVERS IN LINED BOXES

Butter Knife.................doz.	10.96	each	0.80
Butter Knife, Plain Box........doz.	8.32	each	.60
Butter Spreaders.............doz.	10.44	six	4.40
Sugar Spoon.................doz.	10.44	each	.75
Sugar Spoon, Plain Box........doz.	7.80	each	.55
Cream Ladle.................doz.	15.64	each	1.00
Gravy Ladle.................doz.	21.90	each	1.50
Soup Ladle, Medium..........doz.	57.34	each	4.00
Jelly Server.................doz.	19.58	each	1.50
Flat Server (Pierced).........doz.	33.90	each	2.40

S. H. CUTLERY (French Style Blades)

Dinner Knife.................doz.	10.00	doz.	7.20
Breakfast Knife...............doz.	10.00	doz.	7.20
Dinner Knife, Stainless........doz.	16.56	doz.	12.00
Breakfast Knife, Stainless......doz.	16.56	doz.	12.00
2-Piece Carving Set, 6-inch			
Blade, Stainless, Lined Box...doz.	62.64	set	3.75

H. H. CUTLERY (French Style Blades)

	List		Consumer
Dinner Knife.................doz.	$24.40	doz.	$17.50
Breakfast Knife...............doz.	24.40	doz.	17.50
Dinner Knife, Stainless........doz.	27.42	doz.	19.60
Breakfast Knife, Stainless......doz.	27.42	doz.	19.60
2-Piece Carving Set, 6-inch			
Blade, Stainless, Lined Box..doz.	110.16	set	6.60

SETS IN LINED BOXES

Sugar Spoon and Butter Knife...doz.	19.20	set	1.50
2-Piece Baby (Short Handle)....doz.	17.76	set	1.30
3-Piece Child's, Flat or Steel			
Knife....................doz.	28.80	set	2.00

TWELVE-PIECE KNIFE AND FORK SETS

12-E Dinner Set, S. H. Knives...set	9.16		7.10
12-C Breakfast Set, S. H. Knives.set	9.16		7.10
12-ES Dinner Set, S.H. Kvs...St..set	12.44		9.50
12-CS Breakfast Set, S. H. Knives,			
Stainless.................set	12.44		9.50
12-AS Dinner Set, H.H. Kvs., St..set	17.88		13.30
12-BS Bkfst. Set, H.H. Kvs., St...set	17.88		13.30

INTERNATIONAL SILVER CO.

1930 Catalog

Shakespeare Pattern

STRATFORD
SECTIONAL SILVERPLATE
FACTORY "C"
INTERNATIONAL SILVER CO.

SHAKESPEARE

Sugar Spoon and
Butter Knife
In Lined Box
List, $1.60 set
Consumer, $1.50 set

Orange or
Grape Fruit Spoons
In Lined Box
List, $3.59 six
Consumer, $3.00 six

Gravy Ladle
In Lined Box
List, $1.83 each
Consumer
$1.50 each

Cold Meat, Salad
or Serving Fork
In Lined Box
List, $1.48 each
Consumer, $1.25 each

Baby
Spoon
(Bent Handle)
In Lined Box
List, $0.74 each
Consumer, $0.65 each

Berry, Salad or
Serving Spoon
In Lined Box
List, $2.39 each
Consumer, $2.00 each

Individual Salad Forks
In Lined Box
List, $5.74 six
Consumer, $4.80 six

Butter Spreaders
In Lined Box
List, $5.22 six
Consumer
$4.40 six

Cream Ladle
In Lined Box
List, $1.31 each
Consumer, $1.00 each

Jelly Server
In Lined Box
List, $1.63 each
Consumer
$1.50 each

Oyster or Seafood Forks
In Lined Box
List, $3.78 six
Consumer, $3.20 six

Shakespeare
Tea Spoon
Actual Size

Knife and Fork Set
(Dinner Set)
Solid Handle Knives, Flat Forks
List, $9.16 set; Consumer, $7.10 set
S. H. Stainless, *List*, $12.44 six
S. H. Stainless, Consumer, $9.50 set

STAPLES IN PLAIN BOXES		List		Consumer
Tea Spoons	doz.	$4.16	doz.	$3.50
Dessert or Oval Soup Spoons	doz.	8.32	doz.	7.00
Table or Serving Spoons	doz.	8.32	doz.	7.00
Dinner Forks	doz.	8.32	doz.	7.00
Breakfast or Luncheon Forks	doz.	8.32	doz.	7.00
SPOONS IN LINED BOXES				
Baby (Bent Handle)	doz.	8.88	each	0.65
Baby (Short Handle)	doz.	8.88	each	.65
Berry, Salad or Serving	doz.	28.70	each	2.00
Bouillon		9.12	six	3.50
Coffee	doz.	4.70	six	1.85
Coffee, Plain Box	doz.	4.16	six	1.75
Five o'Clock Tea	doz.	4.70	six	1.85
Five o'Clock Tea, Plain Box	doz.	4.16	doz.	3.50
Iced Drink or Parfait		8.10	six	3.25
Iced Drink or Parfait, Plain Box	doz.	7.60	six	3.15
Orange or Grape Fruit	doz.	7.18	six	3.00
Round Bowl Soup		8.88	six	3.60
Round Bowl Soup, Plain Box	doz.	8.32	doz.	7.00
FORKS IN LINED BOXES				
Baby (Short Handle)	doz.	8.88	each	0.65
Tea		7.82	six	3.35
Tea, Plain Box		7.42	doz.	6.50
Cold Meat, Salad or Serving	doz.	17.74	each	1.25

		List		Consumer
Oyster or Seafood	doz.	$7.56	six	$3.20
Salad, Individual	doz.	11.48	six	4.80
SERVERS IN LINED BOXES				
Butter Knife	doz.	10.96	each	0.80
Butter Knife, Plain Box	doz.	8.32	each	.60
Butter Spreaders	doz.	10.44	six	4.40
Sugar Spoon	doz.	10.44	each	.75
Sugar Spoon, Plain Box	doz.	7.80	each	.55
Cream Ladle	doz.	15.64	each	1.00
Gravy Ladle	doz.	21.90	each	1.50
Soup Ladle, Medium	doz.	57.34	each	4.00
Jelly Server	doz.	19.58	each	1.50
Flat Server (Pierced)	doz.	33.90	each	2.40

S. H. CUTLERY (French Style Blades)

		List		Consumer
Dinner Knife	doz.	10.00	doz.	7.20
Breakfast Knife	doz.	10.00	doz.	7.20
Dinner Knife, Stainless	doz.	16.56	doz.	12.00
Breakfast Knife, Stainless	doz.	16.56	doz.	12.00
2-Piece Carving Set, 6-inch				
Blade, Stainless, Lined Box	doz.	62.64	set	3.75

H. H. CUTLERY (French Style Blades)

		List		Consumer
Dinner Knife	doz.	$24.40	doz.	$17.50
Breakfast Knife	doz.	24.40	doz.	17.50
Dinner Knife, Stainless	doz.	27.42	doz.	19.60
Breakfast Knife, Stainless	doz.	27.42	doz.	19.60
2-Piece Carving Set, 6-inch				
Blade, Stainless, Lined Box	doz.	110.16	set	6.60

SETS IN LINED BOXES

		List		Consumer
Sugar Spoon and Butter Knife	doz.	19.20	set	1.50
2-Piece Baby (Short Handle)	doz.	17.76	set	1.30
3-Piece Child's, Flat or Steel Knife	doz.	28.80	set	2.00

TWELVE-PIECE KNIFE AND FORK SETS

			List		Consumer
12-E	Dinner Set, S. H. Knives	set	9.16	set	7.10
12-C	Breakfast Set, S. H. Knives	set	9.16	set	7.10
12-ES	Din. Set, S. H. Kvs., St.	set	12.44	set	9.50
12-CS	Bkfst. Set, S. H. Kvs., St.	set	12.44	set	9.50
12-AS	Dinner Set, H. H. Knives, Stainless	set	17.88	set	13.30
12-BS	Breakfast Set, H. H. Knives, Stainless	set	17.88	set	13.30

INTERNATIONAL SILVER CO.

Tudor Plate

Barbara and Bridal Wreath Patterns

ONEIDA COMMUNITY

DINNER FORK

SPOONS (six in box)		Consumer	List
Tea . . . . Per Doz.	$ 3.00	$ 3.60
Dessert or Oval Bowl Soup . . . . Per Doz.	6.00	7.20
Table . . . . Per Doz.	6.00	7.20
Soup, Round Bowl . . . . Per Doz.	6.00	7.20
Cream Soup . . . . Per Doz.	6.00	7.20
Five O'Clock Tea or Sherbet . . . . Set of 6	1.50	1.80
Iced Drink . . . . Set of 6	2.50	3.00
Sugar . . . . Each	.50	.60
Berry or Serving . . . . Each	1.50	1.80
★Baby (Bent Handle) . . . . Each	.50	.60
Baby (Straight Handle) . . . . . . Each	.50	.60

FORKS (six in box)			
Dinner . . . . Per Doz.	6.00	7.20
Dessert or Entree . . . . Per Doz.	6.00	7.20
Grille . . . . Per Doz.	6.00	7.20
Cocktail or Oyster . . . . Set of 6	2.50	3.00
Salad or Pastry . . . . Set of 6	3.25	3.90
Cold Meat or Serving . . . . . . Each	1.00	1.20
Pickle or Olive . . . . Each	.75	.90
Baby (Straight Handle) . . . . . Each	.50	.60

KNIVES (Mirror Stainless Blades)			
Dinner, Hollow Handle, Streamline . Per Doz.	15.00	18.00
Grille, Hollow Handle, Streamline . Per Doz.	15.00	18.00
Dinner, Embossed Handle . . . . . Per Doz.	8.00	9.60
Dessert, Luncheon or Breakfast, Embossed Handle . . . . Per Doz.	8.00	9.60

KNIVES (Stainless Blades)			
Dinner, Hollow Handle . . . . . . Per Doz.	20.00	24.00
★Grille, Hollow Handle . . . . . . Per Doz.	20.00	24.00

KNIVES (Plated Blades)			
Dinner, Embossed Handle . . . . . Per Doz.	6.90	8.28
Dessert, Luncheon or Breakfast, Embossed Handle . . . . Per Doz.	6.90	8.28
Butter . . . . Each	.50	.60
Individual Butter or Cheese . . . . Set of 6	3.00	3.60

KNIFE AND FORK SETS (6 Mirror Stainless Knives and 6 Forks) Priced, per set			
Dinner or Grille Knives, Hollow Handle Streamline and Forks	10.50	12.60
Dinner Knives, Emb. H. and Forks	7.00	8.40
Dessert, Luncheon or Breakfast, Embossed Handle and Forks	7.00	8.40

CARVER (Mirror Stainless Blade Knife)—For Steak or Game			
2-Piece, Hollow Handle . . . . . . Per Set	5.00	6.00

MISCELLANEOUS			
Salad Dressing or Small Ladle . . . . Each	1.00	1.20
Serving or Gravy Ladle . . . . Each	1.25	1.50
Small Server (Jelly Server) . . . . . Each	.75	.90
Round Server, Pierced . . . . Each	1.50	1.80
Pastry Server, Pierced . . . . Each	2.00	2.40

SETS			
Butter and Sugar . . . . Per Set	1.00	1.20
2-Piece French "Table Serving" . . . Per Set	3.00	3.60
★Baby (Bent Spoon and Fork) . . . Per Set	1.00	1.20
Baby (Straight Spoon and Fork) . . . Per Set	1.00	1.20
★Child's (Spoon, Fork and Emb. Knife) Per Set	1.50	1.80

1936 Catalog. Left, Barbara Design. Right, Bridal Wreath.

See Price Guide — Group 3

TUDOR PLATE
By the makers of Community Plate
Duchess Design

STAINLESS

DUO SERVICE TRAYS—With Dinner Knives

29 Pieces (set for 6)	Retail	List
Embossed Hdle., Stainless	$17.75	$ 22.92
Embossed Handle., Plated	15.00	19.32
Hollow Handle, Stainless	21.75	28.10

34 Pieces (set for 8)	Retail	List
Embossed Hdle., Stainless	$23.00	$29.64
Embossed Handle, Plated	19.25	24.80
Hollow Handle, Stainless	28.25	36.52

COLOR-MODE FREE CHESTS
With Dinner Knives

29 Pieces (set for 6)	Retail	List
Embossed Hdle., Stainless	$16.75	$21.30
Embossed Handle, Plated	14.00	17.70
Hollow Handle, Stainless	20.75	26.50

34 Pieces (set for 8)	Retail	List
Embossed Hdle., Stainless	$21.75	$27.76
Embossed Handle, Plated	18.25	22.98
Hollow Handle, Stainless	27.25	34.72

25 YEAR REPLACEMENT
GUARANTEE

SPOONS
Six in Box—Priced per Dozen

	Retail	List
Tea	$3.50	$4.36
Dessert	7.00	8.72
Table	7.00	8.72
Soup, R. B.	7.00	8.72

FORKS
Six in Box—Priced per Dozen

	Retail	List
Dinner	$7.00	$8.72
Dessert	7.00	8.72

KNIFE AND FORK SETS
6 Stainless Blade Knives and 6 Forks

Priced, per set	Retail	List
Embossed Handle Dinner Knives	$10.00	$12.84
Hollow Handle Dinner Knives	14.00	18.06
Hollow Handle Dessert or Breakfast Knives	14.00	18.06

KNIFE AND FORK SETS
6 Plated Blade Knives and 6 Forks

Priced, per set	Retail	List
Embossed Handle Dinner Knives	$ 7.25	$ 9.26
Embossed Handle Dessert Knives	7.25	9.26
Hollow Handle Dinner Knives	13.50	17.42
Hollow Handle Dessert Knives	13.50	17.42

KNIVES (Stainless Blades)

Priced, per dozen	Retail	List
Embossed Handle Dinner	$13.00	$16.92
Hollow Handle Dinner	21.00	27.36
Hollow Handle Dessert	21.00	27.36

KNIVES (Plated Blades)

Priced, per dozen	Retail	List
Embossed Handle Dinner	$7.50	$9.76
Embossed Handle Dessert	7.50	9.76
Embossed Handle Fruit	7.50	9.76
Hollow Handle Dinner	20.00	26.08
Hollow Handle Dessert	20.00	26.08

1931 Catalog

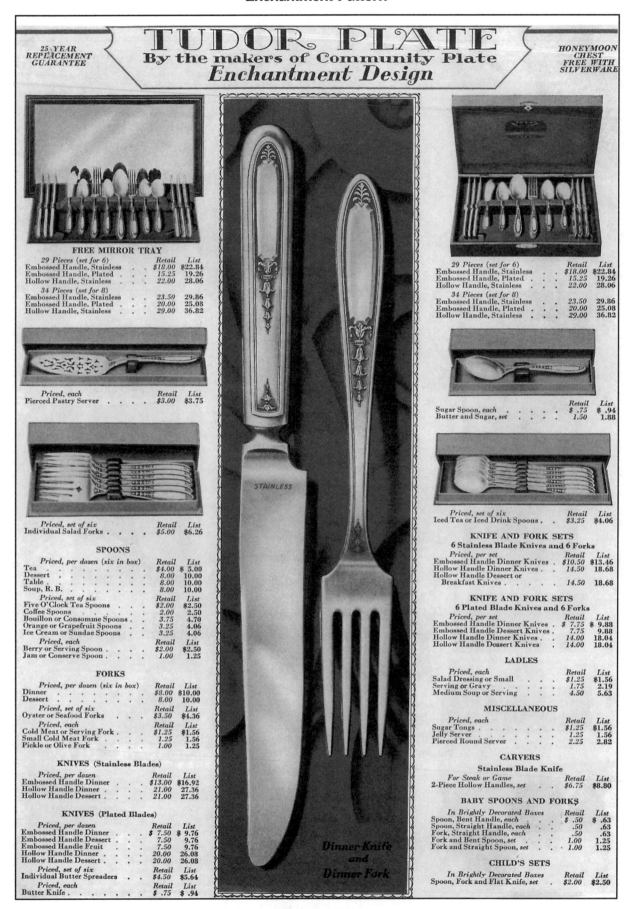

TUDOR PLATE
By the makers of Community Plate
Enchantment Design

25 YEAR REPLACEMENT GUARANTEE

HONEYMOON CHEST FREE WITH SILVERWARE

FREE MIRROR TRAY

	Retail	List
29 Pieces (set for 6)		
Embossed Handle, Stainless	$18.00	$22.84
Embossed Handle, Plated	15.25	19.26
Hollow Handle, Stainless	22.00	28.06
34 Pieces (set for 8)		
Embossed Handle, Stainless	23.50	29.86
Embossed Handle, Plated	20.00	25.08
Hollow Handle, Stainless	29.00	36.82

	Retail	List
Priced, each		
Pierced Pastry Server	$3.00	$3.75

	Retail	List
Priced, set of six		
Individual Salad Forks	$5.00	$6.26

SPOONS

Priced, per dozen (six in box)	Retail	List
Tea	$4.00	$ 5.00
Dessert	8.00	10.00
Table	8.00	10.00
Soup, R. B.	8.00	10.00

Priced, set of six	Retail	List
Five O'Clock Tea Spoons	$2.00	$2.50
Coffee Spoons	2.00	2.50
Bouillon or Consomme Spoons	3.75	4.70
Orange or Grapefruit Spoons	3.25	4.06
Ice Cream or Sundae Spoons	3.25	4.06

Priced, each	Retail	List
Berry or Serving Spoon	$2.00	$2.50
Jam or Conserve Spoon	1.00	1.25

FORKS

Priced, per dozen (six in box)	Retail	List
Dinner	$8.00	$10.00
Dessert	8.00	10.00

Priced, set of six	Retail	List
Oyster or Seafood Forks	$3.50	$4.36

Priced, each	Retail	List
Cold Meat or Serving Fork	$1.25	$1.56
Small Cold Meat Fork	1.25	1.56
Pickle or Olive Fork	1.00	1.25

KNIVES (Stainless Blades)

Priced, per dozen	Retail	List
Embossed Handle Dinner	$13.00	$16.92
Hollow Handle Dinner	21.00	27.36
Hollow Handle Dessert	21.00	27.36

KNIVES (Plated Blades)

Priced, per dozen	Retail	List
Embossed Handle Dinner	$ 7.50	$ 9.76
Embossed Handle Dessert	7.50	9.76
Embossed Handle Fruit	7.50	9.76
Hollow Handle Dinner	20.00	26.08
Hollow Handle Dessert	20.00	26.08

Priced, set of six	Retail	List
Individual Butter Spreaders	$4.50	$5.64

Priced, each	Retail	List
Butter Knife	$ .75	$ .94

STAINLESS

Dinner Knife and Dinner Fork

	Retail	List
29 Pieces (set for 6)		
Embossed Handle, Stainless	$18.00	$22.84
Embossed Handle, Plated	15.25	19.26
Hollow Handle, Stainless	22.00	28.06
34 Pieces (set for 8)		
Embossed Handle, Stainless	23.50	29.86
Embossed Handle, Plated	20.00	25.08
Hollow Handle, Stainless	29.00	36.82

	Retail	List
Sugar Spoon, each	$ .75	$ .94
Butter and Sugar, set	1.50	1.88

Priced, set of six	Retail	List
Iced Tea or Iced Drink Spoons	$3.25	$4.06

KNIFE AND FORK SETS
6 Stainless Blade Knives and 6 Forks

Priced, per set	Retail	List
Embossed Handle Dinner Knives	$10.50	$13.46
Hollow Handle Dinner Knives	14.50	18.68
Hollow Handle Dessert or Breakfast Knives	14.50	18.68

KNIFE AND FORK SETS
6 Plated Blade Knives and 6 Forks

Priced, per set	Retail	List
Embossed Handle Dinner Knives	$ 7.75	$ 9.88
Embossed Handle Dessert Knives	7.75	9.88
Hollow Handle Dinner Knives	14.00	18.04
Hollow Handle Dessert Knives	14.00	18.04

LADLES

Priced, each	Retail	List
Salad Dressing or Small	$1.25	$1.56
Serving or Gravy	1.75	2.19
Medium Soup or Serving	4.50	5.63

MISCELLANEOUS

Priced, each	Retail	List
Sugar Tongs	$1.25	$1.56
Jelly Server	1.25	1.56
Pierced Round Server	2.25	2.82

CARVERS
Stainless Blade Knife

For Steak or Game	Retail	List
2-Piece Hollow Handles, set	$6.75	$8.80

BABY SPOONS AND FORKS

In Brightly Decorated Boxes	Retail	List
Spoon, Bent Handle, each	$ .50	$ .63
Spoon, Straight Handle, each	.50	.63
Fork, Straight Handle, each	.50	.63
Fork and Bent Spoon, set	1.00	1.25
Fork and Straight Spoon, set	1.00	1.25

CHILD'S SETS

In Brightly Decorated Boxes	Retail	List
Spoon, Fork and Flat Knife, set	$2.00	$2.50

1931 Catalog

Fantasy, Fortune & Elaine Patterns

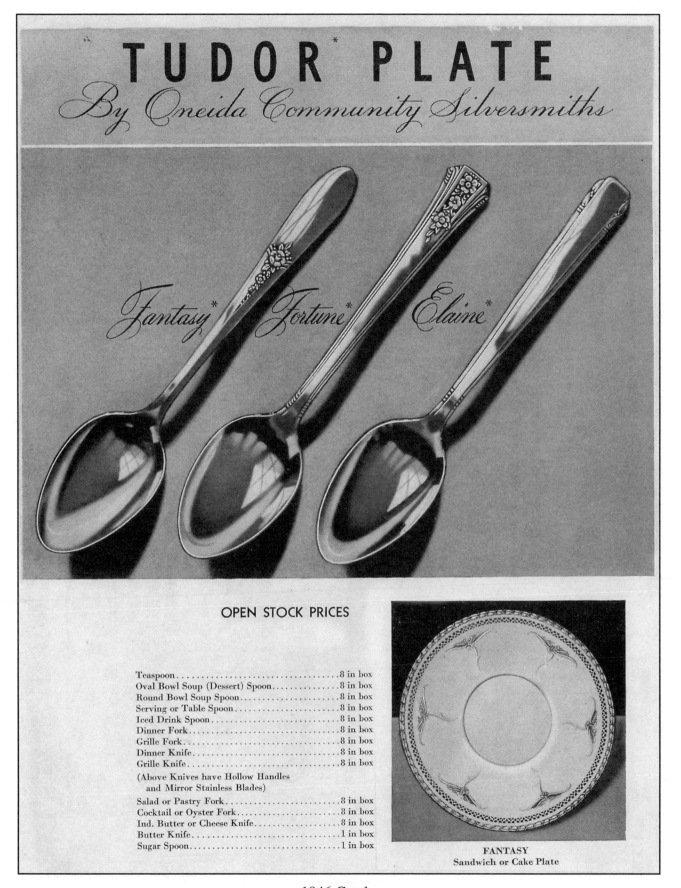

TUDOR*PLATE
By Oneida Community Silversmiths

Fantasy *Fortune* *Elaine*

OPEN STOCK PRICES

Teaspoon. . . . . .8 in box
Oval Bowl Soup (Dessert) Spoon. . . . . .8 in box
Round Bowl Soup Spoon. . . . . .8 in box
Serving or Table Spoon. . . . . .8 in box
Iced Drink Spoon. . . . . .8 in box
Dinner Fork. . . . . .8 in box
Grille Fork. . . . . .8 in box
Dinner Knife. . . . . .8 in box
Grille Knife. . . . . .8 in box
(Above Knives have Hollow Handles
  and Mirror Stainless Blades)
Salad or Pastry Fork. . . . . .8 in box
Cocktail or Oyster Fork. . . . . .8 in box
Ind. Butter or Cheese Knife. . . . . .8 in box
Butter Knife. . . . . .1 in box
Sugar Spoon. . . . . .1 in box

FANTASY
Sandwich or Cake Plate

1946 Catalog

See Price Guide — Group 3

June Pattern

ONEIDA COMMUNITY

Replacement Guarantee

●

SPOONS (six in box)

		Consumer	List
Tea	Per Doz.	$ 3.00	$ 3.60
Dessert or Oval Bowl Soup	Per Doz.	6.00	7.20
Table	Per Doz.	6.00	7.20
Soup, Round Bowl	Per Doz.	6.00	7.20
Cream Soup	Per Doz.	6.00	7.20
Five O'Clock Tea or Sherbet	Set of 6	1.50	1.80
Iced Drink	Set of 6	2.50	3.00
Sugar	Each	.50	.60
Berry or Serving	Each	1.50	1.80
Baby (Bent Handle)	Each	.50	.60
Baby (Straight Handle)	Each	.50	.60

FORKS (six in box)

Dinner	Per Doz.	6.00	7.20
Dessert or Entree	Per Doz.	6.00	7.20
Grille	Per Doz.	6.00	7.20
Cocktail or Oyster	Set of 6	2.50	3.00
Salad or Pastry	Set of 6	3.25	3.90
Cold Meat or Serving	Each	1.00	1.20
Pickle or Olive	Each	.75	.90
Baby (Straight Handle)	Each	.50	.60

KNIVES (Mirror Stainless Blades)

Dinner, H. H., Streamline	Per Doz.	15.00	18.00
Grille, H. H., Streamline	Per Doz.	15.00	18.00
Dinner, Embossed Handle	Per Doz.	8.00	9.60
Dessert, Luncheon or Breakfast, Embossed Handle	Per Doz.	8.00	9.60

KNIVES (Stainless Blades)

Dinner, Hollow Handle	Per Doz.	20.00	24.00
Grille, Hollow Handle	Per Doz.	20.00	24.00

KNIVES (Plated Blades)

Dinner, Embossed Handle	Per Doz.	6.90	8.28
Butter	Each	.50	.60
Individual Butter or Cheese	Set of 6	3.00	3.60

KNIFE AND FORK SETS
(6 Mirror Stainless Knives and 6 Forks)
Priced, per set

Dinner or Grille Knives, H. H. Streamline and Forks	10.50	12.60
Dinner Knives, Emb. H. and Forks	7.00	8.40
Dessert, Luncheon or Breakfast Knives, Emb. H. and Forks	7.00	8.40

CARVER
(Mirror Stainless Blade Knife)—For Steak or Game

2-Piece, Hollow Handle	Per Set	5.00	6.00

MISCELLANEOUS

Serving or Gravy Ladle	Each	1.25	1.50
Pastry Server, Pierced	Each	2.00	2.40

SETS

Butter and Sugar	Per Set	1.00	1.20
2-Pc. French "Table Serving"	Per Set	3.00	3.60
Child's (Spoon, Fork and Emb. Knife)	Per Set	1.50	1.80
Baby (Bent Spoon and Straight Fork)	Per Set	1.00	1.20
Baby (Str. Spoon and Fork)	Per Set	1.00	1.20

Retail Dealers receive 2% Additional Dealer Discount for orders of $25.00 or more.

IND. BUTTER KNIFE

BERRY SPOON

FIVE O'CLOCK TEA SP.

ICED DRINK SPOON

GRAVY LADLE

CREAM SOUP SPOON

SUGAR SPOON

BUTTER KNIFE

◆ *June Design*

TEASPOON

DINNER FORK

DINNER KNIFE

1936 Catalog

Madelon Pattern

Madelon Design

DINNER KNIFE

DINNER FORK

TEASPOON

ONEIDA COMMUNITY
TUDOR PLATE

SPOONS (six in box)

		Consumer	List
Tea	Per Doz.	$ 3.00	$ 3.60
Dessert or Oval Bowl Soup	Per Doz.	6.00	7.20
Table	Per Doz.	6.00	7.20
Soup, Round Bowl . . .	Per Doz.	6.00	7.20
Cream Soup	Per Doz.	6.00	7.20
Five O'Clock Tea or Sherbet	Set of 6	1.50	1.80
Iced Drink	Set of 6	2.50	3.00
Sugar	Each	.50	.60
Berry or Serving	Each	1.50	1.80

FORKS (six in box)

Dinner	Per Doz.	6.00	7.20
Dessert or Entree	Per Doz.	6.00	7.20
Grille	Per Doz.	6.00	7.20
Cocktail or Oyster . . .	Set of 6	2.50	3.00
Salad or Pastry	Set of 6	3.25	3.90
Cold Meat or Serving . . .	Each	1.00	1.20
Pickle or Olive	Each	.75	.90

KNIVES (Mirror Stainless Blades)

Dinner, H. H., Streamline .	Per Doz.	15.00	18.00
Grille, H. H., Streamline .	Per Doz.	15.00	18.00
Dinner, Embossed Handle	Per Doz.	8.00	9.60
Dessert, Luncheon or Breakfast, Embossed Handle .	Per Doz.	8.00	9.60

KNIVES (Stainless Blades)

Dinner, Hollow Handle .	Per Doz.	20.00	24.00
Grille, Hollow Handle .	Per Doz.	20.00	24.00

KNIVES (Plated Blades)

Dinner, Embossed Handle	Per Doz.	6.90	8.28
Dessert, Luncheon or Breakfast, Embossed Handle .	Per Doz.	6.90	8.28
Butter	Each	.50	.60
Individual Butter or Cheese	Set of 6	3.00	3.60

KNIFE AND FORK SETS
(6 Mirror Stainless Knives and 6 Forks)
Priced, per set

Dinner or Grille Knives, H. H. Streamline and Forks	10.50	12.60
Dinner Knives, Emb. H. and Forks . .	7.00	8.40
Dessert, Luncheon or Breakfast Knives, Emb. H. and Forks	7.00	8.40

CARVER
(Mirror Stainless Blade Knife)—For Steak or Game

2-Piece, Hollow Handle .	Per Set	5.00	6.00

MISCELLANEOUS

Serving or Gravy Ladle . .	Each	1.25	1.50
Pastry Server, Pierced . . .	Each	2.00	2.40

SETS

Butter and Sugar	Per Set	1.00	1.20
2-Pc. French "Table Serving"	Per Set	3.00	3.60

Retail Dealers receive 2% Additional Dealer Discount for orders of $25.00 or more.　　　52 Madelon

SALAD FORK

BERRY SPOON

FIVE O'CLOCK TEA SP.

ICED S

COLD MEAT FORK

GRAVY L

SEAFOOD FORK

CREA SOU SPOO

PIERCED PASTRY SERVER

SUGAR SPOON

CARVING SET

BUT KN

1936 Catalog

TUDOR PLATE
By the makers of Community Plate
Mary Stuart Design

DUO SERVICE TRAYS—With Dinner Knives

29 Pieces (set for 6)	Retail	List
Embossed Hdle., Stainless	$17.75	$ 22.92
Embossed Handle, Plated	15.00	19.32
Hollow Handle, Stainless	21.75	28.10
34 Pieces (set for 8)	Retail	List
Embossed Hdle., Stainless	$23.00	$29.64
Embossed Handle, Plated	19.25	24.80
Hollow Handle, Stainless	28.25	36.52

COLOR-MODE FREE CHESTS

With Dinner Knives

29 Pieces (set for 6)	Retail	List
Embossed Hdle., Stainless	$16.75	$21.30
Embossed Handle, Plated	14.00	17.70
Hollow Handle, Stainless	20.75	26.50
34 Pieces (set for 8)	Retail	List
Embossed Hdle., Stainless	$21.75	$27.76
Embossed Handle, Plated	18.25	22.98
Hollow Handle, Stainless	27.25	34.72

**25 YEAR REPLACEMENT
GUARANTEE**

SPOONS

Six in Box—Priced per Dozen

	Retail	List
Tea	$3.50	$4.36
Dessert	7.00	8.72
Table	7.00	8.72
Soup, R. B.	7.00	8.72

FORKS

Six in Box—Priced per Dozen

	Retail	List
Dinner	$7.00	$8.72
Dessert	7.00	8.72

KNIFE AND FORK SETS

6 Stainless Blade Knives and 6 Forks

Priced, per set	Retail	List
Embossed Handle Dinner Knives	$10.00	$12.84
Hollow Handle Dinner Knives	14.00	18.06
Hollow Handle Dessert or		
Breakfast Knives	14.00	18.06

KNIFE AND FORK SETS

6 Plated Blade Knives and 6 Forks

Priced, per set	Retail	List
Embossed Handle Dinner Knives	$ 7.25	$ 9.26
Embossed Handle Dessert Knives	7.25	9.26
Hollow Handle Dinner Knives	13.50	17.42
Hollow Handle Dessert Knives	13.50	17.42

KNIVES (Stainless Blades)

Priced, per dozen	Retail	List
Embossed Handle Dinner	$13.00	$16.92
Hollow Handle Dinner	21.00	27.36
Hollow Handle Dessert	21.00	27.36

KNIVES (Plated Blades)

Priced, per dozen	Retail	List
Embossed Handle Dinner	$7.50	$9.76
Embossed Handle Dessert	7.50	9.76
Embossed Handle Fruit	7.50	9.76
Hollow Handle Dinner	20.00	26.08
Hollow Handle Dessert	20.00	26.08

1930 Catalog

Queen Bess Pattern

TUDOR PLATE
By the makers of Community Plate
Queen Bess Design "I"

Dinner Knife

STAINLESS

Dinner Fork

Tea Spoon

Table Spoon

FREE MIRROR TRAY

29 Pieces (set for 6)	Retail	List
Embossed Hdle., Stainless	$18.00	$22.84
Embossed Handle, Plated	15.25	19.26
Hollow Handle, Stainless	22.00	28.06
34 Pieces (set for 8)		
Embossed Hdle., Stainless	23.50	29.86
Embossed Handle, Plated	20.00	25.08
Hollow Handle, Stainless	29.00	36.82

HONEYMOON FREE CHEST

29 Pieces (set for 6)	Retail	List
Embossed Hdle., Stainless	$18.00	$22.84
Embossed Handle, Plated	15.25	19.26
Hollow Handle, Stainless	22.00	28.06
34 Pieces (set for 8)		
Embossed Hdle., Stainless	23.50	29.86
Embossed Handle, Plated	20.00	25.08
Hollow Handle, Stainless	29.00	36.82

25 YEAR REPLACEMENT GUARANTEE

SPOONS

Six in Box—Priced, per dozen

	Retail	List
Tea	$4.00	$5.00
Dessert	8.00	10.00
Table	8.00	10.00
Soup, R. B.	8.00	10.00

FORKS

Six in Box—Priced, per dozen

	Retail	List
Dinner	$8.00	$10.00
Dessert	8.00	10.00

KNIFE AND FORK SETS
6 Stainless Blade Knives and 6 Forks

Priced, per set	Retail	List
Embossed Handle Dinner Knives	$10.50	$13.46
Hollow Handle Dinner Knives	14.50	18.68
Hollow Handle Dessert or		
Breakfast Knives	14.50	18.68

KNIFE AND FORK SETS
6 Plated Blade Knives and 6 Forks

Priced, per set	Retail	List
Embossed Handle Dinner Knives	$7.75	$9.88
Embossed Handle Dessert Knives	7.75	9.88
Hollow Handle Dinner Knives	14.00	18.04
Hollow Handle Dessert Knives	14.00	18.04

KNIVES (Stainless Blades)

Priced, per dozen	Retail	List
Embossed Handle Dinner	$13.00	$16.92
Hollow Handle Dinner	21.00	27.36
Hollow Handle Dessert	21.00	27.36

KNIVES (Plated Blades)

Priced, per dozen	Retail	List
Embossed Handle Dinner	$7.50	$9.76
Embossed Handle Dessert	7.50	9.76
Embossed Handle Fruit	7.50	9.76
Hollow Handle Dinner	20.00	26.08
Hollow Handle Dessert	20.00	26.08

1931 Catalog

See Price Guide — Group 3

Large quantities of this Betty Crocker premium silver were produced. Introduced in 1946, it is designated as "II" to distinguish it from another pattern.

Skyline Pattern

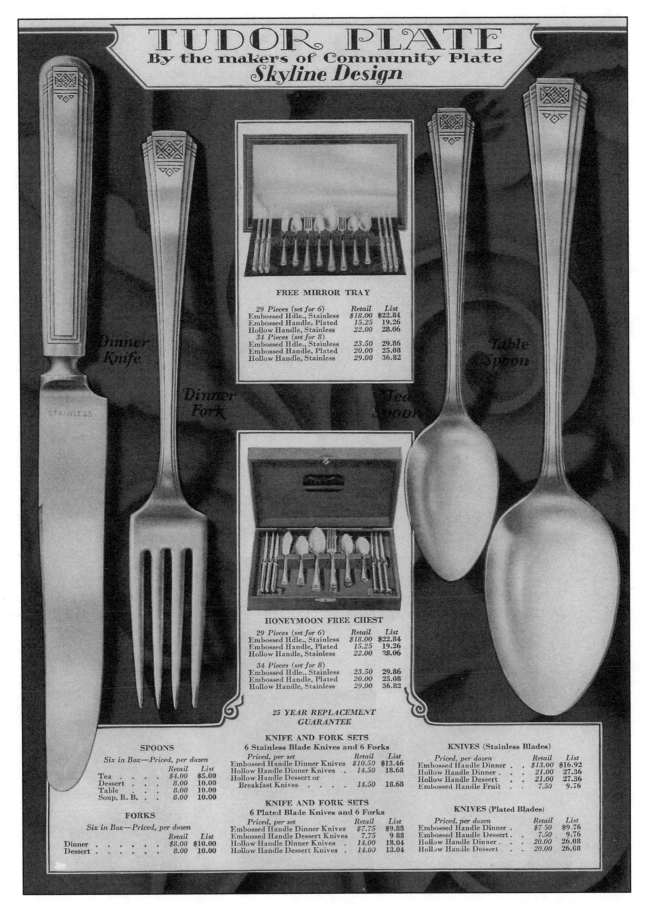

TUDOR PLATE
By the makers of Community Plate
Skyline Design

Dinner Knife

Dinner Fork

Table Spoon

Tea Spoon

STAINLESS

FREE MIRROR TRAY

29 Pieces (set for 6)	Retail	List
Embossed Hdle., Stainless	$18.00	$22.84
Embossed Handle, Plated	15.25	19.26
Hollow Handle, Stainless	22.00	28.06
34 Pieces (set for 8)		
Embossed Hdle., Stainless	23.50	29.86
Embossed Handle, Plated	20.00	25.08
Hollow Handle, Stainless	29.00	36.82

HONEYMOON FREE CHEST

29 Pieces (set for 6)	Retail	List
Embossed Hdle., Stainless	$18.00	$22.84
Embossed Handle, Plated	15.25	19.26
Hollow Handle, Stainless	22.00	28.06
34 Pieces (set for 8)		
Embossed Hdle., Stainless	23.50	29.86
Embossed Handle, Plated	20.00	25.08
Hollow Handle, Stainless	29.00	36.82

25 YEAR REPLACEMENT GUARANTEE

SPOONS

Six in Box—Priced, per dozen

	Retail	List
Tea	$4.00	$5.00
Dessert	8.00	10.00
Table	8.00	10.00
Soup, R. B.	8.00	10.00

FORKS

Six in Box—Priced, per dozen

	Retail	List
Dinner	$8.00	$10.00
Dessert	8.00	10.00

KNIFE AND FORK SETS
6 Stainless Blade Knives and 6 Forks

Priced, per set	Retail	List
Embossed Handle Dinner Knives	$10.59	$13.46
Hollow Handle Dinner Knives	14.50	18.68
Hollow Handle Dessert or		
Breakfast Knives	14.50	18.68

KNIFE AND FORK SETS
6 Plated Blade Knives and 6 Forks

Priced, per set	Retail	List
Embossed Handle Dinner Knives	$7.75	$9.83
Embossed Handle Dessert Knives	7.75	9.83
Hollow Handle Dinner Knives	14.00	18.04
Hollow Handle Dessert Knives	14.00	13.04

KNIVES (Stainless Blades)

Priced, per dozen	Retail	List
Embossed Handle Dinner	$13.00	$16.92
Hollow Handle Dinner	21.00	27.36
Hollow Handle Dessert	21.00	27.36
Embossed Handle Fruit	7.50	9.76

KNIVES (Plated Blades)

Priced, per dozen	Retail	List
Embossed Handle Dinner	$7.50	$9.76
Embossed Handle Dessert	7.50	9.76
Hollow Handle Dinner	20.00	26.08
Hollow Handle Dessert	20.00	26.68

1931 Catalog

See Price Guide — Group 3

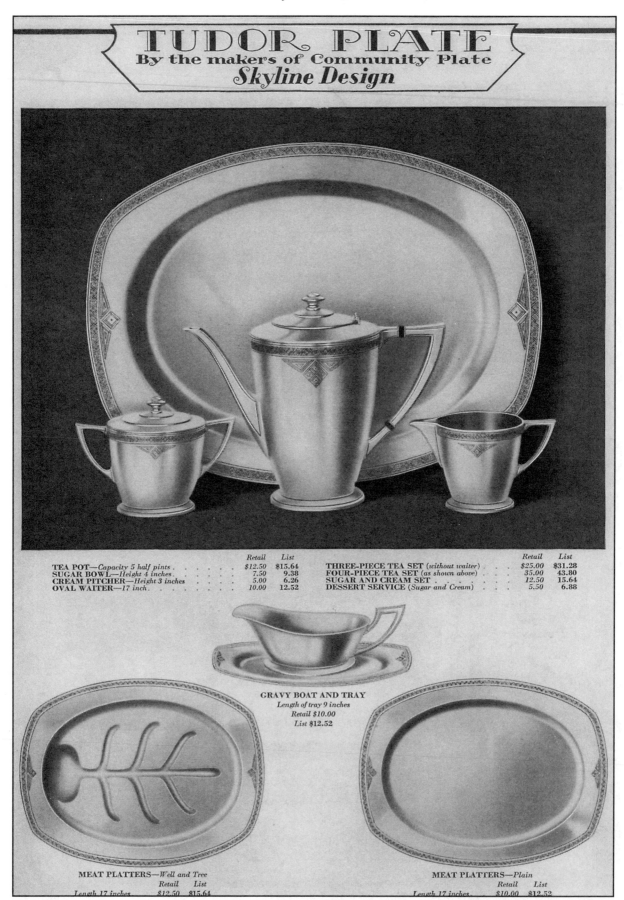

TUDOR PLATE
By the makers of Community Plate
Skyline Design

	Retail	List		Retail	List
TEA POT—Capacity 5 half pints	$12.50	$15.64	THREE-PIECE TEA SET (without waiter)	$25.00	$31.28
SUGAR BOWL—Height 4 inches	7.50	9.38	FOUR-PIECE TEA SET (as shown above)	35.00	43.80
CREAM PITCHER—Height 3 inches	5.00	6.26	SUGAR AND CREAM SET	12.50	15.64
OVAL WAITER—17 inch	10.00	12.52	DESSERT SERVICE (Sugar and Cream)	5.50	6.88

GRAVY BOAT AND TRAY
Length of tray 9 inches
Retail $10.00
List $12.52

MEAT PLATTERS—*Well and Tree*			MEAT PLATTERS—*Plain*		
	Retail	List		Retail	List
Length 17 inches	$12.50	$15.64	Length 17 inches	$10.00	$12.52

1931 Catalog

Universal Silver

Empress, Farmington & Saybrook Patterns

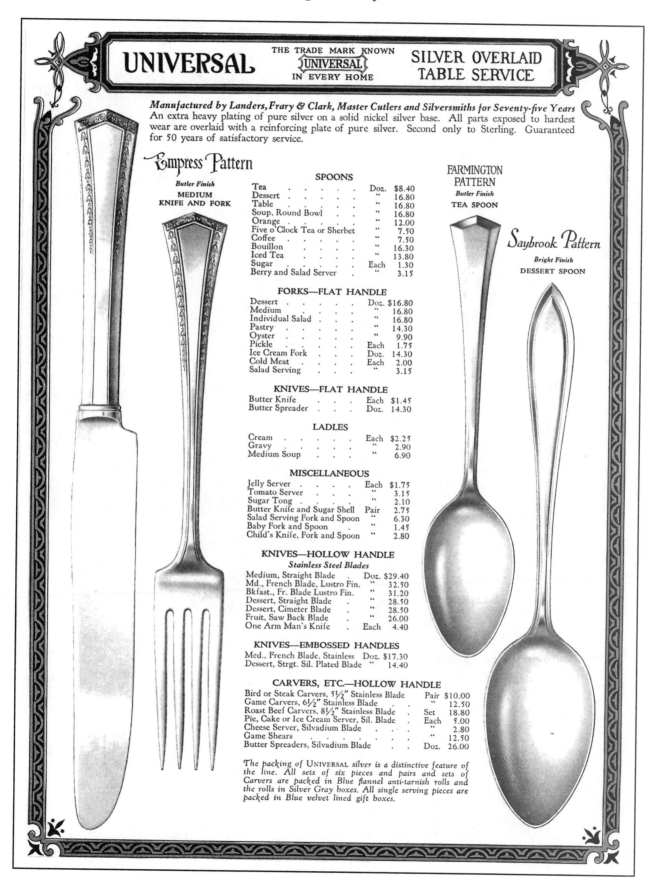

UNIVERSAL THE TRADE MARK KNOWN [UNIVERSAL] IN EVERY HOME **SILVER OVERLAID TABLE SERVICE**

Manufactured by Landers, Frary & Clark, Master Cutlers and Silversmiths for Seventy-five Years
An extra heavy plating of pure silver on a solid nickel silver base. All parts exposed to hardest wear are overlaid with a reinforcing plate of pure silver. Second only to Sterling. Guaranteed for 50 years of satisfactory service.

Empress Pattern

Butler Finish
MEDIUM KNIFE AND FORK

SPOONS

Tea	Doz.	$8.40
Dessert	"	16.80
Table	"	16.80
Soup, Round Bowl	"	16.80
Orange	"	12.00
Five o'Clock Tea or Sherbet	"	7.50
Coffee	"	7.50
Bouillon	"	16.30
Iced Tea	"	13.80
Sugar	Each	1.30
Berry and Salad Server	"	3.15

FORKS—FLAT HANDLE

Dessert	Doz.	$16.80
Medium	"	16.80
Individual Salad	"	16.80
Pastry	"	14.30
Oyster	"	9.90
Pickle	Each	1.75
Ice Cream Fork	Doz.	14.30
Cold Meat	Each	2.00
Salad Serving	"	3.15

KNIVES—FLAT HANDLE

Butter Knife	Each	$1.45
Butter Spreader	Doz.	14.30

LADLES

Cream	Each	$2.25
Gravy	"	2.90
Medium Soup	"	6.90

MISCELLANEOUS

Jelly Server	Each	$1.75
Tomato Server	"	3.15
Sugar Tong	"	2.10
Butter Knife and Sugar Shell	Pair	2.75
Salad Serving Fork and Spoon	"	6.30
Baby Fork and Spoon	"	1.45
Child's Knife, Fork and Spoon	"	2.80

KNIVES—HOLLOW HANDLE
Stainless Steel Blades

Medium, Straight Blade	Doz.	$29.40
Md., French Blade, Lustro Fin.	"	32.50
Bkfast., Fr. Blade Lustro Fin.	"	31.20
Dessert, Straight Blade	"	28.50
Dessert, Cimeter Blade	"	28.50
Fruit, Saw Back Blade	"	26.00
One Arm Man's Knife	Each	4.40

KNIVES—EMBOSSED HANDLES

Med., French Blade, Stainless	Doz.	$17.30
Dessert, Strgt. Sil. Plated Blade	"	14.40

CARVERS, ETC.—HOLLOW HANDLE

Bird or Steak Carvers, 5½" Stainless Blade	Pair	$10.00
Game Carvers, 6½" Stainless Blade	"	12.50
Roast Beef Carvers, 8½" Stainless Blade	Set	18.80
Pie, Cake or Ice Cream Server, Sil. Blade	Each	5.00
Cheese Server, Silvadium Blade	"	2.80
Game Shears	"	12.50
Butter Spreaders, Silvadium Blade	Doz.	26.00

The packing of UNIVERSAL silver is a distinctive feature of the line. All sets of six pieces and pairs and sets of Carvers are packed in Blue flannel anti-tarnish rolls and the rolls in Silver Gray boxes. All single serving pieces are packed in Blue velvet lined gift boxes.

FARMINGTON PATTERN

Butler Finish
TEA SPOON

Saybrook Pattern

Bright Finish
DESSERT SPOON

1835 R. Wallace

Anjou (Victoria) Pattern

Tea Spoon, Full Size

Dessert Spoon Full Size

Dessert Fork, Full Size

8284
8285
8286
8287
8288
8289
8290
8291
8292
8293
8294
8295
8296
8283

It will be mutually advantageous if customers will kindly use the order blanks which are enclosed in this Catalogue, and by ordering Christmas goods at the earliest possible moment, while our stock is full and complete, possible disappointments may be avoided. We prepay mail and express charges on purchases, and engrave initials without extra charge.

Victoria Triple Silver Plated Table Ware

The "Victoria" is a Triple Silver Plated bright polished pattern, and combines design, finish and wearing qualities of the highest character. We will replace any articles that fail to wear satisfactorily.

The Tea Spoon, Dessert Spoon and Dessert Fork are shown full size. The other articles directly above are shown one-third actual size.

8276	Tea Spoons	Dozen	$3.00	8286	Pie Server, Hollow Handle	Each $1.75
8277	Dessert Spoons	Dozen	5.00			
8278	Table Spoons	Dozen	6.00	8287	Orange Knives, Hollow Handles, Saw Back Blades	Doz. 10.00
8279	Dessert Forks	Dozen	5.00			
8280	Table Forks	Dozen	6.00	8288	Butter Knife	Each .75
8281	Dessert Knives, Hollow Handles	Dozen	9.00	8289	Coffee Spoons	Dozen 3.00
				8290	Fruit Knives, Hollow Handles	Dozen 9.00
8282	Table Knives, Hollow Handles	Dozen	10.00	8291	Gravy Ladle	Each 1.00
				8292	Oyster Forks	Dozen 3.00
8283	Soup Spoons, Round Bowls	Dozen	6.00	8293	Berry Spoon	Each 1.00
				8294	Sugar Spoon	Each .75
8284	Carving Set, Knife, Fork and Steel		6.75	8295	Orange Spoons	Dozen 2.75
8285	Cold Meat Fork	Each	1.00	8296	Oyster Ladle	Each 1.50

ADDITIONAL ARTICLES, NOT ILLUSTRATED

8297	Cake Knife, Hollow Handle	Each	$1.75	8300	Cheese Scoop	Each $2.00
8298	Ice Cream Knife, Hollow Handle	Each	2.25	8301	Game Carving Knife and Fork, Hollow Handles	2.25
8299	Soup Ladle	Each	2.00	8302	Cream Ladle	Each .50

We sell half dozens at dozen rates.

1907 Catalog. Anjou was sold as Victoria by the firm 1890 Jennings Bros.

See Price Guide — Group 1

332

Astoria Pattern

"R. WALLACE 1835" SILVER-PLATED TABLE WARE.

On this and the following page we show the new Astoria pattern of "R. Wallace 1835" silver-plated table ware. This trade mark advertised extensively over the United States is a guarantee of the highest possible excellence in silver plate. After exhaustive tests we have selected this brand, from the many good ones, as the best, the one combining in the highest degree design, finish, and wearing qualities.

The Astoria and Joan patterns have a beauty of design and richness of die work equalled by few sterling silver patterns. We give our *unqualified guarantee* as to their wearing qualities. We also show on this page Pearl Handle knives with triple plated (12 dwt.) steel blades. These knives are of fine quality in every respect. The table and dessert knives have sterling silver ferules.

Pieces on this page are shown full size, those on the opposite page one-half size. Initials only (script) will be engraved free. Old English, 5 cents per letter.

Knives cannot be engraved.

PEARL HANDLE KNIVES.

6000	Table Knives, per doz.		$18.00
6001	Dessert Knives, per doz.		14.00
6002	Fruit Knives,	" "	8.50

ASTORIA PATTERN.

6003	Tea Spoons, per doz.	2.50
6004	Dessert Spoons, per doz.	4.00
	pair	.75
6005	Dessert Forks, per doz.	4.00
6006	Table Spoons, per doz.	4.50
	pair	.90
6007	Table Forks, per doz.	4.50
6008	Soup Spoons	4.50
6015	Olive Fork	.50
6016	Salt Spoon	.25
6017	Berry Spoon	1.10
	gilt	1.35
6018	Cucumber Server	1.10
6019	Pie Knife	1.25
	gilt	1.60
6020	Sardine Server	.75
6021	Cake Fork	.75
	gilt	1.00
6022	Jelly Knife	.85
	gilt	1.00
6023	Pie Server, hollow handle	1.50
6024	Orange Spoons, per doz.	2.75
6025	Large Cold Meat Fork	.85
	gilt	1.00
6026	Pickle Fork	.55
6027	Horse Radish Spoon	.40
6028	Butter Knife	.50
6029	Large Cheese Scoop	.85
6030	Bouillon Spoons, per doz.	4.00
6031	Berry Forks, per doz.	2.75
6032	Butter Spreaders, per doz.	4.00
6033	Cream Ladle	.65
	gilt	.85
6034	Mustard Spoon	.30
6035	Lettuce Fork	.90
6036	Gravy Ladle	.85
	gilt	1.10
6037	Cheese Scoop	.75
6038	Cold Meat Fork	.55
6039	Oyster Forks, per doz.	3.00
6040	Coffee Spoons, " "	2.35
6041	Preserve Spoon	.80
	gilt	1.00
6042	Sugar Spoon	.45
	gilt	.55

PIECES NOT ILLUSTRATED.

6043	Salad Set, fork and spoon, in satin-lined box	2.75
6044	Fish Set, knife and fork, in satin-lined box	3.50
6045	Child's Set, knife, fork, and spoon, in satin-lined box	1.00
6046	Crumb Knife	2.00
6047	Oyster Ladle	1.75
	gilt	2.25
6048	Soup Ladle, large	2.25
	gilt	2.75
6049	Ice Cream Server	1.75
6050	Asparagus Server	2.00
6051	Hollow Handle Table Knives, per doz.	10.00
6052	Hollow Handle Dessert Knives, per doz.	9.00

All pieces except tea, dessert, and table spoons, and forks, are put up in satin-lined boxes. Half dozens sold at dozen rates.

6000 Table Knife.

6001 Dessert Knife.

6007 Astoria Dessert Fork.

6002 Fruit Knife.

6003 Astoria Tea Spoon.

1903 Catalog

See Price Guide — Group 1

Astoria Pattern

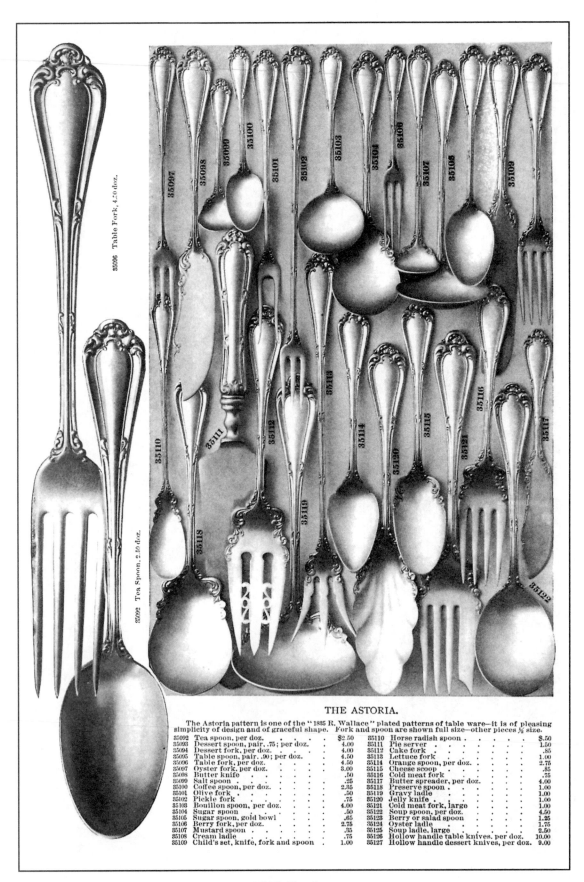

35096 Table Fork, 4.50 doz.

35092 Tea Spoon, 2.50 doz.

THE ASTORIA.

The Astoria pattern is one of the "1835 R. Wallace" plated patterns of table ware—it is of pleasing simplicity of design and of graceful shape. Fork and spoon are shown full size—other pieces ⅝ size.

35092	Tea spoon, per doz.	$2.50	35110	Horse radish spoon	$.50
35093	Dessert spoon, pair .75; per doz.	4.00	35111	Pie server	1.50
35094	Dessert fork, per doz.	4.00	35112	Cake fork	.85
35095	Table spoon, pair .90; per doz.	4.50	35113	Lettuce fork	1.00
35096	Table fork, per doz.	4.50	35114	Orange spoon, per doz.	2.75
35097	Oyster fork, per doz.	3.00	35115	Cheese scoop	.85
35098	Butter knife	.50	35116	Cold meat fork	.75
35099	Salt spoon	.25	35117	Butter spreader, per doz.	4.00
35100	Coffee spoon, per doz.	2.35	35118	Preserve spoon	1.00
35101	Olive fork	.50	35119	Gravy ladle	1.00
35102	Pickle fork	.75	35120	Jelly knife	1.00
35103	Bouillon spoon, per doz.	4.00	35121	Cold meat fork, large	1.00
35104	Sugar spoon	.50	35122	Soup spoon, per doz.	4.50
35105	Sugar spoon, gold bowl	.65	35123	Berry or salad spoon	1.25
35106	Berry fork, per doz.	2.75	35124	Oyster ladle	1.75
35107	Mustard spoon	.55	35125	Soup ladle, large	2.50
35108	Cream ladle	.75	35126	Hollow handle table knives, per doz.	10.00
35109	Child's set, knife, fork and spoon	1.00	35127	Hollow handle dessert knives, per doz.	9.00

1903 Catalog

BAIRD-NORTH COMPANY, GOLD AND SILVER SMITHS, SALEM, MASS.

THE FLORAL PATTERN OF "R. WALLACE 1835" PLATED WARE.

A new creation, and unquestionably the handsomest and richest design ever made in silver plate
All pieces are in the heaviest triple plate—the "R. Wallace 1835" quality of triple plate.   This trade
mark is a guarantee of its wearing qualities.   The knife, fork and spoon are shown in full size –those
pieces shown reduced are one half scale.   It is in the soft gray finish.

35039	Dessert knife per doz. $9.50	35015	Lettuce fork .	$1.00	35027	Olive fork . .	$.60
35040	Dessert fork, each .50,	35016	Cold meat fork .	1.00	35028	Berry fork, per doz.	3.50
	per doz. 5.00	35017	Coffee spoon, per doz.	3.00	35029	Soup spoon, per doz.	6.00
35041	Tea spoon, each .35,	35018	Butter spreader, per		35030	Oyster fork, per doz.	3.50
	per doz. 3.00		doz.	5.00		Pieces not illustrated.	
35042	Table knife, per doz. 10.50	35019	Butter knife .	.75	35031	Soup ladle . .	3 00
35013	Table spoon, per pair, 1.25	35020	Child's set . .	1.35	35032	Pie knife . .	1.75
	per doz. 6.00	35021	Orange spoon, per doz.	4.00	35033	Cucumber server .	85
35044	Table fork, each .65,	35022	Berry or salad spoon	1.50	35034	Cheese scoop .	1.00
	per doz. 6.00	35023	Sugar spoon .	.65	35035	Preserve spoon .	1.00
35045	Dessert spoon, per pair 1 00	35024	Sugar spoon with gold		35036	Mustard spoon .	.40
	per doz. 5.00		bowl . . .	.75	35037	Sardine fork .	.85
35013	Sugar tongs . . 1.00	35025	Gravy ladle .	1.35	35038	Cake fork . .	1.00
58014	Ice cream spoon, doz. 4.00	35026	Cream ladle . .	1.00			

Floral Pattern

Patented 1902 – 1903. Left to right: 10⅕" hollow handle bread knife, 4⅛" chocolate spoon, 11⅕" fish serving knife, 7" ice tongs.

See Price Guide — Group 1

Floral Pattern

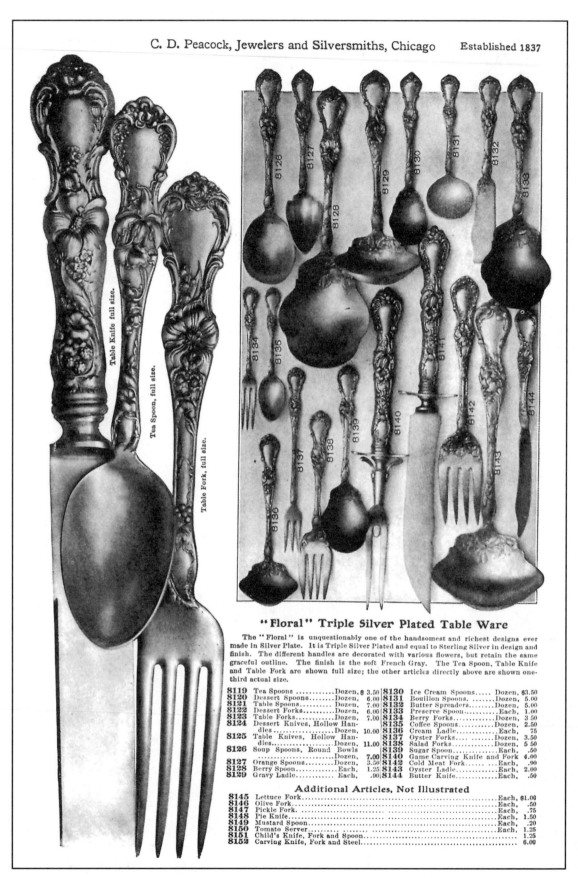

C. D. Peacock, Jewelers and Silversmiths, Chicago   Established 1837

Table Knife full size.

Tea Spoon, full size.

Table Fork, full size.

"Floral" Triple Silver Plated Table Ware

The "Floral" is unquestionably one of the handsomest and richest designs ever made in Silver Plate. It is Triple Silver Plated and equal to Sterling Silver in design and finish. The different handles are decorated with various flowers, but retain the same graceful outline. The finish is the soft French Gray. The Tea Spoon, Table Knife and Table Fork are shown full size; the other articles directly above are shown one-third actual size.

8119	Tea Spoons ....Dozen,	$ 3.50	8130	Ice Cream Spoons..... Dozen,	$3.50
8120	Dessert Spoons.......Dozen,	6.00	8131	Bouillon Spoons. .....Dozen,	5.00
8121	Table Spoons......... Dozen,	7.00	8132	Butter Spreaders.......Dozen,	5.00
8122	Dessert Forks.........Dozen,	6.00	8133	Preserve Spoon.........Each,	1.00
8123	Table Forks...........Dozen,	7.00	8134	Berry Forks...........Dozen,	3.50
8124	Dessert Knives, Hollow Handles........Dozen,	10.00	8135	Coffee Spoons.........Dozen,	2.50
8125	Table Knives, Hollow Handles........Dozen,	11.00	8136	Cream Ladle..........Each,	.75
			8137	Oyster Forks..........Dozen,	3.50
8126	Soup Spoons, Round Bowls ....Dozen,	7.00	8138	Salad Forks...........Dozen,	5 50
			8139	Sugar Spoon...........Each,	.50
8127	Orange Spoons........Dozen,	3.50	8140	Game Carving Knife and Fork	4.00
8128	Berry Spoon..............Each,	1.25	8142	Cold Meat Fork....... ...Each,	.90
8129	Gravy Ladle............ Each,	.90	8143	Oyster Ladle..........Each,	2.00
			8144	Butter Knife...........Each,	.50

Additional Articles, Not Illustrated

8145	Lettuce Fork...Each,	$1.00
8146	Olive Fork..Each,	.50
8147	Pickle Fork. ....Each,	.75
8148	Pie Knife...Each,	1.50
8149	Mustard Spoon...Each,	.20
8150	Tomato Server...Each,	1.25
8151	Child's Knife, Fork and Spoon.......................................	1.25
8152	Carving Knife, Fork and Steel..	6.00

1907 Catalog. Also sold as "Florida" by Mermod Jaccard and King of St. Louis.

Left to right: 10" pastry/pie server, 5½" bonbon, 4⅜" nut pick, 4¹³⁄₁₆" egg spoon, 9⅕" ice serving spoon. *Collection of Karen Fisher.*

See Price Guide — Group 1

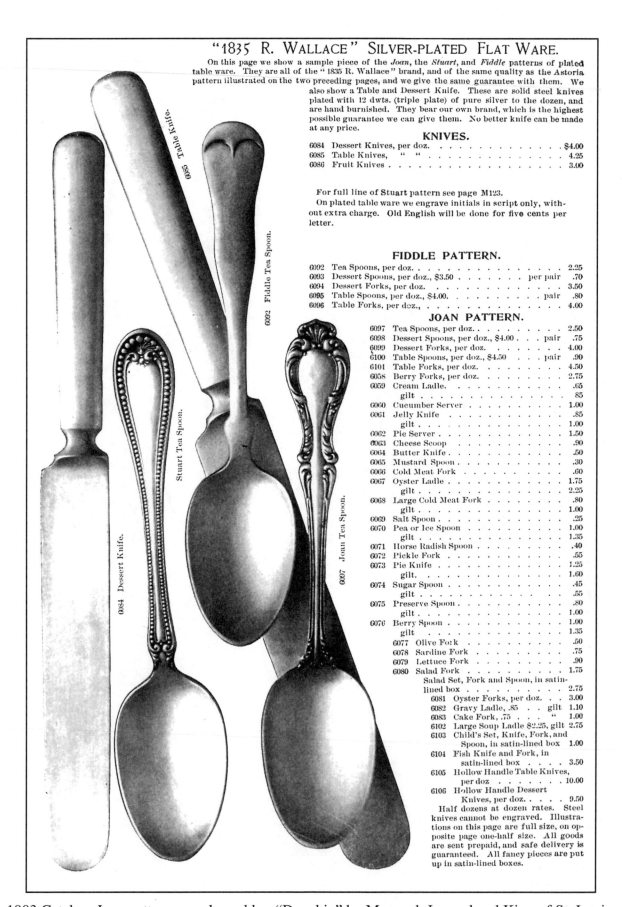

"1835 R. WALLACE" SILVER-PLATED FLAT WARE.

On this page we show a sample piece of the *Joan*, the *Stuart*, and *Fiddle* patterns of plated table ware. They are all of the "1835 R. Wallace" brand, and of the same quality as the Astoria pattern illustrated on the two preceding pages, and we give the same guarantee with them. We also show a Table and Dessert Knife. These are solid steel knives plated with 12 dwts. (triple plate) of pure silver to the dozen, and are hand burnished. They bear our own brand, which is the highest possible guarantee we can give them. No better knife can be made at any price.

KNIVES.

6084	Dessert Knives, per doz.	$4.00
6085	Table Knives, " "	4.25
6086	Fruit Knives	3.00

For full line of Stuart pattern see page M123.

On plated table ware we engrave initials in script only, without extra charge. Old English will be done for five cents per letter.

FIDDLE PATTERN.

6092	Tea Spoons, per doz.	2.25
6093	Dessert Spoons, per doz., $3.50 . . . . . per pair	.70
6094	Dessert Forks, per doz.	3.50
6095	Table Spoons, per doz., $4.00. . . . . . pair	.80
6096	Table Forks, per doz.,	4.00

JOAN PATTERN.

6097	Tea Spoons, per doz.	2.50
6098	Dessert Spoons, per doz., $4.00 . . pair	.75
6099	Dessert Forks, per doz.	4.00
6100	Table Spoons, per doz., $4.50 . . . pair	.90
6101	Table Forks, per doz.	4.50
6058	Berry Forks, per doz.	2.75
6059	Cream Ladle.	.65
	gilt	.85
6060	Cucumber Server	1.00
6061	Jelly Knife	.85
	gilt	1.00
6062	Pie Server	1.50
6063	Cheese Scoop	.90
6064	Butter Knife	.50
6065	Mustard Spoon	.30
6066	Cold Meat Fork	.60
6067	Oyster Ladle	1.75
	gilt	2.25
6068	Large Cold Meat Fork	.80
	gilt	1.00
6069	Salt Spoon	.25
6070	Pea or Ice Spoon	1.00
	gilt	1.35
6071	Horse Radish Spoon	.40
6072	Pickle Fork	.55
6073	Pie Knife	1.25
	gilt	1.60
6074	Sugar Spoon	.45
	gilt	.55
6075	Preserve Spoon	.80
	gilt	1.00
6076	Berry Spoon	1.00
	gilt	1.35
6077	Olive Fork	.50
6078	Sardine Fork	.75
6079	Lettuce Fork	.90
6080	Salad Fork	1.75
	Salad Set, Fork and Spoon, in satin-lined box	2.75
6081	Oyster Forks, per doz.	3.00
6082	Gravy Ladle, .85 . . . gilt	1.10
6083	Cake Fork, .75 . . . "	1.00
6102	Large Soup Ladle $2.25, gilt	2.75
6103	Child's Set, Knife, Fork, and Spoon, in satin-lined box	1.00
6104	Fish Knife and Fork, in satin-lined box	3.50
6105	Hollow Handle Table Knives, per doz	10.00
6106	Hollow Handle Dessert Knives, per doz.	9.50

Half dozens at dozen rates. Steel knives cannot be engraved. Illustrations on this page are full size, on opposite page one-half size. All goods are sent prepaid, and safe delivery is guaranteed. All fancy pieces are put up in satin-lined boxes.

Labels on flatware: 6085 Table Knife. 6092 Fiddle Tea Spoon. Stuart Tea Spoon. 6084 Dessert Knife. 6097 Joan Tea Spoon.

1903 Catalog. Joan pattern was also sold as "Dauphin" by Mermod, Jaccard and King of St. Louis.

Fiddle & Joan Patterns

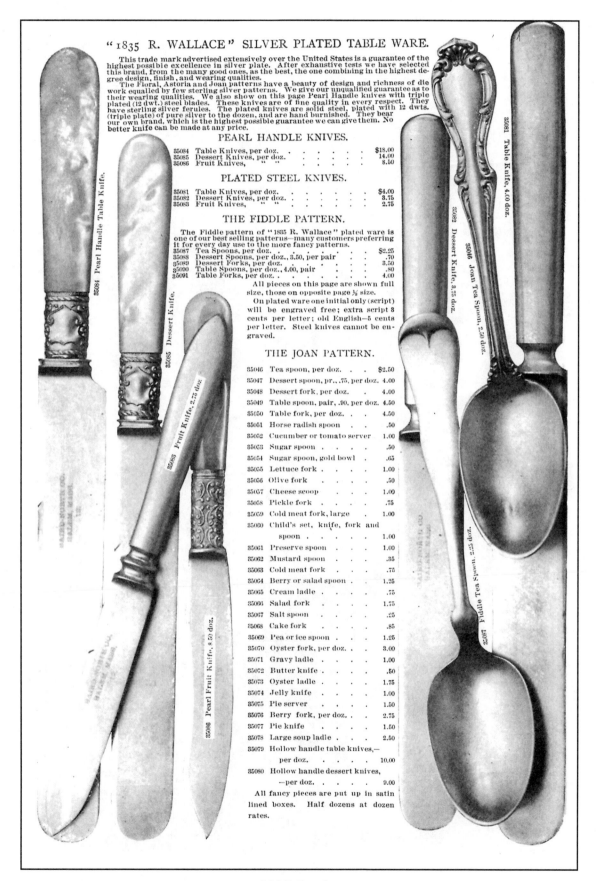

"1835 R. WALLACE" SILVER PLATED TABLE WARE.

This trade mark advertised extensively over the United States is a guarantee of the highest possible excellence in silver plate. After exhaustive tests we have selected this brand, from the many good ones, as the best, the one combining in the highest degree design, finish, and wearing qualities.

The Floral, Astoria and Joan patterns have a beauty of design and richness of die work equalled by few sterling silver patterns. We give our unqualified guarantee as to their wearing qualities. We also show on this page Pearl Handle knives with triple plated (12 dwt.) steel blades. These knives are of fine quality in every respect. They have sterling silver ferules. The plated knives are solid steel, plated with 12 dwts. (triple plate) of pure silver to the dozen, and are hand burnished. They bear our own brand, which is the highest possible guarantee we can give them. No better knife can be made at any price.

PEARL HANDLE KNIVES.

35084	Table Knives, per doz.	$18.00
35085	Dessert Knives, per doz.	14.00
35086	Fruit Knives, " "	8.50

PLATED STEEL KNIVES.

35081	Table Knives, per doz.	$4.00
35082	Dessert Knives, per doz.	3.75
35083	Fruit Knives, " "	2.75

THE FIDDLE PATTERN.

The Fiddle pattern of "1835 R. Wallace" plated ware is one of our best selling patterns—many customers preferring it for every day use to the more fancy patterns.

35087	Tea Spoons, per doz.	$2.25
35088	Dessert Spoons, per doz., 3.50, per pair	.70
35089	Dessert Forks, per doz.	3.50
35090	Table Spoons, per doz., 4.00, pair	.80
35091	Table Forks, per doz.	4.00

All pieces on this page are shown full size, those on opposite page ½ size.

On plated ware one initial only (script) will be engraved free; extra script 3 cents per letter; old English—5 cents per letter. Steel knives cannot be engraved.

THE JOAN PATTERN.

35046	Tea spoon, per doz.	$2.50
35047	Dessert spoon, pr., .75, per doz.	4.00
35048	Dessert fork, per doz.	4.00
35049	Table spoon, pair, .90, per doz.	4.50
35050	Table fork, per doz.	4.50
35051	Horse radish spoon	.50
35052	Cucumber or tomato server	1.00
35053	Sugar spoon	.50
35054	Sugar spoon, gold bowl	.65
35055	Lettuce fork	1.00
35056	Olive fork	.50
35057	Cheese scoop	1.00
35058	Pickle fork	.75
35059	Cold meat fork, large	1.00
35060	Child's set, knife, fork and spoon	1.00
35061	Preserve spoon	1.00
35062	Mustard spoon	.35
35063	Cold meat fork	.75
35064	Berry or salad spoon	1.25
35065	Cream ladle	.75
35066	Salad fork	1.75
35067	Salt spoon	.25
35068	Cake fork	.85
35069	Pea or ice spoon	1.25
35070	Oyster fork, per doz.	3.00
35071	Gravy ladle	1.00
35072	Butter knife	.50
35073	Oyster ladle	1.75
35074	Jelly knife	1.00
35075	Pie server	1.50
35076	Berry fork, per doz.	2.75
35077	Pie knife	1.50
35078	Large soup ladle	2.50
35079	Hollow handle table knives,— per doz.	10.00
35080	Hollow handle dessert knives, —per doz.	9.00

All fancy pieces are put up in satin lined boxes. Half dozens at dozen rates.

Labels on items: 35084 Pearl Handle Table Knife. · 35085 Dessert Knife. · 35083 Fruit Knife, 2.75 doz. · 35086 Pearl Fruit Knife, 8.50 doz. · 35081 Table Knife, 4.00 doz. · 35082 Dessert Knife, 3.75 doz. · 35046 Joan Tea Spoon, 2.50 doz. · 35087 Fiddle Tea Spoon, 2.25 doz.

1905 Catalog

See Price Guide — Group 1

Joan Pattern

1905 Catalog

Joan Pattern

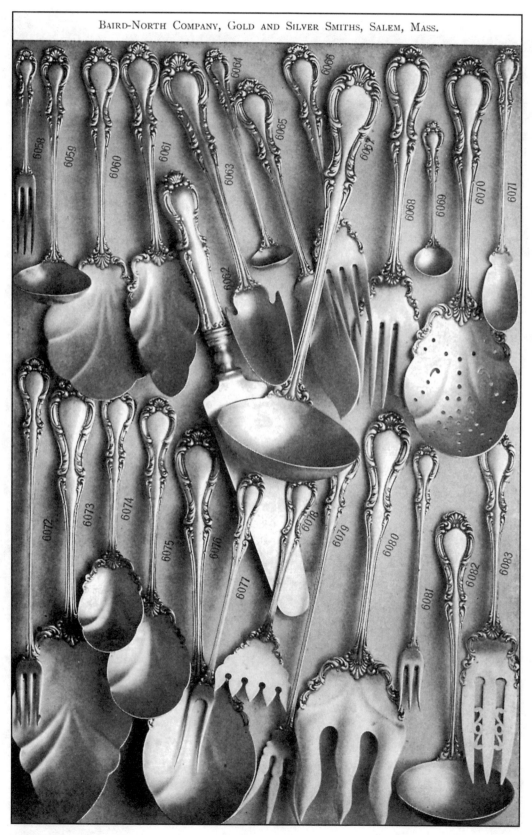

BAIRD-NORTH COMPANY, GOLD AND SILVER SMITHS, SALEM, MASS.

1905 Catalog

See Price Guide — Group 1

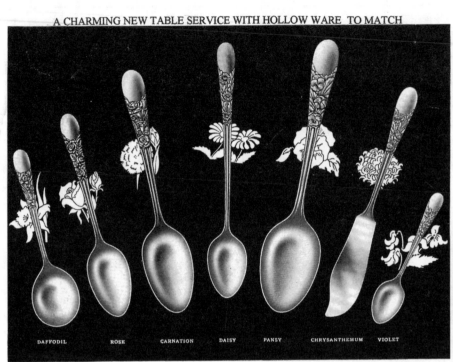

A CHARMING NEW TABLE SERVICE WITH HOLLOW WARE TO MATCH

DAFFODIL · ROSE · CARNATION · DAISY · PANSY · CHRYSANTHEMUM · VIOLET

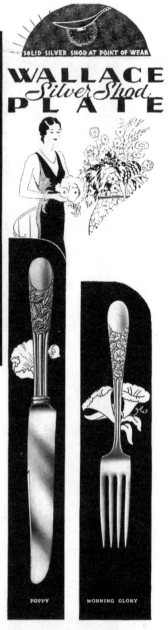

SOLID SILVER SHOD AT POINT OF WEAR

WALLACE *Silver Shod* PLATE

POPPY · MORNING GLORY

Instead of one there are nine floral decorations in one gleaming service. The soup spoon, for example, has a carnation design, the dinner fork a poppy, tea spoon boasts a rose . . . and so on. The fundamental design is of course the same, only the flower varies . . . disarmingly refreshing. New and different . . . So charming on the table . . . Flowers always fit. This pattern is **solid silver** shod, too.

SPOONS	Retail	List
Tea, *silver shod* (Rose)...............doz.	$8.00	$9.60
Dessert or Oval Soup, *silver shod* (Carnation)........................doz.	16.00	19.20
Table, *silver shod* (Pansy)..............doz.	16.00	19.20
Soup, Round Bowl, *silver shod* (Carnation) doz.	16.00	19.20
*Cream Soup or Cereal (Rose).......doz.	13.00	15.60
*After Dinner Coffee (Violet)........six	3.75	4.50
*Bouillon or Consomme (Daffodil)....six	5.75	6.90
Iced Beverage (Daisy)..............six	5.75	6.90
*Orange or Grape Fruit (Rose)........six	5.75	6.90
*Sugar (Rose)....................each	1.50	1.80
*Berry or Serving (Pansy)...........each	2.25	2.70

FORKS		
Grille, *silver shod* (Daisy)..............doz.	16.00	19.20
Dinner, *silver shod* (Poppy)...........doz.	16.00	19.20
Dessert, Luncheon or Breakfast, *silver shod* (Morning Glory)................doz.	16.00	19.20
*Salad or Pastry, individual, (Chrysanthemum)........................six	6.50	7.80
*Cocktail or Oyster (Violet).............six	5.00	6.00
*Cold Meat or Serving (Poppy).......each	2.25	2.70

KNIVES—Hollow Handle—Mirror Stainless Blade		
Grille (Daisy)....................doz.	26.00	31.20
Dinner (Poppy)..................doz.	26.00	31.20
Dessert, Luncheon or Breakfast (Morning Glory)......................doz.	26.00	31.20

KNIVES—Solid Handle—Mirror Stainless Blade	Retail	List
Dinner (Poppy).................doz.	$12.00	$14.40

KNIFE AND FORK SETS
(6 Mirror Stainless Knives and 6 Forks)

Dinner Knives, (Poppy) Hollow Handle, and Dinner Forks, (Poppy), *silver shod*......set	21.00	25.20
Dessert, Luncheon or Breakfast Knives (Morning Glory), Hollow Handle, and Dessert, Luncheon or Breakfast Forks (Morning Glory), *silver shod*............set	21.00	25.20
Grille Knives (Daisy) Hollow Handle, and Grille Forks (Daisy), *silver shod*......set	21.00	25.20
Dinner Knives (Poppy), Solid Handle, and Dinner Forks (Poppy), *silver shod*.....set	14.00	16.80

CARVING SET—Hollow Handles, Stainless Blade and Tines.

*Steak or Bird (Poppy), 2 pieces..........set	6.00	7.20

MISCELLANEOUS

*Butter Knife or Server (Chrysanthemum) each	$1.50	$1.80
*Sugar Tongs (Violet)................each	1.75	2.10
*Cake Server, Hollow Handle (Morning Glory)........................each	3.25	3.90
*Round Server, Pierced (Carnation)....each	2.25	2.70
*Jelly or Small Server (Rose)...........each	1.50	1.80
*Gravy or Serving Ladle (Carnation).....each	2.25	2.70
*Butter Spreaders (Daffodil)...........six	6.00	7.20

In fancy gift box.

1936

MATCHING "NINE FLOWER" HOLLOW WARE

	Retail	List
3-Piece Tea Set and Waiter (illustrated)...	$40.00	$48.00
Coffee, 8¾ in. high, 6 cups (2½ pints)....	15.00	18.00
Sugar, gold lined, 4¼ in. high, 12 oz.......	7.50	9.00
Cream, gold lined, 4¼ in. high, 10 oz......	7.50	9.00
Waiter, 13 in. dia......................	10.00	12.00
2-Piece Dessert Set, gold lined: Sugar, 4¼ in. high, 12 oz.; Cream, 4¼ in. high, 10 oz....	15.00	18.00
Bread or Roll Tray, 10 in. dia.............	6.00	7.20
Double Vegetable Dish, 11 in. long........	15.00	18.00
2-Piece Gravy Set: Boat, 8 oz.; Tray, 8 in. long.............................	9.50	11.40
Meat Dish, plain, 16 in. long.............	12.50	15.00
Meat Dish, well and tree, 16 in. long.......	18.00	21.60
Pitcher, 9½ in. high, 4¼ pints............	15.00	18.00
Candlestick, 10 in. high..............pair	12.00	14.40
Beverage Mixer, 12¼ in. high, 56 oz.......	18.00	21.60
Also: 8-Piece Set (Mixer, 6 cups, oval Waiter).............................	46.00	55.20

1936 Catalog. A charming new table service with hollow ware to match.

BAIRD-NORTH COMPANY, GOLD AND SILVER SMITHS, SALEM, MASS.

104 Dessert Fork.

101 Dessert Knife.

103 Dessert Spoon.

THE STUART.

One of the new patterns of "R. Wallace, 1835" silver plated table ware. This trade mark, advertised extensively over the United States, is a guarantee of the highest possible excellence in silver plate. After exhaustive tests we have selected this brand, from the many good ones, as the best, the one combining in the highest degree, design, finish and wearing qualities.

The Stuart has a beauty of design, and richness of die work equalled by few sterling silver patterns. We give our unqualified guarantee as to its wearing qualities.

The knives shown have hollow handles and the finest Triple plated (12 dwt.) steel blades.

The pieces shown reduced size are three times as long as illustrations.

100	Table knives, hollow handles, doz.	$10.00	120	Coffee spoons, doz.	$1.50
101	Dessert knives, hollow handles, doz.	9.50	121	Ice cream slicer, hollow handle	2.50
102	Tea spoons, doz.	2.50	122	Butter knife	.50
103	Dessert spoons, pair .75, doz.	4.00	124	Cold meat fork	.85
104	Dessert forks, doz.	4.00	125	Lettuce fork	1.00
105	Table spoons, pair .90, doz.	4.50	126	Jelly knife	.85
106	Table forks, doz.	4.50	127	Salad fork	1.75
107	Soup spoons, doz.	4.50	128	Cake fork	.85
108	Mustard spoon	.35	129	Preserve spoon	.85
110	Sugar spoon	.50	139	Same, with gold bowl	1.15
138	Same, with gold bowl	.65	130	Berry or salad spoon	1.00
111	Berry forks, doz.	2.75	140	Same, with gold bowl	1.35
112	Cheese scoop	.90	131	Oyster ladle	1.75
113	Pickle fork	.60	132	Gravy ladle	1.00
114	Sardine fork	.75	141	Same, with gold bowl	1.25
115	Pie server, hollow handle	1.65	133	Cream ladle	.65
116	Butter spreaders, doz.	4.00	142	Same, with gold bowl	.85
117	Cucumber server	1.00	134	Child's set, knife, fork and spoon,	
118	Horse radish spoon	.50		in box	1.00
119	Oyster forks, doz.	3.00	135	Olive fork	.50

All fancy pieces are put up in satin-lined boxes. Half dozens sold at dozen rates. Initials only (script) will be engraved free. Old English, 5 cents per letter.

1916 Catalog

Williams Bros. Mfg. Co.

Vineyard Pattern

8½" cold meat fork, 9⅜" berry spoon. Circa 1907, also marked
"Rockford S.P.Co., Lakeside Brand, Our Very Best." Montgomery
Ward sold this pattern as "Concord."

See Price Guide — Group 1

Wm. Rogers & Son

Alhambra Pattern

NICKLE SILVER, SILVER SOLDERED, HOLLOW HANDLE KNIVES AND FORKS

No. **31424** Medium knives, Alhambra pattern, French gray finish.......... $25.00
No. **31425** Medium forks, Alhambra pattern, French gray finish............ 25.00

No. **31426** Dessert knives, Alhambra pattern, French gray finish........... $23.33
No. **31427** Dessert forks, Alhambra pattern, French gray finish........... 23.33

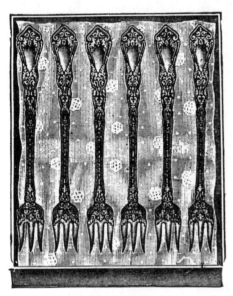

SIX OYSTER FORKS
Alhambra pattern, French gray

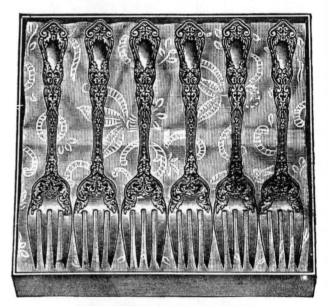

SIX INDIVIDUAL SALAD FORKS
Alhambra pattern, French gray

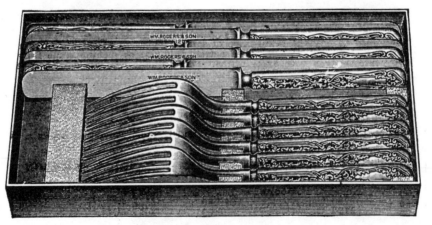

KNIFE AND FORK SET
Alhambra pattern, French gray

1913 Catalog

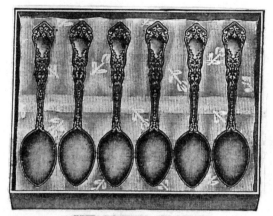

SIX COFFEE SPOONS
Alhambra pattern, French gray
No. 32713 Silver bowls...........per set $2.32
No. 32714 Gold bowls...........per set 4.62

BERRY SPOON
Alhambra pattern, French gray
No. 32709 Silver bowl...................each $2.40
No. 32710 Gold bowl...................each 3.30

12 DWT. SOLID HANDLE KNIVES AND FORKS
No. 31420 Medium knives, Alhambra pattern, French gray finish...........$10.00
No. 31421 Medium forks, Alhambra pattern, French gray finish........... 10.00
No. 31422 Dessert knives, Alhambra pattern, French gray finish.............$9.67
No. 31423 Dessert forks, Alhambra pattern, French gray finish............. 9.67

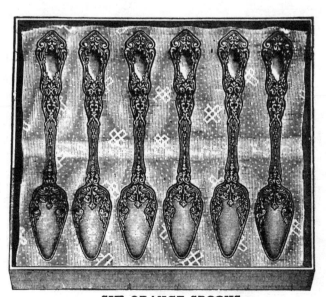

SIX ORANGE SPOONS
Alhambra pattern, French gray
No. 32696 Silver bowls................per set $3.60

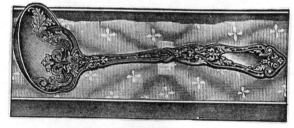

LADLES

Alhambra pattern, French gray
No. 32701 Cream, silver bowl.............each $1.35
No. 32702 Cream, gold bowl.............each 1.95
No. 32703 Gravy, silver bowl.............each 1.80
No. 32704 Gravy, gold bowl.............each 2.70
No. 32705 Medium silver bowl.............each 4.80
No. 32706 Medium, gold bowl.............each 8.00

1913 Catalog

See Price Guide — Group 1

Alhambra Pattern

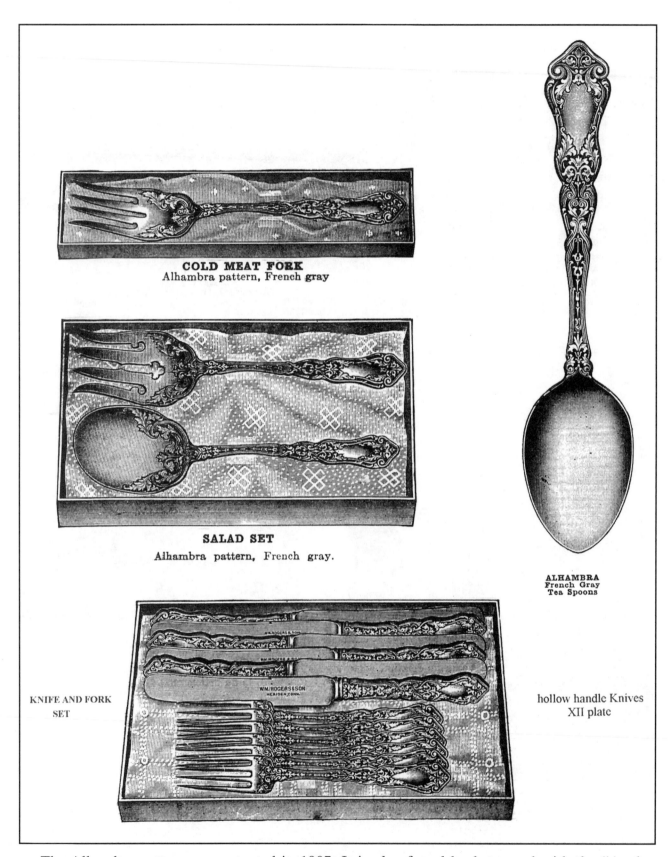

COLD MEAT FORK
Alhambra pattern, French gray

SALAD SET
Alhambra pattern, French gray.

KNIFE AND FORK SET

ALHAMBRA
French Gray
Tea Spoons

hollow handle Knives
XII plate

The Alhambra pattern was patented in 1907. It is also found backstamped with the "Anchor Rogers" mark. Cardinal is a similar pattern that was introduced in 1907 by 1835 Wallace & Son Mfg. Company.

Arbutus was patented in 1908. It is quite similar in design to Orange Blossom, a pattern also made by Wm. Rogers & Son. A quick way to distinguish the two: Orange Blossom has a patent date on the reverse but Arbutus does not. Arbutus orange/citrus spoons were produced in great quantities. The serving pieces are beautiful and greatly sought after. Some pie servers will have the imprint of a buggy on the blade; these pieces were given away by the Banner Buggy Company. The hollow handle knives are very difficult to find, and the hollow handle forks are next to impossible to obtain. Even the solid handle knives are scarce. Many Arbutus collectors fill in with pearl handle knives. It is possible that upwards of fifty different pieces were produced in Arbutus.

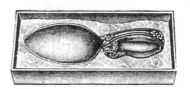

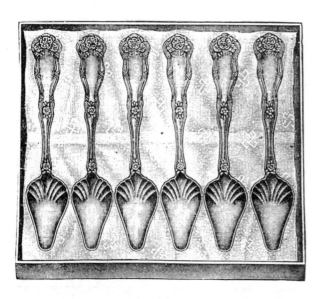

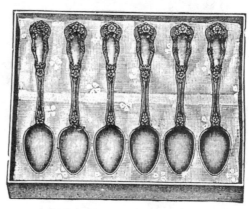

SIX COFFEE SPOONS
Plain bowls.........per set **$2.48**
Gold bowls.........per set **4.07**

WM. ROGERS & SON
WARRANTED 12 DWT.

12 DWT. SOLID HANDLE KNIVES AND FORKS

Medium knives, Arbutus pattern, bright or gray finish
Medium forks, Arbutus pattern, bright or gray finish

Dessert knives, Arbutus pattern, bright or gray finish
Dessert forks, Arbutus pattern, bright or gray finish

See Price Guide — Group 1

NICKLE SILVER, SILVER SOLDERED, HOLLOW HANDLE KNIVES AND FORKS

Medium knives, Arbutus pattern, bright or gray finish   Medium forks, Arbutus pattern, bright or gray finish

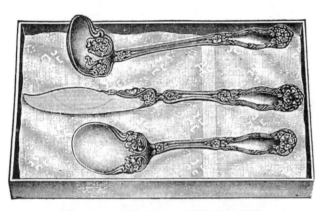

THREE PIECE COMBINATION SET
One Cream Ladle, Butter Knife, Sugar Shell

PIE OR CAKE SERVER
Hollow handle

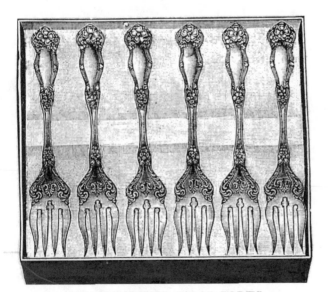

SIX INDIVIDUAL SALAD FORKS

COLD MEAT FORK

1913 Catalog

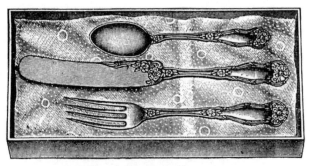

THREE-PIECE CHILD'S SET
Knife, Fork and Spoon

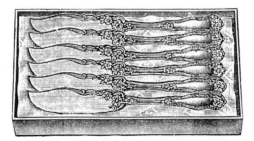

SIX BUTTER SPREADERS

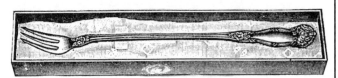

PICKLE FORK

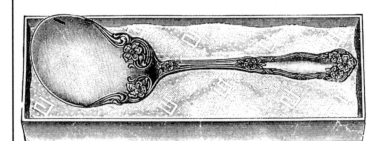

BERRY SPOON

No. **33202** Silver bowl...........................each **$2.13**
No. **33203** Gold bowl............................each **2.92**

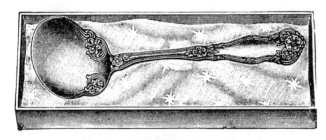

LADLES

No. **33190** Cream, silver bowl.............each **$1.20**
No. **33191** Cream, gold bowl..............each **1.74**
No. **33192** Gravy, silver bowl.............each **1.60**
No. **33193** Gravy, gold bowl..............each **2.38**
No. **33194** Medium, silver bowl..........each **4.23**
No. **33195** Medium, gold bowl...........each **5.25**

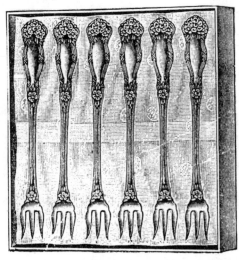

SIX OYSTER FORKS

No. **33204** Silver tines..........per set **$3.33**
No. **33205** Gold tines..........per set **4.92**

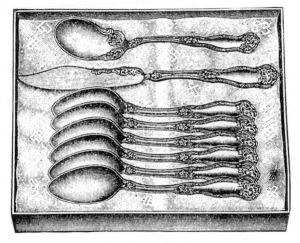

EIGHT-PIECE SET
Six Tea Spoons, one Butter Knife, one Sugar Shell

1913 Catalog

Beauty Pattern

French Gray Finish and Bright Shield

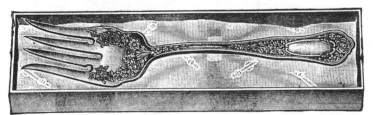

COLD MEAT FORK

No. **32673**   Silver tines.....................each **$1.50**
No. **32674**   Gold tines.......................each 2.08

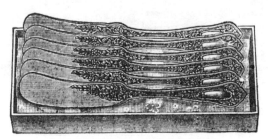

SIX BUTTER SPREADERS

No. **32693**   Silver blades........per set **$5.20**

NICKLE SILVER, SILVER SOLDERED, HOLLOW HANDLE KNIVES AND FORKS

No. **31416**   Medium knives, Beauty pattern, French gray finish.............$25.00
No. **31417**   Medium forks, Beauty pattern, French gray finish..............25.00
No. **31418**   Dessert knives, Beauty pattern, French gray finish............$23.33
No. **31419**   Dessert forks, Beauty pattern, French gray finish.............23.33

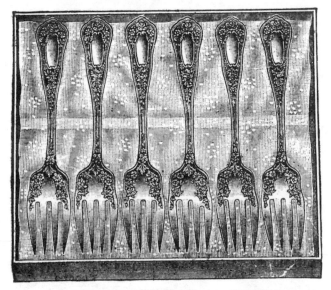

SIX INDIVIDUAL SALAD FORKS

No. **32692**   Silver tines................per set **$5.70**

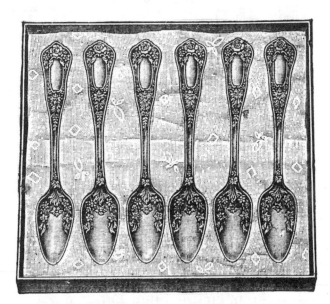

SIX ORANGE SPOONS

No. **32694**   Silver bowls................per set **$3.60**

1913 Catalog

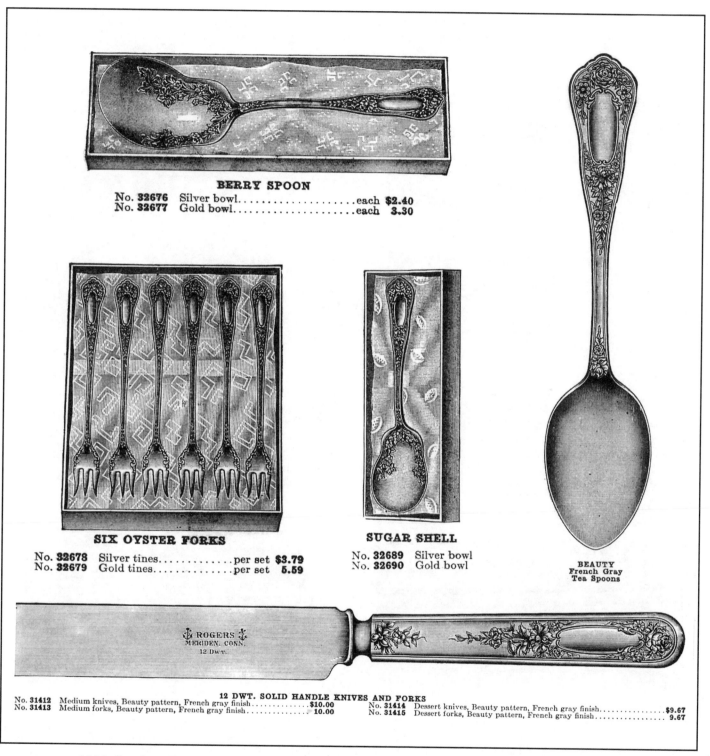

BERRY SPOON

No. **32676** Silver bowl.....................each **$2.40**
No. **32677** Gold bowl.......................each **3.30**

SIX OYSTER FORKS

No. **32678** Silver tines.............per set **$3.79**
No. **32679** Gold tines..............per set **5.59**

SUGAR SHELL

No. **32689** Silver bowl
No. **32690** Gold bowl

BEAUTY
French Gray
Tea Spoons

12 DWT. SOLID HANDLE KNIVES AND FORKS

No. **31412** Medium knives, Beauty pattern, French gray finish.............$10.00
No. **31413** Medium forks, Beauty pattern, French gray finish.............10.00
No. **31414** Dessert knives, Beauty pattern, French gray finish...............$9.67
No. **31415** Dessert forks, Beauty pattern, French gray finish.................9.67

1913 Catalog. Patented 1909. Also found backstamped with the "Anchor Rogers" mark.

See Price Guide — Group 1

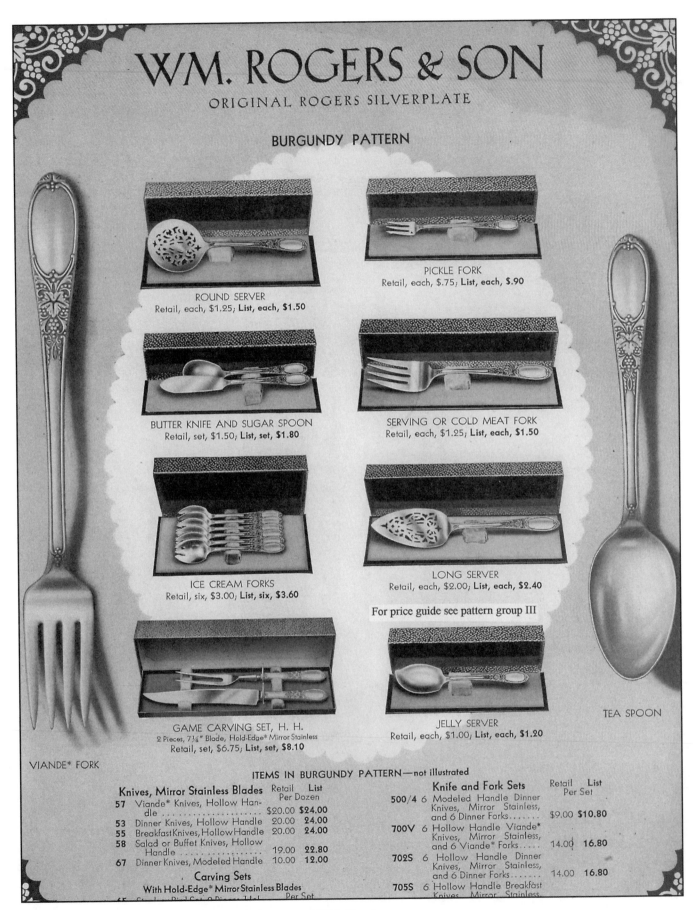

WM. ROGERS & SON
ORIGINAL ROGERS SILVERPLATE

BURGUNDY PATTERN

ROUND SERVER
Retail, each, $1.25; **List, each, $1.50**

PICKLE FORK
Retail, each, $.75; **List, each, $.90**

BUTTER KNIFE AND SUGAR SPOON
Retail, set, $1.50; **List, set, $1.80**

SERVING OR COLD MEAT FORK
Retail, each, $1.25; **List, each, $1.50**

ICE CREAM FORKS
Retail, six, $3.00; **List, six, $3.60**

LONG SERVER
Retail, each, $2.00; **List, each, $2.40**

For price guide see pattern group III

GAME CARVING SET, H. H.
2 Pieces, 7¼" Blade, Hold-Edge* Mirror Stainless
Retail, set, $6.75; **List, set, $8.10**

JELLY SERVER
Retail, each, $1.00; **List, each, $1.20**

TEA SPOON

VIANDE* FORK

ITEMS IN BURGUNDY PATTERN—not illustrated

Knives, Mirror Stainless Blades	Retail	List Per Dozen
57 Viande* Knives, Hollow Handle	$20.00	$24.00
53 Dinner Knives, Hollow Handle	20.00	24.00
55 Breakfast Knives, Hollow Handle	20.00	24.00
58 Salad or Buffet Knives, Hollow Handle	19.00	22.80
67 Dinner Knives, Modeled Handle	10.00	12.00

Carving Sets
With Hold-Edge* Mirror Stainless Blades Per Set

Knife and Fork Sets	Retail	List Per Set
500/4 6 Modeled Handle Dinner Knives, Mirror Stainless, and 6 Dinner Forks	$9.00	$10.80
700V 6 Hollow Handle Viande* Knives, Mirror Stainless, and 6 Viande* Forks	14.00	16.80
702S 6 Hollow Handle Dinner Knives, Mirror Stainless, and 6 Dinner Forks	14.00	16.80
705S 6 Hollow Handle Breakfast Knives, Mirror Stainless,		

1936 Catalog

Daisy Pattern

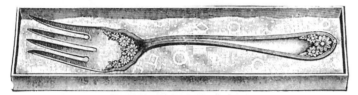

COLD MEAT FORK

No. **33177**   Silver tines.....................each **$1.33**
No. **33178**   Gold tines.......................each **1.87**

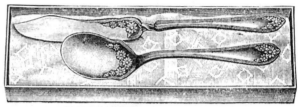

BUTTER KNIFE AND SUGAR SHELL

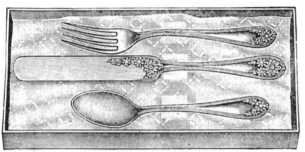

THREE-PIECE CHILD'S SET
Knife, fork and spoon

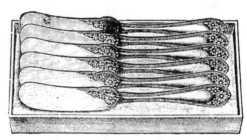

SIX BUTTER SPREADERS

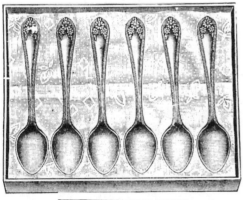

SIX COFFEE SPOONS
Silver bowls.................per set
Gilt bowls..................per se

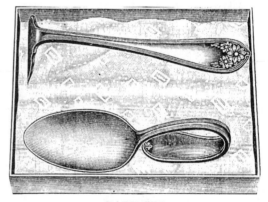

BABY SET
One baby spoon, one food pusher

1913 Catalog. Plain or gray finish.

See Price Guide — Group 1

Daisy Pattern

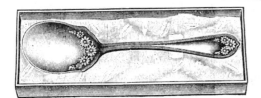

SUGAR SHELL

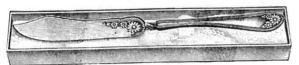

BUTTER KNIFE

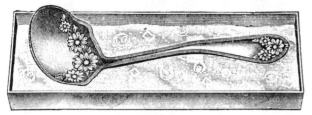

LADLES

No. 33170	Cream, silver bowl............each	$1.20
No. 33171	Cream, gold bowl............each	1.74
No. 33172	Gravy, silver bowl............each	1.60
No. 33173	Gravy, gold bowl............each	2.38
No. 33174	Medium, silver bowl............each	4.23
No. 33175	Medium, gold bowl............each	5.25

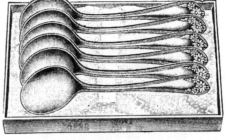

SIX BOUILLON SPOONS

Every article of silver plated Flatware made by Wm. Rogers & Son is extra heavily plated with pure silver on the highest grade nickel silver base, and is guaranteed by the manufacturers to give satisfaction.

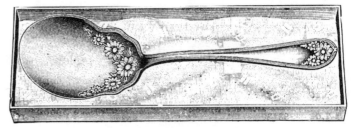

BERRY SPOON

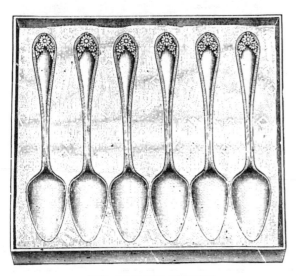

SIX ORANGE SPOONS

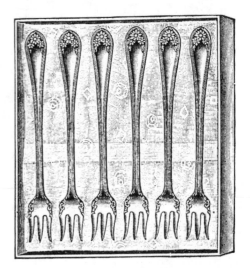

SIX OYSTER FORKS

1913 Catalog. Plain or gray finish.

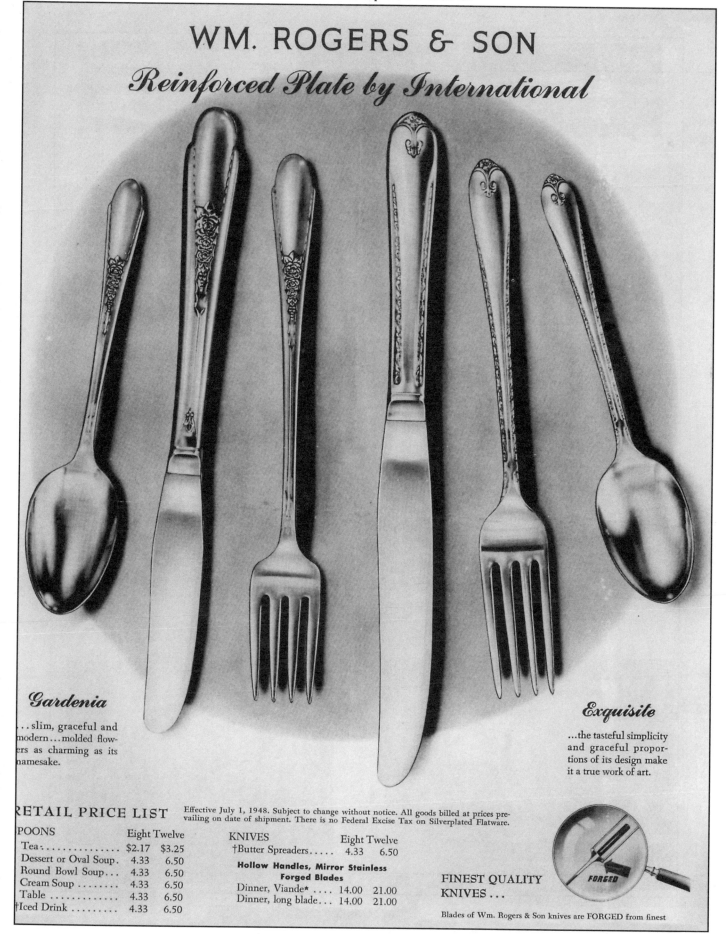

WM. ROGERS & SON
Reinforced Plate by International

Gardenia

...slim, graceful and modern...molded flowers as charming as its namesake.

Exquisite

...the tasteful simplicity and graceful proportions of its design make it a true work of art.

RETAIL PRICE LIST

Effective July 1, 1948. Subject to change without notice. All goods billed at prices prevailing on date of shipment. There is no Federal Excise Tax on Silverplated Flatware.

SPOONS	Eight	Twelve
Tea.............	$2.17	$3.25
Dessert or Oval Soup .	4.33	6.50
Round Bowl Soup...	4.33	6.50
Cream Soup	4.33	6.50
Table	4.33	6.50
†Iced Drink	4.33	6.50

KNIVES	Eight	Twelve
†Butter Spreaders.....	4.33	6.50
Hollow Handles, Mirror Stainless Forged Blades		
Dinner, Viande★	14.00	21.00
Dinner, long blade...	14.00	21.00

FINEST QUALITY KNIVES ...

Blades of Wm. Rogers & Son knives are FORGED from finest

FORGED

Gaiety Pattern

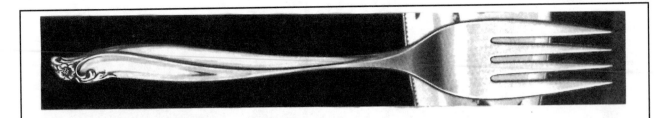

GAIETY — Wm. Rogers & Son Silverplate

Retail

No. 2135 Center Bowl, Pierced, Diameter,
12½ inches $12.50

GAIETY — Wm. Rogers & Son Silverplate

No. 2194 Cracker 'N Cheese Dish. Dia.
14½ inches. Removable wooden cutting block . Retail $12.00

GAIETY — Wm. Rogers & Son Silverplate

Retail

No. 2112 Length, 12 inches $16.50

GAIETY — Wm. Rogers & Son Silverplate
Round Tray

Retail

No. 2170 Diameter, 10 inches .... $ 9.00
No. 2171 Diameter, 12½ inches 11.00
No. 2172 Diameter, 15 inches 13.50

GAIETY — Wm. Rogers & Son Silverplate — Round Tray

No. 2170   Diameter, 10 inches .... Retail $ 9.00

GAIETY — Wm. Rogers & Son Silverplate

Retail

No. 2126 Buffet Tray, Diameter, 15 inches $13.50

1962 Catalog

GAIETY — Wm. Rogers & Son Silverplate

No. 2113 Attached Tray, Capacity 16 ozs. Retail **$11.00**

GAIETY — Wm. Rogers & Son Silverplate

No. 2112/S All Purpose Dish, Length, 12 inches .... Retail **$12.00**

GAIETY — Wm. Rogers & Son Silverplate — Gallery Tray

No. 2171G Diameter, 12½ inches .... Retail **$12.50**
No. 2172G Diameter, 15 inches .... Retail **15.00**

GAIETY — Wm. Rogers & Son Silverplate
Oval Waiter, Chased

No. 2180 Length, 17 inches, Overall length, 21 inches ... Retail **$21.00**

GAIETY — Wm. Rogers & Son Silverplate

No. 2142 Cake Stand. Diameter, 14 inches,
Height, 4 inches .... Retail **$16.50**

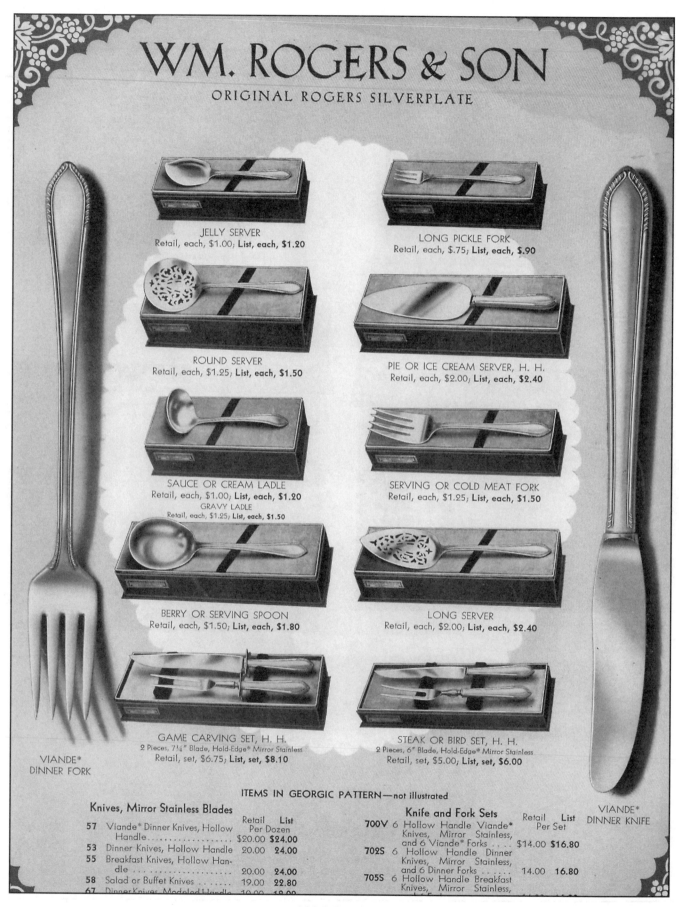

WM. ROGERS & SON
ORIGINAL ROGERS SILVERPLATE

JELLY SERVER
Retail, each, $1.00; List, each, $1.20

LONG PICKLE FORK
Retail, each, $.75; List, each, $.90

ROUND SERVER
Retail, each, $1.25; List, each, $1.50

PIE OR ICE CREAM SERVER, H. H.
Retail, each, $2.00; List, each, $2.40

SAUCE OR CREAM LADLE
Retail, each, $1.00; List, each, $1.20
GRAVY LADLE
Retail, each, $1.25; List, each, $1.50

SERVING OR COLD MEAT FORK
Retail, each, $1.25; List, each, $1.50

BERRY OR SERVING SPOON
Retail, each, $1.50; List, each, $1.80

LONG SERVER
Retail, each, $2.00; List, each, $2.40

GAME CARVING SET, H. H.
2 Pieces, 7¼" Blade, Hold-Edge* Mirror Stainless
Retail, set, $6.75; List, set, $8.10

STEAK OR BIRD SET, H. H.
2 Pieces, 6" Blade, Hold-Edge* Mirror Stainless
Retail, set, $5.00; List, set, $6.00

VIANDE*
DINNER FORK

VIANDE*
DINNER KNIFE

ITEMS IN GEORGIC PATTERN—not illustrated

Knives, Mirror Stainless Blades

		Retail Per Dozen	List
57	Viande* Dinner Knives, Hollow Handle	$20.00	$24.00
53	Dinner Knives, Hollow Handle	20.00	24.00
55	Breakfast Knives, Hollow Handle	20.00	24.00
58	Salad or Buffet Knives	19.00	22.80
67	Dinner Knives, Modeled Handle	10.00	19.00

Knife and Fork Sets

		Retail Per Set	List
700V	6 Hollow Handle Viande* Knives, Mirror Stainless, and 6 Viande* Forks	$14.00	$16.80
702S	6 Hollow Handle Dinner Knives, Mirror Stainless, and 6 Dinner Forks	14.00	16.80
705S	6 Hollow Handle Breakfast Knives, Mirror Stainless,		

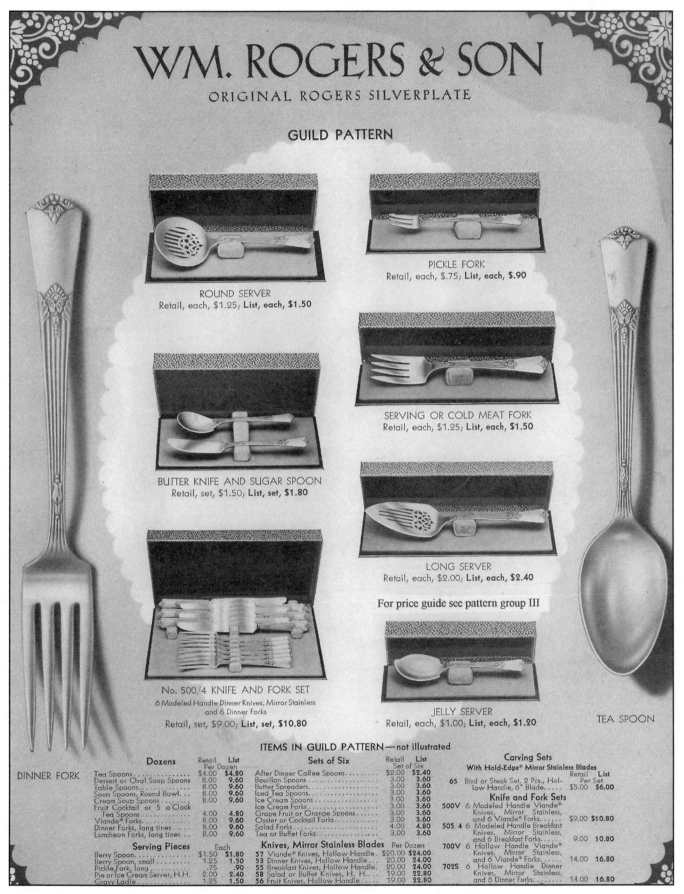

WM. ROGERS & SON
ORIGINAL ROGERS SILVERPLATE

GUILD PATTERN

ROUND SERVER
Retail, each, $1.25; List, each, $1.50

PICKLE FORK
Retail, each, $.75; List, each, $.90

SERVING OR COLD MEAT FORK
Retail, each, $1.25; List, each, $1.50

BUTTER KNIFE AND SUGAR SPOON
Retail, set, $1.50; List, set, $1.80

LONG SERVER
Retail, each, $2.00; List, each, $2.40

For price guide see pattern group III

No. 500/4 KNIFE AND FORK SET
6 Modeled Handle Dinner Knives, Mirror Stainless
and 6 Dinner Forks
Retail, set, $9.00; List, set, $10.80

JELLY SERVER
Retail, each, $1.00; List, each, $1.20

DINNER FORK

TEA SPOON

ITEMS IN GUILD PATTERN—not illustrated

Dozens	Retail Per Dozen	List
Tea Spoons	$4.00	$4.80
Dessert or Oval Soup Spoons	8.00	9.60
Table Spoons	8.00	9.60
Soup Spoons, Round Bowl	8.00	9.60
Cream Soup Spoons	8.00	9.60
Fruit Cocktail or 5 o'Clock Tea Spoons	4.00	4.80
Viande* Forks	8.00	9.60
Dinner Forks, long tines	8.00	9.60
Luncheon Forks, long tines	8.00	9.60

Serving Pieces	Each	
Berry Spoon	$1.50	$1.80
Berry Spoon, small	1.25	1.50
Pickle Fork, long	.75	.90
Pie or Ice Cream Server, H.H.	2.00	2.40
Gravy Ladle	1.25	1.50

Sets of Six	Retail Set of Six	List
After Dinner Coffee Spoons	$2.00	$2.40
Bouillon Spoons	3.00	3.60
Butter Spreaders	3.00	3.60
Iced Tea Spoons	3.00	3.60
Ice Cream Spoons	3.00	3.60
Ice Cream Forks	3.00	3.60
Grape Fruit or Orange Spoons	3.00	3.60
Oyster or Cocktail Forks	3.00	3.60
Salad Forks	4.00	4.80
Tea or Buffet Forks	3.00	3.60

Knives, Mirror Stainless Blades	Per Dozen	
57 Viande* Knives, Hollow Handle	$20.00	$24.00
53 Dinner Knives, Hollow Handle	20.00	24.00
55 Breakfast Knives, Hollow Handle	20.00	24.00
58 Salad or Buffet Knives, H. H.	19.00	22.80
56 Fruit Knives, Hollow Handle	19.00	22.80

Carving Sets
With Hold-Edge* Mirror Stainless Blades

		Retail	List Per Set
65	Bird or Steak Set, 2 Pcs., Hollow Handle, 6" Blade	$5.00	$6.00

Knife and Fork Sets

			Retail	List
500V	6	Modeled Handle Viande* Knives, Mirror Stainless, and 6 Viande* Forks	$9.00	$10.80
505/4	6	Modeled Handle Breakfast Knives, Mirror Stainless, and 6 Breakfast Forks	9.00	10.80
700V	6	Hollow Handle Viande* Knives, Mirror Stainless, and 6 Viande* Forks	14.00	16.80
702S	6	Hollow Handle Dinner Knives, Mirror Stainless, and 6 Dinner Forks	14.00	16.80

1936 Catalog

See Price Guide — Group 3

WM. ROGERS & SON

GUILD SERVICE

5320/21/26. BEVERAGE SET (Mixer, 6 Cups and 16-inch Tray).... **$44.00**
5320. Beverage Mixer, 1½ Quarts capacity..................................... $12.00
5321. Cocktail Cups, ...each 3.00
5326. Tray for Beverage Set, 16-inch.. 14.00

5304
SANDWICH PLATE
Diameter, 10½ inches
$5.50

5319
CASSEROLE, Round
Pyrex lining and cover, Capacity
3 pts.
$7.00

5315
RELISH DISH
Diameter, 14 inches
5 Compartments
Removable Glass Linings
$12.00

For price guide see pattern group III

5325
BON-BON
Diameter
7 inches
$4.50

5317
BON-BON
(low base)
(Not illustrated)
$3.00

5306/7
DESSERT SET
(Sugar, Creamer and Tray), $15.00
5307. Dessert Set (Sugar and Creamer), $10.00
5306. Tray for Dessert Set......... 5.00
Length, 11 inches,

5322
ICE BOWL
Diameter, 6 inches
$7.00

5323. ICE TONGS, $1.50

5316
SALT AND PEPPER
Height, 5¾ inches
$5.00 Pair

5310
CANDLESTICK
Height, 4 inches
$5.00 Pair

5309
CENTERPIECE
Diameter, 13 inches
Silver Plated Double Mesh
Flower Holder
$15.00

5310
CANDLESTICK
Height, 4 inches
$5.00 Pair

5324
CHILD'S CUP
$2.50

NEW! *Juliette*

ROMANCE IN SILVER...

Classic in outline...the smooth surfaces accented by delicately carved flowers from the bride's bouquet to bloom forever in glowing silver

1966 Catalog

See Price Guide — Group 3

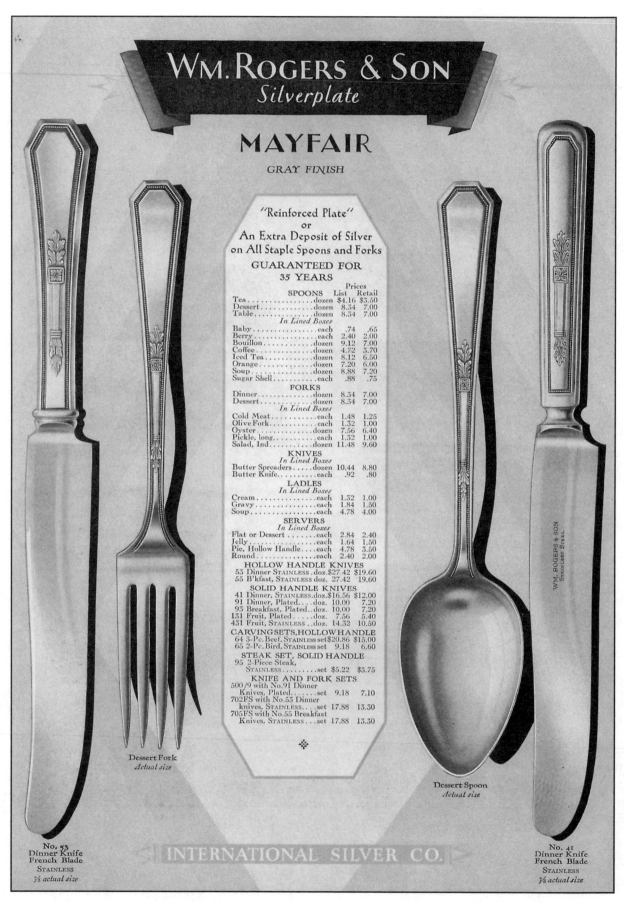

WM. ROGERS & SON
Silverplate

MAYFAIR
GRAY FINISH

"Reinforced Plate"
or
An Extra Deposit of Silver
on All Staple Spoons and Forks
**GUARANTEED FOR
35 YEARS**

		Prices	
SPOONS		List	Retail
Tea	dozen	$4.16	$3.50
Dessert	dozen	8.54	7.00
Table	dozen	8.54	7.00
In Lined Boxes			
Baby	each	.74	.65
Berry	each	2.40	2.00
Bouillon	dozen	9.12	7.00
Coffee	dozen	4.72	3.70
Iced Tea	dozen	8.12	6.50
Orange	dozen	7.20	6.60
Soup	dozen	8.88	7.20
Sugar Shell	each	.88	.75
FORKS			
Dinner	dozen	8.54	7.00
Dessert	dozen	8.54	7.00
In Lined Boxes			
Cold Meat	each	1.48	1.25
Olive Fork	each	1.32	1.00
Oyster	dozen	7.56	6.40
Pickle, long	each	1.32	1.00
Salad, Ind.	dozen	11.48	9.60
KNIVES			
In Lined Boxes			
Butter Spreaders	dozen	10.44	8.80
Butter Knife	each	.92	.80
LADLES			
In Lined Boxes			
Cream	each	1.32	1.00
Gravy	each	1.84	1.50
Soup	each	4.78	4.00
SERVERS			
In Lined Boxes			
Flat or Dessert	each	2.84	2.40
Jelly	each	1.64	1.50
Pie, Hollow Handle	each	4.78	3.50
Round	each	2.40	2.00
HOLLOW HANDLE KNIVES			
53 Dinner Stainless	doz.	$27.42	$19.60
55 B'kfast, Stainless	doz.	27.42	19.60
SOLID HANDLE KNIVES			
41 Dinner, Stainless	doz.	$16.56	$12.00
91 Dinner, Plated	doz.	10.00	7.20
95 Breakfast, Plated	doz.	10.00	7.20
151 Fruit, Plated	doz.	7.56	5.40
451 Fruit, Stainless	doz.	14.52	10.50
CARVING SETS, HOLLOW HANDLE			
64 3-Pc. Beef, Stainless	set	$20.86	$15.00
65 2-Pc. Bird, Stainless	set	9.18	6.60
STEAK SET, SOLID HANDLE			
95 2-Piece Steak, Stainless	set	$5.22	$3.75
KNIFE AND FORK SETS			
500/9 with No.91 Dinner Knives, Plated	set	9.18	7.10
702FS with No.53 Dinner knives, Stainless	set	17.88	13.30
705FS with No.55 Breakfast Knives, Stainless	set	17.88	13.30

No. 53
Dinner Knife
French Blade
STAINLESS
⅞ actual size

Dessert Fork
Actual size

Dessert Spoon
Actual size

WM. ROGERS & SON
STAINLESS STEEL

No. 41
Dinner Knife
French Blade
STAINLESS
⅞ actual size

INTERNATIONAL SILVER CO.

1931 Catalog

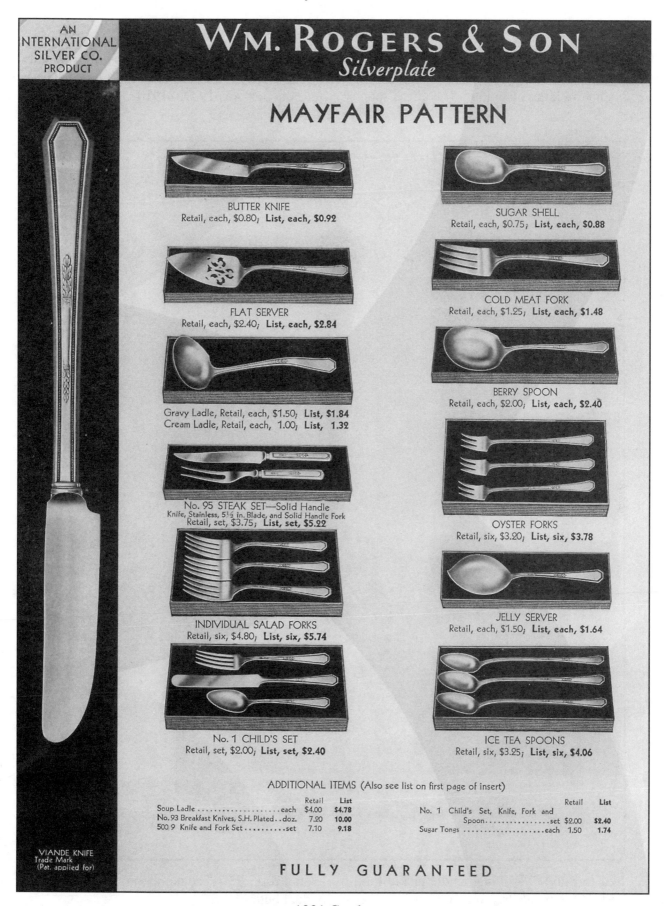

MAYFAIR PATTERN

AN INTERNATIONAL SILVER CO. PRODUCT

WM. ROGERS & SON
Silverplate

Wm. Rogers & Son

BUTTER KNIFE
Retail, each, $0.80; **List, each, $0.92**

SUGAR SHELL
Retail, each, $0.75; **List, each, $0.88**

FLAT SERVER
Retail, each, $2.40; **List, each, $2.84**

COLD MEAT FORK
Retail, each, $1.25; **List, each, $1.48**

Gravy Ladle, Retail, each, $1.50; **List, $1.84**
Cream Ladle, Retail, each, 1.00; **List, 1.32**

BERRY SPOON
Retail, each, $2.00; **List, each, $2.40**

No. 95 STEAK SET—Solid Handle
Knife, Stainless, 5¼ in. Blade, and Solid Handle Fork
Retail, set, $3.75; **List, set, $5.22**

OYSTER FORKS
Retail, six, $3.20; **List, six, $3.78**

INDIVIDUAL SALAD FORKS
Retail, six, $4.80; **List, six, $5.74**

JELLY SERVER
Retail, each, $1.50; **List, each, $1.64**

No. 1 CHILD'S SET
Retail, set, $2.00; **List, set, $2.40**

ICE TEA SPOONS
Retail, six, $3.25; **List, six, $4.06**

ADDITIONAL ITEMS (Also see list on first page of insert)

	Retail	List
Soup Ladle ....each	$4.00	$4.78
No. 93 Breakfast Knives, S.H. Plated..doz.	7.20	10.00
500.9 Knife and Fork Set ....set	7.10	9.18

	Retail	List
No. 1 Child's Set, Knife, Fork and Spoon.................set	$2.00	$2.40
Sugar Tongs ....each	1.50	1.74

FULLY GUARANTEED

VIANDE KNIFE
Trade Mark
(Pat. applied for)

1931 Catalog

See Price Guide — Group 3

Orange Blossom Pattern

This pattern was a California Fruit Growers Exchange promotion. Forty-six different items were produced, some in large quantities. The citrus spoons are the easiest pieces to find. The hollow handle forks and knives are very desirable but scarce. The year of introduction was 1909 – 1910.

Left to right: 8¹⁄₁₆" long handle pickle fork, 6¼" salad fork, 5¹⁵⁄₁₆" sugar spoon, 7⅜" orange knife, 6" orange/citrus spoon. Bottom: 5¹¹⁄₁₆" individual butter knife.

Orange Blossom Pattern

6⅞" round bowl soup spoons, 7⁹⁄₁₆" ice tea spoons. The soups are hard to find, and the ice teas are considered rare.

See Price Guide — Group 1

Wm. Rogers & Son

Patented 1901. Left to right: 8⁹⁄₁₀" pie server, 7²⁄₅" dinner fork, 8¹⁄₁₀" tablespoon, 10³⁄₅" soup ladle.

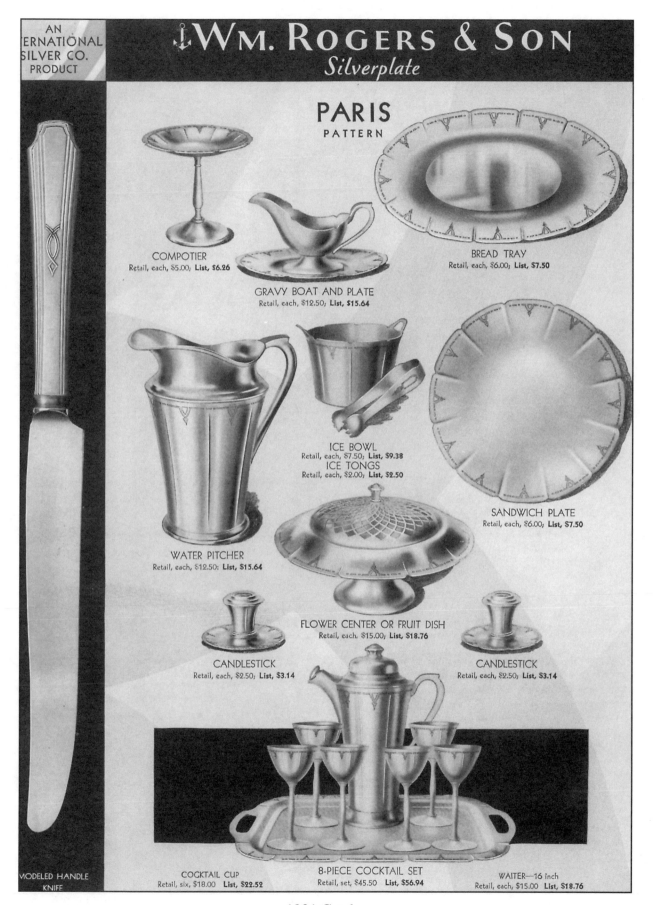

WM. ROGERS & SON
Silverplate

AN INTERNATIONAL SILVER CO. PRODUCT

PARIS PATTERN

COMPOTIER
Retail, each, $5.00; **List, $6.26**

GRAVY BOAT AND PLATE
Retail, each, $12.50; **List, $15.64**

BREAD TRAY
Retail, each, $6.00; **List, $7.50**

WATER PITCHER
Retail, each, $12.50: **List, $15.64**

ICE BOWL
Retail, each, $7.50; **List, $9.38**
ICE TONGS
Retail, each, $2.00; **List, $2.50**

SANDWICH PLATE
Retail, each, $6.00; **List, $7.50**

CANDLESTICK
Retail, each, $2.50; **List, $3.14**

FLOWER CENTER OR FRUIT DISH
Retail, each, $15.00; **List, $18.76**

CANDLESTICK
Retail, each, $2.50; **List, $3.14**

COCKTAIL CUP
Retail, six, $18.00; **List, $22.52**

8-PIECE COCKTAIL SET
Retail, set, $45.50; **List, $56.94**

WAITER—16 inch
Retail, each, $15.00; **List, $18.76**

MODELED HANDLE KNIFE

1931 Catalog

See Price Guide — Group 3

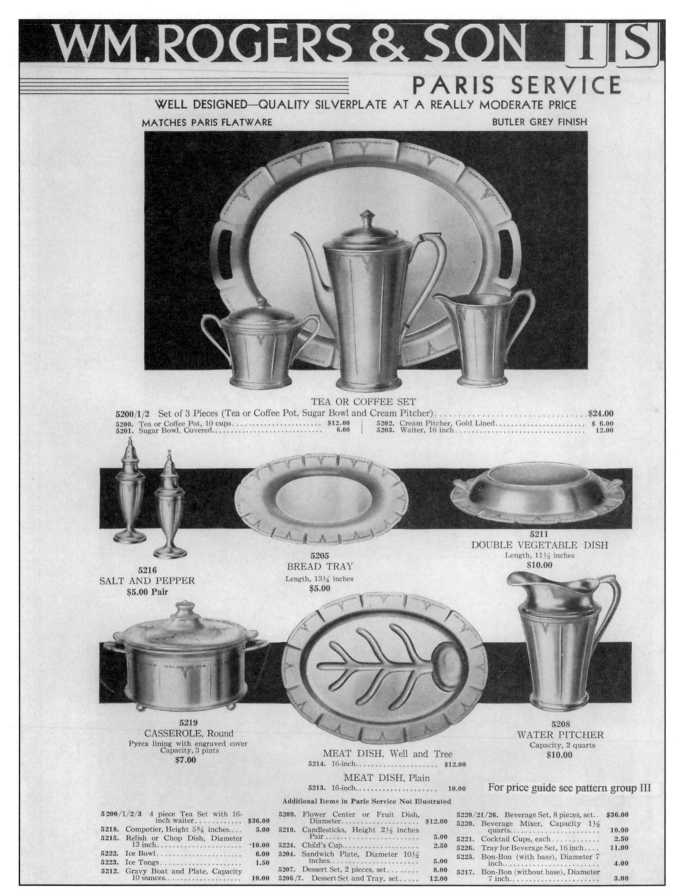

WM. ROGERS & SON I S

PARIS SERVICE

WELL DESIGNED—QUALITY SILVERPLATE AT A REALLY MODERATE PRICE

MATCHES PARIS FLATWARE   BUTLER GREY FINISH

TEA OR COFFEE SET

5200/1/2   Set of 3 Pieces (Tea or Coffee Pot, Sugar Bowl and Cream Pitcher) $24.00

5200.	Tea or Coffee Pot, 10 cups	$12.00	**5202.** Cream Pitcher, Gold Lined	$ 6.00
5201.	Sugar Bowl, Covered	6.00	**5203.** Waiter, 16 inch	12.00

5216
SALT AND PEPPER
$5.00 Pair

5205
BREAD TRAY
Length, 13¼ inches
$5.00

5211
DOUBLE VEGETABLE DISH
Length, 11½ inches
$10.00

5219
CASSEROLE, Round
Pyrex lining with engraved cover
Capacity, 3 pints
$7.00

MEAT DISH, Well and Tree
5214. 16-inch $12.00

MEAT DISH, Plain
5213. 16-inch 10.00

5208
WATER PITCHER
Capacity, 2 quarts
$10.00

For price guide see pattern group III

Additional Items in Paris Service Not Illustrated

5200/1/2/3 4 piece Tea Set with 16-inch waiter	$36.00	**5209.** Flower Center or Fruit Dish, Diameter	$12.00	**5220/21/26.** Beverage Set, 8 pieces, set..	$36.00
5218. Compotier, Height 5⅝ inches....	5.00	**5210.** Candlesticks, Height 2½ inches Pair	5.00	**5220.** Beverage Mixer, Capacity 1½ quarts	10.90
5215. Relish or Chop Dish, Diameter 13 inch	·10.00	**5224.** Child's Cup	2.50	**5221.** Cocktail Cups, each	2.50
5222. Ice Bowl	6.00	**5204.** Sandwich Plate, Diameter 10½ inches	5.00	**5226.** Tray for Beverage Set, 16 inch	11.00
5223. Ice Tongs	1.50	**5207.** Dessert Set, 2 pieces, set.......	8.00	**5225.** Bon-Bon (with base), Diameter 7 inch....................	4.00
5212. Gravy Boat and Plate, Capacity 10 ounces	10.00	**5206/7.** Dessert Set and Tray, set.....	12.00	**5217.** Bon-Bon (without base), Diameter 7 inch..................	3.00

1936 Catalog

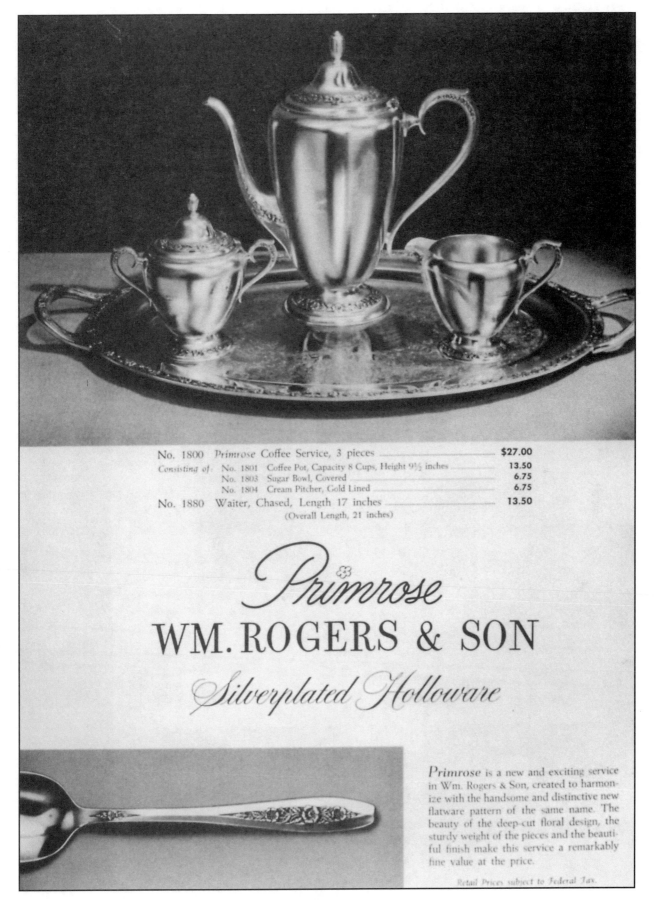

No. 1800   *Primrose* Coffee Service, 3 pieces _____ $27.00

Consisting of: No. 1801   Coffee Pot, Capacity 8 Cups, Height 9½ inches _____ 13.50

No. 1803   Sugar Bowl, Covered _____ 6.75

No. 1804   Cream Pitcher, Gold Lined _____ 6.75

No. 1880   Waiter, Chased, Length 17 inches _____ 13.50

(Overall Length, 21 inches)

Primrose
WM. ROGERS & SON
Silverplated Holloware

Primrose is a new and exciting service in Wm. Rogers & Son, created to harmonize with the handsome and distinctive new flatware pattern of the same name. The beauty of the deep-cut floral design, the sturdy weight of the pieces and the beautiful finish make this service a remarkably fine value at the price.

Retail Prices subject to Federal Tax.

1953 Catalog

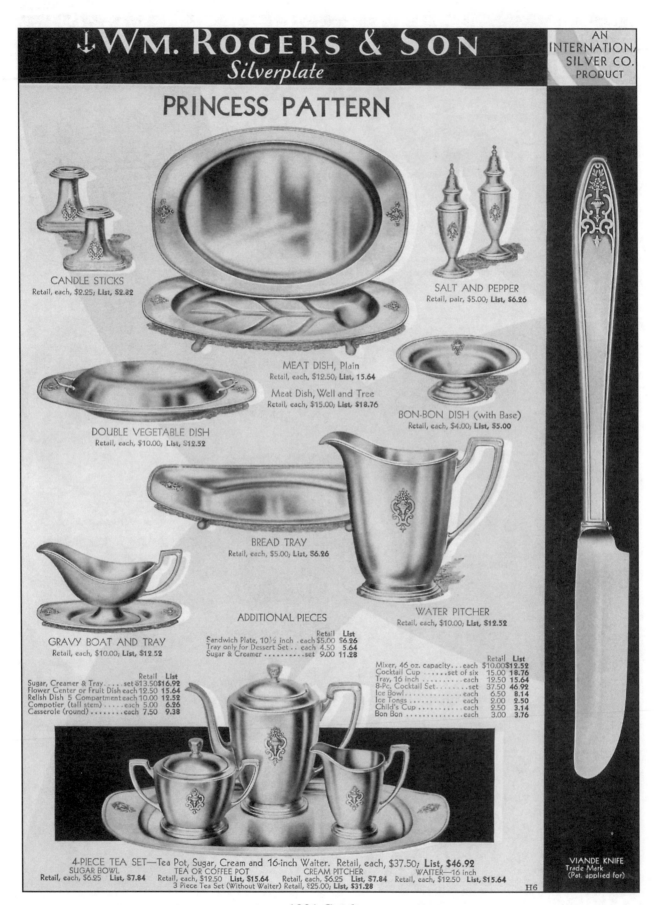

WM. ROGERS & SON
Silverplate

AN INTERNATIONAL SILVER CO. PRODUCT

PRINCESS PATTERN

CANDLE STICKS
Retail, each, $2.25; **List**, $2.82

SALT AND PEPPER
Retail, pair, $5.00; **List**, $6.26

MEAT DISH, Plain
Retail, each, $12.50; **List**, 15.64
Meat Dish, Well and Tree
Retail, each, $15.00; **List**, $18.76

BON-BON DISH (with Base)
Retail, each, $4.00; **List**, $5.00

DOUBLE VEGETABLE DISH
Retail, each, $10.00; **List**, $12.52

BREAD TRAY
Retail, each, $5.00; **List**, $6.26

WATER PITCHER
Retail, each, $10.00; **List**, $12.52

GRAVY BOAT AND TRAY
Retail, each, $10.00; **List**, $12.52

ADDITIONAL PIECES

	Retail	List
Sandwich Plate, 10½ inch .. each	$5.00	$6.26
Tray only for Dessert Set .. each	4.50	5.64
Sugar & Creamer .... set	9.00	11.28

	Retail	List
Sugar, Creamer & Tray .... set	$13.50	$16.92
Flower Center or Fruit Dish each	12.50	15.64
Relish Dish 5 Compartment each	10.00	12.52
Compotier (tall stem) ..... each	5.00	6.26
Casserole (round) .... each	7.50	9.38

	Retail	List
Mixer, 46 oz. capacity...each	$10.00	$12.52
Cocktail Cup ......set of six	15.00	18.76
Tray, 16 inch ....each	19.50	15.64
8-Pc. Cocktail Set........set	37.50	46.92
Ice Bowl...............each	6.50	8.14
Ice Tongs .... each	2.00	2.50
Child's Cup .... each	2.50	3.14
Bon Bon .... each	3.00	3.76

4-PIECE TEA SET—Tea Pot, Sugar, Cream and 16-inch Waiter. Retail, each, $37.50; **List**, $46.92

SUGAR BOWL
Retail, each, $6.25 **List**, $7.84

TEA OR COFFEE POT
Retail, each, $12.50 **List**, $15.64

CREAM PITCHER
Retail, each, $6.25 **List**, $7.84

WAITER—16 inch
Retail, each, $12.50 **List**, $15.64

3 Piece Tea Set (Without Waiter) Retail, $25.00; **List**, $31.28

H6

VIANDE KNIFE
Trade Mark
(Pat. applied for)

1931 Catalog

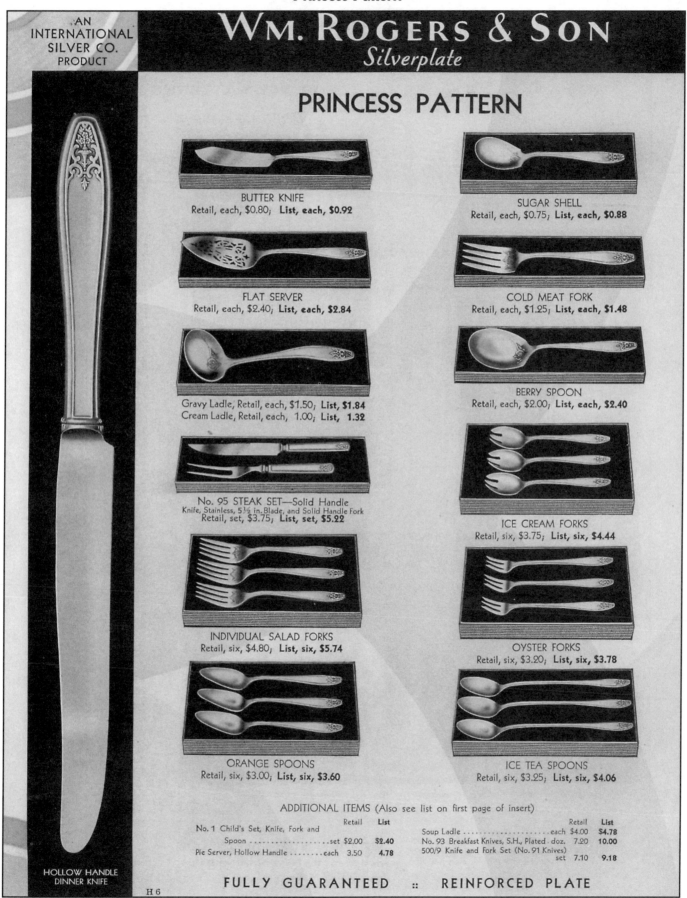

Spring Flower Pattern

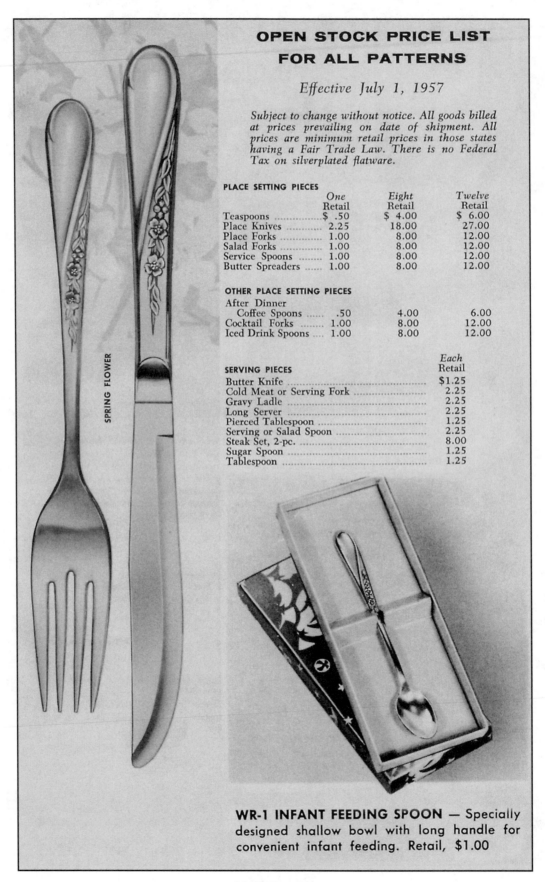

SPRING FLOWER

OPEN STOCK PRICE LIST
FOR ALL PATTERNS

Effective July 1, 1957

Subject to change without notice. All goods billed at prices prevailing on date of shipment. All prices are minimum retail prices in those states having a Fair Trade Law. There is no Federal Tax on silverplated flatware.

PLACE SETTING PIECES

	One Retail	Eight Retail	Twelve Retail
Teaspoons	$ .50	$ 4.00	$ 6.00
Place Knives	2.25	18.00	27.00
Place Forks	1.00	8.00	12.00
Salad Forks	1.00	8.00	12.00
Service Spoons	1.00	8.00	12.00
Butter Spreaders	1.00	8.00	12.00

OTHER PLACE SETTING PIECES

After Dinner Coffee Spoons	.50	4.00	6.00
Cocktail Forks	1.00	8.00	12.00
Iced Drink Spoons	1.00	8.00	12.00

SERVING PIECES

	Each Retail
Butter Knife	$1.25
Cold Meat or Serving Fork	2.25
Gravy Ladle	2.25
Long Server	2.25
Pierced Tablespoon	1.25
Serving or Salad Spoon	2.25
Steak Set, 2-pc.	8.00
Sugar Spoon	1.25
Tablespoon	1.25

WR-1 INFANT FEEDING SPOON — Specially designed shallow bowl with long handle for convenient infant feeding. Retail, $1.00

1957 Catalog

Spring Flower Pattern

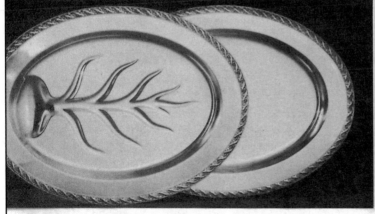

Spring Flower

No. 2000/7   Tea and Coffee Service 7 pieces.....Retail; $130.00

		Retail
No. 2001	Coffee Pot	$15.00
	Capacity 9 cups, Height 10¾ inches	
No. 2002	Tea Pot	15.00
	Capacity 9 cups, Height 10 inches	
No. 2003	Sugar Bowl, Covered	11.25
No. 2004	Cream Pitcher, Gold Lined	11.25

		Retail
No. 2005	Waste Bowl, Gold Lined	$ 5.00
No. 2006	Kettle	32.50
	Capacity 58 oz., Height 13½ inches	
No. 2092 F	Waiter, Chased, Footed	40.00
	Length 22 inches, Overall Length, 28½ inches	

No. 2010/16   Well and Tree Platter.........$10.00
     Length 16 inches
No. 2009/16   Meat Dish.............................9.00

No. 2026   Buffet Tray Retail, $10.00
     Diameter 15 inches, Pierced, Chased

1958 Catalog

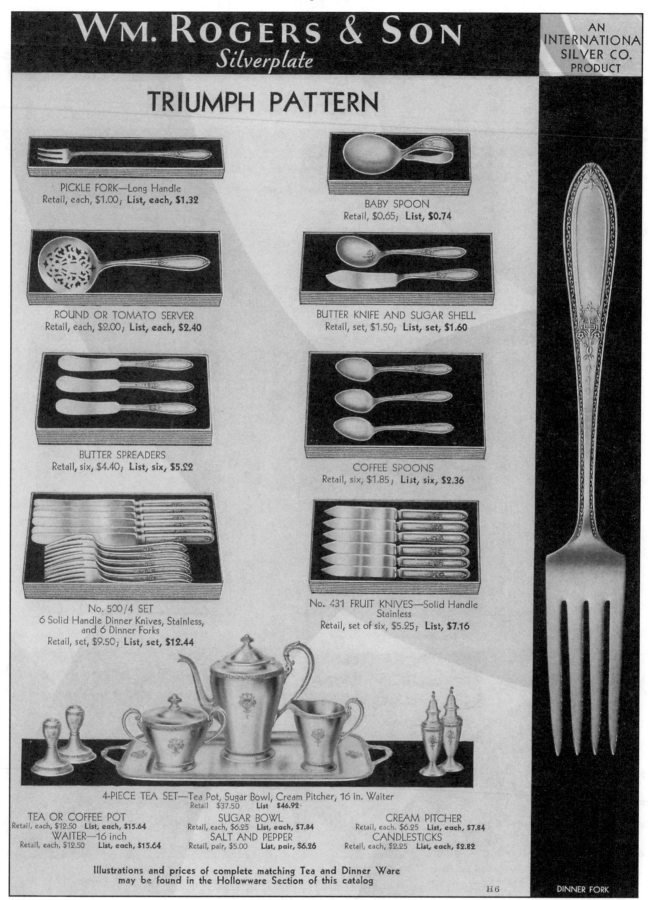

WM. ROGERS & SON
Silverplate

AN INTERNATIONAL SILVER CO. PRODUCT

TRIUMPH PATTERN

PICKLE FORK—Long Handle
Retail, each, $1.00; **List, each, $1.32**

BABY SPOON
Retail, $0.65; **List, $0.74**

ROUND OR TOMATO SERVER
Retail, each, $2.00; **List, each, $2.40**

BUTTER KNIFE AND SUGAR SHELL
Retail, set, $1.50; **List, set, $1.60**

BUTTER SPREADERS
Retail, six, $4.40; **List, six, $5.22**

COFFEE SPOONS
Retail, six, $1.85; **List, six, $2.36**

No. 500/4 SET
6 Solid Handle Dinner Knives, Stainless, and 6 Dinner Forks
Retail, set, $9.50; **List, set, $12.44**

No. 431 FRUIT KNIVES—Solid Handle Stainless
Retail, set of six, $5.25; **List, $7.16**

4-PIECE TEA SET—Tea Pot, Sugar Bowl, Cream Pitcher, 16 in. Waiter
Retail $37.50 **List $46.92**

TEA OR COFFEE POT
Retail, each, $12.50 **List, each, $15.64**

SUGAR BOWL
Retail, each, $6.25 **List, each, $7.84**

CREAM PITCHER
Retail, each, $6.25 **List, each, $7.84**

WAITER—16 inch
Retail, each, $12.50 **List, each, $15.64**

SALT AND PEPPER
Retail, pair, $5.00 **List, pair, $6.26**

CANDLESTICKS
Retail, each, $2.25 **List, each, $2.82**

Illustrations and prices of complete matching Tea and Dinner Ware may be found in the Holloware Section of this catalog

H 6

DINNER FORK

1931 Catalog

WM. ROGERS & SON
Silverplate

AN INTERNATIONAL SILVER CO. PRODUCT

TRIUMPH PATTERN

BREAD TRAY
Retail, each, $5.00; List, $6.26

FLOWER CENTER
Retail, each, $12.50; List, $15.64

COMPOTIER
Retail, each, $5.00; List, $6.26

CASSEROLE
Retail, each, $7.50; List, $9.38

CANDLESTICKS
Retail, each, $2.25; List, $2.82

CHILD'S CUP
Retail, each, $2.50; List, $3.14

DESSERT SET
Retail, set, $13.50; List, $16.92

ICE BOWL
Retail, each, $6.50; List, $8.14
ICE TONGS
Retail, each, $2.00; List, $2.50

GRAVY BOAT & PLATE
Retail, each, $10.00; List, $12.52

RELISH DISH
Retail, each, $10.00; List, $12.52

ADDITIONAL PIECES

	Retail	List
Sandwich Plate, 10½ in.. each	$5.00	$6.26
Tray only for Dessert Set . each	4.50	5.64
Sugar & Creamer ....set	9.00	11.28

	Retail	List
Water Pitcher.........each	$10.00	$12.52
Double Vegetable Dish ..each	10.00	12.52
Meat Dish, Plain, 16 in...each	12.50	15.64
Meat Dish, Well & Tree, 16 in ea.	15.00	18.76
Salt & Pepper ....pair	5.00	6.26

	Retail	List
Bon Bon (without base)..each	$3.00	$3.76
Mixer, 46 oz ....each	10.00	12.52
Cocktail Cup ......set of six	15.00	18.76
Tray, 16 inch ....each	12.50	15.64
8-Pc. Cocktail Set.......set	37.50	46.92
Bon Bon (with base)......each	4.00	5.00

4-PIECE TEA SET—Tea Pot, Sugar, Cream and 16 inch Waiter. Retail, set, $37.50 List, $46.92

SUGAR BOWL
Retail, each, $6.25 List, $7.84

TEA OR COFFEE POT
Retail, each, $12.50 List, $15.64

CREAM PITCHER
Retail, each, $6.25 List, $7.84

WAITER—16 inch
Retail, each, $12.50 List, $15.64

3 Piece Tea Set (without Waiter) Retail, $25.00 List, $31.28

H 6

HOLLOW HANDLE DINNER KNIFE

Victorian Rose Pattern

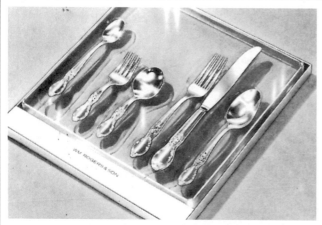

WR-6 ABC Silver Set—Fills children's needs from 1 to 10 years.   Retail **$7.00**

VICTORIAN ROSE—Wm. Rogers & Son Silverplate
Attached tray, Capacity, 8 ozs. ....   Retail **$12.50**

VICTORIAN ROSE—Wm. Rogers & Son Silverplate

		Retail
No. 1915	Candlestick, Height, 9 inches ...pair	$18.00
No. 1916	Candelabrum, Height, 12½ inches	
	Spread, 12⅝ inches ....each	25.00

VICTORIAN ROSE
Wm. Rogers & Son Silverplate

No. 1917 Footed, Ice guard, Retail
Capacity, 2 qts. $22.50

VICTORIAN ROSE — Wm. Rogers & Son Silverplate

		Retail
No. 1945	Punch Bowl, Capacity, 1½ gallons	
	Diameter, 13¼ inches	$40.00
No. 1974	Tray, Diameter, 17⅝ inches	25.00
No. 1947	Ladle (no tax)	7.50
No. 1946	Punch Cups (dozen) Duncan &	
	Miller Glass	12.50

1964 Catalog

See Price Guide — Group 3

VICTORIAN ROSE—Wm. Rogers & Son Silverplate—
Covered Casserole, Footed

No. 1962   Capacity, 1½ qts. Diameter, 11¼ inches. Removable Pyrex
liner...Retail $17.50

WM. ROGERS & SON® SILVERPLATE

Open Stock Price List for all Patterns July 1, 1965. Retail prices shown
are those quoted to consumers on direct inquiry and subject to change
without notice. All goods billed at prices prevailing on date of
shipment.

PLACE SETTING PIECES

	Retail One	Retail Eight	Retail Twelve
Teaspoons	$ .75	$ 6.00	$ 9.00
Place Knives	2.50	20.00	30.00
Place Forks	1.50	12.00	18.00
Salad Forks	1.50	12.00	18.00
Service Spoons	1.50	12.00	18.00

OTHER PLACE SETTING PIECES

	Retail One	Retail Eight	Retail Twelve
Cocktail Forks	$1.50	$12.00	$18.00
Iced Drink Spoons	1.50	12.00	18.00

SERVING PIECES

	Retail Each			Retail Each
Butter Knife	$1.50	**L**	Pierced	
Cold Meat or			Tablespoon ...	1.50
Serving Fork	2.50	**M** † Serving or Salad		
Gravy Ladle	2.50		Spoon	2.50
*Long Server	2.50	**N**	Sugar Spoon ..	1.50
		O	Tablespoon	1.50

*Not Available in Gaiety or Juliette
†Not Available in Gaiety

VICTORIAN ROSE—Wm. Rogers & Son Silverplate

VICTORIAN ROSE—Wm. Rogers & Son Silverplate
Silent Butler, 6 x 6 inches ..... Retail $15.00

Tea and Coffee Services

VICTORIAN ROSE — Wm. Rogers & Son Silverplate

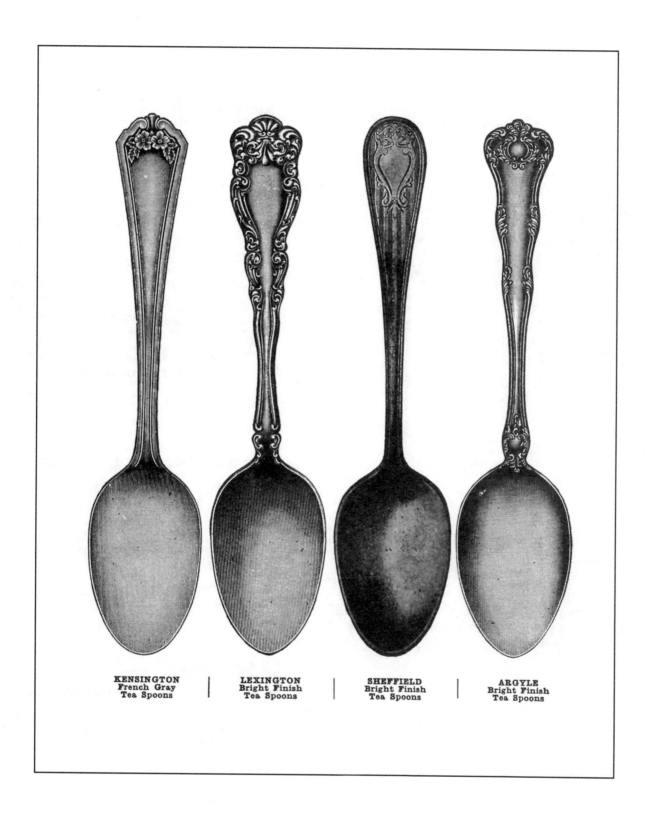

KENSINGTON
French Gray
Tea Spoons

LEXINGTON
Bright Finish
Tea Spoons

SHEFFIELD
Bright Finish
Tea Spoons

ARGYLE
Bright Finish
Tea Spoons

See Price Guide — Group 1

Wm. Rogers (Eagle Brand)

Berwick Pattern

OLIVE SPOON
Berwick pattern.   French gray
No. 32043   Gold bowl..............each **$1.71**
No. 32044   Silver bowl............each   1.30

SIX ORANGE SPOONS
Berwick pattern.   French gray.

SUGAR TONGS
Berwick pattern.

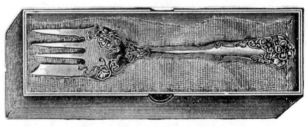

SIX INDIVIDUAL SALAD FORKS
Berwick pattern.   French gray.
No. 32019   Silver tines................per set **$5.95**
No. 32020   Gold tines.................per set   **8.45**

COLD MEAT FORK
Berwick pattern.   French gray.

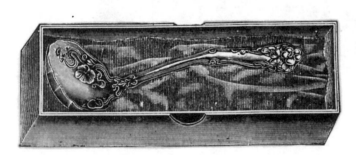

BERWICK PATTERN.   French gray .

No. 32002	Cream Ladle.	Silver bowl................each	**$1.45**
No. 32003	Cream Ladle.	Gold bowl..................each	**2.05**
No. 32004	Gravy Ladle.	Silver bowl................each	**1.90**
No. 32005	Gravy Ladle.	Gold bowl..................each	**2.80**
No. 32006	Oyster Ladle.	Silver bowl................each	**4.10**
No. 32007	Oyster Ladle.	Gold bowl..................each	**5.10**
No. 32008	Medium Ladle.	Silver bowl................each	**5.00**
No. 32009	Medium Ladle.	Gold bowl..................each	**6.25**

BABY SPOON
Berwick pattern.   French gray.
No. 32025...each **$0.80**

Patented 1904. 1913 Catalog

PIE SERVER
Berwick pattern.   French Gray.

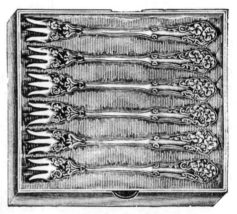

SIX OYSTER FORKS
Berwick pattern.   French Gray.

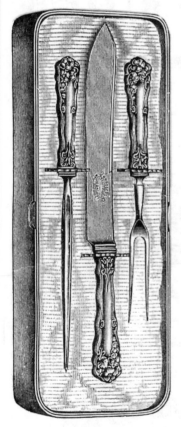

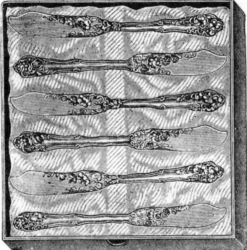

SIX BUTTER SPREADERS
Berwick pattern.   French Gray.

CHILD'S SET
Berwick pattern. French Gray.

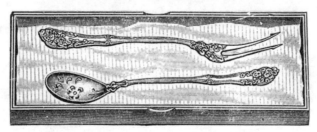

**THREE-PIECE CARVING
SET**
Berwick pattern. French Gray.

PICKLE FORK AND OLIVE SPOON
Berwick pattern.   French Gray.

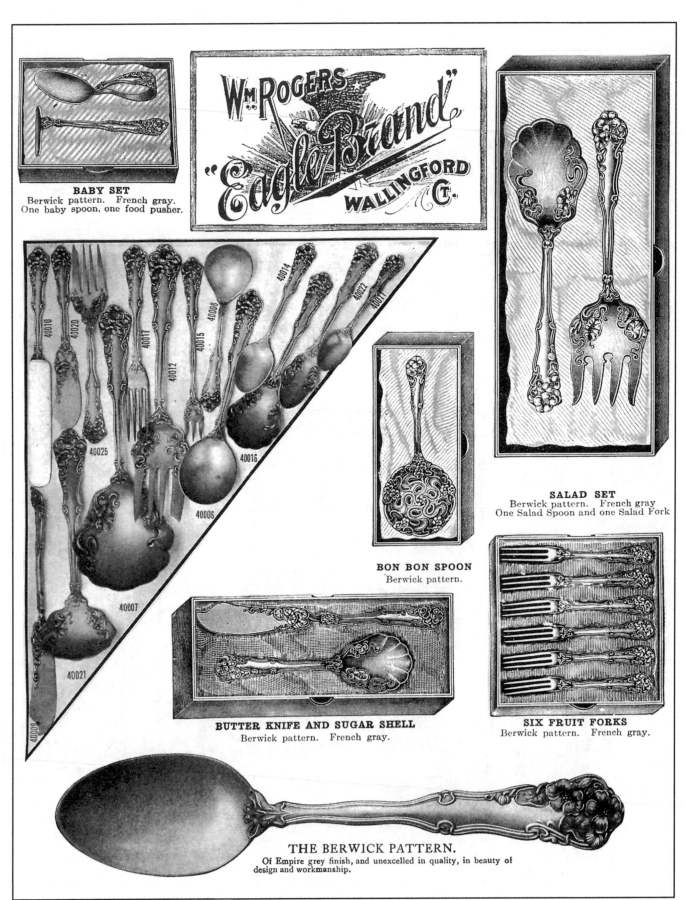

BABY SET
Berwick pattern. French gray.
One baby spoon, one food pusher.

Wm Rogers "Eagle Brand" WALLINGFORD Ct.

SALAD SET
Berwick pattern. French gray
One Salad Spoon and one Salad Fork

BON BON SPOON
Berwick pattern.

BUTTER KNIFE AND SUGAR SHELL
Berwick pattern. French gray.

SIX FRUIT FORKS
Berwick pattern. French gray.

THE BERWICK PATTERN.
Of Empire grey finish, and unexcelled in quality, in beauty of
design and workmanship.

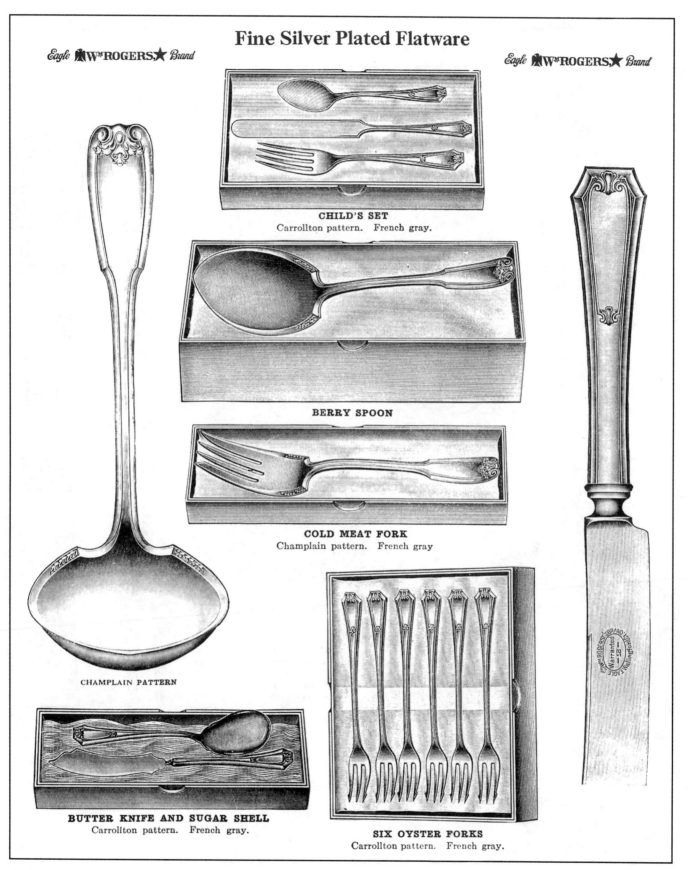

Fine Silver Plated Flatware

Eagle **Wᵐ ROGERS ★** *Brand*

Eagle **Wᵐ ROGERS ★** *Brand*

CHILD'S SET
Carrollton pattern. French gray.

BERRY SPOON

COLD MEAT FORK
Champlain pattern. French gray

CHAMPLAIN PATTERN

BUTTER KNIFE AND SUGAR SHELL
Carrollton pattern. French gray.

SIX OYSTER FORKS
Carrollton pattern. French gray.

1913 Catalog

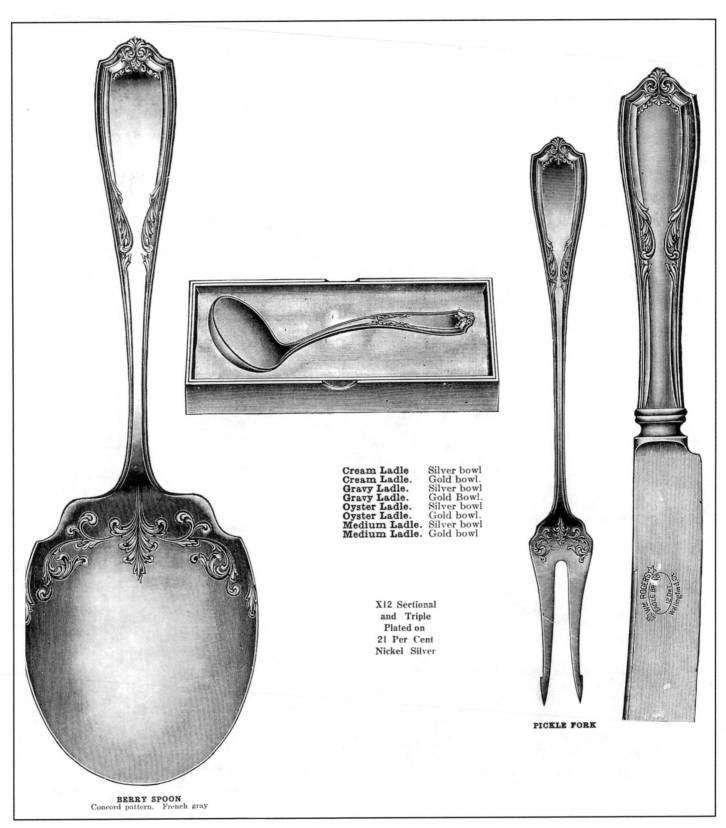

Cream Ladle.   Silver bowl
Cream Ladle.   Gold bowl.
Gravy Ladle.   Silver bowl
Gravy Ladle.   Gold Bowl.
Oyster Ladle. Silver bowl
Oyster Ladle. Gold bowl.
Medium Ladle. Silver bowl
Medium Ladle. Gold bowl

X12 Sectional
and Triple
Plated on
21 Per Cent
Nickel Silver

PICKLE FORK

BERRY SPOON
Concord pattern. French gray

1913 Catalog

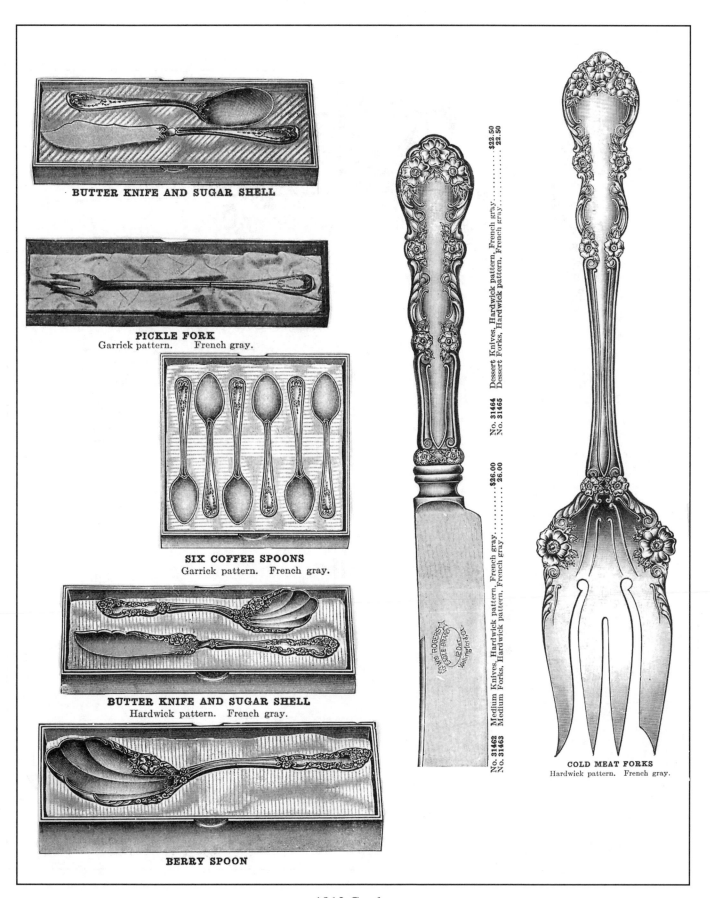

BUTTER KNIFE AND SUGAR SHELL

PICKLE FORK
Garrick pattern.   French gray.

SIX COFFEE SPOONS
Garrick pattern.   French gray.

BUTTER KNIFE AND SUGAR SHELL
Hardwick pattern.   French gray.

BERRY SPOON

No. 31464   Dessert Knives, Hardwick pattern, French gray........ $22.50
No. 31465   Dessert Forks, Hardwick pattern, French gray........ 22.50

No. 31462   Medium Knives, Hardwick pattern, French gray........ $26.00
No. 31463   Medium Forks, Hardwick pattern, French gray........ 26.00

COLD MEAT FORKS
Hardwick pattern.   French gray.

1913 Catalog

See Price Guide — Group 1

Melrose Pattern

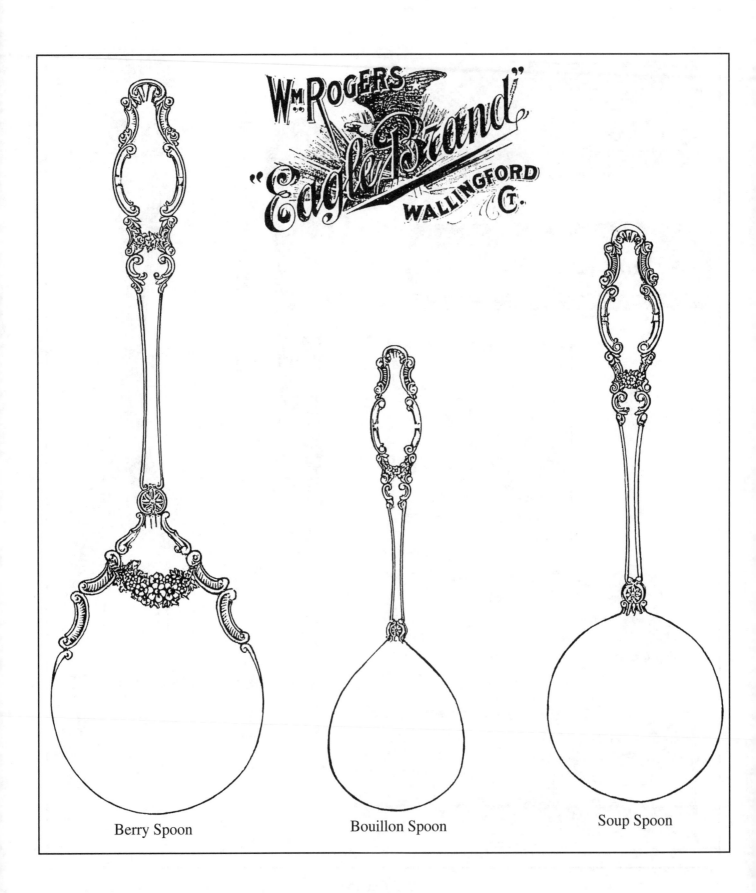

Berry Spoon   Bouillon Spoon   Soup Spoon

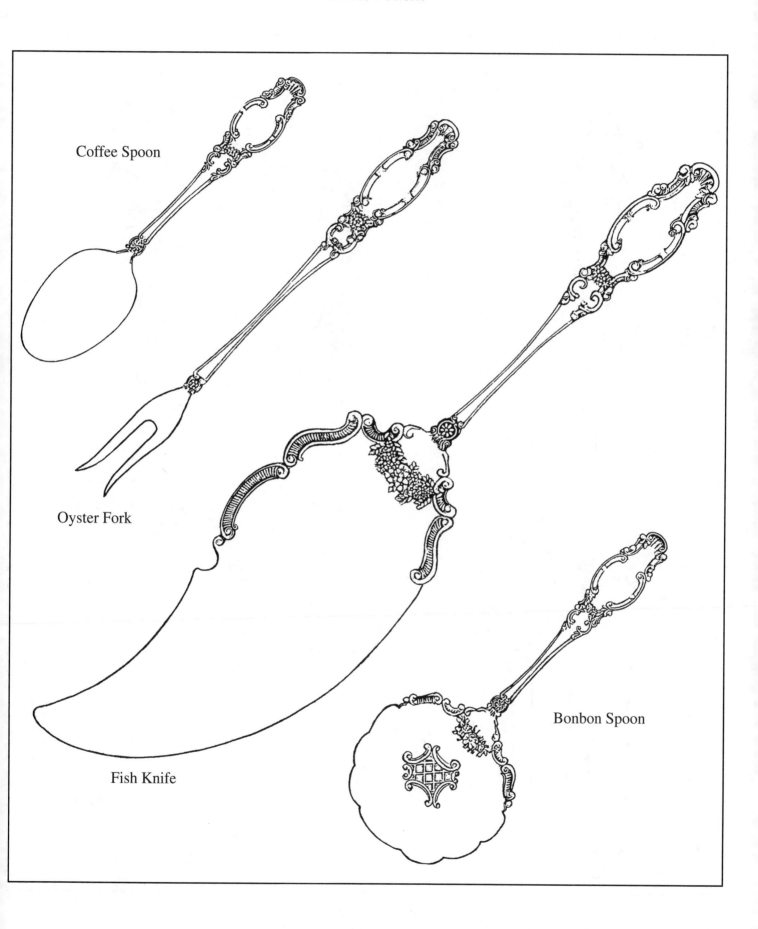

Coffee Spoon

Oyster Fork

Fish Knife

Bonbon Spoon

Melrose Pattern

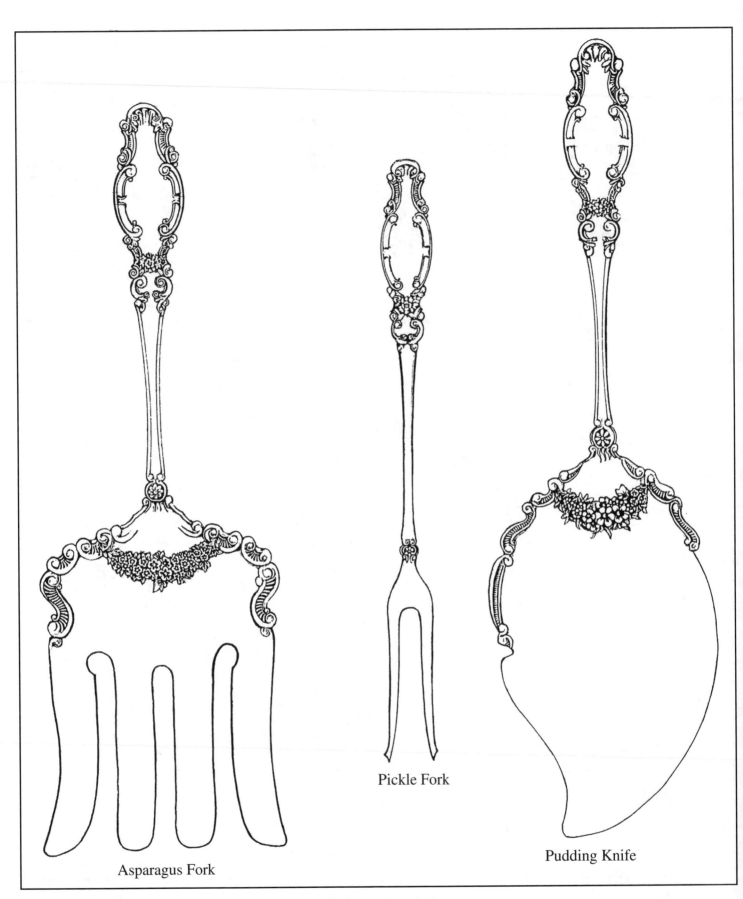

Asparagus Fork

Pickle Fork

Pudding Knife

Items shown actual size.

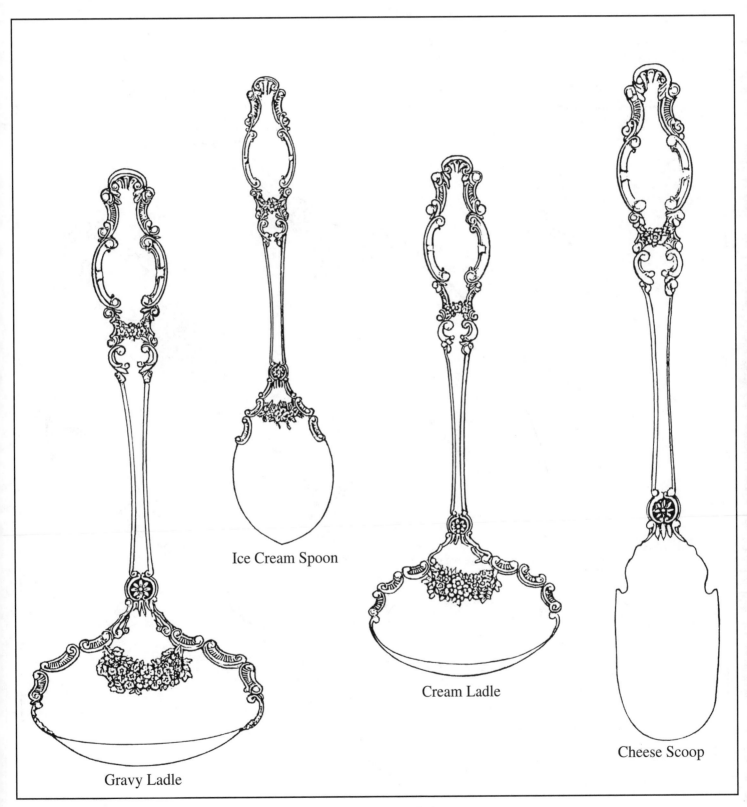

Ice Cream Spoon

Cream Ladle

Cheese Scoop

Gravy Ladle

Items shown actual size.

See Price Guide — Group 1

Melrose Pattern

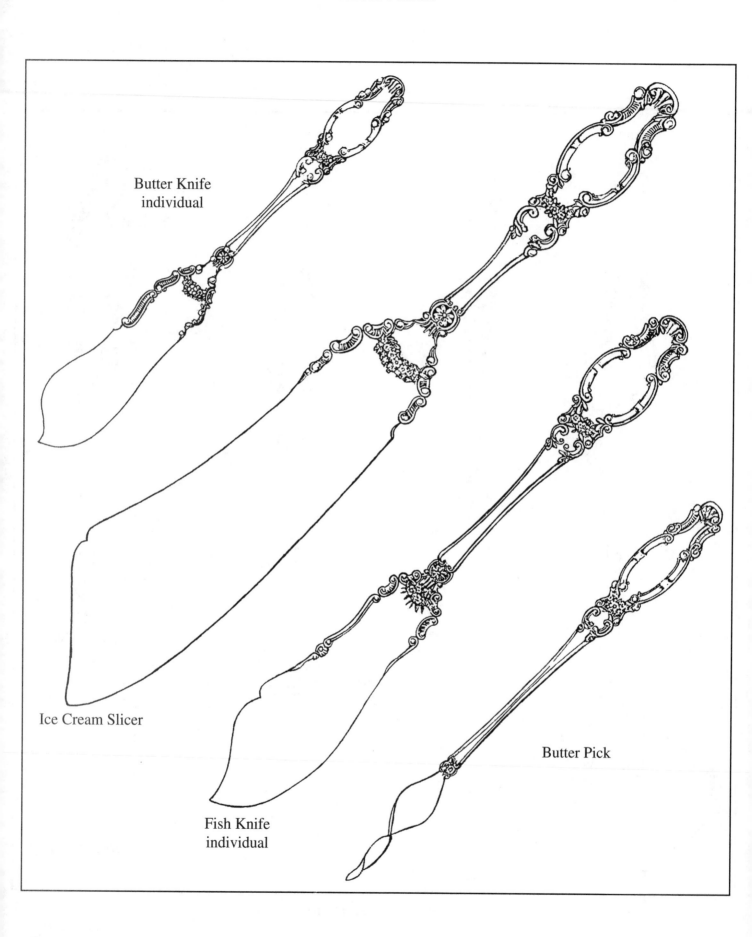

Butter Knife
individual

Ice Cream Slicer

Fish Knife
individual

Butter Pick

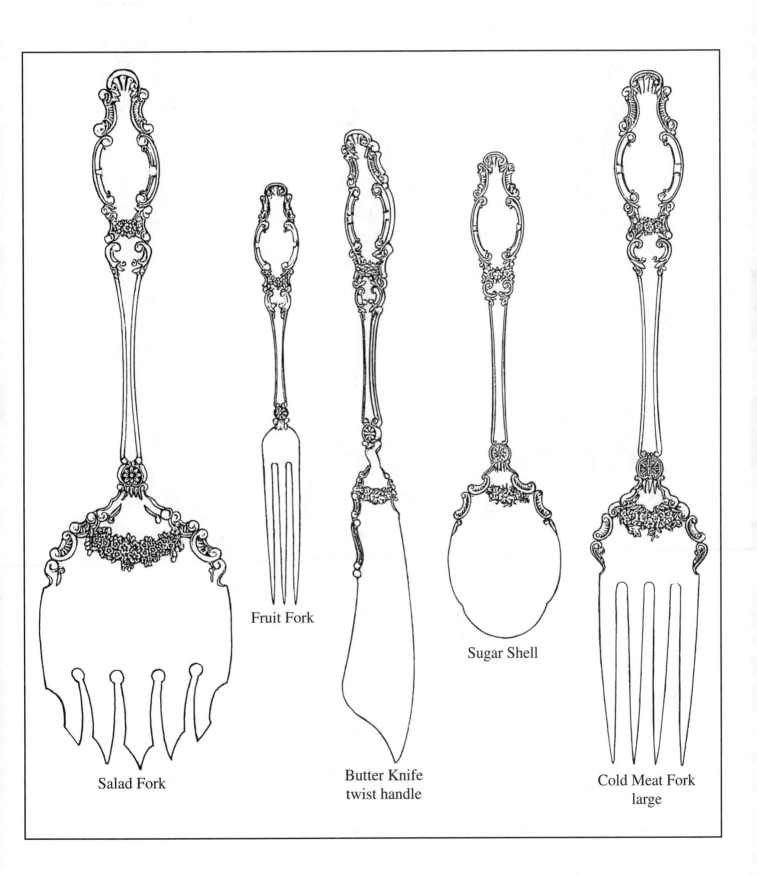

Salad Fork

Fruit Fork

Butter Knife
twist handle

Sugar Shell

Cold Meat Fork
large

See Price Guide — Group 1

Melrose Pattern

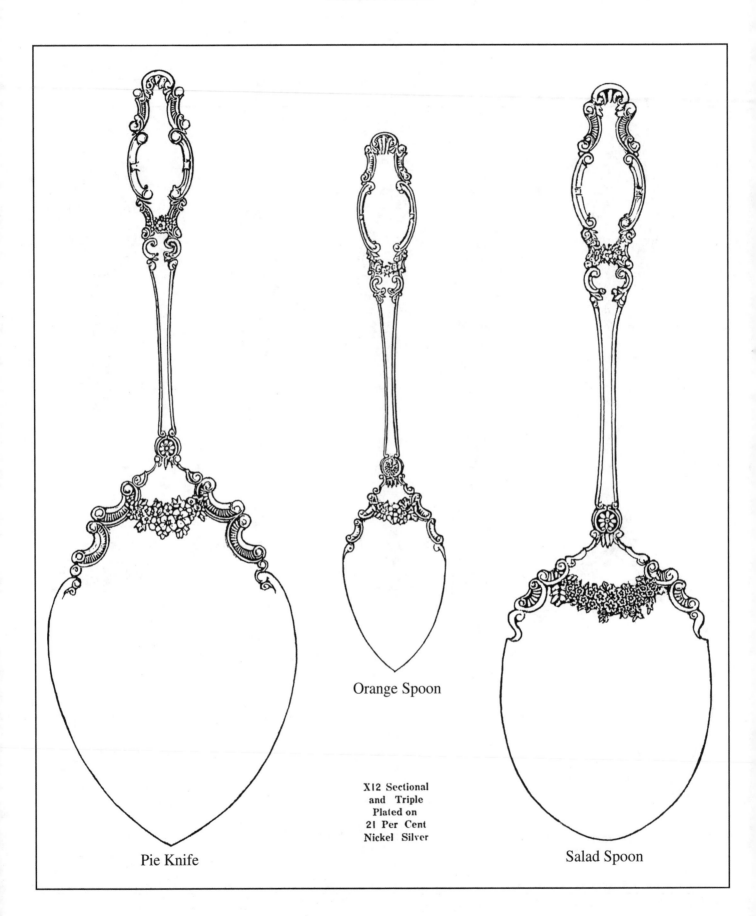

Pie Knife

Orange Spoon

X12 Sectional
and Triple
Plated on
21 Per Cent
Nickel Silver

Salad Spoon

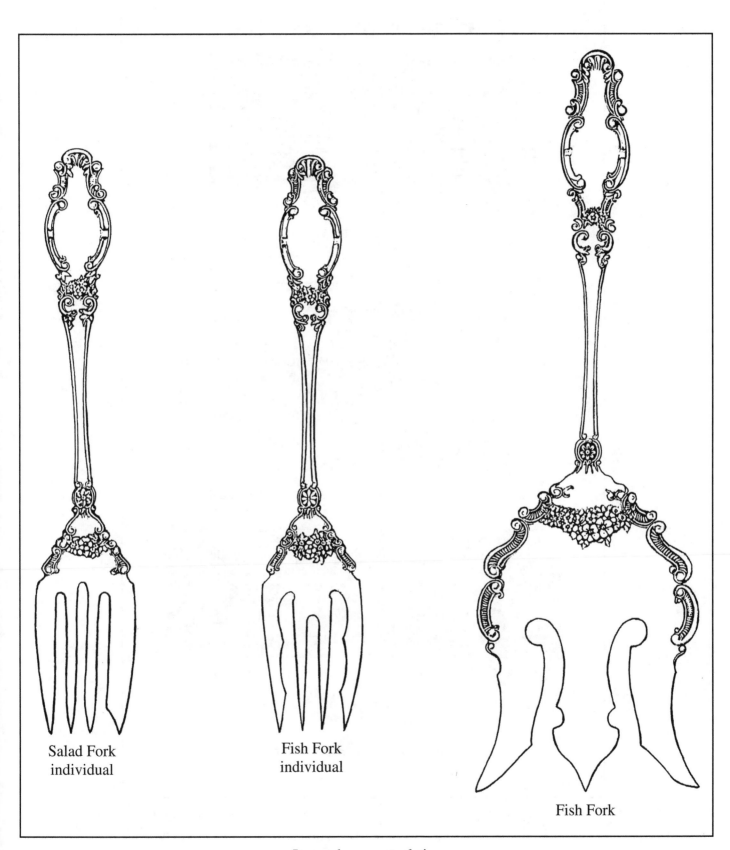

Salad Fork
individual

Fish Fork
individual

Fish Fork

Items shown actual size.

See Price Guide — Group 1

Yale Pattern, patented 1894

| No. **32037** | Silver bowl | each | $1.50 |
| No. **32038** | Gold bowl | each | 4.05 |

TOMATO SERVER
Yale pattern.

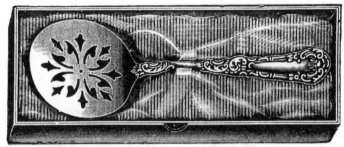

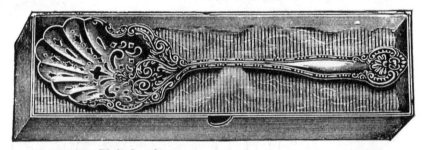

| No. **32039** | Plain bowl | each | $2.50 |
| No. **32040** | Gold bowl | each | 3.10 |

ICE SPOON
York Pattern.

York Pattern, patented 1900

1913 Catalog. York is an extremely beautiful pattern. The ice spoon shown is a very desirable piece. York was made in sterling and may also be found with other backstamps such as the Star Rogers & Bros.

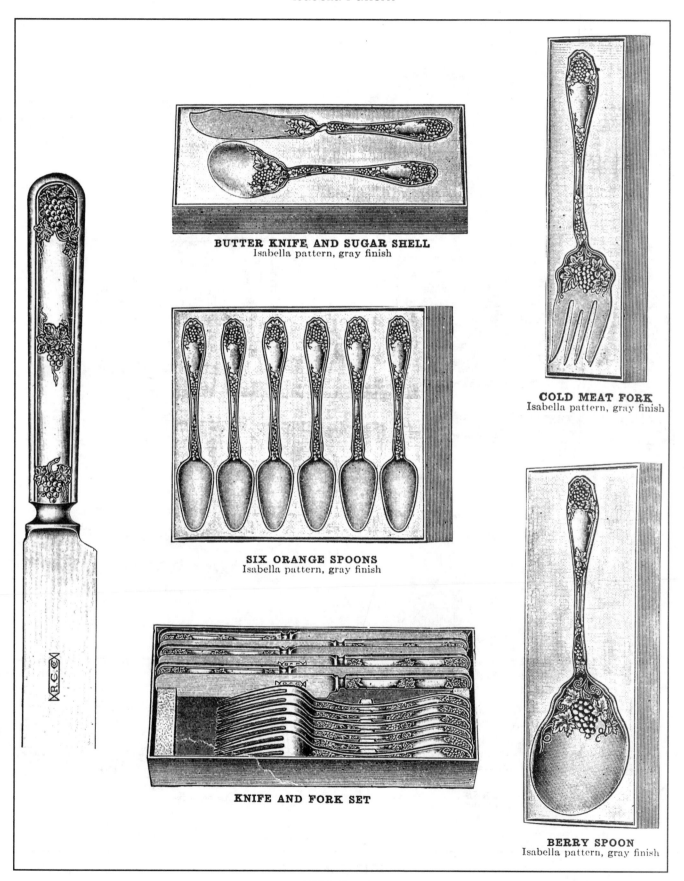

BUTTER KNIFE AND SUGAR SHELL
Isabella pattern, gray finish

COLD MEAT FORK
Isabella pattern, gray finish

SIX ORANGE SPOONS
Isabella pattern, gray finish

KNIFE AND FORK SET

BERRY SPOON
Isabella pattern, gray finish

1913 Catalog

See Price Guide — Group 1

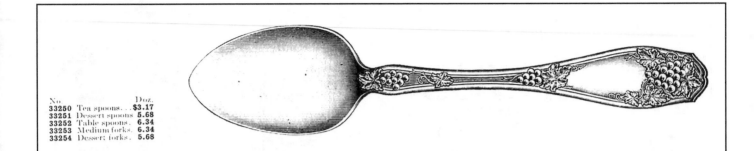

No.		Doz.
33250	Tea spoons	$3.17
33251	Dessert spoons	5.68
33252	Table spoons	6.34
33253	Medium forks	6.34
33254	Dessert forks	5.68

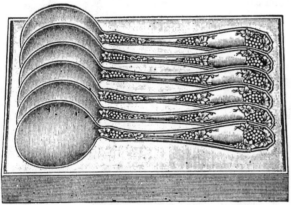

SIX SOUP SPOONS
Isabella pattern, gray finish

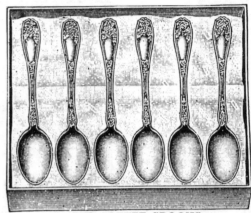

SIX COFFEE SPOONS
Isabella pattern, gray finish

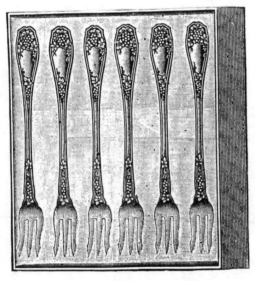

SIX OYSTER FORKS
Isabella pattern, gray finish

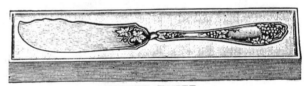

BUTTER KNIFE
Isabella pattern, gray finish

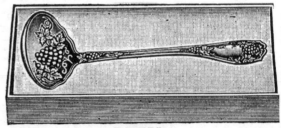

LADLES
Isabella pattern, gray finish

Cream, silver bowl
Gravy, silver bowl
Medium, silver bowl

1913 Catalog

Jubilee Pattern

Early 1950s. Left to right: 9⅕" dinner knife, 7⁷⁄₁₀" Viande fork, 6⅘" individual salad fork, 7⅖" long bowl soup spoon, 8⁹⁄₁₀" cold meat serving fork. Bottom: 6¹⁄₁₀" teaspoon.

See Price Guide — Group 3

Revelation is also found marked American Silver Company. Introduced 1938.

COLD MEAT FORK

THREE-PIECE CHILD'S SET

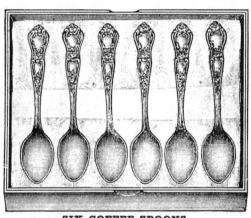

SIX COFFEE SPOONS

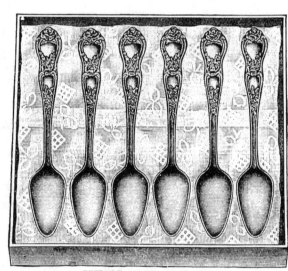

SIX ORANGE SPOONS

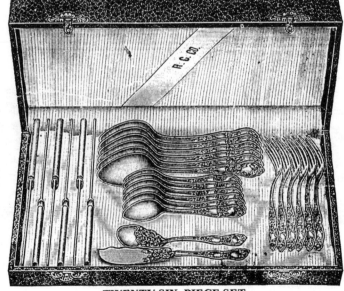

TWENTY SIX PIECE SET

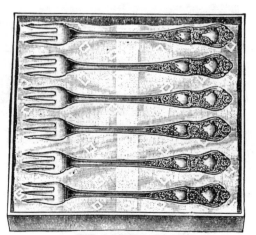

SIX OYSTER FORKS

1913 Catalog

Rose Pattern

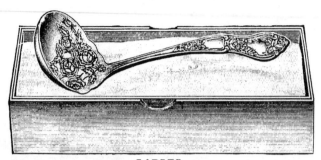

LADLES

No. 33278	Cream, silver bowl	each	**$1.03**
No. 33279	Gravy, silver bowl	each	1.25
No. 33280	Medium, silver bowl	each	3.50

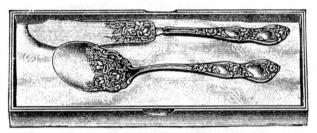

BUTTER KNIFE AND SUGAR SHELL

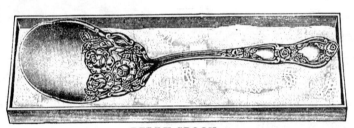

BERRY SPOON

No. **33282**   Silver bowl.............................each **$1.47**

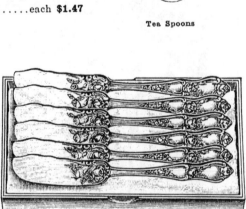

Tea Spoons

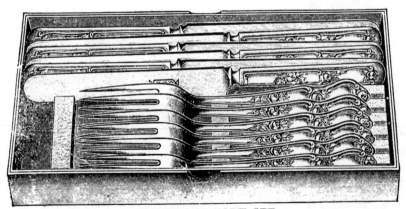

KNIFE AND FORK SET

Six solid handle medium knives, six spoon handle medium forks.

No. **33287**   Per set.....................................**$6.73**

SIX BUTTER SPREADERS

1913 Catalog

Wm. A. Rogers (Horse Shoe Brand)

Arundel Pattern

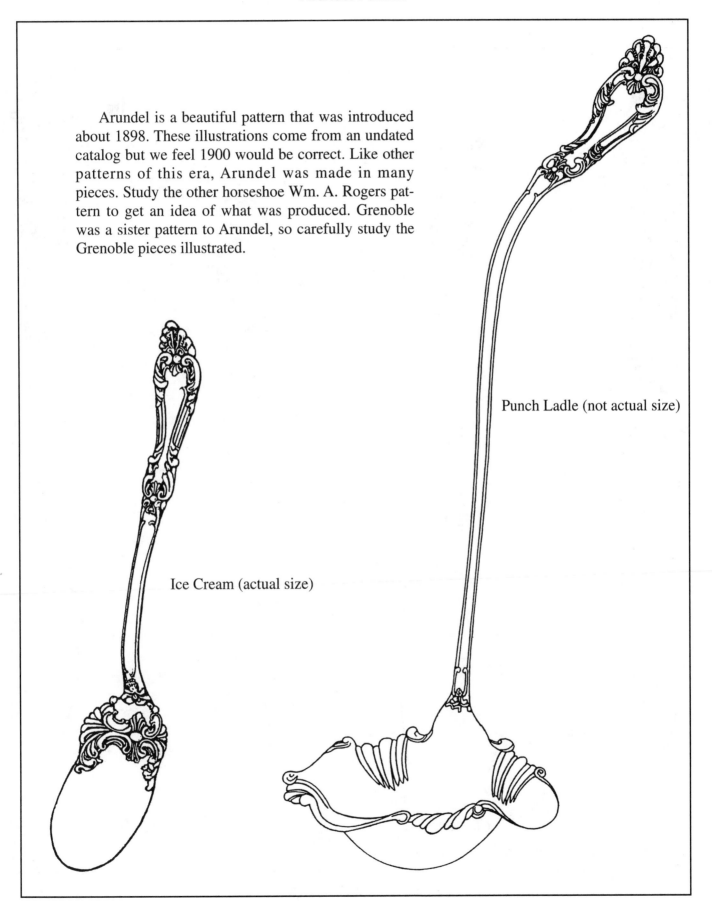

Arundel is a beautiful pattern that was introduced about 1898. These illustrations come from an undated catalog but we feel 1900 would be correct. Like other patterns of this era, Arundel was made in many pieces. Study the other horseshoe Wm. A. Rogers pattern to get an idea of what was produced. Grenoble was a sister pattern to Arundel, so carefully study the Grenoble pieces illustrated.

Punch Ladle (not actual size)

Ice Cream (actual size)

See Price Guide — Group 1

Arundel Pattern

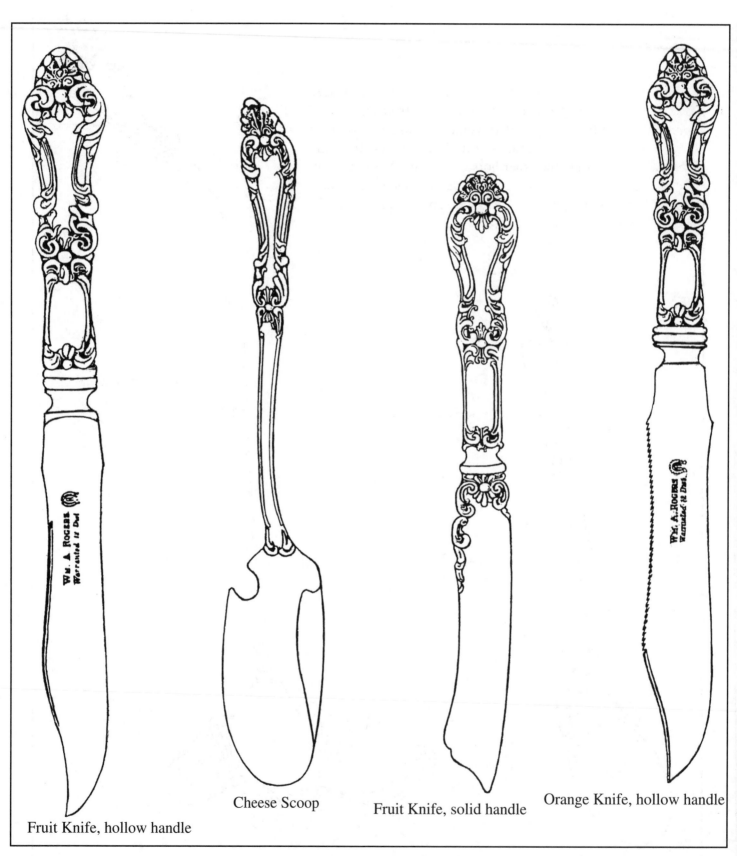

Cheese Scoop

Fruit Knife, solid handle

Orange Knife, hollow handle

Fruit Knife, hollow handle

Items shown actual size.

Arundel Pattern

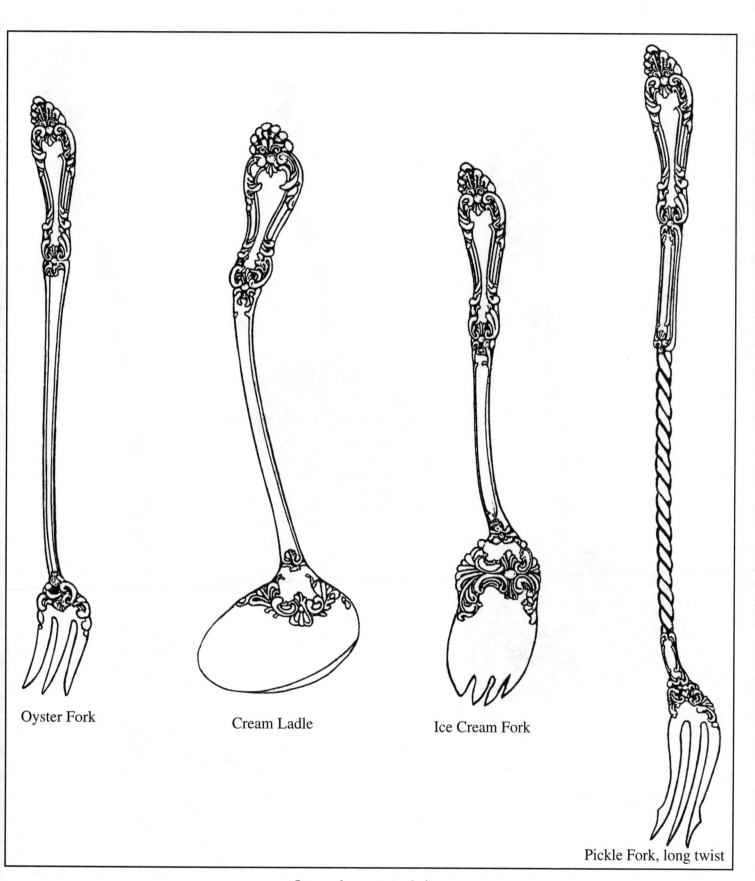

Oyster Fork

Cream Ladle

Ice Cream Fork

Pickle Fork, long twist

Items shown actual size.

See Price Guide — Group 1

Glenrose Pattern

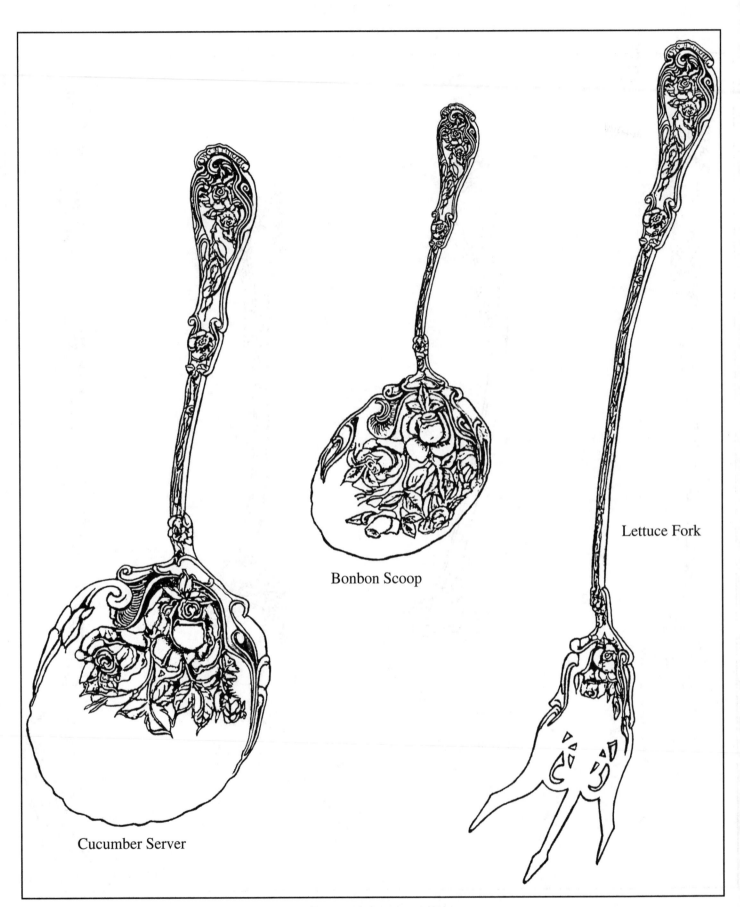

Bonbon Scoop

Lettuce Fork

Cucumber Server

1908.

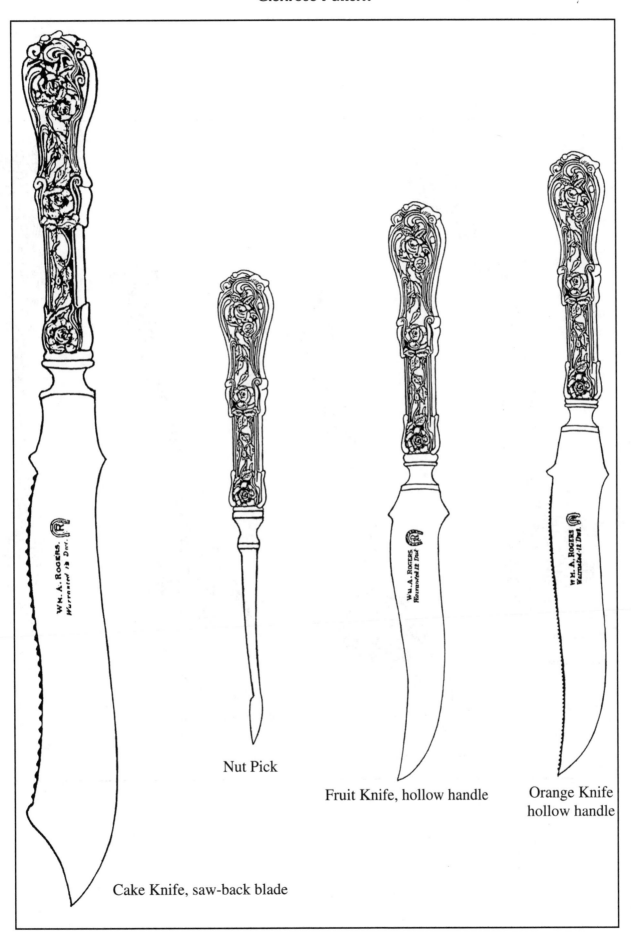

Nut Pick

Fruit Knife, hollow handle

Orange Knife
hollow handle

Cake Knife, saw-back blade

Glenrose Pattern

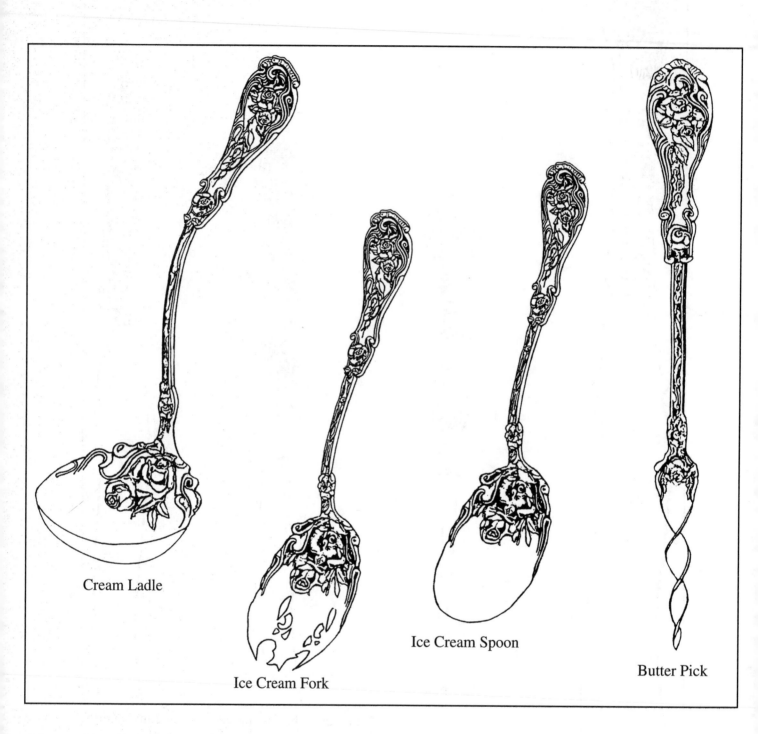

Cream Ladle

Ice Cream Fork

Ice Cream Spoon

Butter Pick

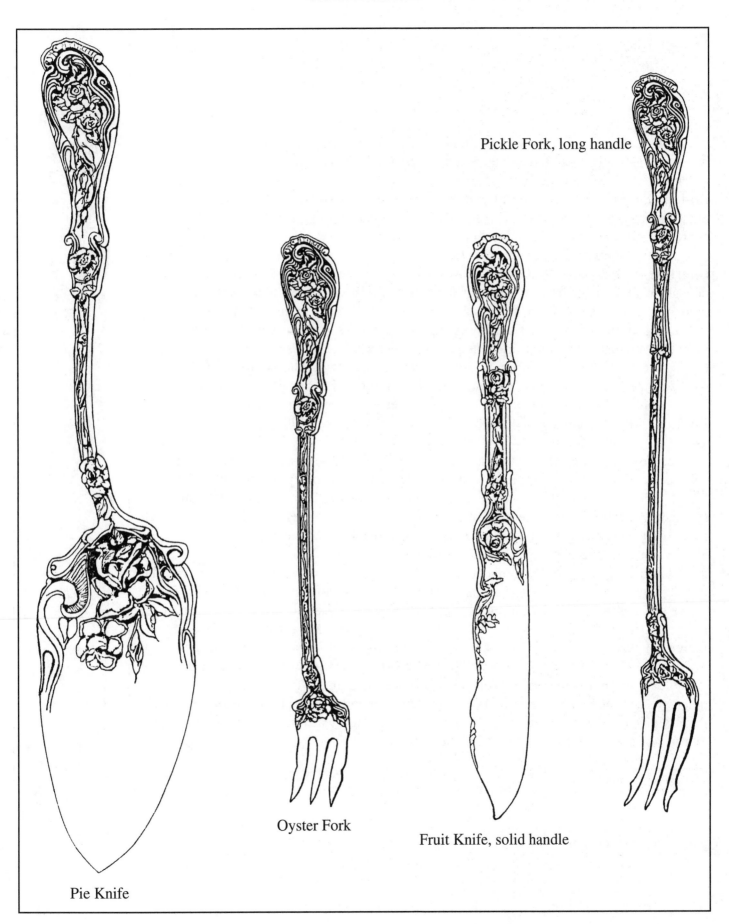

Pickle Fork, long handle

Oyster Fork

Fruit Knife, solid handle

Pie Knife

Grenoble Pattern

Wm. A. Rogers first produced Grenoble in 1905 – 1906. This same pattern was also marketed as the Japanese Lily by the Boston wholesale firm of McLean, Black and Company, Inc. Japanese Lily was made expressly for them by Wm. A. Rogers and was available only in the French Gray sterling finish. This consisted of a heavy deposit of pure silver on each piece at the point of most wear. McLean, Black advertised this pattern as "extra heavy A-1 plate." When marketed as the Grenoble pattern, the buyer had an option in some pieces of the French Gray or gold plate finishes. Additionally, pieces of Grenoble have Rockford S.P. Co. stamped on the back.

Rockford also sold the pattern as Gloria. Some Grenoble serving pieces can be found with a handle of pearl, and are factory-made pieces. Various pieces came in silk-lined boxes and were sold as sets. These were attractively packaged and advertised as gift items. Some sets contained items that were never sold singularly. These sets held six each of small items like nut picks, individual butter spreaders, and individual berry forks.

Occasionally a Grenoble twenty-six piece set is found in its original Wm. A. Rogers box. These table sets had six each of the hollow handle dinner knives, flat

handle regular dinner forks, teaspoons, dessert spoons (long bowl), one sugar shell, and one twist-handle master butter knife. The dessert-size twenty-six piece set was also made, costing a dollar less.

The largest Grenoble carving set is the roast, sometimes listed as a dinner carving set. The smaller carving set was a combination steak/bird utensil. Unlike the 1847 Rogers Bros. patterns which sport three different size carving sets, Grenoble seems to have only two. The smaller version was available with or without the sharpener. These sets were expensive, the roast costing ten dollars in 1906.

The child's set was boxed as a gift item. The knife was one piece, flat handled, with a fancy blade. It is possible that some sets were sold with a pearl handled knife, which considerably increased the price.

Also expensive in Grenoble was the fish set, the largest fork selling for $6.60. Do not confuse the fish serving fork with the smaller salad serving fork. The accompanying fish knife with the large fancy blade is hard to find. Six fish forks were boxed with it. Several salad sets were made in Grenoble, some of the cheaper sets having a cold meat fork coupled with a berry spoon.

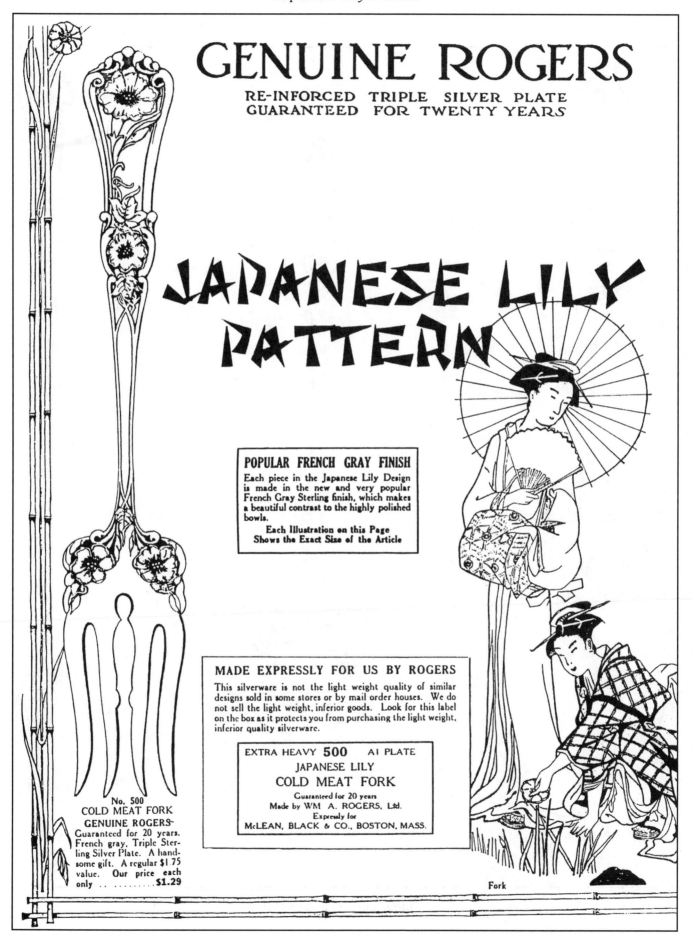

GENUINE ROGERS
RE-INFORCED TRIPLE SILVER PLATE
GUARANTEED FOR TWENTY YEARS

JAPANESE LILY PATTERN

POPULAR FRENCH GRAY FINISH

Each piece in the Japanese Lily Design is made in the new and very popular French Gray Sterling finish, which makes a beautiful contrast to the highly polished bowls.

Each Illustration on this Page Shows the Exact Size of the Article

MADE EXPRESSLY FOR US BY ROGERS

This silverware is not the light weight quality of similar designs sold in some stores or by mail order houses. We do not sell the light weight, inferior goods. Look for this label on the box as it protects you from purchasing the light weight, inferior quality silverware.

EXTRA HEAVY **500** A1 PLATE
JAPANESE LILY
COLD MEAT FORK
Guaranteed for 20 years
Made by WM. A. ROGERS, Ltd.
Expressly for
McLEAN, BLACK & CO., BOSTON, MASS.

No. 500
COLD MEAT FORK
GENUINE ROGERS
Guaranteed for 20 years. French gray, Triple Sterling Silver Plate. A handsome gift. A regular $1.75 value. Our price each only **$1.29**

Fork

See Price Guide — Group 1

Grenoble Pattern

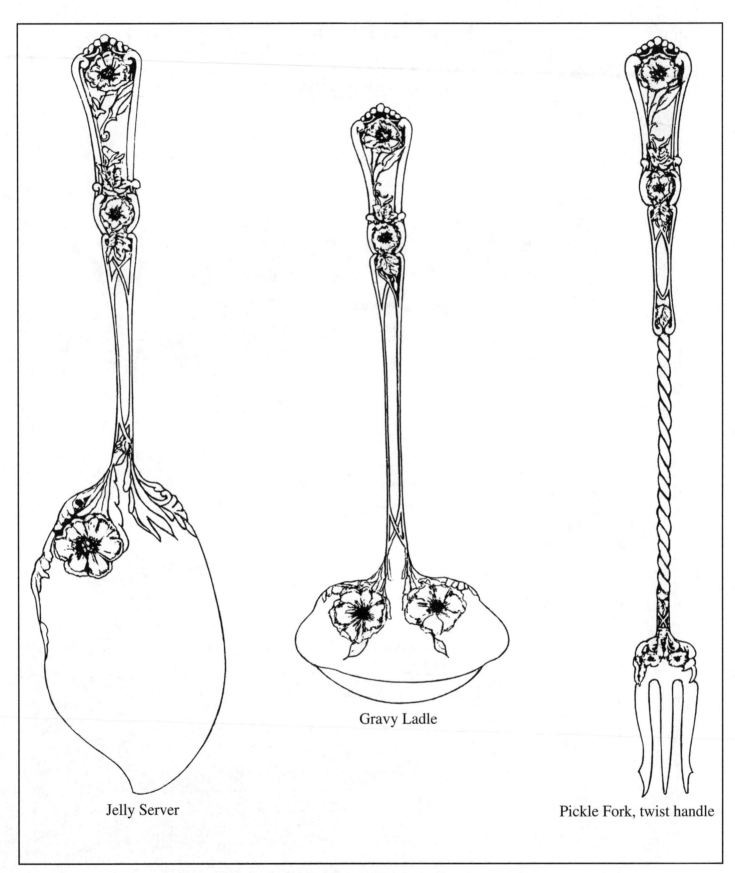

Jelly Server

Gravy Ladle

Pickle Fork, twist handle

Items shown actual size.

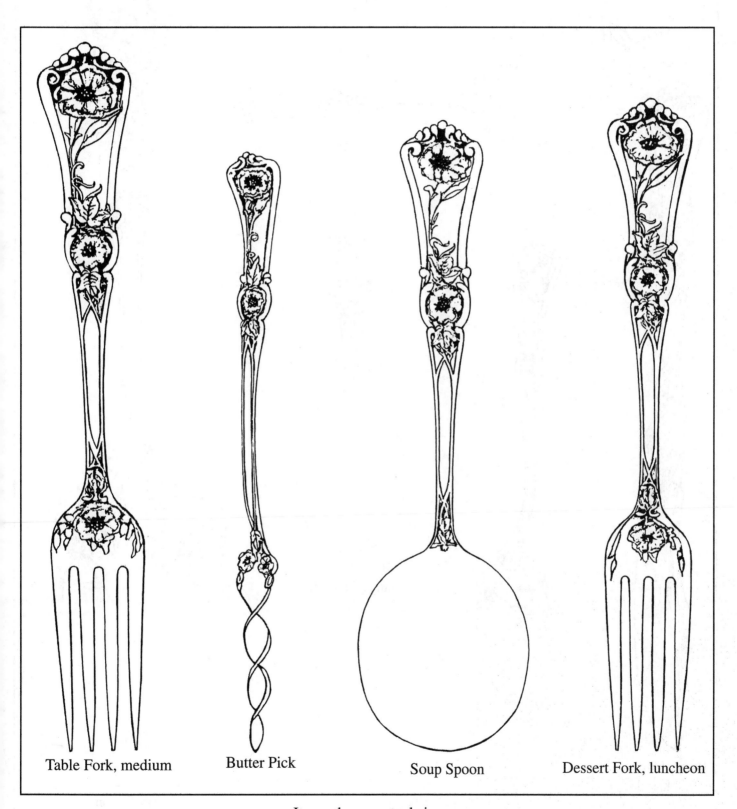

Table Fork, medium   Butter Pick   Soup Spoon   Dessert Fork, luncheon

Items shown actual size.

Grenoble Pattern

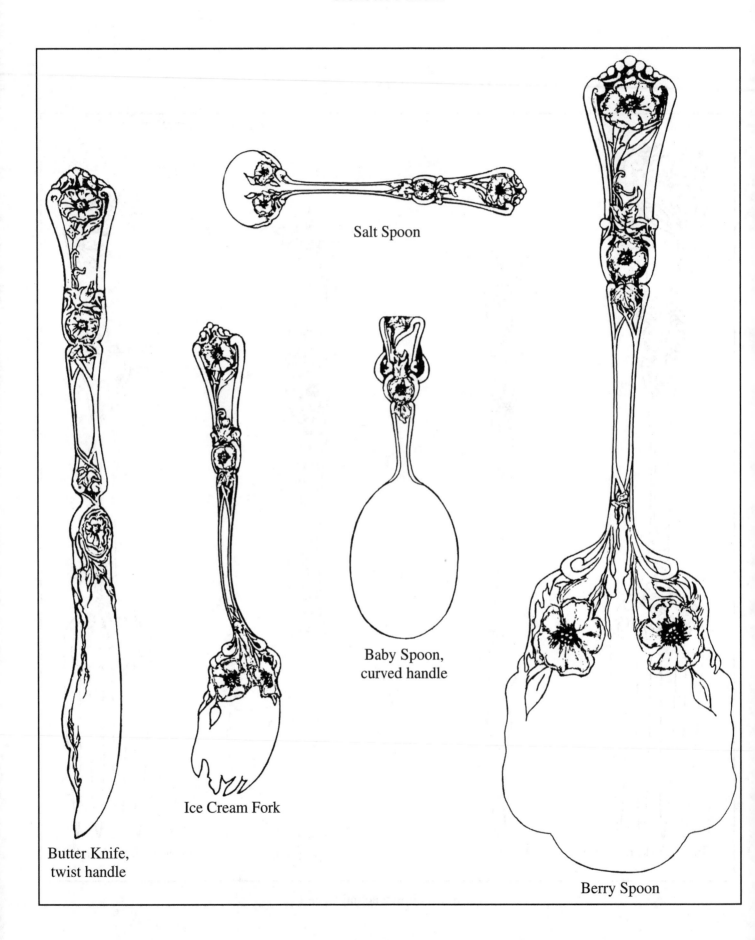

Salt Spoon

Baby Spoon,
curved handle

Ice Cream Fork

Butter Knife,
twist handle

Berry Spoon

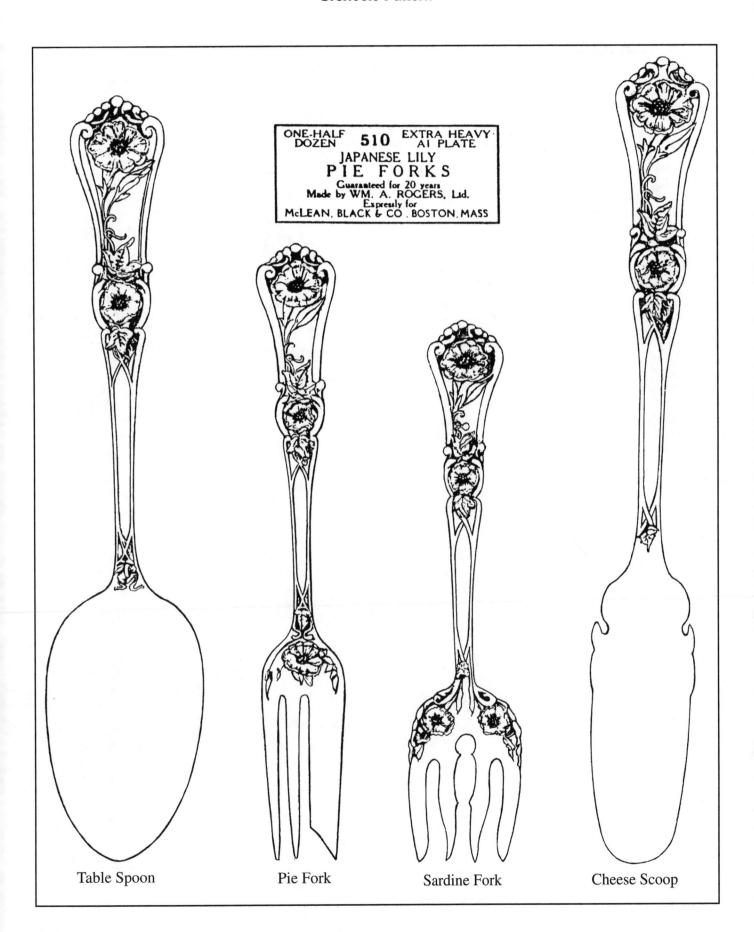

ONE-HALF
DOZEN **510** EXTRA HEAVY
AI PLATE
JAPANESE LILY
PIE FORKS
Guaranteed for 20 years
Made by WM. A. ROGERS, Ltd.
Expressly for
McLEAN, BLACK & CO., BOSTON, MASS

Table Spoon   Pie Fork   Sardine Fork   Cheese Scoop

Grenoble Pattern

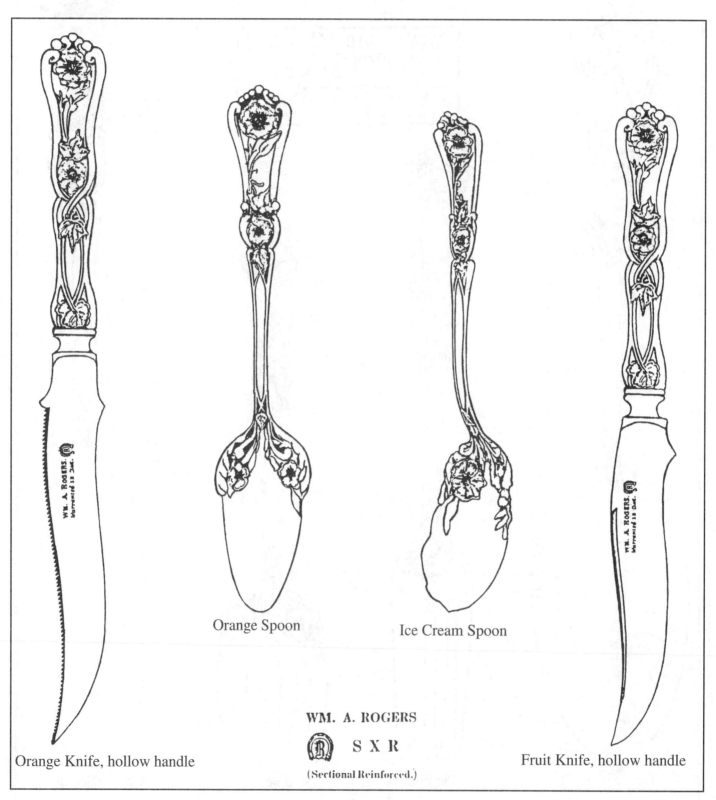

Orange Spoon

Ice Cream Spoon

Orange Knife, hollow handle

Fruit Knife, hollow handle

WM. A. ROGERS

S X R

(Sectional Reinforced.)

Items shown actual size.

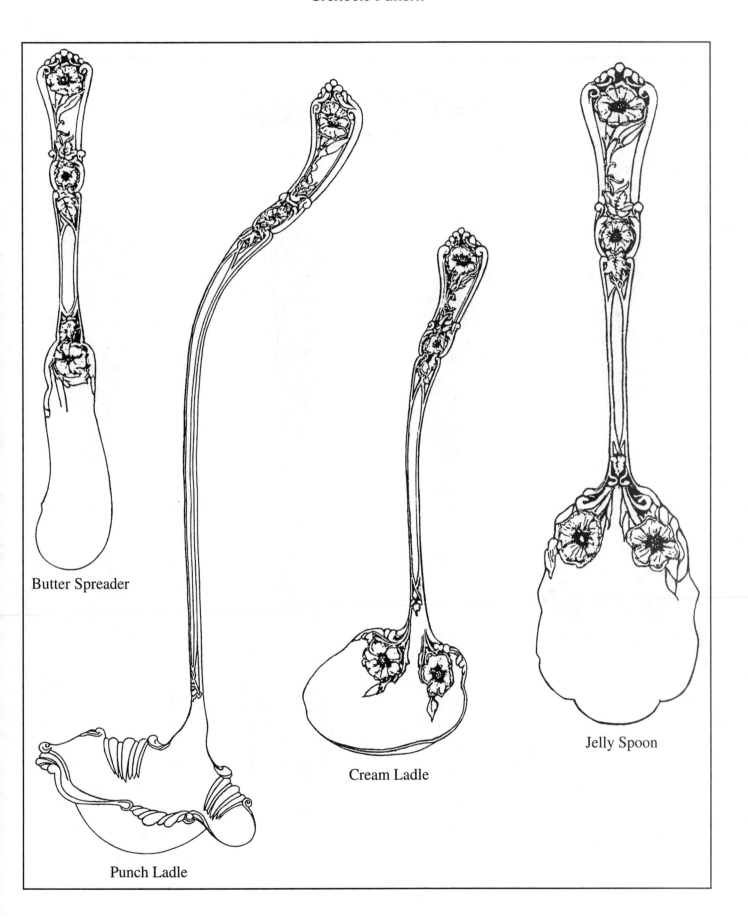

Butter Spreader

Punch Ladle

Cream Ladle

Jelly Spoon

Grenoble Pattern

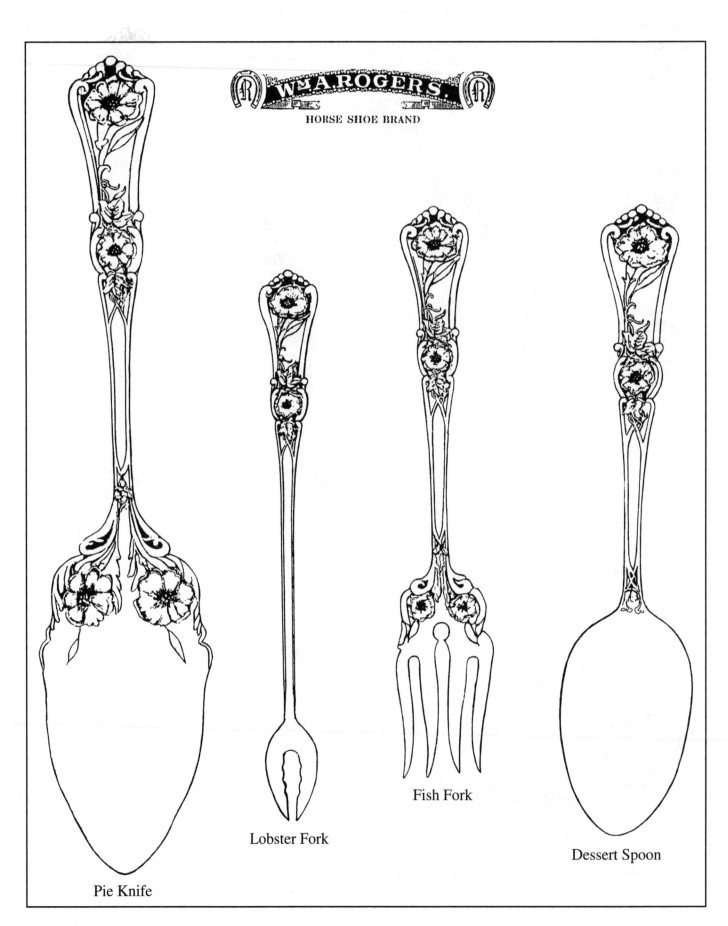

HORSE SHOE BRAND

Lobster Fork

Fish Fork

Dessert Spoon

Pie Knife

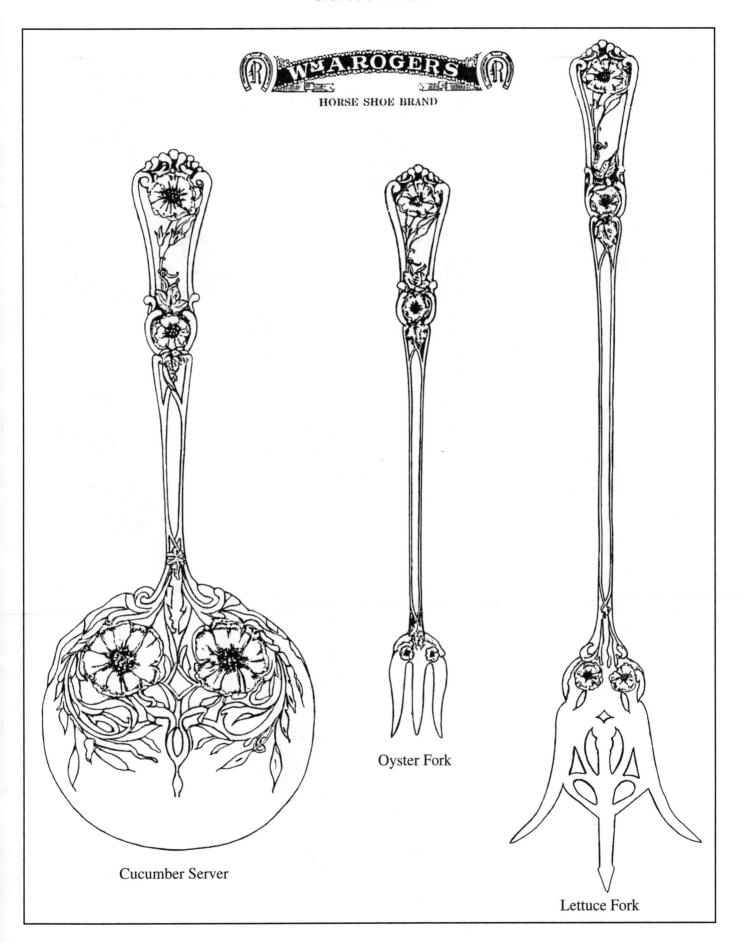

Cucumber Server

Oyster Fork

Lettuce Fork

Grenoble Pattern

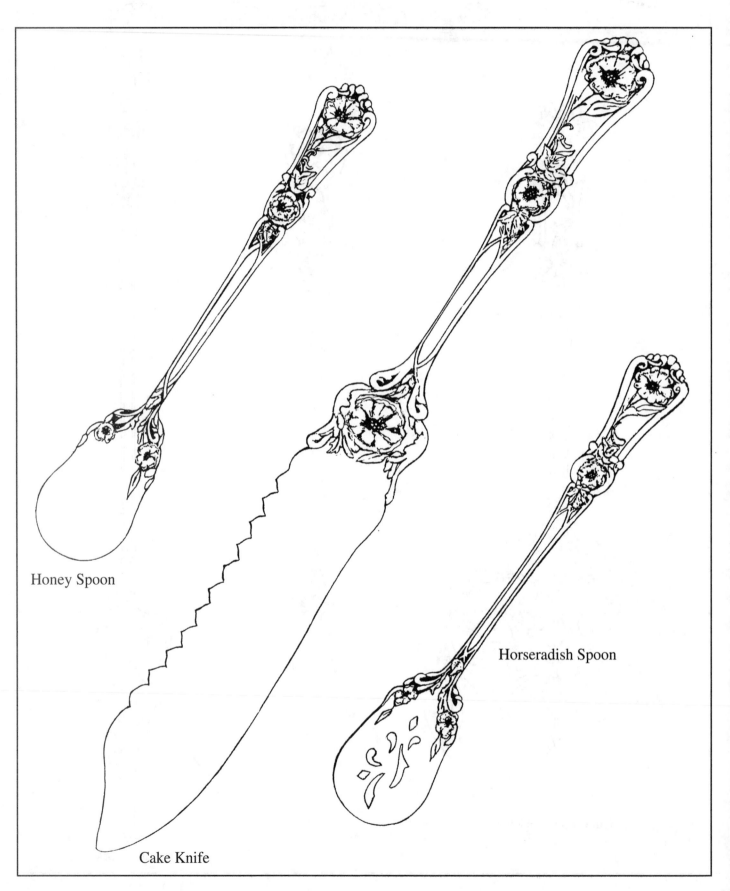

Honey Spoon

Cake Knife

Horseradish Spoon

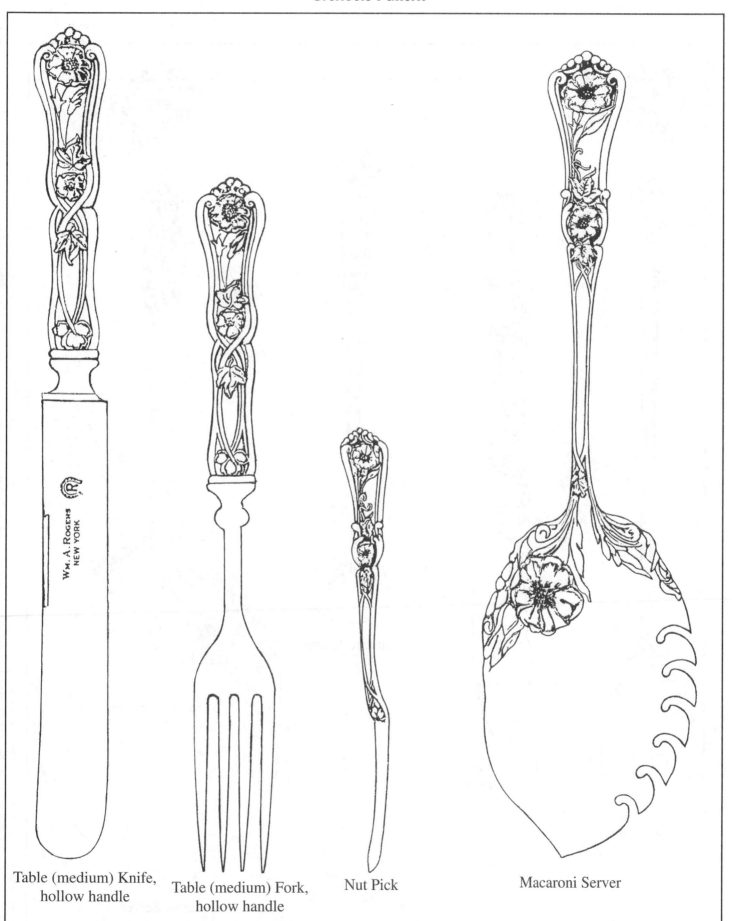

Table (medium) Knife,
hollow handle

Table (medium) Fork,
hollow handle

Nut Pick

Macaroni Server

See Price Guide — Group 1

Grenoble Pattern

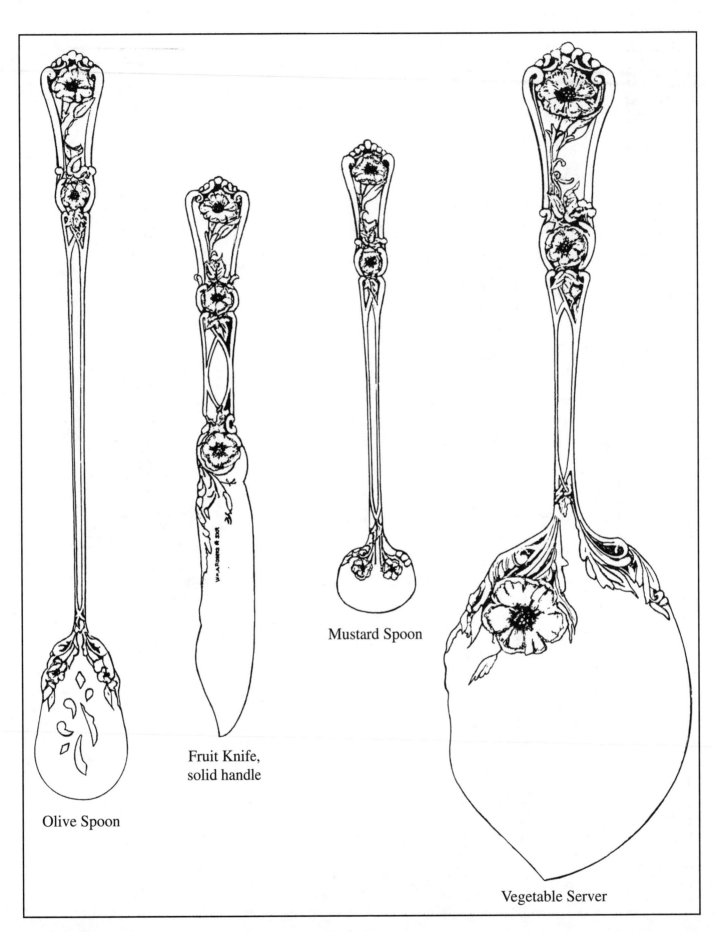

Olive Spoon

Fruit Knife,
solid handle

Mustard Spoon

Vegetable Server

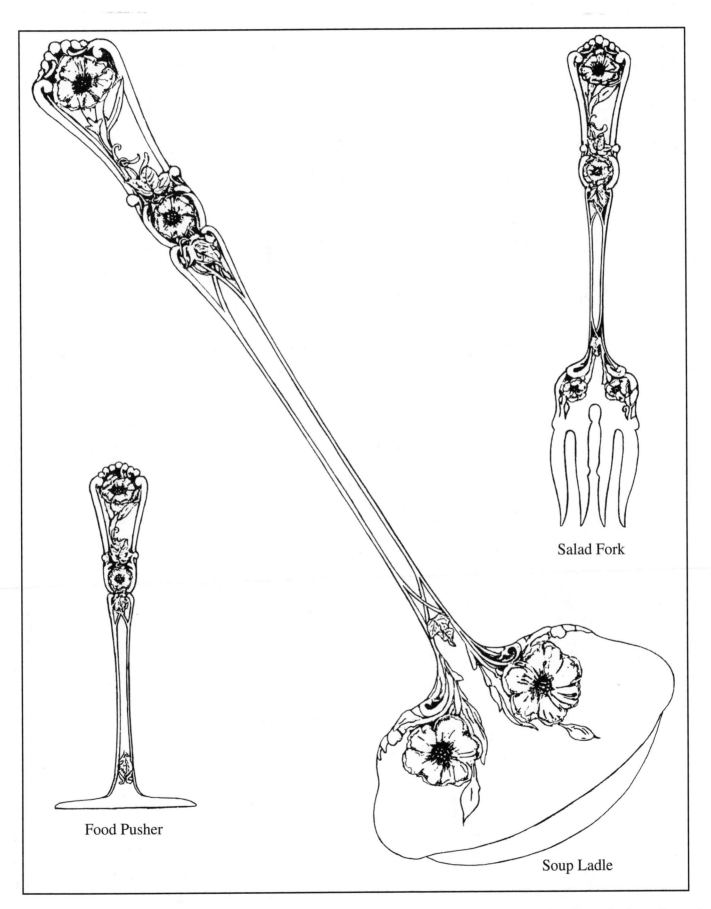

Salad Fork

Food Pusher

Soup Ladle

See Price Guide — Group 1

Grenoble Pattern

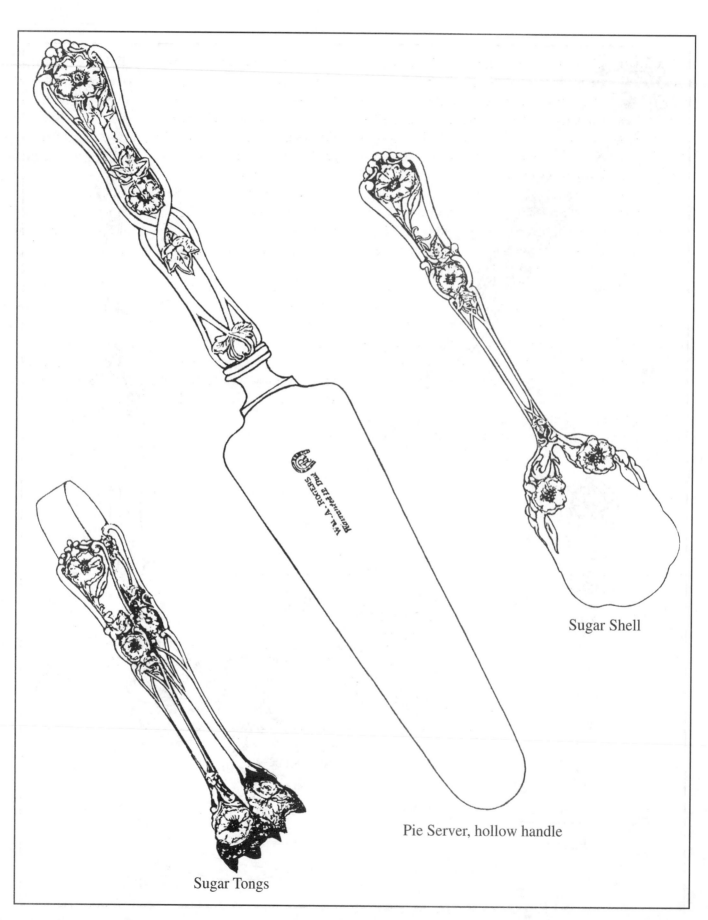

Sugar Shell

Pie Server, hollow handle

Sugar Tongs

Hanover Pattern

Hanover was introduced about 1901. McLean, Black and Company Inc., a wholesale firm located in Boston, Mass., marketed this pattern as Poppy. It is a large, interesting pattern and still possible to assemble as a set. A great deal of Hanover was sold in boxed sets. There are at least four different salad sets consisting of various combinations of pieces such as salad or berry spoons and fish, salad, or cold meat forks. Berries and fruits were an important part of the American diet around the turn of the century and the silver manufacturers made special items for these foods. Hanover had a cream set consisting of a cream ladle, sugar shell, and butter knife. The berry set sported six individual berry forks and one large berry spoon. An oyster ladle and six bouillon spoons made up the bouillon set. Other sets were the pie (six pie forks and the large pie knife) and coffee (twelve coffee spoons, cream ladle, and sugar tongs).

At least three different large Hanover ladles were made for soup: the oyster, medium, and individual.

The Hanover child's set was available with either a pearl handle knife or the silver one that had the Hanover design on the handle. Some children's sets featured a plain steel knife. The 1904 list shows five different children's sets. The pierced salad fork was sold in a boxed set with six individual salad forks. This was an expensive set for its time — about $7.00. This same fork was also sold singularly in a gift box, but we feel its cost limited sales and production. This particular piece is considered quite a prize in any Hanover collection.

The crumb knife was made in limited quantity, retailing for about $4.00. The price for the Hanover punch ladle was approximately $8.00. The large fish knife and fork were about $3.50 each. Gilded bowls were available with many of these large pieces at extra expense. In addition to the gold finish, Hanover was produced in a bright finish and also a French Gray.

Fish Knife

See Price Guide — Group 1

Hanover Pattern

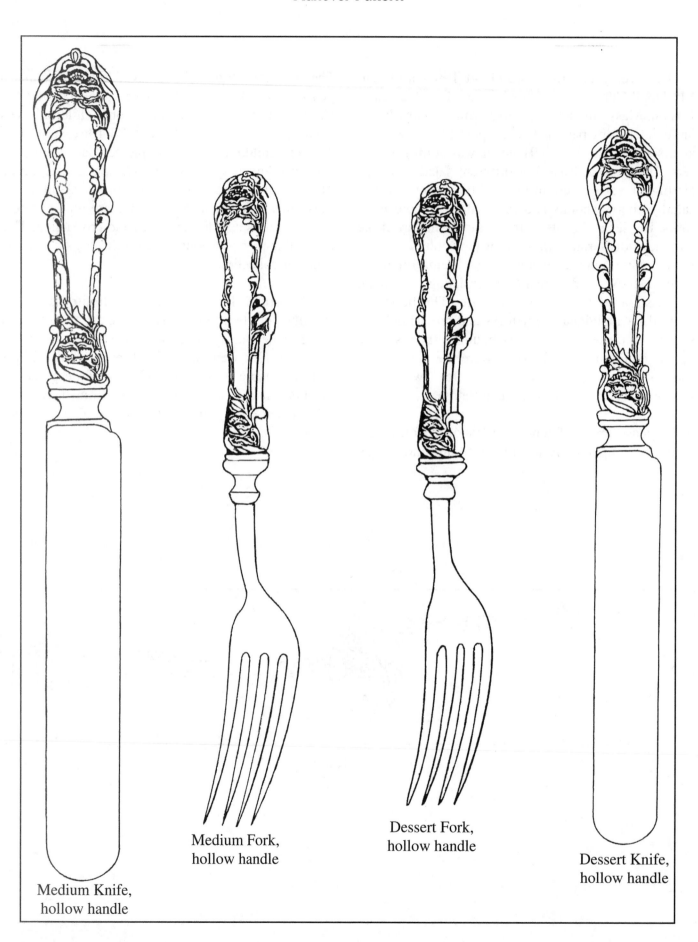

Medium Fork,
hollow handle

Dessert Fork,
hollow handle

Dessert Knife,
hollow handle

Medium Knife,
hollow handle

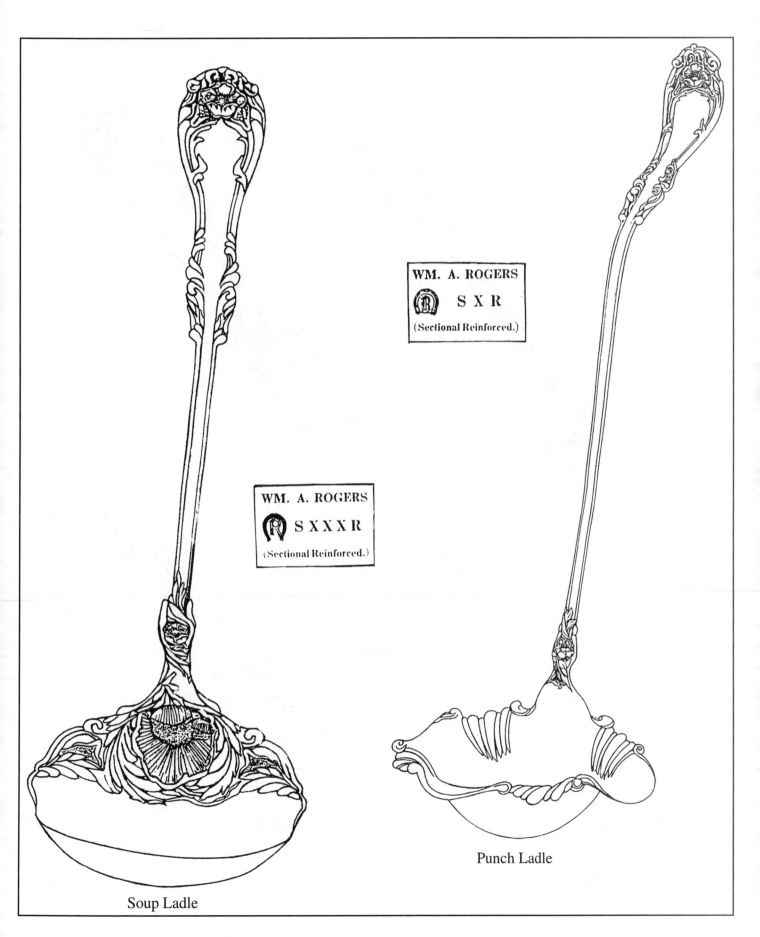

WM. A. ROGERS

SXR

(Sectional Reinforced.)

WM. A. ROGERS

SXXXR

(Sectional Reinforced.)

Punch Ladle

Soup Ladle

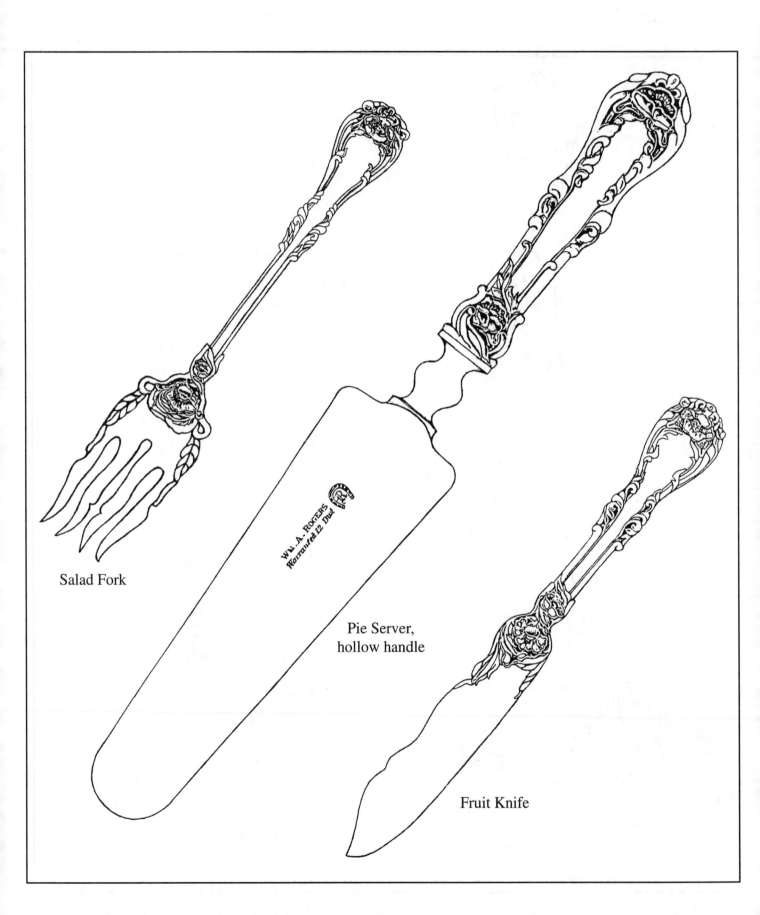

Salad Fork

Pie Server,
hollow handle

Fruit Knife

Hanover Pattern

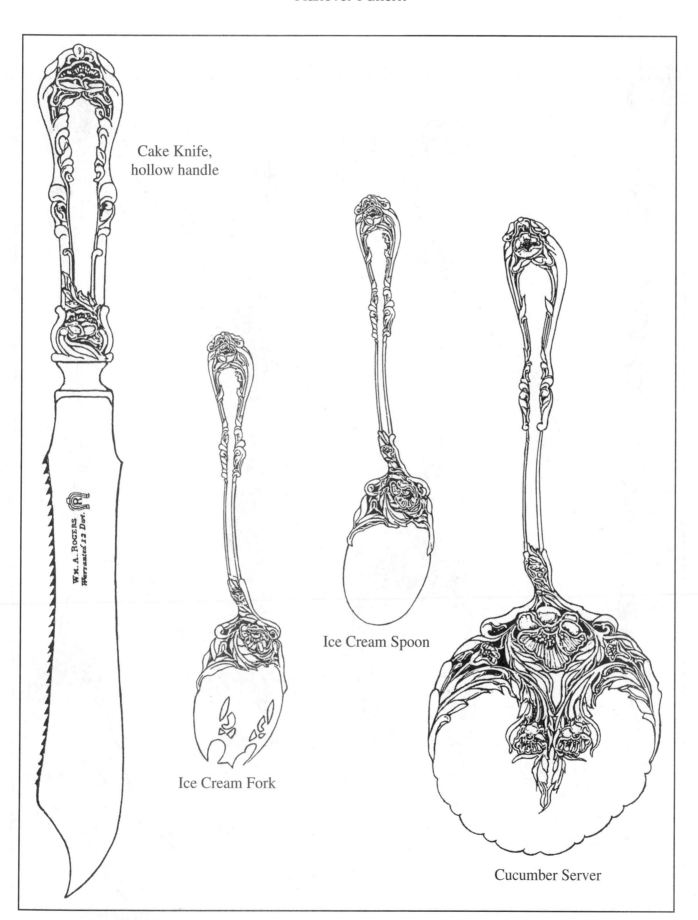

Cake Knife,
hollow handle

Wm. A. Rogers
Warranted 12 Dwt.

Ice Cream Spoon

Ice Cream Fork

Cucumber Server

See Price Guide — Group 1

Hanover Pattern

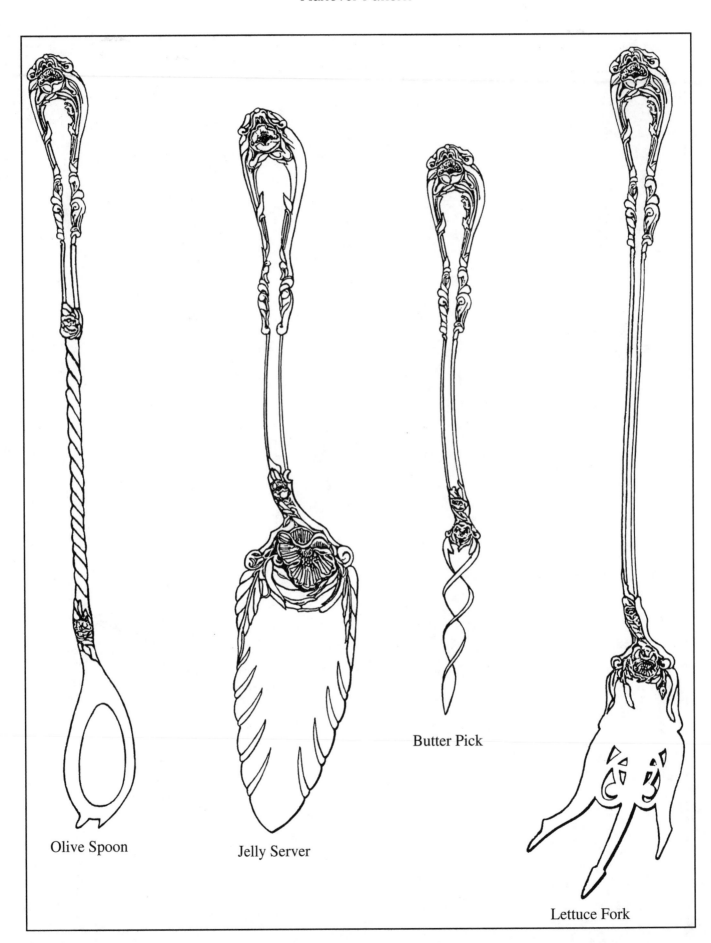

Olive Spoon

Jelly Server

Butter Pick

Lettuce Fork

Hanover Pattern

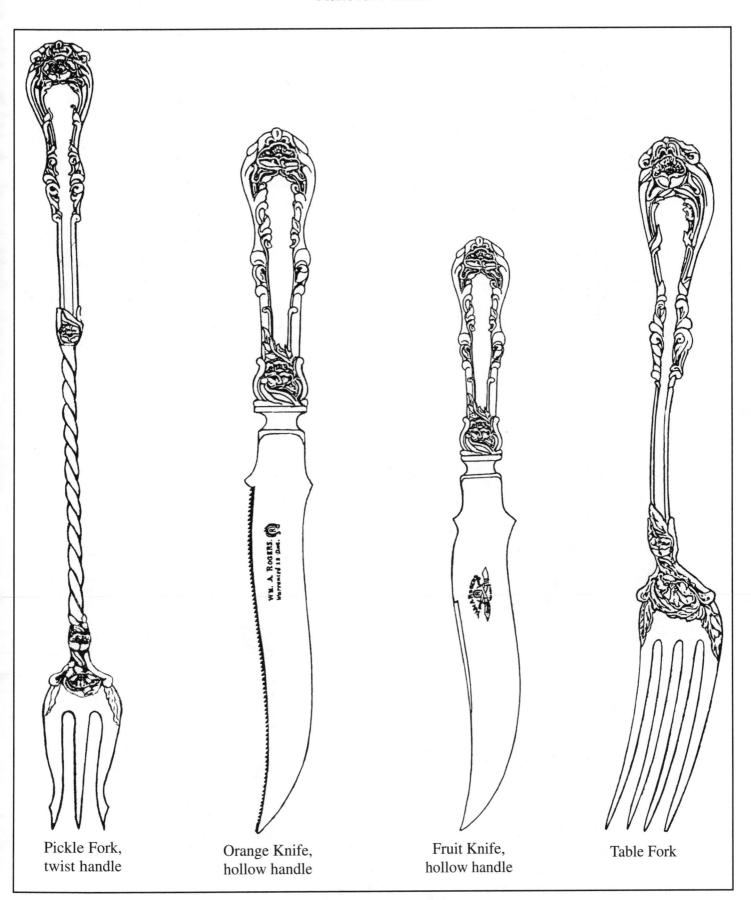

Pickle Fork,
twist handle

Orange Knife,
hollow handle

Fruit Knife,
hollow handle

Table Fork

Items shown actual size

See Price Guide — Group 1

Hanover Pattern

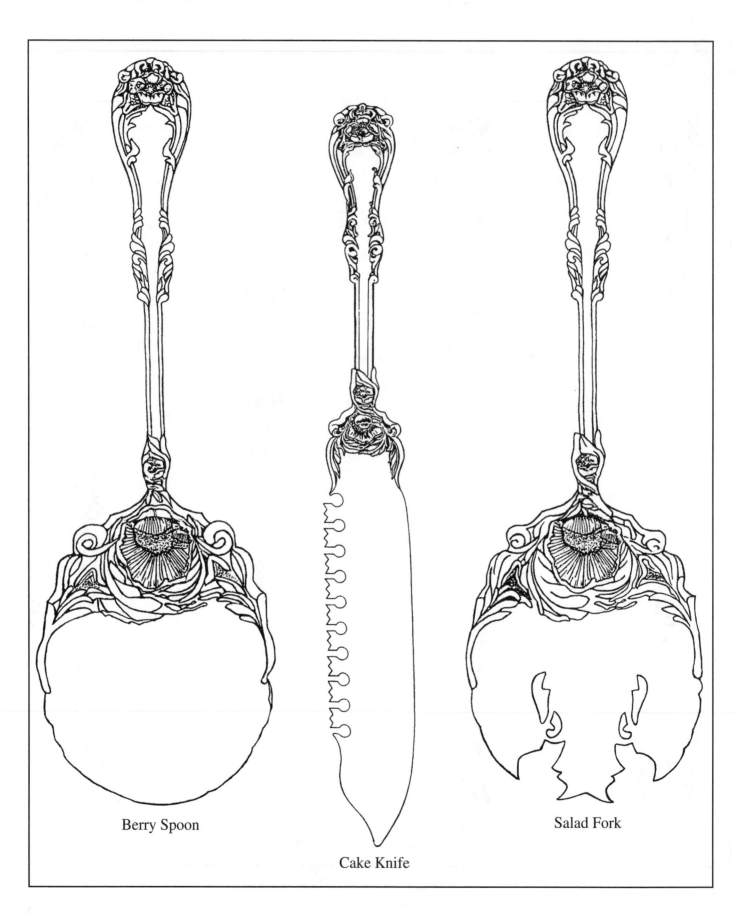

Berry Spoon

Cake Knife

Salad Fork

Hanover Pattern

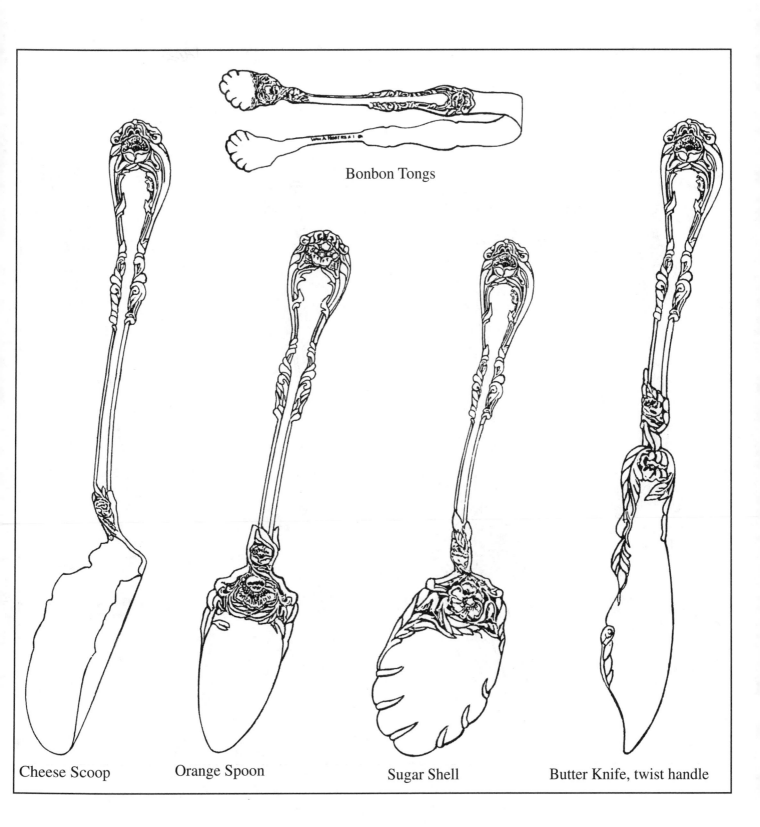

Bonbon Tongs

Cheese Scoop

Orange Spoon

Sugar Shell

Butter Knife, twist handle

Hanover Pattern

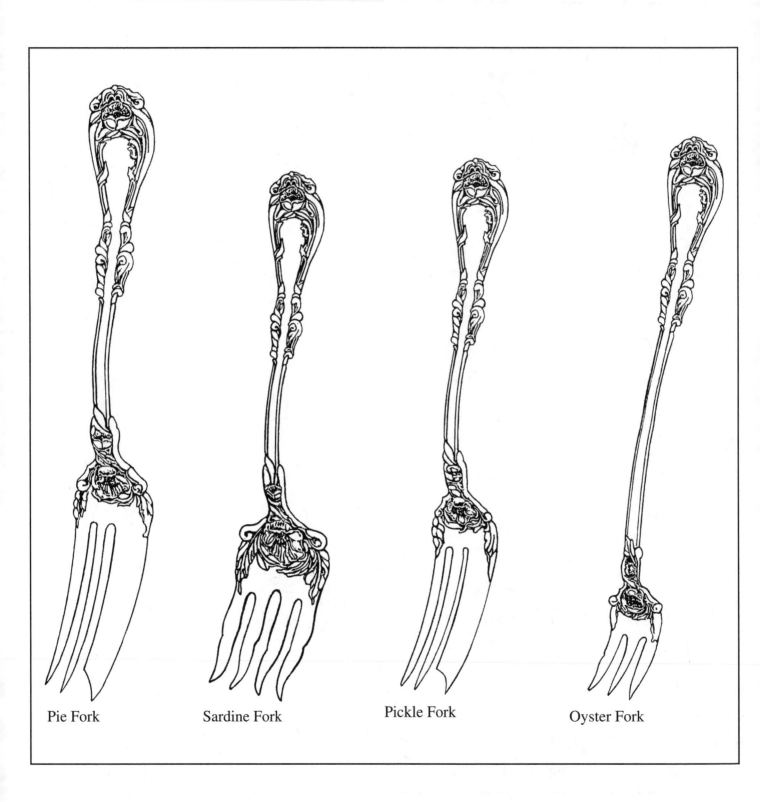

Pie Fork

Sardine Fork

Pickle Fork

Oyster Fork

Patented 1910. 8" ice tea spoon and 5⅞" teaspoon. A beautiful grape pattern that is hard to find in good condition. Hollow handle knives are almost impossible to find.

See Price Guide — Group 1

Marcella Pattern

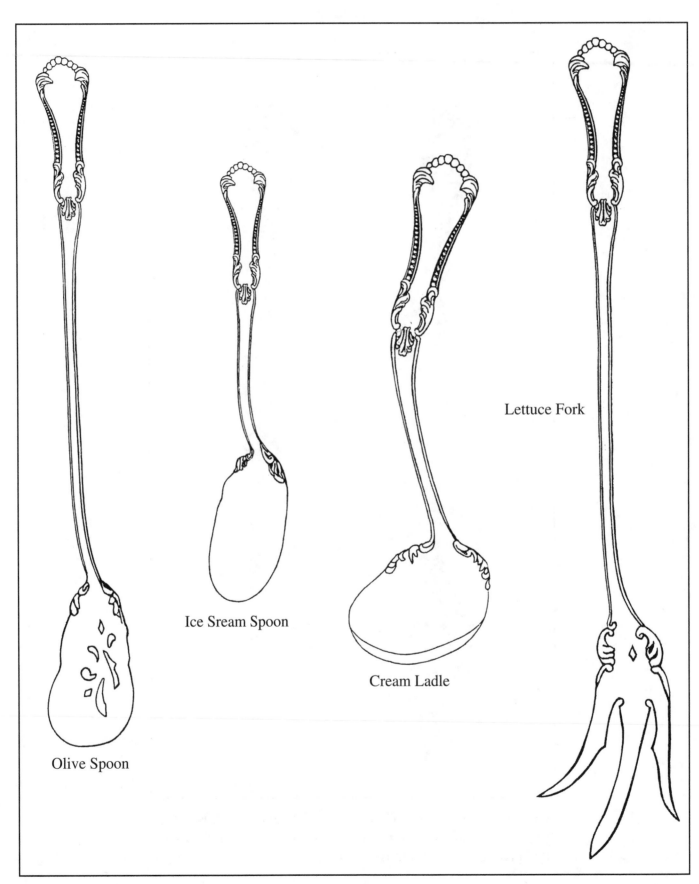

Olive Spoon

Ice Sream Spoon

Cream Ladle

Lettuce Fork

Marcella is also found backstamped Rockford S. P. Co., and 1880 Pairpoint Mfg. Co.

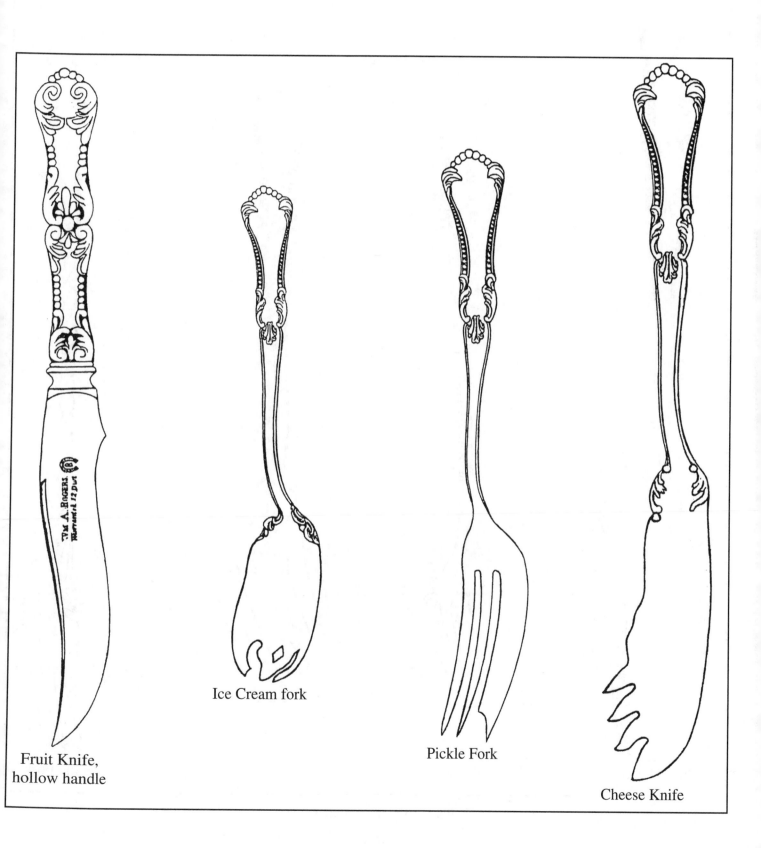

Fruit Knife,
hollow handle

Ice Cream fork

Pickle Fork

Cheese Knife

See Price Guide — Group 1

Marcella Pattern

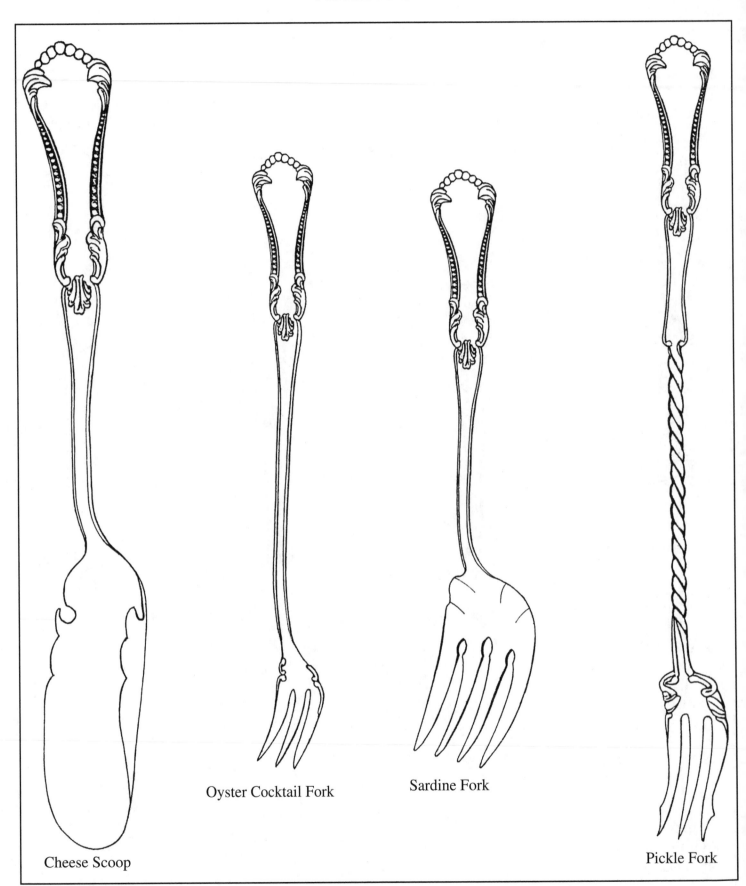

Cheese Scoop

Oyster Cocktail Fork

Sardine Fork

Pickle Fork

Items shown are actual size.

Warrick Pattern

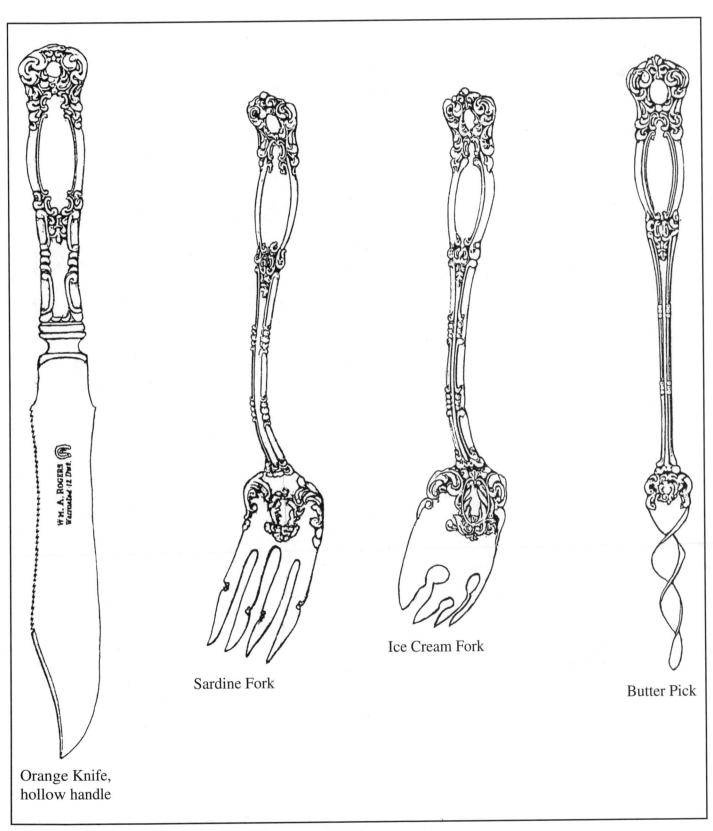

Orange Knife,
hollow handle

Sardine Fork

Ice Cream Fork

Butter Pick

Year 1901. Items shown are actual size.

See Price Guide — Group 1

Warrick Pattern

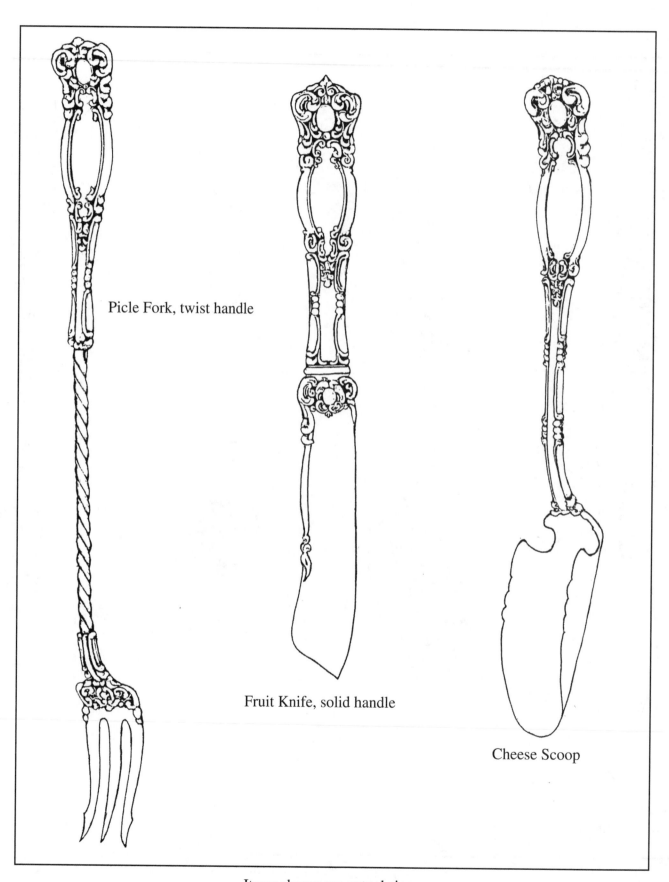

Picle Fork, twist handle

Fruit Knife, solid handle

Cheese Scoop

Items shown are actual size.

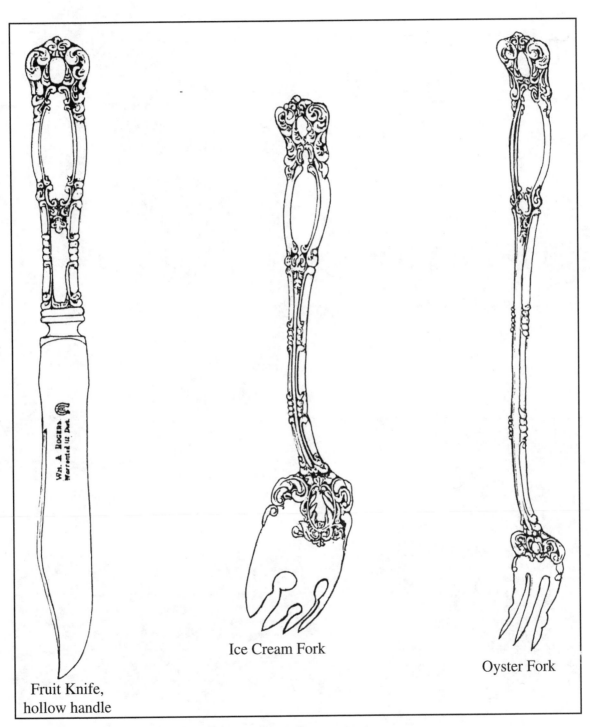

Fruit Knife,
hollow handle

Ice Cream Fork

Oyster Fork

Items shown are actual size.

Wm. A. Rogers (W.R. Brand)

Carnation Pattern

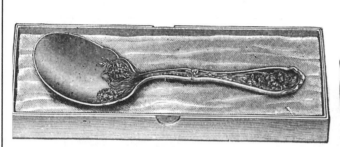

BERRY SPOON
Carnation Pattern.   French Gray.

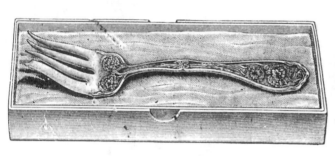

COLD MEAT FORK
Carnation Pattern.   French Gray.

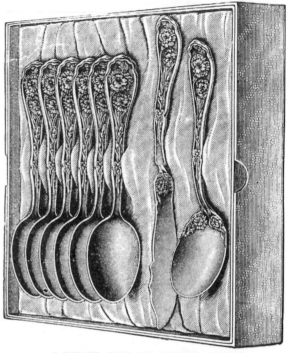

8-PIECE SET IN LINED BOX
Carnation Pattern.   French gray.
Six tea spoons, one sugar shell, one butter knife.

CARNATION PATTERN
French Gray
No. 33240 Cream Ladle.   Silver bowl.................each **$1.05**
No. 33241 Cream Ladle.   Gold bowl.................each **1.40**

CARNATION

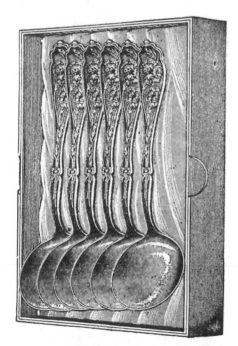

SIX SOUP SPOONS
Carnation Pattern.   French Gray.

CHILD'S SET
Five-piece.   Carnation Pattern.   French Gray.

1913 Catalog

Medium Knives, Carnation pattern, French gray finish............$8.00
Medium Forks, Carnation pattern, French gray finish............8.00

No. 31398 Dessert Knives, Carnation pattern, French gray finish............$7.70
No. 31399 Dessert Forks, Carnation pattern, French gray finish............7.70
Double Silver Plated Wm. A. Rogers W. R. Brand

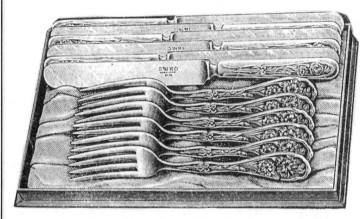

12-PIECE SET IN LINED BOX
Carnation Pattern. French gray.
Six medium knives, six medium forks.

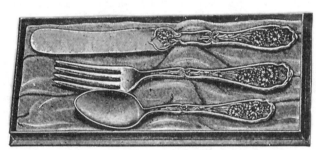

CHILD'S SET
Carnation Pattern. French Gray.

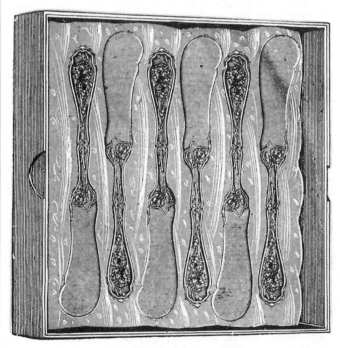

SIX BUTTER SPREADERS
Carnation Pattern. French Gray.
No. 33234 Per set............................$3.00

SIX OYSTER FORKS
Carnation Pattern. French Gray
No. 33232 Silver Tines....................per set $2.95
No. 33323 Gold Tines......................per set 4.00

1913 Catalog

COLLECTOR BOOKS

I n f o r m i n g   T o d a y ' s   C o l l e c t o r

For over two decades we have been keeping collectors informed on trends and values in all fields of antiques and collectibles.

DOLLS, FIGURES & TEDDY BEARS

4631	**Barbie Doll** Boom, 1986–1995, Augustyniak	$18.95
2079	**Barbie Doll** Fashion, Volume I, Eames	$24.95
4846	**Barbie Doll** Fashion, Volume II, Eames	$24.95
3957	**Barbie** Exclusives, Rana	$18.95
4632	**Barbie** Exclusives, Book II, Rana	$18.95
6022	The **Barbie Doll** Years, 5th Ed., Olds	$19.95
3810	**Chatty Cathy** Dolls, Lewis	$15.95
5352	Collector's Ency. of **Barbie** Doll Exclusives & More, 2nd Ed.,Augustyniak	$24.95
2211	Collector's Encyclopedia of **Madame Alexander** Dolls, Smith	$24.95
4863	Collector's Encyclopedia of **Vogue Dolls**, Izen/Stover	$29.95
5904	Collector's Guide to **Celebrity Dolls**, Spurgeon	$24.95
5599	Collector's Guide to **Dolls of the 1960s and 1970s**, Sabulis	$24.95
6030	Collector's Guide to **Horsman Dolls**, Jensen	$29.95
6025	**Doll Values**, Antique to Modern, 6th Ed., Moyer	$12.95
6032	**Madame Alexander** Collector's Dolls Price Guide #27, Crowsey	$12.95
6033	**Modern Collectible Dolls**, Volume VI, Moyer	$24.95
5689	**Nippon Dolls** & Playthings, Van Patten/Lau	$29.95
5365	**Peanuts Collectibles**, Podley/Bang	$24.95
6026	**Small Dolls of the 40s & 50s**, Stover	$29.95
5253	Story of **Barbie**, 2nd Ed., Westenhouser	$24.95
5277	**Talking Toys** of the 20th Century, Lewis	$15.95
2084	**Teddy Bears, Annalee's & Steiff** Animals, 3rd Series, Mandel	$19.95
5371	**Teddy Bear** Treasury, Yenke	$19.95
1808	Wonder of **Barbie**, Manos	$9.95
1430	World of **Barbie** Dolls, Manos	$9.95
4880	World of **Raggedy Ann** Collectibles, Avery	$24.95

TOYS & MARBLES

2333	Antique & Collectible **Marbles**, 3rd Ed., Grist	$9.95
4559	Collectible **Action Figures**, 2nd Ed., Manos	$17.95
2338	Collector's Encyclopedia of **Disneyana**, Longest, Stern	$24.95
5900	Collector's Guide to **Battery Toys**, 2nd Edition, Hultzman	$24.95
4566	Collector's Guide to **Tootsietoys**, 2nd Ed., Richter	$19.95
5169	Collector's Guide to **TV Toys** & Memorabilia, 2nd Ed., Davis/Morgan	$24.95
5360	**Fisher-Price Toys**, Cassity	$19.95
5593	Grist's Big Book of **Marbles**, 2nd Ed.	$24.95
3970	Grist's Machine-Made & Contemporary **Marbles**, 2nd Ed.	$9.95
5267	**Matchbox Toys**, 1947 to 1998, 3rd Ed., Johnson	$19.95
5830	**McDonald's** Collectibles, 2nd Edition, Henriques/DuVall	$24.95
5673	Modern **Candy Containers** & Novelties, Brush/Miller	$19.95
1540	Modern **Toys** 1930–1980, Baker	$19.95
5920	**Schroeder's Collectible Toys**, Antique to Modern Price Guide, 8th Ed.	$17.95
5908	**Toy Car** Collector's Guide, Johnson	$19.95

FURNITURE

3716	American **Oak** Furniture, Book II, McNerney	$12.95
1118	Antique **Oak** Furniture, Hill	$7.95
3720	Collector's Encyclopedia of **American** Furniture, Vol. III, Swedberg	$24.95
5359	Early **American** Furniture, Obbard	$12.95
1755	Furniture of the **Depression Era**, Swedberg	$19.95
3906	**Heywood-Wakefield** Modern Furniture, Rouland	$18.95
1885	**Victorian** Furniture, Our American Heritage, McNerney	$9.95
3829	**Victorian** Furniture, Our American Heritage, Book II, McNerney	$9.95

JEWELRY, HATPINS, WATCHES & PURSES

4704	Antique & Collectible **Buttons**, Wisniewski	$19.95
1748	Antique **Purses**, Revised Second Ed., Holiner	$19.95
4850	Collectible **Costume Jewelry**, Simonds	$24.95
5675	Collectible **Silver Jewelry**, Rezazadeh	$24.95
3722	Collector's Ency. of **Compacts**, Carryalls & Face Powder Boxes, Mueller	$24.95

4940	**Costume Jewelry**, A Practical Handbook & Value Guide, Rezazadeh	$24.95
5812	Fifty Years of Collectible **Fashion Jewelry**, 1925–1975, Baker	$24.95
1424	**Hatpins** & Hatpin Holders, Baker	$9.95
5695	**Ladies' Vintage Accessories**, Bruton	$24.95
1181	100 Years of Collectible **Jewelry**, 1850–1950, Baker	$9.95
4729	**Sewing Tools** & Trinkets, Thompson	$24.95
6038	**Sewing Tools** & Trinkets, Volume 2, Thompson	$24.95
6039	Signed Beauties of **Costume Jewelry**, Brown	$24.95
5620	Unsigned Beauties of **Costume Jewelry**, Brown	$24.95
4878	Vintage & Contemporary **Purse Accessories**, Gerson	$24.95
5696	Vintage & Vogue Ladies' **Compacts**, 2nd Edition, Gerson	$29.95
5923	**Vintage Jewelry** for Investment & Casual Wear, Edeen	$24.95

INDIANS, GUNS, KNIVES, TOOLS, PRIMITIVES

1868	Antique **Tools**, Our American Heritage, McNerney	$9.95
5616	Big Book of **Pocket Knives**, Stewart	$19.95
4943	Field Guide to Flint **Arrowheads & Knives** of the North American Indian	$9.95
2279	**Indian Artifacts** of the Midwest, Book I, Hothem	$14.95
3885	**Indian Artifacts** of the Midwest, Book II, Hothem	$16.95
4870	**Indian Artifacts** of the Midwest, Book III, Hothem	$18.95
5685	**Indian Artifacts** of the Midwest, Book IV, Hothem	$19.95
6132	**Modern Guns**, Identification & Values, 14th Ed., Quertermous	$14.95
2164	**Primitives**, Our American Heritage, McNerney	$9.95
1759	**Primitives**, Our American Heritage, 2nd Series, McNerney	$14.95
6031	Standard **Knife** Collector's Guide, 4th Ed., Ritchie & Stewart	$14.95
5999	**Wilderness** Survivor's Guide, Hamper	$12.95

PAPER COLLECTIBLES & BOOKS

4633	**Big Little Books**, Jacobs	$18.95
5902	**Boys' & Girls' Book** Series	$19.95
4710	Collector's Guide to **Children's Books**, 1850 to 1950, Volume I, Jones	$18.95
5153	Collector's Guide to **Chdren's Books**, 1850 to 1950, Volume II, Jones	$19.95
5596	Collector's Guide to **Children's Books**, 1950 to 1975, Volume III, Jones	$19.95
1441	Collector's Guide to **Post Cards**, Wood	$9.95
2081	Guide to Collecting **Cookbooks**, Allen	$14.95
5825	Huxford's **Old Book** Value Guide, 13th Ed.	$19.95
2080	Price Guide to **Cookbooks** & Recipe Leaflets, Dickinson	$9.95
3973	**Sheet Music** Reference & Price Guide, 2nd Ed., Pafik & Guiheen	$19.95
6041	Vintage **Postcards for the Holidays**, Reed	$24.95
4733	**Whitman Juvenile Books**, Brown	$17.95

GLASSWARE

5602	Anchor Hocking's **Fire-King** & More, 2nd Ed.	$24.95
4561	Collectible **Drinking Glasses**, Chase & Kelly	$17.95
5823	Collectible **Glass Shoes**, 2nd Edition, Wheatley	$24.95
5897	Coll. **Glassware from the 40s, 50s & 60s**, 6th Ed., Florence	$19.95
1810	Collector's Encyclopedia of **American Art Glass**, Shuman	$29.95
5907	Collector's Encyclopedia of **Depression Glass**, 15th Ed., Florence	$19.95
1961	Collector's Encyclopedia of **Fry Glassware**, Fry Glass Society	$24.95
1664	Collector's Encyclopedia of **Heisey Glass**, 1925–1938, Bredehoft	$24.95
3905	Collector's Encyclopedia of **Milk Glass**, Newbound	$24.95
4936	Collector's Guide to **Candy Containers**, Dezso/Poirier	$19.95
5820	Collector's Guide to **Glass Banks**, Reynolds	$24.95
4564	**Crackle Glass**, Weitman	$19.95
4941	**Crackle Glass**, Book II, Weitman	$19.95
4714	**Czechoslovakian Glass** and Collectibles, Book II, Barta/Rose	$16.95
5528	Early American **Pattern Glass**, Metz	$17.95
6125	**Elegant Glassware** of the Depression Era, 10th Ed., Florence	$24.95
3981	Evers' Standard **Cut Glass** Value Guide	$12.95
5614	Field Guide to **Pattern Glass**, McCain	$17.95
5615	Florence's **Glassware Pattern Identification** Guide, Vol. II	$19.95
4719	**Fostoria**, Etched, Carved & Cut Designs, Vol. II, Kerr	$24.95
3883	**Fostoria Stemware**, The Crystal for America, Long/Seate	$24.95

5261	**Fostoria Tableware**, 1924 – 1943, Long/Seate	$24.95
5361	**Fostoria Tableware**, 1944 – 1986, Long/Seate	$24.95
5604	**Fostoria**, Useful & Ornamental, Long/Seate	$29.95
5899	**Glass & Ceramic Baskets**, White	$19.95
4644	**Imperial Carnival Glass**, Burns	$18.95
5827	**Kitchen Glassware** of the Depression Years, 6th Ed., Florence	$24.95
5600	Much More Early American **Pattern Glass**, Metz	$17.95
5915	**Northwood Carnival Glass**, 1908 – 1925, Burns	$19.95
6136	Pocket Guide to **Depression Glass**, 13th Ed., Florence	$12.95
6023	Standard Encyclopedia of **Carnival Glass**, 8th Ed., Edwards/Carwile	$29.95
6024	Standard **Carnival Glass** Price Guide, 13th Ed., Edwards/Carwile	$9.95
6035	Standard Encyclopedia of **Opalescent Glass**, 4th Ed., Edwards/Carwile	$24.95
4732	**Very Rare Glassware** of the Depression Years, 5th Series, Florence	$24.95
4656	**Westmoreland Glass**, Wilson	$24.95

POTTERY

4927	**ABC Plates & Mugs**, Lindsay	$24.95
4929	**American Art Pottery**, Sigafoose	$24.95
4630	**American Limoges**, Limoges	$24.95
1312	**Blue & White Stoneware**, McNerney	$9.95
1959	**Blue Willow**, 2nd Ed., Gaston	$14.95
4851	Collectible **Cups & Saucers**, Harran	$18.95
5901	Collecting **Blue Willow**, Harman	$19.95
1373	Collector's Encyclopedia of **American Dinnerware**, Cunningham	$24.95
4931	Collector's Encyclopedia of **Bauer Pottery**, Chipman	$24.95
4658	Collector's Encyclopedia of **Brush-McCoy Pottery**, Huxford	$24.95
5034	Collector's Encyclopedia of **California Pottery**, 2nd Ed., Chipman	$24.95
3723	Collector's Encyclopedia of **Cookie Jars**, Book I, Roerig	$24.95
4939	Collector's Encyclopedia of **Cookie Jars**, Book III, Roerig	$24.95
5748	Collector's Encyclopedia of **Fiesta**, 9th Ed., Huxford	$24.95
3961	Collector's Encyclopedia of **Early Noritake**, Alden	$24.95
3812	Collector's Encyclopedia of **Flow Blue China**, 2nd Ed., Gaston	$24.95
3431	Collector's Encyclopedia of **Homer Laughlin China**, Jasper	$24.95
1276	Collector's Encyclopedia of **Hull Pottery**, Roberts	$19.95
3962	Collector's Encyclopedia of **Lefton China**, DeLozier	$19.95
4855	Collector's Encyclopedia of **Lefton China**, Book II, DeLozier	$19.95
5609	Collector's Encyclopedia of **Limoges Porcelain**, 3rd Ed., Gaston	$29.95
2334	Collector's Encyclopedia of **Majolica Pottery**, Katz-Marks	$19.95
1358	Collector's Encyclopedia of **McCoy Pottery**, Huxford	$19.95
5677	Collector's Encyclopedia of **Niloak**, 2nd Edition, Gifford	$29.95
3837	Collector's Encyclopedia of **Nippon Porcelain**, Van Patten	$24.95
1665	Collector's Ency. of **Nippon Porcelain**, 3rd Series, Van Patten	$24.95
5053	Collector's Ency. of **Nippon Porcelain**, 5th Series, Van Patten	$24.95
5678	Collector's Ency. of **Nippon Porcelain**, 6th Series, Van Patten	$29.95
1447	Collector's Encyclopedia of **Noritake**, Van Patten	$19.95
4951	Collector's Encyclopedia of **Old Ivory China**, Hillman	$24.95
5564	Collector's Encyclopedia of **Pickard China**, Reed	$29.95
3877	Collector's Encyclopedia of **R.S. Prussia**, 4th Series, Gaston	$24.95
5679	Collector's Encyclopedia of **Red Wing Art Pottery**, Dollen	$24.95
5618	Collector's Encyclopedia of **Rosemeade Pottery**, Dommel	$24.95
5841	Collector's Encyclopedia of **Roseville Pottery**, Revised, Huxford/Nickel	$24.95
5842	Collector's Encyclopedia of **Roseville Pottery**, 2nd Series, Huxford/Nickel	$24.95
5917	Collector's Encyclopedia of **Russel Wright**, 3rd Editon, Kerr	$29.95
4713	Collector's Encyclopedia of **Salt Glaze Stoneware**, Taylor/Lowrance	$24.95
5370	Collector's Encyclopedia of **Stangl Dinnerware**, Runge	$24.95
5921	Collector's Encyclopedia of **Stangl Artware**, Lamps, and Birds, RUnge	$29.95
3314	Collector's Encyclopedia of **Van Briggle Art Pottery**, Sasicki	$24.95
4563	Collector's Encyclopedia of **Wall Pockets**, Newbound	$19.95
2111	Collector's Encyclopedia of **Weller Pottery**, Huxford	$29.95
5680	Collector's Guide to **Feather Edge Ware**, McAllister	$19.95
3876	Collector's Guide to **Lu-Ray Pastels**, Meehan	$18.95
3814	Collector's Guide to **Made in Japan Ceramics**, White	$18.95
4646	Collector's Guide to **Made in Japan Ceramics**, Book II, White	$18.95
2339	Collector's Guide to **Shawnee Pottery**, Vanderbilt	$19.95
1425	**Cookie Jars**, Westfall	$9.95
3440	**Cookie Jars**, Book II, Westfall	$19.95

5909	**Dresden Porcelain** Studios, Harran	$29.95
5918	Florence's Big Book of **Salt & Pepper Shakers**	$24.95
2379	Lehner's Ency. of **U.S. Marks** on Pottery, Porcelain & China	$24.95
4722	**McCoy Pottery**, Collector's Reference & Value Guide, Hanson/Nissen	$19.95
5913	**McCoy Pottery**, Volume III, Hanson & Nissen	$24.95
5691	**Post86 Fiesta**, Identification & Value Guide, Racheter	$19.95
1670	**Red Wing Collectibles**, DePasquale	$9.95
1440	**Red Wing Stoneware**, DePasquale	$9.95
6037	**Rookwood Pottery**, Nicholson & Thomas	$24.95
1632	**Salt & Pepper Shakers**, Guarnaccia	$9.95
5091	**Salt & Pepper Shakers** II, Guarnaccia	$18.95
3443	**Salt & Pepper Shakers** IV, Guarnaccia	$18.95
3738	**Shawnee Pottery**, Mangus	$24.95
4629	Turn of the Century **American Dinnerware**, 1880s–1920s, Jasper	$24.95
3327	**Watt Pottery** – Identification & Value Guide, Morris	$19.95
5924	**Zanesville Stoneware** Company, Rans, Ralston & Russell	$24.95

OTHER COLLECTIBLES

5916	Advertising **Paperweights**, Holiner & Kammerman	$24.95
5838	Advertising **Thermometers**, Merritt	$16.95
5898	Antique & Contemporary **Advertising Memorabilia**, Summers	$24.95
5814	Antique **Brass & Copper** Collectibles, Gaston	$24.95
1880	Antique **Iron**, McNerney	$9.95
3872	Antique **Tins**, Dodge	$24.95
4845	Antique **Typewriters & Office Collectibles**, Rehr	$19.95
5607	Antiquing and Collecting on the **Internet**, Parry	$12.95
1128	**Bottle** Pricing Guide, 3rd Ed., Cleveland	$7.95
3718	Collectible **Aluminum**, Grist	$16.95
4560	Collectible **Cats**, An Identification & Value Guide, Book II, Fyke	$19.95
5060	Collectible **Souvenir Spoons**, Bednersh	$19.95
5676	Collectible **Souvenir Spoons**, Book II, Bednersh	$29.95
5666	Collector's Encyclopedia of **Granite Ware**, Book 2, Greguire	$29.95
5836	Collector's Guide to **Antique Radios**, 5th Ed., Bunis	$19.95
3966	Collector's Guide to **Inkwells**, Identification & Values, Badders	$18.95
4947	Collector's Guide to **Inkwells**, Book II, Badders	$19.95
5681	Collector's Guide to **Lunchboxes**, White	$19.95
5621	Collector's Guide to **Online Auctions**, Hix	$12.95
4652	Collector's Guide to **Transistor Radios**, 2nd Ed., Bunis	$16.95
4864	Collector's Guide to **Wallace Nutting Pictures**, Ivankovich	$18.95
1629	**Doorstops**, Identification & Values, Bertoia	$9.95
5683	**Fishing Lure** Collectibles, 2nd Ed., Murphy/Edmisten	$29.95
5911	**Flea Market Trader**, 13th Ed., Huxford	$9.95
4945	**G-Men and FBI Toys** and Collectibles, Whitworth	$18.95
6029	**Garage Sale & Flea Market Annual**, 10th Ed.	$19.95
3819	**General Store** Collectibles, Wilson	$24.95
5912	The **Heddon** Legacy, A Century of Classic **Lures**, Roberts & Pavey	$29.95
2216	**Kitchen Antiques**, 1790–1940, McNerney	$14.95
5991	**Lighting Devices** & Accessories of the 17th – 19th Centuries, Hamper	$9.95
5686	**Lighting Fixtures** of the Depression Era, Book I, Thomas	$24.95
4950	The **Lone Ranger**, Collector's Reference & Value Guide, Felbinger	$18.95
6028	Modern **Fishing Lure** Collectibles, Lewis	$24.95
2026	**Railroad** Collectibles, 4th Ed., Baker	$14.95
5619	**Roy Rogers and Dale Evans** Toys & Memorabilia, Coyle	$24.95
5919	**Schroeder's Antiques Price Guide**, 20th Ed., Huxford	$14.95
5007	**Silverplated Flatware**, Revised 4th Edition, Hagan	$18.95
6040	**Star Wars** Super Collector's Wish Book, Carlton	$29.95
6139	Summers' Guide to **Coca-Cola**, 4th Ed.	$24.95
5905	Summers' Pocket Guide to **Coca-Cola**, 3rd Ed.	$12.95
3892	**Toy & Miniature Sewing Machines**, Thomas	$18.95
4876	**Toy & Miniature Sewing Machines**, Book II, Thomas	$24.95
3977	Value Guide to **Gas Station Memorabilia**, Summers & Priddy	$24.95
4877	**Vintage Bar Ware**, Visakay	$24.95
5925	The **Vintage Era of Golf Club Collectibles**, John	$29.95
6010	The **Vintage Era of Golf Club Collectibles** Collector's Log, John	$9.95
6036	**Vintage Quilts**, Aug, Newman & Roy	$24.95
4935	The **W.F. Cody Buffalo Bill** Collector's Guide with Values	$24.95

This is only a partial listing of the books on antiques that are available from Collector Books. All books are well illustrated and contain current values. Most of these books are available from your local bookseller, antique dealer, or public library. If you are unable to locate certain titles in your area, you may order by mail from COLLECTOR BOOKS, P.O. Box 3009, Paducah, KY 42002-3009. Customers with Visa, Discover or MasterCard may phone in orders from 7:00–5:00 CST, Monday–Friday, Toll Free 1-800-626-5420, or online at www.collectorbooks.com. Add $3.00 for postage for the first book ordered and 50¢ for each additional book. Include item number, title, and price when ordering. Allow 14 to 21 days for delivery.